The Piozzi Letters

John Stockdale, "The Bookselling Blacksmith, one of the King's New Friends." Caricature by Thomas Rowlandson. (Reprinted by permission of the Trustees of the British Museum, Department of Prints and Drawings.)

The Piozzi Letters

Correspondence of
Hester Lynch Piozzi, 1784–1821
(formerly Mrs. Thrale)

Volume 3
1799–1804

EDITED BY
Edward A. Bloom
AND
Lillian D. Bloom

NEWARK: University of Delaware Press
LONDON AND TORONTO: Associated University Presses

© 1993 by Associated University Presses, Inc.

All rights reserved. Authorization to photocopy items for internal or personal use, or the internal or personal use of specific clients, is granted by the copyright owner, provided that a base fee of $10.00, plus eight cents per page, per copy is paid directly to the Copyright Clearance Center, 27 Congress Street, Salem, Massachusetts 01970. [0-87413-392-0/93 $10.00 + 8¢ pp, pc.]

Associated University Presses
440 Forsgate Drive
Cranbury, NJ 08512

Associated University Presses
25 Sicilian Avenue
London WC1A 2QH, England

Associated University Presses
P.O. Box 39, Clarkson Pstl. Stn.
Mississauga, Ontario,
L5J 3X9 Canada

The paper used in this publication meets the requirements of the American National Standard for Permanence of Paper for Printed Library Materials Z39.48-1984.

Library of Congress Cataloging-in-Publication Data
(Revised for volume 3)

Piozzi, Hester Lynch, 1741–1821.
   The Piozzi letters.

   Includes bibliographical references and indexes.
   Contents: v. 1. 1784–1791 —v. 2. 1792–1798—
v. 3. 1799–1804.
   1. Piozzi, Hester Lynch, 1741–1821—Correspondence.
2. Authors, English—18th century—Correspondence.
3. London (England)—Intellectual life—18th century.
I. Bloom, Edward Alan, 1914–   . II. Bloom,
Lillian D.   III. Title.
PR3619.P5Z48   1988   828'.609 [B]   87-40231
ISBN 0-87413-115-4 (v. 1 : alk. paper)
ISBN 0-87413-360-2 (v. 2: alk. paper)
ISBN 0-87413-392-0 (v. 3: alk. paper)

Printed in the United States of America

Contents

List of Illustrations 7
Introduction 9
Short Titles for Major Manuscript Repositories 27
Short Titles for Hester Lynch Piozzi's Manuscripts and Books 29
Short Titles for Secondary Sources 33
Names and Abbreviations of Major Figures in the Piozzi
 Correspondence 41
Editorial Principles 43

Letters, 1799–1804 47

Index 488

Illustrations

John Stockdale, caricature by Rowlandson	Frontispiece
Maria Anne Fitzherbert, by Condé after Cosway	68
Richard Brinsley Sheridan, by Hall after Reynolds	114
David Garrick, by Dance-Holland	133
Thomas Cadell, by Meyer and Evans after Beechey	208
Samuel Rogers, by Meyer after Hoppner	254
Hannah More, by Edouart	272
Daniel Lysons, by Dance	378
Samuel Lysons, by Lawrence	379
Samuel Johnson, by Reynolds	406
The Prince of Wales, by Cosway	452
The Prince of Wales, by Humphrey after Gillray	454
Sophia Lee, by Ridley after Lawrence	466
The Ladies of Llangollen, by Lynch	470
Plas Newydd, near Llangollen, by Walton	471

Introduction

1

In 1799, Hester Lynch Piozzi looked forward to a time of literary excitement and self-fulfillment. Tested by her second marriage, she summoned an inner strength that fortified her against the notoriety imposed by would-be censors. They tried to dehumanize her as a monster-mother who had entered into a vulgar marriage to satisfy her sexual passion. But both the marriage and its publicity served her well, each in its own way. The gossip made her smart but, never bashful, she welcomed attack as preferable to indifference.

In Gabriel Piozzi, moreover, she found the lover-husband, whom in her obedient Thrale years she could only fantasize. Piozzi emerged as a companion and a friend who, because he did not fathom the mannered proprieties of British gentility and of feminine self-effacement, helped her cast them aside. He perhaps did not perceive the intensity of her creative compulsion. But since his own sensibility centered on music—its composition and performance—he doubtless encouraged the aspiration toward utilizing her artistry as an expression of drive and power. Gabriel Piozzi was soft and gentle but he toughened his wife into undertaking what she thought would be the most creative adventure of her maturity—*Retrospection*.

She anticipated that the two-volume work, published in 1801, would impose direction on her intellectual life, and reward her with a happy and profitable reception. After all, she could recall that *British Synonymy* in 1794 had both disgruntled readers and well wishers; for the most part it was favorably received, except for the sly intimation that it plagiarized from a similar unpublished work by Samuel Johnson. As an instance, the *Monthly Review* commented with assumed objectivity: "It has been supposed, or rather suggested by envy, that Mrs. Piozzi had in her possession fragments of a work on Synonymy by the late Dr. Johnson,—but, we believe, totally without foundation. The lady frequently cites Dr. Johnson's opinions on subjects which he had discussed in conversation, and which probably were heard only by herself and family; if she had chosen to arrogate to herself the honour of these, there was not the least chance of her being detected." Having planted the seed, the *Monthly Review* figuratively abandoned it to flower or die in a public forum.[1]

Three Warnings to John Bull before He Dies, a hastily devised propaganda exercise in conventional pamphlet form, had only a slim sale in 1798, but it made a bold intellectual statement without compromise. To Hester Lynch Piozzi it was a *succès d'estime*. And even if *Retrospection* were to fall short of the plaudits she hoped for it, she could call upon her already tried courage and her defiant vanity which, whether in anger or petulance, quickened the depth of her personality.

When the composition of *Retrospection* was comfortably under way, the Piozzis decided to send for John Salusbury, the son of Gabriel's younger brother Giambattista. As she confided in *Thraliana*, the decision was her husband's; she acceded because in their married life, he made few decisions and even fewer requests. Her plan for "Mr Piozzi's Baby—The Little Italian Boy is come over; & we have placed him with Mr Davies who keeps a University as he calls it for Young Students under 12 Years old—This infant was just 3 [actually he was 5]— when he touch'd English Ground [late in November 1798] I understand."[2] To her he was nameless, ageless, indeed faceless, in a boarding school at Streatham. Near but not interferingly so, John Salusbury was a Piozzi child and hence not her immediate responsibility. He spent an occasional school holiday with his uncle and adoptive aunt but usually he was held at a distance while he lived at school.

Because she made no effort to learn his exact age, she assumed (along with most of her contemporaries) that the toddler-exile had been frightened by the imminence of the French during the first Italian campaign, that he had to learn the ways of the English, and that he could be manipulated as a weapon to bring her daughters into conventional acquiescence. Her plan for "Mr Piozzi's Baby" was calculated. He would be educated and naturalized, and then, she wrote, "we will see if He will be more grateful, & rational, & comfortable than Miss Thrales have been to the Mother they have at length *driven to desperation.*"[3]

At first the boy meant little to her except as a rescued waif; only later (again without realistic assessment of the individual) did she fashion an ideal of the man he would become. He did not in fact betray her or let her down; he simply did not share or understand her triumphal vision by which he bested the Miss Thrales.

In the meanwhile she regarded him—if she regarded him at all—as a distant presence while she concentrated on writing a history of the western world from the time of Christ to the beginning of the nineteenth century. Not until her project was begun did she describe it, somwhat coyly, to her eldest daughter. On 11 February 1796, she admitted to the imperious Queeney: "Well! 'tis a Sign my Spirits are not low, for last Monday I begun upon a Literary Work of no inconsiderable Magnitude. Its Title would be anticipated if I let any body know it, but when we meet I shall tell it you under promise of Secrecy, and shew you as far as it will be gone by that Time: But I do not work hard."[4]

The pose of insouciant author did not disguise her diligence; on the contrary she played no amateur game with the book. In August 1800, Lord Henry Petty stopped at Brynbella, later telling Hayward about his visit: "I remember [Madame Piozzi] taking me into her bed-room to show me the floor covered with folios, quartos, and octavos, for consultation, and indicating the labour she had gone through in compiling an immense volume she was then publishing, called

'Retrospection.' She was certainly what was called, and is still called, blue, and that of a deep tint, but good humoured and lively though affected."[5]

Even before Petty's one-day stay at Brynbella, she felt the pressure of time in the spring of 1799: intellectually she forced a single-minded concentration on *Retrospection*, "my great Book & prepare for the Time of Publication . . . in A Year & half I must (if alive) take it with me quite finished to London—for in March 1801 It should be out—& he who runs against Time has an Antagonist not subject (like himself) to Casualties."[6]

She never considered *Retrospection* an easy task, although she probably romanticized it as a knock-wood celebration of life that staved off the finality of death. Realistically she knew that the work needed a professional scholar with access to source materials, that it called for a scrupulous proofreader and indexer. Still shrouding the subject of her book in mystery, she jokingly boasted to Queeney of her pretentious folly for "undertaking a Work which should be written in All Souls College Oxford that I might have Books at hand, just where I have no Books to consult."[7]

About a week later, on 16 April, she could no longer maintain silence, revealing to her confidante the methodology of her *chef d'oeuvre*. "My Book will be a Summary of Events for the whole 1800 Years interspersed with Reflections &c. and a Table of immense Length in the last of four 8vo. Volumes with the Names of all Cities mentioned in the Course of the Work, as called by Ancients and moderns; French, Italian, English, and Latin—Some Rivers *to run thro'* besides—and the whole to have for its Title Retrospection. You see I have given myself Time enough to do it in, for it *should* not come out till exactly this Time *four* Years: but Gibbon is more indispensable than any Thing in this stage of the Business, 'piu necessario che il Pane' as Mr Piozzi says of what he cannot do *without*."[8]

By the summer of 1800, Hester Lynch Piozzi urged her friends John Gillon and the Reverend Leonard Chappelow to negotiate for a publisher from whom she would demand £1,000 for the copyright. Yet Robinson, who had published *British Synonymy*, rejected it. She then had her "agents" approach John Stockdale with her proposal for an honest profit as the measure of her worth. He, however, made a counter offer, which at first she thought perverse, if not downright simplistic. He would give her a half interest in the profits of the publication, he paying all the expenses of printing, bookkeeping, and advertising. On 3 November she signed a contract and by 14 November she was—as she told Chappelow with pleasurable exaggeration—buried under proofs.

Retrospection was nastily reviewed, most of the critics finding the author a presumptuous quasi-historian, who proffered neither verified facts nor relevant commentary. More than harsh, they launched a vendetta, irate that a woman dared to work so vast a canvas. To whet their attacks and justify their sneers, they ignored the introduction that spelled out her intention. It is as if they sought to rewrite her book for scholarly direction and to insinuate a masculine patina.

She had made no false claims for *Retrospection*. She admitted in the introduction that the history was subjective, colored by her personal background and the dictates of her class. She went one step further to confess that it was abridged history compelled by a time of crisis: the rampage of French armies where they chose to fight. "To an age of profound peace and literary quiet I should have considered such an abridgment as insulting: to our disturbed and busy days abridgments only can be useful. No one has leisure to read better books."[9] Her confessional modesty does not beguile; nor does it camouflage her special pleading on behalf of hit-or-miss knowledge. Without doubt she rationalized her technique, but as she saw *Retrospection,* it had a dualistic purpose. It provided a learning experience for young people and a provocative digest for adults who had squandered their earlier historical interests and wished to retrieve them.

She never resolved this focal purpose that contradicted itself. Shortly after the book appeared, its criticism fell into categories. The author stood pilloried for writing informal or anecdotal history, for being insufficiently serious, and for punctuating her narrative with jests and amusing materials. Such criticism forgot that she herself never intended to plumb "the deep current of grave history [that] rolls her full tide majestick, to that ocean where Time and all its wrecks at length are lost." Hers, she admitted, was only a "flashy Retrospect, a mere *jet d'eau*" that cooled "the hearts of an autumnal day with its light-dripping fall, and form[ed] a rainbow round."[10]

She intimated that she never sought comprehensive inclusion. To aim at such totality would have been hubristic, a profanation of God and his creation. With all the self-effacement she could muster, she acknowledged that "[t]his work . . . is at best a fragment: but what else shall we find in the most finished labours of man? The biography of one particular sovereign is a mere fragment, broken off from his own dynasty. The revolutions of a peculiar state form but a larger fragment: one piece, one page, torn from the great book, the general account of all mankind; which is itself at last no other than one species, one genius rather, among those uncounted millions that animate and people the earth, air, and water, of our terraqueous globe. That globe a fragment too, a trifling spot, of which the most exact and faithful narration would be found but a short chapter in the grand history, the universal volume of our Creator's works, containing the changes and chances of systems without number, rolling in illimitable space, at distances not to be judged of by humanity."[11]

Deeply religious, Hester Lynch Piozzi deemed *Retrospection* an act of piety. As part of the divine system, people, she implied, could see only in bits and pieces, that the sanctified "plurality of worlds" was reduced by human myopia to an incomplete fraction of one. She also believed in the pietistic function of history, one design "ultimately [pointing] out the inadequacy of a life without Christ, illustrating the pitiful failure of the hopes of the flesh and the pride of men."[12] Like Gibbon, whose knowledge she admired and whose skepticism she abhorred, she professed much in the spirit of a Christian "Croaker" that history showed no movement toward perfectibility; human nature, try as it might, could never conceal its grossness. History in her *jet d'eau* demonstrated a long chain not of endeavor but of absurdities—ugliness, ineptitude, and cruelty.

Certainly there are serious philosophical lapses and aesthetic misalliances in *Retrospection.* Perhaps large-scale anecdotal history written by a novice represents not merely a contradiction in terms but in the end becomes a self-defeating process. She chose her sources haphazardly, garnering whatever lay at hand. Sometimes she drew upon authorities who for all their one-time trendiness had degenerated into clichés or had been discredited. But she seemed not to know that source materials rose and fell in fashion, that they had a vulnerable lifespan.

The two volumes—each at one guinea—sold rapidly at first but not for long. As soon as the *Critical Review*—a verbal Jack Ketch—appeared in May 1801, *Retrospection* was doomed without the right of appeal. "To the learned, it must appear as a series of dreams by an old lady; and many of the mistakes are so gross, as not to escape the general reader. . . . Far less is it fit for the perusal of youth, of either sex; since the numerous errors, and the air of sufficiency with which they are written, might leave impressions difficult to be eradicated by the genuine page of history."[13] The *Critical Review* blamed Hester Lynch Piozzi for everything that violated the established pattern of objective historical research: for womanhood, for blunders of fact, for all typographical errors, and for failure to index. The blunt axes of the reviewers swung wide, striking from high to low and maiming all that lay between.

Like many other jousters who had dared less, she lost. *Retrospection* remained her last major effort, patronized as a "pretty piece of female patch-work."[14] All in all the critics decreed by fiat a grim end to a literary career.

2

Even after the manuscript of *Retrospection* had been turned over to Stockdale, the author had neither the leisure nor the tranquility to enjoy the relaxation and euphoria that sometimes follow accomplishment. Indeed she faced a different crisis, a legal problem fomented by the daughter she most respected and feared, one joined in by the three others. On 10 March 1800, she noted in *Thraliana*: "Miss Thrales make a new Attack on our Property, & menace to take away the Oxfordshire Estate—they see we dislike Law, & take unjust Advantages. I believe they are themselves afraid of losing all their own Substance to Gov^t so they fly upon us."[15] That is, Queeney's lawyers rightly claimed that Crowmarsh, "the Oxfordshire Estate," had been bequeathed to her by Henry Thrale and that her mother unknowingly had been pocketing income from Crowmarsh since 1781. The lawyers for both sides—perhaps because of Queeney's icy decorum or because of their own common sense—dropped the matter when they realized that litigation required yet another involved and expensive interpretation of the snarled Thrale will.

If the squabble adds little else to the history of Hester Lynch Piozzi, it does offer some insight into the mysterious association between mother and daughters. What brought them together and separated them were distrust played out by both sides under cover of mutual politesse as a form of aggression. The three eldest daughters never forgot that their unmotherly mother had virtually abandoned them to the care of an unknown governess when she married Gabriel Piozzi; they never forgot the bleakness of the Thrale ménage, where they were pushed into an undefined background by her sparkling chatter with great men, her flamboyant but precise dress, her innumerable pregnancies, or her disciplined arrogance.

The diminutive author felt exhausted by the task of writing *Retrospection*, of completing it on time despite the threat of Queeney's lawsuit. Yet she rarely allowed fatigue to show, or other weaknesses for that matter. In February 1801, Hannah More wrote to the Reverend Thomas Sedgwick Whalley: "Your lively friend, Mrs. Piozzi is our next neighbour [in Great Pulteney Street, Bath], and the expense of strength and spirits which two such quartos would suppose, have not one whit diminished her gaiety, animation, and cheerfulness."[16] In January 1803 a Welsh neighbor met her on the way to Wynnstay, the seat of Sir Watkin Williams Wynn in Denbighshire; startled by her joyous vitality, he saw her " 'skipping about like a kid, quite a figure of fun, in a tiger skin shawl, lined with scarlet, and only five colours upon her head-dress—on the top of a flaxen wig a bandeau of blue velvet, a bit of tiger ribbon, a white beaver hat and plume of black feathers—as gay as a lark.' "[17]

Instinctively she knew how to live for the day, her good humor often spilling forth spontaneously. Yet for long periods she thought of herself as a handwringer. Her husband's vulnerability to gout, which once amused her as a proper Englishman's ailment, had become recurrent and increasingly debilitating. Each year from 1798 to 1801, he had suffered a relapse. By 1803 and probably for the remainder of his life, he was crippled, mobile for the most part only "in a Bath rolling Chair."[18] At the end of 1804 Mrs. Piozzi again detailed for Queeney her husband's torment: "Mr. Piozzi has but just done Shrieking, and 'tis hoarseness, not happiness makes him leave off *now*. A Succession of 3 frightful Abcesses in 3 different Parts of his Feet, have set Opiates and Pacifiers all at Defiance; and kept him nine Days without our daring to move him, or change his linen or his Bed. Two Men, Two Women and myself did however accomplish it on the 10th Morning when he was kept with the utmost Difficulty by dint of Wine and Cordials, from bursting in our Arms with Rage and Pain united."[19] She had come a long way from being the woman who in 1781 adhered to the convention that the "Sisterhood" lacked emotional rigor to attend funerals, even of husbands or of beloved sons. But now, some twenty years later, she had accepted the horror of Gabriel Piozzi's sickroom, with its stench and the screams of a man who found temporary quiet in "strong Madeira" and in hysterical delirium—the mind's reluctance to live with pain.

Her grief over the critical bashing of *Retrospection*, the tawdry if courteous struggles with her daughters, the unspoken realization that her husband was slipping toward death—often more drunk than sober—all this real sorrow was moderated in her letters by restraint that obviated public lamentation. Although they respected her anxiety, the recipients of her letters wanted less a display of personal problems than a decorous but witty stage for the analysis of the world's affairs and of events that affected British well-being.

The rules established by this epistolary "coterie" were never defined, but Mrs. Piozzi knew and obeyed them instinctively. The "coterie"—the term and usage were hers—consisted for the most part of friends who shared similar backgrounds, temperaments, political philosophies, and even class identities. In their letters they were undemonstrative but companionable, united culturally in an ethic that matched effusiveness with vulgarity. Any differences among them faded into the uniqueness of the group, a band of the elect who only rarely took the side of dissent. No subject needed to be spelled out; a debate could begin *in medias res*. A hint could be understood; a discreet blank mentally filled in but usually left unsaid.

The events between 1799 and 1804, the year of Napoleon's coronation, went beyond faction or party loyalty, even adherence to class values. Rather they were of sufficient importance to justify lengthy if allusive discussion because they tested the structure of Great Britain and its moral underpinnings. Of importance were the questions of Britain's involvement in the slave trade purportedly necessary in a trade war with France and in the creation of a colonial empire; of union with Ireland; or of the peace established at Amiens and its dissolution; of the French empire that emerged fully blown in 1804. Each of these problems evaded facile answers and Mrs. Piozzi. Her opinions not cast in granite, she altered them with time and circumstance. Sometimes she tried to anticipate Pitt or his successor Henry Addington on an executive problem but failed; or she turned away from them both as time-servers and relied instead on prophecy or arcane biblical statement.

Yet, on the whole, she remained a realist, usually not denying what she saw and heard and felt. All about her in North Wales were the poor cottagers in the unnatural spring of 1799. "No grass grows at all, Sharp cutting Frosts and steady Continuance of Cold operates so that no Duck will sit—no Bird will sing. The poor farmers Horses drop down dead in the Carts, unable to drag Weight for want of Food—Cattle perish, & Sheep run from their Lambs—100 Ewes perished in the Neighborhood of Abergelley from the Severity of this unparallel'd Season—What will become of us? Mr Pitt cares not—he has a Majority in ye House—indeed in ye Nation, for carrying on ye War." She did not blink away the possibility that "a Victory abroad" spelled starvation "at Home. Well! I am of King David's Mind: any thing rather than flee before our Enemies—let us as he says fall into the Hands of God, not into the Hands of Men—but I really expect a Famine."[20]

The poor continued as a ubiquitous presence, the victims of grain scarcity and the inflated prices of corn factors. Their suffering cried out for alleviation and parliamentary action. Mrs. Piozzi was not sure that legislative action would answer their needs, but she did what she could to help her tenants, the sine qua non of the bountiful mistress of Brynbella. On the Piozzis' return from Bath close to 10 March 1800, she confessed obliquely that personalized hands-on charity eased the guilt of the rich: "we have ye Happiness of having fed 30 poor Families this Winter, which without us *must have perished*. The Oatmeal is 2 Guineas o' Hobbet—every thing else in proportion: Some poor people in Caernarvonshire have subsisted only on Grains & Buttermilk. Tremendous Times!! The Soup Establishment however is a Good one, & rich ffolks *do* appear to take no small portion to keep their Cottagers from starving."[21] Her birthday also allowed her to preside as a "Benefactress" of the poor. On 27 January 1804 the day was "kept very chearfully . . . & all the little Children of the Village & Cottages in our

Parish to the amount of 60 as I remember, came & eat Plumb Pudden, 40 *very good* Girls & Boys, had 6ᵈ each for singing & saying their Catechism so well . . . all very comfortable, very happy indeed."²²

Repugnant to many Britons—but certainly not to the shipping magnates of Bristol and Liverpool—was the slave trade. Early efforts to abolish that trade which began in the House of Commons in 1788, drowned in vehement debate. On 12 May 1789, William Wilberforce, for example, reintroduced the problem of the slave trade in a long parliamentary speech. For more than three hours he spoke with the sanction of strange political allies, Fox and Pitt. Nevertheless, the cause itself came to nothing under repeated attacks of colonial planters and ship owners engaged in the actual transport of slaves. Oratorically they argued that abolition concealed the potential ruin of Britain and her military machine. With few alternatives, the abolitionists schemed for time. In effect, those who favored the slave trade and its expansion defeated Wilberforce and his mismatched supporters. "From 1792 to 1800 the cause of Abolition had lost ground. From 1800 to 1804 it had seemed to slumber. Of that retrocession the main cause had been the ferment of Revolutionary France, and the fears that ensued in England."²³

Hester Lynch Piozzi morally abetted abolitionist activity in Britain although with less intensity than did the "Saints," those members of the evangelical Clapham sect who saw the slave trade as a desecration of God's creatures. In June 1788, she by implication sneered at unnamed William Wilberforce who—she charged—abandoned the fight for abolition because he had been "made ill by eating Strawberries or even Turtle."²⁴ By 19 December 1794, she overtly described to Queeney her pleasure that the slaves "at last *are* liberated" in the French colonies. Yet she chafed that such "philanthropy" originated in an edict of the revolutionary Convention rather than in a law passed at the bar of the House of Commons.²⁵

Her anxiety intensified when she assumed that the blacks might translate their little-understood freedom into violence and revenge. Her worry was perhaps augmented by an "Extract of a letter from Martinico, Oct. 14," published in the *St. James's Chronicle* (13–16 December 1794). "A sad destiny has attended all the French aristocrats, men and women, with many infants, too horrid to relate; the whole, to the number of five hundred, with their hands tied behind them were placed, in a ditch dug out for the express purpose; were fired upon by an equal number, and immediately after the discharge of musquetry, the ditch was filled up. . . . The French seem determined to emancipate their slaves, and with pain I observe that system gains ground."

Her distress over the unpredictable behavior of freed slaves yielded quickly to a consistent proabolitionist position. In *British Synonymy* she defined the verb "to manumit," illustrating it with a defense of the "Saints" and their religious argument on behalf of emancipation. To manumit "implies the power of doing an act with our own hands, and must shortly become useless; for who can Manumit when servitude shall be no more? When the human soul however is Set Free from all corporeal temptations, by the dissolution of that body which contains it, how will theirs rejoice that have from pure motives, from honest and general principles contributed towards Emancipating the Blacks, and Delivering them from Slavery!"[26]

When Addington's government succeeded Pitt's in 1801, the abolitionists expediently postponed their fight. The king opposed an end to Britain's investment in the slave trade. The Addington ministry on this issue—as well as several other members of parliament—upheld the strong objections of George III. As a monarchist, Hester Lynch Piozzi in 1801 kept silent on the subject. Even two years earlier, she had suggested (after reading Mungo Park's *Travels in Africa*) a qualified, if sophistical, rationale for Britain's slave trade. About June 1799 she wrote to a friend in Beaumaris, admitting that she had picked up nothing new from Park's book except a single idea. He had, she acknowledged, "cured me of my Uneasiness for those African Slaves that arrive *safe* at our Sugar Islands. They are really in a State of Preferment to the situation awaiting them at home, and from which they can for ought I see scarcely escape. The Ships they are conveyed in to the other Hemisphere are horrible Dungeons indeed; I hope some Method will be found to get them over with less Hazard and more Ease to themselves."[27] At about the same time—1799 or 1800—she had written about the antislavery forces to which all the world now wished success over "the interest of private [mercantile] individuals."[28]

What she left unstated were certain incontrovertible statistics: that by the end of the eighteenth century British merchants had cornered the slave trade market and that half the slaves reaching the Americas were transported chained to one another in British ships. She deplored the immorality of the slave trade, siding for the most part with conservative abolitionists. She would, however, curtail only with reluctance British commerce during the war with France. If the slave trade continued a powerful economic weapon against the enemy, then she would wait for a time of "lasting peace" to denounce such trade.[29]

Essentially hers was a vague humanitarian objection to the slave trade. What she possessed in compensation was a religious conviction that it trampled upon God's design of the human body and spirit.

3

The controversy over the profitable slave trade raised scruples among a literate British minority. But most people, tired of the war and food shortages, gave little thought to a problem in conveniently abstract morality. Moreover, few individuals ever saw a slave ship or the conditions under which slaves were carried as cargo from Africa to British colonies in the Americas. Certain radical corresponding societies—at least so labeled in the eighteenth century—pointed to the traffic as a social evil created by the rich for the benefit of the rich. But as a political issue with economic overtones, it remained remote from the daily struggle of most English lives.

More pressing to the British, especially to those with property and voting rights, was the existence of a chaotic and rebellious Ireland which since 1798 constituted an ever-present menace to the mother country. Readers of the English press understood that no peace existed for them as long as the Irish lived in turmoil. For example, on 12 March of that year, the police raided a meeting of the Leinster directory of United Irishmen at Oliver Bond's house in Dublin and arrested twelve leaders. On 21–23 May at Maidstone in Kent, Arthur O'Connor and the Reverend James Quigley, both of them members of the outlawed United Irishmen, were hastily tried and found guilty. (Quigley, apparently the ringleader, was hanged on 7 June.) As a reaction to these two events, a United Irish rebellion began at Leinster. Fighting and insurrectionary activity continued through the last week in May so that by the thirtieth the town of Wexford was occupied by the insurgents, who held it until 21 June when they were defeated at Vinegar Hill, near Enniscorthy.

The military failures of the United Irishmen at New Ross, county Wexford, at Ulster (6–7 June), and at Ballynahinch, county Down (13 June), prompted them to seek foreign help. On 22 August 1798, as an instance, about one thousand French troops under General Jean Humbert landed at Kilcumin, near Killala. After holding out for about two weeks, Humbert capitulated to Cornwallis at Ballinamuck. In less than a month a small French squadron led by James Napper Tandy—almost ridiculous as a fighting unit—made a brief landing on Rutland Island. This "invasion" also effected nothing. That the Irish rebellions failed, that executions by the English were numerous, that all too many bridges were decorated with impaled Irish heads, exacerbated the sectarian bitterness of 1798. The acrimony between both sides was real enough. It convinced the ministry, and perhaps Pitt first of all, that the Dublin parliament of wealthy Protestant landowners no longer represented the whole of the Irish nation. Ever pragmatic, Pitt sought to convince enough Irish M.P.s that the Dublin parliament worked contrary to their interests, since it symbolized a divided country that would in all likelihood further agrarian looting and burning. Expanding property values and full rent rolls would elude the landowners who, given the political situation, faced only economic depression.

Two men, the elderly English Marquess Cornwallis and the young Irish Viscount Castlereagh, had the task of proving to the Dublin parliament that it was self-destructive, running counter to the values of the national Church of Ireland and the interests of the landed gentry. Yet in January 1799 the first bill of union failed to pass in Dublin; opposition to it grew powerful among country members who spoke for Protestant landlordism and for those Dublin "professional classes [who] feared for their livelihoods if the city lost the legal and administrative benefits accorded to a European parliamentary city."[30]

The government in Westminster set about to override the veto, "partly by propaganda and persuasion, partly by trying to gratify the crudely personal objectives of many peers and M.P.s."[31] By such methods it secured a majority in both houses of the Irish parliament on 1 August 1800. The British Act of Union, passed on 2 July, had led the way. Union became a fact on 1 January 1801. About one hundred Irish members of the Commons went to Westminster. With the maneuvering of Castlereagh, Irish textile manufacture received twenty years of modest protection before full trade between the countries was achieved. The Churches of Ireland and England were joined, strengthening the national religion in numbers.

Despite minimal benefits handed out to individuals and institutions, Irish union had only a nominal reality. It "was a constitutional job carried for British convenience, bought with British determination and mostly British cash. It did nothing to solve the underlying tensions and contradictions of Irish society."[32] Left unresolved was the single question that alone could have promised a peaceful Ireland—the matter of Catholic emancipation.

In 1799, Hester Lynch Piozzi closely followed the parliamentary debate over union with Ireland. When parliament convened in January, the government's support of union was attacked with such vehemence that the motion was tabled for the rest of the session. This constituted a near turning point in her political loyalties. She for the moment abandoned Pitt and sided with antiministerial Tory forces led by Henry Addington as speaker of the House of Commons.

In this same year she considered the Irish (especially the rebels) as savages and fools. She saw no contradiction in this view; more to the point, she saw no justice in their cause or in their insurrectionary conspiracies. In 1799 they were potentially inept traitors, dupes of the French, according to the *True Briton* of 9 March 1799 as well as the *London Chronicle* of 14–16 March, and justifiably the butts of jest. One such joke was told to her by the usually gentle Leonard Chappelow: "3 English Gentlemen in the inside of the coach invite the [Irish] fool to take the 4th Seat.—National pride obliges him to *keep,* as he thinks in a superior place.—Tis dreadfully cold—and snows.—He does not care for that. He will not be happy—he tumbled from the roof of the coach—which Left Him behind—he Lost his road—a direction post told him the way to London—I'll receive no direction—he turned back—and went to the Devil—allez vous en—" (Ry. 562.58).

Hester Lynch Piozzi replied seriously (less with an eye on Ireland than on France) to Chappelow's letter and his anti-Gaelic joke. "As to the Dispute concerning Ireland it enrages me— —If by letting them Alone and saying *Allez vous en* we should not degrade our*self* as a Nation, and give France an Advantage over us, I should not care how long it was before we *intreated* Paddy to take a warm front Seat in Britannia's State Coach, but now it seems necessary almost to *force* the Union they pretend to despise: and make them happy tho' we *break their Hearts* as 'Squire Western says in Tom Jones."[33]

As a "Croaker," she simply did not perceive the depth of the Catholic commitment to emancipation; but she suspected that the bill of Union, such as the one pushed forward by Pitt in 1800, would not placate the United Irishmen or even those conservative "Hibernians" who frowned upon antiestablishment activity. On the contrary, as early as mid-February 1801, she anticipated "fierce Deeds in Ireland." Actually, there were only minor skirmishes during this winter. The "fierce Deeds" did not erupt until the summer of 1803 with the uprising led by the Protestant Robert Emmet. On 28 July *The Times* reported "that an extraordinary Riot had taken place in [Dublin] on Saturday night [23 July], in which Lord Kilwarden, the Chief Justice of the King's Bench, lost his life. It is stated, that his Lordship was in his carriage, accompanied by his nephew (the Reverend Richard Wolfe) and two daughters, when he was attacked by the assassins. His nephew . . . shared his fate; but the young Ladies escaped."

Once again the insurrection flourished, seemingly without cause or direction. The rebels were defeated by the king's troops; Emmet and nineteen other prisoners who had participated in the Dublin conspiracy were tried in August and September. Eighteen, including Emmet, were executed.[34] Between 1798 and 1803, the English never mitigated their policy of dealing with Irish conspirators except to step up the frequency of rebel court martials. If blame were to be fixed for the Emmet uprising, the English were prepared to point to France as the instigator. As *The Times* on 29 July speculated: "There can be no doubt, from all the circumstances of this rebellion, that it was produced by the influence of the enemy. Nor do we think it would be carrying conjecture too far, to suppose, that the six French ships which lately took their station in the outward water of Brest Harbour, were designed, if an opportunity could be obtained, to co-operate with the Irish rebels." This inference did not originate with *The Times*; on the contrary, it had become a comfortable English cliché since 1798 that freed the country of ministerial harshness or of an unwillingess to negotiate the differences that sparked hostilities.

In Hester Lynch Piozzi's mind no distinction existed between French infamy and Irish copycat treachery, whatever the year. She had tagged France "our Enemy"—implacable and ruthless, dedicated to provoking war and insurrection among the Irish rebels. Her condemnation of France went far beyond any one political state. France was the villain, whether a democratic, mob-driven terror or a predynastic country headed by a First Consul elected for life and selfcrowned as emperor on 2 December 1804.

4

England and France, with allies or without, had fought each other for almost a decade. Pitt hankered for peace although two serious peace initiatives had already failed. The first in 1795–96 could not pacify Austrian and French belligerence. The second embassy, headed by Lord Malmesbury, seemed to make tentative progress despite the fact that both sides wrangled over disputed territory. The *coup d'état* of 18 Fructidor reasserted temporarily Jacobin dominance in the Directory and Malmesbury left with an ultimatum for England. Peace, he reported to Pitt, had become an impossibility unless Britain relinquished all her conquests while acknowledging those of France.[35]

England suffered in the financial war with France. The British national debt increased from four and one half million in 1793 to forty-four million pounds in 1797. Pitt, without alternative, raised taxes with paradoxically ruthless rationality. In 1797 he trebled the "assessed taxes" on luxuries, like servants and carriages. He proposed an income tax in his 1798 budget address and collection began in 1799. The British accepted the tax, assuming with patriotic stoicism that it was a wartime measure only. When Pitt was succeeded by Addington, the latter's peace feelers in 1801–2 were bolstered by a wishful palliative that if peace came the income tax would vanish.

On 1 October 1801, Great Britain and France signed "Preliminaries of Peace." *The Times* on 10 October determined to give the "Preliminaries" a luminous halo, stressing commercial advantages that would accrue to England like the retention of Ceylon in the Indian Ocean and of *"St Trinidada"* in the West Indies; the neutrality of the Cape of Good Hope as a free port. While *The Times* editorialized positively, more mercantile interests expected more aggressive concessions than the "Preliminaries" granted. The continent remained closed to trade, as in the past, by protective tariffs as difficult to bear as the financing of the war. Lord Fitzwilliam in parliament fulminated against the "Preliminaries" and the treaty itself as a deception. Similarly, George Canning derided both for "gross faults and omissions . . . weakness and baseness, and shuffling and stupidity."[36]

Addington suffered the abuse because he understood British public opinion. Almost any peace proposal, however defective, promised relief to a people exhausted by war, overtaxed, and caught in an inflationary spiral with no apparent end in sight. The prime minister listened to the advocates of peace even though he knew that the peace of Amiens (27 March 1802) was abortive. While he could not predict its staying power, he nonetheless built up the militia by 75,000 occasional troops, maintained sufficient military forces in the West Indies in order to retake it an opportune time the colonies already ceded by treaty.

HLP was a reluctant peacemonger in October 1801. But she seemed ready to accept the "Preliminaries" with the same wariness implied by *The Times*. She looked upon them as an experiment worth the risk. Indeed, as we have seen, she found the war hard on her poor cottagers and ironically on the neighboring gentry who needed the financial respite a peace offered. In a letter to Penelope Pennington on 9 October 1801, she put a happy face on the "Preliminaries." As a person who had once protested too much, she wrote: "The Terms are certainly in no sense disgraceful—and since we have been saying so repeatedly 'Let us heal our own Wounds, limit our own Expences, and care no longer for Allies who 'tis sure care not for us.'" Never above special pleading, she continued: "I pronounce our Ministers fully justified to *this* Country for quitting their post and leaving every *other* Country to the Fate they would none of them resist." She emphasized that "the Gold and Silver and Rubies and Rice from Ceylon, sweetened by sugar from Trinidad will keep Great Britain in perfect good humour. . . . Let us light up our Windows and be merry."

Her tenuous euphoria did not, however, last out even the letter, which ended in a statement of cynical wonder. "Little did I dream seven Years ago of seeing Peace proclaimed between Great Britain and the *Consular* State of Europe—Little could I *ever* have dreamed that I should see Venice annihilated, Genoa forgotten; Piedmont's Alpine Barrier insufficient to keep out Invasion even in the Depth of Winter—And old Rome divided against herself—dropping into her Enemies' Mouth almost with Invitation."[37]

The Peace of Amiens had been signed in early spring 1802. Although many conservatives thought it a short-term expedient, the peace itself won immediately popular support. The Foxites rejoiced; the government's peace policy was approved in the Commons by a vote of 276 to 20. On 1 June England celebrated "a General Thanksgiving for the return of Peace with a service at Westminster Abbey and at St. Margaret's."[38]

By early May 1803, her "quiet" changed to vigorous flag waving. Tension between England and France had become so strained that Lord Whitworth, Britain's ambassador to France, had been recalled and on the seventh the *Courier* reported that André Andreossi, his French counterpart, would return to Paris. By the tenth the same newspaper conceded reluctantly that the peace could not be preserved, that war would be renewed, as it was to be on 16 May.

While writing to the Reverend Leonard Chappelow on 7 July 1803, she expressed relief that the fragile peace of Amiens was no more. "We shall now have a *lasting* peace, when Peace is again made. [She could not anticipate the Hundred Days or the fact that she would wait more than a decade for her '*lasting* Peace.'] France will convince herself that Britain possesses an unyielding Spirit—and will torment her no more if upon this Occasion she proves true to her own Honour." To establish the validity of her epistolary rhetoric, she accepted the burden of the "new" taxes introduced by the second Pitt ministry in June 1803: those "offensive" levies on *West India* produce and on income or property "for the necessary defence of our country" (*The Times*, 29 June). She made still another contribution more personal and so more significant than that of paying taxes. She wrote once more for the public, this time a broadside entitled *Old England to her Daughters*. An anonymous publication, it was signed "Poor Old England" and was "Printed for R. Faulder, New Bond Street [by J. Brettell, Printer]—Price 1d. or 9d. per Dozen." Consisting of two columns, it probably appeared in bookshops about June 1803.[39]

Her attitude toward these new taxes—"offensive" enactments, she called them—was one of resignation. Perhaps like the editors of *The Times* on 28 June, she believed that "A Tax upon Income is evidently the fairest of all possible imposts, since a man is thus called upon to pay only a moderate proportion out of what he *actually receives*." All these innovative sources of revenue—to which by early autumn were added annual duties on inhabited houses and on windows, on male servants, on carriages, on horses used for recreation, on house dogs, on armorial bearings—all these levies were created to sustain a victorious military establishment.[40]

Hester Lynch Piozzi never questioned the "necessary defence of Britain" against Bonaparte's aggression. For that reason she had chided a politely muttering Chappelow as early as 7 July 1803 with what she called a rule and an example. "I hope we shall all of us pay our taxes chearfully, and give a great Example to Europe of one Nation not contented to sell her Sons for Slaves to Buonaparte. . . . Dear Mr. Piozzi can neither fight nor fly, but he must make his Purse his Substitute; and no Man is more loyally attached to the Throne and Government of England—Don't you remember how he entered his Income higher than there was any need to do, once before? and would not appeal when advised to [do] it."[41]

In the course of fourteen months Addington's peace proved no more popular than Pitt's war. But the no-nonsense Addington stood firm against verbal assault. He used his time to escalate Britain's military preparedness: early in 1803 it was good enough for the prime minister to declare war on France, purportedly surprising Bonaparte, who himself eagerly awaited the renewal of hostilities after he had paved the way for new political splendor as emperor and founder of a dynasty.[42]

5

In 1804 HLP concerned herself with two details of French life. Late in the preceding year English newspapers began to report rumors of an invasion of Britain led by Bonaparte, that he was in consultation about the means of effecting his menaces against England.[43]

She was never quite sure when the threat no longer had reality. In a letter to "Philosopher" Lloyd, dated 14 June 1804, she jokingly dismissed the French as invaders: "I feel half ashamed to intrude on your agreeable Pursuits, with my Letter; But you live in the Country enough to know and feel one's Avidity for News concerning the great Mart of Intelligence—London: when I no longer expect to hear Talk of Impossible Descents of *French Imperialists*. They will perhaps be quieter now under an hereditary Sovereign; who having made himself a permanent Interest in the Country he has acquired—I will be less disposed to put his Subjects upon Impracticable Schemes, and poyson them for not succeeding."[44] But a month later, writing to Lady Williams of Bodelwyddan, she reversed herself: she believed that Bonaparte had to make good on his promise to the French, and particularly to his army—that theirs was the "long-promised right to the Plunder of London."[45]

What surprised Hester Lynch Piozzi most in 1804 was the number of anti-Bonaparte conspiracies that sprang up and the ruthlessness with which Joseph Fouché, the minister of police, discovered and suppressed them: the royalist plot planned by the young Chouan Georges Cadoudal, Pichegru, and Moreau in late February; the kidnapping of the duc d'Enghien from neutral territory, his mock trial, and his execution.[46] Only one other alleged conspiracy delighted her. On 18 June 1804, she wrote to Chappelow, reworking an editorial surmise of *The Times* on 13 June 1804: "It seems to be a principle with the French Emperor to remove, by one way or other, all his former Revolutionary friends. The Republican spirit is certainly not suited to a man who has just dissolved a Republic. Bonaparte, therefore, has . . . very consistently ordered Carnot, Sieyes, Garat, Coulon, Gregoire, and Lanjaunais to reside on their respective estates in the country until further orders; which will probably remove them altogether out of the country."

She singled out from this list just two names—Carnot and Garat—to make a silent plea for the possibility of poetic justice. She gloated in her letter: "You ask me what I think of The French. . . . Carnot. . . . who proposed tanning Human Hides,—and Garat—who carried the sentence of Death to Louis seize, both sent into banishment by the new Emperor."

She for the most part ignored the titles bestowed upon or seized by Bonaparte, whether that of General, First Consul, Consul for Life. The title of Emperor she applied ironically, embellished by the adjective "new." Just as consistently she referred to him as the Tyrant or the Despot. She saw 1804 as a year which challenged all faith and rational belief, all secular right and wrong.

"*What* would these Essayists have said had they seen the French decapitate a blameless King, abolish all Religion—make Barracks of their Palaces, and Brothels of their Churches;—set up 5 distinct Constitutions in 5 Years; drive head long into every *possible*—almost every *impossible* Impiety; worshipping A Strumpet under the Name of The Goddess of Reason without Restraint, Abolishing the Sabbath at home, and making successful War against a whole Continent abroad?

"What would they have said? And what would they have predicted from such Sights?

"Scarcely *could* they have <inferred> the exaltation of a petty Chieftain from Corsica into the Seat of absolute Sway over all France, and his Coronation as their Emperor."[47]

Notes

1. 15:243.
2. *Thraliana* 2:992-93.
3. *Ibid.*, 2:984.
4. *Piozzi Letters* 2:317 n. 2.
5. A. Hayward, *Autobiography / Letters and Literary Remains / of Mrs. Piozzi (Thrale)*, 2 vols., 2d ed. (London: Longman, Green, Longman, and Roberts, 1861), 1:345-46.
6. *Thraliana* 2:966.
7. Hester Lynch Piozzi to Hester Maria Thrale, 7 April 1796 (Bowood Collection); James L. Clifford, *Hester Lynch Piozzi (Mrs. Thrale)*, 2d ed. with a new introduction by Margaret Anne Doody (Oxford: Clarendon Press, 1987), pp. 393-94.
8. Bowood Collection; quoted in part by Clifford, p. 394.
9. *Retrospection* 1:vii.
10. *Ibid.*, 1:viii.
11. *Ibid.*, 1:ix.
12. Doody, p. xliii.
13. *Critical Review* 32 (1801):28.
14. See *GM*, pt. 2 (1801):603; Mrs. Piozzi's retort to the *Critical Review*. Another example of the antifeminist attack may be found in the *European Magazine* 39 (January-June 1801): 188-93, 271-76, especially p. 188.
15. *Thraliana* 2:1003 and n. 4.
16. The Reverend Hill Wickham, ed. *Journals and Correspondence of Thomas [Sedgwick] Whalley, D.D.*, 2 vols. (London: Richard Bentley, 1863), 2:188.
17. Hayward 1:346-47.
18. Clifford, p. 408.
19. Hester Lynch Piozzi to Hester Maria Thrale [31 December 1804] (Bowood Collection), in *Piozzi Letters* 3:484.
20. *Thraliana* 2:996-97.
21. *Ibid.*, 2:1002.
22. *Ibid.*, 2:1048.
23. Earl Stanhope, *Life of the Right Honourable William Pitt*, 4 vols., 3d ed. (London: John Murray, 1867), 2:34-35, 4:202.
24. *Piozzi Letters* 1:264 and n. 10. Hester Lynch Piozzi was wrong about Wilberforce's presumed gourmet indulgences. He was dangerously ill in the winter and spring of 1788.
25. *Piozzi Letters* 2:218.
26. *British Synonymy; or, An Attempt at Regulating the Choice of Words in Familiar Conversation*, 2 vols. (London: G. G. and J. Robinson, 1794), 1:193.
27. Hester Lynch Piozzi to Anne Poole [ca. June 1799] (Yale University Library), in *Piozzi Letters* 3:106.

28. *Retrospection* 2:483.

29. For the gradual abolition of the the British slave trade after 1806, see Hester Lynch Piozzi to the Reverend John Roberts [November–December 1813] (Princeton University Library); to John Williams II [ca. 10 August 1814] (Ry. 6 [1813–21]). See also *Slavery and British Society, 1776–1846*, ed. James Walvin (Baton Rouge: Louisiana State University Press, 1982), pp. 49–68.

30. Eric J. Evans, *The Forging of the Modern State / Early Industrial Britain 1783–1870* (London and New York: Longman, 1983), pp. 96–98; *A New History of Ireland*, ed. T. W. Moody, F. X. Martin, F. J. Byrne, 9 vols. (Oxford: Clarendon Press, 1982), 8:290–91.

31. *The Course of Irish History*, ed. T. W. Moody and F. X. Martin (Cork: Mercier Press, 1967), p. 247.

32. Evans, p. 98.

33. Hester Lynch Piozzi to the Reverend Leonard Chappelow [15 February 1799] (Ry. 561.161); see *Piozzi Letters* 3:66.

34. Stanhope 4:71–75; *GM* 73, pt. 2 (1803); 686–87; also Hester Lynch Piozzi to the Reverend Leonard Chappelow, 30 July 1803, in *Piozzi Letters* 3:66.

35. Evans, p. 79.

36. *Cambridge Modern History (Napoleon)*, ed. A. W. Ward, G. W. Prothero, Stanley Leathes, 13 vols. (Cambridge: University Press, 1902–11), 9:76; J. Holland Rose, *William Pitt and the Great War* (London: G. Bell, 1911), p. 471.

37. See also Hester Lynch Piozzi to the Reverend Leonard Chappelow, 17 September 1801 (Ry. 561.114); *Piozzi Letters* 3:324.

38. *Courier*, 2 June 1802.

39. The manuscript of *Old England to her Daughters* (Ry. 629.19) is at the John Rylands Library of the University of Manchester.

40. See the "Abstract" from the Assessed Tax Act in the *Morning Chronicle*, 20 October 1803.

41. See Hester Lynch Piozzi to the Reverend Leonard Chappelow, 17 November 1803 (Ry. 561.126), in *Piozzi Letters* 3:436.

42. David G. Chandler, *The Campaigns of Napoleon* (London: Weidenfeld and Nicolson, 1966), p. 304.

43. *Morning Chronicle*, 1 and 3 November, 26 December 1803, and 2 January 1804; Hester Lynch Piozzi to the Reverend Robert Gray, 9 January 1804 (Hayward 2:262); to the Reverend Leonard Chappelow, 25 January 1804 (Ry. 561.129); to Lady Williams, 20 February 1804 (Ry. 2 [1802–6]).

44. National Library of Wales, MS 12421 D. 56.

45. Hester Lynch Piozzi to Lady Williams, 14 July 1804 (Ry. 2 [1802–1806]).

46. For the Cadoudal plot, see Hester Lynch Piozzi to the Reverend John Roberts, 16 March 1804 (Princeton University Press). See also *The Times*, 21 March 1804. For the trial of the duc d'Enghien, see Hester Lynch Piozzi to Lady Williams, 12 April 1804 (Ry. 2 [1802–6]) and to Penelope Sophia Pennington, 16 April 1804 (Princeton University Library).

47. Princeton University Library: a random reflection dated simply "1804."

Short Titles for Major Manuscript Repositories

Barrett — The Barrett Collection of Burney Papers, British Library, London, 43 vols., Egerton [Eg.] 3690–3708

Berg — The Henry W. and Albert A. Berg Collection, New York Public Library, New York City

Bodleian — Bodleian Library, Oxford University

Bowood Collection — The Bowood Collection of Thrale-Piozzi letters in the possession of the marquis of Lansdowne, Bowood House, near Calne, Wilts.

Brit. Mus. Add. MSS — British Museum [now British Library] Additional Manuscripts

C.R.O. — County Record Office[s], England, Wales, and Ireland

Harvard University Library — Houghton Library at Harvard University

Historical Society of Pennsylvania — Historical Society of Pennsylvania, Philadelphia

Huntington Library — Henry E. Huntington Library, San Marino, California

Hyde Collection — The Donald and Mary Hyde Collection at Four Oaks Farm, Somerville, New Jersey; and at the Houghton Library, Harvard University

N.L.W. — National Library of Wales, Aberystwyth

N.P.G.	The National Portrait Gallery, Trafalgar Square, London
Osborn Collection	James Marshall and Marie-Louise Osborn Collection at the Beinecke Rare Book and Manuscript Library, Yale University
Peyraud Collection	The Paula F. Peyraud Collection of Piozzi letters and marginalia, Chappaqua, New York
Pforzheimer Library	The Carl H. Pforzheimer Library, New York City
The Pierpont Morgan Library	The Pierpont Morgan Library, New York City
Princeton University Library	Firestone Library at Princeton University
P.R.O.	Public Record Office, Chancery Lane, London
Ry.	The John Rylands University Library of Manchester, England
Victoria and Albert	Victoria and Albert Museum Library, London
Yale University Library	The Beinecke Rare Book and Manuscript Collection at Yale University

Locations of miscellaneous collections of Piozzi manuscripts not listed above are identified at the foot of each relevant letter under *"Text."*

Short Titles for Hester Lynch Piozzi's Manuscripts and Books

"Account Books" "[Gabriel Piozzi's] Accounts, 1784–1792," Drummond's Bank, Charing Cross, London.

Anecdotes *Anecdotes of the Late Samuel Johnson, LL.D., During the Last Twenty Years of His Life.* London: Printed for T. Cadell, 1786.

"Appeal" "Mrs. Piozzi's Appeal against the *Critical Reviewers*," *Gentleman's Magazine* 71, pt. 2 (July 1801): 602–3.

British Synonymy *British Synonymy; or, An Attempt at Regulating the Choice of Words in Familiar Conversation.* 2 vols. London: Printed for G. G. and J. Robinson, 1794.

"Children's Book" For "The Children's Book or rather Family Book" from 17 September 1766 to the end of 1778 (Hyde Collection), see Mary Hyde, *The Thrales of Streatham Park.* Cambridge and London: Harvard University Press, 1977.

"Commonplace Book" "The New Commonplace Book." Random entries made by HLP after the completion of *Thraliana*, the first entry written at Brynbella in 1809 and the last in 1820 at Penzance (Hyde Collection).

Florence Miscellany *Florence Miscellany.* Florence: Printed for G. Cam, Printer to His Royal Highness. With Permission, 1785. Hester Lynch Piozzi contributed the preface and nine poems.

French Journals *The French Journals of Mrs. Thrale and Doctor Johnson.* Edited by Moses Tyson and Henry Guppy. Manchester: Manchester University

	Press, 1932. Hester Lynch Thrale's *French Journal* (1775) includes pp. 69–166; Hester Lynch Piozzi's *French Journey* (1784), pp. 191–213; Samuel Johnson's *French Journal* (1775), pp. 169–88.
"Harvard Piozziana"	"Poems and Little Characters, Anecdotes &c. Introductory to the Poems." 5 MS vols., 1810–14, for John Salusbury Piozzi Salusbury. Harvard University Library, MS Eng. 1280.
"Italian and German Journals"	"Italian and German Journals, from 5 September 1784 to March 1787," 2 MS notebooks (Ry. 618).
"Journey Book"	"Journey through the North of England and Part of Scotland, Wales, &c." 1789 (Ry. 623).
Letters	*Letters to and from the Late Samuel Johnson, LL.D.* 2 vols. London: Printed for A. Strahan and T. Cadell, 1788.
"Lyford Redivivus"	"Lyford Redivivus or A Grandame's Garrulity." [Signed by] "An Old Woman" [1809–15] (Hyde Collection).
"Memoirs"	Autobiographical Essays: For Sir James Fellowes, December 1815. Thirty-six MS pages bound into Johnson's *Letters*. Princeton University Library, for William Augustus Conway, May 1819. Eleven MS pages bound into *Observations*. Hyde Collection. See also Mrs. Piozzi to the Proprietors of the *Monthly Mirror*, 17 June 1798. Huntington Library, MSS 20831, and vol. 2, *The Piozzi Letters*.
"Memorial"	"Memorial of H. L. Piozzi against John Cator Esq." [autumn 1792]. John Rylands Library, MS Ry. 611, and Appendix, vol. 2, *The Piozzi Letters*.
Merritt	*Piozzi Marginalia*. Edited by Percival Merritt. Cambridge: Harvard University Press, 1925.
"Minced Meat for Pyes"	"Minced Meat for Pyes" (ca. 1796–1820), a scrapbook of verse and prose (portions in

Merritt). Harvard University Library, MS Eng. 231F.

Observations — *Observations and Reflections made in the Course of a Journey through France, Italy, and Germany.* 2 vols. London: Printed for A. Strahan and T. Cadell, 1789.

Old England — *Old England to her Daughters. Address to the Females of Great Britain.* [Signed by] "Poor Old England," penny broadside. London: Printed by J. Brettell for R. Faulder, ca. June 1803.

Retrospection — *Retrospection: or A Review of the Most Striking and Important Events, Characters, Situations, and their Consequences, which the last Eighteen Hundred Years have Presented to the View of Mankind.* 2 vols. London: Printed for John Stockdale, 1801.

"Thrale Estate Book" — "Accounts of the Estate of Henry Thrale, also Guardian Accounts with the four Thrale Daughters." MS in Hyde Collection.

Thraliana — *Thraliana: The Diary of Mrs. Hester Lynch Thrale (later Mrs. Piozzi), 1776–1809.* Edited by Katharine C. Balderston. 2d ed. 2 vols. Oxford: Clarendon Press, 1951. The original MS, 6 vols., is at the Huntington Library, San Marino, California.

Three Warnings — *The Three Warnings.* Kidderminster: Printed by John Gower, 1792. This work appeared originally in Anna Williams, *Miscellanies in Prose and Verse* (1766).

Three Warnings to John Bull — *Three Warnings to John Bull before He Dies. By an Old Acquaintance of the Public.* London: R. Faulder, 1798.

"Una and Duessa" — "Una and Duessa, or A Set of Dialogues upon the most Popular Subjects." 149 MS pages. April to July 1791. John Ryland Library, MS Ry. 635.

"Verses 1" — "Collection of Hester Lynch Piozzi's MSS Poetry." 140 leaves, of which 60, i.e., 120

	pages, contain HLP's original poetry (Hyde Collection).
"Verses 2"	"Collection of Hester Lynch Piozzi's MSS Poetry." 34 pages of Hester Lynch Piozzi's verse plus 19 blank pages (Hyde Collection).
Welsh Tour	Mrs. Thrale's Unpublished Journal of her Tour in Wales with Dr. Johnson, July–September, 1774. In A. M. Broadley's Doctor Johnson and Mrs. Thrale, pp. 155–219. London and New York: John Lane, 1910.

Short Titles for Secondary Sources

We have used standard encyclopedias, school and university rosters, biographical dictionaries, law lists, peerages, armorials, baronetages, knightages, medical and clerical rosters, town and city directories, almanacs, and so forth. Along with these we have consulted annual army and navy lists; *Boyle's Court Guide; Royal Kalendar;* the Reverend William Betham, *The Baronetage of England,* 5 vols. (1801–5); the numerous editions of Burke's *Peerage and Baronetage* as well as Burke's *Landed Gentry;* Burke's *Royal Families of the World,* 2 vols. (1977); Burke's *Irish Family Records* (1976); George Edward Cokayne, *The Complete Peerage,* revised by Vicary Gibbs, et al., 13 vols. (1910–59); *The Complete Baronetage,* 6 vols. (1900–1909); W. A. Shaw, *The Knights of England,* 2 vols. (1906); Howard M. Colvin, *A Biographical Dictionary of British Architects, 1660–1840* (1954; 1978); Joseph Haydn and Horace Ockerby, *The Book of Dignities,* 3d ed. (1894); Gerrit P. Judd IV, *Members of Parliament, 1734–1832* (1955); Sir Lewis Namier and John Brooke, *The House of Commons, 1754–1790,* 3 vols. (1964).

These works will be cited only when specifically appropriate.

AR	*The Annual Register, or a View of the History, Politics, and Literature. 1758–.* (See Mrs. Piozzi to Mrs. Pennington, 4 August 1794, n.10.)
Baronetage	Cokayne, George Edward, ed. *Complete Baronetage.* 6 vols. Exeter: W. Pollard, 1900–1909.
Bayle	*The Dictionary Historical and Critical of Mr. Peter Bayle.* 2d ed. 5 vols. London: Printed for J. J. and P. Knapton [etc.], 1734–38.
Boaden	Boaden, James. *Memoirs of Mrs. Siddons, Interspersed with Anecdotes of Authors and Actors.* 2 vols. London: Henry Colburn, 1827.
Boswell's Johnson	*Boswell's Life of Johnson.* Edited by George Birkbeck Hill and L. F. Powell. 6 vols. Oxford: Clarendon Press, 1934–64.

Broadley	Broadley, A. M. *Doctor Johnson and Mrs. Thrale*. London and New York: John Lane, 1910.
Brooke	Brooke, John. *King George III*. New York: McGraw-Hill, 1972.
Campbell	Campbell, Thomas. *Life of Mrs. Siddons*. 2 vols. London: Effingham Wilson, 1834.
Chandler	Chandler, David G. *The Campaigns of Napoleon*. London: Weidenfeld and Nicolson, 1966.
Chapman	Chapman, R. W., ed. *The Letters of Samuel Johnson, with Mrs. Thrale's Genuine Letters to Him*. 3 vols. Oxford: Clarendon Press, 1952.
Clifford	Clifford, James L. *Hester Lynch Piozzi (Mrs. Thrale)*. 2d ed. Reprinted with corrections and additions. Oxford: Clarendon Press, 1968, 1987 (with a new introduction by Margaret Anne Doody).
Corr. George IV	*The Correspondence of George, Prince of Wales, 1770–1812*. Edited by A. Aspinall. 8 vols. New York: Oxford University Press, 1963–71.
Décembre-Alonnier	[Joseph] Décembre–[Edmond] Alonnier. *Dictionnaire de la Révolution française, 1789–1799*. 2 vols. Paris [1866–68].
Diary and Letters	*Diary and Letters of Madame d'Arblay*. Edited by Charlotte Barrett. 7 vols. [1842–46.] London: H. Colburn, 1854.
Dodsley	*A Collection of Poems in Six Volumes by Several Hands*. [Edited by Robert Dodsley.] London: Printed by J. Hughs, for J. Dodsley, in Pall-Mall, 1765.
Doody	Doody, Margaret Anne. *Frances Burney: The Life in the Works*. New Brunswick, New Jersey: Rutgers University Press, 1988.
Early Journals	*The Early Journals and Letters of Fanny Burney*, vol. 1 (1768–73). Edited by Lars E. Troide. Oxford and Montreal: Oxford University Press; McGill-Queens University Press, 1988–
English Poets	Johnson, Samuel. *Lives of the English Poets*. Edited by

George Birkbeck Hill. 3 vols. Oxford: Clarendon Press, 1905.

Farington   *The Diary of Joseph Farington.* Vols. 1–6 edited by Kenneth Garlick and Angus D. Macintyre. Vols. 7–16 edited by Kathryn Cave. New Haven and London: Published for the Paul Mellon Centre for Studies in British Art, Yale University Press, 1978–84.

Genest   Genest, John. *Some Account of the English Stage, from the Restoration in 1660 to 1830.* 10 vols. Bath: Printed by H. E. Carrington and sold by Thomas Rodd, Great Newport Street, London, 1832.

GM   *The Gentleman's Magazine.* Edited by Sylvanus Urban. London, 1731–1907.

Hawkins   Hawkins, Sir John. *The Life of Samuel Johnson, LL.D.* 2d ed. Revised and corrected. London: J. Buckland [etc.], 1787.

Hayward   Hayward, A., ed. *Autobiography, Letters and Literary Remains of Mrs. Piozzi (Thrale).* 2d ed. 2 vols. London: Longman, Green, Longman, and Roberts, 1861.

Hazen   Hazen, Charles Downer. *The French Revolution.* 2 vols. New York: Henry Holt, 1932.

Hemlow   Hemlow, Joyce. *The History of Fanny Burney.* Oxford: Clarendon Press, 1958.

Highfill   Highfill, Philip H., Jr., Kalman A. Burnim, and Edward A. Langhans. *A Biographical Dictionary of Actors, Actresses, Musicians, Dancers, Managers & other State Personnel in London, 1660–1800.* Carbondale and Edwardsville: Southern Illinois University Press, 1973–.

Hodson   Hodson, V. C. P. *List of the Officers of the Bengal Army 1758–1834.* 4 pts. London: Constable; Phillimore, 1927–47.

Howell   *Epistolae Ho-Elianae, The Familiar Letters of James Howell.* Edited by Joseph Jacobs. 2 vols. [1645–55.] London: David Nutt, 1892.

Hyde	Hyde, Mary. *The Thrales of Streatham Park*. Cambridge and London: Harvard University Press, 1977.
Hyde-Redford	The Hyde Edition of *The Letters of Samuel Johnson*, volumes 1–3, edited by Bruce Redford (Princeton, N.J.: Princeton University Press, 1992–)
Idler	*The Idler and the Adventurer*. Edited by W. J. Bate, John M. Bullitt, and L. F. Powell. Vol. 2 of *The Yale Edition of the Works of Samuel Johnson*. New Haven and London, 1963.
Jerningham	*The Jerningham Letters (1780–1843)*. Edited by Egerton Castle. 2 vols. London: Richard Bentley and Son, 1896.
Jesse	Jesse, J. Heneage. *Memoirs of the Life and Reign of King George the Third*. 2d ed. 3 vols. London: Tinsley Brothers, 1867.
Johns. Misc.	*Johnsonian Miscellanies*. Edited by George Birkbeck Hill. 2 vols. Oxford: Clarendon Press, 1897.
Johns. Shakespeare	*Johnson on Shakespeare*. Edited by Arthur Sherbo. Vols. 7–8 of *The Yale Edition of the Works of Samuel Johnson*. New Haven and London, 1968.
Journals and Letters	*The Journals and Letters of Fanny Burney (Madame d'Arblay)*. Edited by Joyce Hemlow et al. 12 vols. Oxford: Clarendon Press, 1972–84. Especially vol. 7, edited by Edward A. Bloom and Lillian D. Bloom (1978); vol. 8, edited by Peter Hughes et al. (1980): vols. 9–10, edited by Warren Derry (1982).
Knapp	Knapp, Oswald G., ed. *The Intimate Letters of Hester Piozzi and Penelope Pennington 1788–1821*. London, Toronto, and New York: John Lane; Bell and Cockburn, 1914.
Lefebvre	Lefebvre, Georges. *The French Revolution*. Vol. 1, *From its Origins to 1793*, translated by Elizabeth Moss Evanson. Vol. 2, *From 1793 to 1799*, translated by John Hall Stewart and James Friguglietti. London: Routledge and Kegan Paul; New York: Columbia University Press, 1962–64.
Lloyd	Lloyd, J[acob] Y. *The History of the Princes, the Lords Marcher, and the Ancient Nobility of Powys Fadog, and the

	Ancient Lords of Arwystli, Cedewen, and Meirionydd. 6 vols. London: T. Richards [Whiting], 1881–87.
London Stage	*The London Stage 1660–1800.* Edited by William Van Lennep, Emmett L. Avery, Arthur H. Scouten et al. 5 vols. in 11 and index. Carbondale: Southern Illinois University Press, 1960–79.
McCarthy	McCarthy, William. *Hester Thrale Piozzi: Portrait of a Literary Woman.* Chapel Hill: University of North Carolina Press, 1985.
Mangin	[Mangin, Edward.] *Piozziana; or, Recollections of the Late Mrs. Piozzi, with Remarks.* London: Edward Moxon, 1833.
Manvell	Manvell, Roger. *Sarah Siddons: Portrait of an Actress.* London: Heinemann, 1970.
Marshall	Marshall, John. *Royal Naval Biography.* . . . 4 vols. London: Longman, Hurst, Rees, Orme, and Browne, 1823–35.
Nichols	Nichols, John. *Illustrations of the Literary History of the Eighteenth Century.* 8 vols. [7 and 8 by John Bowyer Nichols.] London: Nichols, Son, and Bentley, 1817–58.
Oxford Proverbs	*The Oxford Dictionary of English Proverbs.* 3d ed. Revised by F. P. Wilson [1970.] Oxford: Clarendon Press, 1982.
Parliamentary History	*The Parliamentary History of England from the earliest Period to the Year 1803, from which last-mentioned Epoch it is continued downwards in the work entitled "Hansard's Parliamentary Debates."* 36 vols. London: Printed by T. C. Hansard [etc.], 1806–20.
Pastor	Pastor, Baron Ludwig Friedrich August von. *The History of the Popes, from the Close of the Middle Ages.* 40 vols. London: J. Hodges [etc.], 1891–1953.
Peerage	Cokayne, George Edward. *The Complete Peerage of England, Scotland, Ireland, Great Britain and the United Kingdom.* 2d ed., rev. and enl. Edited by Vicary Gibbs et al. 13 vols. London: St. Catherine Press, 1910–59.
Poems	*Poems.* Edited by E. L. McAdam, Jr., with George

	Milne. Vol. 6 of *The Yale Edition of the Works of Samuel Johnson*. New Haven and London, 1964.
Prayers	*Diaries, Prayers, and Annals*. Edited by E. L. McAdam, Jr., with Donald and Mary Hyde. Vol. 1 of *The Yale Edition of the Works of Samuel Johnson*. New Haven and London, 1958.
Queeney Letters	*The Queeney Letters*. Edited by the marquis of Lansdowne. London: Cassell; New York: Farrar & Rinehart, 1934.
Rambler	*The Rambler*. Edited by W. J. Bate and Albrecht B. Strauss. Vols. 3–5 of *The Yale Edition of the Works of Samuel Johnson*. New Haven and London, 1969.
Redford	Redford, Bruce. *The Converse of the Pen*. Chicago and London: University of Chicago Press, 1986.
Repertorium	Winter, Otto Friedrich. *Repertorium der diplomatischen Vertreter aller Länder seit dem Westfälischen Frieden (1648)*, vol. 3, 1764–1815. Graz-Köln: Verlag Hermann Böhlaus, 1965.
Rothenberg	Rothenberg, Gunter E. *Napoleon's Great Adversaries: The Archduke Charles and the Austrian Army, 1792–1814*. Bloomington: Indiana University Press, 1982.
Sale Catalogue	1. *Streatham Park, Surrey. A Catalogue of the . . . Household Furniture . . . a Collection of Valuable Paintings . . . also the Extensive and Well-Selected Library . . . the genuine Property of Mrs. Piozzi . . . will be sold by Auction, by Mr. Squibb, on the Premises, on Wednesday the 8th of May, 1816, and Four following Days (Sunday excepted)*. 2. *Collectanea Johnsoniana. Catalogue of the Library, Pictures, Prints, Coins, Plate, China, and other Valuable Curiosities, the Property of Mrs. Hester Lynch Piozzi, Deceased, to be sold by Auction, at the Emporium Rooms, Exchange Street, Manchester, by Mr. Broster, on Wednesday, [September 1823] the 17th instant, and [six] following days, Saturday and Sunday excepted. Chester*.
Seward, *Anecdotes*	Seward, William. *Anecdotes of Some Distinguished Persons, Chiefly of the Present and Two Preceding Centuries*. 4 vols. and supplement. 2d ed. London: T. Cadell, Jr., and W. Davies, 1795–96.

Seward Letters	*Letters of Anna Seward: Written between the Years 1784 and 1807.* 6 vols. Edinburgh: Archibald Constable and Co.; London: Longman, Hurst, Rees, Orme, and Brown, William Miller, and John Murray, 1811.
Shakespeare	*The Riverside Shakespeare.* Boston: Houghton Mifflin, 1974.
Siddons Letters	Burnim, Kalman A. "The Letters of Sarah and William Siddons to Hester Lynch Piozzi in the John Rylands Library." *Bulletin of the John Rylands Library* 52 (1969–70): 46–95.
Spectator	*The Spectator.* 8 vols. London: Printed by H. Hughs for Payne, Rivington [etc.], 1789. This is Hester Lynch Piozzi's copy, bought in 1794, with her marginalia (Peyraud Collection).
Stanhope	Stanhope, Philip Henry, fifth earl. *Life of the Right Honourable William Pitt.* 4 vols. 3d ed. [1867] New York: AMS Press, 1970.
Tilley	Tilley, Morris Palmer. *A Dictionary of the Proverbs in England in the Sixteenth and Seventeenth Centuries.* Ann Arbor: University of Michigan Press, 1950.
Walpole Correspondence	*The Yale Edition of Horace Walpole's Correspondence.* Edited by W. S. Lewis et al. 48 vols. in 49. New Haven, 1937–83.
Warton	Warton, Thomas. *The History of English Poetry, from the Close of the Eleventh to the Commencement of the Eighteenth Century.* 4 vols. London: J. Dodsley [etc.], 1774–81.
Watson	Watson, J. Steven. *The Reign of George III, 1760–1815.* Oxford: Clarendon Press, 1960.
Welsh Journey	Johnson, Samuel. *A Journey into North Wales, in the Year 1774.* In *Boswell's Johnson* 5:427–61.
Wheatley	Wheatley, Henry B. *London Past and Present.* 3 vols. London: John Murray; New York: Scribner and Welford, 1891.
Wickham	Wickham, The Reverend Hill, ed. *Journals and Correspondence of Thomas [Sedgwick] Whalley, D.D.* 2 vols. London: Richard Bentley, 1863.

Names and Abbreviations of Major Figures in the Piozzi Correspondence

AL	Alexander Leak (1776–1816)
CB	Charles Burney (1726–1814)
CMT } CMM }	Cecilia Margaretta Thrale (1777–1857); in 1795 Mrs. Mostyn
DL	The Reverend Daniel Lysons (1762–1834)
EM	The Reverend Edward Mangin (1772–1852)
FB } FBA }	Frances "Fanny" Burney (1752–1840); in 1793 Mme d'Arblay
GP	Gabriel Piozzi (1740–1809)
HLS } HLT } HLP }	Hester Lynch Salusbury (1741–1821); in 1763 Mrs. Thrale; in 1784 Mrs. Piozzi
HMP } HMS }	Harriet Maria Pemberton (1794–1831); in 1814 Mrs. Salusbury; in 1817 Lady Salusbury
HT	Henry Thrale (1728 or 1729–81)
JB	James Boswell (1740–95)
JF	James Fellowes (1771–1857); in 1809 Sir James, knight
JMM	John Meredith Mostyn (1775–1807)
JSPS	John Salusbury Piozzi Salusbury (1793–1858); in 1817 Sir John, knight
JW	John Williams (1794–1859); in 1830 Sir John, second baronet; in 1842 Sir John Hay-Williams
LC	The Reverend Leonard Chappelow (1744–1820)
Ly W	Margaret Williams (1768–1835) of Bodelwyddan; in 1798 Lady Williams
MF	Marianne Francis (1790–1832)
MW	Margaret Williams (1759–1823) of Bath
PSW } PSP }	Penelope Sophia Weston (1752–1827); in 1792 Mrs. Pennington
Q	Hester Maria "Queeney" Thrale (1764–1857); in 1808 Lady Keith
RD	The Reverend Reynold Davies (1752–1820)
RG	The Reverend Robert Gray (1762–1834)

SAT	Susanna Arabella Thrale (1770–1858)
SJ	Samuel Johnson (1709–84)
SL	Samuel Lysons (1763–1819)
SS	Sarah Siddons (1755–1831)
ST } SH	Sophia Thrale (1771–1824); in 1807 Mrs. Hoare
TSW	The Reverend Thomas Sedgwick Whalley (1746–1828)
WAC	William Augustus Conway (1789–1828)

Genealogical Abbreviations

cr.	created
fl.	flourished
M.I.	monumental inscription

Editorial Principles

Manuscript Sources

All letters are arranged chronologically. Mrs. Piozzi's correspondence creates few textual problems since she prided herself on her penmanship and wrote with a strong hand. We have transcribed literally, changing only what we believe would detract from clarity. We have retained original spellings, capitalization, and punctuation. Certain accidentals—the omission of a period or a closing parenthesis—are silently emended. Superior letters are lowered. Her intermittent use of an elision to form a past tense—a usage that she came to see as outmoded—is normalized: e.g., "defer'd" becomes "deferred." Most abbreviations—except in a few instances or in addresses and postmarks—are expanded.

Mrs. Piozzi's paragraphing can puzzle. Occasionally she follows normal practice by dropping a line and then indenting. At other times to indicate a new paragraph she merely extends a space on the same line. Sense usually dictates where a visibly uncertain paragraph begins. Dashes, similarly, are hard to decipher since her lines for that mark can be of any length or even appear as a seemingly extended ellipsis. Dashes, consequently, are transcribed as "—" or, when elongated to suggest emotional response, as "——."

The writer's address is shown at the upper right of the letter along with the date. The complimentary close and signature for each letter are presented in run-on fashion with slash marks to indicate line breaks or divisions. At the foot of each letter are provided, where available, repository, address of recipient, and postmark. Franked letters are marked as such.

Pertinent complementary correspondence usually appears in notes in order to explain obscurities, clarify cryptic remarks, or solve problems. In a few instances, however, when Mrs. Piozzi answers a letter—say, of Sarah Siddons, Leonard Chappelow, Joseph Cooper Walker, or Daniel Lysons—point-for-point, we incorporate in the body of the text the letter that initiated or continued the correspondence.

Generally, square brackets "[ ]" signal such defects in the holographs as blots, tears, seals, oversights. In addition, when a date of composition is conjectural, it is enclosed in square brackets and annotated. Angle brackets "< >" indicate places where a printed date, as in a postmark, a word, or a phrase is blurred. When warranted by the context, emendations are made within the appropriate square or angle brackets.

Printed Sources

Texts are reprinted literally although erroneous datings and obvious misprints are corrected with explanations when necessary, and certain typographical eccentricities, such as the arbitrary and inconsistent use of small capitals in words and phrases, are not reproduced.

We have consistently used the names of Welsh counties as HLP would have known them. Since 1974, however, following reorganization under the Local Government Act (1972), the new county of Clwyd, e.g., was created from Flintshire, most of Denbighshire, and the Edeyrnion district of Merioneth. Similarly, the new county of Gwynedd was formed out of Anglesey, Carnarvonshire (or Caernarfonshire), the rest of Merioneth, and the Conwy valley in Denbighshire.

The Piozzi Letters

Letters, 1799–1804

TO THE REVEREND LEONARD CHAPPELOW

[ca. 6 or 7 January 1799][1]

The Brawn and the Books and the Turkey and the Boy are all Subjects of a thousand Thanks to Dear Mr. Chappelow;—*all are safe.* The Brawn nearly devoured, the books invitingly useful and desireable, The Turkey outweighing every Body's Turkey, and the Boy active and well proportioned, intelligent and merry-hearted—almost beyond anybody's Boy. I think we shall do very nicely, Health and long Life alone are wanting; and *those,* these Salutary Waters would supply, but the Interested 'Pothecaries beseech one not to drink them because the Weather is too cold or too hot or some Nonsense. I must not however go freeze myself to Stone any more. Such Tricks did no Mischief Seven Years ago,— but It does not suit the *Autumnal* Equinox.

My Master has a bad Heel, otherwise pretty well; I have more need of Laudanum than he, the People plague me so. Mr. Ray says he has heard heavy Censures on me for saving this poor Innocent Baby Nephew of Mr. Piozzi's from Destruction——Comments as if I meant to disinherit my own beautiful and deserving Daughters, and give *all to him.* People are exceedingly premature in their Comments, and very unkindly ready with their Censures (quoth I). Little is the *all I have to bestow* compared to theirs and their Father's noble Fortunes: nor had I reason to think they esteemed that little as of any Value. To no Mortal did I ever say that I would *give him all*: He comes here for Refuge, for Instruction, for Education——I will give him the best of each which my Country affords—In his Country I met with generous Treatment, and the Kindness experienced from his Uncle I will endeavour to repay to *him.* With proper leading, driving &c. he will want nothing from the beautiful and deserving Ladies I'm perswaded: You never saw a little Creature sharp and busy and tidy and helpful so at 5 years old. He can put on and off his own clothes, tye them all up in his little Bag and see that nothing is lost: and when he is a *General Officer* he tells me he will go back to Brescia and scold them well if they have not taken care of the *white Hens he left them in Charge*.[2]

Poor Rogue! he has seen early Service; and gave me yesterday a very clear Account of the battle he saw somewhere——in the Square he says——between French and Germans; how their Legs were broken—and the Surgeons tyed them up with Bandages &c.[3] I asked him if they loved the French at Brescia——my Mama hates them says he because they dirtied Count Fenarolis fine House[4]—— (*Citizen* Fenaroli I mean—)—and threw his best Pictures out at Window.[5]

This Gossiping Stuff will shew you at once the State of their Country and the Character of the Child.

Now for a Bath Joke

Says the Prince of Wales to his Friend Sir John Lade—We hear that Buonaparte has actually driven four Beys out of Egypt. *Four* Bays! exclaims Sir John—why that's no Wonder! I can myself—upon a Pinch—drive *Six in* <*harness*>⁶

All this while we know nothing certain about these Beys except what's told us in the intercepted Letters, and those I have scarce Time to read as I ought to do.⁷ Mr. Gillon is come among us, and Mr. and Mrs. Pennington from Bristol. Mr. Ray left our Society soon; my Notion is that all these Reports and Conjectures (tho he would not tell me so) arise from pretty Mrs. O'Brien, friend to Susanna Thrale and Niece to Mr. Macnamara of Streatham:⁸ They were all enraged because We let the House to Mr. Giles instead of *presenting* it to our Daughters who had once as you know refused our Offer of living in it for nothing. Mr. Macnamara likes young Neighbours, and Mrs. O Brien is zealous for her Friends and I suppose all comes from that Quarter originally, but it shall not give me a Moment's Disturbance or turn my Course of Ideas one Inch.

Adieu / Dear Sir and continue to love / our Master and his H: L: P.

I wish these Folks had your Urticaria—then would they *tingle* themselves a little, and feel how they liked it.

Text: Ry. 561.160. *Address*: Rev: Mr. Chappelow.

1. HLP's letter was written at Bath near the end of the first week in January, for LC answered it on Thursday, the 10th (Ry. 562.57). "I have now," he wrote, "a Letter before [me] from you without any date.—but the first Line of it is a complete Specimen of *Heterogeniety*. Brawn, Books, Boys and Turkies."
2. LC responded to HLP's description of her daughters' hostility to JSPS. According to LC, on the 10th: they "have behaved so ill to you, that one of the great pleasures they have deprived you of has but by few been attended to.—Whats that?—The pleasure every one must derive at the declining period of Life from the circumstance of having some one younger than themselves, to receive at their death with gratitude what we cannot [take] with us to the grave.—Your Children if they do *not* forfeit it, have undoubtedly the first claim, even if they do not want it, but if they do not want it you are more than justified in scrutinizing their merits with a strict Eye—and acting accordingly.—I hope your boy will never be what he talks of, a general officer, unless he is a Church Militant—this *smells episcopally.*"
3. The fighting that JSPS witnessed occurred largely in July 1796. The Austrian general Peter Quasdanovitch (fl. 1796) commanded the westward column (about eighteen thousand men) of Würmser's offensive in Italy. With considerable effort Quasdanovitch defeated Sauret's division north of Lonato and seized Brescia, including armament and French casualties. But by 1 August Augereau's troops had driven the Austrians from Brescia.

See also HLP to PSP, 10 January 1798, n. 1.

4. According to JSPS's baptismal record (Ry. Ch. 1247), his godfather was conte Luigi [Lewis] Fenarole (d. 1810).
5. JSPS saw or was told not only of the military struggles between the French and the

Austrians but also of the democratic uprising at Brescia early in 1797. Of the latter, *The Times* on 13 April 1797 reported: "The Revolution of Brescia . . . does not appear to have been effected in so easy and peaceful a manner, as that of Bergamo. A part of the inhabitants having joined the Venetian troops, a battle ensued between them and the Revolutionists, who being reinforced by 1500 inhabitants of Brescia, forced their opponents to retreat. The Revolutionary <Influenza> has spread as far as Peschiera, where a Tree of Liberty has been erected."

6. See HLP to PSP, 14 September 1798, n. 2. In Jesse 3:481, Sir John is described as "a notorious sporting character of the day." His favorite pastimes were harness racing and gambling. Cf. [Charles Piggott], *The Jockey Club, or a Sketch of the Manners of the Age*, 2d ed. (1792), pp. 85–87.

7. According to *The Times*, 11 December 1798, the reference is to the "Intercepted Correspondence from the Army of Gen. Buonaparte in Egypt." About to be published, the collection is "not only interesting on account of the confession of the persons employed on the expedition, respecting the miserable conditions of the army, and the universal disgust which prevails in being sent to such an inhospitable country; but the introduction contains some very pertinent observations on the motives which induced the Directory to set it on foot.

"The Correspondence was intercepted at different periods, by the Turkish and English ships of war. It consists of official and private letters. . . .:" *The Times* printed extracts from these letters on 11, 13, 14, and 29 December. For the published collection, see *Copies of Original Letters from the Army of General Bonaparte in Egypt, intercepted by the Fleet under the Command of Admiral Lord Nelson. With an English Translation* (London: J. Wright, 1798). For an abridgment, see *GM* 69, pt. 1 (1799): 413–14.

8. For Margaret O'Brien, see HLP to Robert Ray, 23 July 1798, n. 5.

TO THE REVEREND ROBERT GRAY

> No. 43, Great Pultney Street, Bath
> Fryday, 11th Jan. 1799.

Home is the place for *happiness*, though leaving it a moment produces *pleasure*; and dear Mr. Gray will not be found deserting his post, or slumbering on his stand, should the call of enquiry sound forth. It grieves me not a little to hear the Dissenters cry out,[1] and see the Socinians sneer at the supineness of our orthodox clergy.[2] My health has permitted me to go but twice to church in this town yet, and never did I listen to more eloquent discourses than were pronounced those two times; but every book one borrows breathes democracy; every mouth opens against Church establishments; every play, every novel discourages subordination, and militates against conjugal fidelity and filial reverence. The batteries against religion are scarcely masked ones; her outworks give way, and good people cluster close into the citadel. I feel amazed and shocked at the strange process made since I was here before,—not made by *vice*; *that* has perhaps been nearly the same for ever,—but by shameless avowal of all which was once concealed, and desire of justifying what till now was always condemned.

Text: Hayward 2:250–51.

1. In *GM* 68, pt. 2 (1798): 750–52, a letter to Mr. Urban vindicates the charge of the bishop of Sarum to the clergy of his diocese. Therein he "forcibly recommends exertions to resident ministers, for the confronting of the fantastical doctrines of our modern Dissenters, or rather Reformers."

The letter itself attacks the growing body of Methodists as subverters of church and state at all levels of society. As they "gain proselytes . . . our resident Clergy, supinely afraid of departing from their accustomed routine of duty, perceive a gradual decrease in their flock."

The letter writer suggests that the Methodists are determined to erode Anglican authority "for what [they deem] the progress of *[their] true evangelical mission*."

2. HLP's fear of Socinianism (or of deism or agnosticism) was supported at this time by a controversy involving three printed works. The review of the controversy appears in *GM* 68, pt. 1 (1798): 42–48. See Andrew Fuller, *Socinianism indefensible on the Grounds of its moral Tendency; containing a Reply to Two late Publications; the one, by Dr. Toulmin, intituled, "The practical Efficacy of the Unitarian Doctrine considered;" the other, of Mr. Kentish, intituled, "The Moral Tendency of the genuine Christian Doctrine"* (1797).

TO THE REVEREND LEONARD CHAPPELOW

No. 43 Great Pulteney Street Bath
Queen's Birthday [18 January] 1799.

Dear Mr. Chappelow

You are very partial to me and my Book and will be very partial to our little Boy when you see what a sharp-witted active Creature 'tis. All his Ideas *now* are military, but he will make a Scholar too I dare say; for he learns English apace, and accommodates himself to every new Situation with chearful Good humour never seeming to regret what has been left behind: If we can but live to *launch* him, he will *swim*.

In two Years from this Day the heavy Work of Retrospection will get out of Dock; if things continue in their present State I mean, and no strange Event happens to close my last Volume; but here we are hoping and listening for News and making Lies, and raising Phantoms, and fabricating Conjectures of every possible Form and Shape and Colour, because The Ice keeps all close at the great River's Mouth which from its *White* Appearance in Winter Season I suppose, was originally denominated by the Romans Albis and thence Elbe.[1]

You are always complaining of a bad Memory, yet had the Kindness to recollect our Chat concerning Strigil and Strigilis![2] I am much obliged by that and by all your very friendly Remembrances. Fret not about the Turkey which will find its way hither in due Time—and if it does not——I hate *Kitchen* Griefs as I call them—There are Griefs enough which one must attend to, in the Parlour and Drawing room.[3]

Mr. Maynard seems a pleasing Man, I have not seen his Lady,[4] our dear Master's everlasting Confinement is such a Drawback upon all the Comforts of

Life! Yet he hopes to be well soon and run to London with the Child; fix him at Davies's, and then see our good Tenant Mr. Giles &c. 'Tis vexatious that all that should be done before you get to Hill Street.

Well no matter! We have hope of seeing Siddons here—Siddons her own Self—See her on the Boards where I saw her first, with an Admiration that has gone on increasing ever since the Year 80 to this Hour. It will be a great Delight.[5]

Mrs. Pennington is with us and we pass many a comfortable Hour in Chat, and People drop in, and Time rolls away and my Health mends: but I see and feel plainly that Democratic Principles are gaining Ground *tacitly* every hour——tho such are their consequences that your old Acquaintance Miss Weston—now Pennington—shewed me a Lady with whom She had that Moment finished a Rubber of Whist, who was one of the Prisoners at Wexford that heard the fatal Clock Strike, and the Bell toll for their own Execution.[6]

A little Miss too not *eight* years old attracting my Notice by her Beauty one Morning at the pump Room; her Friends informed me She was an Epileptic Patient here at Bath, in Consequence of Fright at seeing her Papa—a Protestant Clergyman—savagely murdered: and She forced by the Assassins to pull his Bowels out with her own Hands.

fill up the Blank
These are the Fruits of that ——————— Tree,
which Madmen are I know not how
impelled to plant in this only quiet
Country!!!

God bless you my Dear Sir and cure your Urticaria if you can—if you can*not*, Think but what others suffer, and we shall soon learn to laugh at Mr. Piozzi's Gout, Your Nettle Rash, and the *Stingers* who delight in tormenting Your / ever Obliged and Faithful / H: L: Piozzi.

Mr. Gillon is here and desires me to add his Compliments.——Mrs. Piozzi has not told Mr. Chappelow that Mrs. Pennington (as Miss Weston) always remembers him with peculiar Esteem and Respect.—How delighted I am to find our Friend as kind, as entertaining and charming as ever, after Six long years of Seperation!

Text: Ry. 560.85. *Address*: Rev: Mr. Chappelow.

1. Known to the Romans as Albis, the Elbe marked the farthest Roman advance into Germany under Drusus in 9 B.C.
HLP's statement recognizes the military inaction in central Europe at the beginning of 1799. The czar had broken with the Allies; Prussia remained neutral with leanings toward France. In Germany the rulers of Bavaria and Württemberg and the elector of Mainz had promised subsidies, which at this time remained just that. Austria, the dominant Allied leader on the Continent, suffered financially; her war effort was further stalled by administrative inefficiency with newly appointed generals less capable than their prede-

cessors (e.g., Kray for Archduke Charles in December 1798, and an aged General Melas for Suvórov).

2. When LC was last at Brynbella, he and HLP discussed and disagreed about the terms *strigil* and *strigilis*. On 10 January (Ry. 562.57), he wrote to correct his initial error and end the debate. "When I was Librarian at Trinity College Cambridge, I had the keeping of Curiosities.—foolishly one antique was I believe ticketed—a Strigil.—anglecizing the word.—this word dwelt upon my Tongue.—and as it is not a classical word to be met with in the poets—I thought it was grammatically thus—Nom: case—strigil—Gen: Strigilis.—but I now find You was right—The Nominative is Strigilis as well as the second case."

Their discussion had centered on the English *strigil*, a form of scraper, and its derivation from the Latin *strigilis*.

3. HLP responds to LC's comment in his letter of the 10th: "I am as mad as a march hare.—My foolish Servant Norfolk—by mistake sent 2 Turkies to Macknamara.—one of which should have gone to Bath for you.—"

4. LC had asked HLP to deliver his enclosed letter, now missing, to a Mr. and Mrs. Maynard, who after many years in Italy now lived in Bath.

Anthony Lax Maynard (d. 1825) of Chesterfield, Derbyshire, and Harlsey Hall, Yorkshire. He had married Dorothy, youngest daughter of the Reverend Ralph Heathcote, rector of Morton, Derbyshire, and vicar of Sileby, Leicestershire.

5. For SS in Bath, see HLP to PSP, 11 November 1798, nn. 3 and 4.

The Thrales, accompanied by FB, came to Bath in March 1780 to aid HT's convalescence after a serious illness. There, sometime in April, she saw SS perform for the first time. The role was that of Belvidera in *Venice Preserved*. See *Thraliana* 1:432–36; *Diary and Letters* 1:351.

6. Irish rebels had entered Wexford on 30 May 1798. Many Protestants who had lived there managed to escape but others were imprisoned. "The majority of the [Catholic] population received the insurgents with unequivocal signs of joy, and largely participated in the atrocities and massacres which ensued."

HLP refers to two such atrocities against Protestants, which—if they occurred—might have been "perpetrated under the direction of one Thomas Dixon, a ferocious ruffian," who was able to influence the most "fanatical of the rebels."

For the details of the massacre, see *AR* 40 (1798): 118, 126–31, and chap. 7. The executions on 20 June began at two in the afternoon. "At seven in the evening ninety-seven persons had been massacred, when the bloody work was interrupted by a report that general Moore had been victorious, and that Vinegar-hill was surrounded by the King's troops."

TO LADY WILLIAMS

Bath Sunday
10: February 1799

I have my dearest Lady Williams strangely forgotten—of what Nature my last Letter was, and what we talked of in it. 'Tis ten to one I shall repeat some of the Nonsense over again—but you are a partial and excusing friend.

Mr. Piozzi has left me for awhile and gone to London with his little Boy, but I expect him back again tomorrow.[1] A most agreable Friend and very old Acquaintance kindly condemned herself to stay with me till his return, and as we once lived much together, and have been parted by Life's various Currents now for these last seven Years;—no Chat is ever wanting.[2] Sweet Mrs. Siddons too—by Accidents unfavourable enough for her, lucky for *us*; has past a Week or two here among all her *earliest* Admirers,[3] and will have such a Benefit tomorrow as may convince her She's admired *still*, altho' the Profits must fall miserably short of that great Theatre in Drury Lane.[4]

Mr. Moreton and Mr. Andrews too which last Friend frees this Cover, are among us;[5] and form with her and a few more, a sort of little comfortable Coterie which meets those Nights we are not at the Play——but from which Politics are completely banished by mutual Agreement and Consent.

Indeed Dear Madam if we would be happy—*That Topic* must be driven away from every *Evening* Conversation. The *Morning* Visitants and Public Newspapers bring in such Store of Melancholy Intelligence, that all wise People seem resolved to drown Remembrance of *past—and Fear of future* Horrors in the 1st Glass of Wine drank after dinner—leaving the later Hours of the four and Twenty open to other Subjects.

Oh how your ladyship's kind heart would melt to hear the horrid Tales from Italy! Poor Conte di Fron[6]—late Turinese Ambassador comes now and then to disburthen his Sorrows on us—and more lamenting his King's Misfortunes than his own[7]—tells how that hapless Prince knelt on the Ground in vain before the unfeeling General of the French Forces—begging a Brother's Life[8]——while that Commander lately a low Attorney of some Country Town, shewed him thus humbled to his Brother Officers and made the Scene a Matter of Encouragement for France to persist in her Resolves against Crowned heads.

This was Sardinia's King,——The Royal Family of Naples suffered but little less:[9] chased from their Capital and driven on Board our Ships where Storms pursued them till with the Fright and Sickness *one* Prince died in the Vessel, and I am told the Life of another Child is since despaired of.[10]

Poor Villa Albani that you read of in my superficial Book, which says not half of what its Praise deserved——shews how the *Roman* Territory is treated:[11] they have in the strictest Sense levelled it quite to Ground; and the two beautiful Pillars made of What they in that country called *Paglia* Marble—a Straw coloured Stone almost inestimable—being too big to carry easily away—the French rolled heavy Weights—and *broke them all to Pieces.*

'Tis nonsense tho' to lament Stocks and Stones when my poor little Boy from Lombardy said as I walked with him across our Market——*These are* Sheep's Heads are they not Aunt? I saw a Basket of *Men's heads* at Brescia. His perfect recollection of such Horrors will be however quickly lost at School, where a new Set of Play fellows speaking a Tongue wholly new to him—besides the little necessary Application to Business—will I hope and trust in a few Months wholly obliterate these Sad Ideas and substitute others less unpleasing in their Room. As he was by lucky Chance baptized too in Compliment to *me*—*John Salusbury* five Years ago—when happier Days smiled on his Family;——He will be known in England by *no other* and it will be forgotten he is a foreigner: A lucky Circumstance for one who is intended to work his Way among our Islanders, by Talents, Diligence, and Education.

Have you dear Madam heard another Story? How Nelson's brave Defence of

Italy is not—tho' warm and tender—quite disinterested. 'Tis said a Neapolitan Lady holds *him* Captive,[12] and very Sorry am I for his Wife, who looks so pretty and seems so happy with her husband's Father here; The People quite delight to look on them, and clapped one Night when they came into the Playhouse.

We have had a Sad Loss of Miss Williams, She is gone to Town before the Benefit, for which She would have made good Interest: Mr. Madocks left Bath long ago, and I have heard no more of him.[13] Mrs. Leo will come hither without doubt, if any thing bad happens at Llannerch—but while there is Life there is Hope.[14]

Never, no Never was there known in England so cold a Winter; It freezes now as if the Weather was but just *set in*, and I believe even *that Circumstance* one of our peculiar blessings——because there [part of a sentence missing] Scarlet Clokes too——or short Riding Coats——or Spencers very expensive and magnificent, and chiefly made of Velvet are much in request: and some like Clokes of blue Velvet with deep black Lace very well adapted to the Season.

But 'tis Time to have done gossiping so, and release your Ladyships Eyes and my own. I will end with my best Regards to my Dear little Friend the young Squire of Bodylwyddan, whom I dearly love: and my Maid Allen (who met me at Shrewsbury) hopes he has not quite forgotten the Respect *She* bears him——her earliest Enquiries after those concerning our *own* family were for *him*.

Adieu Dear Ladies both——and kind Sir John; and may they never be less partially kind to their / Obliged and faithful / H: L: Piozzi.

Text: Ry. 1 (1796–1802). *Address*: Lady Williams / Bodylwyddan / St. Asaph / Flintshire / N.W. *Postmark*: Franked by hand: Bath February Tenth 1799 MP free Andrews.

1. In what remains of a letter to Ly W on 14 January 1799, HLP had written: "We have got [JSPS] here since I wrote last, and as his Uncle's Gout promises to mend quickly, he will take him to School [at Streatham] next month—(—for as *our* John has nothing but his Talents and Education to depend upon, *he must be a Scholar,* and we will try hard to make him a very good one." See Clifford, p. 392.

2. Probably PSP.

3. After SS's initial performance in Bath this season, the *Bath Chronicle* on Thursday, 31 January, wrote: "We do not recollect ever to have seen the Theatre of this city so completely crouded as it was last night, nor so brilliant an audience as it displayed. The attraction indeed was great—Mrs. Siddons in *The Grecian Daughter.* When we recollected that this excellent actress had been originally transplanted from Bath, we felt additional pleasure at seeing her once more on the Thespian boards of this city. . . . We do not hesitate to say that her performance was perfection; and he who could see unmoved that natural display of interesting passion which Mrs. Siddons's Euphrasia exhibited, must have been more or less than man."

4. As advertised, "Mrs. Siddons's Night" was to be Saturday, 9 February (*Bath Chronicle*, 7 February), but in view of her extended stay, the "Night" was pushed ahead to 11 February.

5. Thomas Reynolds–Moreton (1776–1840), cr. earl of Ducie and Baron Moreton of Tortworth (1837). His wife was Frances, née Herbert (d. 22 August 1830), daughter of the 1st earl of Carnarvon.

Miles Peter Andrews, a second-rate dramatist and leader of fashionable society, was Member of Parliament for Bewdley (1796–1814). (See HLP to SL, 17 November 1787, n. 5.)

6. The son of the statesman *Giuseppe Francesco* Gaetano San Martino di San Germano (1712–64) and his Spanish wife, Maria *Christina* Teresa Ferrero Fieschi di Masserano (1714–65), Emanuele Filippo (1748–1813), styled conte di Front, was a Sardinian diplomat. He served as minister plenipotentiary to Portugal (1785–87) and as an official in his country's embassy in London, 1788–99, 1802–12 (from 1805 onward as minister plenipotentiary).

For this information we are indebted to the Archivio di Stato di Torino.

7. For Carlo Emanuele IV, see HLP to LC, 30 September 1796, n. 4.

By 1798 the French government, which had for some time wanted Piedmont, forced Carlo Emanuele to abdicate and retire to Sardinia.

8. Carlo Emanuele had an ailing brother, *Maurizio* Giuseppe Maria (1762–99); knight, Order of the Annunziata; duke of Montferrato; captain-general of the army in 1780. He was to die at Alghero, Sardinia, on 1 or 2 September, within nine months of Sardinia's defeat.

9. In January the French under Championnet reached Naples, were fought off by the *lazzaroni* until the 20th. On the twenty-third the Parthenopean republic was proclaimed. Ferdinando fled in panic with his family and court to Palermo on board Nelson's ships.

10. The king of Naples and Queen Marie Caroline had with them three sons. Of the three *Alberto* Maria, born at Naples 2 May 1792, died at sea 24 December 1798.

The king and queen also had with them their four unmarried daughters. The child "despaired of"—but not because of the flight—was Maria *Isabella*, born at Naples 2 December 1793 and died there, 23 April 1801.

11. The villa, not far from the Porta Salara, was built ca. 1760 by the architect Carlo Marchionne for Cardinal Albani. Magnificent with its opulent use of marble and with gardens overlooking the Sabine Mountains, the villa was renowned for its many collections of antiquities that the cardinal had gathered.

Although the building was not destroyed (it was sold in 1866 to the Prince Torlonia), its collections were ravaged. Two hundred ninety-four pieces of choice sculpture were seized by Bonaparte and carried off to Paris, where they remained until 1815. (A few pieces are still at the Louvre.)

HLP responds to an exaggerated rumor that "the destruction of the Villa of Cardinal Albani . . . was a subject of regret to every lover of the arts. So complete was the ruin effected by revolutionary vengeance, that the very shrubs which ornamented its delicious gardens, were rooted up and sold." See *AR* 40 (1798): 31; also *Observations* 2:125–26 and *Retrospection* 2:525.

12. The "Neapolitan Lady" was Emma Hamilton, whom Nelson met in the summer of 1793 when he was sent to Naples in the *Agamemnon* to transport a convoy of Neapolitan troops to Toulon. Her association with Nelson probably began with his return to Naples in September 1798, after the battle of the Nile.

His "brave Defence of Italy" was in part manipulated by Lady Hamilton and, more vigorously, by the Neapolitan queen. He outdid the loyalty of the country's most royalist subjects, except in the ranks of the *lazzaroni*. From September 1798 to July 1800 and later, he was prepared to deploy his squadron for Marie Caroline, the "Dear Queen" of his letters to Lady Hamilton.

13. John Edward Madocks (1760–1806) owned Fron Iw, near Llandyrnog, in Denbighshire. His presence in HLP's letters at this time is best explained in the following letter to Margaret Owen [ca. 12 February 1799].

14. For Daniel and Letitia Leo, see HLP to Q, 23 February 1794, n. 3. Daniel Leo died in 1803, his wife in 1801.

TO MARGARET OWEN

[Bath]
[ca. 12 February 1799]

My dear Miss Owen
   wants a Chit Chat Letter, and a Chit Chat Letter She shall have: Dear Mr. Piozzi is in London—carrying the Boy to Mr. Davies's School. We left his worthiest Admirers at Shrewsbury, and much has he regretted since we had him about again, that Dr. Goodinge did not hear him sing, as he has since been able.[1]
   I will give him the Musical Commands at his Return.
   We have got charming Siddons here among us, and Mr. Moreton and Mr. Andrews from London and many a pretty Evening do we spend: but Mrs. Madocks's will be a feeling Loss next Summer——I hear indeed Vronew is not likely to be inhabited soon again.[2] Its last Sweet Mistress had somewhat tender Health, and they would drag her over those Mountains into Merionethshire because Mr. Madocks hated to Sing without her Accompanyment &c. So She miscarried——as I think I told you——and died here of the Consequences some Months after. The Margravine[3] came and took her pretty Babies home, her Brother[4] was at the Balls and Theatres and every thing till just before She died—expressing Vexation tho' at being delayed in a Place *not then quite fashionable*: her Husband gay, good humoured, and light hearted—Sees all upon the favourable Side—and so People say he will soon marry again—of Lady Stawel I hear nothing at all, good or bad.[5] Poor Mrs. Madocks expired in a mean Lodging, a Shoemaker's Shop I think in Milson Street and was buried by her own Ancestors.[6]——I forget the County. What seems most remarkable to *me* was her Aunt's Husband, a Clergyman Mr. Johnstone, the moment he was told of her Death by oft repeated Epileptic Fits——fell into one *himself*, and so continued, exactly in the manner *She* had done, *till he died too*: four days after a Lady——for whom he never had expressed any peculiar Care, Affection, or Regard.[7]
   But the Burials here at Bath never were so frequent, the Bells tolling every Day and all Day long.
   This Weather was expected to do Good among the Invalides but nobody seems well as I see yet; and if the Cold would cure us, here's enough on it.
   The French are however well employed in Italy, they will avoid coming hither where nothing can be got but Blows: and they will not leave any Place unpillaged whose Spoils may serve as useful for the furnishing of Fleets to help our Enemies in Ireland.
   I'm sorry for the Duke of Leeds's Death:[8] The King has lost in him an able Counsellor, Society—a very pleasing Man: and my Heart recollects him as a Play-fellow——I feel quite grieved for my own Part though in these later Years we very seldom met——ten Years ago I used to spend the Evenings with Mrs. Lewis often in his Company.—
   Miss Ormsby has you say nothing to do now but be married[9]——some rich Young Ladies find that Matter difficult, but She I hope will make it easy to her, and diffuse Happiness thro' all her Circle of Friends and of Relations.

12 February 1799 59

    This Place is more beautiful than ever—finer Streets, Newer Squares,[10] London looks dirty and *Commercial* to it; Bath is the head Quarters of Pleasure and Gayety: our Stone Buildings give it such an Air of Cleanliness I wonder Ladies should not prefer it to a Town where the People write me word no Carriage can be drawn without four Horses——no not a *Hackney Coach*.

    Are you not sorry for the King of Naples! to lose his little Boy by fear and Sickness hurried away so from his own Capital! And *they do say* now that Lady Nelson may be a little sorry if She pleases, for that her Husband's *warm Feelings* for Italian Distress—springs from Love of a fair Neapolitan Lady——No wonder! *That* has been evermore the *Siren's Coast*. Would you desire more or better Scandal?

    Meanwhile the World is hasting rapidly to Ruin and its original Chaotic State. Every Country is shaken, every Government battered or undermined—or both. Your old Friend Honoria Piggott passed an Hour with me this Morning in old Family Talk—past, present, and to come seemed dismal tho' and yet I think we parted not displeased with each other.[11]

    Mr. Ormsby must get his *Heel* to *heal* up as my Master's does——but there yet remains as Mr. Hay the Surgeon[12] says a Quarry of Chalk behind. Have you heard that Mrs. Leo will soon be a Widow? Mr. Chappelow must get himself ready. Adieu Dear Friend and continue to love / Your own H: L: Piozzi.

Text: National Library of Wales: Brogyntyn MS 38.

    1. Thomas Goodinge (ca. 1746–1816) received a doctorate in canon law (1778) from Oxford. He was a successful preacher and schoolmaster. By 1789 he had become rector of Cound in Salop, living for the most part in or near Shrewsbury.

    2. Elizabeth (1768–99), daughter of William Craven (1738–91), sixth baron Craven (1769), had married in 1792 John Edward Madocks.

She had died in Bath on 3 January, following a miscarriage caused by "scrawling over our Welsh mountains last Year for a Frolic with Lady Stowell" (*Thraliana* 2:993, n. 5, derived from a Bowood letter to Q, 4 January).

    3. The dramatist and travel writer Elizabeth (1750–1828), daughter of Augustus, fourth earl of Berkeley, had married William, Lord Craven (30 May 1767), and separated from him in 1780. Less than three weeks after his death, she married on 13 October 1791 Christian Frederick (1736–1806), Margrave of Brandenburgh-Anspach and Bayreuth. See *Thraliana* 2:730.

    4. Elizabeth Madocks had three brothers, of whom the two eldest were army officers: William Craven (1770–1825), seventh baron Craven (1791), cr. Viscount Uffington and first earl of Craven (1801); Henry Augustus Berkeley Craven (1776–1836); Keppel Richard Craven (1779–1851).

    5. Mary (1760–1804), second daughter of first viscount Curzon, had married 1 July 1779 Henry Stawell (1757–1820), sixth baron Stawell of Somerton. Lady Stawell had served as lady-in-waiting to the Princesses Augusta and Elizabeth.

    6. Elizabeth Madocks was buried by the Cravens, probably at Uffington, Berks.

    7. Thomas Crane Johnstone (1756–99), originally of Kidderminster, Worcs. A distant relative of Elizabeth Madocks, he had matriculated at Saint Alban Hall, Oxford (1785), receiving his B.A. (1793) and becoming rector of Aston Bottrell in Salop.

    8. For the duke of Leeds, see HLP to Sophia Byron, 7 October [1788], n. 3. He died 31

January. According to Farington (4:1189), "He kept late hours, till three or four in the morning, & gamed, so as to distress Himself, which together caused him to be restless uneasy, & probably greatly affected his constitution. The complaint which carried him off was, a mortification in the bladder." Others, however, say he died of erysipelas.

9. Owen Ormsby (1749–1804) had married Margaret (d. 1806), eldest daughter and eventually heiress of William Owen, of Porkington, Salop. Their only child, Mary Jane (1781–1869), inherited through her mother much of the Godolphin property. For the amount of the inheritance, see P.R.O., Prob. 11/1446/591; also Farington 5:2420.

10. According to *The Bath and Bristol Guide*, 4th ed. (post 1769), pp. 11–12, the architect Wood was responsible "not only [for] building Queen-Square, and several Streets contiguous, but the Grand Parade, Pierpont-Street, Duke-Street, &c. And just before his Death, he settled a Plan for erecting a Grand Building call'd the King's Circus, which is in Part finish'd; and a Street leading to it call'd Gay-Street, is quite completed.

"King's-Mead-Street, King's-Mead-Square, Avon-Street, Beaufort-Square, and several Buildings adjoining, were all built within those thirty Years, tho' not under any particular Person's Direction. . . .

"The Houses in Lady-Mead, which leads from Walcot-Street (in the Parish of St. Michael's) toward the Parish of Walcot, have been built within a few Years; and a new Row of Buildings are now erected just above it, call'd Bladud's Buildings."

11. Honour (1735–1816) was the daughter of Robert Pigott (d. 1770) of Chetwynd, Salop.

12. Alexander Hay (1732–1801), Bath apothecary and surgeon.

TO HESTER MARIA THRALE

Bath Tuesday Night
12: February [1799].

In spite of Winds and Snows and Frosts your darling Letter got hither the 3d Day after its Date:[1] but *here's a* Night in which the Newfound Land Dog himself would not I think venture out. *Famine of Felicity* has however driven some fearless Ladies forth in Search of *Pleasure*—and there was a nice Musical Party at Mrs. Coote and Lysaght's where *we* were expected:[2] but I sit still, unable and unwilling to brave the Storm. Among our desperate Chairmen *Unus et hic audax*—as Leander says to Hero of the Bonny Boat-men at Abydos,[3]—offered to take me safely unto Brock Street; but Mr. Piozzi and I have undressed and resolved to listen after falls of Chimneys—here in our own house.

It is a dreadful Winter: but my heart tells me that the Cold saves us from *greater Calamity*.

Poor Lady Nelson whom last Week we looked upon as the happiest of our present Race of human Beings, some of us now regard with Compassion—since it has been said that her brave Husband tho' warm and tender in Defence of Italy, is not however wholly *disinterested*: a lovely Neapolitan holds the Victor in *her* Chains I'm told—let us see if Lord St. Vincent succouring Lisbon will be caught in a like Snare,[4] and renew the Old Ballad of the Spanish Lady.[5] He will I trust have *his* Ship freighted soon with the old crazy Queen of Portugal[6]—Things do go on ripening apace—Yet Hannah More says, notwithstanding all She sees, and hears, and understands; that Affairs will take a *Crane-neck Turn*, (that's her Expression:) and strike us all with Wonder, Joy, and Gratitude.

Mr. Piozzi persists that *Il Vento è forte—ma cambierà*. That's *his* Expression; Doctor Randolph only wonders we do not mend our Manners when God's Judgments do so manifest themselves around us:[7] and *I* stand amazed at the Hope and Confidence they all three entertain——Mrs. Pennington is my Comfort, I have effectually converted *her* and Lady Orkney to *my* way of Thinking,———and both of them wish they had never heard me mention it.

So now if you please we will talk about the *Abraxas*[8] which *Word* being of base Latinity I trust revolted Dr. Burney at the onset—and not being encouraged I went no farther with him into the Subject:[9] but those *steady Scholars* will be often found neglectful of what would not disgrace them to know: They keep polishing and brightening the *Key* of Knowledge, but think not of opening the *Door* with it;[10] and so you and I run up our Rope Ladder and climb in at Window sometimes, and bring away a bit of Plunder—and if our Rope does not break and we fall down and disgrace ourselves—*we* look wise for a Moment, and *they* look foolish.

Mean Time I found a Friend who had it *all ready for Call*——little Mr. Gray of Farringdon who wrote the Key to the Old Testament, preached the Bampton Lectures one Year, and printed his Travels.[11] He possessed good Eyes too, and could discern upon Your elegant Impression——since I wrote last——The Figures which till then I never made out; They are a Cock, a Ram, a Man, and A Horse he says—and we wanted to think them emblematical of the four Seasons of the Year or the four Times of the Day. The word Constantia or Constantius Chlorus is written round, so that He certainly avowed the Possession on't;[12] but what you say is strictly true concerning Early, and Demi Converts carrying them about close concealed as Royalists in France kept their King's Effigies cut in Seal-Handles, Tobacco Stoppers &c.[13] You must have seen them often. Orthodox Christians in those Dangerous Days had the two first Letters of our blessed Saviour's Name *thus* ☧ in a Monogram; and those who embraced the Basilidian Mode carried Abraxas or Abracax, or Abraſas, for so 'twas written *sometimes* with a Greek Sigma.

The Idea of the World being created by seven Angels seems to have originated from the Seven Golden Candlesticks expressive of the *Seven* Spirits which Stand before God's Throne ruling as *They* supposed, the *seven* Planets represented by the Seven Metals which as you know in Chymistry bear *their* Names—*Sol, Luna,* &c.[14] The Number *Seven* has a Thousand Mystic Ideas attendant on it Since God was pleased to say that he rested on the *Seventh* Day from the Great Work of Creation.[15] There seems to have been an old Heretical Custom of using that Number for Divination of future Events: witness Balaam's insisting on Balak's sacrificing *seven* Bullocks and seven *Rams* upon *seven* Altars every Time he went in Search of Events which might in Anticipation delight the King of Moab.[16]—— And I can *myself* remember here in England, that when Conjurors or Quack Doctors came to a Country Town, they always proclaimed themselves a *seventh* Son—doubtless because such was *David, the Man after Gods own Heart*.[17] I do not mean that the Conjurors knew *that* was the Reason; but that from the Days of King David such a Traditionary Notion had kept itself alive in the World even till this present Century, and so Cheats, Impostors and such fellows took the Advantage.

I wonder if this strange Letter will come safe!!

The Storm seems to increase instead of lessening.——You will see more and more dreadful Shipwrecks:[18] I hope you bought the dear Dog which saved the drowning People[19]——his Master will grudge paying Tax some Day and *hang him.*——Don't you remember Mrs. Chapone's Story of a Man bringing to Doctor Desagulieres[20] for Purpose of Dissection, the faithful Cur which once he owed his Life to? ? ? Was the poor Newfoundlander *Yours,* he would be safe.

When you said Suffolk Coast was Fertile in Amber I forgot to ask whether it was the fossil or Ambergris, that strangest of all Substances?—being as I have somewhere read—The Sum of a Tree, hardened by the Sun, purified by the Waves, and when analysed is found to contain [not] a *Vegetable* Oyl——but a *Mineral* Acid. I think 'twas from Dr. Johnson's Lips I once wrote down those particulars, but they are strongly imprinted on my Memory.[21]

You say very comically what a valuable Subscriber I am to Bull![22] And the Compliment is kind as well as flattering—but Bull hates the very Sight of me the while, because I come to his Shop at 8 or 9 o'Clock in the Morning always—the only Leisure hour the Man has from Readers who sit round his Table all Noon, and Footmen who ferret after him for Novels all Night—: and I make him clamber for me and reach Books which do not answer, and then he has to mount the Steps again, and so we go on: I have not routed after Spanheim yet, but I will see if he has got the Ecclesiastical History[23] the first Morning my Legs will stand under me; tomorrow I believe 'twill be impossible.

We are all here raving mad about Sweet charming Siddons, who has given us Three Nights and we expect three more. For my own Part when I reflect 'twas here I saw her first, and first admired her with Admiration which for Nineteen Years has now gone on increasing, I am inclined to weep even without a Word of the Tragedy, to think She should be still *Alive* to draw these Crouds, and I Alive to make one yet amongst them: so many chances against both of us—and so many of hers! and *my* Companions of that Day—numbered among the Dead—would one not weep for Joy and Gratitude!! So many lost, and we *so* spared! Besides that She's a finer Actress now, a finer Woman too than She was in the Year 1780 when We were all at Bath before. *That* seems surprising too—yet so it is.[24]

But I will *not* fill my Frank as well as my Letter, that I will not: tho' Mr. Piozzi makes me add his best Regards to you and to your Sisters. He ran to London with his little Boy whom he has put to School with Mr. Davies while the clear Frost lasted—and the Journey did him no harm it seems; he came back before the Week was out, for Siddons' Benefit.

So now you *shall* be released, and God bless you; and do not set out for Town till the Land Floods abate: They will be prodigious no doubt after these heavy Rains and such a Snow to melt away beside.

12 February 1799

Write me once again before you go to yours and Susan and Sophy's / Affectionate Mother H: L: P:

Text: Bowood Collection. *Address*: Miss Thrale / Lowestoffe / Suffolk. *Postmark*: Bath February Thirteenth 1799 M. P. <Andrews>.

1. HLP was mindful of exceptionally severe storms, floods, and hurricanes, which plagued England from the 8th through the 11th of February. See *AR*, "Chronicle," 41 (1799): 6–7.
2. Mary Coote lived at 8 Brock Street as early as 1791. Within two years she and Ann Lysaght (1743–1812) were listed as the ratepayers for the house. By 1814 both their names had disappeared from the "Walcot Parish Poor Rate Books" (Bath, Guildhall). See also "Walcot Burial Register" (C.R.O., Somerset).
3. Leander to Hero in Ovid's *Heroides* 18.9.
4. John Jervis, made commander in chief of the Mediterranean fleet in late 1795, had become an English hero in 1797 for his role in the victory of 14 February over a superior Spanish fleet off Cape St. Vincent, Portugal. (See HLP to Q, 21 December [1796], n. 7.) He was therefore gazetted to an earldom, the king choosing for him the title of St. Vincent, which he signed for the first time on 16 July 1797.

In 1799, Portugal (at war with France since 1793) was continually harassed by the French Directory and the Spaniards. See, e.g., *The Times*, 4 March 1799. HLP assumed that when the Portuguese monarchy surrendered, the Royal Family would be conveyed into exile by the fleet under St. Vincent's command.

5. See "The *Spanish* Lady's Love," in *A Collection of Old Ballads*, 3 vols. (London: J. Roberts and D. Leach, 1723), 2:191–94. The ballad consists of sixteen eight-line stanzas, beginning: "Will you hear a *Spanish* Lady, / How she woo'd an *English* Man . . ."

HLP was facetious. Now sixty-four, Lord St. Vincent was exhausted by his naval adventures and by the pressures of his command, which he shared with Q's friend, Lord Keith. In fact, the older man relinquished his command on 15 June.

6. Maria I (1734–1816) was titular queen of Portugal from 1777 until her death. She apparently became insane shortly after the deaths of her uncle-husband Pedro III in 1786 and her eldest son, José, in 1788. Her only surviving son, Dom João (1767–1826), was acting regent of Portugal from 10 February 1792 until he was formally declared prince regent on 15 July 1799. (He became king at Rio de Janeiro on 6 February 1818, but returned to Portugal in 1821.)

The queen's insanity had long been known to the English and was often ridiculed. Thus, the *Morning Post*, 19 October 1795, wrote: "The Queen of Portugal is still *insane.—* This accounts for her obstinacy in persevering in the War against France."

7. For Francis Randolph, now rector of Corston and one of the proprietors of the Octagon Chapel (and later of Laura Chapel), see HLP to PSW, 29 August [1791], n. 9.

8. HLP explains the abraxas and its personal associations in "Harvard Piozziana," vol. 4.

"Monsignior Ennio Visconti the great Antiquarian gave me an Abraxas Gem [i.e., a Labrador stone] set in a Seal; it exhibits the Bull's Head, Ram, and Eagle—Mystic Emblems! The Word Aion in one of the Horns. Lady Keith gave me an Abraxas Gem set in a Ring of larger Size, and of no greater Dignity. It once apparently belonged to no less A Man than Constantine Chlorus. The word Abraxas is an odd one—Abrasax seems mingled of Persic and low Latin Abra *White* and *Saxum* a *Stone*. Abracax as often Old Doctor MacLean, and Dr. Gray—Old Testament Gray as they call him, told me most about this curious Matter, and the Supplement to a Gentlemans Magazine 1786 adds some curious Specimens from Mr. Towneley's Musæum. The Cock's Head means the Sun—always he was sacred to Apollo: Esculapius in Heathen Days, and Salutes the Rising Day under all Dispensations." See also "Minced Meat for Pyes" (2:17).

"Abraxas, a word probably first used by the Basilidians . . . and engraved on certain stones, called on that account abraxas stones. The Greek letters *abraxas* make up the number 365, and the Basilidians gave the name to the 365 orders of spirits which emanated in succession from the supreme being. These orders were supposed to occupy 365 heavens, each fashioned like but inferior to that above it, the lowest being the abode of the spirits who formed the earth and its inhabitants, to whom was committed the administration of its affairs. In addition to the word *abraxas* the stones often have cabbalistic figures engraved on them." *Encyc. Brit.* (1797). For the etymology of *abraxas*, also *abrasax*, and *abracadabra*, see *Oxford Dictionary of Etymology* (1966); cf. *Thesaurus Linguae Latinae* (1900–4).

9. For Charles Burney, Jr., and the reasons for HLP's hostility, see her letters to Sophia Byron, 8 June 1788, n. 6, and 8 June [1789], n. 7.

10. See Luke 11:52. While Luke addresses lawyers, HLP has in mind Charles Burney, Jr., whom she classified among the "quasi-scholars": "ye have taken away the key of knowledge: ye entered not in yourselves, and them that were entering in ye hindered." For Charles Townley [Towneley], see HLP to Sophia Byron, 11 August [1788], n. 15.

11. When RG published *A Key to the Old Testament and Apocrypha* in 1790, he was identified on the title page as "Late of St. Mary Hall, Oxford." Shortly thereafter he was presented to the vicarage of Faringdon, Berkshire. In 1794 he produced *Letters during the Course of a Tour through Germany, Switzerland, and Italy, in the Years 1791 and 1792,* under the imprint of F. and C. Rivington. In 1796 he was appointed Bampton lecturer, and his discourses were issued by the Rivingtons in the same year as *Sermons on the Principles upon which the Reformation of the Church of England was established.*

12. As HLP remembered the inscription, the name was Aurelius Valerius Constantius (Chlorus) (250–306, at York). He was a distinguished officer and governor whose primary task was to recover Britain from the usurper Carausius (assassinated A.D. 293), self-proclaimed emperor of Britain.

13. For effigies of Louis XVI mysteriously imprinted on the Labrador stone, see HLP to PSP [ca. 24 December 1802]; to LC, 25 January 1803.

14. See Rev. 1:12, 20.

15. Gen. 2:2.

16. Num. 23:1.

17. Acts 13:22.

18. The storms that struck Bath were duplicated throughout the country.

"After a week's continued snow and frost, early on Saturday morning [the 9th], the night being very tempestuous, the wind suddenly changed to the Southwest, and brought on a very rapid thaw, which being accompanied on Sunday by a heavy rain, produced the greatest flood on our river that has been experienced since 1774; Monday night, when at the highest, it was more than ten feet above its usual level" (*Bath Chronicle,* 14 February).

19. Probably a Suffolk incident reported by Q in a missing letter.

20. John Theophilus Desaguliers (1683–1744), French-born, was brought to England and educated at Christ Church, Oxford (B.A., 1710; M.A., 1712). A lecturer in experimental philosophy, he moved to London in 1712; within two years he became F.R.S. as demonstrator and curator.

21. While HLP combines some of the qualities of *amber* and *ambergris* as they are detailed in SJ's *Dictionary,* the description is hers, coming close to that in Diderot's *Encyclopédie.*

22. According to the Bath directory for 1800: John Bull, bookseller, owned a circulating library, 6 Lower Walks.

23. [Friedrich Spanheim, 1632–1701] *Friderici Spanhemii . . . Opera, quatenus complectun-*

tur Geographiam, Chronologiam, et Historiam Sacram atque Ecclesiasticam utriusque temporis, 3 vols. in 2 (vols. 2 and 3 ed. J. a Marck) (Leyden, 1701–3).

24. When SS left Bath, the newspapers commented:
"Our theatre experienced a great loss last week in the departure of Mrs. Siddons. . . . It is pleasing, however, to reflect, that both the publick and the actress must have been equally gratified by this *transient* exertion of her talents on the stage, from which she originally migrated" and for which she earned more than £500. SS's last performance was on 26 February, a benefit for Mr. Dimond. Her earnings for this night were the "unprecedented sum" of £163 (*Bath Chronicle*, 7 March 1799; *Morning Herald*, 9 March 1799).

The play was *George Barnwell* and "the theatre was crowded to excess—some persons, who could not gain admission in the Gallery, and had probably tickets, made so great a noise, that the first scenes of the play could not be heard—it was expected that when Mrs. Siddons made her app. the noise would cease, but it did not, and she was obliged to retire—when the tumult subsided, the play was begun again from the 1st speech" (Genest 7: 459). See Clifford, p. 183, for SS in 1780.

TO THE REVEREND LEONARD CHAPPELOW

No. 43 Great Pultney Street
Bath—Fryday Morning
[15 February 1799][1]

I was glad to receive *any* Letter from you dear Mr. Chappelow because we both thought it very long since we had heard of, or concerning Your Welfare. The Overturn and Blow upon the Head was a vile Accident, and I am sorry for it[2]—A propòs Lord Kirkwall seems to have recovered [from] his completely——He came to Bath only for three Days, but failed not to call on *us*; Mr. Gray of Farringdon came only for *two* Days, and dined one of those Days with us:[3] so we have all the Civilities we can wish——and my Master has no Gout *now,* and tho' he ran to London with his little Boy, caught no Fall going or returning, but said twas *a very pleasant Journey.* The young Traveller still more hardy than his Uncle, felt no Sensations but those natural to his Age; Delight in Change of Places and Faces. He is both safe and happy under Care of Mr. Davies who has Companions and Instructions just Suitable to his Capacity: I hope he will do very well.

We are all here raving Mad about Dear charming Siddons who attracts Crouds to our Theatre three Times o'Week as if She had been never seen before. I *have* asked her what you bid me,[4] and She commissioned me to tell you——(but to request you would never say a Word upon the Subject to any human Creature for various and cogent Reasons—) That *Nothing* does her any Good——or produces any but a momentary Relief——That Anxiety of Mind increases it almost to Distraction but that She has Martyred herself with unavailing Remedies, and will try *no more.* Since Maria's Death it has returned upon her terribly, and She is as lean as yourself; but very beautiful, and light and graceful in her Figure.

'Tis odd I should have two of my best Friends plagued so; but we passed yesterday Evening together, and She was half asleep all the while with Laudanum taken externally and internally for this horrid Torment—poor Soul!

So now *swear* to me you *will not tell*; but say Mrs. Siddons is here and acting divinely, which is the strictest Truth: and that She looks better than ever, which is the strictest Truth likewise: Confession of Illness is to *her* a Ruin——Say not that anything ails her for Heaven's Sake.

As to the Dispute concerning Ireland it enrages me[5]——If by letting them Alone and saying *Allez vous en* we should not degrade our*self* as a Nation, and give France an Advantage over us, I should not care how long it was before we *intreated* Paddy to take a warm front Seat in Britannia's State Coach, but now it seems necessary almost to *force* the Union they pretend to despise:[6] and make them happy tho' we *break their Hearts* as 'Squire Western says in Tom Jones.[7]

Pray is it true that while the Bath River rose by the melting Snow to an unheard of height, and while poor Mouse Trap hall was inundated in the manner you mention[8]——an Earthquake was observed to shake the Isle of Wight? 136 Acres of which were swallowed in the Sea?[9]

Such are the Popular Concussions and strange Occurrences in the *Political World*, that People seem unmoved at whatever happens in the *natural* one: and to speak Truth the odd Supineness of all Kings, Princes, and Governors whilst their Thrones are cracking and crumbling from under them is much more unexampled than an Earthquake.

Do you drink Water still Dear Sir, and eat plain Meat? I believe that is a good Plan for your general Health, and keeps the Stomach as it should be. You tell us nothing of Lady Bradford; her Friends the Recluses are well[10]——I saw Miss Harriet Bowdler an Intimate of theirs last Night at Mrs. Siddons's.[11]

Have you read the new Plays upon the *Passions*? They are much talked of—— That on *Hatred* is a most extraordinary Performance; The Author wholly unknown: but I fancy *Scotticisms* may be discerned that will point towards Detection by and by.[12] Let me know what Pamphlets beat the Bell in London now, though I have no Time to study. For *that* indeed the Summer is best adapted and I shall soon go home fresh to my Work after this long Vacation.

Now Adieu and write us a kind Letter soon. My Master sends a thousand best Regards with those of Dear Sir Yours &c. / H: L: P.

Text: Ry. 561.161.

1. HLP's letter was written on Friday, 15 February, in response to LC's of 12 February (Ry. 562.58).
2. In his letter of the 12th, LC had lamented:
"Miseries upon miseries so said Job.—On Wednesday Last I left my Ash Wednesday prayers at Weston, to accompany Mr. Simpson Lord Bradfords 2d Son to London—in consequence of a Summons from the Duke of Portland—who said the most anxious wish of his political Life was the Union with Ireland.—We travelled night and day—and Lost but one 1/2 hour, not stopping a moment till we were overturned at 4 'Clock in the Thursday morning in a dreadful snowdrift 4 miles this side of Chappel House—I was

undermost and got a dreadful blow on my head—which has ached ever since.—We got here [Berkeley Square] at 6 'Clock, and at 8 Mr. Simpson went to the House." See also HLP to LC, 10 March 1799.

John Simpson (1763–1850) assumed by act of parliament the surname and arms of Simpson (his mother's maiden name). He was at this time M.P. for Wenlock (1784–85, 1794–1820).

William Henry Cavendish, later Cavendish–Bentinck (1738–1809), third duke of Portland. He became much interested in Ireland when he served as viceroy there in 1782.

3. "Mr. Gray of Farringdon came to Bath purposely on a Visit to *me* I believe; his Curiosity was excited by what he had heard of *Retrospection*: I read him what I could of it—I should be glad to get his Corrections before we print—We must shut up this Farrago now & *mind the great Affair*" (*Thraliana* 2:994).

4. Frequently when LC had to confront a problem, he suffered from his "old Tormentor the Urticaria. . . . I was covered from Top to Toe [following his return to London].—Do for God Sake ask Mrs. Siddons how she does.—Has she received any assistance from internal or external applications?"

5. HLP refers to the debate over union with Ireland. When Parliament convened in January, the government-sponsored proposal was attacked with such vehemence that the motion was tabled for the remainder of the session. Not until 1800 did the ministry have majority support. The British Act of Union passed on 2 July and the Irish act on 1 August. The union became a fact on 1 January 1801.

6. HLP's image is drawn from a joke told her by LC on 12 February. "3 English Gentlemen in the inside of the coach, invite the [Irish] fool to take the 4th Seat.—National pride obliges him to keep, as he thinks, in a superior place.—This dreadfully cold—and snows.—He does not care for that. He will not be happy—he tumbled from the roof of the Coach—which Left him behind—he Lost his road—a direction post told him the way to London—I'll receive not direction—he turned back—and went to the Devil—allez vous en—" (Ry. 562.58).

7. In bk. 18, chap. 8, Squire Western, responding to Sophia's refusal to marry Blifil, informs Squire Allworthy: "I have packed her up in chamber again, and tomorrow morning down she goes into the country, unless she consents to be married directly, and there she shall live in a garret upon bread and water all her days; and the sooner such a b—— breaks her heart, the better, though d——n her, that I believe is too tough. She will live long enough to plague me."

8. In his letter of 12 February, LC had written: ". . . my small habitation [in Hill Street] has been overwhelmed in Snow—Cart Loads were removed when it began to Thaw.—But yet we could not get the frozen snow from the Gutters which obstructing the deluge of rain we had on Sunday night inundated Us completely—and my House was filled with water in every room."

9. According to *AR*, "Chronicle," 41 (1799): 7:

"An awful phenomenon occurred in the Isle of Wight: a large tract of land, containing 130 acres, with a dwelling–house and other edifices upon it, occupied by farmer Hervey, was suddenly separated from the adjoining ground, and propelled forwards towards the sea; leaving in the place which it before occupied a stupendeous gulph or chasm that instantly filled with water."

The report was suspect, John Gillon 15 February commenting: ". . . and the History of the dreadful Earthquake in the Isle of Wight, you have heard of, must be, as you conjecture the Dream of a Day, or a trumped up Story" (Ry. 577.15).

10. The Ladies of Llangollen: the Hon. Sarah Ponsonby (ca. 1755-1831) and Lady Eleanor Butler (ca. 1745-1829). See HLP to Q, 10 March, 1796, n. 16.

11. Harriet Bowdler, i.e., Henrietta Maria (1754–1830), was the daughter of Thomas and Elizabeth Stuart Bowdler of Ashley, near Bath; the sister of John (*Reform or Ruin*) and Thomas (ed. *Family Shakespeare*).

Living at 2 Park Street, Bath, Harriet Bowdler had written two volumes of religious

Maria Anne Fitzherbert. Portrait by Richard Cosway, R. A.; engraved by John Condé (1792). (Reproduced by permission of the Trustees of the British Museum, Department of Prints and Drawings.)

Poems and Essays (Bath, 1786). For her *Sermons on the Doctrines and Duties of Christianity,* see HLP to LC, 30 July 1803, n. 17.

12. The Scottish poet and dramatist Joanna Baillie (1762–1851) published anonymously in 1798 the first volume of *Plays on the Passions,* "A Series of Plays; in which it is attempted to delineate the stronger passions of the mind, each passion being the subject of a tragedy and comedy." The volume contained *Basil,* a tragedy on love; *The Trial,* a comedy on love; *De Monfort* (sometimes *De Montfort*), a tragedy on hatred.

TO THE REVEREND LEONARD CHAPPELOW

Bath
[ca. 20 February 1799][1]

I am all of your Mind about public Affairs Dear Mr. Chappelow, There is no Trust to be put in Princes:[2] They seem all in a Confederacy to pull down their own Palaces and pick the Cement out of the Thrones they sit on. 'Tis a strange Moment——and so *sickly* too.

We have a kind of contagious Diarrhœa going about here, owing possibly to the stagnant Waters after such unexampled Floods of Rain. Your Friend Mrs. Fitzherbert has been at the point of Death——I know not *now* how near She is to Recovery[3]—but I was fainted away twice one Morning from Violence of the Disease, and frighted my Husband and kind Mrs. Pennington——A propòs *She* too is tortured with the *Urticaria*.

Dear Siddons acts here three Days in every Week; and no Prince molests her as I see. Bath wants not Arrivals to fill it; The Throng of People in our Pump Room is immense, but I shall give up my Morning Ranelagh[4] soon and return to Brynbella where the Air is dry and the Water rolls away, leaving no Stagnation to cause putrid Vapours. Write me another letter though, before we go; and do send the Enclosed to Mrs. Holman who I hear is not well, and I am really sorry.[5] Poor Lady Bradford is greatly to be pitied, She will *now* I fear, never perfectly recover her Spirits.

The Irish will not long stand out, but from forced Marriages sometimes spring Divorces——my fear is lest they never should be friendly.

Have you read the new Plays written to illustrate the *Passions*? Pray find out who is Author of so new a Device——but there are stranger Books than these. I read a Pamphlet this Morning which says the *Sun is a Body of Ice*——Is it not Time to go home and tell my Neighbours what is going forward? If you hear any *amusing* tales such as *Earthquakes* &c. pray favour us with the Communication and accepting all our true Regards / Believe me / Dear Sir ever yours / H: L: Piozzi.

Text: Ry. 561.166.

1. LC immediately answered HLP's letter, dated [15 February 1799]. With this present letter she responded to his, now missing. Hers was written before 26 February, when SS left Bath but sufficiently after the 15th to allow for the exchange of two letters between Bath and London.

Moreover, the flooded Avon began to recede only on 13 February. The water ("as high as the bellies of horses"), which inundated houses and the Bristol road, could not have become stagnant for several days. (See the *Bath Chronicle*, 14 February.) HLP's letter was therefore written ca. 20 February.

2. Ps. 146:3.

3. When Maria Anne Fitzherbert ended her liaison with the Prince of Wales, she took pains to avoid him. She sold the lease of Marble Hill and took up residence at Castle Hill, Ealing. She gave up visiting Brighton and instead often wintered in Bath. In February she was so seriously ill that a newspaper assumed that "'She *had died* at Bath.'" See Christopher Hibbert, *George IV / Prince of Wales* (N.Y., Evanston, San Francisco, London: Harper and Row, 1972), pp. 170-71.

4. See HLP to PSW, 10 July 1789, n. 1.

5. Jane Holman, née Hamilton, who had married 12 February 1798, miscarried a year later. See HLP to the Miss Thrales, 18 [April 1793], n. 4.

TO THE REVEREND LEONARD CHAPPELOW

Brynbella
10: March 1799.

My dear Mr. Chappelow

has shewed us so many kindnesses—I am Sure he will pay 8d. with all possible Good humour for the Pleasure of knowing we are got home safe and Sound before this *second* Snow threatens our young Trees with a long White Night Cap as if Christmas was coming back at Easter. If I had known where any of Your Members of Parliament resided, I should not however have directed this Letter to No. 12—but they are all Young Men and fly about, and one knows not where to shoot a Cover at them.

If you go—as was your Intention to Streatham Park, beg Mr. Davies to write now and then and say how the little Boy does, and how he comes on: we have had but one Letter from the University since our *Student* had *Chambers* there, and then the Abbè *forgot to name him.*

Mrs. Fitzherbert's Knocker was tyed up when we left Bath, but 'twas said that no Danger remained; you See Lady Derby has brought a Baby very well after all, and We hear in the Country that Mrs. Mostyn and her Son prosper exceedingly. She sent the old Nurse who has lived with Miss Thrale these 15 Years and is now at Llewessog on a Visit——to see *this Place* while we were at Bath. The Gardiner and his Wife walked over it with her of Course[1]——and Lord Bless me! says the Woman—"what Fools must the Owners be to build such a Seat which they *never can live to enjoy!!!* but they have sent for an heir from Italy it seems; so *no matter.*"

Poor Italy!! Its last Breath of Independance seems *expired* with Naples: I wish

10 March 1799 71

Vesuvius would revenge its Cause at last, and swallowing up the City save it the Disgrace of falling under French Dominion.[2]

Buonaparte sending home for Actors and Dancers is admirable:[3] can any Man have a harder *Part* to *play* than himself? Dear Siddons made a nice Shining Time at Bath. She left Cecilia there under Custody of Miss Lees;[4] but She is not the Cecilia you remember admiring: Her height and long slight slim form, fright such of her Friends as were agonized about Maria, whom She resembles to a terrifying Exactness. No one *hopes* She will reach 21 Years old.[5] Her charming Mother told me Slyly, that if anything ever *did* do her good for that *horrid tingling* She and you are tormented with; it was the Baths of Mineral Water She washed in while among us this last Month: but it often gets quieted for a Time I find—— and then returns.—Let us hear my good Sir how *You* are, and how the little Darling Book gets forward.[6] *My* Stuff has stood like one of the Mile Stones in our high Road—covered with Snow all this Time; but I will begin on All Fool's Day— (if I live so long)——and set resolutely to work upon't. My Master will find Amusement among his Workmen &c. but we miss Your Company terribly. Lord Kirkwall is *now* not the worse for his Blow that Night, but the Effects did not go off soon. It was the last good Assembly——Poor Mrs. Wynne[7] and her one-Armed Consort could not make out eight Friends——and so the whole Thing dropt after we came away.

The Ladies at Llangollen will be very angry that we did not call; but the Truth is we were obliged to be at home *to a Day,* and dared not venture being dug out of the Snow *again* upon those Mountains; so we ran thro' Shrewsbury never stopping to break a short Cake even with dear Miss Owen, and drove to Brynbella by the Wrexham Road.

Tell me some News foreign and Domestic, and say if poor Seward be yet alive:[8] Mr. Graves of Claverton[9]—Shenstone's Mr. Graves,[10] called on me at Bath to tell that he was dying.—Merry is gone too—our Florence Miscellany Companion;[11] <To>*us ces Morts ont vecu*; Take Care of yourself and accept our Kindest Regards / from the hand of H: L: Piozzi.

Text: Ry. 560.75. *Address*: Rev: Mr. Chappelow / No. 12 / Hill Street / Berkeley Square / London. *Postmark*: DENBIGH E MR 12 99.

   1. For Tibson, see HLT to FB, 20 May 1784, n.6. She was accompanied by Thomas Davies, Brynbella's gardener, and his new wife, the former Mrs. Beckwith.
   2. On 24 January, "there was an eruption of Mount Vesuvius, which had been tranquil for five years past. This phenomenon, which had hitherto been regarded as an indication of the anger of their favourite saint [Januarius], in the present temper of the Neapolitans [now supporters of their conqueror Championnet], was constructed into a favourable omen. The blood of the saint flowing at the same time . . . confirmed by another miracle this sudden revolution in Naples" (*AR* 41 [1799]: 154, 155).
   3. On 17 January *The Times* reported, "the French have not only erected a Theatre, but a Concert Room, and Gardens, like our Vauxhall, at Cairo, where fire–works and music entertain the company in the evening in the Parisian stile." On 6 March the same newspaper announced that "Several French Actors have received passports from the Minister of the Marine, in order to proceed to Egypt, to perform in the theatre established by Buonaparte at Grand Cairo."

4. Five-year-old Cecilia Siddons was sent to Belvidere School, conducted by Harriet and Sophia Lee. See HLP to SL, 17 November 1787, n. 7; to PSW, 5 September [1791].

5. For Maria Siddons's illness, see HLP to PSP: 27 March, n. 3; 14 September, n. 3; 4 October, n. 1; 22 October, n. 1 (all in 1798).

6. For LC's planned poetic interpretation of the animal kingdom, see HLP to LC, 3 June 1796.

7. Anna Maria Wynn, the mother of JMM and the widow of Edward Watkin Wynn, an army officer who died suddenly in 1796.

8. William Seward was to die of an "asthmatic" heart condition, complicated by dropsy, in Dean Street, Soho, on 24 April.

9. A poet and novelist best known for *The Spiritual Quixote*, Richard Graves (1715–1804), an Oxonian, was ordained in 1740. Moving about until 1748, he was presented by William Skrine (ca. 1722–83) to the rectory of Claverton, near Bath, in 1748.

Meeting HLP in Bath was inevitable, for Graves walked to that city almost daily from his parish. He admired HLP and on 1 February sent her a poem in heroic couplets upholding her reputation against "a most impudent insult on so respectable a character." See the MS in the Butler Library, Columbia University; *Thraliana* 2: 994.

10. William Shenstone (1714-63) had been a close friend of Graves when they were both at Pembroke College, Oxford. They met frequently at Claverton between 1744 and 1763.

HLP admired Shenstone for his poetry and his landscaping of the Leasowes. See her "Stanzas written . . . at Shenstones Leasowes," in "Verses 1," p. 38. The three stanzas begin: "To Shenstone in his Grot retired / My truest praise I'll pay."

11. In 1798 a corpulent and inactive Robert Merry was living in Baltimore. On 14 December of that year, while walking in his garden, he had a paralytic stroke and died within three hours.

TO PENELOPE SOPHIA PENNINGTON

Brynbella
Sunday March 10: 1799.

First of Friends in Every Sense of the Word, Dear and kind Mrs. Pennington! What a charming Letter have you written me! And how consoling it was to receive such a Compensation—altho' a small one for the Converse I have so great Reason to regret.

Our Journey was excellent and mended on us every Stage, till the Sun lighted up our lovely Vale of Clwydd, and never seen before the Moment of our ascending the last Hill—has smiled upon us ever since.

I shall not begin Work till after Easter, we have enough to employ us now in surveying our sweet Place and recounting the *Braave Alteraations* as the Fool said to Mr. Whalley. There are indeed no *Chickens to peck*, but soon there will be; and though tis a Sharp Frost I hope much Benefit both to Health and Agriculture from the dry Season, so necessary after those heavy Rains. That A Peck of March Dust should be worth a King's Ransom was an Old Proverb familiar in your good Mother's Day;[1] and Kings being fallen in Value now, I suppose The *Dust* rises in Estimation.

Are not you sorry for the poor Tricked and betrayed, but ever courageous Neapolitans? of which those were happiest who left their Dead Bodies in the

Street defending their lovely City to the last. Vesuvius seems to have half a Mind to save further disgrace on that Country, and will perhaps swallow it up—*from* the French, or *with* the French—who knows?

Well! I got dear Doctor Randolphs Blessing, and a kind Squeeze by the Hand of his amiable Lady,[2] before we left Bath: and then I resolved to mind my own Business and let the Public think of its own Affairs.—They mingle so with *mine* however, that I cannot separate them as Siddons does: her little Girl seemed bent upon shewing me that Day we dined at Miss Lees and made our Partenza—— How well you were versed in the knowledge of her Family Character. She is sure enough no common Child, no healthy Child, and no Good humoured Child; If she remains at Belvedere House She will not long be a spoiled Child: for those Ladies—*have the way*—and will make her a charming Creature! *We Parents* meantime seldom think our Nestlings *can* be *improved*; it is therefore very *seldom*— (never I think)—that we feel obliged to those who bring our Babies into what the World calls *good Order*. I should think it Happiness for Cecilia to remain where She is——and Felicity for Miss Lees to return her safe home again in April. If I read her Fortune aright, She will be taken to Marlborough Street this next Spring. Pray let me know if I have lived long enough near Norwood to understand the Gypsie Trade and predict pretty Girl's Fortunes nicely.[3]

Mrs. Mostyn sent the Old Nurse I told you of, over here in a Post Chaise——to see Brynbella while we were away——What a place! exclaimed She; and what Fools the Builders to plan a Thing it is impossible they should live to finish;—But they have an Heir now—come from Italy I find.

This is the only Domestic News which could interest *you*, and I know Dear Mr. Pennington is kind enough to care about whatever concerns us and our little Boy. Pray give him and Mrs. Weston our True Loves and Compliments and believe me with truest Esteem and tenderest Regard / Your much obliged Friend and Faithful Servant / H: L: Piozzi.

Text: Princeton University Library. *Address*: Mrs. Pennington / Dowry Square / Hot Wells / Bristol. *Postmark*: DENBIGH.

1. Very popular in the sixteenth and seventeenth centuries, the proverb about the "Peck" or "bushel" of early spring dust suggests a time of good seeding that follows upon a dry March.
2. Mary Randolph, née Randolph (1745–1809), was the daughter of Thomas (1701–83), archdeacon of Oxford and president of Corpus Christi College; the sister of John (1749–1813), bishop of London.
3. Norwood, a village near Streatham, was once notorious as "a principal haunt of gypsies." Victims of local prejudice, they were stigmatized as thieves and fortunetellers. One remaining vestige of their presence is the name "Gypsy Hill." See also HLP to Q, November 19[–20]1794.

TO HESTER MARIA THRALE

Brynbella
19. March 1799.

Your Letter my Dearest Girl followed us hither from Bath—where Miss Lees promised to take Care of our Correspondencies after the *Hegyra*—so Mahomets Disciples call the *Flight* I think. We fled from Pultney Street because of heavy Rains which gathered such a World of Stagnant Water under our House and round it, I really felt more than half afraid lest something might happen in Consequence of such putrid Vapours. Many Knockers too were tyed up; The little Contagious Diarrhea—which Mrs. Fitzherbert stopping by Laudanum endangered her Life—seemed to be gaining Ground; and we thought it was better come home to a pure dry Air; and bright cold, Spring Weather among our Snowtopt Mountains. Besides that my Holydays were out, and 'tis good to begin Work *early* when one recollects dear Dr. Johnson's Observation "that those who run against Time encounter an Antagonist not Subject to Casualty or Accident."[1]

I'm glad you made your Journey to London so agreeable; I never saw Cambridgeshire, Ely, or the Counties of Norfolk and Suffolk:—or Kings College Chapel, nearer than from the Warren Hill Summerhouse in Offley Park, Hertfordshire, whence on a clear Day we could easily discern the Flag flying on any particular Occasion—so extensive and distinct was that Prospect. Alnwick, Northumberland,[2] exhibits a minute, but perfect Resemblance of the beautiful Structure you so justly admire—in the Repository her Husband built for His Duchess—last of our old Percies and Plantagenets.[3] It contains a magnificent *Cenotaph.*[4]—The *Body* was deposited in Henry 7ths Chapel at Westminster and her Pedigree in a right Line from *Charlesmagne* is drawn out upon White Marble and forms an elegant Ornament to the Place.[5] I will however make an Effort to see the lovely Model whence Alnwick Chapel was copied before I die—for 'tis too silly to leave a World after residing in it half a Century and know nothing of what one has left behind.

Your Father—a good Oxonian,[6] used to despise the Colleges at Cambridge,— and swear that our Almshouse at Newington near the Borough Stones End—was as handsome an Edifice as any of them.[7]

Poor Ickworth will be long before it sees its Master:[8] The Bishop likes Italy better than home I fancy—but being *forced* upon a foreign Residence may possibly cure his Passion.[9] The Loss of that Ship Load of Rareties which Sir William Hamilton had been so long and so judiciously collecting, is still a grater Calamity to the Lovers of Virtù than the taking Lord Bristols Pack<et>—but every thing belonging to that hapless Country seems hastening to an <end.>[10]

Oh! truly did I tell them a Dozen Years ago that it was *22 o'Clock* with old Rome even *then*——and our latest Accounts from Lombardy having brought us word that the Dear Marquis of Araciel, Abate Bossi, and other of our truly intimate Friends are dead[11]—makes *us* care less and less for what *further* is to happen in the most charming Part of nearly-ruined Europe.

Death of Acquaintance does really *pursue* one, or more properly *surround* one on every Side: Sweet Mrs. Madox is a cruel Deprivation here, so is Mr. Pennant whom I made my Dictionary; and Llannerch Park is likely soon to be broken up. Poor Merry the celebrated Della Crusca found Death in America and old Mr. Graves of Claverton—*Immortal* Mr. Graves—who wrote the Spiritual Quixote, and was (a thousand years ago) the favourite Correspondent of Shenstone—called on me at Bath to say that Seward was dying.—I hope *that* News was not true, for 'tis a melancholy Thing—as Floretta found it in Dr. Johnson's Tale—to outlive Lovers and Haters, and Friends and Foes; and find ones' self surrounded by those with whom one has no Ideas in common,—no Care for Applause nor no Strife of Competition.[12]

Do you take an Interest in these new Plays written (as the Author says) with intent to exemplify the Progress of the Passions? They attracted our Notice at Bath very forcibly though never acted. *I* said the Character of Jane de Montfort was like *my* Mother's Character—and Sally Siddons said it was like *her* Mother's Character.—Pray read the Dramas, they are no common Things; they will repay your Trouble. No one of our Society knew who it was that wrote them, we *all* made Guesses and I guessed Fanny D'Arblaye; but there were those who said *no Woman* was capable of such Performances. *I* think however with Metastasio *Noi possiam quando a noi piace*[13] and my Heart tells me that *no Man* wrote these Plays.—or the Preface.

I hope you will find the Town in high Good Humour with Mr. Holman's new Piece[14]—a Votary of Fame only, he will perhaps get into the *Road to Riches*[15] and such is his Estimation in the World that even his own Rival Authors seemed pleased with his Success——What an Account of a Man! What a Trait is *that!!* but he is an excellent Creature.

I seldom talk in my Letters of Domestic Arrangements—*Kitchen Griefs* as I call them: Mrs. Beckwith's Conduct however amazed even *me* who am not easily astonished at Proofs of human Depravity. She married the Gardiner but just in Time it seems, and is ready to lye In at 3 Months End. A poor meek, mortified, unhealthy, unhappy, but completely *Ladylike* Person as She appeared to me; and as She really *was* in Birth and Manners: but too much Opium, and too many Modern Novels were certainly the Cause.

I am glad to hear my Streatham Neighbour Lord Deerhurst is likely to be at length rewarded for that *chearful* Endurance of Affliction so very uncommon and in my Mind so very near *meritorious*. One has heard so many People grumbling over *good* Fortune, that the Sight of a Man bearing Blindness and narrow Means of living, as *he* did;[16] always excited in me particular Esteem; and now I am informed he is likely to die rich, and leave his Children happily provided for—I was really much pleased with the news.[17] When Things were at the worst between Lord Coventry and him,[18] he never would speak or hear others speak disrespectfully of his Father I remember—and the Thoughts of such Conduct now, will help heal the Breach. But Mr. Piozzi's Baisemains must be added to my best Wishes for you all, remaining evermore / affectionately Yours H: L: P.

Text: Bowood Collection. *Address*: Miss Thrale / Great Cumberland Street / Oxford Road / London. *Postmark*: DENBIGH 22 MR 99.

1. "Pope," *English Poets* 3:117.

2. "Alnwick Castle contains about five acres of ground within its Outer Walls, which are flanked with sixteen Towers and Turrets. . . ."
"The Castle properly consists of three Courts or Divisions; the entrance into which was defended with three strong massy Gates." The castle was further embellished with portcullises, draw-bridges, prisons. "Under each of the Prisons was a deep and dark Dungeon. . . . That of the Inner Ward is still remaining in all its original horrors." See *A Description of Alnwick Castle, Northumberland* (Alnwick: Printed by J. Catnach, 1796), pp. 15, 18.

Founded by the Romans and further built upon by the Saxons, "the Castle and Barony of Alnwick came into the possession of the Percies [in 1309]. . . . Immediately on this acquisition, the Lord Henry de Percy began to repair the Castle; and he and his successors, afterwards Earls of Northumberland, perfected and completed both this citadel and its outworks." See *A Description of Alnwick Castle, Northumberland* (Alnwick: W. Davison, 1846), pp. 5–7; George Tate, *The History of the Borough, Castle, and Barony of Alnwick*, 2 vols. (Alnwick: Henry Hunter Blair, 1866–69), 2:357.

3. Sir Hugh Smithson of Stanwick (ca. 1714–86) succeeded his father-in-law, Algernon Seymour (1684–1750), seventh duke of Somerset (1748) and first earl of Northumberland (1749). Upon the latter's death, Smithson took his seat as earl of Northumberland and by act of Parliament (12 April 1750) assumed the name of Percy in lieu of Smithson. In October 1766, he was created Earl Percy and duke of Northumberland of the third creation.

In July 1740 he had married Lady Elizabeth (or Lady Betty), née Seymour (1716-76). She succeeded her father (7 February 1749/50) in the barony of Percy as *suo jure* Baroness Percy. By virtue of this title, Lady Elizabeth could claim descent not only from the Percy line but from Mary (d. ca. 1361), daughter of Henry Plantagenet, earl of Lancaster and grandson of Henry III. She had married in 1334 Henry (d. 1368), third Lord de Percy of Alnwick (1351/52).

4. HLP refers to Alnwick Castle's chapel, "under [whose] great east window is an elegant Cenotaph of statuary marble, erected to the memory of Elizabeth, the first Duchess of Northumberland. . . . At one end of the Cenotaph are the arms of the Duchess, and at the other the arms of the Duke her husband. On the top are a lion and unicorn couchant, and between them, on a small tablet is [an] inscription Sacred to the Memory of Elizabeth Percy . . . Heiress of the Ancient Earls of Northumberland." See the 1846 *Description*, pp. 20-21.

5. The duchess was interred with her parents in the family vault in the chapel of Saint Nicholas, Westminster Abbey. Her monument is an amalgam of ancient Roman monumental style and that which dominated the reigns of Elizabeth I and James I.

In the center is a pyramid surmounted by a flaming vase and having at its base an antique fluted mable sarcophagus. Within the confines of an elliptical arch below the sarcophagus is the following inscription in gold letters on black marble: "Near this place lies interred, / Elizabeth Percy Duchess of Northumberland, / In her own right / Baroness Percy, Lucy, Poinings, Fitz–Payne, Bryan, and Latimer. . . ."

6. HT matriculated at University College in June 1744, aged fifteen. He left without a degree to make a grand tour of Europe with William Henry Lyttelton, later Lord Westcote.

7. In Southwark.

8. Ickworth House in the parish of West Suffolk, near Bury St. Edmunds, was the seat of the Hervey family and the earls of Bristol.

9. On 20 August 1798, *The Times* (under dateline Florence, 20 May) commented: "You have no doubt heard of the arrest of this celebrated and *eccentric* Prelate. The circumstances which gave rise to it were the following:—In consequence of his fine collection of pictures, statues, &c. having been put into a state of *requisition* by the French *connoisseurs*, on their triumphal entry into Rome, his Lordship, instead of yielding to this *fraternal* mark of the attachment of the *Great Nation,* immediately sent dispatches to the

English Minister [in Florence], and to Sir Wm. Hamilton at Naples, containing a ludicrous account of the French troops in Italy. . . . One of these letters, which also contained a violent attack on the unprincipled ambition of the French Directory, and of the sordid views of all their Generals, Buonaparte himself not excepted, unfortunately fell into the hands of the enemy. . . . In consequence of which the Bishop was arrested at Ferrara, as a *spy*, and for some time was kept in close confinement." He was, however, soon allowed to go "to Milan, where he now resides, attended by a body guard of *chosen* Republicans."

On 12 March 1800 *The Times* reported that the bishop had "returned to Rome. It seems a scandal he should not be obliged to reside in his diocese. If his Lordship prefers Italy, he should resign his Bishopric."

10. Sir William had formed an important collection of Greek vases, most of them discovered in 1789 and 1790 in tombs in the Two Sicilies. Wishing to sell the collection, he sent it to England aboard the *Colossus*, a seventy-four gun ship of the line returning from the Battle of the Nile, which was wrecked off the Scilly Isles on 10 December 1798 (*The Times*, 19 December). Eight cases of the vases were lost but sixteen were rescued. These were bought by Thomas Hope in 1801 for forty–five hundred guineas.

For Sir William Hamilton, see HLP to Q [ca. 25 March 1796], n. 7.

11. Both died in 1798. For Giuseppe, marchese de Araciel, see HLP to William Parsons, 4 August 1786, n. 2; for Abate Giuseppe Bossi, see her letter to SL, 7 December 1784, n. 6.

12. While still innocent and illusioned, Floretta (like the fairy, Lady Lilinet of the Blue Rock) believed that "every reasonable being must love that which having never offended, could not be hated, and having no power to hurt, could not be feared." But with experience comes the bitterness of disillusion, alienation, and loss. Floretta's "friends, her enemies, her admirers, her rivals dropped one by one into the grave, and with those who succeeded them she had neither community of joys nor strife of competition." *The Fountains: A Fairy Tale*, in Anna Williams' *Miscellanies in Prose and Verse* (London: T. Davies, 1766), pp. 116, 140. For HLT's self-identification as Floretta, see G. J. Kolb, ed. *Rasselas and Other Tales* (1990), pp. 215–18.

13. HLP's deliberate variation of Metastasio's phrase from *Gioas re di Giuda*, pt. 2, line 333: "Quando a te piace" (spoken by Giojada to Ismaele).

14. Holman's *The Votary of Wealth* opened at the Covent Garden, 12 January. It appeared eleven times in January, six in February, two in March, and once each in June and September.

15. HLP's quip upon the fact that Holman acted the leading role of Harry Dornton in Holcroft's *Road to Ruin* (1792).

16. Lord Deerhurst (1758-1831), at nineteen, angered his father by marrying without his consent Lady Catherine Henley (d. 9 March 1779), daughter of the earl of Northington.

Shortly after the death of Lady Catherine, Lord Deerhurst, while hunting near Wooton in Oxfordshire, tried to jump a " 'five-barred gate.' His horse fell on him and Deerhurst's 'right eye was beat into his head, his nose broke and laid flat to his face,' and he was 'much mangled [and] reported dead' " (*London Chronicle*, 21 November–7 December 1780) (pp. 496, 513, 542). The report of his death was premature, but he was blinded. See *GM* 79, pt. 2 (1809): 892; *Walpole Correspondence* 33: 242 n.11.

17. As reported in the *True Briton*, 25 April:

"The reconciliation which has recently taken place between the Earl of Coventry and his son, Lord Deerhurst, was effected by the Hon. Mr. Coventry, eldest son of the Earl's present wife, and in a manner that puts the character of that Gentleman in the most amiable point of view. The Earl desired that Lord Deerhurst would bring all his family to this interesting meeting; and this long–desired and long–talked of interview had such an effect upon the feelings of Lord Deerhurst's second son, that he fainted away with excess of gratification."

18. Lord Deerhurst's father was George William Coventry (1722-1809), sixth earl of Coventry (1751); an Oxonian, he was M.P. (Tory) for Bridport (1744–47); for Worcestershire (1747–51); lord lieutenant and *custos rotulorum* of Worcestershire (1751–1808).

TO THE REVEREND LEONARD CHAPPELOW

Brynbella
Monday 19: March 1799.

Dear Mr. Chappelow

I hope this will find you quite well of the Cough and Cold which has attacked every body this Season, and which we have lost by change of Air completely.[1] It was very friendly of you to let the Ladies know we could stop nowhere——God knows we were enough wanted at home.[2] Our Gardiner's Wife is almost ready to *lye In* it seems, and the whole Environs talk loudly of her Conduct: one has a Sad Life with these Men and Maids——but who can help it? 'Tis better than being Man and Maid ones' self. You are very kind and very Comical about our little Boy.[3] His Arrival has worked no Reformation in our *other* Connections as yet however; for Lady Orkney, Lady Williams, Lady Blaquiere——*all* the Neighbours, even from Plâsnewydd have either come, or sent, or both—to welcome us home;[4] while Mostyns alone remain mute. I hear *He* is so full of the Notice he received from the Prince of Wales, that no *other* Company can please him:—They are hasting to London *now* 'tis said, that the Acquaintance may not be lost for want of due Cultivation.[5]

Doctor Thornton will be a valuable Friend if he can cure the Urticaria.[6] I know poor Siddons's Torture *well*, but tis *outside* some *times*, and I have seen it all in *Stings like yours*; and then it would go *in* She said and put her in worse Agony than even *that* puts *you*.[7]

These united Irishmen will give Government the *Urticaria*;[8] we may backen the Treason by *one* Medicine, and drive it *in* by another, but I see no *Cure* likely to take Place: People flatter themselves however, and 'tis cruel to convince them that all is relapsing into Chaos——yet what is likely to stop the Progress of such Ruin?——Buonaparte's Players at Grand Cairo, and Barringtons Rope Dancers at Botany Bay——(for he too has set up a Theatre)[9]——I should rely on just as firmly as on Francis the Emperor, and his easily-corrupted Officers.[10]

Well! I will go to work and mind my own Business, and when you are about once more, and Mrs. Clay has cured you[11]——you will do me a kind Turn in asking or finding out what Annual Register it is that tells—from Sir Joseph Banks[12]—and by his Authority——a strange Tale of *Sudara* an Indian Idea that People of a certain Cast upon the Banks of the Ganges——now and then bring forth a Crocodile at the same Birth with a Child; that the Crocodile lives in the River and his *Relations* throw in Presents to him.

I could not have dreamed all this; I *read* it once, and never could find it more. A young Girl told Sir Joseph Banks that She herself had an *Uncle* a Crocodile and She called him *Blue King* I remember. Such a Story wild as it appears cannot be my Invention, That I read it *some*where I will make Oath; nor was the Matter wholly new to me neither when I *did* read it——and I can get nobody to listen or believe now: and my Recollection does not serve me where to get at it again: *do find it me out*.[13]

Make a thousand kind Compliments to Mrs. Clay for us, She is a very charming Lady; but if you get well quicker at her House than ours, we shall be very jealous. Why will you not point me out some Members of Parliament to whom I might direct under Cover and save you these Eightpenny Expences.

Lord Deerhurst's Reconciliation was known at Worcester, and the People there seemed glad——They *know* Lady Coventry's Son, and have only *heard* of my Lord's.[14] I am the most peevish Explainer possible of these Matters, yet am honestly rejoyced that my old Streatham Neighbour's long and chearful Endurance of Misfortune is likely to be at length rewarded. He always *did* love his Father, and never spoke, or would patiently hear others speak disrespectfully of him.

Cecilia Mostyn is big with Child again they tell me, and grown fat besides, and looks exceedingly well, and is packing up for *Town*, and for *Ton* and for all fine Things of Course.[15]

Every body asks for You; Sir John and Lady Williams perpetually—Lady Orkney quite anxiously, and instead of coming hither—You are visiting *Lord Lonsdale*.[16] Oh do tell why dear Siddons acts at Drury Lane again;[17] I thought She and Sheridan were *two* about the Money Stuff: has he paid her the long Arrears I wonder, or how is it?[18] You will hear *all* who *live* in the *living* World.

Have you read the new Dramas written to evince the Progress of the Passions? Pray read and tell me who is the Author. When I was at Bath, every body was guessing, and probably every body guessed wrong. I thought 'twas Mrs. D'Arblaye, Cy devant Fanny Burney. Poor Merry's Death afflicts me.

Does Mrs. Fitzherbert recover? Adieu my Dear Sir. Accept my Master's true Regards with those of Yours sincerely / H: L: P.

You must make haste to North Wales——Mrs. Leo will soon be at Liberty. Her Husband is given over by the *Regulars* and lives only by some Quack Medicine called Tickell's Other.[19] He chased out our gentle Friend Mr. Moore—and sent for Thomas of St. Asaph——Then drove *him* away, and could scarcely be decently civil to Dr. Curry from Chester who told him he would never come again[20]——But the worst of all was Throwing his Crutch at his poor Old Wife, who being blind could not see her Danger, and being lame could not *runaway*.

Such is to *her* the *Irish Union* it seems.

Adieu!

Text: Ry. 560.76. *Address*: Rev: Mr. Chappelow / at Mrs. Clay's / Highgate / Middlesex. *Postmark*: DENBIGH 10 o'Clock MR 22 99 <   > E MR 22 99.

1. HLP responds to LC's letter, 15 March (Ry. 562.59), which he begins by complaining of "a dreadful Cough the consequence of a North east wind."
2. LC had "told the Ladies at Llangollen that [HLP] could not stop a moment even at Shrewsbury—that [she] went by Wrexham and was necessitated to be to a day at Brynbella."
3. LC, who mentioned planning to visit "the Brescian" at the Reverend Reynold Davies's school at Streatham, referred to HLP's "Son and Hero," hopeful that he would "as an Englishman enjoy Brynbella and the vale of Clwyd."
4. Among the neighbors who welcomed the Piozzis was a guest of Lady Orkney of

Lleweni: i.e., Eleanor, née Dobson (1756–1831), wife of John Blaquiere, or De Blaquiere (1732–1812), at this time a baronet (cr. 16 July 1784). Their daughter Anna Maria (1780–1843) was to marry 18 August 1802 John, Viscount Kirkwall (1778-1820) of Lleweni. See *GM* 72, pt. 2 (1802): 781.

Representing Plas Newydd were Robert Watkin Wynn (or Wynne) and his wife, Anne Sobieski, née Dod. See HLP to Q, 27 April 1796.

5. When CMM with her husband and sisters were at Streatham Park in the summer of 1797, Arthur Murphy invited the Prince of Wales to visit there. See *Thraliana* 2:973 n.3.

HLP's scorn of the prince remained largely private. When reading *Spectator* 358 [1789 ed.], on the abandonment of good taste, she wrote: "The nearest Thing to this (that ever I saw) was the Prince of Wales pouring a Bottle of Champagne forcibly down a Waiters Throat once at Ranelagh" (5:253).

Mostyn's association with the Prince of Wales brought him the appointment of "Sheriff of Denbigh 17 March 1801." See P.R.O., *Lists of Sheriffs for England and Wales* (1963).

6. Robert John Thornton (ca. 1768–1837) studied at Guy's Hospital medical school, receiving his M. B. from Cambridge in 1793 and his M. D. from Saint Andrews in 1805. In 1797 he had begun his London practice, which soon became large.

7. HLP replies specifically to LC's comment: "paying a sick visit the other day to Lord Lonsdale—I met accidentally with [his] Physician a Dr. Thornton—who says he can cure Urticaria.—I told him I had oiled my skin—You are nearly right says he.—Neats foot oil I recommend. I have found great relief indeed—and so I told Mrs. Siddons whom I met the other day—but it seems from a moments conversation I had with him that Mrs. Siddons's complaint is quite different to the common urticaria—hers is internal—and but sometimes external.—"

8. A select committee was convened 23 January. On 15 March it printed its report, which allegedly proved "systematic design, long since adopted and acted upon by, France, in conjunction with domestic traitors [the United Irishmen], and pursued up to the present moment with unabated perseverance, to overturn the laws, constitution, and government, and every existing establishment, civil or ecclesiastical, both in Great Britain and Ireland; as well as to dissolve the connexion between the two kingdoms, so necessary to the security and property of both." See *AR*, "Appendix to the Chronicle" 41 (1799):150–52.

9. Irish–born George Barrington, whose real name was Waldron (b. 1755), a pickpocket, was first convicted in 1777 and frequently thereafter. In 1790 he was transported to Botany Bay and in time made superintendent of the convicts.

The governor in charge of Botany Bay sanctioned a theater at Sydney: the actors were convicts and the price of admission was meal or rum. The first play presented (16 January 1796) was Young's *The Revenge*. Barrington wrote a prologue best known for its ironical couplet: "True patriots we, for be it understood, / We left our country for our country's good." See *D.N.B.*

10. HLP was suspicious of Franz II because he signed the Treaty of Campo Formio and because as a result he agreed to the congress at Rastatt (or Rastadt) in which the various states of the Holy Roman Empire and France participated.

11. For Jane Clay, see HLP to LC, 18 September [1797], n. 8.

12. Joseph Banks (1743–1820), naturalist and explorer, cr. baronet (1781). In May 1766 he was elected F.R.S. and in November 1788 became the Royal Society's president, a post which he held until his death. He was honored with the order of the Bath 1 July 1795 and sworn of the privy council 29 March 1797. In 1802 he was to become a member of the National Institute of France.

HLP probably recalls *AR*, "Natural History" 24 (1781):39–52, which provides *"An Account of the Ganges and Burrampooter Rivers. By James Rennell . . . communicated by Joseph Banks . . . from Vol. LXXI of the Philosophical Transactions"* (pp. 87-114). The article, however, did not provide HLP with the information she outlined.

13. In all likelihood HLP read of the East Indian myth in *An Account of the Voyages undertaken by the order of His present Majesty for Making Discoveries in the Southern Hemisphere*

. . . *drawn up from the Journals which were kept by the Several Commanders, and from the Papers of Joseph Banks, Esq.*, by John Hawkesworth, LL.D., 3 vols. (London: W. Strahan and T. Cadell, 1773), 3:756-58. Many years later she recorded it in her copy of Dodd's Bible when reading Gen. 12:15.

The superstition holds "that women, when they are delivered of children, are frequently at the same time delivered of a young crocodile as a twin to the infant.... These crocodile twins are called *Sudaras.*" The same account includes a story told to Banks by a young female slave, that her dying father charged her to go to the river daily and feed his crocodile *sudara*. See *The Endeavor Journal of Joseph Banks: 1768–1771*, ed. J. C. Beaglehole, 2 vols. (The Trustees of the Public Library of New South Wales. In association with Angus and Robertson [1962] 1963), 226-27.

14. After the death of his first wife, Lord Coventry married on 27 September 1764 Barbara, née St. John (d. 1804). Their son, who brought about the reconciliation of Viscount Deerhurst and his father, was either John (1765–1829) or Thomas William (ca. 1779–1816).

Lord Deerhurst was the son of the earl of Coventry and Mary, née Gunning (1732–60).

15. CMM's second son was Henry Meredith, born in London in early autumn 1799.

16. James Lowther (1736–1802), M. P. for the counties of Cumberland, Westmorland, etc., was elevated to the peerage, 24 May 1784, with the titles of Baron Lowther, Viscount Lowther, earl of Lonsdale, etc.

17. According to the *True Briton*, 18 March:

"Mrs. Siddons resumed her situation on Saturday last [the 15th] at this place in the Character of *Lady Randolph*. Her excellence in this Character is too well known to demand the homage of Criticism. It is sufficient to say, that she exerted all her powers with unabated zeal, and made her usual appeal to the hearts of her Auditors.—"

18. Sally Siddons on 19 January had written to PSP: "I wonder if Mr. Sheridan has any notion that she is really at last determined to have no more to do with him." The quarrel was once more about money. See Manvell, p. 248.

19. Letitia Leo (d. 1801) predeceased her husband Daniel by two years. See HLP to Q, 23 February 1794, n. 3.

Tickell's Other was the "Ethereal Anodyne Spirit," a quack medicine concocted by William Tickell, a Bath surgeon.

20. HLP probably refers to Honoratus Leigh Thomas (1769–1846), originally of Hawarden, Flintshire. After receiving his diploma from the Corporation of Surgeons, 16 October 1794, he volunteered for medical service in the army. By 1799 he had begun to establish a successful London practice in surgery and medical consultation.

The other doctor was William Currie (ca. 1749–1834), of Boughton Hall, Chester. He was affiliated with the Chester Infirmary (1773–90 and 1800).

TO THE REVEREND LEONARD CHAPPELOW

Brynbella
31: March 1799.

You are very kind always My Dear Mr. Chappelow, and very comical about the Gardener; he and his Lady's Conduct seem indeed as if they both had been deep read in Boccacio. I shall be glad of the Romance you mention, but 'twas not there I saw the Story of Sudara: Catherine of Russia's Life is likewise necessary to me—
—If you are good natured enough to send me these Books, put up a Hundred decent Pens with them, for tho' you say I write so very neatly; nothing have I but

Skewers. La belle *Catherine* was a Student of *Boccacio* too, but there is no doing without her Life——let it be the *English* one, for your Friend Mr. Moore wishes to borrow it—and he does not read French.¹ Àpropos he has no Heart of the Oyling Scheme: it will shut all your Pores he says and produce something worse than Urticaria.²

I am delighted that Mr. Whalley and You have met again, and made me *tertiam quid*. His Wife is not much *older* than himself I believe, and looks *younger*;³ She was a crooked Woman when he married her, but not an old one at all, and her first Husband was well known to have adored her.⁴

I care not how much you talk about me with dear Mr. Whalley, but why are my Affairs to be arranged so at Mr. Macnamara's? He had more need settle concerning his Duke of Bedford's Intentions than mine,⁵ for they are of more Consequence: and if *his* succeed,——I shall have no Estate to leave I fear⁶—— and poor John Salusbury has little Cause to rejoyce in his Change of Country: unless a good English Education may benefit him, and give Power to gain that Fortune and Consequence in Life which his good Grace seems studious (by The Tales we are told) to fling away. What you have to relate of Mr. Piozzi is most excessively to *his* Credit I am sure: he has been a good Steward to the Ladies in every Respect, and nothing you say of *us* at Streatham, will be concealed from *them*.

By the way our poor Master here has got the Gout again, and every Creature in this Country has sent Howdyes except the Family at Llewessog. I have a Touch of Rheumatism too, but do not mean to gratify Mr. Macnamara's Curiosity concerning my Will and Testament, or Mr. Lyson's concerning My last Dying Speech and Confession yet awhile: my Parentage and Education they may all learn from that Monthly Mirror Book.⁷

Of all Biographical Anecdotes none ever struck me more forcibly than the one saying how Hannah More *la Devote* was the Person who Educated fair *Perdita la Pecheresse*:⁸ I asked if it has any foundation in Truth—and She owned it as a Fact. You shall have one, little known to the World—of H: L: P; and make what Comments you will upon it.

'Tis that when my little Welsh Estate first came into my Hands—I went to Mr. Scrase at Brighthelmstone and made him arrange Matters so by Will or Deed of Settlement I think they called it—or some thing; to secure My Husband Mr. Thrale as my *sole Heir*, tho' I had then by him Two Sons and several Daughters all alive. He knew nothing of the Transaction till Scrase told it him a year after: He was gone somewhere when I went to Sussex——which I only add to assure you that I was not under his *Influence*——and as to Mr. Scrase, tho' he was the *Family's* Friend—not mine:⁹ he admonished me against the Measure.—and now when you have all said "She was an odd Woman and loved her Husbands"—Even drink her health, and talk of something else.

Here is enough to talk of: Tell me about the 98 Worthy Gentlemen catched up in Red Lyon Street:¹⁰ They should not have held their Treacherous Meetings at *the Royal Oak*, it was unlucky to *them*; and saved our Monarchy a Second Time.¹¹ This nonsense is not worthy Mr. Walter;¹² he is a fine Writer himself, and his Reflexions in Wednesday's Paper were most beautiful;¹³ but when I have Leisure from *old* Rascalities to think on *New*——I will send you my Thoughts for him most freely. These eightpenny Letters *do* afflict me tho; and you should have more Stuff if it were cheaper——notwithstanding 'tis my bounden Duty now to mind My Book, which if I once neglect, no Faeries will finish for me. *'Tis long since Delia and her Train were here.*[14]

Adieu then Dear Mr. Chappelow and if you are kind enough to send me the Books you mention, ask one Priddy an Oylman in Poland Street if he has anything coming down for us[15]——(he had a while ago,) and these Things may come with them——or else send them by a cheap Carriage some how, not Mail Coach——directed to Care of Mr. John Williams Grocer in the High Street Chester.[16] They will come safe—but you must let me pay for them / Accept our united Regards and believe / me ever yours H: L: P.

Hodgkins says the Mail Coach is best and Hodgkins is a Wise Man, [17] but his Master will not be of that Mind when he pays the Carriage.

Text: Ry. 560.77. *Address*: Rev: Leonard Chappelow / No. 12: / Hill Street / Berkeley Square / London. *Postmark*: DENBIGH AP 2 99.

1. HLP wished the following: Jean Henri Castéra, *The Life of Catherine II, Empress of Russia*. An enlarged translation from the French [*La Vie de Catherine II, Imperatrice de Russia*, 2 vols. (Paris, 1797)], 3 vols. (London: Longman and Debrett, 1798).
   For the superstition of Sudara, see HLP to LC, 19 March 1799, n. 13.
2. John Moore, the Denbigh apothecary of Vale Street. See HLP to PSW, 15 September 1792, n. 3.
3. For Elizabeth (Sherwood) Whalley, née Jones, see HLP to SL, 17 September 1784, n. 11.
4. John Withers Sherwood (1736–70), barrister.
5. Daniel Macnamara (1720–1800) was the duke of Bedford's steward in Streatham. See HLP to PSP, 26 April 1793, n. 4.
6. HLP was perpetually at war with the duke of Bedford, the causes altering with his attacks on the Pitt ministry or Tory interest.
   At this time she was offended by his assault upon the income tax bill, which came before Parliament early in January. He argued against "the principle of taxing income. It had been the general practice of taxation, to levy as great a portion as possible of the sum wanted upon articles of luxury and consumption: and, so long as that practice could be continued, it would never be considered as materially unjust in its operation. Although the whole community might not pay towards it in equal proportion, still, as it was optional, it could not be considered as fundamentally wrong. If it was abandoned, it would be a confession, that we could not go on in the most equitable course of taxation." See *AR* 41 (1799): 186–87.
7. See HLP to Thomas Bellamy [4 May 1798] and n. 2; to the Proprietors of the *Monthly Magazine*, 17 June 1798; John Gillon to HLP, 13 July 1798.
8. HLP alludes to the *Memoirs of Perdita*, by Mary Robinson (1784), wherein the one-time mistress of the Prince of Wales acknowledged that she had been taught at the Miss Mores' school in Bristol and had been taken to her first dramatic performance by the sisters.
   Mary Robinson, née Darby (1758–1800), had been born in Bristol. When she was fifteen, she married an articled clerk named Thomas Robinson who, because of extravagance, was imprisoned for debt along with his wife and baby daughter. After being

released, she sought the aid of Garrick, who arranged for her debut as Juliet at the Drury Lane in 1776.

On 3 December 1779 *The Winter's Tale* was produced at the same theater by royal command. Mrs. Robinson appeared as Perdita, her beauty entrancing the Prince of Wales. Within a few weeks and after a written promise to give her £20,000 upon his coming of age, she became his mistress. The relationship did not last long and in a few months she was bought off with a capital sum of £5,000 and an annual pension of £500.

9. For Charles Scrase, see Elizabeth Montagu to Elizabeth Handcock Vesey [25] July 1784, n. 3; HLP to Q, 4 June 1785, n. 24.

10. From the *London Chronicle*, 9–12 March:

"The persons taken into custody at the Royal Oak, in . . . Red–Lion–square, on Sunday night, seventeen in number, after their examination at the Duke of Portland's office, were all, except one, sent to Clerkenwell and Tothilfields prisons, together with the landlord of the house. They are accused of having assembled as United Irishmen. They were brought in coaches. . . .

"Thirty other persons, who are said to be of the same description, were yesterday brought up to the Police Office in Marlborough–street, and committed to prison. They were taken out of a house in St. Giles's."

11. King Charles II is supposed to have hidden in an oak tree near Boscobel House in Salop following his defeat by Cromwell on 3 September 1651, at Worcester, some twenty-five miles away. The royal escape from the oak tree is celebrated 29 May. See John Brand, *Observations on the Popular Antiquities of Great Britain*, 3 vols. (London: Henry G. Bohn, 1849), 1:23-76.

12. Either John Walter (1739–1812), founder of *The Times*, who gave up the management of the newspaper in 1795; or, more likely, his son John II (1776–1847), who was recalled from his studies at Trinity College, Oxford, to begin his association with *The Times*.

13. HLP refers to the author of *The Times* editorial, not of Wednesday but of Thursday, 14 March, on the subject of the Red Lion conspiracy.

Using the conspiracy as a springboard, the writer effects a panegyric upon a government ever vigilant against treason. He concludes: "It is to the unvaried system of politics which the Ministers of Great Britain have pursued in suppressing sedition, that we are indebted for our present state of internal tranquility."

14. See Milton, *Paradise Lost* 9.387.

15. Jacob Priddy, Italian Warehouse, 14 Poland Street, Soho. He had been the proprietor there from ca. 1790 to 1819. He was succeeded by Samuel Priddy, who in 1820 removed the establishment to 1 Charles Street, Manchester Square.

16. See HLP to Q, 23 February 1796, n. 1.

17. For Samuel Hodgkins, the butler at Brynbella, see HLP to Q, 1 August 1793.

TO PENELOPE SOPHIA PENNINGTON

Brynbella
5: April 1799.

My Dear Mrs. Pennington's Letters are always delightful[1] and the little gleam of Sunshine given by the Arch Duke's Victory—strikes across the middle of your last—*So* prettily![2] *So* like the darting Brightness that illuminates our Valley just now——with gloom and gathering Storm all round it.[3]

But I would not have you so sure my kind Friend that all will be decided before we meet again. No, No; although this vile 1799 be *pregnant* with Events, I can't perswade myself She'll be *delivered* exactly at *nine Months End*. Mrs. Jackson knows *these* Matters better than *you* do, by *Experience*—tell her I say so with my best Regards and Mr. Piozzi's.[4]

You see *her* Conjectures about the Play were right after all: Mrs. Radcliffe owns herself Author as Susan Thrale writes me word——and Jane de Montfort will come out immediately[5]—She says not a Syllable of Mr. Whalley's Performance.[6] Lord bless me my Dear! his unfortunate Niece cy devant Fanny Sage, sent to me Yesterday for 20£ and said she was *detained*, (for debt I trow) at our poor petty Town of St. Asaph two Miles off.[7] A tall ill looking Man on Horseback brought the Letter, but will not I hope revenge my refusal of his Lady's Request, when Dumouriez shall have set all the wild Irish at full Liberty:[8] I was half afraid sure enough, yet little disposed to give what would make 40 honest Cottagers happy, to a gay Lass whom I never liked in her *best Days*, and who never had any Claims on *my Friendship* which She now talks so loudly of.

Well! and your little favourite John Salusbury! Susanna Thrale has been to Streatham on purpose I fancy to gratify hers and her Family's Curiosity:—So She saw a little boy with My *Name*, and my Husband's *Face*——and I know not which was the greatest Recommendation of the *two*,—to her.

All this Paper filled—and not a word of our ever-tortured Master! He has been 16 or 17 Days now in strict Confinement with this vile Gout again, as if the Bath Fit had never taken Place. His Looks and Appetite however are not impaired—— and now I have him fast and know *where to find him*—I may work at the Book. Here is no Weather to tempt one out at all, no Blushes and Blooms—We shall have Summer burst out all at once and lose our Spring completely.

With regard to Public Affairs, our Domestic Traytors terrify me most; but if French Valour should by this late Victory get into Discredit abroad, perhaps it would not be so much the *Ton* to imitate their Proceedings here at home, and we should remember Hannah More's Prediction of the *Crane-neck Turn*.[9] If they *can* be made to *run*——they will find no Place that will receive them I believe——All honest Men and Women too are their natural Enemies—and a Grison Girl said to a Gentleman I know something of, "Why dear Sir what should we sit still for, like figures made of Papier maché till our Houses are burned down, our Parents mangled, and our free Will violated! Better go out with the Troops, and sell our Lives at least at as high a Price as we can." The same Gentleman wrote his Sister word that the high Roads were covered with *female Corpses*, which he galloped over.[10]

These are—far as my Reading goes,—new Notions and new Occurrences. I will get me the Book you mentioned. Is not Adolphus a Jew Merchant? How long has *he* been a Writer?[11]

Sweet Siddons's Name is in every Day's Paper I see, her Friends in Cumberland Street say little about her tho'[12]——Did their Intimacy cease with the frail Life of pretty Maria?

Give our kind Love to Mr. Pennington whose Hospitality and Kindness we feel so very sensibly.—How go your *Kitchen* Griefs? Does Frank stay with you? Our Mrs. Beckwith that married the Gardiner will not wait I hear

Till *Nine Times shall Cynthia fill her Silver Horn* &c.[13]

They will have a Cottage full presently as we are told. And now dear Friend farewell, and present our best Remembrances to Mrs. Jackson: has She read Mr. Whalley's Play, and what does She think of it?

This Weather will be favourable at worst, and he will not have *Fevers* to contend with as Mr. Greatheed had, when his Regent came out the second Time.[14]

Once more Adieu! and write now and then; for you *must* hear something more than meets of the Ear of / Your ever truly faithful / H: L: P.

Text: Princeton University Library. *Address*: Mrs. Pennington / Dowry Square / Hot Wells / Bristol. *Postmark*: DENBIGH.

1. HLP answers PSP's letter, dated 31 March (Ry. 567.79).
2. PSP had written: "The Blessing of To Day however is *good* News; a complete defeat gained by the Arch duke [Charles] and his Austrians over Jourdan and his Army."
Both women referred to a battle fought 21–22 March between the army of the Danube, commanded by Jourdan and his opponent, the archduke. The *Gazette de France* reported from Strasbourg (as of 26 March): " 'The contest was maintained with great perseverance on both sides, and the loss was very great. Our army, which was much inferior to that of the Austrians, *has lost some ground.*' " From this excerpt, *The Times* (5 April) speculates "that the Archduke Charles was completely successful."
3. PSP had written of quickening military affairs:
"The Clouds seem to gather and blacken from every Quarter and I can only supplicate the Being 'who rides the whirlwind and directs the Storm' [Nah. 1:3] to indue my Mind with submission and Fortitude to meet the Evils that seem but too likely to burst upon us.—*This* Summer I think will be the Crisis, and that the Fate of this Country, in common with others, will be nearly decided 'ere the period *returns* at which *we* hope to *meet* again.—That is, I think we shall nearly have surmounted our Dangers, or find them advanced upon us in such a manner, as to render the future a matter of tolerably certain conjecture."
4. Eliza Jackson was visiting PSP at Clifton, according to the latter. For Mrs. Jackson, see HLP to PSW, 11 February 1791, n. 6.
5. Kemble's adaptation of Joanna Baillie's *De Monfort* did not appear for a year, opening with Kemble and SS at the Drury Lane only on 29 April 1800.
6. After a ten-day delay occasioned by the illness of two performers, TSW's *The Castle of Montval* opened at the Drury Lane on 23 April with SS as the Countess of Montval. It held the boards for a total of eight performances, until 22 May.
7. After her divorce from William Townsend Mullins, Frances Elizabeth (charged with adultery) married the Reverend Robert Boyle Sullivan, who was to die at La Flèche, ca. 1824.
For Frances Elizabeth Sage, see HLP to TSW, 5 January [1789].
8. HLP believed Dumouriez to be untrustworthy. Having turned once against the French in 1793, he could turn again she assumed, this time on behalf of the French and of England's still rebellious Irish subjects.
9. See HLP to PSP, 29 May 1799, n. 3; Ly W, [19] March 1804.
10. The anecdote emphasized the anti-French spirit that animated the Grison country, conquered by the French on 17 March and soon forced into the Helvetic Republic. See *AR* 41 (1799): 250.
11. PSP had recommended the work of John Adolphus (1768–1845) of German extrac-

tion, later a barrister-at-law, particularly his anti-Jacobite *Biographical Memoirs of the French Revolution*, 2 vols. (London: T. Cadell and W. Davies, 1799).
    See also Farington 8:3146 for a description of Adolphus's legal career, which began in 1807.
    12. A reference to HLP's three eldest daughters and to SS's intimacy with Thomas Lawrence.
    13. HLP's variation on John Gay, "When the pale Moon had nine times fill'd her Space/ The pregnant Goddess. . . ." (*Trivia*), 2.135–36.
    14. See HLP to TSW, 5 January 1789, n. 7.

TO THE REVEREND REYNOLD DAVIES

                                                    Brynbella Fryday
                                                    5: April 1799.

I thank you for your Letter dear Mr. Davies—It was Time to write—Judge of my Amazement when we perceived the first Intelligence of little Salusbury conveyed to us by Susan Thrale of all people. She tells me too what your Epistle confirms; that pretty Mrs. O'Bryan is grown Thin, and has the Jaundice.[1]—Lest She should think however that all Beauty is *her own* now, I sent her this old French Epigram which I dare say Mr. Macnamara remembers—and which is the more Apropos, as another Friend writes me word that his Niece is going soon to be married.

            Iris! quelle Metamorphose!
            Mon Œil ne vous reconnoit point,
            Qu'est devenu votre Embon point
            Et ce Teint de Lis et de Rose!
            Voyant dans le Miroir un si grand Changement,
            Profitez au plûtôt de l'Avertissement
            Que les justes Dieux vous fournissent:
            Voici le Sens de la Leçon,
            Ainsi que les *Épics*—quand les *femmes jaunissent*
            C'est le vray Tems de la *Moisson*.[2]

            Iris! Alas my pretty Dear!
            What Metamorphosis is here!
            From plump to lean so quickly grown,
            The Lilies too and Roses flown!
            Call for your Glass—and haste t'obey
            This Warning sent from Heav'n,—to say
            "That Ceres takes her rip'ning Tint
            "Just as the Husbandman is sent;
            "Then wait but Three Months more at farthest,
            "You've just turn'd *Yellow* for the *Harvest*.

And now Farewell Dear Mr. Davies, and I wish you a *merry Christmas*; for except at that Season, such Weather as we have now, did I never see. One cannot stir out; so nursing a Gouty Husband, and turning French Epigrams afford small proof either of Wit or Virtue.—There is nothing else to be done; unless pelting you with Eightpenny Letters be permitted:—and my Excuse for that Sport, you have taken away. Do not let our dear Streatham Neighbours forget us, they will never have a Friend so near who knew their Value better—and our Parrot will not leave *us* unreminded even of *Sweet Doctor Perney*.[3]

I rejoice that you have so *limed* the little Boy—*liming* goes before *taming* as the Bird-catchers say:[4] I should suppose young Apreece[5] and Bourdieu[6] would be fine Decoys for such a Flutterer. The Chicken Pox is a good Thing well got over: of all infantile Ailments I feel most horror at Thoughts of the Hooping Cough—It nearly cost Cecilia Mostyn her Life.[7]

Mr. Chappelow was a Water drinker when we met last and when we parted; yet he talks of dining with Mr. Macnamara. Well! I make no promises, but if I see any more such Rareties as I had a Glimpse of last Week;—Your Man shall have a Ride to the Inn—where that Mutton was left—and Streatham shall witness that Fish of an uncommon Excellence haunt our Welsh Shores. Adieu!

Oh, but Mr. Piozzi says this hard Weather ought to have *some* good Consequences, and that while he is buying Hay at five guineas here in Wales, Jacob is surely selling it as dear in Surrey: Be so kind as enquire—*do;* for the Beasts must have fodder even in *Your* fine Part of the World,—No Grass can grow while these cutting Winds continue.——May they but bring us some Good News to keep our hearts warm at least.——How long are we to live I wonder on this last *seventimes Fricassee'd Victory*![8]

Write now and then to Your faithful Friend, Servant, and Constituent / H: L: Piozzi.

I'm glad methinks Lord Deerhurst is so happy.[9]

Text: Peyraud Collection. *Address*: Rev. Mr. Davies / Streatham / Surrey. *Postmark*: Holywell 10 o'Clock AP 8 99.

1. For Margaret O'Brien, see HLP to Robert Ray, 23 July 1798, n. 5.
2. For the verses "sur une fille qui avoit la jaunisse," attributed to [Bernard] de la Monnoie (1641–1728), see [Gilles Ménage], *Ménagiana*, 4 vols. (Paris: Chez la Veuve Delaune, 1729), 4:189–90.
3. For John Anthony Perny, see HLP to PSP, 15 [December 1793], n.3.
4. See Tilley, B380 and 394.
5. Thomas George Apreece (1791–1842), second baronet of Washingley (1833), county Huntingdon.
6. HLP had learned of William Bourdieu from RD's letter dated 4 December 1798: "I am—we are all extremely impatient about seeing [JSPS]. . . . Perhaps most of all a little student (William Bourdieu) who is four years and six months old. William Bourdieu who asks if the little fellow who cannot speak English has a tongue. W: B: who has no mother assures the Housekeeper he loves her next to his Papa and Aunt Mary &c. He is not a little afraid of being supplanted by the little Stranger" (Ry. 573.6).

William, a schoolmate of JSPS at "Streatham University," was probably the son of John Bourdieu, a successful barrister, originally of Coombe House, Croydon, a "noble mansion." The boy's mother, Anne, was buried in the Croydon church in 1798. See Edward Wedlake Brayley, *The History of Surrey,* 5 vols. (Dorking: Robert Best Ede; London: David Bogue, 1844), 4, pt. 1, 16.

7. For CMT's illness in 1783, see *Thraliana* 1:560, 563 and n. 2, 564 and n. 2.

8. HLP refers to Nelson's destruction of the French fleet in the battle of the Nile on 1 August 1798. For her earlier celebration of this British victory, see HLP to RG, 14 October 1798, n. 3; to PSP 22 October, n. 3; to LC, 17 December; to Ly W, 18 December, n. 3.

9. Peggy, Lady Deerhurst, was again pregnant, delivering her ninth child, Barbara, on 15 July 1799. See "Christenings 1756–1812, St. Leonard's Church, Streatham" (Greater London Record Office); HLP to PSP 11 February 1794, n. 11.

TO THE REVEREND LEONARD CHAPPELOW

                                                         Brynbella
                                                  10: April 1799.

The best Pen in the whole Packet Dear Mr. Chappelow—and they are very good ones too——not excellent enough to sing or say or write the Praises of your kind Friendship.[1] Catherine's Life is not only useful to me now, but *will* be necessary and the little Romance which I had more than half forgotten is a more curious Performance than I thought it was.

No Smoke without some Fire say those who seek for Subjects of Intrigue; no Smoke without some Fire says Mr. Walter when he hears of the Arch Duke's dubious Victories.[2] I am perswaded that the French have lost Ground: as for Buonaparte if the Turks can contrive to rid the World of its Scourge by their *compendious* Methods and *summary* Justice,[3] 'tis a better Thing by far than sending him to England to Dine with Sir Francis Burdett &c. and receive Civilities from one half the Country out of Admiration, and the other half out of Ostentation.[4] Let him go to his kindred Crocodiles by the nearest Method *is my Prayer.*

How good is Mr. Gray to remember me! and kind Mr. Whalley, to whose Play I wish Success most sincerely——I now see tis *that* has driven Siddons back to Drury Lane. She never writes herself to any one——it is *her way* never to write, so one goes merely by Conjecture but I am sure tis that. Tell me if you go to see it how far good Fortune goes before——and Fame flies after with a Laurel as Prior says.[5] Oh I sent a French Epigram on Mrs. O'Bryan's Jaundice and its Impromptu Translation the other Day to Davies when I wrote about the Dear little Boy.[6] Would you believe that Susan Thrale rode down to Streatham last Week—The Pretence a Visit to Mr. Macnamara's Niece now She is Ill—but the true Reason I conceive merely *to see that Child*—and so the Curiosity was gratified; and our Piccolino was produced, with *My Name* and my *Husband's Face*——I wonder which would be the *greatest Recommendation!* If any more astonishing fine Smelts such as I once saw here this Spring, offer themselves again——I'll get my Neighbours Favour for *myself* though.——We call those Fish *Sparlings* in this

Country, and tis the right Name; Lemery says *Eperlanus:*[7] how does Linnæus denominate them?[8] and why are they twice—ay three Times as large in the Dee as in the Thames?[9] I think if old Vitellius had once heard of them, he would have come to Conway or to Chester.[10]

Our Spring has been exceeding coarse and rough—Scarce can a Primrose put its head out yet,

> Or the pale Plum foretell a fruitful Year,
> While blushing Almonds cloth'd in Pink appear.[11]

Rule and *Example* you know Dear Mr. Chappelow——according to the honest Laugh we had about the Pimple on that poor Man's Nose. It was *his* Brother died at the Cape a while ago, and I heard another of them was gone since; but People have a vile Trick of dying every where; altho' Susanna writes me word how Murphy our good old Friend is quite recovered from that dreadful Illness—— Saved I imagine by past Temperance, leaving the Constitution strong and firm to battle with Disorders in *the last Act.* Seward I doubt has broken his Habit up by use of Medicine——exhausting the Succours of Illness during Health, till they have no Effect—and he dies Dropsical.[12] You say nothing of poor Lady Bradford; She goes on in the same Way I fear——Let the *great Constitution* stand fast: 'tis a trying Time, but the *nine* Ships ought to make at least a *nine* Days Wonder.[13] One of our unpleasant Characteristics of these Days is the Ingratitude which we regard Success with. No Victory seems to be followed of late Years with any Consequences somehow—either at home—*or abroad.*

This is a shocking Way of thanking You for all your favours, all your kind Expressions—Your Geese are Swans indeed,[14] when you make such a Wonder of <Your &c.> / H: L: Piozzi.

Tell me *do* when You have been to Streatham and write sometimes, and let us not as Hamlet says *burst in Ignorance:*[15] I am dying to hear something of the Conspirators.[16]

Text: Ry. 560.78. *Address:* Rev: Mr. Chappelow / No. 12 / Hill Street / Berkeley Square / London. *Postmark:* DENBIGH E AP 12 99.

---

1. In his letter of [13] April (Ry. 562.60), LC noted: "The best pens are 12s. per hundred.—They are hard—brown plumed Hudson bay wild Quills."

2. HLP refers to *The Times*'s editorial of 27 March that announced Austria's declaration of war against the French on 12 March.
"While the Scales of Europe tremble upon the Banks of the *Lech* and the *Danube,* and the public eye is turned to that great collision, from whose first shock will start the general ruin and subversion, or the renovation and safety of mankind, it is some consolation to see the partial mischiefs and local calamities of the world, suspended and adjourned for a moment." Everything, according to the editorial, waits "till the general fate and common interests of the world shall have been decided upon the frontier of *Suabia.*"

3. Since September 1798, the Turks had fought the French. Supported by a British squadron, they began to assemble an army in Syria for the invasion of Egypt. Conse-

quently, Bonaparte set off for Syria in February 1799 with fewer than fifteen thousand men. HLP hoped for a collision there, with the Turks victorious.

Moreover, she was also aware that on 1 March united Turkish and Russian forces had seized "the town and forts of Corfu, together with the artillery, provisions, stores, ammunition, and all other public effects." See *GM* 69, pt. 1 (1799): 338–39.

4. Francis Burdett (1770–1844), fifth baronet (1797), was impressed by radicalism during a visit to Paris in the early days of the Revolution. By marrying Sophia, née Coutts, in 1793, he was able to become (by purchase) M.P. for Boroughbridge (1796). In that capacity he stood for everything political that HLP excoriated: i.e., he denounced the war with France and Pitt's suspension of habeas corpus.

5. *The Ladle*, lines 35–36: "Mars standing by asserts his Quarrel: / And Fame flies after with a laurel."

6. See HLP to RD, 5 April 1799.

7. Louis Lémery (1677–1743) in his *Traité des Aliments* (Paris, 1702), translated two years later into English, wrote that "A Smelt in Latin, is called Eperlanus, à Perlâ, a Pearl, because 'tis like it in Colour. They call is also *Viola marina*, because it smells like Violet" (*A Treatise of Foods, in General*, p. 239).

8. Linnaeus refers to the smelt as "Salmo *Eperlanus*," noting that "In Scotland, and in some parts of England, this species is called the Spirling or Sparling." See *Elements of Natural History; being an Introduction to the Systema Natural of Linnaeus*, 2 vols. (London: Cadell and Davies; William Creech, 1801, 1802).

9. The Dee flows through North Wales and Chester.

10. Aulus Vitellius (15–69 A.D.), a Roman emperor and glutton. See Suetonius, *De Vita Caesarum*, bk. 7, especially the biography of Vitellius and the description of a dinner given him by his brother: two thousand fish and seven thousand birds were served (sec. 13).

11. Probably HLP's couplet, a variation to suit the season, familiar "precept and example" as used by schoolmasters.

12. Murphy had no threatening illness now. Quoting Pope, he described his own situation: "Taught, half by reason, half by mere decay, / To welcome death, and calmly pass away" (*Essay on Man* 2.259–60). According to Jessé Foot, Murphy lived a relatively abstemious life. He ate and drank little, for the most part seeming tranquil and orderly in his habits of pleasure and work. See *The Life of Arthur Murphy, Esq.* (London: J. Faulder, 1811), pp. 433–35, 442–43. For Seward's death, see HLP to LC, 10 March, n. 8.

13. HLP here recalls that as early as April 1797 "Lord Bridport's squadron"—as part of the Channel Fleet—was "to have nine fresh ships for his ensuing cruize; making in the whole 23 sail of the line." See, e.g., the *Bristol Gazette*, 6 April 1797. With this expanded squadron, Lord Bridport was to blockade the French fleet and protect the British coast against French depredations.

14. See Tilley, G369.

15. *Hamlet*, 1.4.46.

16. That is, the United Irishmen. HLP anticipated Pitt's address on 19 April, which in part emanated from the Select Committee's report (15 March) and the Red Lion Square conspiracy. He proposed that anyone who continued after a specified date to be a member of the "Corresponding Society," the "United Irishmen," or "United Englishmen" be subject to penalty, varying from a fine to imprisonment or transportation. He urged further that the licenses required for lecture rooms be applicable also to debating societies; that the proprietors of printing presses be certified; that every book or paper bear the name and residence of its printer. His proposals passed both Houses with little opposition. See Stanhope 3:182.

TO JAMES ROBSON[1]

Brynbella
16: April 1799.

You are excessively good to me in writing so Dear Mr. Robson, and I take the earliest Opportunity of thanking you for administering such a timely Cordial. If the Archduke can once bring French Valour into Disgrace upon the Continent—our Blockheads here at home will cease to admire and tread in their Steps with a Meanness of Imitation no more to be paralleled—than it is to be pardoned by me. Pray send me the Account of this Conspiracy to destroy the King *under the Royal Oak:* likewise a Book or Pamphlet by one of our Scribbling Sisterhood, called a Tale of other Times. I am told there's Merit in it and the Author poor.[2]

Believe me my good Sir nothing could give Mr. Piozzi and me so much pleasure as the friendly Visit you half promise us——if Mr. Grey should suffer me to be disappointed of his Company, although nothing better should be held out to him as a Lure, it would grieve me very sensibly:—but how Sir Thomas Clarges can be the Bishop of Durham's Nephew is beyond my Skill to fathom.[3]

Mr. Piozzi is just come out from his Chamber where the Gout confined him three Weeks; and I am exceedingly glad of it, because now he will be quite at his best when you come hither, and able to go about and make Cicerone for us. He has been happily permitted to save one Child out of his ruined Family—a Baby five Years old——But although much has been lost, Hope is not yet extinguished: This glorious News rekindles the Idea which has remained alive thro' many a painful Year in my Husband's heart; that his Country will even Yet prove a Sepulchre to French Vain Glory——and that a Sure though tardy Vengeance waits them, in that horribly-injured Peninsula.[4]

Dear Mr. Drake—of the Diplomatique Corps[5]—helped to keep that Notion warm, by his Assurances to Mr. Piozzi of the Hatred and hope of Revenge entertained all over Italy towards these Modern Vandals.

I am glad the Government employs such Loyal Subjects and able heads as my old Friend and Acquaintance Mr. Robson[6] who is very kind in remembering as such / his very faithful Servant / H: L: Piozzi.

Text: Butler MS Collection, Columbia University. *Address:* James Robson Esq. / Bond Street / London. *Postmark:* DENBIGH   E AP 17   99.

1. For James Robson, the New Bond Street bookseller, see HLP to SL, 26 February 1785, n. 8.
2. Jane West (1758–1852) wrote *A Tale of the Times*, 3 vols. (London: T. N. Longman and O. Rees, 1799). It was published on 14 March and sold for 12s. On 21 May, the *True Briton* advertised, "This Day is Published, The Second Edition. . . . The Writer of these Volumes has before received the praise of the British Critic, for great ingenuity, and a correct knowledge of the human character. She now appears before the Public with more exalted claims, as the strenuous advocate of Religion and good Morals, and the powerful enemy of unsound and vicious principles, however disguised or denominated."
Jane West, who had married Thomas (d. 1823), a yeoman farmer in Northamptonshire, attended to the household and dairy, but she was not poor, as she was often said to be.

See Nichols, *Illustrations of the Literary History of the Eighteenth Century,* 8 vols. (London: J. B. Nichols and Sons, 1848), 7:88–89 n.

3. Thomas Clarges (ca. 1780–1834), fourth and last baronet (1782), of Aston, near Stevenage, Herts. At this time young Clarges, preparing for Oxford, was being tutored by RG.

Sir Thomas was a great-nephew of Bishop Shute Barrington. That is, his grandfather, Thomas Clarges (1721–53), had married Anne, daughter of John, first Viscount Barrington, and sister of Shute Barrington.

4. The "glorious News" is Jourdan's decisive defeat by Archduke Charles at Stockach in Swabia in late March.

In Italy the French were also being beaten. Despite more than 160,000 troops in the field, they were too scattered to be effective. The Austrians, backed by some 18,000 Russians under Suvórov, overpowered the French commander in chief, Schérer, and Moreau. The Allies were to seize the bridgehead at Cassano and capture Sérurier with 3,000 troops on 27 April. They were able to enter Milan and take Turin.

5. Francis Drake (d. 1821) served early in his career in Denmark and later was envoy extraordinary and minister plenipotentiary in various German States. See *GM* 91, pt. 1 (1821): 94.

6. Perhaps a reference to the appointment of Robson as high bailiff of the city and liberty by the dean and chapter of Westminster, ca. 1797.

TO THE REVEREND LEONARD CHAPPELOW

Brynbella
Mayday 1799

Dear Mr. Chappelow

Tis an unmerciful Thing to write long Letters full of Enquiries, yet what else can ours contain? The Facts we have to relate are only how my Master had the Gout in his Hand *last* Week, and in His Foot *this* Week;—How my Shoulder pained me in April and my Elbow in May: how poor old rough Fox died a while ago, and how a Cow Calf was born this Morning which If I lived nearer Windsor I should long to make King George a Present of,——so *peculiar* is her Beauty and Elegance: the Colour a light Brown shading to white in the Face; curled Forehead like a Bull, but never will have Horns.

How different are the Facts *you* have to relate who live in the Front Box of that vast Theatre *London!* which one day presents a Tragedy full of Conspirators, The Catastrophe *somewhat uncertain;* one Day a Comedy crouded with Intrigue, and finishing in *Divorce:*—another Time a Farce of Quackery or Foolery of some new Kind, The wonderful Child or learned Pig, Gyants or *Androides:*——where little Things are great to *little* Men.[1]

I hear however that London is not the only large and Civilized Town in our Hemisphere; *now.* A new World is discovered—We are told——in the very Heart of Africa,[2] where Mr. *Davies* says there are *Schools,* the *Sheffield* People tell that there are *Files* and curious *Steel Instruments;* The *Wits* find out that there are Men *of Letters*——but nobody being Interested about Religion and Government—Two Things that are going fast out of Fashion——not a Word seems to be spoken about *Them*.³ If I was admitted to ask Questions upon the Subject, I should enquire if they *eat Pork at Houssa*?⁴ If they *do*——They must have been descended from the Inhabitants of old Numidia when 'twas a Roman Province I suppose, and sometimes supplied even Italy with Wheat.⁵ There was a terrible Slaughter of them by the Vandals, and consequent Migration of such as could escape: This was about the Year 484 when all Men were too much engaged in *Self* Defence to observe what became of their <Betters>; if these have any Arts——they must have retained and transmitted them on from that Time. A large Sea of Salt Water Mediteranean Lake has been descried⁶——and Davies bid *me* ask *You* who Mr. Brown was, that relates these Wonders. Our Friend Moore of Denbigh knew him in Cumberland many years ago—a young Man—full of Curiosity and empty of Money—desirous to provide Knowledge for himself, but impatient of that Controul necessary to its Acquisition in a regular way.

Pick me up all the Intelligence You can dear Mr. Chappelow——I have no Time to read Quarto Volumes, yet cannot bear to be bursting in Ignorance of such Important Discoveries.

The Arch Duke Charles's Fame will reach even these People soon I think—his Victories are very rapid and closely followed up. Swarroff will find nothing to do but free Tuscany,—The Venus will be got to Paris tho' before he can rescue her I think;⁷ and Paris will be no safe Residence for any thing in *human Shape*, when once their Ill Success renders their Tyrants despicable as well as odious.⁸ I do expect a dreadful Blow-up, a tremendous Explosion at Paris.

My vexatious Book tyes me down so that I can hardly find Time to ask or hear; but take Compassion of me *do,* and Send me a long Letter, and accept all I can give: the truest and kindest wishes of Your very / Sincere Servants and Friends at / Brynbella.

Mr. Leo is gone to Bath without his Wife, and Mr. Mostyn is gone to London without his Wife; I wish you would come o'courting in their Absence.

Text: Ry. 560.79.

1. See, e.g., the following advertisement:
"That Wonderful Infant, Master Parker, a Child of only 4 years and a half old, will make his first appearance on Monday, the 22d inst. at Hanover-Square Room." Described as an "Infant Phænomemon," he was talented in music and declamation and was introduced to members of the Royal Family. The "Father to this wonderful Child" sold tickets at No. 40, Great Suffolk-street, Charing Cross (*The Times,* 17 April).
For the divorce of Lord and Lady Abercorn, see HLP to PSP, 11 November 1798, n. 5; for the learned pig, see HLP to Q, 22 April 1785, n. 23.
"The Androides, or Animated Mechanism" were exhibited at "No. 38, Norfolk-street, Strand." Designed for young people, the exhibition "consists of a Spelling Figure, a Writing and Drawing Automaton; the Telegraph, which clearly explains that useful invention; the Fruitery; the Liquor Merchant, and the Highland Oracle." The price of admission was 2s. for boxes and 1s. for gallery seats. See *The Times,* 26 March, 6 and 26 April.
2. HLP refers to the discoveries of William George Browne (1768–1813), a well-known traveler of Cumberland lineage. Having taken an Oxford degree in 1789, he planned an exploration of Africa, which originated in Alexandria in January 1792. After traveling

through Egypt, Syria, and Asia Minor, he returned to England in 1798; the next year he published *Travels in Africa, Egypt, and Syria, for the Years 1792 to 1798*. During a subsequent Mideastern journey, begun in 1812, Browne was murdered. For his discovery of the "new World," see *Thraliana* 2:996.

3. In Dar-Fûr Browne had seen "wire, brass, and iron," as well as sword blades and firearms. Files were probably available, since he notes that certain African tribes filed their teeth (pp. 302-3, 347n.)

Among the "Men of Letters in Kahira," Browne praises "the more liberal among the Mohammedan ecclesiastics" for their knowledge of law and literature; and "the Mohammedan merchants . . . who have visited various parts of the empire, and who have learned to think that all wisdom is not confined to one country or one race of men" (pp. xii-xiii).

4. Hausa (sometimes incorrectly written Haussa, Houssa, or Haoussa) denominates a people of several states constituting about a half million square miles in western and central Sudan, from the Niger in the west to Bornu in the east. In the latter part of the fourteenth century Islam was introduced into the Hausa states and gradually influenced traditional beliefs and culture, such as the proscription of pork. See, e.g., A. J. N. Tremearne, *Hausa Superstitions and Customs* (London: John Bale, Sons, and Danielson, 1913); J. H. Greenberg, *The Influence of Islam on a Sudanese Religion* (New York: J. J. Augustin, 1946).

5. HLP assumed that if the inhabitants of Hausa were not Mohammedans, then they were descended from the people of Numidia, the Roman name for that part of Africa north of the Sahara (corresponding roughly with modern Algeria).

Numidia had been under Roman control ever since the first Punic War in the third century B.C. The control continued for approximately six hundred years, the area becoming gradually Christianized and agriculturally rich. This civilization and prosperity ended with the coming of the Vandals in 428 and of the Arabs in the eighth century.

6. In chap. 4, "Terané to the Natrôn Lakes," Browne describes a number of seemingly interconnected saline lakes. "How thick the substance of natrôn is in the lake, I did not accurately determine, but those employed to collect it report that it never exceeds a cubit, or common pike; but it appears to be regenerated as it is carried away" (pp. 40-41).

7. For the Venus de Medici at the Uffizi, see HLP to LC, 21 July 1796, n. 7.

8. Because of French military losses in Swabia and Italy, HLP anticipated that the Directory would be discredited and France thrown into turmoil.

After the coup d'état of 30 Prairial (18 June 1799), two directors, La Revelliére-Lépeaux and Merlin, were forced to resign. The retirement of Reubell a short time earlier also shook the Directory. His place was filled by Sieyès. The new directors, Gohier and Moulin, were honest but incompetent and narrow-minded. Barras remained greedy and vicious. The fifth director, Pierre Roger Ducos, an ex-Girondist, was expedient. By November (18 and 19 Brumaire, An VIII), the Directory gave way to the Consulate with Bonaparte (first consul), Cambacérès, and Lebrun.

TO JOHN GRIFFITH[1]

3: May by the *Kalendar*
3: March by the *Weather*
1799.

Dear Mr. Griffiths

Accept our best regards and do not reject our Solicitations for Hay: but out of true Neighbourly Charity keep us all you can spare because our Horses here are starving—while The old Stacks in Surry are selling at 3£.11s. Would it not make a Man wild? Mr. Piozzi is really quite out of humour about it, and threatens to send my *Favourites* all off to England.² Do Dear Mr. Griffith be kind enough to stop their Journey, for Love of yours and Mrs. Griffiths's Obedient H: L: P.

We *can't* send for it till next Week. Oh *do* keep it for us.

Text: National Library of Wales, MS 4734 B.

1. When Hugh Griffith died in 1795, the estate and lands of Brynodol (along with leased Piozzi lands) went to his eldest son, John (1753–1830). High sheriff of Carnarvonshire (1813), he had married Margaret, née Owen (d. 1841), of Clenennau.
For the Griffith family and the Piozzi lands in the parishes of Tydweiliog and Llangwadl, see HLP to Hugh Griffith, 19 September 1789, nn. 1 and 2.
2. The scarity of hay at Brynbella resulted from a severe winter in Flintshire and a chilly spring. "No grass grows at all, Sharp cutting Frosts and steady Continuance of Cold operates so that no Duck will sit—no Bird will sing. The poor Farmers Horses drop down dead in the Carts, unable to drag Weight for want of Food—Cattle perish, & Sheep run from their Lambs" (*Thraliana* 2:996).

TO THE REVEREND LEONARD CHAPPELOW

Brynbella
7: or 8: of May 1799.¹

Dear Mr. Chappelow
I thank you for your short Letter, tis better than none, and do now God bless you pick me up some Intelligence about my Daughters: I *know* their Knocker in Cumberland Street has been tyed up——and I wrote last Wensday——This is Tuesday——to intreat any one of them to write because I felt sincerely and seriously unhappy. Not a Scrap have I had in answer tho' my Letter was both tender and anxious: I fear Miss Thrale is ill,——pray find out how and what and how *little* not how *much* She ails, for how can I help being miserable?²

Mr. Lloyd is a most amiable Man,³ I hope you will often meet, and often talk together of Natural History and Philosophy sometimes,—and sometimes of H: L: Piozzi and her Book——for I am working hard; pleasing myself one Day with hopes of Success,—frighting myself another Day with Fears lest it should not succeed.

Have you looked at the new Work of Mr. Such a one Sir? Says a Bookseller to Boisrobert—the merry Favorite of Cardinal de Richelieu——It has been talked on now *Twenty Years*—Ay that I have, replies Boisrobert; and I can assure you my good Friend——That it will not be talked on any more, after *Twenty days* at farthest.⁴ Horresco referens.⁵ If such should *my* Case be!! Well! here is tremendous Weather to be sure. 'Tis difficult for you in Hill Street to imagine *how* cold, and *how* unpropitious is this Season. No Hedges green except where a Gooseberry Bush or Elder peeps by Chance—no Hens sitting——a dead Silence in the

Woods and scarce a solitary Swallow skimming the Pools where no Insect Life allures them. How very dismal! but worse than dismal the Consequences among our wretched Cottagers whose Horses drop down even in the Empty Carts for very weakness, and the poor Ewes run from their Lambs. I never saw such a Spring: Beef at 6*d*.½ the Pound *here* where it sold for 2*d*.¾ just four Years ago— and Wheat rising apace. Not a Lock of Hay for Money, and no Grass likely to grow.[6] Mr. Piozzi turns to the Newspapers for Comfort, and rejoyces in the Deliverance of his own immediate Country from *their* Devourers.[7]

When will our wise Fellows here at home be Sick of French Follies and French Principles? They cannot *now* admire their Acts of Valour; and I trust a short Time will shew them as miserable at home as they are detestable abroad. Sure France herself will rise upon her Tyrants and bury them under the Ruin they have caused. Till that Event takes Place, The People's Brains will not be *re-settled*. You see they are disposed now to resist the Authority of Parliament, and call the Report of Parliament *itself*—*A Libel on the Immaculate* Characters of their Triumivirate Took, Hardy, and Thelwall.[8] What a strange Thing is this! what an unexampled Audacity! O do pray leave me not in Ignorance of the Result. The Report of the Secret Committee which was sent *me* had nothing of these Worthies in it— —The chief Business was about the Mutiny I think. God send our Sailors stanch and steady notwithstanding all their Arts; and if this vile blighting howling Easterly Wind blows us a brave Victory, and early News of it; we will not repine even tho' it *does* famish our Cattle and ruin our corn.——King David chose Famine or Pestilence as a Punishment rather than *flee before his Enemies* I remember; and said—(like a Man who deserved to be *Solomon's* Father)—Let us fall into the hands of God and not into the hands of Men.[9]

Mr. Whalley may be happy Things went no worse than they did at the Theatre—There is a Revolution in Taste as well as in every Thing else.[10] When will the People have run their Folly out of Breath? She has had her *Head* a long time methinks. I hope when You get a Day for Streatham *my* Name will not be forgotten among my old neighbours; I hope little Dear will remember me too;— —when we were at Bath, and he had scarce any English,—he used to call me *Merry Lady*. Miss Lee,—not Harriett but Sophia Lee, is in London; with a very lovely little Girl of her own bringing up: an Orphan Daughter of Tickell the Wit,[11] who married a Sister of the first Mrs. Sheridan,[12] and threw himself out of the Window at Hampton Court.[13] I wish some rich Man would fall in Love with *her,* as Mr. Sympson did with my pretty Cousin Charlotte Hughes[14]——You should *see* this smiling Lass, and put her in Fashion with the Ton Folks. *Tickell's Other* is all the Mode now; and you never saw any more *delicately dephlegmated* than my little amiable Bath Belle.

So if you won't write long Letters—I *will,* and go on hoping till I get one full of Intelligence: but I would rather hear good of Cumberland Street than even of Lord Bridport——for tho' The Ewes run from their Lambs 'tis only because they are starving;—My Lambs run from *me* Yet I can't help *Baa*ing after them / whilst H: L: Piozzi.

Accept our true Love my Dear Sir and Addio!

Text: Ry. 560.80. *Address:* Rev: Mr. Chappelow / No. 12 / Hill Street / Berkeley Square / London. *Postmark:* Strand Unpaid Penny Post; 7 o'Clock 10 MY 99 NIGHT.

1. Since the letter was written on a Tuesday, it may be dated 7 May.
2. Q's illness was probably influenza, followed by mild depression. By mid-June, she was "better, & going on a Trip to Scotland—not a Marriage Trip but to see ye Country; She's right enough: it's an exceedingly interesting Journey. wherever She goes, God bless her" (*Thraliana* 2:998).
3. John Lloyd of Wigfair.
4. François le Métel de Boisrobert (1589–1662), abbé de Châtillon-sur-Seine, poet, dramatist, and wit. He was a favorite of Cardinal du Perron, the queen mother (Marie de Medici), and of Richelieu. His facility in repartee and practical jokes made him useful to Richelieu as a jester, a man "passionné pour la comédie" (*Ménagiana* 1:22–27; 2:162, 358; 3:78–85).
5. *Aeneid* 2.204.
6. As a member of the landed gentry who farmed a sizable portion of her estate, HLP always worried about the weather, either for her own interests or those of the poor about her. The climate early in June was "so *very* remarkable. . . . After ye longest Winter & coldest Spring and sickliest Season possible—The Hay at a *Peny* o'Pound—the Beef at 10^d the Mutton at 8^d in Denbigh Market. . . . What will become of us? . . . We shall wish ye Mountain to fall on us perhaps in Preference of what's to come" (*Thraliana* 2:997).

HLP was so distraught by scarcities and consequent rising prices that she even faulted Pitt for indifference.

7. Field Marshal Alexander Vasilievitch, Count Suvorov-Rimnisky (1729–1800) was recalled to service during the War of the Second Coalition. In 1799 he was sent to command Russian troops in North Italy. He had three quick victories: against Moreau at Cassano, against Macdonald at the Trebbia, and against Joubert at Novi. These successes undid almost all of the work of Bonaparte's first Italian campaign (1796–97). See *Thraliana* 2:997.
8. HLP refers to the "Report of 3 May Sitting of Court of King's Bench" (see, e.g., the *Morning Herald*, 4 May):

"Mr. Erskine said he rose . . . to move for a rule to shew cause why a criminal information should not be brought against Mr. John Wright, a Bookseller in Piccadilly, for a . . . libel, reflecting upon the character of Mr. John Horne Tooke. . . . The libel, which was published under the title of the Secret Committee of the House of Commons, stated the result of former Secret Societies, and that bills of indictment had been found, in 1794, against Thomas Hardy and eleven others, three of whom, namely Thomas Hardy, John Horne Tooke, and John Thelwall, were tried and acquitted." Nevertheless, Wright's pamphlet implied that these three men were guilty of subversion, and Erskine asked whether it would be the prerogative of "a common Bookseller, in the ordinary course of his trade, to hold forth the individuals of the country in a light that must excite all mankind against them. . . . Lord Kenyon asked what the pamphlet was? If it was really the Report of the Committee of the House of Commons, the Court could not hear it called a gross and flagitious libel. . . . If the pamphlet complained of was really not the Report of the House of Commons, but falsely pretended to be so, on that ground the Court would grant the rule. . . . His Lordship concluded by desiring Mr. Erskine to take his rule, on the ground that the Report was not the Report of the Committee of the House of Commons."

9. 1 Chron. 21:11–14; 2 Sam. 24:13–14.
10. Sally Siddons informed PSP on 29 April that TSW's *Castle of Montval*, while not judged "a 'standing' play, was pretty well received. 'My Mother really acts most divinely in it, and looks as beautiful as possible' " (Manvell, p. 249).

PSP encapsulates varying attitudes toward TSW's tragedy. In a letter to HLP, 25 May

(Ry. 567.81), she writes: "Dear Mr Whalleys Play excites very different Feelings. . . . It has been more favorably received by the Public than was expected, I fancy owing to charming Siddons *great exertions."*

11. Elizabeth (1781–1860) was the daughter of Richard Tickell (1751–93), a pamphleteer and dramatist, and Mary, née Linley (ca. 1756–87). Tickell was the grandson of Thomas Tickell, Addison's editor (1721); and Sheridan's brother-in law.

Elizabeth was to marry Ebenezar Roebuck (d. 1807), a civil servant in Madras, and secondly a young merchant named John Simpson. Forced by circumstances, the Simpsons (with six of Elizabeth's children by her first marriage) emigrated to Canada. See J. F. Meehan, *More Famous Houses of Bath and District* (Bath: B. and J. F. Meehan, 1906), p. 24.

12. Elizabeth Ann Linley (d. 1792) was the first wife of Richard Brinsley Sheridan.

Both Elizabeth Ann and Mary were part of the large family of Thomas Linley (1732–95), director of public concerts at Bath. The family was so musical that CB once referred to them as "the nest of nightingales." For Thomas Linley, see the M.I. at Wells Cathedral.

13. After his marriage to Mary Linley in 1780, Tickell had a grant of rooms in Hampton Court Palace for his political services. He took as his second wife the eighteen-year-old daughter of Captain Ley of the *Berrington* East Indiaman. She was dull-witted, had a small dowry but expensive tastes. See Farington (1:90) for a description of the suicide and its reasons: "Distressed circumstances and an apprehension of being arrested, it is said was the cause of this momentary phrenzy."

14. See HLP to PSP, 10 August 1793, n. 12; 27 March 1798, n. 6.

TO THE REVEREND LEONARD CHAPPELOW

Brynbella
22: May 1799.

I am glad my Dear Mr. Chappelow that the folks in London live so merrily: If naval Success is added to the Landed Triumphs of the Confederate Powers, we shall be quite wild with Joy no doubt. In the mean while here is the most horrible Storm that even *Equinoctial* Gales ever excited. The Waves run Mountains high[1]—We see from our Windows White Breakers that would Startle even old Sir Edward Hawke;[2] and how are our Ships to fight and conquer, and carry home their Prizes thro' such a Tempest I wonder!!

We never insure any House: one may live a long Life without fear of *Burning* unless by a *Fever;* and I think you are in no danger even of that——while you keep the Post Miss Owen assigned you in the *Cold Stream. Fire, Water, Woman are Man's ruin* however, so 'tis not amiss to be careful.[3]

Do you see Murphy advertising Poems and dedicating them to pretty Girls?[4] He is the only Bird who sings this unpropitious Season:——About *Bees* too! why he should have inscribed Verses upon Bees to a Cambro Briton, who would have sent him a Dozen of *Metheglin* as a Reward, The Beverage of old British Bards. "Fill out Cupbearer the Horn of Heroes! Fill out the *mellifluous* Drink to the Poet who sits at Llewellyn's right hand &c. &c."[5] I count the Dedication of such a Work to a Brewer's Daughter, *deplacè* unless he had sent it her in the *Honey Moon*. Joking apart, They are exquisitely pretty Lines, and 'tis a Comfort to see him so *alive*. Miss Thrale is got quite well dear old Mr. Jones writes me word;[6]

and has sent round her Cards of Thanks for obliging Enquiries. I should not be so merry else: by the way he complains heavily that She *left him out,* tho' he both called and sent.

I am delighted that you *like* our little Boy and hope the Time will come that you will *love* him. Could I *but* live to see this John Salusbury a fine Fellow, and accounted one of the first Scholars at Eton; I really should think it a prodigious Happiness——and Yet a Lad is not fairly *launched* into the World till he quits the University——leaving Christ Church with *Eclat* for the Bustle of active Life.

His cy devant Country seems likely to be cleared of its Oppressors now—*They* cleared it of every thing else I suppose before.

> When the Beesom of Reformation
> Which should have made clean the Floor;
> Swept all the Wealth out of their Nation
> But left them of Dirt good Store.[7]

Have you read Duppa's Journal of their Proceedings while at Rome. I propose getting it by Heart by and by[8]——That if I should be ever tempted to pity the French who fall in Swarroff's hands, the Thoughts of such Depredation as they committed *there,* may Steel my Heart against compassionating them.

With regard to the Radstat Business it appears to be private Assassination for mere purpose of Plunder.[9]

Adieu Dear Sir, and go to your Book sometimes, and do not *forget* the Daughters of *Memory* herself,[10] in the Croud of Engagements London offers your Acceptance; and do not forget us neither; and our Farm &c. Why the Lease of Bachygraig will be out soon, and we *ought* to double our Rent almost, but no such good Fortune awaits us, for that vile Edward Jones who never (as you expressed it) carried a *Spoonful* of Manure to many of our Fields, will leave it in such a Condition that People will scarce *take it at all*.[11]

Fare well! and pray for better Times, and be happy this Nonsense costs nothing from Yours ever Sincerely / H: L: Piozzi.

My Master sends you his best Regards——Mostyn is come back to his Wife I hear: but I hear likewise that they mean leaving this Country for *Good* as the People say. God send it may not be for Ill. We have never seen *them* since we saw *you*, not even by Accident: I hope She will get happily thro' her Lying in, but will not subject myself as last year to be driven almost from her door.[12]

If you hear of her Sister's coming down to attend her, do let me know: for I shall not hear it from them if it is so.

Text: Ry. 560.81. *Address:* Rev: Mr. Chappelow / No. 12 / Hill Street / Berkeley Square / London. *Postmark:* 8 o'Clock MY 24 99 MORN.

    1. For the rains and gale-force winds, see *Thraliana* 2:997.
    2. Edward Hawke (1705–81), cr. Baron Hawke of Towton (1776), began his naval career as a volunteer in 1720. In perhaps the boldest of his many sea battles, he defeated Conflans at Quiberon Bay, 20–21 November 1759, in heavy weather. For this action, when

he captured five ships and ran several others aground, he was thanked by the Commons and given a pension of £1,500 (later increased to £2,000). Retiring from active sea duty in 1762, he became first lord of the admiralty (1766–71); admiral of the fleet (1768).

3. The allusions mentioned in this paragraph must have been discussed by LC in his last letter, which is now missing.

4. Murphy's translation of *The Bees. A Poem from the fourteenth book of [Jacques] Vanière's Praedium Rusticum* (London, 1799).

The book is dedicated to SAT. "I Here present to you the production of a very young Poet. . . . The work was finished several years ago, in the season of youth, when the famous *Italian* and *French* writers of Latin Poetry engaged my attention. Lately indeed, for the amusement of some vacant hours, I revised the Translation with all the care in my power. . . . As soon as I had retouched the whole, I was on the point of consigning it once more to obscurity, when it occurred to me that the subject might afford you some entertainment. I therefore resolved to send it into the world, and to adorn it with your name. . . .

"Shall I betray my own secret? The fact is, I am rather selfish on this occasion; I mean to gratify my pride, by declaring in this public manner, that I am favoured by you and your amiable sisters with a degree of politeness and attention, which it has never been in my power to deserve." The dedication continues with a short panegyric on HT.

5. Cf. the poem *Hirlas*, by Owain Cyfeiliog, prince of Powys (ca. 1130–97), which described the large drinking horn (*hirlas*) used to commemorate a battle against the English at Maelor (i.e., Denbigh and Flint counties). The poem was translated by the Reverend Evan Evans (1731–88) in a volume called *Some Specimens of the Poetry of the Antient Welsh Bards* (London: R. and J. Dodsley, 1764), pp. 8–13.

HLP has paraphrased and conflated numerous incremental parallels: e.g., "Fill, Cupbearer, fill with alacrity the horn of Rhys, in the generous prince's hall"; "Fill thou the yellow-tipped horn, badge of honour and mirth, full of frothing meath," etc.

6. For John Jones of Mitcham in Surrey and London, see HLP to Charlotte Lewis, 8 December 1790, n. 3.

7. HLP quotes st. 5 of "Rebellion given over Housekeeping." The ballad was first published in 1660 to observe the downfall of the commonwealth and the restoration of Charles II. It was reissued in 1688 to celebrate the overthrow of James II.
See *The Pepys Ballads*, ed. Hyder Edward Rollins, 8 vols. (Cambridge: Harvard University Press, 1929–32), 4:3–7, No. 164.

8. Richard Duppa (1770–1831), *A Journal of the Most Remarkable Occurrences that took Place in Rome, upon the Subversion of the Ecclesiastical Government, in 1798* (London: G. G. and J. Robinson, 1799). The *Journal* is essentially an account of French vandalism and depredations at Rome, beginning with the "Death of Gen. Duphot" and moving on to "The Planting of the Tree of Liberty on the Capitol" (chap. 3), "The Dismission of the Pope" (chap. 4), "The Sacking of the Vatican Palace" (chap. 5), etc.

9. The congress of Rastatt, which opened in December 1797, intended to rearrange the map of Germany by providing compensation for those princes whose lands on the left bank of the Rhine had been seized by France. As the French delegates left Rastatt in April 1799, they were waylaid and two were assassinated by Hungarian soldiers for unknown reasons. See the *Oracle*, 16 May.

10. HLP's reminder that LC should not forget his own poetry.

11. Edward Jones and his wife, Eleanor, née Owens, were tenants of Bachygraig from shortly before 1784 until the summer of 1800. There three of their children were born: Esther (1784); Edward (1787); and Manice (1788). There two of their older children died: Peter (1793) and Samuel (1794). See the Tremeirchion parish registers, C.R.O., Clwyd.

12. When CMM's John Salusbury was born in August 1798, HLP had to wait about three months to see her first grandchild (*Thraliana* 2:990, n. 2).

HLP learned about the birth of CMM's second son, Henry Meredith (Harry), from SAT, who on 4 September wrote tersely that CMM "was brought to bed of a Boy on Sunday last [1 September], and is as well as can be expected" (Ry. 553.25).

TO PENELOPE SOPHIA PENNINGTON

> Wensday—*29:* May 1799
> not one *Oak in Leaf*

On the very Evening of the Day I receive Your last kind Letter Dear Friend—I write to acknowledge both.[1] The *Home* Post will tell you nothing you like Tho' except that our Accounts of little Salusbury are all good——but *poor Uncle* is always having a bad Foot, and as you say if it were not for the comfortable News from Italy he would be low enough.

This blowing blighting Weather ruins us all; my poor Cottagers are sick with Agues chiefly and Dropsies: with broken hearts too poor Things! when their Horses drop under even Empty Carts—for full ones they cannot drag.

Our Hay here has been as *one Peny* o'Pound, our Beef at *ten Pence:* This approaches very near to Famine, but may justly be termed Scarcity; and the same dreadful Wind which retards the growth of all Vegetation, and restrains the hand of Industry in *our own Island*—has driven our protecting Fleet from Cadiz Harbour, and let the French and Spaniards form a Junction.[2]

Meanwhile charming Hannah More was right in her Conversation as in her Book; there *has been* a Crane Neck *Turn* as she expressed it, and Things are certainly mending on the Continent.[3] If Ireland should come to her Senses and *unite* with us in Abhorrence of French Principles and French Seducers, who could promise them Assistance and never carry it, but go on another Scheme while the Rebels *there* were waiting the Fleet's Arrival——It might be lucky that Lord Bridport *did* let them escape.[4]

Poor Fellow! how you do hate that Man![5] very comically! and very unreasonably indeed——for when we saw him he was—as the Phrase is—out of his *Element;* and looked to be sure something like a *Fish out of Water;* but I never heard anything amiss of him in my Life, and believe he will not be found at the critical Moment to carry *Two Faces under a Hood.*[6]

Have You Seen Doctor and Mrs. Randolph lately? What do they say about these *Riflers of Sweets* that we hear so much of? Bath has been a Scene of odd *Robberies* by gay Lotharios—*who scorn to ask the lordly owners leave.*[7]

It makes me only Laugh, but I trust Hannah More would say like Benvolio—No Coz, rather *weep.*[8] Glorious Creature! how She writes! finding new Reasons to enforce old Virtues: and adorning her Sacred Sentiments with Brilliancy that throws *Rays* round all her Periods.[9]

It would be doing her too much wrong to suppose *her* capable of regarding the Nonsense talked against her by Misses mad to see their Mammas reading the New Book with Approbation, and looking at *them* over their Spectacles at every interesting Passage. *She* must be invulnerable to Wounds from such weak hands sure. The old Heroes in Homer——

> By *Pallas* guarded thro' the dreadful Field:
> Saw *Swords* beside them *innocently* play,
> While *Darts* were bid to turn *their points away.*[10]

All they can say and do, only contributes to shew how greatly such a Book was wan[ted].

Mr. Whalley's Thinking he has contributed to Siddon's Fame is pretty enough: She thinks *her* Contribution useful to him no doubt.[11] The Writer of Pizarro is censured for giving *her* Part to Mrs. Jordan.[12]——

I saw with Pleasure Miss Allingham's Marriage in the Papers:[13] her Conduct to our charming Friend at Bath, was very pretty if your recollection retains it.

The Intelligence concerning Mrs. Radcliffe's having written that Play on hatred seems to have been premature. Oh how your Account of Mrs. Jackson's Domestic Situation presses Hannah More's Book upon one's Heart![14] The Italians have a Proverb to say that there are only three Things worth caring about: La Salute, L'Anima, and la Borsa. One's Soul, one's Health and one's Purse. *We risque all three* to make our fair Daughters *accomplished*. Doctor Johnson said that whoever found their Mothers admired and reverenced by that Circle which forms a little *Silkworm World* round every Individual; would add their Admiration and Reverence, merely because they saw other people pay them theirs. I cared (says he) nothing for *my* Parents, because nobody cared for them.[15]—Mrs. Jackson's Children cannot make that *their* Excuse: She has been a Woman—since I have known her—particularly *petted* by her friends, and those Friends have been People eminent for good Taste and good Sense.

Are the Canterbury Tales come out yet?[16] Nobody has sent them *me*, and I will not write again to Harriet Lee till I have read them. Sophia is in Town with her little Protegé [Elizabeth Tickell]——

> Who if She cannot conjure down
> The Pale Moon from the Sapphire Sky
> May draw Endymion from the Moon[17]

perhaps—and I really wish her good Luck.

Tickell's Ætherial Spirit is a new Medicine much in Fashion, it is so finely *dephlegmated* the Apothecaries say:[18] I think there is as much pure Spirit, and as little *Phlegm* about the tiny Bath Belle as can be imagined. Some rich Man will *take* her I hope.

Have you felt an Interest in these African Discoveries? They are Things of prodigious *Curiosity*—rate them at the lowest:[18] I think very seriously about them for my own Part, but none of my Correspondents seem caring much concerning that Subject unless 'tis Miss Thrale from whom I get about 4 or 5 Letters in a Year——and She has been ill this Spring——So has everybody. I watch the Weather cock all Day but the cold Blight continues. The Leaves which *try* to come out, look like fryed Parsley round a Dish of Soles. Do not *you* be sick, but be blythe and console Dear Mr. Pennington and give him my Master's true Regards with those of your H: L: P.

Text: Princeton University Library. *Address:* Mrs. Pennington / Dowry Square / Hot Wells / Bristol. *Postmark:* DENBIGH.

1. HLP here responds to two of PSP's letters, dated 20 April and 25 May (Ry. 567.80, 81).

2. According to the *Morning Herald*, 2 May: "Dispatches were yesterday received at the Admiralty from Admiral Lord Bridport, containing an account of the French Fleet having put to sea from Brest on the morning of the 26 ult. On that day his Lordship, with the principal part of the Channel Fleet, was blown considerably to the Westward by a strong gale from the N.E., of which circumstance the enemy took advantage, and their escape from port being also favoured by very thick weather, they were not perceived by any of our ships, except the Flora frigate." See n. 4.

3. Hannah More had recently published a much acclaimed book, *Strictures on the Modern System of Female Education. With a View of the Principles and Conduct Prevalent among Women of Rank and Fortune,* 2 vols. (London: Thomas Cadell, Jr., and William Davies, 1799).

On 14 March HLP had recorded in *Thraliana* (2:995) the same optimistic metaphor for Allied strategy in the European conflict: "Hannah More says there will be even yet a *Crane-Neck Turn* as She calls it." By analogy, that is, Miss More stressed the superior maneuverability of Allied forces on sea and land.

The figure of speech was inspired by a mechanical apparatus well known to eighteenth-century travelers. As described by the London coachmaker William Felton: "Cranes are the strong iron bars, to which are united the hind and fore part of a carriage on each side. They are made of a crooked form, resembling, at the fore part, that of a crane's neck, for the purpose of admitting the fore wheels to pass under unobstructed, whereby ground is saved in turning, which gives to carriages made with them a great advantage, as they can be used with more freedom in narrow confined places" (*A Treatise on Carriages,* 2 vols. [London: Felton, 1794]), 1:111.

4. Lacking military intelligence to guide him and suspecting a French attempt on Ireland, Lord Bridport ordered the Channel Fleet to range for the next month along the coast from Mizen Head to Achill Head. During this exercise, however, the French fleet was in the Mediterranean.

5. On 25 May PSP had written: "Our Joy [in Allied continental victories] is a little checked by Fears excited on account of that formidable Fleet, which Lord Bridport has *again suffered to escape him.* I read nothing but *ill luck* in that Man's dull, inanimate Countenance when I saw him at Bath and always said, if ever this Country felt a *vital Blow* in her *Navy* it would be through his Inanity and Torper."

6. For the derivations of the metaphors, see *Oxford Proverbs,* pp. 264 (F318), 237 (F10).

7. See Nicholas Rowe, *The Fair Penitent,* 2.2: "Rifle the sweets, and taste the choicest fruits, / Yet scorn to ask the lordly owners leave."

8. *Romeo and Juliet,* 1.1.182.

9. PSP and HLP were captivated by More's *Strictures on Female Education,* PSP describing it in both her letters as "the nearest thing to *Perfection* on the Subject that human Talents can ever produce."

10. Pope's translation of the *Iliad* 4.632–33. The two last lines should read:

> Might Darts be bid to turn their Points away,
> And Swords around him innocently play. . . .

11. See HLP to LC, 7 or 8 May 1799, n. 9.

12. HLP is reporting a rumor based on a constant fact: namely, SS's financial struggles with Sheridan. See HLP to LC, 25 September 1799.

13. The tragic actress Maria Caroline Allingham on 18 April had married Samuel Ricketts of Clare Street, Bristol. She accompanied him to Surinam, South America, where he became a planter. She died there 9 April 1811.

The Times, 20 April, and *GM* 69, pt. 1 (1799): 346, reported the marriage, identifying the actress, who had made her London debut at the Covent Garden, as being "of the Bath Theatre."

14. For Eliza Jackson's unruly sons, see HLP to Charlotte Lewis, 9 May 1791, n. 1. PSP had written of them on 20 April 1799:
"Mrs. Jacksons is really a very acute and very ingenious Mind.—Her Conversation was a great relief to me amidst the total dearth of Intellect and Intelligence that prevails in this place. . . . I am sorry to find we have been much mistaken in one Axiom respecting this good Lady whose Children we used you know always to say, however disagreeable to others, she must certainly have attached in the closest Bonds of Affection to *herself*.—Alas! far other wise! She complains of the most *unfeeling*, disrespect, neglect and disobedience!—"

15. See, e.g., *Rasselas,* chap. 26; *Rambler* 149; *Anecdotes,* p. 26–28.

16. The third volume of the *Canterbury Tales* by Harriet and Sophia Lee was published in 1799 by G. G. and J. Robinson. It consists of two novellas: "The Officer's Tale" and "The Clergyman's Tale." See HLP to PSP, 17 July 1799, n. 4.

17. In *The Children's Book or rather Family Book begun 17: Septr 1766* (Hyde, p. 197), HLT on 16–20 December 1777 had written:

> ———to draw down
> The Pale Moon from the frighted Sky
> She'll draw Endymion from the Moon.

We suggest the lines are HLT's, based on the description of the relationship between Endymion and the Moon in Lucian's *Dialogues of the Gods,* no. 11; and her recollection of the two following Shakespearian lines: "To pluck bright honour from the pale-fac'd moon" (*The First Part of Henry IV,* 1.3.202) and "Peace, ho! the moon sleeps with Endymion, / And would not be awak'd" (*The Merchant of Venice,* 5.1.108–9).

For the possibility that the lines may be a conflation of the above two Shakespearian metaphors, we are indebted to Sidney T. Fisher (*Notes and Queries* 223 [April 1978]:162).

18. See HLP to LC, 19 March 1799, n. 19.

19. See *Thraliana* 2:996 n. 2: "The Discovery of ye new World in Africa [as described by William George Browne] seems a strange Thing . . . have we dug out the ten lost Tribes at last? I hope so."

TO ANNE POOLE

[Brynbella]
[ca. June 1799][1]

My dearest Anna Poole must exert her kindness now and forgive my not writing sooner: The Rain quenched all my Spirits, and Mr. Piozzi's perpetual Gout kept me constantly employed. We had Friends here besides all this, Mr. and Mrs. Gray—and Sir Thomas Clarges[2];—and now we have Mr. Chappelow and Mr. Lygon[3] and Mr. Gillon[4] *Your futur;* and Lady Alleyne and her charming Daughters called here today[5]——The *first* Day we have strayed even a Mile from home; how amiable they are! and they talked of you, and of good Mr. Griffith,[6] and mentioned your partiality for Brynbella and its Inhabitants.

We have had a strange Summer of it: constant Wet Weather, and some consequent Ill Health. We have now a faint Repetition of the once really felt Alarm, concerning the Invasion of Ireland by the French.[7] I hope that Tranquillity they have lately so much boasted is not a false or Ill-founded one; I *hope* that if the French *do* land, they will have no Success.

We have seen nothing since we left Bath and of Course can tell nothing that you do not know better. Beaumaris has been quite the *Beau Monde* this Year; and I feel now that you should be writing *me* the Letters of Information. Hannah More's beautiful Book upon female Education is quite the prettiest of all the Literary Novelties;[8] She has so much Virtue and Piety levigated so admirably by Wit and by a consummate Knowledge of Modern Manners; that the Gayest Person living may like her Work, and the wisest Person living may profit by it.

Mungo Parke's Travels into Africa, another composition which calls out the Public Notice this Year, pleases me less: It tells so *very* little that one did not know before, and is so unsatisfactory somehow! I thought to gain a Thousand new Ideas from such *new Ground:*[9] he has given me but one; he has cured me of my Uneasiness for those African Slaves that arrive *safe* at our Sugar Islands. They are really in a State of Preferment to the Situation awaiting them at home, and from which they can for ought I see scarcely escape. The Ships they are conveyed in to the other Hemisphere are horrible Dungeons indeed; I hope some Method will be found to get them over with less Hazard and more Ease to themselves.[10]

Does your amiable Friend Mrs. Williams of Tros or Avon interest herself in what passes around her more than She used to do? or does She shut herself up with you and her Children, resolving to be good and happy herself—Think little of the rest of the World. I hope her health continues mending, if it yet wants any Emendation: She will delight in Miss More's Strictures.[11]

Sir Robert and Lady Williams are not yet got to Anglesey I trust; There must be a little of the world seen, and 'twas too late for the London season: They are probably at some crouded Watering Place.[12] We were told that the Bishop of St. Asaph pronounced the Marriage Ceremony on that Occasion in a Manner peculiarly impressive:[13] I am glad He did; The Runners away who are married how they can, and *where* they can, slip thro' their Engagements the more easily,——perhaps the more pardonably, (in a slight Degree); from never hearing their Duty told them by unquestionable Authority.[14] Sir Robert Williams has got a Wife of apparently very good Principles, *Polish* enough, and I think no *Varnish:* Miss Hughes was always one of my favourites. Our dear Friends at Bodylwyddan are in an anxious Situation. Sir John broke the small bone of his Leg by a fall much too soon after his lovely Wife's Delivery[15]——and poor Mrs. Williams has had a great Tryal of her Courage besides that you know.[16]

Mrs. Bagot has been Ill too—*very* Ill,[17] but Doctor Thackeray went back to Chester to day, and left all safe.[18]

Adieu! my Dear Miss Poole here is not half Paper enough for me to enumerate The Friends I wish to accept my Regards. Distribute them prettily and take the largest Share yourself / from yours ever / H: L: P.

Text: Yale University Library. *Address:* Miss Anne Poole / Castle Street / Beaumaris / Anglesea. *Postmark:* DENBIGH.

1. This letter can be dated ca. June 1799. By 7 June (Ry. 577.23), HLP received a copy of Hannah More's "fine Book [sent to her by Gillon] about young Ladies & their Education." More specifically, in June HLP acknowledged her depression caused by the lingering rain in North Wales and GP's illness (*Thraliana* 2:997; 1000 n. 3). Mungo Park's *Travels* was published about 1 May. RG and his wife visited Brynbella for a week in June (*Thraliana* 2:999).

2. For Sir Thomas Clarges, see HLP to James Robson, 16 April 1799, n. 3.

3. William Beauchamp Lygon (ca. 1782–1823), second earl Beauchamp (1816). An Oxonian, he became B.A. (1804), M.A. (1808); M.P. for Worcestershire (1806–16). He had come to Brynbella as a friend of Sir Thomas Clarges.

4. HLP was again matchmaking. Like many of such efforts, this to unite Anne Poole and John Gillon came to nothing. For the latter, see HLP to LC, 30 August 1798, n. 13.

5. Lady Alleyne (d. 1800) had been born Jane Abel, daughter of Abel Alleyne of Barbados (her husband's paternal uncle). In 1786, she became the second wife of Sir John Gay Alleyne (1724–1801), originally of Barbados, and created baronet (6 April 1769). She was probably accompanied by her four eldest daughters: Mary Spire (d. 1862); Jane Gay (d. 1836); Rebecca Braithwaite (d. 1846); Christian Dottin (d. 1873).

6. For Richard Griffith, rector of Llandegfan cum Beaumaris, see HLP to Anne Poole, 8 January 1798, n. 9.

7. HLP consistently feared a French invasion of Ireland. At this time, however, she drew upon last year's news. On 16 September a small French force under James Napper Tandy (1740–1803) had made a brief landing on Rutland Island, county Donegal. From 12–20 October a French invasion squadron under Commodore Bompard was engaged outside Lough Swilly by a British squadron under Sir John Borlase Warren. Seven of the ten French ships were captured. (Wolfe Tone was arrested on landing at Buncrana, county Donegal, 3 November.)

8. See HLP to PSP, 29 May 1799, n. 3.

9. About 1 or 2 May 1799, Mungo Park's *Travels in the Interior Districts of Africa: performed under the direction and Patronage of the African Associations, in the years 1795, 1796, and 1797* was published. See HLP to LC, 8 or 9 June 1798, n. 10.

10. For Park on slavery, see *Thraliana* 2:1000; "Introduction" 3:17.

11. In July 1792 Margaret Hughes (d. 1821), eldest daughter of the Reverend Edward Hughes, married Owen Williams (ca. 1764–1832), eldest son of Thomas and Catherine Williams of Llanidan, Anglesey. In the last seven years Margaret Williams had borne two sons: Thomas Peers (1795–1875) and Owen Edward (b. January 1798).

HLP refers to Margaret Williams allusively. She is "Tros or Avon," across the river, because she had left North Wales to live in Temple House, Berkshire, near Great Marlow, which her husband was to represent in ten parliaments from May 1796 onwards. HLP's recommendation of More's *Strictures . . . on Female Education* indicates her hope that the Williams's third child would be female.

12. Sir Robert Williams (1764–1830), of Nant and Caerau, had been in the First Regiment of (Grenadier) Guards and participated in the siege of Valenciennes (1793). He succeeded to the baronetcy (19 August 1794). He was to serve as M.P. for Carnarvonshire (1790–1826) and for Beaumaris (1826) until his death.

On 11 June 1799 Sir Robert married Anne (1775–1837), second daughter of the Reverend Edward Hughes.

13. For Lewis Bagot, Bishop of St. Asaph, from 1790 until his death, see HLP to LC, 15 September 1794, n. 9; to Q, 8 September 1798, n. 2.

14. A snide allusion to the elopement of the Mostyns in 1795.

15. For Ly W's three children, see HLP to the Ladies of the Williams family, 27 March 1798, n. 1.

16. Ly W's mother, Eleanor, née Hughes (d. 13 May 1810), was the widow of Hugh Williams (1741–68) of Ty Fry, Pentreath, Anglesey. She suffered from a slowly developing cancer. See HLP to JSPS, 7 November 1808; *North Wales Gazette*, 17 May 1810.

17. Mary Bagot, née Hay, was the niece of the earl of Kinnoul. Despite Dr. Thackeray's optimism, she died on 17 August 1799 at St. Asaph. See *GM* 69, pt. 2 (1799): 726.

18. For Dr. William Makepeace Thackeray of Chester, see HLP to LC, 23 August 1794, n. 7.

TO THE REVEREND LEONARD CHAPPELOW

Brynbella
2: July 1799.

Is any thing the matter that you never write? I should be very sorry. We have had our amiable Friend Mr. Gray here for a Week and His Lady and Sir Thomas Clarges[1] and my perverse Master kept his Bed all the while and so they missed Music at home, Invitations from Neighbours abroad, and as the People call it—Society.—but we had some pretty friendly Chat, and I shewed him the *The Great Book of Knowledge* in *good Time*!!derm[2] And he was very good natured about it, and I hope will kick it forward if it ever lies dormant in the Path he drives over. But as Bath Season is yet distant, I am athirst for News;——Do pray write soon, and hang Franks, your Letters pay their own Postage. Tell what will happen when Abbè Sieyes is Dictator of France; I expect that Event to take place every Day.[3] Why does not the old House of Bourbon come forward now their Friends are on the Frontiers: and make a fair Experiment whether the Nation at large desires——or detests the Idea of their Restoration.[4] They had *better* call their own King home at any rate——for if they do *not*, Sieyes will *Sell* them I suppose—Great Britain *purchase*——and the Emperors *enjoy*.[5]

Miss Thrale is going to Scotland I understand—just when the Emigrant *Princes* leave it: So Gretna Green will not unite her to *Them*; and Mr. Thrale's Daughters seem to think no *common* Mortals worthy their Attention.[6]

The *new* Lodger in Pall Mall[7] having turned out the *Old* one puts me in Mind of an Imitation I used to be very fond of—Horace's Audivere Lyce.

> The Gods have had Pity at length on my Prayer,
>   They have heard me at length Mother Waning;
> Tho' grown an Old Woman you romp drink and swear,
>   While nothing is left but complaining.
>
> You invoke with a Voice that now tremblingly squeaks,
>   Brisk Cupid—tho' sure of Denial;
> He leaves you and basks in the blossomy Cheeks
>   Of Miss Gubbins that Plays on the Viol.[8]
>   &c. &c.

But do tell me how all that Nonsense *is*? and what the People meant by the *Spectre* Story? We live in the Basket here, and only catch a Glimpse of passing Follies as they fly over our heads.[9] The best Jeu de Mots here is a *Sentiment* drank at Gentlemens houses in our Vale of Clwydd.

> *Rex Lex* et *Pontifex;*
> A Toast no honest heart rejects;
> The *King* in Safety all protects,
> The *Church* to future Bliss directs,
> But Knaves who seek our State to vex,
> May *Law* provide for all their Necks.

Perhaps you have heard this before: It was new to me when Dr. Myddelton flashed it off the other day.[10] Doctor Myddelton is the Man that People say resembles you, and we called him Mr. Chappelow's *Double.*

I know not however who is like Dear Mr. Chappelow in true Friendship and Kindness for us and all that belongs to us. It was very pretty to go and give Salusbury a kiss and a Half Crown so. Poor Fellow! I should hope he might *make* Friends in a generous Nation like ours, where he has no *Natural* one: he must be very good and very diligent——a Single Skiff so *in gurgite vasto*!![11] but I wont be lowspirited——We *may* live to launch him, Who knows! his Friends in Italy no longer afraid to write freely, begin describing their past Sorrows with a pathetic Pen; and say that the Carnage has been beyond Credibility in these obstinately-defended Battles, lost at length by the French.

While Matters are going on to our Wish however on the Borders of Provence,[12] I fear Macdonald's Junction with Moreau will deluge the old Romagna with Blood once again:[13] Things are not settled *there* at all: and that Inflammation which is brought to A Head and broken in the *Knee* of Italy's luckless Peninsula, will gather again in the Calf of the Leg I fear. Buonaparte's Expedition is not compleatly counteracted either; so far as I can understand the Accounts we have lost very fine young Men there both Officers and Soldiers; and till the French General is killed in Battle, or beheaded by the Turks I count nothing of our Success.[14]——His coming Prisoner to England will do less good than harm: I hated the folly of making *Fêtes* for Dumouriez and the Dutch Enemy *DeWinter;*[15] And *This* Man's appearance in London will only set People *raving mad.*

Adieu dear Sir and do write very soon, and say you are well, and have conquered *Your* Urticaria, or that you are in the way to conquer it——as near as Europe is to be clear from *her Urticaria* The French.

Here is fine seasonable Weather at last, and the Swallows who build in the Cornice of our House, *come to the Ground* every day; I see them *now* and [then] pick something (I know not what) which they carry up to their Nests.

Once more Adieu! and believe that no one is more sincerely yours than Mr. Piozzi and Your much Obliged Servant / H: L: P.

Text: Ry. 560.82. *Address:* Rev: Mr. Chappelow / No. 12. / Hill Street / Berkeley Square / London. *Postmark:* Streatham Unpaid Penny Post; 12 o'Clock JY < > 99 NOON.

---

1. For the visit to Brynbella of RG and his wife, accompanied by the former's pupil, see *Thraliana* 2:997 n. 3; HLP to Robson, 16 April.
2. The manuscript of *Retrospection.*

3. Sieyès had become a member of the Directory in the spring of 1799, when Jean-François Reubell was forced to resign. See HLP to PSP, 1 August 1798, n. 11.

4. There was to be a royalist insurrection on 18 Thermidor, Year VII (5 August 1799), in Haute-Garonne and the nearby cantons, under the leadership of baron Antoine Rougé and comte Jules de Paulo. For a short while Toulouse was surrounded but the outbreak was isolated.

The house of Bourbon did not "come forward." The comte d'Artois, who had been living in Scotland, was now to move no farther than Baker Street in London. The prince de Condé, probably the most militant of the Bourbons, was at this time to leave Russia, moving to Prague 24 August, to Constance 7 October, and to England 20 March 1800.

Louis XVIII now enjoyed the uncertain protection of Czar Paul at Mittau in Courland. He left there in 1801, remaining on the Continent until the French victories at Austerlitz, Jena, Eylau, and Friedland forced him to England in 1807.

For victorious Allied military action in Switzerland and Piedmont, see *The Times*, 22, 26, and 27 June.

5. HLP's mordant allusion to the British practice of providing subsidies for all members of the French Royal Family once in Great Britain. The comte d'Artois's portion was the loan of Holyrood Palace (near Edinburgh) and a £500 monthly allowance; the duc de Berri's monthly stipend was £300, and that of Louis XVIII in 1807 £600. See Margery Weiner, *The French Exiles, 1789–1815* (London: Murray, 1960), p. 137.

6. The comte d'Artois, who lived in Holyrood Palace, Edinburgh, attracted many of the émigré nobility and their families who had belonged to the Royal Court. Among them were vicomte Walsh de Sérrant, comte Eugène de la Ferronays, comte de Vaudreuil, the ducs d'Uzès, de Maillé, de FitzJames, de Lorges, de Duras, de Choiseul, de Castries, de Chartres. See Weiner, pp. 50, 83, 132–33, 138.

7. John Gillon had written to HLP on 7 June (Ry. 577.23):

"Your Information as to the Pall-Mall Rake I am sorry to say is a mistaken one. *Au Contraire*, He has just taken a House for the pretty Miss Honor Gubbins, whom you may recollect having seen at Bath. It is a great Pity! His Wife, I think, looks handsomer than ever she did; and as I understand is truly amiable. It is charming to see how she has taught her little Daughter to kiss her Hand, from the Coach Window, to every one she passes in the Park. It was mistakenly surmised that the Queen encouraged the Breach; for she has been paying her a Visit at Blackheath. . . . The Life that he has led has impaired his Health. He looks very ill."

For Honoria or Honor Gubbins, see HLP to PSP, 17 July 1799, n. 6.

8. HLP's "imitation" of Horace's *Carmina* bk. 4, "Ode 13," lines 1–8.

9. LC was to admit that he knew "nothing of the Spectre—for want of Stimulus I suppose the prince was low spirited; and thought he saw The devil in some shape or other. 'Tis all one. He has been ill, but is now better" (Ry. 562.61).

More specifically, HLP alluded to cryptic items in the *Morning Herald*, 9 and 10 May.

"The preposterous rumour of a *vision* having been seen by an illustrious Personage, has spread itself far and wide, and has been shaped into the various tales of '*raw head, and bloody bones,*' agreeably to the taste, and genius of the several reciters." And:

"The story of the *Royal Ghost*, whatever may have been its origin, has at least a curious *transit*, like that of Mercury, so as delusively to appear in the *disk* of the Georgium *apparens* when this *vision* in reality, appertained alone to a *planet* of somewhat inferior elevation, which, on this occasion, has been dexterously concealed by an *artificial eclipse*."

Cf. Pope, *Essay on Man* 1.13: ". . . . shoot Folly as it flies."

10. See HLP to LC, 15 September 1794, n. 1. The Reverend Robert Myddelton in 1794 married May, née Ogilvie (d. 1823). A son, Ogilvie John, born recently to the Myddeltons, died before the end of 1799.

11. HLP's conflation of two images: *The Vanity of Human Wishes*, line 238, and the *Aeneid* 1.118 (cf. 3.197, 6.741).

12. HLP learned of military activities from an "Address" made by the citizens of Grenoble to French officialdom. The "Address" reported, e.g., in the *True Briton* (18 June),

announced "that the City of *Turin* had not only fallen into the hands of the Austrians, but that [they] were at the same time Masters of the City of *Suza,* a distance of not more than one day's march from France. . . . this Address of the Inhabitants of *Grenoble* . . . throws more light on the state of affairs in *Italy* than any other document, and leaves nothing of any importance to be communicated by the *Hamburgh* Mails that can arrive for this long time."

13. The French generals to whom HLP referred are Jacques-Étienne-Joseph-Alexandre Macdonald (1765–1840), duc de Tarente; and Jean-Victor Moreau (1763–1813).

Defeated in separate battles by the combined Austrian and Russian forces (particularly the latter), they were nevertheless able to achieve a "Junction." Toward the end of July, Macdonald (after a defeat at the Trebbia), together with his army now reduced to about thirteen- or fourteen-thousand men, joined Moreau in the environs of Genoa. The "Junction," however, accomplished little tangible good for the French. See *AR* 41 (1799): 291.

14. The Turks' obstinate defense of Acre—assisted by Sir Sidney Smith's capture of the vessels bringing the French siege artillery—forced Bonaparte to begin his retreat to Egypt on 20 May.

Exhilarated also by having forced Bonaparte to raise the siege at Acre and by having gained a victory at Jaffa, the Turks pursued the French into Egypt. Their exhilaration ended when they were defeated at Aboukir on 25 July.

15. HLP resented the attention in England to Dumouriez, whom she still regarded as an enemy, or to de Winter, the Dutch admiral defeated by Duncan at Camperdown in October 1797. Newspapers like the *Morning Herald* (23 January; 23 March; 10 April) printed accounts about Dumouriez, now living in Swabia under the protection of the Austrians. In fact, negotiations by the British government were under way to bring the general to England, where by 1800 he was given a pension and asylum.

Jan Willem de Winter (1761–1812) had become a sentimentalized hero of English art. Thus, "the sketch of Mr. Copley's new picture, which he exhibited on Thursday last to the Court of Common Council," depicted the capitulation of the Dutch admiral. See the *Morning Herald,* 10 April. De Winter was also the subject of a painting (No. 862) by Samuel Owen for an exhibition at the Royal Academy (*Morning Herald,* 1 May 1799). See also HLP to PSP, 3 December 1803, n. 3.

TO THE REVEREND LEONARD CHAPPELOW

Brynbella
Monday 15: July 1799.

Dear Mr. Chappelow
It is ridiculous to make you pay for a Letter like this—which only says—and only *can* say we shall be always glad and very glad to see you. I can arrange no Plans, nor certify in the least concerning Weather, or *Gout* which gives no more notice than Weather——but Mr. Gray's Visit was a Solace not a Trouble to *me;* I was only grieved that we could do no more to amuse him. Mr. Piozzi ought to be well now till Winter, and take his long Fit *then* at Bath: but there is no Insurance Office for these Matters. Your Company will make us amends if the Equinoctial Gales *should* blow as the Midsummer Gales are *blowing now.*

The Sea is boyling with Rage at this Moment, and the Winds roar like November: I never saw such a Year.

You bring no Friends with you as appears on reading your Letter a second Time; why then this Ceremony?[1] Come and see us—and rejoyce with us in the Good News——if the good News and Cause of rejoycing continues:[2] should any thing check the Transport we now feel in poor Dear Italy's Deliverance and approximation of quiet hours—come and condole with us. It may be good Weather in September. We have a Proverb here

> Winter till May
> Summer till New year's day—

but the Summer is not come yet, perhaps it will be here by Michaelmas——no Fears of *Snows* however; we have less *Snow* here than in England.

Adieu, the Post waits and I can just say how sincerely we are Yours, and that no Place contains truer Friends and Servants to Dear Mr. Chappelow / than does / Brynbella.

Text: Ry. 560.83.

1. In his letter of 12 July (562.61), LC introduced the probability of a visit to Brynbella. On 31 July (Ry. 562.62) he promised to be at Brynbella on Monday, 5 August.
2. HLP responds to LC's description (12 July) of Macdonald's defeat at the Trebbia: ". . . to day I read the particulars of the Severest Engagement we have had this campaign.—How gloriously every thing goes on.—General Ross writes word to Sir Robert Gunning, that the battle lasted 4 days.—from the 18 to the 22, on the 23 Suwarroff rested and on the 24 marched off to find Moreau—who by this time has shared the same fate with Macdonald.—The seat of War we see evidently will be removed into the Heart of France—and I make no doubt but that Suwarroff will march to Paris."
While LC was too enthusiastic and premature, his rejoicing marked not only Macdonald's defeat at the river Trebbia but earlier allied victories at the battles of Magnano (5 April) and Cassano (27 April), which led to Suvórov's entry into Milan and to his seizure of Turin.

TO PENELOPE SOPHIA PENNINGTON

Brynbella
Wensday 17: July 1799.

Your Letter Dearest Mrs. Pennington is like yourself—full of true Friendship, honest Loyalty and sound Criticism: Freedom from *Prejudices*—as Principles are called now o'Days—we must not come to *you* for.[1] My Master has the Gout from Time to Time but as he has nothing else we must be content; *Our* Country loves him dearly, and his own will soon begin to breathe again, and in due Time recover. I do believe you were right in that *unjustifiable* Conjecture of yours concerning the Death of those Deputies at Radstadt.[2]

You have heard me speak of Mr. Moore with Esteem, he sayd the same Thing as you did at the same Moment, and I now begin to fear you were both right—

but *Retrospect* of past Ages can show no Perfidy beyond *that*, if so it should prove upon Investigation. The Arch Duke now seems to act with his Hands untied, and cooperates with Swarrow in every thing:[3] yet I suspect something behind the Curtain still; The Emperor is willing enough to see Italy freed—but does not want Louis dixhuit on his Throne again I suppose, whereas the Russians and English are trying to accomplish that Purpose with all their might: and no lasting Peace can be obtained but by his Restoration. We shall see how 'twill End.

You are droll indeed in your Account of the new Canterbury Tales, I have not read them yet;[4] Mr. Gillon will bring them himself he says.[5] When Romances first were Written They went by Name of—Incredibilities——but People soon found out that Fiction looks best, the more She endeavour to resemble Truth. It grows however a mighty Tedious Thing after a certain Age to keep filling one's Head with flitting Dreams so——turning one's Mind into a magic Lanthorn for Shadows and Ombres Chinoises to pass over. If Incredibilities are desireable, *We* can hear enough of Mr. and Mrs. Mostyn—as that Lady told you at some Place that Mrs. *Moyston* as She called her, made all the Talk—*and so She does God knows*.

Well! any nonsense but *dishonourable* Nonsense—*disgraceful* Folly, such as Honoria Gubbins has Exhibited. You know I always said she looked like a Bacchante Girl, but She admired nothing except *Siddons* I remember;—In good Time.[6]

Dear charming Siddons! How triumphantly must She have looked in the first and last Scene of Pizarro![7] And what a happy Contrast Sheridan has made between her artificial Character, and Cora's natural one![8] Yet I cannot seriously approve of a *Heroic* Tragedy in *Prose*. *Domestic* Tragedy, George Barnwell, or the Gamester, or the Stranger, would lose the Interest they now gain in our hearts if they spoke any *but* Colloquial and Domestic Language;[9] Poetry is made on purpose to adorn the lofty Sentiments of Rolla:[10] and Cora's Song is the sweetest Thing in the whole Play,—only because 'tis *Verse*.[11]

Poor Cora! She is not of *your* Mind that Love is of no Consequence compared with a hundred other Things—and that She should have completely no *other* Idea present to *her Mind*, makes her so natural, so interesting and so adorable. What is stranger than Love itself—and Love is strange enough too,—is that one should never have done admiring that *selfish* Passion when represented in Works of Fancy. I remember an old Alderman of London[12] who when there was loud Talk of Invasion 20 Years ago or more said among a Dozen people once at my House

"Well! I care not for my Part if the *Island* was *devoured* tomorrow, so as My Wife and Child were safe, and I had enough to keep them with."

This *Patriotic* Sentiment met with no Approbation at all from an *old Alderman in real Life*, Yet this is the Sentiment that Cora expresses all thro' five Acts, and not only her Auditors in the Pit and Boxes but Rolla himself likes her the better for it.[13]

So you see Fiction may resemble Truth in some Things while if Truth resembles Fiction we hiss her out of Doors.

Poor dear Old Mr. Jones is very bad—and like to die, or has been like to die, and I am very sorry indeed; for though there's but little Poetry or Criticism about

Richard Brinsley Sheridan. Portrait by Sir Joshua Reynolds; engraved by John Hall (1791). (Reproduced by permission of the Trustees of the British Museum, Department of Prints and Drawings.)

old Mr. Jones he is a good Friend and a valuable Member of Society and wishes well to My Master and to me: If I had been near Mrs. Mackay I might have heard all the Story of Sir Harry Englefield and Mrs. Crewe to great Advantage, but here am I left in the Basket.[14]

Mr. and Mrs. Sullivan certainly were in this Neighbourhood together, whether they have parted since or not; and they had a Niece of his with them, and they were much liked at St. Asaph till People found out who and what they were. He was said to be a *Clergyman*——Is he in Orders or no? Sure Fanny Sage's Life must be beyond all the Novels ever written, When will she finish her mad Career? People hereabouts admired her *Accomplishments,* but said there was very little Beauty to boast.

The World is foolisher than Wise People would think, and wickeder than good People would believe: It grieves me to see that charming Hannah More has omitted to mention the *Attitude* Master put about the Misses of last Year by their Educators.[15]

Mrs. Siddons goes to Edinburgh I hear, but by what you say of Sally—I trust She cannot be of the Party:[16] Miss Thrale is in Scotland, and will have the Pleasure of seeing her—as I saw her at Bath.

No Letter have I ever received from Marlbro' Street but one—and *That* was from the Master of the Mansion.[17] Dear Friend Adieu! and love *my* Husband, and give our truest and tenderest good Wishes to *your own* Husband, and bid Colonel Barry[18] continue to remember / Your Affectionate / H: L: P.

Compliments to Mrs. Weston.

The Little Boy comes next Week, next Month I mean with Davies.

Text: Princeton University Library. *Address:* Mrs. Pennington / Dowry Square / Hot Wells / Bristol. *Postmark:* DENBIGH E JUL 18 99.

    1. HLP responds to PSP's letter of 3 July (Ry. 567.82).
    2. On 25 May (Ry. 567.81), PSP had written: "I entertain a perswasion on [the Rastatt assassination] that does not seem to strike any one else. *I firmly believe* it is an Act of *French* Policy and that it was, somehow, perpetrated by *French Agency,* tho perhaps the Fact can never be traced or known, to give a *new Impulse* to their People, which is evidently much wanted—and the ridiculous *Pantomime* they are acting over on the occasion, with their illiberal and absurd *accusations* of the Arch Duke confirm me in the opinion.—Their *pre-judging* him so *unfairly* and also declaring every measure he *can* take either to find out, or punish the offenders *will be of no avail*—proves the Fact against *Them.*"
    PSP's interpretation of the events at Rastatt was not unique. The Directory exposed its envoys to needless danger and this fact supported the farfetched view that it tried to win popularity for the war out of French blood. To this day, however, there is no verifiable explanation of the assassination.
    3. The two generals, victorious at this time in separate theaters of war, were frequently compared. In the *Oracle* on 22 May, e.g., "Suwarrof stands *six feet four inches,* and is proportionably corpulent; whilst the Archduke Charles is only *five feet one inch,* and as thin as a lath; but their *Souls* are alike heroic, ardent, and determined on rescuing the world from a Monster!"

Contrary to such reports and HLP's statement, Charles proved incapable of cooperating with his Russian allies under Suvórov.

4. On 3 July, PSP had commented: "Have you seen the 3d Vol. of Canterbury Tales?—Without pretending to be Critical, I cannot think these productions at all likely to advance the Reputation of the fair Writers in any point of View.—It strikes me that these two last Tales are most particularly Characteristic of the Women.—Harriet's has a most *flimzy foundation* with here a patch of Embroidery and there a few Silver Spangles.—While Miss Lees runs *so wild* in the Fields of *tender Romance* that probability and *Morality* are equally lost sight of."

The third volume includes "The Officer's Tale. *William Cavendish,*" by Harriet (pp. 1–194); "The Clergyman's Tale. *Henry,*" by Sophia (pp. 195–522).

5. On 28 June (Ry. 577.24) John Gillon had accepted an invitation to visit Brynbella, promising to bring the third volume of the *Canterbury Tales.*

6. Honoria, or Honor Gubbins (d. 1807), born in Ireland, had recently become a subject of gossip that swirled about the Prince of Wales.

7. When *Pizarro* opened on 24 May, its first night was not a success, although it drew a large crowd. After certain alterations and omissions made for its second night, the play quickly took hold, earning £30,000 in sixty nights. For contemporary reviews of the play, see *The Dramatic Works of Richard Brinsley Sheridan,* ed. Cecil Price, 2 vols. (Oxford: Clarendon Press, 1973), 2:631–40.

Within a month *Pizarro's* financial success startled Jane Holman, who wrote to HLP on 23 June (Ry. 555.94): "What do you think of Mr. Sheridan's luck in making such sums of money of a play very little other than a translation [of Kotzebue's *Die Spanier in Peru*]? I assert the fact boldly—for Miss Thrale told me she had read in the original German, the play whence Pizarro is taken—that, with the exception of curtailments, there is but very slight variation between it and Mr. Sheridan's alteration. Yet he is (I hear) to have £500 for his copyright! We were at the first representation, and were fatigued by the enormous length of the performance; which was not over till a quarter before twelve—however, I understand it is now judiciously cut to a moderate length. Drury Lane is to remain open till July, on account of the houses attracted by this piece."

8. The role of Elvira, as SS played it, suggested a figure heroic in her passions, her courage, and then her penitence. Thus writing of Elvira's opening scene (and the same qualities might be attributed to her in the final one, 5.4), the *Oracle* for 25 May argued that she, "who first appeared a few minutes before, the enfeebled slave of passion, assumes a dignity and resolution, which even shook the tyrant for a moment."

Cora, who was played by Mrs. Jordan (not successfully), typifies the woman devoted without question to her husband, Alonzo, and their child.

9. *The London Merchant, or the History of George Barnwell* (1731), by George Lillo; *The Gamester* (1735), by Edward Moore; *The Stranger* (1798), by Benjamin Thompson, altered from Kotzebue's *Menschenhass und Reue* (1789).

10. Although Cora was once betrothed to the great Peruvian warrior Rolla, he gives her up because in the spirit of noble self-sacrifice he realizes her love for Alonzo. This spirit was consistently maintained in the character and in Kemble's depiction.

11. Appearing in 5.1, it is entitled simply "Song." It consists of six stanzas of varying length, beginning "Yes, yes, be merciless, thou Tempest dire; / Unaw'd, unshelter'd, I thy fury brave." The music was written by Michael Kelly (ca. 1764–1826).

12. Probably Thomas Sainsbury. See HLP to Q, 7 July 1787, n. 2.

13. When Cora first appears (2.1), she fixes her dominant quality in "the pious supplication of the trembling wife, and mother's heart." She addresses her husband: "Oh! my Alonzo! daily, hourly, do I pour thanks to Heaven for the dear blessing I possess in [my child] and thee."

14. Henry Charles Englefield (1752–1822), seventh baronet (1780); antiquary and scientific writer; F.R.S. (1778); F.S.A. (1779). A Roman Catholic, he moved at will in Whig circles that supported Catholic emancipation, where he would meet Charles Fox, e.g.,

and Frances Anne Crewe, née Greville (1748–1818), the wife of John (1742–1829) later Baron Crewe (1806), who was an active M.P. for forty-eight years.

15. The work not mentioned by Hannah More was that of Charlotte Palmer (fl. 1780–97), *Letters on several Subjects, from a Preceptress to her Pupils who have left School. Addressed chiefly to real Characters, and designed for the Use of Young Ladies from Sixteen to Twenty Years of Age* (London: E. Newbery, 1797).

16. On 3 July, PSP had reported that the Siddons family (or at least SS and Sally) "set off for Scotland early Sunday Morning [29 June].—She Plans to be all this Summer in Edinburgh.

"Poor Sally never escapes an attack of her tormenting Complaint at the end of every Fortnight, and wrote me She was just on the Eve of it, when they set out.—What an Existence!!—all is quiet with respect to Mr. Lawrence."

For the association of the artist Thomas Lawrence with Maria, Sally, and SS, see Manvell, chap. 6; HLP to PSP, [29] April 1798, n. 3., *Thraliana* 2: 992 n. 4.

17. The letter from William Siddons is missing.

18. For Colonel Barry, see HLP to PSW, 11 June 1789, n. 2.

TO JOHN LLOYD

Brynbella, Thursday
18: July 1799.

My dear Sir

Imperious Business makes me the Plague of *your* Life and of that kind Friend to whom the inclosed is addressed——I am a most expensive Correspondent to him, let him pay but *one* Penny for this Epistle at least.[1]

The News mends every Day and the French fall now as fast as they mounted: I think their Ballon is burst now sure enough, and hope nothing will happen to catch them safe before they drop to Ground.[2]

Astlys Jones in their Circus Advertisements prove my Notion right concerning Pizarro, and their crouded houses evince the preference People give to Show over Language[3]——'Tis not so here in the Country; where folks believe their *Ears* rather *too much:* Did they wait for the *Eyes* to confirm many Reports I think they would not spread so.

Come soon among us Dear Sir and bring Pardon with You for all the Trouble you have had with Your / H: L: Piozzi.

Text: National Library of Wales MS 12421D. *Address:* John Lloyd Esq. / Member of Parliament / Garden Court / Temple / London. *Postmark:* DENBIGH JY 20 99.

1. HLP's enclosed letter, which replied to John Gillon's of 13 July (Ry. 577.25), is missing.

2. The alliance in 1799 between the czar of Russia and the Austrian emperor had altered military affairs on the Continent. The troops of both countries appeared in strength on the Adige. Ferdinando was back in Naples under the protection of Nelson and the British fleet. The French in Italy had been driven northward from Naples to Rome

and from Rome to Florence. Suvórov had virtually mastered northern Italy. Macdonald was defeated at the Trebbia; Joubert defeated and killed at the battle of Novi. Milan and Turin belonged to the Allies, as did Mantua. In Germany the French were forced to recross the Rhine.

3. From *The Times*, 13 July (advertisement): "This present Saturday, July 13, will be presented . . . an entirely New Operatic Ballet of Action, interspersed with Song, Dance, and Chorus, composed, written, and arranged by Mr. Astley, jun. called Rolla and Cora; or The Virgin of the Sun: from the German of Kotzebue, and the literal Translation of Miss Plumtre [Anne Plumptre, 1760–1818]. . . . In the course of the Piece will be pourtrayed the exact Procession which preceded Ataliba, Inca of Quito, when, in full Assembly, Rolla was declared his Heir! Also, the Solemn Procession of Priests and Priestesses, &c. from the House of Stars to the Temple of the Sun, from whence Pizarro collected his riches; with the destruction of that Idolatrous Temple, and the total Abolition of Peruvian Superstition."

TO ELIZABETH GRAY

Brynbella
20th. July, 1799.

It was exceedingly kind of you my dear Mrs. Gray to tell me when, and how safely you got home: Mr. Piozzi and I both felt half uneasy that the letter was so long in coming.[1] The Ladies at Llangollen were kind in remembering me without resentment of my apparent neglect. I shall now say they deserved the visit. We have however really *not* deserved the vacant uncomfortable sensation occasioned by your departure, and 'twas hard upon poor Jones to miss you all; for I trust his conversation pleasures at Oswestry are few.—[2]

—Llangollen and the Leasowes exhibit, as places of seclusion, the most characteristick difference imaginable, one so sublimely, the other so beautifully tranquil.[3] You will like the first best to look at, the last to live in. Yet the Leasowes are always to be *had* somehow, no tenant keeps them long; Travellers *fancy* themselves enamoured of the place which has been of late often taken by men of business, who believe they could effectually bury all their cares in so sweet a solitude. Unluckily they bury their only ideas there, and soon feel the necessity of rekindling the Fire of Life by London chat.

If one must live alone I would rather it should be at Llangollen, but the general taste is against me: was that place empty tomorrow, few would strive for it.—

Ask Mr. Gray if <King> Richard Coeur de Lion gave the Bishops Armour when he bestowed it on *other* Heroes;[4] the Bishop of Beauvais I remember whose name was Dreux and is I believe Father of the Drax family, fought him hand to hand, but I recollect not his *device* as it was called, yet tis most like he wore one for distinction's sake in the field, and that the Pope was well acquainted with it; because our surly Sovereign sent him the armour,[5] bidding him see now and know whether this be thy son's coat or not as Joseph's brethren said to their father.[6]

Cardinal Ruffo is reviving old modes in the South of Italy now, and the tide seems completely turned against the French.[7] Will the Great Nation be sold quietly by the Abbé Sieyes to the best bidder I wonder, or will these vaunting liberty boys let Swarroff come to Paris and prescribe their future Government?—

The sundial is putting up; I shall be very proud of his verses on it[8] tho' I do not promis<e> to bury *my Heart* under as Sir William Temple did, for love of his own motto.[9]

Mr. Piozzi is much as you left him, he does not bear fatigue at all otherwise very well: we are to dine out tomorrow for the first time, and I am afraid it will prove a painful operation.

His best regards with mine wait yours and Mr. Gray's acceptance; with every possible wish for every possible happiness to your darlings. Compliments to Sir Thomas Clarges and to Lady Clarges[10] who you mention as if on a visit at your house. Pray prevail on Mr. Gray to let me hear when the Family *increases*.[11] You may have many *nearer* and many more useful friends but none more truly your faithful and obedient servants than those you left at / Brynbella.

Text: Hyde Collection (Copy).

1. For Elizabeth Gray, see HLP to LC, 21 February 1797, n. 4. She had written to HLP on 11 July [1799] (Ry. 558.86).
2. Probably the attorney Lewis Jones (fl. 1775–1829), who in 1828 served as Oswestry town clerk. See Tibnam's *Directory* (1828), C.R.O., Salop.
3. From the cottage of the Ladies of Llangollen, purchased in 1780 and named by them Plas Newydd, the vista pleased the romantic-minded. Behind the cottage to the northeast were the Eglwyseg mountains; "the sublime cone of Dinas Bran, the ruined castle on its top . . . further east ran the menacing striations of the Trevor rocks; to the south the range of the Berwyn mountains. Behind the cottage the land dropped steeply to a delicious miniature ravine with a mountain stream flowing through it, while the back windows gave a view over the chimney-pots of Llangollen itself," the church and its graveyard. See Elizabeth Mavor, *The Ladies of Llangollen* (London: Michael Joseph, 1971), pp. 56–57.
For the Leasowes, see HLP to Sophia Byron, 4 September 1787, n. 6.
4. The armor that Richard I bestowed not merely on bishops but on others as well is described in *Retrospection* 1:313. "To reward those who fought bravely by his side, the privilege of what is now called *coat armour* was invented. The half moons [i.e., Turkish crescents] were bestowed on those who had subdued infidels, wearing that badge of Mahometanism, and gryffons adorned the shields of such as seized a saracen so called. Our monarch's battle-axe was named *mate gryphon*."
5. Among the branches of the House of France is that of the now extinct family of Dreux. It originated with Robert, comte de Dreux, fifth son of Louis VI, who married ca. 1152 Agnès de Baudiment, Dame de Braine, from whom he procured what was to be a hereditary coat of arms for his family.
Their son was Philippe de Dreux (d. 1217), bishop of Beauvais. A courageous warrior, he was taken prisoner by the English near Milly ca. 1196 and brought to England. The pope asked for Beauvais's return, calling him his spiritual son. But the request was refused. Only after King Richard's death could the bishop be ransomed ca. 1202 and returned to France.
No apparent connection exists between the families of Dreux and Drax. The latter were anciently seated in Yorkshire and in HLP's time in Charborough and Bere Regis, Dorset.
6. Gen. 37:32.
7. Fabrizio Ruffo di Bagnara (1744–1827) was named *chierico di camera* for Pius VI, and then general treasurer of the apostolic chamber. He became a cardinal in 1791.

In December 1798, after the French invasion of Naples, he accompanied the royal family to Sicily. About February, he landed in Calabria with seven men, lacking money or arms, and began the process of recovering the kingdom of Naples for Ferdinando. Aided by an anti-Jacobinical insurrection of peasants, he was able to lead a movement that restored Naples to the king.

8. RG's verse was "Umbra tegit lapsas [lapsus] præsentique imminet Horæ, / Dum Lux, dum lucis semita—Virtus agat," or " 'Ere yet the threat'ning Shade oerspred the Hour, / Hasten bright Virtue and exert thy Pow'r" (*Thraliana* 2:999).

9. Sir William Temple (1628–99) wrote in his will: "I desire my body may be interred at Westminster Abbey, near those two dear pledges gone before me . . . and I desire and appoint that my heart may be interred six feet under ground, on the south-east side of the stone dial, in my little garden at More Park." See Thomas Peregrine Courtenay, *Memoirs of the Life, Works, and Correspondence of Sir William Temple, Bart.*, 2 vols. (London: Longman, Rees, etc., 1836), 2:485–86.

10. Louisa Clarges, née Skrine (1760–1809), was the widow of Thomas Clarges (1751–82), third baronet of Aston, Herts. (1759), and M. P. for Lincoln (1780–82). Their son Thomas (ca. 1780–1834), fourth and last baronet, was a pupil of RG (*Thraliana* 2:997 n. 3). For Lady Clarges's later misfortunes, see HLP to Q, 17 January 1806, n. 28.

The elder Thomas's will, signed 8 December 1782, was proved 13 January 1783 (P.R.O., Prob. 11/1099/7); Lady Clarges's will, signed 13 January 1809, was proved 31 August 1809 (P.R.O., Prob. 11/1501/613).

11. The increasing Gray family finally consisted of nine sons and five daughters, many of whom were in such frail health that by 1831 only six were alive. See Audrey Brooke, *Robert Gray, First Bishop of Cape Town* (Cape Town, Johannesburg: Oxford University Press, 1947).

TO PENELOPE SOPHIA PENNINGTON

Brynbella
21: August 1799.

My Dear Friend

Your Letter is like yourself, wise and kind, and I am willing to join in your Wish for early meeting this Year—but not for an early Winter.[1] Oh, little do you *Townsfolk* know how prejudicial is this Weather to Country Farmers, Labourers, &c. The Shoemaker and his Apprentice at Bristol make so many more Boots and Clogs, and some Bath Chairmen get a few Shillings extra:—but *my* honest Neighbours have but just barely *Bread* in the *strictest* Sense; mere Bread, and that made of Barley too for their Families during such Winters as this cruel Summer will infallibly produce: Mr. Piozzi and I shall scarce be suffered to get thro' the Village they will so cling, and cry round us; and beg we will stay another Month, another Week, &c.

When the Gardiner came Yesterday scratching his head and saying There would be no *Wall Fruit* this year, I could hardly answer him civilly, but I *did* say for Gods Sake think about the Hay and Corn, and hang the fine People and their Wall Fruit.

The Produce of whole Meadows may be seen swimming down our over-flooded River to the Sea this Moment, and carrying with it the Subsistence of Hundreds of Innocents.

May this fine Expedition make amends for all![2] It *will* if Peace and Abatement of necessary Exertion be its Consequences. English Pride will be bravely swelled that's certain, if we can thus give Law and Order and Happiness to Europe. Are such Blessings within Hope? People *say* they are almost within *Grasp*. Meanwhile let us try to live that we may see these good Days; Mrs. Bagot the Bishops Wife's Death has affected my Spirits strangely:[3] I got a pain in my Stomach on the *Instant* Allen told me the News, and it has never wholly left me since:—She dined here in high Spirits on our Wedding Day Three Weeks ago, and expired on Saturday Morning. The Ton Men and Ton Women bear these Things without Concern, and prove that Fashion can do more than Philosophy towards hardening one's heart, but my Nervous Fingers shake while I write about it—Mrs. Madox! Mrs. Bagot! *close* Neighbours, and pleasing Acquaintance whom we were in the habit of seeing familiarly and often—I am greatly shocked at their Loss.

To divert Thought I took up the Canterbury Tales which Mr. Gillon had just brought me:[4] Harriet's Management of the *pretty Mamma* making the Man miserable so unconsciously is very good—and in *this Age* scarcely violates Probability. The other Story is too romantic—and the Ghost part too inartificial, one sees it could be only Carey: for Love It abounds but little with *That* I think. Julia keeps her Passion very quiet, one is most interested about Agnes and Carey.[5]

Real Life meanwhile affords stranger Occurrences than any Novel can shew. Mr. Conant the London Magistrate[6] told Mr. Gillon who told us the following Tale not a fortnight ago. Some little London Shopkeepers sent out their Girl of 11 Years old with a Baby 8 *Months* old in her Arms, upon some Errand I forget what, but no further off than the short Street's End. A Young Woman genteely dressed stopt the Girl and begged her to cross over and ask the Price of a gay coloured Hankerchief hanging at a Window promising that she would hold the Infant till his Sister returned. When She came back however both little Boy and young Woman were vanished, and the Girl ran back half wild to her Parents and told the Story. They flew from their Counter in Search of the Thief and desperate with Rage and Terror exhibited to the Neighbours a certainty that the Shop might be easily plundered while their Distress employed every Thought— accordingly the *Man* returning home at Night, found his poor Dwelling robbed of many valuable Articles while the Girl to whom all this Confusion was owing, had hid herself under the Bed for fear of a Beating, and the Father was perswaded *She* too was lost.

The Mother parting from her Husband who had wandered over six Parishes swore She would never see home again without her Baby, and remained out the whole day and the whole Night in search. Morning found her much exhausted at a Chandler's Shop Door in Edgeware Road, and when it opened, She went in to buy a Bit of Cheese: a little Wench went in with her, and the Mistress of the House seeing her Anguish kindly asked the Cause. I've lost my Child said She, my dear little Boy—My Mommy has found one says the Wench, and don't know what to do with it.

They ran together to a Green Stall and found Baby safe in that Woman's Possession; who said a Young *Gentlewoman* had pretended to buy Sellery of her, and while She went backwards to look for some, threw down the Infant and was seen no more.

Mr. Conant was applied to and found a Cause for all. The well dressed Lady was a Chambermaid who having had a Child by her Master made him pay for its Maintenance altho' it died during the 1st Week; and he, tired of repeated Calls for Money, resolved that hapless Day to *see* his *Son:* Molly had nothing for it but to borrow one, and when the Purpose was served—to rid her hands on't: and no Novel can bring to A Reader's Fancy more perfect Distress than those poor Parents suffered. Their Girl however who lay concealed till Mother and Brother returned, told her Tale so well that a Subscription was raised, and all went better than before in the little Shop in Silver Street, Carnaby Market.

So instead of our best Compliments to Dr. and Mrs. Randolph,[7] instead of Affectionate Regards to Mr. Pennington or Bon Mots of our little John Salusbury; here's a Page from the Romance of *real Life*, unadorned by Your True Friend H: L: Piozzi, and for this you will pay 8*d*.

Text: Princeton University Library. *Address:* Mrs. Pennington / Dowry Square / Hot Wells / Bristol. *Postmark:* DENBIGH.

    1. HLP is responding to PSP's letter of 5 August (Ry. 567.83) in which the latter hoped that next winter she and HLP would be "sitting by a good Fire and chatting over the past and the present once more together."
    2. Pitt had planned an expedition against Holland, now the Batavian Republic. It consisted of thirty thousand British troops and about fifteen thousand Russians, who were to land in the province of North Holland and march to Amsterdam. The duke of York had the chief command with Lord Chatham as one of his major generals. See HLP to LC, 25 September 1799, n. 4.
    3. For Mary Bagot, see HLP to Q, 17 September 1794, n. 7. According to *GM* 69, pt. 2 (1799): 726, she had died 17 August at Saint Asaph.
    4. Before departing for Brynbella, John Gillon awaited the close of the London opera season on 3 August. By the 8th he was in Worcester and planned "to Morrow to make gradual Approaches to Brynbella" over roads "deep and bad, and ill suited to [his] little open Carriage; which is not remarkable for Strength" (Ry. 577.28). He arrived at Brynbella ca. 10 August, and departed on the 23d. By the 24th he was in Liverpool with plans to stop at Manchester and Birmingham before his return to London (Ry. 577.29).
    5. In "The Officer's Tale" by Harriet Lee, the *"pretty Mamma,"* discarding her husband Cavendish and her son, assumes the name of Mrs. Mordaunt. This same son later discovers the secret of Mrs. Mordaunt, who was *"The divorced wife of Mr. Cavendish!* Gracious God! this then was the secret calamity, the long-hidden sorrow that silently consumed his father's heart" (3:169).
Sophia Lee's "The Clergyman's Tale" takes place in part in the wild but romantic scenery of North Wales and on the battlefields of Canada. The main characters are the quiet Julia Pembroke; Henry, who adores her; Cary, the world traveler who adopts "the pure and simple habits of" the Brahmins of the Ganges; and the long-suffering but "angelic Agnes." All these and many other characters are involved in a complex plot of near-disaster that ends happily.

6. Nathaniel Conant (1745–1822) was placed in the commission of the peace for Middlesex in 1781. One of the first to suggest the idea of the newly established police force in 1792, he was appointed a magistrate at Great Marlborough Street (1793–1813). He became chief magistrate of the Bow Street Court and was knighted. See *GM* 92, pt. 1 (1822): 371.

7. The Randolphs had been mentioned in PSP's recent letters because they "have been in Residence at Bristol for the last five Weeks (of which Cathedral he is a Prebend)."

TO JOSEPH COOPER WALKER

Brynbella near Denbigh. N. Wales
31. August 1799.

Sir[1]

When any Apology is necessary, The truest is always the best. Your kind and flattering Letter never reached me till last Week—Mr. Piozzi and I have had no House in or near London these two Years, and my Daughters say they never observed that your obliging Application to me had lain half a Year about *their* Apartments.

The moment I received it, Lady Eleanor Butler lent me your beautiful Work; and I have been reading little else since I opened it.[2]

If there are any Faults in that Work, there are Beauties enough to render them wholly undiscernible by me; whose Acquaintance with the Subject though much limited before, is now at least sufficiently encreased to taste the Charms you so well know how to heighten. My own familiarity with Italy has led me much more to Knowledge of its *Manners* and "What before us lies in daily Life" as Milton says,[3] than to any desirable Intimacy with its early Literature; We shall however find equal Occasion to rejoyce in having lived long enough to see the Theatre of *your* Studies, and *my* numerous Friendships cleared from that worse than Vesuvian Eruption of unexpected Barbarism with which the French lately oppressed and crushed it—to the Despair of future Antiquarians, who will I trust be at Loss to settle what was destroyed by ancient, and what by modern Vandals.

I feel gratified at hearing that we were remembered upon the lovely Borromæan Islands.[4]—Those sweet Scenes have left their yet unworne Impression strongly on *my* Memory and spoyled me for a Residentiary of great Cities. In this *most* lovely Country of *our own* Island Mr. Piozzi has built a pretty little Villa like some of those upon the Brenta, and we are tempted to leave it only for the three Winter Months which we chiefly spend at Bath. I must however begin the new Century at London I'm afraid, lest I should like you have to lament those errors of the Press which can be avoided only by close Attendance on the Printers.[5]

Wish me Success Dear Sir, and accept my most sincere Thanks for your friendly Notice of her who remains Your much Obliged and Obedient Servant / Hester Lynch Piozzi.

Text: National Library of Wales MS 14002C. *Address:* Joseph Cooper Walker Esq. / Eccles Street / Dublin. *Postmark:* DENBIGH SE 4 99.

1. Joseph Cooper Walker (ca. 1762–1810) was an Irish antiquary who, suffering from acute asthma, lived for many years in Italy in the hope of relief. He used his time to study Italian literature and Irish antiquities. Upon his return to Ireland he settled in a house called St. Valeri in Bray, county Wicklow, where he stored his art collection and library. There he died on 12 April and was buried two days later in St. Mary's Churchyard, Dublin.
2. HLP had been reading Walker's *Historical Memoir on Italian Tragedy* (1799).
3. *Paradise Lost* 8.193.
4. The "enchanted Islands of Lago Maggiore, where Count Borromeo lent [the Piozzis] his Palace" in the summer of 1786. See Walker's reply on 14 September, n. 1.
5. Like others who followed her progress, HLP was premature in expecting that *Retrospection* would be finished by early 1800. By the summer of 1800 the work was only nearing completion. But more than a year earlier, the *Oracle* on 22 April reported: "Mrs. Piozzi, almost forgotten in the Metropolis, besides building a fine house in *Wales*, is busily engaged in adding another *tier* to the Temple of her *Literary Reputation*."

JOSEPH COOPER WALKER TO HESTER LYNCH PIOZZI

St. Valeri, near Bray (Ireland)
14 September 1799

Madam,

I am honoured with your obliging favour of 31st August and much flattered by your approbation of my very imperfect work. As I was ignorant of your address, it occurred to me to send my letter thro' Mr. Cadell, who had formerly been your printer. Hence, probably, the real cause of the delay.

I have received too much pleasure from your several productions not to rejoice at the object of your intended excursion to London. Whatever your subject may be, I am confident it will receive new graces from your pen. Of your success I cannot doubt. My best wishes shall certainly attend you.

Had you been forgotten on the Borromean Islands, I should have been surprized. To you, Madam, I am indebted for the pleasure which I derived from my visit to that romantic scene. I was drawn to it by the magic of your descriptive powers.[1]

You have chosen an enchanting country for the place of your abode. I think North infinitely superior to South Wales. The latter certainly has many beauties,—but they are rather tame. My hermitage stands in a country that unites in some degree, the charms of both.

Of the accomplishments of your fair friends of the Cottage, I have often heard. I conceive their minds to be "virtue by the graces drest."[2] I hope you are acquainted with the Lady who did me the honor to place my *Memoir* in Lady Eleanor's library.[3] To know her is to admire her. To great elegance and purity of mind, she writes an infinite variety of information, with many personal charms.

You say, Madam, that "your familiarity with Italy has led you much more to knowledge of its *Manners*, than to any desirable intimacy with its early literature." With its early literature I cannot suppose you unacquainted; but certainly your *Observations* exhibit a more finished picture of Italian manners than any that has yet been presented to the public. This too was the opinion of my departed friend, Lord Charlemont, who has resided long in the enchanting country which we so much admire.[4]

As my Memoir was still before you when you wrote, I am not yet without hopes of being honored with your strictures. They might serve me essentially in case the work should ever reach another edition.—I wish I could prevail on your ingenious friend Mr. Parsons, to favor me with some account of his friend, the Marquis Ippol. Pindemonte.[5] Perhaps, Madam, Pepoli, Alfieri, and Monti were known to him also.[6]

The imperfection of my Introduction must have struck you. In order to supply the deficiency in that part of the work, I have undertaken "An Essay on the revival of the Drama in Italy."[7] I have already analyzed some Latin dramas of the 14th and 15th Centuries, and am now deeply engaged in the perusal of a curious collection of Rappresentazioni; or Mysteries, of the same period.

I have the honor to remain, Madam, with great respect, / Your much obliged and most obedient humble Servant / Joseph Cooper Walker.

Text: Ry. 556.158.

1. The description of the islands appears in the section labeled "Milan, 21st June 1786" in *Observations* 2:218–26.
2. See "Verses making Part of an Epitaph on the same Lady," in Dodsley 2:97. "Her Form each beauty of her Mind express'd / Her Mind was Virtue by the Graces dress'd" (lines 11–12).
3. Harriet Bowdler, the literary friend of the "Ladies." Their friendship began at least as early as 1785. See HLP to LC [15 February 1799] n. 11.
4. James Caulfeild (1728–99), fourth viscount Charlemont (1734), cr. earl of Charlemont (1763), was also commander in chief of the celebrated volunteer army of Ireland in 1780.
5. Walker would have known of Parsons' friendship with Pindemonte from the former's "Epistle to the Marquis Ippolito Pindemonte" in *Florence Miscellany,* pp. 24–30, and from *A Poetical Tour in the Years 1784, 1785, and 1786. By a member of the Arcadian Society at Rome.* See HLP to Q, 22 April 1785, n. 18.
6. As part of his continuing work on Italian drama, Walker was interested in firsthand accounts of the dramatists Alessandro Pepoli (1757–96); conte Vittorio Alfieri (1749–1803); Vincenzo Monti (1754–1826).
7. *An Historical and Critical Essay on the Revival of the Drama in Italy* was to be published at Edinburgh in 1805.

TO THE REVEREND LEONARD CHAPPELOW

Brynbella
Wednesday 25: September 1799.

No Letters having arrived here for you dear Mr. Chappelow, I shall write you one myself before the 1st of October calls you up to Town and makes it difficult to get my Cover *freed*——for with all this *Liberty* they tell us of, I miss the Comfort of *Franks*, and *franking* terribly.[1] How must the Revenue be increased since I sate down every Saturday Night to direct Letter Cases for *Constituents*, and have done Six Dozen at a Time very often.[2] You who like old Times less than new, will cry Shame upon such fraudful dealings, and praise our present disinterestedness and Virtue. I hope some of it has been shewn in India, and that our Triumphs there will be unpolluted by Rapacious Avarice.[3] Meanwhile *Cold Water* seems to have been thrown on our Dutch Expedition:[4] they will come home again soon I suppose, saying *Adieu Canaux, Canards, Canaille;* but tho' the Land of *Frogs* is the Subject, I wish not to be quite a *Croaker*. Pray write from London, and say what's the Reason alleged for Mrs. Siddons's Secession? Pizarro being advertised without her, seems a Strange Thing, and I do not above half like it.[5]

Miss Thrale too wrote word you know that I might direct to Glasgow, and so I did; but have heard no Tydings of her arrival there, and I do not half *like that*. When You are got to Hill Street I shall hear some thing of everybody and every thing. Mrs. Bridgeman will be in an agony no doubt,[6] because of these blundering Irish Fellows who will never have done Pike making——When shall we be *married* to them in earnest I wonder! They will bear away the *Ring* upon the *Lance* presently, like the Heroes in an Old Tournament.

Mrs. Strickland ventured not to cross the Rivers but went round from Chester by Land to Liverpool: Her Letters express much good humour, both with her Children and her Friends; among whom She now reckons Mr. Chappelow. Lady Orkney has a mind to go away a while from Llewenny, and live in Cumberland for Change of Scene and Cheapness——They are under Water now, and the Corn all Swimming: We had a famous Assembly notwithstanding and sadly regretted Your non appearance.

Mr. Piozzi keeps on grumbling but is not laid up yet: I think the Fit waits till we get to Bath; where we shall claim your kind Promise of adding to our social Comforts.——

I am working away pretty hard to lighten my next Summer's Burthen; being perswaded the less one leaves to a future Time the better, for a Thousand Reasons——besides the great Reason of all—that such Time may never come. Your *Sun* has illuminated us a long while now,[7] and we are much obliged to you; but there seems a strange Stagnation of Accounts from Italy and Switzerland——The Cause of which I guess not.[8]

Paris too, the Papers led us to imagine was become a Focus of Confusion and of Heated Spirits; but nothing has so long transpired thence——one feels weary of wondering what they can be about.[9]

My great Dependance is on You for *News: Scandal* I shall purvey from other Quarters; I never can get you to tell even true Tales of *Ladies*. Farewell however; and pursue Your kind Occupation of consoling your Friends till October reminds you of *yourself* a little, and the Dear Book which will have Friends and Enemies in plenty; as doubts not its true Admirer, and Your own / Exceedingly Obliged and Faithful Servant / H: L: Piozzi.

Accept my Master's *best*.

Text Ry. 560.84.

1. HLP's access to franks was temporarily halted, for Parliament had been convened unexpectedly on 24 September and members were in London.
2. For HT as M.P. for Southwark (1765–81), see HLP to PSW, 6 August 1791, n. 7.
3. HLP refers to the British triumph in India, when the government sent an army of thirty thousand men commanded by General Harris into Mysore. The British defeated Tippoo in several encounters and besieged him in Seringapatam. On 4 May the city was taken by assault and, with Tippoo fallen, the war ended. The whole of Mysore was now in the gift of the governor general, who divided it among the East India Company, the Nizam, and the Peishwah.
4. On 27 August a British force landed in Holland, defeated the Dutch troops, and reduced the Helder fort. Additionally, the Dutch fleet in the Texel—thirteen ships of the line and some smaller frigates—capitulated.
Sir Ralph Abercromby, entrenched at the Zype, awaited the duke of York, who arrived mid-September with the main division of the Russians from the Baltic and three more brigades of British troops, numbering thirty-three thousand in all. On 19 September, the Allied army advanced in four columns. One column of Russians, either without instructions or disobeying them, outran their supply lines and were driven back in disorder. The success of the other columns was thus nullified. See Stanhope 3: 195–98.
5. The absence of SS's name from the advertisements was prompted by the haggling between William Siddons and Sheridan over her compensation. Financial arrangements were not to be concluded until November, when SS agreed to appear once more in *Pizarro*. (Sheridan knew the popularity of his play depended on SS as Elvira.) Although she secured no advance payments—one of the stipulations—she performed on 11 December and then intermittently until 18 February 1800.
6. On 12 July (Ry. 562.61), LC had written: "I met Mrs. Bridgeman [at Horton] and 3 or 4 of her Littel ones—You know the Father is doing military duty in Ireland."
For Lucy Elizabeth and Orlando Bridgeman, see HLP to Sophia Byron, 2 June [1788], n. 7. The Bridgemans in 1799 had four sons born between 1789 and 1795.
7. LC subscribed to the London *Evening Sun*—founded 1 October 1792 by George Rose et al.—copies of which he frequently sent to HLP. Journalistically enterprising and readable, the *Sun* sustained a vigorous Tory bias on behalf of the Pitt ministry. For a long time it was an important competitor of another administration mouthpiece, the *Courier*. See Stanley Morison, *The English Newspaper 1622–1932* (Cambridge: At the University Press. 1932), p. 198; H. R. Fox Bourne, *English Newspapers*, 2 vols. (London: Chatto and Windus, 1887), 1:288, 355, 368.
8. Defeated in many parts of Italy and Germany in 1799, the French nevertheless maintained their ascendancy in Switzerland. About 4 June, Archduke Charles, having crossed the Rhine into Switzerland, fought the first battle of Zurich, the French led by Masséna. But by 10 July, the Austrian emperor ordered Charles to halt combat until relieved by Suvórov's corps from Italy and Russian auxiliary corps from Germany under Korsakov. Only on 17–18 August did Charles combine with Korsakov to attack French

positions. By 25–26 September the allied effort failed and Charles removed most of his troops to Germany. See HLP to PSP, 17 October 1799, nn. 1, 3, 9.

9. HLP was impatient; she had only to wait for the revolution of 18 Brumaire (9 November), when the Directory was overthrown and a new constitution framed, which vested the executive government in three consuls. The first consul was Bonaparte.

TO JOSEPH COOPER WALKER

Brynbella near Denbigh N. W.
8: October 1799.

How kind is the Letter and how admirable are the Verses of Dear Mr. *Walker* detto il *Pellegrini!*[1] I rejoyce to see one Poet still pleased with the Praise of *Ingenuity*. Mr. Parsons and I do not correspond, nor am I apprized of his Direction, but if any body can tell what became of the Cavalier Ippolito Pindemonte in this last general Concussion, it must be *he;* for they were very intimate. Vittorio Alfieri I never saw but once, he had a high Reputation for poetical Powers—but they were in those Days wholly devoted to the Amusement of the Princesse de Stolberg.[2]

You have chosen a charming Subject to work upon.—I shall long for the Book of *Rappresentazioni* as sincerely as Pope Innocent 4th did to see our Chester Plays in Henry 3d's Time when he sent his Favourite Fool over to enjoy the *Holye Sportes* he was denyed to see by Distance.[3]

Count Meltzi a Milanese by Birth and Grandee of Spain has told me such Stories of these Mystic Representations as would fill a Volume:[4] but tis long since I lost Sight of that very accomplished Nobleman, and though Correspondence with Italy is easier now than it was when all their Fingers were tied up tight to that horrid Tree of Liberty——It is not yet Holyday among them——Championnet seems still moving on;[5] and altho' the Spell which held them all Root bound and Branch bound like Phaeton's old Maiden Sisters[6]—*is loosed*—It is not absolutely *broken* I believe.

Meanwhile as it is completely in your Way will you Sir be kind enough to tell me why *Argine* is written under one of the Queens in the old French Cards?[7] Is it because the Word is an Anagram of *Regina?* They are not called *Reines* but *Dames* in the Play at a Table and the Italians set them still lower, only *Donne*.

I want Information on another Subject——Why the Pretender's Emblem was a *White* Rose?[8] Margaret Daughter to Henry 7th by Elizabeth of York had equal claim to *both* the Red and White[9]—but her Father's preference of *his own* family[10] appears in all old Verses made upon her Marriage into Scotland: where the *lusty fresche Rose of cullour Reid* seems to be always taking Place, and the Lineage carefully exalted over the *pale Lily*—a Preference of *Tudor* to *Valois* I suppose.[11]— The 10th of June was alike favourable to *either* and the Pretender did not claim by a *female* Line—if White represented the Females, as it did in the Contest between York and Lancaster. I *must* have heard why his Rose was *White*, but have forgotten.[12]

Are You safe in your Sweet Retirement? and free from Fears of Disturbance and Distraction! *When the Winds rise worship the Echo* is an old Piece of Advice:[13] We have *here* only the *Echo* of those noisy Contests which I think will never have done shaking poor harrassed Europe, and here we shall pass the remainder of our nearly finished Century if it please God—only going for a little hot Water to Bath in the dead Winter Months.

You see Sir 'tis I who come to you for Knowledge of what passes in my own Country—but no small Light will be thrown on many of our old Customs by your Book, and the Editors of Shakespear will be enlightened too——for in short *every* thing good and bad and wise and foolish *all* came to *us* thro' an Italian Medium. I was shown in the Ambrosian Library at Milan a mighty curious Manuscript by Matteo Palmeri[14]——A Sort of *Pilgrim's Progress* in Terza Rima it appeared to *me*, but I suppose old Bunyan never heard of it.——And some of the Ecclesiastics mentioned that it was heretical—but one always runs about like a Bat in Twilight so (at least I did) that one just *hits* against a Thing and recollects the impression it made upon a future Day when 'tis impossible to repeat it.[15]

La Citta della Vita was the Name of this Poem with which no doubt *you* Sir, are well acquainted, and when Matteo Palmeri lived too; some time about 1460: but the French will doubtless have destroyed that and every thing else of Value before now.—I have an Idea that the *printed* Copy was publickly burned; and that When I just looked at the MS I thought how like our Pilgrim's Progress 'twas: but having nobody to say so to, the Thought faded away.

Farewell Sir and accept my truest Thanks for your so flattering and kind Attention: believing that such kind Regard has not been flung away on Your exceedingly obliged Servant— / H: L: Piozzi.

Text: National Library of Wales MS 14002C. *Address:* John <Joseph> Cooper Walker Esq. / St. Valeri / near Bray / Ireland. *Postmark:* <   >

1. A punning pseudonym for Walker, who traveled with the zeal of a pilgrim looking not for salvation but for health.
2. Louisa (1753–1824) was the daughter of Gustavus Adolphus, prince of Stolberg-Gedern. For three years a canoness of Mons, she left the convent in 1772 to marry Charles Edward Stuart (1720–88), the Young Pretender. She, as the countess of Albany, endured an unhappy marriage for eight years. Determined to end it, she eloped with Alfieri. Their association for two decades was socially sanctioned, both being received in the best circles. For her life after the death of Alfieri in 1803, see Vernon Lee, *The Countess of Albany* (London and New York: John Lane, 1910), and H. M. Vaughan, *The Last Stuart Queen: Louise Countess of Albany* (London: Duckworth, 1910). See also *Walpole Correspondence* 11:270.
3. HLP was to alter the anecdote within the year. In *Retrospection* 1:350, Pope Innocent IV was interested not in the Chester plays but in the elaborate marriage celebrations of Henry III and Eleanor de Provence. Unable to attend, he sent his favorite fool.
The anecdote was based on an uneasy association between the pope (1243–54) and Henry (1207–72), king of England since 1216. It was dominated by Innocent, who forced England to pay large papal subsidies and to allow a preponderance of foreign clergy there. See F. M. Powicke, *King Henry and the Lord Edward*, 2 vols. (Oxford: Clarendon Press, 1947), 1:356–60.
4. Born in Milan, Francesco (1753–1816), conte Melzi d'Eril, traveled in Spain and

throughout much of Italy from 1783 to 1787. What HLP did not know was that he had become a supporter of Bonaparte and was to be made duke of Lodi in 1807.

5. HLP associated Jean-Étienne Championnet (1762–1800) with several of the more brutal French victories in Italy. See *Retrospection* 2:536.

6. HLP refers to Phaethon, the son of the sun god, Helios, and Clymene. Granted permission to drive the chariot of the sun for a day, he allowed the horses to go too high, where they knocked down stars, or to run too close to the earth's surface, where they singed the desert in the Sudan, etc. The earth itself began to burn and to call to Zeus. He himself threw a thunderbolt, and Phaethon, afire, fell into the Eridanus River. His sisters wept so at his death that they were transformed into trees.

7. See Diderot, *Encyclopédie, ou Dictionnaire raisonné des sciences, des arts et des métiers* (Paris, 1752). In the article "Cartes": "Les quatre dames, Rachel, Judith, Pallas, & Argine, anagramme de *regina* (car il n'y a jamais eu de reine appellée *Argine*), expriment les quatre manières de regner, par la beauté, par la piété, par la sagesse, & par le droit de la naissance" (2:711).

8. The paragraph is accurate in its parts but the whole contains a confusing collapse of centuries and royal houses.

The Old Pretender was James (1688–1766), styled by the Jacobites James III of England and VIII of Scotland. His emblem—a white rose (identifiable with "the Cycle of the White Rose")—was the dominant Stuart motif and without relevance to the Wars of the Roses (1455–85), wherein the white rose was associated with the House of York and the red with the House of Lancaster.

9. Margaret (1489–1541) was the eldest daughter of Henry Tudor (1457–1509), who assumed the Lancastrian claim and ascended the throne of England as Henry VIII (1485) after defeating Richard III (1452–85) at Bosworth Field and ending the War of the Roses. Her mother, however, was Elizabeth of York (1465–1503). Margaret, therefore, had "equal claim to both the Red and the White." She married first James IV (1473–1513), king of Scotland; second, Archibald Douglas (1555–88), eighth earl of Angus; third, Henry Stuart (ca. 1495–ca. 1551), later first Lord Methven.

10. For a variety of reasons, Henry VII's "Preference" was for a continuation of the Tudor line through his second son, Henry VIII (1491–1547), king of England (1509–47).

11. Representative of the ballads to which HLP refers are "White Rose & Red" (2:312–19) and "The Rose of Englande" (3:189–94)—("our *King,* he is the rose soe redd, / *that* now does fflourish ffresh and gay. / Confound his ffoes, *Lord,* wee beseeche, / & love his grace both night and day!") See *Bishop Percy's Folio Manuscript / Ballads and Romances,* ed. John W. Hales and Frederick J. Furnivall, 3 vols. (London: N. Trübner, 1868).

12. The 10th of June was significant to the Old Pretender's adherents as his birth date (old style) and indeed the Jacobite White Rose Society continues to observe that anniversary.

13. See HLP to SL, 1 March 1786, n. 4.

14. The Ambrosian Library of Milan, a celebrated collection of printed books, manuscripts, and art objects, owes its existence to the munificence of cardinal Federico Borromeo (1564–1631), archbishop of Milan. Established in 1602 and opened to the public in 1609, it was named in honor of Saint Ambrose, archbishop and patron of Milan. Through the bequest of Borromeo the collection was added to over the years so that when HLP saw it, the library contained about sixty thousand printed books and fifteen thousand manuscripts. A gallery of paintings, statues, antiquities, and medals, many of which are rare, is annexed to the library. Larousse, *Grand Dictionnaire universel du XIXe siècle;* see also HLP to Q, 5 January 1785.

15. *La città di vita* (an imitation of Dante's *Commedia*) was composed between 1455 and 1464 by Matteo Palmieri (1405–75), apothecary, orator, writer, and Florentine statesman, who had been introduced to the Platonic tradition by Georgios Gemistos Plethon [Georgius Gemistus Pletho] (ca. 1355–1452). The poem was annotated by a friend high in the church hierarchy and illustrated by a painting attributed by Vasari to Botticelli [but

probably painted by Francesco Botticini, 1446–98]. The picture and poem were both condemned as heretical and hidden from the public until mid-eighteenth century. About 1557 they had been moved from the Casa del Proconsolo to the Laurentian library in Florence. See Walker to HLP, 29 October 1799, n. 8.

TO PENELOPE SOPHIA PENNINGTON

Brynbella
17: October 1799.

Do you know Dear Mrs. Pennington that Mrs. Randolph and I are in Correspondence? We are indeed—and tis all about Bath, and Laura Place—and No. 1 and Christmas Holydays, and our Dear Friend from Dowry Square——and not a Word of the dismal—the more than Dismal Gloom which these last Accounts from abroad have thickened round us once again on approach of foggy November——There *was* a nice consoling Gleam a while ago that deceived *some* People and delighted *all:* but tis clouded over again, and those that see thro' the Mist have better Eyes than Mine.[1] In the mean Time Helen Williams's old Acquaintance General Moore is a fine Fellow,[2] and our Welsh Folks fight like Tygers: I have Cousins in Holland more than one, and I hear well of them all.[3]

But you must not expect us to pass *Weeks* at Bristol, you must *not* indeed now: It suits *no*way; and you are above silly Etiquette of *"I wont come to your House unless you come to my House"* &c. *Last* Year we had not met for such Ages, that the first Place we *could* meet in was the best, but now; *let it be as it used to be.* Apropos to that Phrase We have got old *Abbess* again,[4] and She likes Wales, and does not whine after her Daughters—and *so tis as it used to be.*

Give our true Love to our very dear and amiable Mr. Pennington and assure him that no House is so desirable to visit at as *his*. But *my* Masters health is much more *uncertain* than *his* is;[5] and no one can guess if once we were *in*—when we should be *out* again: and 'tis no Joke to take a House at Bath and then be confined at the hot Wells.

Now pray *pray* do not alarm your own head nor your Husband's about his Danger when he catches Cold: He was in *no* Danger more than *I* was in when my poor Pulse was lowered down to nothing and my Voice gone——and the kind Doctor felt afraid to tell me of the little Speck in my Throat.

How good you *all* were! and how charming your Society!——Don't repeat your Invitation I conjure you: for we *could* not refuse it and *indeed* it would suit none of us——but *Hodgkins,* who has been seized with a Vomiting of Blood poor Fellow! and frighted us sadly—he is a valuable Appendage to our Household——and will not I hope be lost.[6]

Miss Powell will make herself and you comfortable, it was a good Thing you had such a Companion at such a Moment—Is She a Croaker like you and I?[7] When Things go worse than our dear Sophia expected, they must be in a fine

Way sure: and even *You* thought poor Italy safe[8]——*We* are at this Instant trembling from Apprehension that the French will fall upon Milan, and make an Example of those that called in their Enemies.[9]

I'm glad my little Boy is far away from them all: I think you will find Him improved—unless He falls off this half-Year, and begins to change his nice little Teeth &c.: —Im glad Mr. Mcgwire and Mr. Richard Greatheed are well,[10] when does young Bertie come home to <*illuminate*> us? All the Jacobins will be *up* now, and happy I suppose, but let them remember we have taken Surinam in one Continent, Seringapatam in another.[11]—The Money is ours, and the Commodities (which their Friends the French *must* buy,) are all ours; and the very Warehouses in every Port Are too little to hold our Riches. Few of them are Thinkers deep enough to know that Wealth at such a Moment as *this*, is a mere Invitation to Plunder; and I wish not to remind *them* of so fatal a Truth, tho' I scruple not to tell it to *you*. While it can purchase Russians to find *them* in Employment, The Money is useful however, and well bestowed: and I would rather hire foreign Troops with it than send out our own, who will be necessary when the War *draws nearer*.[12] And I feel sorry the Ministers did not make more bustle in London about the Capture of Surinam—for it is undoubtedly fair to rejoyce when *we* reap solid Advantages from a War, whence no other Country—not even that of the Victors—gain any Advantages *at all*.

Said I well and wisely?

Mrs. Siddons's Situation does not please me—for *her* sake; for my own tis well enough for we are the more likely to meet at Bath. Being at Doncaster so late in the year is a dull Thing indeed; I wish She had some Method of getting paid at Drury Lane—because *Seceders* if they are not called back to their Seats, only look Silly:[13]——and when Mr. Garrick Left London for his Health one Year when in the fulness of Public Favour; I remember he was disgusted at his Return to find the Receipts of the Theatre had suffered nothing at all during an Absence he thought would have broken all our Hearts.[14]

Adieu my valuable Friend—present us kindly and tenderly to Mr. Pennington and Thankfully to pretty Miss Powell for her Remembrance of / Your faithful and Obliged / H: L: P.

Text: Princeton University Library. *Address:* Mrs. Pennington / Dowry Square / Hot Wells / Bristol.

1. See, e.g., the *True Briton*, 12 October:
"We yesterday received *Paris Papers* to the 8th inst. The Victory obtained by the Archduke, near *Manheim*, as well as the capture of the place, and of 2000 Men, is fully confirmed; but these advantages have been dearly bought, and we shall long have to regret that the Archduke should . . . have left Massena an opportunity of being victorious in *Switzerland*. This has unfortunately happened. On the 25th ult. the French made a general attack in that Country . . . and obtained some advantages over the Russians and the Austrians. The following day was still more fatal to the latter; they were driven from *Zurich* [the second battle of Zurich], and if we may believe the French accounts, completely routed."

For further bad military news, see nn. 3, 9.

2. John Moore (1761–1809), was the son of Dr. John Moore of Glasgow. Commissioned

David Garrick. Pencil drawing by Sir Nathaniel Dance-Holland (1771). (Reproduced by permission of the National Portrait Gallery.)

in 1776, he rose in rank until in 1798 he was a major general. In 1799 he was ordered to Holland, where he was wounded at Egmont-op-Zee.

3. On 19 September the Allies were defeated in Holland. By 2 October, however, they renewed their attack on French and Dutch positions. The Russians did not advance in sufficient time, and though the English gained the victory, they lost two thousand killed and wounded. Another battle, on the 6th, produced further casualties but no conclusive end. See Stanhope 3:197–200; *AR* (1799):301–11; HLP to LC [ca. 2 December], n. 4.

Possible HLP relatives with the Allied forces in Holland were: Lieutenant Colonel Sir Stapleton Cotton (1773–1815), sixth baronet (later viscount Combermere); Lieutenant Lynch Cotton (fl. 1796–1809); Lieutenant Thomas Salusbury (fl. 1791–1805), of Cotton Hall and Llanwern, county Monmouth.

4. HLP lured Joyce Abbiss away from Thomas Pownall's service to preside again as housekeeper at Brynbella. See HLP to PSP, 18 December 1795, n. 3.

5. HLP learned from PSP, 6 October (Ry. 567.84), that William Pennington had suffered for about two weeks from a sore throat and fever. Lowered resistance was thought responsible for an attack of gout.

6. For the Piozzi butler, Samuel Hodgkins, see HLP to Q, 1 August 1793, n. 8.

7. For Jane, or "Jenny" Powell, now PSP's guest at the Hotwells, see HLP to PSW, 2 November 1789.

8. On 6 October PSP had predicted: "That the French will be completely expelled from Italy . . . because the Italians have the good Sense and right feeling to be *unanimous* and *decided* in their abhorrence of them and their Principles."

9. *The Times* on 12 October had reported the French victory at the second battle of Zurich. On the 14th it quoted French sources: "*Suwarrow* is completely beaten. We have taken from him 10,000 prisoners. . . . This victory is decisive." While the French triumph in Switzerland threatened northern Italy, the Italians remained unmolested.

10. Thomas MacGuire (1733–1803), a Londoner, entered Westminster School in 1743, Gray's Inn in 1754. Once admitted to the bar, he emigrated to America, becoming attorney general of North Carolina in 1767 and a member of His Majesty's council for the province of North Carolina in 1774. Taken prisoner by the colonists in 1781, he was soon released and—at the conclusion of the War of Independence—returned to England.

For Richard Wilson Greatheed, see HLP to Ann Greatheed[b], 2 April [1788], n. 3.

11. On 16 October, *The Times* (citing the *London Gazette* of the previous day) reported "that the Colony of Surinam surrendered to his Majesty the 20th inst. [of August] and that the British troops took possession of Fort New Amsterdam, the principal fortress, on the following day."

12. In June the ministry had sent to Parliament a treaty, agreeing that the Russians "should employ an army of forty-five thousand men, and that England should assign to [the czar] the sum of 225,000*l.* as preparation money, and 75,000*l.* monthly, besides a further payment at the conclusion of a peace made by common assent" (Stanhope 3:184).

13. According to PSP on 6 October: "Dear Siddons writes me word, She cannot get a Shilling from Sheridan and that it is quite uncertain where she shall pass the Winter.—Kemble says the Sids *might* get their Money, as he does, if they would persue the *same* means;—without it however she seems now resolved not to return to Drury Lane. Her letter was dated the end of <last> month from Doncaster, where she was playing for the Races.—"

14. Perhaps HLP refers to Garrick's two-year sojourn on the Continent (1763–65). See George Winchester Stone, Jr., and George M. Kahrl, *David Garrick / A Critical Biography* (Carbondale and Edwardsville: Southern Illinois University Press, 1979), p. 320.

JOSEPH COOPER WALKER TO HESTER LYNCH PIOZZI

St. Valeri, Bray
29th October 1799

Madam,

Your obliging favor of 8th instant would have been acknowledged long ere this, had I not been much occupied and much indisposed. Permit me now to offer you my best thanks which, be assured, are not the less sincere for being late.

I am so warm an admirer of Alfieri, that I [can] almost envy you the pleasure of having even once enjoyed his society. Is his person as gigantic as his mind? Does the same strength of expression prevail in his conversation that we find in his dramas? Did the Princesse de Stolberg rival "the mountain nymph, sweet Liberty,"[1] of whom he was once enamoured.

Your anecdote of Innocent 4th is extremely curious. It is, I believe, omitted by my departed friend Pennant in his highly amusing account of the Chester plays.[2] If my memory does not deceive me, the antiquity of these rude pieces has been lately questioned.[3]

Count Meltzi would be a treasure to me on the present occasion. If you were to behold my table at this moment, you would pity me. It is strewed over with Rappresentazioni in all the horrors of blackletter.[4] I am now entirely confined to the *edifying* conversation of Saints and Martyrs, who, tho' very good sort of people, are very indifferent company.

Your conjecture, dear Madam, in regard to the word *argine*, is extremely ingenious, and, I believe, equally well founded. I think, with you, it is an anagram of *Regina*. But I shall embrace the first opportunity of consulting Daines Barrington's dissertation on Cards.[5] My attention too shall be directed to your other enquiry. On all occasions I shall be happy to meet your wishes.

Our Obligations to Italy are infinite,—indeed I am entirely of your opinion that "every thing good and bad, and wise and foolish came to us thro' an Italian medium." The fertility and versatility of the Italian genius is astonishing. Of this fertility and versatility we have availed ourselves. We have borrowed,—improved,—and are, I fear, ungrateful.

Permit me, dear Madam, to ask if you think with the Commentators of Shakespeare, that he was ignorant of Italian?[6] Do you suppose he could have been unacquainted with a language so prevalent in his time as *that* of Italy? Where did he find the story of Othello, if Giraldi Cinthio's novel did not wear an English garb when he wrote his play?[7] Who supplied him with the Italian words and phrases which he so often uses, and always so aptly applies?

You are perfectly right in supposing that Matteo Palmeri lived about 1460. The dedication of his *Cicta di Vitta* (Città della Vita) is dated 1466.[8] I regret I did not examine this poem minutely. The author took for his model the *comedia* of my favourite Dante,—one of the most wonderful effusions of the human mind. That Bunyan heard of this poem is not probable, but it is, I believe, certain that had he seen it, he could not have read it. The idea of Bunyan's work originated in his own vigorous mind. Had *that* mind been highly cultivated, Bunyan would probably rank with or very near Dante.—Palmeri's poem was condemned because the author, "visvigliò una dell'Eresie d'origene"—

You kindly ask am I safe in my retirement?—I think I am. Yet disaffection still prevails around me. The spirit of Sedition still haunts our mountains. I have, however, no fears. The state of my health demands pure air, and while I listen to the sweet strains of the swans of the Po and Arno, I smile at danger.

You will find Bath delightful in the dead winter months. I speak from experience. I have passed some pleasant days in that gay city. But should I ramble again, it is to Florence I would direct my steps. Perhaps I may yet be so fortunate as to meet Mrs. Piozzi on the banks of <the> Arno!

Permit me to ask whether you have ever met with an Italian translation (or rather imitation) of *Romeo and Juliet*? La Tragedià Veronese which I saw at Florence, was not then printed. I am sorry you did not see the Italian *Lear*.[9]

If you admire Mr. Roscoe (and I think you must) I am sure you will be pleased to hear that he is now employed on the Life of Leo X.[10] What a charming work is his Lorenzo de' Medici![11] If I were married, his *Nurse* (from Tansillo)[12] should always lie on the toilet of my wife.

Addio—I have the honor to remain, / Madam, / with great respect, / Your much obliged, / and most obedient humble Servant / J. C. Walker.

If you ever read Novels, I hope you admire those of my friend, Mrs. Smith—[13]

If Miss Brooke's *Reliques of Irish Poetry* (published by the Robinsons in Paternoster Row)[14] have found their way into your library, or into that of Lady Eleanor Butler, it would gratify me to learn your opinion of the effusions of our early Bards.

Text: Ry. 557. 221. *Address:* Mrs. Piozzi, / Brynbella, / Denbigh, / N. *Wales*—. *Postmark:* CHESTER.

1. Walker's metaphor "mountain nymph" is from Milton's *L'Allegro,* line 36, and applied to Lady Ligonier.
She was Penelope (1749–1814), the daughter of George Pitt (ca. 1722–1803), first baron Rivers. She had married on 16 December 1766 at the British embassy in Paris Edward Ligonier (1740–81), a distinguished army officer who succeeded to the Irish peerage as Viscount Ligonier (1770) and was created Earl Ligonier of Clonmel (1776).
Lady Ligonier's affair with Alfieri began ca. 1771 and lasted until 1775. Early in their relationship she was divorced, the charge being adultery with the Italian. Lord Ligonier fought a duel with Alfieri on 7 May 1771 in Green Park.

2. Pennant in *A Tour in Wales* 1:137–45 writes about the Chester Cycle with a caveat: "I refer the reader to [Warton's] amusing history of the rise and progress of [the Chester plays]; and confine myself to a few specimens of the gross and ridiculous exhibitions of the times; when the audience listened with the fullest admiration and devotion" (pp. 138–39).
Comparing such a reaction to that of the Romans who watched "the farces in their days of honest simplicity" (p. 139), Pennant then described the guilds that performed in these plays, chosen for their appropriateness. Thus, the tanners acted in the *Fall of Lucifer;* the drapiers in the *Creation of the World;* the water leaders and drawers of the Dee in the *History of the Deluge,* etc.

3. Essentially summarizing Warton's conclusions, Edmond Malone late in the century wrote: "The Chester Mysteries . . . originally composed in 1328, were revived in the time of Henry the Eighth (1533), and again performed at Chester in the year 1600. . . . The last Mystery, I believe, ever represented in England, was that of *Christ's Passion*, in the reign of king James the First [1603–25]." Malone had also admitted: "I am unable to ascertain when the first Morality appeared, but incline to think not sooner than the reign of king Edward the Fourth (1460)."

See Warton 2:178–80, 206–9; Malone, *An Historical Account of the Rise and Progress of the English Stage, and of the Economy and Usages of our Ancient Theatres,* in *The Plays and Poems of William Shakespeare,* 10 vols. (1790), 1²: 3 ff., 23–24, 26.

4. In sec. 4 of *An Historical and Critical Essay on the Revival of Drama in Italy* (Edinburgh: Mundell and Son; London: Longman et al., 1805), Walker describes "Rappresentazioni, or Mysteries, of the fifteenth century" (pp. 75–99). He uses the term as a synonym for "Festa, Storia, Misterio, or Esempio; for by all these denominations the species to which we allude was distinguished. This rude drama was uniformly founded upon subjects drawn either from holy writ, or from the lives of the saints, or the martyrs. In its construction, neither unity of time nor place were observed; nor was the action usually broken by divisions of acts or scenes. . . . The argument was delivered in a short *annuzia*, or prologue, by an angel, who strictly enjoined silence *(silentio! state chete);* and a moral, following from the subject, concluded the piece" (pp. 76–77).

5. Daines Barrington, "Observations on the Antiquity of Card-playing in England." The paper was "Read February 23, 1786" and printed in *Archaeologia: or, Miscellaneous Tracts relating to Antiquity,* vol. 8. Published by the Society of Antiquaries of London (London: Printed by J. Nichols, Printer to the Society, 1787), pp. 134–46. For Barrington, see HLP to LC, 29 June 1796, n. 6; *GM* 70, pt. 1 (1800): 291–94.

6. A long-standing assumption. Gerard Langbaine, e.g., had questioned the depth of Shakespeare's learning, and of his familiarity with French and Italian. SJ likewise expressed uncertainty, yet was finally "inclined to believe, that [the dramatist] read little more than English and chose for his fables only such tales as he found translated." And at best, according to the Reverend Richard Farmer, he "might pick up in the writers of the time, or the course of his conversation, a familiar phrase or two of French or Italian: but his *studies* were most demonstratively confined to *nature* and *his own language."*

See T. W. Baldwin, *William Shakespeare's Small Latine and Lesse Greeke,* 2 vols. (Urbana: University of Illinois Press, 1944), 1:40; "Preface," *Johns. Shakespeare* 7:86; *Shakespeare's Plays and Poems,* third variorum ed. [Edmond Malone and the younger James Boswell], 21 vols. (London: Rivington, etc., 1821), 1:359–60.

7. "The source of *Othello* is a *novella* by Giraldi Cinthio [Giovanni Battista Giraldi, 1504–73], the seventh of the third decade of his *Hecatommithi,* published in Venice in 1565. There was no English translation available and some think Shakespeare read the work in a French version of Cinthio by Gabriel Chappuys (Paris, 1584)." See Riverside *Shakespeare,* p. 1198.

8. See *Libro del poema chiamato citta di vita composta da Matteo Palmieri Florentino. Transcribed from the Laurentian MS XL 53 and compared with the Magliabechian II ii 41. . . .* Preface by Margaret Rooke, Smith College Studies in Modern Languages, vols. 8 and 9 (Northampton, Mass, 1927–28).

On 24 March 1466 Palmieri sent to Leonardo di Piero Dati a letter and a final copy of his poem, to which Dati responded in April with thanks. Walker considers Palmieri's letter a dedication. For these and a few other letters between Palmieri and Dati, see Angelo Mario Bandini, *Catalogus codicum italicorum Bibliothecae Mediceae Laurentinae* (Florence, 1778).

Bandini published Dati's introduction and the first canto of the poem in Florence, 1778; E. Bottari printed the second canto, 1885. See Rooke, pp. vii–viii.

9. There are four early translations of *Romeo and Juliet: Romeo e Giulia,* per Musica, in due Atti, per S. A. S. Monsignore il Principe Eruditario di Brunswick. Composto dal Sanseverino (Berlin, 1773); *Avventure di Giulietta e Romeo,* di Davide Bertolotti (Milano, n.d.); *Romeo e Giulietta,* Romanza Storico di Regnault de Warin. Prima Traduzione Italiana

(Verona, 1812). There was still another translation by Michele Leoni printed in Florence in 1814. See *Observations* (for *Tragedia Veronese*) 1:225; (for *il Rè Lear è sue tre figlie*) 2:73.

10. William Roscoe (1753–1831), *The Life and Pontificate of Leo the Tenth*, 4 vols. (Liverpool: J. M'Creery, 1805).

11. *The Life of Lorenzo de' Medici, called the Magnificent*, 2 vols. (Liverpool: J. M'Creery, 1795). Walker was much indebted to this work for his own analysis of Lorenzo de Medici's literary performances discussed in sec. 4 of *An Historical and Critical Essay*. See n. 4.

12. Roscoe had translated in 1798 from the Italian *La Balia* (1552), *The Nurse, a Poem*. The author was Luigi Tansillo (1510–68). Described "i poemetti didascalici in terzine," *La Balia* exhorted noble ladies to nurse their own children.

13. For Charlotte Smith, popular novelist as well as poet, see HLP to Q, 10 July 1796, n. 16; and to Walker, [30] November [or 1 December] 1799, n. 14.

14. Charlotte Brooke (1740–93), youngest daughter of the novelist and dramatist Henry Brooke (ca. 1703–83), by whom she was educated in the Irish language as well as in literature, art, and music. She published by subscription in 1789 *Reliques of Irish Poetry* (Dublin: George Bonham, 1789), a quarto volume consisting of heroic poems, odes, elegies, and songs translated into English verse by her and others. An octavo edition was published at Dublin (1816), but we have not seen the English edition alluded to. The collection begins with ancient bardic literature and concludes with "An Irish Tale" of her own composition. Many of the Irish originals are included.

Walker had projected a biography of Charlotte Brooke but did not live to complete it.

TO THE REVEREND ROBERT GRAY

Brynbella
October 1799.

Mr. Piozzi is at his best now, and has little to torment him except foxhunters who break his fences, and perpetual showers that hinder his fields from drying so as to admit the wheat which must be sown, or else no bread for next year. . . . Yet tho' he walks out at present and enjoys a gleam of sunshine when it comes, his health is itself a mere gleam of sunshine, and gives him but little power of promising a visit to Berkshire. You must come to us at Bath,—*that* will be best; and we shall have Mr. Chappelow and Mrs. Pennington, and contrive to conclude the old year with tolerable chearfulness. . . . Yet how awful a thought is it that with this next December concludes that date of 17— to which we were all born, and which our fingers have been so long acquainted. Some more extraordinary events will perhaps fill up the twelve or thirteen weeks that remain of the time, and mark the moment with a strong impression. The Italians seem to apprehend their sufferings are scarce over. 'Roma quondam orbis caput, postea Populi Romani Sepulchrum,'[1] has still a load of insects within her, preying on her putrid and neglected carcase. Will they set up a new Pope?[2] If they do, Abbé Maury has *my* vote, and he is *Pierre* Maury;[3] and that will tally neatly enough with my remark how all power ends with the same *name* it began. France has done so exactly. Clovis is Louis,[4] you know, as our Vale of Clwydd is Llwydd and Lloyd . . . and the first Stadtholder of Holland was William.[5] The last wretched creature that made believe *Emperor* of Rome possessed both the names of Romulus and Augustus;[6] but if the last Pope be *Peter,* it will do for *me.*

To be serious, these are terrifying times,—they are indeed. Our little Bishop of St. Asaph thinks the French will set up an *Adepte,* an *Illuminè* man, to profane the papal chair for ever. Perhaps they will. The poor bishop did look very dismal for awhile, and the first Sunday I went to the Cathedral after Mrs. Bagot's death affected my spirits so, that I came home seriously and unfeignedly sick. I have, as you well know, no *Ton* insensibility about me, but I really find those lucky that *have;* because everything shows that reason and religion, good sense in this world and firm trust in a better, have not *half* as much power to calm and smooth appearances as *Ton* has; when sorrow and joy and love and hate are all covered with a coat of fashionable varnish, they cannot struggle as they used to do. So they all lye still and go to sleep.

Speaking ill of our Universities begins to be the mode, I think; and *female* parents, in particular, seem as if one should fancy it pretty in *them* to dislike a place where so much vice is going forward, they say. When one asks them, however, where *less* vice is to be found, or where any virtue is more encouraged, no answer has been prepared. There is at least more learning and more virtue at Oxford than anywhere I suppose; and to say one wishes there were *more,* is what may be urged of every other place with equal propriety. I am still for Eton and Christ Church.[7] The high road is dusty and carriages do run against you, but byways are always worse; and those who suffer by taking indirect paths are apt to regret, and to consider their original destination or choice as cause of their ill-fortune. . . . He who is overturned in the *Grand Chemin* must confess it to be his own fault.

Text: Hayward 2:251–53.

1. Probably HLP's variation of Ovid's *Fasti* 5.93: "hic, ubi nunc Roma est, orbis caput. . . ."
2. Pius VI, a virtual prisoner at the Certosa of Florence, had become mortally ill. Forced by the Directory to leave Florence, the dying pope began to move from place to place until he arrived at Valence on 14 July 1799 as a common prisoner of the French government. He died at dawn, 29 August (Pastor 40:389).
See *The Times,* 13 September, for speculations about the pope's successor.
3. HLP borrows a prophetic assumption, that if the names of the first and most recent holder of power or authority are identical, then the power becomes extinct.
Maury's name was not *Pierre* but Jean-Siffrein (1746–1817). Known as the Abbé Maury, he had trained for his vocation at the séminaire de Saint-Charles at Avignon, then at the séminaire de Sainte-Garde. In 1794 he had been made a cardinal and in 1810 was to become archbishop of Paris.
Pius VI was succeeded by Luigi Barnabá Chiaramonte (1742–1823) as Pius VII (1800–23).
4. Clovis I (ca. 466–511), Frankish king (481–511), founder of the Frankish monarchy.
5. The title *Stadholder* and the office were declared hereditary by Holland and Zeeland in 1672 and by Gelderland, Utrecht, and Overijssel in 1675. The first *Stadholder* was therefore William of Orange (1650–1702), William III of England (1689), and the last was William V, driven out of the Netherlands by the French in 1795.

6. On the basis of literary tradition, HLP assumes that the first "Emperor" of Rome was the Romulus who putatively founded the city ca. 750 B.C., that the "last" was Romulus Augustulus. For the latter, see HLP to Q, 22 May [1796], n. 8. Cf. *Thraliana* 2: 988–89.

7. A summary of HLP's pedagogical plans for JSPS.

TO THE REVEREND LEONARD CHAPPELOW

Brynbella
Sunday Night 2: November 1799.

My Dear Mr. Chappelow

I am very sorry, very sorry *indeed* for the Sufferings of your amiable Relations: Those that have been produced by Speculation I more particularly feel for, as they once came *very near myself:* Tell Mrs. Clay so; it will comfort her to reflect how safely Providence has brought *me* out——I hope and trust She will come out safe too.

The Speculating Men's Minds are magnifying Glasses, and as they see the *Profit* nearer and greater than it really is, while tempted by Avidity and Leisure; So does the Danger appear formidable beyond its real Size, when once the *Swallowed Bone is sticking in their Throat.* It will go down;——and Mr. Clay will *try again* when he's recovered from his Fright of the present Moment.¹

I hope Dundas will *not* try again to set up Stadtholders that are not wanted:² The Pope's restoration,—I mean the restoration of the Ecclesiastical Government at Rome—is of more Consequence to Europe's Tranquility—than a Stadtholder of Holland——and I do not like fighting for *that. My* Advice is to have no War with France——and no Peace with her: but defend our Islands while we *can,* both from her Hostility and Fraternity: protect our Commerce and mend our Manners; and *Let the French abide*——hanging Napper Tandy and every other Rebel without Mercy; no Mad dog is as dangerous as Napper Tandy: we shall never be without Rebels if *he* is suffered to infect us with Principles from whence Rebellion springs, gaining in Height and Danger every day.³

'Tis well you know how to cure the Plague. Our Newspaper says it is on board the Lisbon Fleet homeward bound——A pretty Cargo!⁴ and I'm sure our Merchants would brave the peril by cheating Government and excusing a Weeks Quarantine for 15*s.* or 15£ Gain——a pretty Speculation!

A pretty Cassandra! exclaims dear Mr. Chappelow——but do not let ill News make you sick. When we have got a House at Bath and are fixed there I write a chearfuller Letter. The Ladies of Llangollen claim our Promise, and if we are not blown over their Mountain, my Master who still keeps *on foot* and pretty well, promises to make it good. Such a Storm as blows at *this Moment* never did I see or hear. The Moon shines brightly, and there is no Rain; but *louder* Weather I scarcely can conceive. Perhaps its the Tail of some West India Hurricane: I cannot see the Sea because 'tis late, but The Roar of Elements is tremendous.

Never mind Franks, while we have Eighteen Pence Eight of them will be well spent in a Letter from you. Tell what Humour the Town is in with regard to this failure on the Continent; and what is hoped or feared from the meeting of Parliament.[5] God send some good News before then: It would grieve me to see the Opposition triumph in their Country's Sorrows and in Europe's Danger.

Dear Sir how could you think of Lord Kirkwall standing for our Towns here or Counties?[6] Flintshire *must* be Sir Roger—I mean Sir Thomas Mostyn's;[7] and Miss Myddeltons command the Borough of Denbigh as you do Mouse-Trap hall.[8] Lord Kirkwall is very generous indeed and very good: and has set his Estates at the old Rents, not raising *one Tenant*. But the Wind makes such a Clatter I cannot go on: I began this Letter to divert Fear, but one grows more and more uneasy— —poor Yellow Fox sits trembling under the Tables. I never heard such an outrageous Tempest.

Adieu! and be safer and less afraid than We. The Transports will be all lost to be sure.[9]

Good Night and the Man if we are not blown away will carry this Letter to The Post from / Yours ever / H: L: P.

Text: Ry. 560.86. *Address:* Rev: Mr. Chappelow / No. 12 / Hill Street / Berkeley Square / London. *Postmark:* DENBIGH NOV 6 99.

1. Since LC's letter is missing, it is difficult to determine the specific cause of William Clay's "Fright." A merchant, he had at this time engaged in speculations that threatened insolvency.
   HLP recalls the bone that gave her such a fright some five years earlier. See her letter to PSP, 26 April 1794; *Thraliana* 2:882.
2. Behind the Anglo–Russian military effort in Holland was the ministerial assumption that the Dutch would rebel against the French and secure the return of the Stadholder.
   Like many of her contemporaries, HLP singled out David Dundas (1735–1820), a lieutenant general during the Helder campaign, as the scapegoat for the disastrous expedition to Holland.
3. James Napper Tandy (1740–1803), born in Ireland, had by this time a consistent history of anti-British activity. In 1792, he helped create a military organization in Ireland modeled after the French national guard. To avoid prosecution he escaped to America, where he remained until 1798, and in February of that year went to France. Supported by a French ship and supplies, he sailed for Aran, hoping to start a national revolution. His hopes frustrated, he fled to Hamburg, where French pressure prevented his extradition to England. On 29 September 1799, however, he was returned first to London and then to Dublin. After a series of court cases on various charges related to high treason, he was sentenced to be executed in May 1800. The execution was delayed through the intervention of Bonaparte and English recognition of disputed points of international law. On 14 March 1802 Tandy was to arrive at Bordeaux and finish out his life in France.
4. On 18 October the *Morning Chronicle* reported: "The following calamitous account of the dreadful ravages made by the plague in Morocco, has within these few days been received by his Grace the Duke of Portland.—Government have, in consequence, with a promptitude that does them credit, given orders at all the ports to enforce the quarantine laws with the greatest strictness."
   News of the Lisbon fleet began to appear in the *Morning Chronicle* on 26 October; namely, that "the convoy for England sailed on the 13th inst. from Lisbon under the Zealous, of 74 guns, and the Aurora, of 28 guns." By 1 November the "large fleet" was "off the Isle of Wight." All the ships were "to be fumigated, owing to the orders for putting under strict quarantine all the vessels coming from any part of the Mediterranean."

5. The Anglo–Russian defeat in Holland was reported in the daily press but without exceptional flourishes. The final meetings of the current parliamentary session conveyed equal calm. While Parliament sat in October, the Commons busied itself with routine affairs and put the best face on the matter. Both houses of Parliament adjourned from 12 October to 21 January [*The Times,* 14 October], during which time the burdensome cost of the war was underscored, particularly in Opposition newspapers.

6. Kirkwall, a Tory, had political aspirations. He was to be elected for Heytesbury (1802–6); for Denbigh Borough (1812–18).

7. Thomas Mostyn (1776–1831), sixth baronet (1796); M.P for Flintshire (1796–97, 1799–1831).

8. HLP refers to the two unmarried sisters of Chirk Castle: Charlotte and Harriet. For their other sister, Maria, see HLP to LC, 17 June 1798, n. 3.

9. That is, the ships carrying British and Russian troops from Holland back to England. According to item 5 of the "Articles," signed by representatives of the British and Russian armies on the one hand and of the French and Batavian forces on the other, concluded at Alkmaar, 18 October, all enemy troops had to leave Holland no later than 30 November (*The Times,* 28 October).

TO THE REVEREND REYNOLD DAVIES

Brynbella
9: November 1799.

Not only a Truce, but a complete Cessation of Hostilities Dear Mr. Davies, if ever any Hostilities commenced.[1]

We are all three of one Mind I am sure in desiring the Improvement of little Salusbury, and we seem to be likewise all of a Mind with regard to Your Mode of disposing of him these next Holydays. Mr. Piozzi and I are going to Bath in Three Weeks Time; and though the little Fellow's Company there is exceedingly agreeable to us, Yet we are often from home, and he would be going back instead of forwards certainly.[2]

We shall be happy to think that he is *safe with you,* and do let Hawkins look in his Mouth when the little Teeth are changing: I *must* have the new ones come nice and fine——It is very comfortable to hear he makes himself beloved, our Croydon Friend only repays me; for I took a great fancy to *his Charlotte,*[3] who said "it was a Sad Thing (I remember) that such a pretty Lady as Lady *William* Russell, should go by a *Man's Name.*"[4]

Pray make our proper Compliments there and due Respects, and Thanks for kind Remembrance. Likewise to Mr. Macnamara—We shall see Mrs. O'Bryan next Month I hope.

This very Post shall carry kind Wishes of Happiness to Mr. Ray to whom I owe much Regard indeed[5]——and seven Guineas and a half beside—if every Man came by his Right; I borrowed it at Bath, and he was gone before I paid it. But This Time next Year We hope to be 200 Miles nearer you all, than now.

I trust that Salusbury will decline Musa by then: tell me how far Kerr is before him, and what hope there is of his coming up to his Class-Fellows. Bourdieu is a

Frenchman by Extraction I conclude from the Name[6]——and Kerr is Scotch, of the house of *Ancram* is not He?[7] It is scarce possible that our Titmouse can be as forward as they the first Year, because of the Language, and 'tis astonishing how the Idiom sticks with him, even tho the Accent is gone.

He says Shall I shut again the Door? instead of Shall I shut the Door again? It used to surprize me when I heard him do so——another odd Transposition—— he would say "He bid me Mr. Davies to be a good Boy": instead of Mr. Davies bid me be a good Boy. You see now that all this did not escape me——He will lose it best in an English house to be sure.

Give our true Love to Mr. Embry when you see him, and charge him from me to keep very well, and to pray for us that we may keep well too, and have a happy Meeting This Time Twelvemonth.[8]

Tell me likewise where I should direct any Woodcocks if our Dogs were to stumble over any, that they might not be spoiled as the fine Sparlings were: and *pray pray* some Literary News.

I suppose John Coventry is almost at Top of the University by now[9]——The Time does fly so—'tis dreadful;——and nothing done: except complaining of the Weather, which has been really unexampled—and for such long Continuance. Our poor Neighbours have scarcely got in their Harvest yet; The upper Counties——I guess not why—have done better; but 'tis poor Doings all of it this Year.

Tell dear little John that Frisk sends his Duty to him, and is sorry they are not likely to meet soon:——I feel half sorry too, yet I am sure 'tis a wise Measure. His Parents always write *so* anxiously and make such minute Enquiries for their Darling one pities them from one's heart. But to make him a good Scholar, and as he himself says—*a great Man;* no Sacrifice *on my Part,* nor no Expense shall ever be grudged; as no one can be more Affectionately his Aunt or more faithfully Dear Mr. Davies's Friend and Servant than is / H: L: Piozzi.

Mr. Piozzi sends you Thanks for your Letter. He keeps quite well thank God and is planting 3000 Trees. He begs you will be kind enough to ask Jacob whether Mr. Giles pays the Taxes for us—or we for ourselves; and to bid him write and tell.——Likewise to write word about the Coat he ordered——We hear *so* seldom from Streatham:[10]

Text: Hyde Collection. *Address:* Rev: Mr: Davies / Streatham / Surrey. *Postmark:* DENBIGH 10 o'Clock NO 11 99; E NO 11 99.

1. Prior to 25 October, HLP had complained to RD about the cost of JSPS's tuition and the amount of care he had been given. Her letter is now missing but RD responded to it in two letters: the first was dated 25 October (Ry. 573.13) and the other 6 November (Ry. 573.14).

In the former: "*Be merciful in your charges.* What an admonition! . . . We have attended more closely to John Salusbury than we ever did to student before. At a very serious expence I have taken into the house a preceptress whose labour was for a long while confined to him alone. He is hard at his books for above *eight hours* every day with one of us teachers at his elbow. All say, and Bishop Embry, who is more than all says, it is too much; but Mrs. Piozzi's words are 'Duc invitas ipsa per ora rota' [see Ovid *Fasti* 6.608]. Labour is the characteristic of the university at the expence of one hundred pound per annum. Idleness and extravagance are the characteristics of Eton at the expence of three hundred pounds per annum."

On 6 November, RD wrote: "The substance of my last long Letter amounted to this, that we have bestowed *more* pains on Salusbury than we ever did on student before, that his Bill was the same with all the other Bills, but that my best Friend threatened to become my worst Constituent. Now a truce to Hostilities."

2. HLP's response to RD's question on 6 November:

"What is the plan for his Christmas Holidays? I could with all Humility recommend his passing the Christmas with us. To spend a month this winter at your table will retard his progress in English very much. He will here have a teacher constantly at his elbow, whose labour will be devoted to him alone. In consequence you will see him in the summer furnished with a few Ideas and *completely English*."

3. William Hawkins in 1765 at Southwark had married Elizabeth, née Newman. See *Boyd's Marriage Index*, Miscellaneous, 1751–75. Their daughter Charlotte had been born on 7 February 1776.

In a letter of 2 December 1799 (Ry. 573.16), RD commented that "Hawkins [of Croydon] is the Physician in the establishment."

4. For Lady Charlotte Anne Villiers Russell, wife of Lord William Russell and sister-in-law of Francis, duke of Beford, see HLP to Q, 13 November 1793, n. 3.

5. On 6 November RD had written:

"Your old friend Mr. Ray married this day week a Lady whose name was Barker. She is neither young nor handsome nor rich, but no doubt *has mind*. Nobody here knew her before this marriage. . . . Her friends, I understand, live at Edmonton."

Ann Ray (d. 1841) was to bear three children: Henry Belward; Edmund Barker; Lucy. See Robert Ray's will: P.R.O., Prob. 11/ 1889/ 43. Proved 1 January, 7 February 1838.

6. For William Bourdieu, see HLP to RD, 5 April 1799, n. 5. On 25 October, RD informed HLP that JSPS "is now in class with . . . William Kerr [who] is six months younger but he is much forwarder than Salusbury."

7. HLP refers to the Scottish family of Kerr, who among other titles held the earldom of Ancram and the marquessate of Lothian. The eldest son of the Kerrs was usually named William. But JSPS's classmate came from Northampton. He was named William (b. 1794) after his physician grandfather (1738–1824) and was the son of General John Manners Kerr (1766–1843) and his first wife Isabella, née Errington (d. ca. 1794). See the Reverend J. Charles Cox and the Reverend R. M. Serjeantson, *History of the Church of the Holy Sepulchre, Northampton* (Northampton: William Mark, 1897), pp. 97–99.

8. Edward Embry (1745–1817), rector of St. Paul's, Covent Garden (ca. 1809–1817). For thirty years a curate of that parish and a schoolmaster, he was presented to the rectory of St. Paul's upon the death of the Reverend Dr. Bullock by the duke of Bedford. See *GM* 80, pt. 1 (1810): 482; 87, pt. 1: 281.

HLP had known Embry at Streatham as early as 1777 (*Thraliana* 1:101).

9. The grandson of the sixth earl of Coventry and the son of John Coventry (1765–1829), young John (1793–1871) was to matriculate at Emmanuel College, Cambridge (1812), having migrated from Christ Church, Oxford.

10. In a letter, dated 17 October, HLP directed Weston to order from Tode [a tailor at Golden Square] a coat for GP. It was to be made of dark blue cloth, not so dark as to suggest mourning or so modish as to suggest the foppish dress of those who paraded up and down Bond Street.

TO ROBERT RAY

> Brynbella
> Saturday 9 November 1799

Among the numberless Congratulations You will have received Dear Sir, assure yourself that no one's are more Sincere than mine; I include those of my Husband who bids me add his true and kind Regards.

So you are come into our *Row,* and as *silently* as possible; we never heard a Syllable till this Morning from Mr. Davies. Pray make my best Compliments to your charming Lady, and try to make her love me, because I shall grieve else; and pray make my good Wishes known to your Dear Mama[2] who will never be *Old* Mrs. Ray——whatever pains you take to give her that Distinction. We have had a Dismal Summer——you indeed were courting and never minded the Weather I trow: but *we* protest there never was seen such a one—no nor *heard* neither: for the Storms have been loud beyond anything within my Comprehension. How looks the Town and its Neighbourhood? We are forgetting as forgotten almost; I mind nothing but my Business——a little Pleasure too in the Thoughts of going to Bath next Month and of being 200 Miles nearer to you all this Time next Year if it should please God we were to live so long.

Soon now! how soon shall we change the old Date of 17—— in which we were all born, and with which our fingers have been so long acquainted——Great Events may yet happen before *that* Day, *very* great ones before the Century is closed: yet I have heard of no Occurrence so agreable lately as your Increase of domestic Comfort; There is nothing else in this World worth caring about after all, and that you may be happy in the married State for as many, and twice as many Years as I have been so; will be the Sincere and constant Wish of / Dear Mr. Ray's ever obliged and / Faithful humble Servant / H:L:Piozzi.

I have not forgotten that besides owing you every possible Testimony of my true Esteem, I owe you *seven Guineas and a half* borrowed at Bath[1]——

Text: Princeton. *Address:* Robt. Ray Esq. / at Mrs. Ray's house / Streatham / Surrey. *Postmark:* DENBIGH 10 o'Clock NO 11 99 F NOON; E NOV 11 <   >

1. HLP incurred the debt when Robert Ray brought JSPS to Bath late in December 1798 to meet the Piozzis for the first time.
2. Robert Ray's mother was Sarah (1722–1814) of Streatham. See HLP to PSW, 5 September 1791, n. 7.

TO JOHN GILLON

Brynbella
Monday Morning 18: November 1799.

My Dear Mr. Gillon

If we relinquish all the Claims we ever had——*since the beginning of the World*——(for that's the Phrase I see) upon Mr. Cator;[1] and if we are contented at last with payment of one Half Year of Crowmarsh Estate according to the Sum I received many years before Mr. Cator and Miss Thrale made a Lease at advanced Rent during our Absence, and without our Concurrence; I think he should at least in Compensation or Friendship or what you will, assist us to prevail on Miss Thrale so to sign Newton's Lease as to rid us of all further Torment on *that* Subject. For with your Letter comes one from Mr. Vandercom, expressing the Farmer's Uneasiness and Impatience; and positive Resolution never to pay any *more Rent* till the Lease is signed[2]——If we dismiss this Suit in hope of not being involved in Disputes with our *young Ladies,*——let us not be distressed by them on another Side, where there is less hope of Disputing to Advantage——Mr. Vandercom apparently *expects* us to be tormented, and thinks Perhaps that our known Facility of accommodating, will lay us open to more Impositions. Be this as it may; Do not Dear Mr. Gillon put the papers we send you back out of your Hands *till the Lease is signed*. This Request is made by Mr. Piozzi as well as by myself, and you must excuse Suspicion from such Sufferers.

As to the 136£.6d., you will when received be kind enough to pay it into Hammersley's——but My Husband and I both are more in haste to see Newton's Lease completed, than to receive that trifling Sum; and till The Transaction relative to Oxfordshire is settled——*we make Releases in vain;*——we never shall be *released ourselves* from Trouble and Anxiety.[3]

Let me request from your Friendship this favour——to hold the Papers fast till Farmer Newton is quiet.

The Public Affairs please me no better than the private ones. My advice would be to keep in a *middle* State *medio tutissimus ibis*[4]——with the French, against whom War seems unsuccessful; and Peace dangerous. Let us defend our Coast against Invaders, our Hearts against Seduction, and like my Father's Newfound Land Dog engaged in Battle with a Mastiff;—draw our Antagonist into *the Water* if possible——for that's our Element.

Business as you well know Dear Sir is not *my* Element, yet I must dip into it again just to tell you that Mr. Vandercom seems to think our old Friend Murphy excites the Ladies not to sign this Lease, I rather feared some Influence from Mr. Norris;[5] but however it has happened—The Farmer pleads Miss Thrale's express Promise, and *pleads in vain*. Tho' She certainly did shake the Man by the hand herself *before* Mr. Vandercom's Face, and gave him her Word that when the Lease was ready, She would sign it. It is surprizing to me why they should object: If Mr. Cator raised the Land advantageously to 366£ o'Year, and they approved, why should they disapprove when we raise it to 450£? and why should they think it a good Thing to let Newton go, and have the Farm spoiled by being let to Yearly Tenants? It

Text: Ry. 533.23; an incomplete draft.

1. Behind this letter and statement lie suspicions of Cator that went back to 1792 and a suit against him for £1400 that began in Chancery in Easter term 1797. Embarrassed by proceedings that involved the Thrale daughters, HLP and GP decided to seek a settlement outside of litigation with John Gillon as their representative.
 As early as 22 February 1799, Gillon reported to HLP (Ry. 577.16): "Mr. Vandercom is not to proceed in the Law Suit, which *has been* instituted; but is to apply amicably to Mr. Cator for a fair Settlement. . . . Little Expence will attend Mr. Vandercom's doing this. If he do not succeed, I will myself try if I cannot prevail on Mr. C[ator]."
 On 29 March (Ry. 577.18), Gillon gave HLP an account of his meeting with Cator. "[I] then proceeded to state your Claims, first half a years Rent of the Oxfordshire Estate amounting to £136; secondly the Difference of Interest, in the Sums received in Payment of Timber not having [been] brought to the Credit of the Mortgage, as soon as they should have been; and thirdly your having been paid no more than at the Rate of £1200 a year for three half years, when you should have received £1500 a Year." But, according to Gillon, Cator rejected two of the three claims, agreeing only "to investigate the Claim of the half Years Rent."
 By 27 May (Ry. 577.20) Gillon reported that Cator "would consent to pay the £136, if you and Mr. Piozzi would agree to relinquish all further Claim, and dismiss your Bill. . . . My Opinion is, that it would be adviseable for you to agree to it, if he will agree to pay his *own* Costs." The Piozzis agreed and still Cator delayed.
 There were further legal maneuvers in November. See Gillon's letter to the Piozzis on 15 November (Ry. 577.34). "The Business with Mr. Cator" was finished only on 8 January 1800. See Gillon to HLP, 9 January 1800 (Ry. 577.41).

2. From 1796 through 1831, Thomas Newton (d. ca. 1834) was the tenant of Crowmarsh Battle—its farm and adjoining lands. In 1832 his name disappears from the "Land Tax Assessments" and is succeeded by that of his son William. As late as August 1834, however, Thomas Newton was alive, leasing and owning land (over a hundred acres) throughout the parish of Benson. See "Crowmarsh Battle Land Tax" (C.R.O., Oxfordshire); and in the same office the "Hedges' Collection" (II. a/88).
 The estate of Crowmarsh was identified in the tax records as the property of HLT (from 1785 to 1791), as Q's from 1792 to 1807, as Lady Keith's from 1807 to 1832 (and later).

3. HLP's suppressed frustration was partially allayed by Gillon in his letter of 20 November (Ry. 577.35). "Miss Thrale's Journey has done her wondrous Good. . . . I, fortunately, said nothing on the Subject of the Lease; it being a first Interview. I mentioned only, in the course of Conversation, your Anxiety to hear of her Safety, and your wish to know if the Letter you had written, and directed to her at Glasgow, had found her. She said it had, and that She had had Intentions to write you, and asked me if *I* was soon to write you. I of course said yes, and that I should have a Frank for this Day. So she promised to send me a Letter to forward. . . .
 "I had got thus far in my Letter, when yours of the 18th was brought me, by which I see that the Lease was not signed. I will not Part with the Release, and Order of Dismissal, *until you authorize me*, or until the Lease be executed. You will observe, in the Mean Time, that Term ends in a few Days, and if the Bill be not dismissed before then, nothing can be done in the Business until next Term, and I suppose Mr. C[ator] will defer paying the Money, such is his Caution, until it can be completed. . . .
 "Mr. Vandercom I remember told me, when last I saw him, that Mr. Norris promised him to endeavor to prevail on Miss T: to execute the Lease. I do not think she can have had Time to attend to it, since her Arrival. I will enquire."

4. Ovid *Metamorphoses* 2.137.

5. In the legal dispute over Crowmarsh, Randall Norris acted as lawyer for Q. See Vandercom's letter to GP, dated 6 July 1798 (Ry. 606.56), and Cator to HLP, 12 November 1796, n. 1.

TO THE REVEREND LEONARD CHAPPELOW

Brynbella, Thursday Night
[21 or 28 November 1799][1]

Bad Public and worse private News dear Mr. Chappelow; My Husband is again in Bed with a Gout so like the Rheumatism, that 'tis with Difficulty I perswade my self there is no Mixture of that Torment with the other. Back and Shoulders, Neck and Collar Bone all suffer so that We see neither hope nor Probability of seeing Hawkestone or *Weston,* or *you* or any thing except Mr. Moore whose hollow cautious Step sounding in the Passage is the only Thing I shall *hear* either, for God knows how long. And the Parlour Bed was taken down—where you lay—and every thing prepared for our Journey: Lord Kirkwall asked us to a Sort of Leave-taking Visit at Lleweney and bid me carry his best Compliments to you and express his truest regards——but here am I sending instead of bringing Respects &c. to Weston like my old Friend *quam mallet ferre Salutem.*[2] Mr. Piozzi's disappointment encreases his Pain, and we had sent off some of our Household too, and all goes as badly as one's worst Enemy could wish.

And this sneaking Emperor beside, that we used to see under Joseph 2d's Wing learning *Philosophy;*[3] makes a piteous Figure truly, and contrives to encrease the Triumph of the French without exchanging a Blow.[4]

Things do run very cross and You are afraid of Famine and Insurrection,[5] while my Terrors are chiefly of the Plague: because one knows that for 80 and 90 per *Cent,* half the *Industrious* and *respectable* Traders of our Commercial Country would run the Risque of bringing it any Day of the Week——and no Scourge is comparable to Contagion.[6] Lady Orkney is purchasing Tar and Tobacco as precautions, but I am all for taking lodgings in a Tar Pit.

Never mind Franks—send a Word of Comfort, and say you forgive a Fault we could not help. Lady Bradford I'm sure will pardon what has perhaps lengthened your Stay in Shropshire, and nothing is more certain than we suffer so much now——no Time will be lost in trying to make ourselves Compensation when it can be done with Prudence.

I write from the Bedside in some faint Hope of getting a little Sleep. For the last 50 Hours none has visited / Your anxious and fatigued / H: L: Piozzi.

Text: Ry. 561.159.

1. The Piozzis planned to leave Brynbella for Bath ca. 1 December and were preparing the house for their departure. They were, however, delayed by GP's attack of gout. Since

he was well on 9 November and no mention of illness was made on the 18th, this letter, written on "Thursday Night," may be dated 21 or 28 November.

2. Ovid *Epistulae ex Ponto* 3.5.5 ("quam mallet praesens adferre salutem").

3. In 1784 Franz (Franz II of Germany, 1792–1806; Franz I of Austria, 1806–35) was sent to Vienna to complete his education under the guidance of Joseph II (1741–90), who was childless. The latter found his nephew unattractive and was repelled by the boy's cold and retiring personality. The emperor treated him with an impatient contempt that confirmed Franz's timidity.

See also HLP to PSP, 26 April 1794, n. 3, and 4 August 1794, nn. 10 and 11.

4. Along with many of her contemporaries, HLP blamed Franz for the humiliating treaty and peace of Campo Formio (1797), for the abandonment of the Swiss to the French, and for Archduke Charles' inertia in November, while the bulk of the Austrian army remained concentrated at Donaueschingen.

5. As HLP reported in *Thraliana* 2:1002: "The Quartern Loaf in London is 15^d & Oatmeal *here* bears a Price high as Wheat." According to *AR*, "Appendix to the Chronicle," 41 (1799): 187, the price of wheat in January was 6s. 2d. a bushel. Oats, however, at the beginning of the year were 2s. 5d, becoming by December 4s. a bushel.

6. HLP recorded her fear in *Thraliana* 2:1002 n.3. "The Plague is come from Barbary to Lisbon. Oh Dreadful! America is desolated by the yellow Fever, Fine Times! *I* expect Pestilence in England, but nobody else does; yet I see not what Possibility there is of escaping. If we do not feel Pestilence War and Famine before the century ends, I think 'tis nothing but miraculous Interposition of Providence y^t protects us."

TO JOSEPH COOPER WALKER

Brynbella
[30] November [or 1 December] 1799[1]

How good you are Sir in leaving your Work—a complicated Work like yours too—for half an Hour's Conversation thus with a distant Friend: such Mr. Piozzi and I yet hope to have one Day the honour of calling you.——

Alfieri was rather below than above the middle Size if I remember rightly; Bruys says the same of Prince Eugene in his *Eloge,* and says it is the usual Size of *Great Men.*[2] His Princess was a warm Votary of the *Mountain Nymph;* and miserably impatient till She had broken her Conjugal Fetters and fled where *Vittorio* called.

It must however be a long Time I think before we talk these Matters over on the banks of the Arno. One Sight of plundered Florence and her ruined Gallery,[3] one Look taken of la Biblioteca Laurenziana stript of its valuable Volumes,[4] would so lower our Spirits; we never should arrive at seeing Rome; and viewing the Devastations made there.[5] A Friend informed me yesterday that of Rafaelle's inestimable Transfiguration not two feet are left whole;[6] and if the Jacobins enraged by Buonaparte's Usurpation, resume their energetic Violence, every thing brought to Paris will perish there in one prodigious Ruin.[7]

But I would rather talk about Shakespear whose Knowledge of colloquial Italian seems proved in each Scene of his Taming of the Shrew[8] as his Acquaintance with their Writers may be traced in Othello——No Englishman would have called the Serving Man *Biondello,* who had not known the Customs of the Country: Lucentio's Excuse to him for wearing Tranio's Clothes, and the little Wonder expressed by the Fellow when he hears his Master's false Tale in the First Act, are to me *Confirmations strong* that Shakespeare was even *Intimate* with Italian manners.[9]

I never saw The Tragedia Veronese[10] but am more and more perswaded of every Story coming first from Italy.

Mr. Whalley once related to me a Tale of a petted Valetudinarian longing to eat his Wife's favourite Thrush, and I thought the Fact a true one and Doctor Johnson was delighted with it; and blamed the Woman for gratifying such Depravity of Mind as well as Appetite——Tho' I believe her Tears Served for the Sauce too.

Many years since I lighted on an old black Letter Curiosity called The *Chorle and the Byrde*[11] and it was said to be taken from the Interesting Story of Federigo and his Hawk in Boccacio.[12] If every thing comes out of that Repository, Lydgate was right enough to make *Adam* call him *Cosyn Bochas* in his Mutabilities of Fortune since the Creation of Man. The *Churl* was evidently the Person of whom my Friend made a Modern Story.[13]

Of lately-written Novels certainly few if any Surpass the Orphan of the Castle, Mrs. Smith is a beautiful Writer[14] and as for Mr. Roscoe he has for his Admirers all who read him——The new Work he is engaged in is most Interesting.

We shall spend a Day or two next Week with the Ladies of Llangollen, and I shall enquire for Miss Brooks' Reliques of ancient Poetry.——

St. Patrick's Destruction of the Bards[15] being five or six Centuries anterior to Edward's Cruelty here in Wales,[16] your Reliques must be older than ours——and from the Traditionary Songs &c. I conclude some later Poems have been composed which She has been curious to collect: but I never heard of them. Had the ancient Ballads and Stories narrated by Tale-tellers, and sung by Minstrels and Glee maids been preserved *genuine;* they would have shown the State of Society in past times far beyond all Historic Annals, which have to do more with the *political* State of every Country than its *Manners:* Your Rappresentazioni Dear Sir will be a valuable Present to the Public, but Poggio himself had not harder Work in digging up the Classics than you will find in these old Legends and *Storial Showes:*[17] if you arrange them in Chronological Order. It seems to me as though the *Presepio* of Naples[18] *represented* these *Representatione,* for I fancy the early ones made a whole Town subservient to their Purpose, Milan or Florence: clustering a few Actors on a near Hill dressed up like the holy Family for example—and all the others following with Presents to imitate the *Tre Rè Magi,* or whatever was the Subject of the Entertainment——Fryars some tell us, Pilgrims Voltaire seems to think,[19] begun this curious Device; I am impatient to hear what *you* think and say of it——My own stupid Fancy suggests nothing to me but a *Live Presepio.* But I will detain you no longer than just to say that your obliging Letter was received only this Week tho' dated the 29th of October. I hope ill health will not make your Studies uneasy to you when so much benefit to us all is likely to result from them. I remain with the greatest Esteem Sir Your Most Obliged and humble Servant H: L: Piozzi.

Be pleased to direct *Post Office Bath*.

Text: Peyraud Collection. *Address:* Joseph Cooper Walker Esq. / St. Valeri / Bray / Ireland.

1. HLP had misdated the letter "31 November 1799."
2. The *Éloge historique du Prince Eugène de Savoye*, by François Bruys (1708–38), was published posthumously in *Mémoires historiques, critiques, et littéraires . . . avec la vie de l'auteur, et un Catalogue raisonné de ses ouvrages* [Publiées par Abbé P. L. Joly], 2 vols. (Paris: Hérissant, 1751).
Bruys is better known for his *Histoires des Papes, depuis St. Pierre jusqu'à Benoit XIII, inclusivement*, 5 vols. (La Haye: H. Scheurleer, 1732–34).
HLP's little dissertation was prompted by Walker's curiosity about Alfieri (29 October).
3. See HLP to Q in 1785, 4 June and 26 July; to SL, 14 June and 27 July.
4. See HLP to SL, 14 June 1785.
5. See HLP to Q in 1786, 4 March; to SL, 25 March.
6. An unfounded rumor. On 24 September 1796 the *Morning Chronicle* and the *Oracle* published a "List of [100] Works of Art chosen from the collections of Rome, by the Commissaries of the French Republic, in virtue of the 8th Article of the Armistice, concluded between the French Republic and his Holiness the Pope. From the Museum of the Vatican." Among the hundred were the "Transfiguration" (No. 84) and the "Belvedere Apollo" (No. 1). See HLP to John Ewen, November 1802; *Observations* 2:109–11.
7. See HLP to Q, 30 August and 8 September 1798.
8. Indirectly, HLP may be correct insofar as Gascoigne's *Supposes* (1566)—the source of Shakespeare's Bianca plot—was derived from Ariosto's comedy *I Suppositi* (1509).
9. *The Taming of the Shrew*, 1.1.218–48.
10. See HLP to Q, 4 June 1785, n. 27.
11. *The Churl and the Bird*, trans. John Lydgate from the French (ca. 1370–ca. 1451), printed by William Caxton about 1478. A long, moralizing poem, the original story has been attributed to Petrus Alfonsus, *Disciplina Clericalis*. See Derek Pearsall, *John Lydgate* (Charlottesville: University Press of Virginia, 1970), p. 198; Warton 2:224n.; Thomas Tannero, *Bibliotheca Britannica-Hibernica* (London: Printed by William Bowyer, Impensis Societatis ad Literas Promovendas Institutae, 1748), p. 490.
12. "Federigo degli Alberighi loves and is not loved in return: he wastes his substance by lavishness until nought is left but a single falcon, which, his lady being come to see him at his house, he gives her to eat: she knowing his case, changes her mind, takes him to husband and makes him rich." The ninth story on the fifth day in *The Decameron of Giovanni Boccaccio*, ed. Edward Hutton, 2 vols. (London: J. M. Dent; New York: E. P. Dutton, 1930), 2:48–53.
13. "The Tragedies gathered by John Bochas of all such princes as fell from their estates through the mutability of fortune since the Creacion of Adam until his time. . . . When Adam appears, he familiarly accosts the author [Boccaccio] under the salutation of *Cosyn Bochas*" (Warton 2:62–63). See Lydgate's *Fall of Princes*, ed. Henry Bergen, 4 pts. (Washington, D.C.: The Carnegie Institution of Washington, 1923–27), 1.1.484.
A likely candidate for the modern churl is Jack Brown, the creation of Hannah More as the profligate character in her tale of "The Two Shoemakers."
14. Charlotte Smith, *Emmeline, the Orphan of the Castle*, 4 vols. (London: T. Cadell, 1788).
15. HLP has confused the Druidic priests, who were ousted from authority after the coming of Saint Patrick in 432, with the learned class—the "Filidh"—who included the poets. The pagan Druids, although highly respected and feared as seers and magicians, could not withstand the impact of Christianity. The Filidh, on the other hand, likewise believed to have supernatural (and even deadly satiric) gifts, continued to be influential in Ireland's cultural life.
See J. B. Bury, *The Life of St. Patrick and his Place in History* (London: Macmillan, 1905);

Edmund Curtis, *A History of Ireland* (London: Methuen, 1936), chap. 1.

16. Edward I (1239–1307), king of England (1272–1307), eradicated the autonomous principality of Wales, which under Llewelyn ap Gruffydd grew to include all Welsh lordships and considerable territory recovered from the marcher lords. Edward, determined to crush Llewelyn, invaded Wales in 1277 and seized control. He put down rebellions ruthlessly, slaying Llewelyn and his brother David (1282–83). Welsh resistance after ca. 1294 and for the next hundred years halted.

17. Poggio Bracciolini (1380–1459), an Italian humanist who had recovered many lost works of Roman literature.

18. See *Observations* 2:43–45.

19. See in *Oeuvres Complètes de Voltaire:* no. 4, "Des Quatre Évangiles," *Sommaire Historique,* 30:302–3; "Épiphanie," *Dictionnaire Philosophique,* 18:562–64; "Juifs Ignorants," *Histoire de L'Établissement du Christianisme,* 31:58–59.

TO THE REVEREND LEONARD CHAPPELOW

[ca. 2 December 1799]

Dear Mr. Chappelow

I shall make you forfeit 8*d.* for frightening me so about our little Boy: Jacob [Weston] told us he was exceedingly well and happy, what could induce the Man to go to *you* with a Story of his Sickness? My Comfort is, Your Date is not a recent one: We have had Letters since then from Mr. Davies,[1] and have resolved at his Suggestion to leave the Child at Streatham these Xmas Holydays, because Bath is a bad Place for him, and he is only losing his Time; and as his Master does not leave Surry in the Winter—His Pupil will be best disposed of *there*.

'Tis enough to make folks out of humour Dear Sir, to pay 15*d.* the Loaf and be afraid of fetching Corn from abroad lest the plague should come *too*: but being out of humour will only add to our Sorrows and 'tis best bear them *well;* they will be heavier before they are lighter:——and I always said so.

The Price of Oatmeal here is such as the oldest Man cannot recollect; all our Corn is monopolized and sent to Ireland; our Poor would starve round us but for my Masters Charitable Care, and what is more surprising than all—Oatmeal here is highprized as Wheat, and Water Gruel is grown a Dainty with us.[2]

Do not however mind the Eight pences but write me a kind Letter directed Post office Bath, and get well, and keep well, and learn to *smoke Tobacco* as a Preservative.[3]

Ah Mr. Chappelow! let us see now if Cleanliness and Opulence and Modern Refinements will keep Your fine Town sweet *next Summer,* for this Winter I have no fears; we shall have frost and Snow by and by, and here are fine *Ventilating Winds,* I have heard many a noisy Season, but never one like this.

Are you hard at Work? And are you very angry at being disturbed? You have a right to be angry till you recollect that tis a Punishment for having played the Alarmist about little Salusbury whom—as the Almanacks say by King George—God long preserve. The French will fall on his native Land now again because of our Expedition's unhappy failure[4]——and We have another on foot!!![5]

Adieu tis better be thinking on the Swallows, than on these Vultures of Voracity.

Accept our true Regards and believe me ever &c. / H: L: P.

Text: Ry. 560.87. *Address:* Rev.: Mr. Chappelow / No. 12 / Hill Street / Berkeley Square / London.

1. RD's letter was dated 6 November. See HLP's letter to him, 9 November, n. 2.
2. Because of an inadequate harvest, all grains—and hence bread—rose in price. The plight of the poor, whether in city or country, was so desperate that, e.g., a group gathered in London "for the purpose of alleviating the wants of the industrious poor." Its chairman "recommended an extension of the plan commenced with so good effect, in 1795" whereby "40,000 persons had been relieved by 750,918 meals from soup-shops, at an aggregate expense of 3,476*l*. 8*s*. 10*d*. and concluded by moving resolutions to extend the meritorious establishment." See *AR*, "Chronicle," 41 (1799): 40–41.
3. Probably intended as a witticism. Although there had been some vague conjectures in the Renaissance about the medical properties of tobacco, the *Encyclopedia Britannica*, 3d ed. (1797), treats it as a pernicious plant and adds: "We have been told, that tobacco, when chewed, is a preservative against hunger; but this is a vulgar error; for, in reality, it may more properly be said to destroy appetite by the profuse discharge of saliva" (18: 540).
4. In the *London Gazette* for 23 November, Lt. Gen. Sir James Pulteney (ca. 1751–1811) reported that the last British and Russian troops in Holland had embarked on the 19th. "Every thing belonging to the army was brought off, excepting a small proportion of damaged provisions, a few waggons, and about 300 draught horses of little value. . . . Several large Dutch Indiamen and other ships, which it was impossible for us to remove in their present state, but which might have been fitted out as ships of war by the enemy, were completely disabled and rendered useless for any further purpose." See also *The Times*, 25 November.
5. HLP refers to an abortive expedition to Malta, which had fallen to the French in June 1798. The British, eager to regain the island, were aware of tension between the captors and the natives. On 29 October 1799 *The Times* reported that "the garrison of *Malta* is so reduced by sickness and deaths, as also the number of armed peasants, their assailants, that both parties are compelled to remain on the defensive, until one of them receives a reinforcement sufficient for offensive operations." By 6 November *The Times* stated its concern that Malta would "pass under the Russian yoke. We therefore trust that the wisdom and integrity of his Majesty's Councils will be successfully opposed to any such transfer."

On the same day *The Times* announced that British ships commanded by Captain Alexander Bell had undertaken a blockade of Malta preparatory to landing an expeditionary force there, but the effort proved premature. Not until 4 September 1800 did the French under General Charles-Henri, comte de Belgrand de Vaubois, sue for peace.

TO THE REVEREND LEONARD CHAPPELOW

Henrietta Street Laura Place Bath
Tuesday 12: December 1799.

Dear Mr. Chappelow

You say too true about once pretty Bath; We are here in such a fog one cannot see across the Street, and the Place looks like a Boyling Pot——The Water will make *me* amends however, but if you who never drink it—do actually prefer Twickenham——why I will *not* hold you to your promise. We are in Laura Place, the very Bottom of the Punch bowl, and the house is small.

Davies's Letter telling of our little Dear, has calmed my Spirits concerning *him*,[1] but your Fears of a Famine are catching. All the Accounts of Harvest in Glostershire and other Counties we passed thro' are dreadful, The Barley is out *yet* in many Places——worse than with us in Wales——A propòs to my Care for favourite Dogs it is not half enough, instead of being too much. The rough Terrier Gipsey whom we left safe before the breakfast Room Fire one Morning about a fortnight ago—was *lost* before Dinner Time, and has never been seen since (except once) tho' you may be sure I raised the Country to search for her. That *once* a Farmer near Brynbella saw her on the Drag of a Fox as he supposed, and we think that She followed him into the Earth—and came out no more: The Pointer who accompanied her on this private Hunting Party, was brought home to us next Day;——but poor Gipsey shall I never stroke more.

All things are odd now, and contradictory. We are looking for Peace to the very Man whose Genius and Element is War—and who—had not the World been in a State of Contest and Distraction never would have acted any Part upon it at all.[2] He may perhaps do some Thing yet to amaze us: The Republic is no longer indivisible——he may possibly give the King a Slice, People expect him to play General Monk,[3] but I am inclined to think he loves the *first* Post best, and that he will keep it till a Jacobin Knife tumbles him down from his Pedestal. We have lost all the nice Writing in the Times by dawdling on our Journey. The Ladies of Llangollen are true to their Passion for *you*, and retain their Ardour for News and Prattle. I fretted to think how little entertainment our Conversation could give them for we too were hungry < > of Information and eager to catch at new Books and new Tales. I am reading Miss Starke's interesting Account (such it ought to be) of poor Italy during The French Usurpation:[4] Buonaparte seems to have squeezed the Lemon and thrown away the peel now: Mr. Piozzi entertains hopes that *his* Country's Sorrows are over, and She tells us that much is yet left behind. Meantime You are making Piscatory Eclogues like Sannazarius I suppose instead of minding the steady Book:[5] And I am come hither resolved to keep my Eyes and Ears open to catch all of Intelligence which this Place, The Echo of London—will afford me.

Wish me good Success Dear Sir *et que les Boyaux de* Madame may escape that Effect of the Damps with which you and others threaten Your most faithful / H: L: P.

My Master 'scapes Gout yet, and sends his best. I am much obliged to you for the Tooth brush—*very* much indeed: only you and I know the Value of such Things.

Text: Ry. 560.88. *Address:* Rev: Mr. Chappelow.

1. On their journey from Brynbella to Bath, the Piozzis stopped at Gloucester. Awaiting them at the post office was a letter from RD, dated 2 December, which answered HLP's

queries about JSPS's health. "On the receipt of your Letter I stepped to the Housekeeper's room where your John happened to be standing near Mrs. Plummer. I told her that Mrs. Piozzi feared Salusbury had the plague. He not hearing me distinctly observed 'What! I never heard Mrs. Piozzi was a Plague!' . . . He has a little cold to day which he caught, yesterday from running about without his hat which he is very apt to do. . . . I believe he was forbidden going out of doors for a day or two about a month ago on account of a little cold. When any thing is materially wrong, you may depend upon hearing from me immediately" (Ry. 573.16).

2. An allusion to Bonaparte as First Consul.

3. George Monck or Monk (1608–1670), first duke of Albemarle (1660), was a soldier and politician who served both Cromwell and Charles II.

HLP makes a comparison between Bonaparte and Monck because the two men were seemingly at home with opposing factional forces, with military command and political activity.

4. Mariana Starke (ca. 1762–1838), *Letters from Italy, between the years 1792 and 1798, containing a view of the Revolution in that country, from the capture of Nice by the French Republic to the expulsion of Pius VI. from the ecclesiastical state,* 2 vols. (London: R. Phillips). Published late in 1799, it bears an 1800 publication date.

5. See HLP to LC, 3 August 1786, nn. 8 and 9.

TO PENELOPE SOPHIA PENNINGTON

Thursday
[ca. 12 December 1799][1]

My dear Mrs. Pennington

I hear sad Tales of your Health—yet every one is sure you are mending, and nobody seems quite convinced what we ought to *call* your Complaint. A little Bath Water by and by will restore you; our door has never rested since we came, and I know by Mrs. Randolph and Miss Case too,[2] that the dear Nerves are not *just now* up to a Rattle and a Noise; but pray give me the very *first* news of their recovered Tension, and let us meet and tell each other what and how, and where and when—as we used to do.

The last admirable Letter assures me you are (at least) in the way to be well, the best Writers do not write *so* when they are very sick. You must not however be too angry with People in Power, They certainly are doing their best, and my Master used to be the only Person who scolded the Losers when they went up at Commerce.[3]

We have got a very nice House neither cheap nor dear, but close to the Chapel, No. 4 Henrietta Street. Dr. Randolph looks very well.[4] So does everybody—So they say do we, but I have catched Cold I fancy at Gloster Cathedral for a vile Head ach has possessed me since Sunday, and a Head ach is no usual complaint of mine.

Miss Hannah More is in Agony with a Swelled Face; as usual, She is a sad Invalide.[5] Your Cousins look in full Beauty[6] and little Cecilia Siddons is so improved You would scarce know her. The Lees do not leave Bath this Xmas, *They* complain of this Rye in the Bread exceedingly. It is dreadful on such large

Families as theirs—but I will write no more except Loves and Compliments to kind Mr. Pennington who is ever partial to his Brynbella Friends: Mrs. Weston and I will not despair of meeting again even in *this* World tho' I think now 'twill not be in this Century.

Adieu Dear Soul and write soon. I am all of Your Mind about our lovely Tragic Muse, She is where She ought to be:[7] as for Sally there seems no *present* Danger, and that is all we can say of even the healthiest. 'Tis never the sick Folk that dye[8]—not dear Mrs. Pennington but her flashy Friends——Let us hope that among them will not be counted her / Affectionate / H: L: P.

Text: Princeton University Library. *Address:* Mrs. Pennington / Dowry Square / Hot Wells / Bristol. *Postmark:* BATH.

1. HLP and the ailing GP left Brynbella on Wednesday, 3 December, reaching Gloucester by the 7th and settling into Bath shortly thereafter. HLP's letter to PSP was written ca. 12 December, probably on the same day that she wrote to LC.
2. A friend of PSP, Hester Case (1756–1823), who was visiting Bath, lived in Broad Street, Ludlow (C.R.O., Salop).
3. A popular card game.
4. Laura Chapel was on Henrietta Street, its minister Dr. Randolph.
5. Hannah More, who lived at Laura Place, was now a neighbor of the Piozzis, whose residence was less than a street away.
6. TSW and his wife, Elizabeth.
7. William Siddons believed he had worked out all financial difficulties between SS and Sheridan. Sally, however, writing to PSP on 24 November, thought otherwise. " 'Not a farthing of money has my Father yet touch'd . . . but *he* seems satisfied with his agreement, and that is enough for me' " (Manvell, p. 251). By 22 November SS was back at Drury Lane, performing in *Isabella, or the Fatal Marriage*; in *Jane Shore* (25 November); in *The Stranger* (27 November); and in *Measure for Measure* (29 November). On 11 December she had once more played the role of Elvira in *Pizarro*.
8. See HLP to PSP, 1 June 1797.

TO PENELOPE SOPHIA PENNINGTON

Thursday
20: December [1799]

Put not yourself out of your Way for *us* Dearest Mrs. Pennington, but come and begin the new year with us as you originally intended. My Master will be out of his Room by then, and able in some Measure to amuse your amiable Husband whose Kindness to us merits every possible Attention. Your Bed is kept aired, I only vex that we have no neat Dressing Room for Mr. Pennington, but he must make shift with the Dining Parlour, and Frank (if he brings him) must help make it ready afterwards for Dinner.

We will not quarrel about the Beauties of a *Miss* or about her Accomplishments: The Singing shall be referred to Mr. Piozzi's Judgment——and of the rest, I hear London is soon to decide.

Lady Hesketh[1] will be a valuable Addition to our Society if we can get at her; one of the Miss Mores—my Neighbours here—is dumb just as *She* is: I have got my Voice again and am very glad of it, for a mute Piozzi makes no Sport at all—except in these wondrous Letters which you so kindly extol.

I shall however make this a short one, Mr. Dimond meant no harm I hope; he has gone *so far* of his Journey through life with the Character of a good humoured inoffensive Man, 'twould be pity to stumble *now*.[2]

Be in Spirits and *keep up the Ball* in every Sense of the Expression; and give our true Love to your Family, our Compliments to your Friends / believing me ever / Dear Mrs. Pennington Yours truly / H: L: P.

Text: Princeton University Library. *Address:* Mrs. Pennington / Dowry Square / Hot Wells / Bristol. *Postmark:* BATH [1799].

1. Harriet, née Cowper (1733–1807), married Thomas Hesketh (d. 1778), cr. baronet (1761). She was a cousin and favorite correspondent of the poet William Cowper (1731–1800) and grandniece of William Cowper (d. 1723), first Earl Cowper, lord chancellor.

HLP probably met Lady Hesketh through Charlotte Lewis. On 8 May 1786, the latter wrote to HLP at Milan (Ry. 556.127): "Lady Hesketh had not yet found time to write to you but she I believe intends it for I fancy she has a request to make, which is to procure her some subscriptions for a new translation of Homer, by her Cousin William Cowper, its superior merit to Popes is a more exact imitation of the original in blank verse."

PSP refers to Cowper's translation of the *Iliad and the Odyssey of Homer into blank verse*, 2 vols. (London: J. Johnson, 1791).

2. For William Wyatt Dimond, see HLP to SL, 15 November [1788], n. 2.

TO PENELOPE SOPHIA PENNINGTON

Bath
27: December 1799

Dear Friend

I will have no more of these Letters pass: New year's Day approaching, and we must meet. My Brynbella Turkey indeed which I hoped to treat Mr. Pennington with—has no Mind to wait longer than Sunday when Mr. Greatheed and Mr. Parsons will be the Eaters of it.

Every one is sick—I mean confined by Colds, but I feel most interested in Dr. Randolph's Recovery. His first Sermon of the Year 1800 no wise Person would regret coming 180 Miles to listen to. You will I fear lose Mr. Nugent's Reading and Singing, but French Plays attract you very little.[1]

Come however, and resolve to be as well and as happy as you *can*. Nothing even *you* can say now, will be as desirable as these three Words *I grow better* to yours and Mr. P's / H: L: Piozzi

Text: Princeton University Library.

1. See the advertisement for R. Nugent in the *Bath Chronicle*, 12 December: "Dramatic French Readings at the Lower Assembly Rooms. The First Reading will be on Saturday Morning next the 14th inst., at Half-past Twelve. . . . The Play (by particular Desire) will be the favourite Comedy of La Musicomanie; with Singing, accompanied by the Piano-Forte, &c. Previous to which will be read, One Scene selected from the Comedy of La Fausse Agnes, and one Scene from L'Optimiste. . . . The other Readings will take place on Tuesday, Thursday, and Saturday, in the next Week, and on Monday and Thursday in the following." In fact, the sixth and last reading occurred on Tuesday, 31 December.

TO THE LADIES OF THE WILLIAMS FAMILY

Bath
12: January 1800.

I will not let this month Slip away without sending the Dear Ladies at Bodylwyddan a Letter with a *new Date,* which confounds many People so that they fancy a *new Century* begun, forgetting that Number *one* is the first of all numbers.

We have however much to confound us beside that: Buonaparte's Letter and Lord Grenville's Reply furnish a World of Chat, and the People are so in earnest concerning the Correspondence, that their Politics interfere even with critical Judgment, and they find out how beautifully written that is which best agrees with their Notions of Propriety.[1]

Meanwhile the weather is dull and unwholesome, every Article of Provision risen to double Price——I really speak seriously, almost *every* thing is doubled: and never did I see such Splendid or Expensive Dresses in my Life—or Entertainments half so varied and so costly——A French Emigre read Plays to us in his own Language for a while here—to crowded Audiences, who I fancy could not *all* be supposed to understand him;[2] and we now willingly pay our 5s in a Morn to hear another French Emigre play upon the harp:[3] but you get no more Amusement for a Crown this Year than you get Bread for 6 Pence: a Mouthful of *any* thing is all that is to be had——and the little tiny Bonnets, and the Scanty Petticoats look as if Love of *Quantity* was wholly lost among us——Veils of 20 and 30 Guineas each are absolutely *common Things,* and Black Lace of two or three Guineas a Yard is seen on shoulders that seem wholly *unused* to such Magnificence.—

These are great Contradictions, but there are greater. The Invalide Ladies all tell you how they are in a Course of Hemlock, how they swallow *Opium* by spoonfuls and Ether in large Draughts;—Taking Mercurials they consider as a Slight and occasional Remedy——how long People will last who practise on themselves so boldly, I will not determine——The Bath Pump does for me.——

I live for my own part chiefly in a Literary Set which like Mr. Piozzi and myself are mere Spectators of the Magic Lanthorn, as it Presents various Pictures before our Eyes; and I am sometimes tempted to Cry out as your dear Boy did, the night Sir John performed the Part of Show-Man—"Look Sharp Cousins the Devil will come at the last"—

Meanwhile every Street is full and every House taken, I do not see Mrs. Wynne and Miss Mostyn *this* year, but our Neighbour Leo's new Equipage is among the gayest, and his Laced Liveries among the finest. Mrs. Leo speaks of Her Husband's Health as precarious; but he looks very well, and is said to make Showy Dinners &c.[4]

—Three Months Dissipation is the most my Head will bear: my whole study is to fill that head with modern Intelligence of the living World: but I really do find that living World every Year so much wickeder, and so much foolisher than the last Time I saw it, that each return to Dear Friends and Neighbours at home—— Grows annually more and more precious to Your Ladyship's / Affectionate and Obliged / H: L: P.

Text: Ry. 1 (1796–1802). *Address:* Lady Williams / Bodylwyddan / near St. Asaph / N:W. *Postmark:* BATH.

1. On 25 December 1799, Bonaparte as first consul wrote directly to George III and offered to open peace negotiations. Along with this letter was one by Talleyrand, as minister of foreign affairs, directed to his counterpart, Lord Grenville.
The Cabinet in London agreed that the answer should not come from the king or go to the first consul, that it should be addressed by Grenville to Talleyrand. Accordingly the English minister expressed the king's decision to defer negotiations until "the restless schemes of destruction which had endangered the very existence of civil society were at length finally relinquished." See Stanhope 3:203–4, 210–11; *The Times,* 6, 7, and 8 January 1800; *GM* 70, pt. 1 (1800): 78, 169–70.

2. The price paid to hear Mr. Nugent was 5s. Of his performance the *Bath Chronicle* wrote on 9 January:
"During the last three weeks this city has been amused by the French Readings of Mr. Nugent; and the general applause of a crouded and polite audience is the best criterion of his merit. . . . His delivery of the first act of *Oedipe en Colonne,* with the music of Sacchini, is captivating. His *Musicomanie* and *Richard Coeur de Lion,* are also *chef d'oeuvres.* We hope his engagement in London will not prevent his sort of promise of returning in the spring."

3. On 9 and 30 January, the *Bath Chronicle* advertised: "Mr. Elovis respectfully informs the Public, that his Performance on the Harp will be on Saturday the 25th instant, at one o'clock. . . .
"Tickets 5s. each, to be at the [Lower Assembly] Rooms, at Messrs. Lintern's musicshop, Mr. [John] Bull's library, and of Mr. Elovis, No. 2, South Parade."

4. For Anna Maria Wynn and her daughter Anna Maria Mostyn, see John Meredith Mostyn to HLP, 14 June 1795, n. 4; for Daniel and Letitia Leo, see HLP to Q, 23 February 1794, n. 3.

TO THE REVEREND LEONARD CHAPPELOW

Bath
18: January 1800.

I am exceedingly glad Dear Mr. Chappelow to see your handwriting after such a shocking Accident; It was a Sad Slip, and one wonders it ended no worse. Whether the Century is or is not ended——causes so many Disputes that it spoyls Conversation[1]—a public Topic like a public Mourning levels all Distinction——and those who meant to shew their Wit or their Beauty in its best Dress—are all disappointed. I was appealed to as Casting Vote one Evening last Week—and said it would be the best Way for all the Boys, *Minors*, to be of that Opinion which makes Men of Age at 20 instead of 21. And for all the Girls—Misses; to be against that opinion which calls them 20 the Day after they are 19. 'Tis well we have nothing more serious or less irremediable to occupy our Cares—when Bread is at such a Price, and so many Knockers are tyed up in all populous Towns. Buonaparte too is a Subject of Debate which I doubt not but some Jacobin Dagger will quickly remove; and what follows will perhaps be little better. I begin to despair of Europe's Recovery from her present unequaled Calamity, They came on in a New Mode, a New Form, and the old Methods never will relieve them. If our Continent like those Tragic Heroines which Doctor Johnson used to talk of, is distressed as nothing human ever was yet distressed; She must like them too, be delivered as nothing human ever was delivered.[2] Regular Physicians can administer no Aid where the Nature of the Disease is wholly unknown, or embarrassingly complicated: Cure if Cure comes at all, will be some sudden Appearance that shall tend to unite us at a Stroke. Our Irish Friends here, and they are numerous, seem to think the Storm is not yet laid in their Island, where Preparations of Resistance are made by both Sides, and with unabated animosity as I learn.

Talking of private Affairs is less frightful. Miss Lee carries this Letter to London, whither She goes on a short Visit to Mrs. Siddons, and brings Cecilia your little Friend——(who would not have her foot touched—) back to School with her.[3]

A propos to Cecilias; I am very glad to find Mrs. Mostyn behaves so prudently during her husband's Absence: our Letters from Wales tell us that He has given up his Seat there to his Mother Mrs. Wynne, who once more takes up her Residence at the pretty Place we visited her in;——You will not remember it by its hard Welsh Name;[4]——and that he means when that Affair is settled, to live in or near London, because his Wife likes that place best——*She is not of my Mind.*

Mr. Gillon says the Miss Thrales are gone or going to Brighthelmstone: it looks as if your great Metropolis was thin, and I should be sorry Queen Charlotte's Birthday were ill attended:[5] but Parliament adjourns till February in the hope (no doubt) of a new Revolution in Paris which may silence all Objections to Lord Grenville's Letter.[6]

You tell me no Literary News, nor ever mention Your own Book or mine:[7] but we sleep and wake at opposite hours like the Antipodes upon the Globe. I do nothing now, and you work hard; when Summer comes I shall fag away; and you will go to Weston and Horton and I hope to Brynbella. Will it be possible to make You believe that Return thither is a pleasant Thought to me? The first Bud shall call us home; and I will watch the Tacamahacs, and kiss little Three Legs, and run to see our new Plantation on the Bryn; and make the Cold Water supply the Place of Hot by bathing. If Mrs. Pennington so recovers her Health here that I can leave her in pretty good Spirits, nothing else will make me regret *les Plaisirs bruyans* of Society.

Mr. Piozzi says you must apply to Wright of Piccadilly[8] or to *the very* Man Mr. R[ichar]d Bagshaw, Newsman, Bow Street, Covent Garden—concerning the Paper which you are most welcome to:[9] only sending it safe to us the Moment you have done with it. The enclosed Card will be the Man's Authority. And Farewell / Dear Sir accept our / truest Regards from the Hand of / H: L: Piozzi.

Mrs. Pennington makes me add her Compliments.

Text: Ry. 560.89. *Address:* Rev: Mr. Chappelow / No. 13. / Hill Street / Berkeley Square / London. *Postmark:* 7 o'Clock 20 JA 1800.

1. Whether the century began or ended in 1800 became a matter of dispute in both England and France. "The Astronomer Lalande thus determines the question; which, he says was equally agitated at the end of the last century. . . . 'Many persons,' says he, 'imagine that, because, after having counted 17, they commence 18, that the century must be changed, but this is a mistake; for, when 100 years are to be counted, we must pass from 99, and we arrive at 100; we have changed the 10 before we have finished the 100. Whatever calculation is to be made, we commence by 1, and finish by 100; nobody has ever thought of commencing at 0, and finishing by 99.' Thus, he concludes that the present year 1800 incontestably belongs to the 18th century." See *AR*, "Chronicle," 42 (1800): 6.

2. According to SJ: "To bring a lover, a lady and a rival into the fable; to entangle them in contradictory obligations, perplex them with oppositions of interest, and harrass them with violence of desires inconsistent with each other; to make them meet in rapture and part in agony; to fill their mouths with hyperbolical joy and outrageous sorrow; to distress them as nothing human ever was distressed; to deliver them as nothing ever human was delivered, is the business of modern dramatists. For this, probability is violated, life is misrepresented, and language is depraved." See "Preface" (1765), in *Johns. Shakespeare* 7:63.

3. Sophia Lee proposed to bring Cecilia Siddons from Belvidere School to her parents' house at Great Marlborough Street.

4. John Meredith Mostyn did not turn Segroid over to his mother, whose seat was Llewesog. (After Mostyn's death in 1807 the estate was inherited by his eldest son, John Salusbury.)

5. According to *The Times* (20 January) the birthday was celebrated—as usual—on 18 January by "a grand Gala at Court, which vied in splendour with any we recollect to have seen." This was followed in the evening by a ball. "The King was throughout the evening in close conversation with Mr. Pitt, and from the earnestness apparent, it may be presumed that it related to the second overture from France, received in the morning."

6. Grenville's letter on the 4th to Talleyrand (and indirectly to the first consul) was intended to end the exchange of letters between England and France. But the French minister wrote again, declaring that France all during the Revolution desired peace and

had been driven to war by the hostility of other European powers. On 20 January Grenville restated what he had written earlier.

Parliament opened on 21 January. The correspondence between England and France was presented. The debates both within and outside Parliament accelerated. On 28 January in the Lords and on 3 February in the Commons the conduct of the Pitt ministry in handling the matter of the correspondence was upheld. Stanhope 3: 210–13.

7. At the end of a long and facetious paragraph, LC on 27 January observed: "You say I never mention my Book.—Tho' I cannot report progress—yet I get on most wonderfully—The nature of my present employment is absolutely necessary—My Figure is but in Chalk—and my palate is filling with all the different colours which I shall want in the executive part of The work" (Ry. 562.63).

8. For the bookseller John Wright of 169 Piccadilly, see HLP to PSP, 1 August 1798, n. 2.

9. Richard Bagshaw (fl. 1798–1817), stationer and news dealer at 27 Bow Street in 1800, at 31 Bow Street (1802–13). From 1814 to 1817 he reappears as Bagshaw and Sons, news venders, at 31 Bridges Street, Covent Garden. Between 1818 and 1819 the business was carried on by his sons Thomas and George Bagshaw and between 1820 and 1821 by only the former.

TO THE REVEREND REYNOLD DAVIES

Bath Wednesday
22: January 1800.

I am sorrier for *you* dear Mr. Davies than I am for Mr. Macnamara;—*he* seems to have suffered little or nothing, but you must tell me the particulars another Time.[1]

I am sorry for myself too, We shall all have a Sad Loss——My best Wishes wait on the Ladies.[2] Did you expect this?

Dear little Boy! he has worked hard you Say—I am very glad: My Heart tells me he will be a valuable Creature with God's Blessing and your kind Care.

Let him dance by all means; and let me see him all that a fond Mother can fancy—and a true Friend wish.

My last Letter went by favour of Miss Lee, and there was a Note of Enquiry in that; I enclose another now for Mrs. O'Bryan, who has doubtless been tenderly remembered:[3] Nobody's Uncle disinherits them except Poor Mrs. Piozzi——I will hope better from a Man of Business like our Neighbour——*My* Sir Thomas was a Country Gentleman;[4] They have not—even when equally rich—the same familiarity with Money as has a Man of the *Gown* bred to a Profession: nor the same Notion of making equitable Disposition of their Effects at parting.

John Salusbury will I hope be an active Member of the State he has been so early called to;—I *hope* England and he will have reciprocal Reason to love each other always: and to that End will imbue him with the best Principles of Integrity and Honour, the largest Portion of Knowledge we can get into him. Little Phials must be filled with a Tunning-dish however; Else much learning is spilt by the way, and the fragile Bottle is in danger of bursting. I did not know that as well when I was 25 years old as I know it now——but I began teaching before I had learned; and writing before I had read enough—always;——and that made me do both so Ill. You are better qualified in as much as you have more Experience everyday——Lord Lansdowne is excessively good natured and give[s] me Envelopes every day.[5] Mr. Piozzi encloses you a Cheque with Apologies for the long Date——We are sorry to see the poor little Rogue *has been* Ill, but you were kind in settling all without shaking the Nerves of your / Obliged and faithful / H: L: Piozzi.

When my Master threw down your last Letter——I cried at [its] bad News! It struck to my heart. I never *thought* of Mr. Macnamara; He had lived so long I was in hopes Death had forgotten him. When we come to town next November the little Preceptress shall see I do not forget *her*.[6] Mrs. Pennington begs that Salusbury will remember her Love for him, and *I* beg that you will write directly and say this letter came safe.

Text: University of Texas Library, Stark 610.

1. On 14 January RD had written (Ry. 573.17): "Mr. Macnamara has been within this week very very ill to the great grief of this village, but we have now some grounds for hoping that Sir John Hayes will bring him once more about." But on 20 January RD wrote again: "You will read with sorrow what I write with pain that poor Mr. Macnamara died at a quarter before two this morning" (Ry. 573.18).
2. The widowed Catherine Macnamara and Margaret O'Brien, niece of the deceased.
3. For the failure of Macnamara to remember his niece, see HLP to Robert Ray, 23 July 1798, n. 5.
4. See HLP to Wilshire, 26 April [1791], n. 2. For Sir Thomas Salusbury's will, see HLP to the *Monthly Mirror,* 17 June 1798, n. 15.
5. For William Petty, first marquess of Lansdowne, see HLP to Hugh Griffith, 20 December 1792, and n. 3.
6. For JSPS's "preceptress," see HLP to RD, 9 November 1799, n. 1. She did not always have an easy time with JSPS, for—according to RD on 24 January (RY. 573.19)—the boy "knocked his Preceptress off the chair the other day flat on the ground."

TO THE REVEREND REYNOLD DAVIES

> Bath Tuesday
> 11: February 1800.

Dear Mr. Davies

I have not written because Parliament has called its Members so from Bath and left none to free my Covers: but we think no less of *our* little Boy than those who have *their* little Boys always in Sight. His Opinion about Mr. Macnamara's not having had Time to get to Heaven in a Day, was long considered as wise and Orthodox: The Widow and Mrs. O'Bryan are yet in the like Mind, and consider Purgatory as no bad half-way House for such as do not die *Saints actuellement;* at least I *believe* they think so.[1]

People think less and less of these Matters every day indeed, yet I see not that this World gets happier or better in proportion as it keeps the next wholly out of all Thought.

Let Salusbury be a constant Attendant on Prayers public and private, nor ever sit in the Seat of the Scorner whom of all Men I most abhor.[2] The Comfort is no really good Scholar ever ends in an Infidel—he leaves that to the Wits. We have many of the Sort here, *so* many, and of so many Sorts and *Shades,* that I am half sick and half frighted at them.

You will find me by and by like that Mrs. Argent (Lady Pitches's Maid) who was alarmed for *Master* Dudley's Virtue (the Coachman's Baby 8 months old) whom we used to laugh so about; but I protest 'tis no Joke to see and hear how wicked the folks do grow; and the Reports of Eton's Enormities would terrify any one who did not know the Delight we Talkers have in filling our Mouths with big Words, and stretching our Neighbours Eye-lids with Wonder while we utter them.[3]

Bad as we be however, Paris is *worse* after all She has done and suffered with Intent to mend herself. The nouveau Tableau of that Town written by Mercier[4] exhibits such Scenes as I hoped had never appeared since the Days of Juvenal—
—or Suetonius——Borrow the 3d or 4th Volume and just see how they are going on there:[5] The Volumes are thin things like Magazines with a loose Print and broad Margin, an hour's reading each.

How does our good Bishop Embry?[6] *Nine Times shall Cynthia fill her Silver horn*[7] and we will meet—if it please God—in London; and much Talk and much Consultation will we have about our Dear Boy; and how to give him all the *Good* of Public Education with as little Evil as we can: not sending him to Eton till he is grown even *arrogant* of his own Scholarship, and likely to substitute *Literary Pride* in the Place of grosser Amusements. My Care and yours must be to make him desirous of Praise for Knowledge, he will then despise the Commendations of a Hackney Coachman and neglect the Solicitings of those who tempt him to Vice—
—for tho' People are bad enough, yet I am well perswaded that of the Thousands who go to Old Nick every Day hundreds go to please *their Friends* as they call them—not for their own Gratification.

So here's a long Sermon to the Preacher, A Military Lecture to Hannibal: of *that* I trust the Close was considered as best Part[8]——and of my Discourse the *Benediction* will be most agreeable.

So God bless you good Mr. Davies, and God bless little Dear. / And believe me ever his and Your faithful / &c. / H: L: P.

Mr. Piozzi is very well—our Furlough will be out now in Three Weeks.[9]

Text: Huntington Library MS 1326. *Address:* Rev: Mr. Davies / Streatham / Surrey. *Postmark:* BATH FEB 12 1800.

1. Whatever Macnamara's religious origins, he died as an Anglican and was buried in Saint Leonard's Church, Streatham, on 27 January. See the "Register Book of Burials 1754–1812" of that church, in the Greater London Record Office.

On 29 January RD (Ry. 573.20) described the funeral for HLP: "Mr. Macnamara's corpse was deposited in a vault near your pew [on the south side] between twelve and one on Monday. Nothing could be more simple and better regulated than the burying. It was a walking one, the coffin being borne on men's shoulders. Street and myself walked first. Then followed the corpse, the pall borne by [six men, including Sir Hill Duncan, the Earl of Inchiquin, Lord William Russell, and the Duke of Bedford. These were followed by] Six of his nearest friends or chief mourners two by two. . . . The Service was read by Dr. Bullock, who met us at the Church yard gate. . . . All our students were at the Church on Monday."

2. Ps. 1:1—"seat of the scornful."

3. Among the "enormities," HLP probably recalled a recent notorious episode in which thirty "young Gentlemen of Eton School . . . behaved in a very refractory manner to their Masters." All of the pupils involved were disciplined, although only one—the "son of a Lottery-office-keeper"—was expelled for his part in the escapade. HLP nonetheless regarded Eton as a suitable institution for JSPS's education. See *The Times,* 29 June 1798; HLP to RG, October 1799.

4. HLP refers to Louis-Sébastien Mercier (1740–1814) and his multivolumed *Tableau de Paris,* 1781–88, published in Paris, Hamburg, Neufchâtel, Amsterdam, and London. While his tableaux of city life do not approximate those of Juvenal and Suetonius, he does rely on images of filth to describe a decadent Paris.

5. In volumes 3 and 4 Mercier asserts that the church in Paris is given over to luxury, that theatrical spectacle—particularly the opera—is degenerate, that marriage evokes repugnance, etc. In one of his concluding chapters "Que deviendra Paris," he likens the city to those which have succumbed—"Thebes, Tyr, Persopolis, Carthage, Palmyre" (4:177). Similarly Paris will be destroyed. See 4:179.

6. HLP's response to RD's comment on 14 January (Ry. 573.17): "The Bishop [Embry] can give good advice to young as well as old and is very partial to Salusbury." See also *Boswell's Johnson* 3:248, 518.

7. See HLP to PSP, 5 April 1799, n. 12.

8. See HLP to the Reverend Robert Myddelton, 28 March 1805, n. 2.

9. The Piozzis left Bath 3 March. See "Pocket Book," 1800 (Ry. 616).

TO THE REVEREND LEONARD CHAPPELOW

[Bath, ca. 18–23 February 1800][1]

Dear Mr. Chappelow

We did receive the Paper *as you said,* and it was—*as you said* filled only with Debate. God grant that the whole Hornets Nest may be blown up this next Summer—*as you said.*[2]

Some few lasting Stings we must expect in the Business—Some swelled-up Eyes &c. but gentle as My Nature is, I am contented that they should be blown-up; ay and willing to lend my last Guinea for the Work.[3] Ask what has changed me into such spitting-Cat——I have read the Nouveau Tableau de Paris by Mercier. Pray read it, Pray do.

If you ever go thro' the City call on Robinson and ask when Mrs. Piozzi's Book comes out; or make some of your Literary Friends call and ask——I would be loth to think he forgot it.[4]

Is the Prince better?[5] And does Mr. Pitt's Health mend?[6] A Victory gained by the Chouans would do Mr. Pitt good.[7] Gallant Suarroff will battle Buonaparte I suppose under the Walls of Paris——but will he beat him *there*?[8] Nous verrons. What I see already is the Cold Countenance and dull Looks of the Democratic Gentlemen at the Pumproom. I like Pitt's notion of Citizen Tippoo exceedingly,[9] *his* Character is *White* however compared with French Tyranny, Perfidy &c.

Mr. Pye's Play seems but little admired by what I can learn,[10] You never tell me who is Authour of the new Series of Dramas upon the Passions,[11] *one* of which Kemble brings out this Winter;[12] People now say he wrote it, but of that I believe not a Word. No Heroine of a *Mans* Play was ever a *Sisterly* Character 40 Years old and *more:* some Woman must have been Writer where such a Person is produced, and with Siddons to act it the Effect will be prodigious. Our Pizarro here is sweetly done,[13] and we have a showy Rope Dancer who attracts very full Houses.[14] I shall hate Drury Lane after the dear Bath Theatre and my Friend *Dimond* who is still *brilliant*[15]——*Your* Conversation and that of other agreeable People must make me amends for risquing my health in Smoky London next Year——when like my Countryman Mostyn I find the *Mountain Air* my proper Element as you say. He and his Wife are your Neighbours are they not?

Adieu! here is no News stirring but Expectations of fierce Deeds in Ireland,[16] and a sad Scarcity of Grain:[17] Send us some Events public or private for me to carry home and meditate on at Brynbella whence a Letter will come now and then to say how Sincerely I am Dear Sir / Yours &c. / H: L: P.

Mr. Piozzi and Mrs. Pennington join in a Thousand Compliments.

Text: Ry. 561.162.

1. This letter was written between 18 February, when HLP had seen *Lovers' Vows* at Bath, and 23 February, a day before she again wrote to LC.
2. Newspapers reported the controversy provoked by the British government's rejection of Bonaparte's offer to negotiate a peace. Only slightly less space was given over to discussion of the late expedition to Holland.
3. HLP alludes to the periodic calls for voluntary subscriptions to help finance England's military engagements.
4. HLP was concerned with plans to publish *Retrospection*. Because George Robinson had published *British Synonymy*, she turned to him first of all the booksellers. Indeed, she had begun to send him rough drafts of chapters as early as 1798, but there was no talk of contracts. Now she deputized LC to be her agent in all negotiations relevant to the publication of *Retrospection*.
For George Robinson, see HLP to LC, 21 October 1793 and n. 3.
5. According to *The Times*, 13 January: "The Prince of Wales has been very much indisposed during the last week, the four first days of which he was confined to his bed." Despite recurrent reports of improvement, he continued to ail. "This," wrote *The Times* on 1 March, "has induced his Royal Highness to make an application to the King for leave to go to Lisbon or to Madeira for the recovery of his health. As this permission could not be granted without the consent of Parliament, his Majesty referred the subject to his Ministers," who urged that the prince reconsider his request. The matter was then dropped.
6. *The Times* on 31 January announced, "There is no doubt but Mr. Pitt is much indisposed; and that besides being so hoarse as to be unable to take any part in a debate, he is incommoded with a complaint in the bowels, which has very much weakened him."
7. The Chouans had taken up arms again in 1799 against the French republic. As the

royalist forces, they were divided into six principal bodies, concentrated in Lower Poitou and the Vendée, in Anjou, in Maine, in the Morbihan and Normandie. Countering them was the "Army of England" under General d'Hédouville. Late in November 1799 an armistice was worked out and extended to 21 January 1800.

But by 28 December the first consul decreed that all Chouans who failed to surrender within ten days would be treated as rebels but that those who laid down their arms would be given amnesty. Although organized Chouanerie ended in February the guerillas fought on sporadically through most of 1800.

Despite reports of the continued failures of the Chouans, HLP based her hopes on the continued resistance of Frotté and Bruslart in Normandy. She learned of the capture and execution of Frotté only on 3 March. See *The Times*, 13 and 18 January, 8 February, 3 and 13 March.

8. Suvórov at this time was the source of mixed rumors. Many newspapers asserted that he and his troops had set out for Russia. But other accounts had him consulting with the British for an allied engagement against the French (*The Times*, 28 January).

9. For the epithet "Citizen Tippoo," see *Retrospection* 2:530.

10. Kemble believed that Pye's *Adelaide* had "every claim" to his assistance because the laureate was a "scholar and a critic." But when he performed in it on 25 January—and again on the 27th and 29th—he knew his effort was no more "than a powerful struggle with intractable materials." See Baker, p. 237; *The Times*, 27 January.

11. *Plays on the Passions* was published anonymously in 1798. Almost immediately conjecture arose about authorship. Samuel Rogers reviewed it as the work of a man, and Walter Scott was at first suspected of being the author. As HLP indicates, the guessing game continued. She herself contributed to the game but her choice went always to a woman. But by 24 April 1800, *The Sun* reported that "*De Montfort*, which has hitherto been attributed to Mrs. Hunter, widow of the celebrated John Hunter, and a Lady whose talents fully justified the report, is now ascribed to a Miss Bailey, who, we understand, does not disavow the Work." See also HLP to LC [15 February 1799], n. 12.

12. *De Monfort* [sometimes *De Montfort*] had been written with Kemble and SS in mind. The former was so exhilarated by it that he "altered and adapted [it] to the stage." The play, which opened 29 April, was a *succès d'estime*, intellectuals and women giving it great praise. But one critic declared it "uniformly dull," and the play closed after only eight performances.

13. *Pizarro* opened at the Theatre Royal, Bath, on 6 February and was performed intermittently until 4 March.

14. On 21 January, "Mr. Richer will exhibit a variety of new and unequalled Performances on the Tight-Rope: In the course of which he will introduce the Manual and Platoon Exercise" (*Bath Journal*, 20 January).

According to the *Journal* on 17 February, "Richer's performances were given in his very best manner, and with an elegance and grace which sets competition at defiance. We understand he is to perform one night more [date not specified], at the request of several who could not get admittance."

15. William Dimond performed in the Bath theater while the Piozzis were there. They had seen him play Anhalt in *Lovers' Vows* on 18 February, and they knew that he was to perform the main role in a benefit performance of *The Stranger* on 11 March. See the *Bath Journal*, 17 February and 18 March.

16. HLP alludes to the bickering attendant upon the proposed Act of Union between England and Ireland. The Irish parliament had met for the last time in January 1800. Dublin was hostile to the union, and the Orange lodges sent resolutions against the project. There were minor disorders at this time (*The Times*, 2, 15 January, etc.), but the "fierce Deeds" expected by HLP were not to break out until the summer of 1803 with the uprising led by Robert Emmet.

17. So strongly had scarcity affected the lives of the poor that "A committee was appointed of the house of commons, on the tenth of February, to consider of the most effectual means of remedying any inconveniences that might arise from any deficiency of the last crop of grain, and empowered to report their proceedings, from time to time, to

the house. A similar committee was appointed in the house of peers. The committee of the commons reported on the thirteenth of February." See *AR* 42 (1800): 129.

Both committees recommended "self-denial" and supported Pitt's laissez-faire policy "of abstaining, as a Government, from all interference in the purchase of corn in foreign markets, conceiving that the speculations of private individuals gave the most likely prospect of producing a sufficient supply." See Stanhope 3:220.

TO LADY WILLIAMS

Bath Monday
24: February 1800

My dear Lady Williams

Does my Correspondence much honour in so valuing it; The Prettiest Thing in this Letter will be my Congratulation on the Green Chair and fast Trotter that Promises to bring so Charming a Friend early to Brynbella. It will be very delightful to see home and its lovely Environs again——my Appetite for pleasure is always damped by Three *Weeks* Dissipation and satiated by Three *Months*.—If Miss Williams does not take things moderately this Spring, I shall doubt whether *her* Legacy is or is not a just Cause for Congratulation.[1]

London will be inordinately full and gay, the hours worse and the Suppers better than ever. We are getting fast into such Follies *here* and the Fancy of the Winter has been to stop the Musick when Public Balls are over, and they dare not Play another moment at the Rooms—to take the whole Orchestra away from the Door, and carrying them off, make them Subservient to a private Company at some fine House till Breakfast Time next morning—When at sober Bath—The Town for Invalides, for Green Misses just coming into the World, and Grey Veterans just going out of it——such Tricks are played——What does your Ladyship think is doing at the Metropolis?

Godwin's St. Leon is worth a Place in the Library I am *sure*,[2] and Moore's Mordaunt ought to be good and probably *is* so;[3] We have not read that, we have no Time to read or write either—but Mrs. West's new Novel called A Tale of the Times is very highly, and very justly spoken of, as a Book of excellent Tendency.[4] St. Leon though Godwin's, has no harm in it; the Devil's Claw is at least well concealed: and the Story—as a Story, is incomparable.[5] But there is a comical Thing about the World—its Name the Vagabond, written with *good* humour, and *great* humour too,[6] by way of ridiculing the new philosophers, Especially Holcroft who falling from his Horse a while ago, broke two Ribs;—at which he expressed great Surprize,—Because (said he) I did not *will* to break them; and the Mind ought to regulate the Body.[7]

We have another famous Man 14 Miles from here, who has found out a Secret of medicating Air, so as to give strong Powers to the *Mind:* produce agreable Ideas and I know not what—but People run after him.—No Wonder—and he shuts the Consumptive Patients up in a Stable with four fine Cows, whose Breath they are to draw in night and day.

Beds are accordingly fitted up in the Hovel, and all close shut that the external Atmosphere may not disturb or ventilate the *Smell:* Sir John will agree with me that this Doctor ought at his Time—and Hay so dear—to be monstrously well paid. In Effect these Lodgings are even struggled for at Two and Three Guineas a Night.

But Money seems more plenty than ever——I saw a Robe of Norwich Manufacture Yesternight amazingly Magnificent and asking its Price—16 Guineas was the Reply—but says a Lady near me it cannot be worn *often,* because one should be known by one's Gown. It may answers the Owner be put on 16 Times in different Companies—very *easily;* and nobody would wish to wear it any more.

Wait for the rest of such silly nonsense dear Lady Williams till I come and rejoyce in Your Distance from the Fools and the Follies. Your *Youngest* Daughter will soon have more sense than This, Your eldest Son had more when I left Wales.[8]

Mr. Leo's Servants, gay and flashy like their Master, tell our Servants when they meet, that the Family returns to Llannerch Park the first Week in May, Mrs. Leo is once more out of Danger——and if Things go on so, No hopes of the fine Piano e forte. It is remarkable enough that one never sees them at any Party, tho' every body sees they live showily, and People say they live very Expensively.

Mr. Piozzi's health and his Voice have been better this Winter than I have known them; he has enjoyed the Caresses of a numerous Acquaintance very happily thank God, and will I hope bring back good Spirits, as I am confident he will bring good Will to entertain our True Friends at Dear Bodylwyddan: to every Inhabitant of which your Ladyship must present us with respectful Attachment, containing every possible good Wish for theirs and your continued Happiness.

Sir John De Blaquiere will do well enough;[9] The Irish must make a little Bluster and Bounce, but they will Comply at last——No Room to say how sincerely and Affectionately I have the Honour to remain / ever yours / H: L: Piozzi.

Text: Ry. 1 (1796–1802). *Address:* Lady Williams / at Bodylwyddan / near St. Asaph / Flintshire / N.W. *Postmark:* BATH.

1. For MW, see HLP to Ly W, 18 December 1798, n. 1. Since the letters from Ly W to HLP are missing, it is at this time impossible to determine the nature and the source of the "Legacy."

2. St. Leon: A Tale of the Sixteenth Century, 4 vols. (London: G. G. and J. Robinson, 1799).

3. As Advertised: "In Three Volumes Octavo, Price 1£ 1s. in Boards, Mordaunt. Sketches of Life, Characters, and Manners in various Countries. Including the Memoirs of a French Lady of Quality. By the Author of Zeluco and Edward. Printed for G. G. and J. Robinson, Paternoster-row."

4. *A Tale of the Times,* 3 vols. (London: T. N. Longman and O. Rees, 1799).

5. A friend of Helen Williams (when she had lived in London), Holcroft, Paine, and Horne Tooke, William Godwin had justified the French Revolution. His two-volume *An Enquiry concerning Political Justice* was published by G. G. and J. Robinson in February 1793

and with it he assumed "the Devil's Claw" as the philosophical representative of English radicalism.

6. *The Vagabond, a Novel* was a spoof on the "new philosophers," those rationalistic and/or deistic writers with revolutionary tendencies, such as Holcroft, Godwin, Mary Wollstonecraft, Rousseau, Priestley, Voltaire, Paine, etc. It was published in two volumes in 1799 by author-publisher George Walker (1772–1847) in collaboration with Lee and Hurst. The format emulates the mock learning quest of the young traveler Frederick Fenton, who examines each experience of society—law, philanthropy, political justice, human equality—in the nonsensical terms of the philosophical Dr. Stupeo.

7. The anecdote, probably apocryphal, emerges from the rational, if not always practical, stoicism of Thomas Holcroft (1745–1809), dramatist, novelist, and translator. A frequenter of Debrett's, "he constantly deprecated force, rashness, tumult, and popular violence. He was a friend to political and moral improvement, but he wished it to be gradual, calm, and rational." See *Memoirs of the late Thomas Holcroft, written by himself, and continued to the Time of his Death*. . . . With Commentary by William Hazlitt, 3 vols. (London: Longman, Hurst, Rees, Orme, and Brown, 1816), 2:122.

8. For Ly W's three children, see HLP to the ladies of the Williams family, 27 March 1798, n. 1. On 1 August 1799, she bore another daughter, Margaret (d. 1880).

9. John Blaquiere, cr. Baronet De Blaquiere (1784), began his career as an army officer, becoming a lieutenant colonel in the Seventeenth Dragoons. He had a short diplomatic career, serving as secretary of legation in France (1771–72) and chief secretary to the lord lieutenant of Ireland (1772–77). An M.P. for many years, he consistently supported the union and, as a result, was elevated to the Irish peerage as Baron De Blaquiere of Ardkill (30 July 1800). See also HLP to LC, 19 March 1799, n. 4.

He was known in North Wales (prior to buying an estate near Denbigh) through his visits to the countess of Orkney.

TO THE REVEREND LEONARD CHAPPELOW

Bath
Tuesday [25]: February 1800[1]

Dear Mr. Chappelow

You are very good indeed, however bad the Times may be, and those are no very bad times neither which produce one such true Friends. I do believe and hope and trust that Robinson means to have the Book, and I shall never treat with any other Person till that Faith, Hope, and Trust are found vain.

We set out for Home the Day after tomorrow[2] and when we get there, and I get settled and see how much and how little remains of my Work to do, I will take the straightforward Method and write to him. He saw the first and last Chapters of the first Volume when we were last in London, and for ought that I could observe actually liked them: but Men of his Profession never depend on their own *Taste*, they always put the Cup to somebody's Lips they can depend on: As you kindly recollect the Synonymes and the Trouble I gave You with them, You may likewise remember that they were submitted to Murphy for Perusal, and he knew my Hand Writing. Robinson and he were Friends then, they have quarreled since if I understand rightly;[3] The Journey-Book was pronounced upon by poor Seward.⁴ Your Enquiry however and Commendation and all that has passed will act as A Whetter, and I am much obliged to you.

Poor Mrs. Clay! She is indeed greatly to be pitied. Will her Husband come home soon, and will he come home rich?⁵ And will that comfort her? The Duke of York will have a thousand Applications⁶——A skilful American Trader affords safer *Anchorage* in these Days, than a powerless Prince of the Blood.

Mr. Parsons who brings you this Letter is a Croaker, he apprehends much on *one* side, and I apprehend much on the *other;* my heart tells me the War will end this Campaign, and that Peace abroad and Union at home will come forward with Number 1.⁷——Yet am I not satisfied concerning The State of Europe; scarcity is not confined to our Island; and contagious Diseases, Jacobinical Principles, with many other Misfortunes may perhaps render a Cessation of Hostilities no Cessation of Evil. Besides that the Conduct of our Allies is so little better (for ought I see,) than the Conduct of our Enemies——great Pains must be taken to make one even *wish* them Success.⁸ Selim the 3rd must uncross his Legs and look about him, for I verily expect to live to see a Muscovitish Fleet riding in the Dardanelles.⁹ *Your* Book is pleasanter than mine, it produces no Ideas of Cruelty or Treachery or Folly——everything in its place so prettily; and 'tis such an *odd Thing* to read a poetical Body of Natural History issuing from *Mouse*-Trap hall: The Old Roman Emperors Valens and Valentinian who Delighted in Onomantical Researches,¹⁰ would have found out that *Your* Name composed of a Lyon and a Goat, *must* have graced the Historian of Animated Nature.¹¹ Do you know Buonaparte's Name?—his *Christian* Name?¹² for baptized he was no doubt——by some good Pastor, who little dreamed *that* Child would make and sign the Proclamation he set forth in Ægypt:¹³ Marbœuf is said to be his Father.¹⁴

All this while I have forgot to say that I carried Your Letter myself to Mr. Meyrick's Door, and gave it safely to his Servant.¹⁵

My Master says I must not forget his true and faithful Regards. He will not be easy nor I neither—till you read the new *Tableau de Paris:* a Translation is coming out, but 'tis daily less useful to translate our Languages reciprocally;¹⁶ but that Book is half of it English Words, and the English Works one reads are full of Gallicisms.

Adieu Dear Sir and direct your next to Brinbella near Denbigh N. W. You have been exceedingly good about the Newspaper, as about everything else; we have missed it only one Day I forget when:—*it was last Saturday sennight.*¹⁷

The first Letter you receive from Wales shall tell how Lady Elinor and Miss Ponsonby bear the Union; bear it or not, We *must* be united, and there's an End: Pistols for two or three more Couple perhaps, and then I shall disregard further *Reports:* in full Confidence that their *Flash* is exhausted. / Ever Your truly Obliged / H: L: Piozzi.

My young Ladies are yet at the Seaside, are they not?

Text: Ry. 560.90.

1. HLP dated the letter 24 February; but if written on Tuesday, it should be the 25th.
2. The Piozzis changed their minds, remaining in Bath until 3 March.
3. In the first half of the 1790s Robinson and Murphy, if not friends, were business associates. Murphy represented the bookseller in a copyright case and also worked out the financial details for the sale of *British Synonymy*. See HLP to LC, 21 October 1793 and n. 3.

If a quarrel took place, it arose out of political differences between the two men. Robinson made politics subordinate to a desire to sell a successful book of any persuasion, however "radical." Murphy, on the other hand, was not merely a Tory but was—according to Samuel Rogers—"very rancorous on politics." See Peter William Clayden, *The Early Life of Samuel Rogers* (London: Smith, Elder, 1887), p. 263.

4. HLP's *Observations* was published by Strahan and Cadell (1789).
5. A merchant, William Clay was now "a skilful American trader" since a parliamentary committee "proposed a bounty, to serve as an indemnity, to importers of grain from the Mediterranean and America, before the end of October, if, in consequence of a good harvest, it should decline in price" (Stanhope 3:221).
6. Despite the failure of the expedition to Holland, the duke of York as commander of the army was eulogized by both the Ministry and the Opposition.

See, e.g., *AR* 42 (1800): 107 for Lord Holland's motion on 12 February "that the principal share of the disgrace, with which the expedition was attended, was to be imputed to ministers, and none to the commander, the officers, or the army." See also Stanhope 3:214–15.

7. For the passage of the Act of Union, see HLP to LC [15 February 1799], n. 5.

"Peace abroad" assumed shape with the preliminary negotiations that began between England and France on 21 February 1801, following the fall of Pitt and the onset of the Addington ministry. These negotiations led to the Peace of Amiens, signed on 27 March 1802. See HLP to PSP, 9 October 1801.

8. In need of allies, the English realized they could no longer count on the Russians. On 13 February, therefore, the king informed Parliament that he was cooperating with the emperor of Austria, the elector of Bavaria, and other German princes to bolster the war effort. He then appealed to Parliament for financial support. Four days later, subsequently, Pitt moved for an immediate levy of £500,000, with the expectation of two millions more upon the completion of the treaties.

9. Selim (1761–1808) became Selim III, sultan of the Ottoman Empire from 1789 to 1807. In this latter year he was overthrown and imprisoned by the Janissaries; on 28 July 1808 he was strangled in Constantinople.

For more than a hundred years the rulers of Russia considered Turkey their "lawful prey." Indeed, when Selim became sultan, his country and Russia were at war (the latter abetted by the Austrians). What the two European powers wanted then and managed to obtain were the Turkish provinces in the Danube region.

Now involved in a war against France in Egypt, the Turks were vulnerable at home. If a Russian fleet were to "ride" in the Dardenelles, it would control the approach to Constantinople, the heart of the Turkish empire. See HLP to PSP, 1 May 1800; 3 June 1801, n. 16; *Retrospection* 2:536; Chandler, *Dictionary of the Napoleonic Wars*, p. 407.

10. A Pannonian, Valentinian became Roman emperor in February 364 A.D. A month later at Constantinople, he elevated his brother Valens to rule in the east while he assumed responsibility for the government of the west. Valentinian I died at Brigetio in 375, having proclaimed his son Gratian as emperor in 367. Valens died in 378, defeated at the battle of Adrianople on 9 August.

11. LC's name appears to be derived from Latin *caper* (he goat) and from *leo* (lion). The "Historian" is Oliver Goldsmith, who compiled in eight volumes *An History of the Earth and Animated Nature* (London: J. Nourse, 1774).

12. For the meaning of Bonaparte's Christian name, see HLP to PSP, 31 January 1801, n. 2.

13. See HLP to RG, 14 October 1798, n. 4.

14. Napoleon's father was Carlo Bonaparte (d. 1785), who at the age of eighteen married Maria Letizia Ramolino (ca. 1750–1836), then fifteen. The hospitality of their home in Ajaccio was lavish. Among their guests was Louis-Charles-René, comte de Marbeuf (1712–86), commander in Corsica of the first army of occupation, who secured Napoleon's admittance to Brienne in 1779. When Bonaparte became first consul, speculations about his parentage ran the gamut from Marbeuf to the Man in the Iron Mask.

15. James Meyrick (d. 1818) of 42 Lower Grosvenor Street and Wimbledon, Surrey; Fellow of the Royal Society and Society of Antiquaries.

16. The only recorded translation is *Paris in Miniature; taken from the French picture at full length, entitled Tableau de Paris. . . . together with a preface and a postface.* By the English Limner [J. P. Macmahon] (London: G. Kearsley, 1782; Dublin: T. Walker, et al. 1782).

17. LC arranged to have *The Times* delivered to the Piozzis in Bath. See LC to HLP, 27 January 1800 (Ry. 562.63).

TO PENELOPE SOPHIA PENNINGTON

Brynbella
Sunday 9: March 1800.

I hasten to fulfill my Promise to Dear Mrs. Pennington. We came home but last night, and I wish to say that we are come home well, and find our Household well too; and truly glad of our safe and early return.

The Time past at Shrewsbury was full of Amusement; Miss Owen feasted and fondled us, and called all the People round to feast us and fondle us, and detain us till Thursday which had been long bespoke, and Fryday beside by the charming Cottagers in Llangollen Vale. *They* asked me much after that Mrs. Pennington who writes such beautiful Letters, and insisted on my Describing your Person to them, and said they knew Miss Seward esteemed you highly; though all Intimacy between you was at an End.[1] The unaccountable knowledge those Recluses have of all living Books and People and Things, is like Magic; one can mention no one of whom the private History is unknown to Them——What they told me of Doctor Maclean's Brother was very curious and Interesting[2]—— and from them I obtained the books I had so long searched London and Bath for—in vain. Borrowing is however particularly unpleasing to me so Sir Richard Clayton will be still doing me no small Kindness in procuring them.[3]

Did You see any more of Doctor and Mrs. Randolph? They have a large Portion of my Affectionate Admiration for their uncommon Virtue and Talents. Mr. Hunt of Boreatton too! Oh Dear! what a Man that is! You must read his new Pamphlet,—a Word on the Times to Buyer and Seller.[4] It is Perfect in its Kind to be sure. What I have read there keeps me silent concerning the Weather and the Price of Grain &c. &c. He says Most wisely that it should not be made matter of general Chat, and that for a <thou>sand Reasons.

Let me therefore talk of Mr. Pennington and ask how he does. You may be certain how I do, and what I do. Looking out my Books, setting my Plaies to rights; Ladling out the Soup to 30 Families round: feeding the Dogs with what *they leave,* mixed up with Potatoe Peelings and so forth is mine and my Master's and Abbess's Employment whilst Allen blows her Nose in Consequence of Cold catched in a damp Bed at Worcester—and Thanks God the Evil ends there.

The little Three legged Cur jumps into my Lap, licks my Face, and runs to his Master to tell the good News how the Family is *come home to the Hall* and every body and every Thing looks pleased to see us. Mary's Admiration of her Head-Knot was even more than I counted on, and I have had a civil Letter from Susan Thrale who bids me direct to Cumberland Street and makes Common Place Lamentations concerning the *Times* but *nothing further*——nothing I mean tending towards Confidence or Communication.

We broke our Chaise between Llangollen and Ruthyn—no Wonder! such Roads! 'tis really frightful: but neither Mr. Piozzi or I were hurt.

Here are no Members of Parliament; no Franks of course, so I shall write very seldom: for the joke is a good one two or three Times o'year, but no oftener; when 14d. is to pay for 44 Lines about nothing: and Friendship is a fine thing, but so is fourteen Pence. Miss Lee's Brother happened to find himself at our Inn one Morning while Mr. Hunt was visiting us.[5] They apparently took to each other, and I left them together——Such is the *Chapter of Accidents*.[6]

Take Care of your own health and that of your good Husband; and give my truest Regards to him and assure Mrs. Weston we shall meet again. There is a Lady at Shrewsbury—born the last Day of 1699—and She is very well, and plays upon the Piano e forte as you describe Mr. Whalley's Mother to do;[7] but poor Mrs. Montague's Sun is setting apace I hear. She has left her fine house and retired into a smaller, giving up the Grandeur to her Nephew—and Lady Oakley said the Estate too, but I hope she has had more *Wit than that*.[8] Lady Oakley is very agreeable[9] notwithstanding what Dear Mrs. Fordyce told us:[10] *She* has not given up any Magnificence: I saw her in a Robe embroidered (as She said) with the Wings of an Indian Fly: there is no describing its Beauty or Lustre.

Farewell! I have no Room to say how sincerely I am Yours H:L: Piozzi. Accept Mr. P's best Regards.

Text: Princeton University Library. *Address:* Mrs. Pennington / Dowry Square / Hot Wells / Bristol. *Postmark:* DENBIGH.

1. For the "Intimacy" between PSP and Anna Seward, see HLP to PSP, 1 August [1798], n. 10.
2. Dr. Archibald Maclaine (1722–1804) became co-minister of the English church at the Hague in 1747. After the French invasion of Holland, he resigned his charge in 1796. He settled in Bath and died there. See *GM* 74, pt. 2 (1804): 1172.
   His brother James (1724–50) was known as the "gentleman highwayman." He and an apothecary named Plunket tried to make money by fraud but soon took to the highway. In June 1750 they held up the Salisbury Flying Coach at Turnham Green and then on Hounslow Heath, Lord Eglintoun's coach.
   On 27 July 1750 James Maclaine was arrested. He was tried on 13 September, found guilty and hanged at Tyburn on 3 October.
3. Rather William Clayton (1762–1834), of Harleyford, near Great Marlow, Bucks., and of Alty Cadris, Carmarthen; fourth baronet (1799); M.P. for Great Marlow (1783–90). In 1790 he and his family moved to Marden Park, Surrey.
4. The third edition of Rowland Hunt's pamphlet was advertised in the *Sun*, 18 April 1800: "This Day was published, / Price 4d. on fine Paper, 3d. on common Paper . . . / A

Word on the Times, to those who Buy; also, Five Minutes Advice Before Going to Market, to those who Sell."

It was dedicated to Joseph Carless, Esq., mayor of Shrewsbury, Sir Charles Oakeley, "and the Committee who superintend the Distribution of Provisions to the Poor." It was printed and sold at Shrewsbury by J. and W. Eddowes; "sold also by Messrs. Longman and Rees, Paternoster-row; and Mr. Stockdale, Piccadilly, London; Mr. Cruttwell, and Mr. Hazard, Bath, &c. &c."

5. For George Augustus Lee, see HLP to PSP, 21 October 1795, n. 3.

6. Sophia Lee wrote a three-act opera, *The Chapter of Accidents*, based on Diderot's *Le Père de Famille* (1758). Unable to get it produced, she converted it into a five-act comedy, which was successfully performed on 5 August 1780 at the Haymarket.

7. Mary Whalley was ninety-three years old at this time.

8. By 1798 Elizabeth Montagu was feeble and almost blind. Far from leaving "fine" Montagu House, she was to die there on 25 August 1800 within a month and a half of her eightieth birthday.

She had brought up her nephew Matthew (b. 1762) after his father, Morris Robinson, died in 1777. The young man was her constant companion following the death of her husband in 1775 and took the name of Montagu. All her property, reputedly £10,000 a year, went to Matthew. He had entered Parliament as the member for Bossiney in 1786, was elected for Tregony in 1790, and for Saint Germans in 1806. He succeeded his brother Morris Robinson as fourth baron Rokeby [I.] in 1829 and died 1 September 1831.

9. In 1777 Helena Beatson (d. 1829) had married Charles Oakeley (1751–1826), cr. baronet (1790) for service as governor of Madras and his reformation of the East India Company's financial affairs.

10. Henrietta, née Cummyng (1734–1823), was the widow of the Presbyterian minister Dr. James Fordyce (1720–96), SJ's friend and an eloquent preacher.

TO THE REVEREND REYNOLD DAVIES

Brynbella
Saturday Morning 29: March 1800.

What a Pleasure Dear Mr. Davies to see your handwriting and the Letters beginning with *I only write to congratulate:* I really trembled a little at the *outside* lest we should have been too happy of late and in Danger of Mortification——little Dear will be a good Child however, and give me nothing but Comfort I hope. His Preceptress shall have no Reason to repent her Care——but when does he leave *her* and take his due Seat among the Students? As I would rather his Knowledge was solid than brilliant tho': my Impatience for his shining is far less than my Earnestness to lay a sound Foundation——do Dear Mr. Davies let *our* Boy learn his Grammar and his Catechism in the old steady Style; and leave Philosophy to Mr. Vandercom.

Lord and Lady William will make a good Exchange, and old Bedford house which neither splendid nor commodious neither Ancient nor Modern can do nothing better——than be pulled down I Think.[1]

The Vale of Clwyd affords no Conversation but concerning the Earthquake which ushered in our Fast Day—a slight Concussion, but serving to fright People who never felt such a Thing before. You may believe that Mr. Piozzi and I were not much alarmed.²

We past a nice Week with Miss Owen in our way home, and were feted most kindly and liberally at pretty Shrewsbury——Your *Future* Miss Adelaide Congreve asked what *Token* She should send of her continued and unshaken Fidelity?³ They are a good-humoured Set—Those proud Salopians as they are called——but we did very well at Bath too, and my Health is better than usual.

You may tell Mr. Robinson that he will be a *happy Man* if he gets my big Book for his Thousand Guineas;—and as you love A Joke *You* may tell him too that Tho' I shall not—like the Horse-Dealers *warrant it free from Blemish*—I will venture to pronounce it—as they do—*an easy Goer*. Truth is, my Intents are to finish and bring it to London in November because I should like that it should come out as early in 1801 as possible. We will not quarrel when The Century begins; but *One* will alw[ays] be the first *Number;* and I want Retrospection to make the *first Figure* in it, if we can.

When the ffolks plagued me at Bath about that Nonsense, my Way of quieting 'em was to say that the Young Men should all profess themselves of that Opinion which would make them considered as of Age at 20 Years old instead of 21 while Young Women must as strenuously oppose the People's Notion of calling them 20, when they are but just 19.

I am glad Mr. Murphy is about London. Our Friend Gillon wishes to find and have a Talk with him. Will you find Mr. Gillon at his Silver Smith's Shop Corner of the Adelphi—and tell him where Murphy resides?⁴ We heard he was set out for Bath.

Adieu dear Mr. Davies. This Letter is not worth 4d. much less 8d. but you shall have a prettier another Day.

I have only just Leisure Now to send my truest Love and that of his Uncle to little Salusbury, and hope I shall see him much improved when he receives the next Affectionate kiss from his loving Aunt and your most Faithful Servant / H: L: Piozzi.

The News from *Oxfordshire* (not Vale of Clwyd) is that Miss Thrale claims the Estate *there*, and has sent to *my* Tenant to pay *her* the Rent I have received now just 19 Years.⁵

We expect the same to be done in Surrey⁶ which She says makes *Part* of Oxfordshire: if so Adieu Streatham! But we shall come to a London Hotel in November. Robinson likes Garret Authors best I dare say.

Text: Hyde Collection. *Address:* Rev: Mr: Davies / Streatham / Surrey. *Postmark:* DENBIGH < >.

1. Very much in the news at this time was Bedford House, Bloomsbury, the town house of the dukes of Bedford, erected in the reign of Charles II, for Thomas Wriothesley, earl of Southampton, whose only daughter had married William Lord Russell. The house filled the whole north side of present Bloomsbury Square, and the grounds extended northward to include the southern portion of Russell Square. "The Duke of Bedford having disposed of the materials of Bedford-house for 5 or 6000£, a sale of the furniture,

pictures, etc., by Mr. Christie" began on 7 May 1800 before a crowded audience. See *AR*, "Chronicle," 42 (1800): 12–13, Wheatley 1:143–45.

Once the house was demolished and the avenue of trees in the garden cut down, Bedford Place was created. On it were built between 1801 and 1805 two rows of private houses running north and south, connecting Bloomsbury Square with Russell Square.

For Lord and Lady William Russell, see HLP to Q, 13 November 1793, n. 3.

2. There was a series of minor shocks in North Wales from late March to May. See, e.g., Lady Eleanor Butler to HLP, 16 April [1800]: ". . . some of these Tremendous Storms you mention—have rushed vehemently through our Valley—but made one Stop nor <admitted> any deviations in their furious passage—possibly I was the only one who perceived the Earth quake—It was early in the Morning you mention—I awakened Miss Ponsonby to say—that if there was a Concussion of the Earth in Wales. I experienced a mad moment 'but ere I Spoke it veered' " (Ry. 581.7). See *Thraliana* 2:1004 for a later shock in the first week of May; HLP to PSP [ca. 21 April 1800].

3. Adelaide Sarah was the daughter of John Congreve (d. 7 January 1783), of Shrewsbury, and the granddaughter of Colonel William Congreve, described as being of Shrewsbury when he was made a burgess in 1758. She died unmarried 9 July 1836. See C.R.O., Salop.

4. Murphy's address, according to the *London Directory*, was 10 Saint Martin's Lane.

5. Under the terms of the "Marriage Settlement," 9 and 10 October 1762 (Ry. Ch. 1236), HT entrusted Henry Smith and Robert Salusbury Cotton to oversee the estate of Crowmarsh for ninety-nine years; to divide the income equally between him and HLT. In the event that he predeceased her, she was to receive £400 annually from this property. When he made his will, however, he had either forgotten or neglected to revoke this item of the "Settlement," ordering that Crowmarsh was to go to Q and that she was to receive the rents "for all her natural life."

HLP began to take seriously the impending battle over Crowmarsh when Gillon wrote to her on 14 March (Ry. 577.50): "Miss Thrale . . . told me that . . . she wished me to mention to you the Subject of her Claim to the Oxfordshire Estate; which it was now discovered belonged to her, and not to you. . . . She said she did not wish to quarrel, nor to do a harsh or uncivil Thing, in writing to Newton, to direct him to pay the Rent to her; without your being first apprised of the Business."

6. Although Vandercom, according to Gillon, admitted ambiguities in HT's will concerning Streatham, the attorney thought that HLP in this regard was not favored. That is, she was clearly entitled to a settlement of £30,000 in funds, but not to the real property which, among other estates, included Streatham. Shortly thereafter, however, Vandercom must have reconsidered his initial interpretation, for HLP was reassured that she owned the estate during her lifetime, provided she pay the annual taxes on it (at this time £108). See Gillon to HLP, 21 and 28 April (Ry. 578.57, 58).

TO THE REVEREND LEONARD CHAPPELOW

Brynbella
Monday 21: April 1800.

My Dear Mr. Chappelow will be willing I am perswaded to pay the Small Sum of Eight Pence for a *new* Chapter in *Natural History*. I intended telling you nothing of the Business till every Thing was decided; but Life is short, and the Law is tedious, and we will begin the Tale and end it. Scarce were we returned from Bath and looked over Papers for the *Book*—before a Bunch of Letters surprized and terrified me into a new Agony; when I was made to comprehend that Miss Thrale—the eldest—had written to our Oxfordshire Tenant Mr. Newton charging him not to pay any more Rent to *us*—but to *her;* who had at length examined her Father's Will, and found it would bear her out in the Demand. Accounts from Vandercom accompanying this Inteligence with Menaces that my Daughter would no longer endure patiently the Loss of 400£ o'Year, but make me *refund* all I had wronged her of.

It will be soon refunded: I never wronged her of a Shilling——nor ever had it either in my Power or Inclination to injure her. The Crowmarsh Estate was settled on me at my Marriage with Mr. Thrale, subject to my Pinmoney during his Life, my Joynture after his Death: The Rents and Profits of that Farm have been paid to my *use* now 36 years—to my *orders* 19; and 'tis late to find a Flaw we must own——if at last a Flaw can be found. You see clearly how the Matter stands; While Oxfordshire brought in only 272 Pounds o'Year——it went quietly for *mine,* so it did when raised only to 366£ o'Year; but at present that Master Newton has signed a Lease for 450£—it is *hers* directly. Poor Mr. Piozzi thought he had been very civil to Miss Thrale in never claiming the Arrears; and in taking the odd 50£ per Annum for my Life, instead of insisting on her paying up *in a Sum*——what that Estate has failed to bring all these 19 Years: but She contends that Streatham was to make up that failure, and brings some Expressions forward in support of her Claim.

Mr. Gillon has shewn astonishing and persevering Friendship to us on the Occasion: calling repeatedly in Cumberland Street on my fair Enemy, and prevailing on her at last to lay *her* Case before *one* Counsel, whilst He lays *our* Case before another Counsel; with Intention to prevent this worse than American War, in which Victory itself will make little Amends for the Pain suffered——and in which Defeat would be dreadful.[1] Now write to me soon Dear Sir, and tell me you are sorry.

Tell me likewise if you can, something to make me glad: Tell me that Kleber has eat up Buonaparte,[2] and Sir Sydney Smith has eaten up Kleber:[3] That Sieyès looked round for a *second Course,* and found nothing but a Rope—his *Dessert.*[4]

Every Thing is *new* in these Days, but nothing is *strange.* Mr. Piozzi sees a Pope elected, and expects a King of France presently.[5] 'Tis a good Joke enough that the *Man in the Iron Mask* should be said to be Father or Grandfather to the Grand *Destroyer.*[6] I never heard such Marvels: one would think we were living in the tenth Century, instead of approaching the Twentieth. Scarcity very pinching too, and the Plague threatening:[7] Mercy on us! yet you and I find Leisure to watch Swallows. I saw two this afternoon looking over their old Summer-haunts; it came into my Head they were our Acquaintance of last year——*one* seemed as if *reconnoitering:* just as we shall do in London next November when Houses are empty. My Printer if Davies is to be the Man, would not wish me to be further off him than Argylle Street or its Vicinage:[8] and Habitation *there* would surely be cheap for the three worst Months of Winter. I hear Houses are *now* at an Enormous Price. Mrs. Hughes of Kinmell gives Ten Guineas in old dirty shabby Jermyn Street, St. James's.[9]

What ails our Prince of Wales? is he really Ill, or only Love-sick?[10] Tell me some

London Chat of Literature or Scandal, or any Thing to keep Law Suits and Lawyers out of my Head. They are really Pests of Society——Professors of Quarrell and Contest. We have good Weather for Sowing, but the poor People cannot afford to purchase Corn here, so the Fields must lye uncultivated and Scarcity be prolonged to another Year. The Horses are not able to plough for Weakness, and the Cows give no Milk. People can't afford feeding Poultry, so Eggs are not expected.—And a Labourer's Wages does not suffice to buy *Bread* for his Family. *Welsh* Folks might eat Oats and Barley you'll say; so they *might*: but there is neither Oats nor Barley to be had. Farewell my Dear Sir, accept our True Love and Respects, and write a Kind Word to H: L: P.

Text: Ry. 560.91. *Address:* Rev: Mr: Chappelow / No. 12: / Hill Street / Berkeley Square / London. *Postmark:* DENBIGH E APR 23 1800.

1. Gillon wrote on 14 March (Ry. 577.50): "I told [Q] that I would certainly write to you on the Subject [of Crowmarsh], as she desired it, and that indeed I had done so already; for that, as I had been attending of late to your Interests, you had mentioned this new Matter to me, in a recent Letter, and that I should be candid in telling her, that I had advised you to take the Opinion of eminent Counsel, on your Part, after laying a full and accurate statement of the Case before them, with the *Settlement and the will*, to refer to. . . . I then took my Leave, and rode on to the City to Mr. Vandercom; with whom I had a long Conversation on this untoward Subject. . . . I mentioned to him *Mr. Butler*, the great Conveyancer; whom *I know* to be an *able* and *honorable* man. He said a *better* Counsel could *not* be applied to."

2. Jean-Baptiste Kléber (1753–1800), général de division (April 1794). HLP first became aware of the name as she followed the war in Egypt. He had been wounded in the assault on Alexandria (2 July 1798) but recovered in time to command the forces at El Arish, Jaffa, Acre, and at the battle of Mount Tabor (16 April 1799).

She knew further that Bonaparte before he departed from Egypt on 22 August 1799 "left a letter addressed to general Kleber, with orders that it should not be opened for twenty-four hours after his quitting the land. This letter contained his appointment to the chief command of the army of all Egypt, during the absence of Buonaparte, and an order for conferring the command of Upper Egypt on general Dessaix." See *AR* 42 (1800): 3.

3. HLP at this time recognized Smith as the hero of the British victory at Acre in May 1799, for which he was given the thanks of Parliament, of the City of London, and the freedom of the Levant Company, etc. See HLP to Q, 10 July 1796, n. 5.

4. Abbé Sièyes in 1800 was held responsible for making Bonaparte first consul and for securing the promulgation of the constitution of the year VIII on 25 December 1799. See *AR* 42 (1800): 8–17; chap. 4.

5. On 1 December 1799 thirty-five cardinals met to elect a new pope on the island of San Giorgio Maggiore. On 14 March Gregorio Luigi Barnabà Chiaramonti (1740–1823), a Benedictine of Monte Cassino, became Pope Pius VII.

6. A mysterious, i.e., unidentified, state prisoner in the reign of Louis XIV, confined at Pignerol, on the island of Sainte Marguerite, and finally in the Bastille, wore a mask covered with black velvet.

7. HLP alludes to the report that the corn and bread committee of the Commons introduced on 6 March. They emphasized "the deficiency of the late crops of grain in many parts of the country, particularly in Scotland." They therefore made suggestions "for diminishing the consumption of corn, for encouraging the importation from abroad, and for bringing into extensive use, such substitutes as might supply the place of it." The suggestions quickly became law. *AR* 42 (1800): 135–37.

8. Apparently reconciled to the probability that George Robinson would not produce

Retrospection, HLP now envisaged William Davies as a likely publisher. In fact, John Stockdale was to undertake the task; his printer was Thomas Gillet of Salisbury Square.

9. Mary, née Lewis (1743–1835), married 10 August 1765 the Reverend Edward Hughes (1738–1815), of Kinmel Park, Denbighshire. See HLP to Ly W, 15 June 1815, n. 4.

10. In HLP's mind the prince was as much drunk as "Love-sick." See her poem, which she did not circulate, on the prince's excessive drinking, in "Verses 2," p. 77. It begins: "Of various Ills our Prince complains. . . ."

TO PENELOPE SOPHIA PENNINGTON

[ca. 21 April 1800][1]

What in the World Dear Mrs. Pennington has been doing at Bath? I wrote to Doctor Randolph about a Book of his which I wanted, and His Letter in return has affected me very deeply. Yours gave a hint of something like a Riot, but nobody seems sensible that We live out of the World here and know nothing of what passes in it.[2] The Newspaper we take, tho' it swelled and raved so about Mr. King's Fire,[3] said nothing of *this* or so little we quite disregarded it; and yet Dr. Randolph says that *our* Quarter of the Town was saved by Miracle from being even now a Heap of Cinders.

Thank God we were come home. The Slight Shock of Earthquake that ushered in our Fast Day *here* and frighted many of our Neighbours—not *us:*—is a light Matter compared with Mobs and Insurrections—Let us as King David said of old, fall into the hands of God and not into the hands of Men.[4]

The Noise accompanying even this trifle of a Concussion was such as to alarm Mrs. Griffiths exceedingly:[5] She said it was like a Hundred Carts of Lime Stone overturned close by her Bed. Mr. Piozzi and I never waked to hear or feel it—— Miss Thrale had not then (as now,) kept our Eyes wholly sleepless by a new and violent Attack on our Feelings and property: sending—without Notice or Introduction—to our Oxfordshire Tenant, a Requisition to pay *her* the Rent I have hitherto received for 19 Years since My first Husband's Death in Consequence of the Marriage Settlement signed by him in 1763, confirmed again by Will in 1781, and claimed now AD: 1800 with Threats—to our afflicted Friend Mr. Gillon—of making me refund all I have *unjustly* taken *from my daughters*. It will be soon refunded. No Ass—as Moses says—of theirs did I ever take—nor no Present at their hands for Bribe.[6] How cruel 'tis to sit down and accuse me So!! Miss Thrale says Streatham was given me to make *up* 400£ o'Year, but that Crowmarsh is not liable. Now it will turn out upon Examination that Crowmarsh is *first* liable, and that if my Due from that Estate is not paid me—I have a Right to make *forcible* Entry, and *take* it *without Impeachment of Waste*. This being provided in the Marriage Settlement, I understand *must* be secure; so do not you nor dear Mr. Pennington be uneasy: we shall *lose* nothing but Appetite and Sleep. And I was *so* well after the Bath Waters! and proposed being *so* diligent at the Book—and now nothing but Law and Letters, and Chancery Suits, and false Accusations and every Evil Plague.

21 April 1800

No News from abroad yet—that we can depend upon—will it be good when it arrives?[7] The Times as Dr. Randolph says are signally aweful; and I verily think that Dæmons are roaming about among us, with enlarged Permission both to tempt and terrify. God preserve us! even from our own bad Passions; he only can: *mine* are sometimes ready to run away with me now, for Welsh Blood heats over a Fire of Sharp Thorns thus, till it boyls again.[8] Oh dear how dreadful are these Days! A Lady in this Neighbourhood made a grand Entertainment on the Fast appointed by Government by way of Spiting that Government[9]——They must leave off appointing such Solemnities; The Time is over when they did any Good. You should procure me that Pamphlet of Dr. Beddowes[10] and send it me in a frank sometime, or in *Two* Franks.

Would you believe that when I carried that Book Mr. Gray bought for me—hither—I found out that I had packed up Dr. Randolph's instead of my own; so that he has got two *first* Volumes now of the same Work and we have two *second* Volumes so wisely have I managed.

Pray did you see My Master's old Pocketbook after we came away? He certainly left it behind: it was tyed with a black Ribband—but contained only Memorandums,—and *they,* unintelligible.

I wish Miss Case would tell *me* what they have suffered at Bath, and what they have escaped, for I cannot now make it clearly out: If harm comes to Hannah More we are all undone——*her* Health is a public Concern, yet I forget who is her Physician. Should my Dear Tormenters leave me Life and Strength enough to see You all again, it will be with great Kindness: and pray say sweet Words for me to Mr. Whalley——This Earthquake was not so slight a Thing as I thought it: Some Houses at Conway and Caernarvon were much injured, and it spread a general Alarm—from the *Unfrequency* of the Thing—Yet to People who have lived much in Italy, an Earthquake that did not *wake* one, seems laughable enough. Lady Orkney appears fluttered about it—She is sorry Mrs. Carrick has any thing to afflict her for her *father's* Sake; the Doctor is got well however I hope and trust.[11]

Pray get well yourself and give our truest and tenderest Regards to your good Husband and poor Mrs. Weston who I now begin to fear I shall see no more somehow.

Much may and probably much *will* happen this Summer to give us a little further Insight into what's coming in earnest. The best is our seasonable and Salutary Change of Weather——had we Corn to *sow* The Ground will be in fine Order for putting it in. I am glad Buonaparte sends us no Corn—I was afraid of Contagion in the Sacks, and the Thought of an Expedition to Ægypt and Syria frights us lest some Pestilential Disease should be brought home from Places so constantly infected.[12]

Farewell and love us as you used to do; and take as little Laudanum as you can help; and pity my poor Master who has the Toothach terribly while I am telling you that I am Yours in all true Affection / H: L: P.

Text: Princeton University Library. *Address:* Mrs. Pennington / Dowry Square / Hot Wells / Bristol.

1. PSP herself assigns HLP's undated letter to April 1800. Because its contents are similar to those in a letter to LC, dated 21 April, we assume that the two letters were written about the same time. See Knapp, p. 187.

2. When early in 1800 the price of grain rose sharply, the poor and laboring classes suffered. Protest took the form of riot, arson, and robbery in Bath. Among these was a near-disastrous fire that destroyed a brewery, inflicting losses estimated at £20,000. "Whether the fire was accidental or otherwise, cannot be ascertained.—An anonymous letter, threatening destruction of their premises, &c. has been received by the proprietors of another extensive brewery in this city" (*Bath Chronicle,* 13 March).

Other incidents led the mayor to convene a meeting on 17 March to list "what steps he had already taken to secure tranquillity. . . . In consequence of which the principal housekeepers have enrolled themselves as Constables, and have established a patrole, consisting of six each in the three parishes in the city, and eighteen in the vicinity; who are to patrole from ten at night, to six o'clock every morning, to examine and secure all persons who cannot give a good account of themselves and to prevent sotting and rioting in any of the publick-houses." See the *Bath Journal,* 24 March.

3. James King (1746–1816) was from 1785 to 1805 master of ceremonies at the Bath Lower Assembly Rooms. On 4 February, his house "was destroyed by fire; and the family had hardly time to escape into the street. Mr. K, getting into bed the preceding night, threw back the curtains, which were of calico, and, touching a candle, was instantly in a blaze. He endeavoured to pull them down, and his shirt caught fire. Mrs. K, who was at her toilet nearly undressed, threw herself on him, in hopes of extinguishing the flames. The room was then in a blaze, and she rushed out to apprize the two maid-servants. . . . The door closed after her, and it was with extreme difficulty that Mr. K, who was nearly suffocated, could open it." See *GM* 70, pt. 1 (1800): 174; *Bath Chronicle,* 6 February.

4. See HLP to LC, 7 or 8 May 1799, n. 8.

5. For Mrs. John Griffiths, see HLP to Q, 19 December 1794, n. 10.

6. See 1 Sam. 12:3 (the speaker is Samuel) and Exod. 20:17.

7. Although the war had been renewed, little action took place in Europe. On the Rhine there were sporadic skirmishes. "The Archduke Charles has resigned the command of the Imperial army [to Marshal Kray]; and is gone to Vienna, whence he will set out for Prague, for the benefit of his health. The cause of his Highness's quitting the command . . . it is believed [by many] to be the fruit of political cabal and intrigue at the Court of Vienna." The Austrians were also bogged down in the Piedmontese Alps. See *GM* 70, pt. 1 (1800): 378–79.

8. Variation on proverbial expression: "His Welsh blood is up." Thomas Fuller, *The History of the Worthies of England* [1662], ed. John Nichols, 2 vols. (London: F.C. and J. Rivington, etc., 1811), 2:256.

9. March 12, "being appointed as a day of General Fast [by royal proclamation], was observed with great decorum; the shops were closely shut, and the churches were fully attended.

"Their Majesties and the Princess Elizabeth attended Divine Service at the Chapel Royal. The Sermon was preached by the Rev. Dr. Strachey. . . .

"The Lord Bishop of Oxford preached before the House of Peers at Westminister Abbey."

See *The Times,* 13 March, which described further the participation of the government and the Commons in observances at St. John's church, Westminster; and at St. Margaret's and St. John's Association.

10. Born in Salop, Thomas Beddoes (1760–1808) took his M.D. at Oxford in 1786 and was appointed reader there from 1788 to 1792. About 1793 he began to work on a project for the establishment of a "Pneumatic Institution," i.e., the treatment of diseases by the inhalation of different gases. In 1798 the hospital that he projected was built at Clifton.

The pamphlet was a *Notice of some Observations made at the Medical Pneumatic Institution* (Bristol: Printed by Biggs and Cottle, for Longman and Rees, London, 1799).

11. Andrew Carrick (1767–1837), M.D., of Clifton and Marlwood House, Glos. Begin-

ning his practice in Bristol, ca. 1789, he was to be elected one of the physicians to the Bristol infirmary in 1810 and senior physician in 1816, which rank he held until 1834.

His first wife was Elizabeth, née Hillier (d. Clifton, 10 June 1817); his second was Caroline, née Tudway (1787–1872), whom he was to marry 10 August 1819 at Saint Cuthbert's, Wells (C.R.O., Somerset). See also the *Bristol Gazette*, 12 June 1817 and 22 June 1837; *GM* 111 [8 n.s.] (1837): 100.

For recent earthquakes in Wales, see HLP to RD, 29 March 1800 and n.2.

12. HLP had in mind the treaty of El Arish (in late January 1800) and a question about its ratification. According to *GM* 70, pt. 1 (1800): 267: "The Turks have been successful against the French in [Egypt], and have recaptured El Arisch, after a very severe conflict. Letters from Constantinople also state, that, when the Grand Vizier had advanced within three days' march of Cairo, he received overtures from General Kleber, requiring permission to evacuate Egypt with all his army, and to return to France."

Because the treaty, primarily negotiated by Commodore Sir William Sidney Smith, could not be approved by Lord Keith (as chief command), the war was to resume and require new expeditionary forces.

TO THE REVEREND LEONARD CHAPPELOW

[Brynbella Saturday
26: April 1800]

Dear Mr. Chappelow

I must take one of Lady Elinor's fine Crow Quills and write a small hand because this goes in a frank to Mr. Gillon and costs you but a Peny. Is it not worth a Peny to hear how after almost 40 Years I am likely to lose either Streatham or Oxfordshire Estates?——as the Ladies please. They contend that (by some Flaw in my Marriage Settlement with their Father) my Joynture is a mere Rent Charge on those *two Estates* by him in that Settlement *united* for Payment of 400£ o'Year; I have now for 19 Years since his Death received both——*but my Time is come.* Your good-natured Hand Writing *on* the *Paper* encourages me to write you this Stuff again; indeed if it were *in* the *Paper* that the Piozzis are likely to be chased from their old Covert near Norwood I should neither *wonder* nor *weep*——Such *Huntresses* would *rouse* any one's Spirit—but mine, more into Anger than Sorrow.

They made a Stoop at the Furniture—but House and Goods are left me by Will.—Streatham indeed Miss Thrale says,—is to pay a Part, and Crow Marsh a Part—and make me up 400£ o'Year: I brought Mr. Thrale 10,000£ in the Year 1763.[1] My Mother left me 2,500; my Aunts—600£ I think;[2] and Dr. Wilson—(who translated Thuanus) 300£ more.[3] Mr. Thrale enjoyed this Welsh Estate 11 Years, and cut Timber to amount of 1800£——I call that a 20000£ Fortune——*but it is more;* and my Settlement's *leanness* was compensated by my Husband's generosity, in his testamentary Disposition, or I had made a miserable Bargain: tho' the Ladies try to make People believe that their Papa had a wretched Match of it: *He* did not think so, he left me Streatham which If they persist in treating me *thus*, I will strip to the Skin, sell the Pictures &c. and plough the Ground up. My Welsh Blood boyls at such Treatment. They know that every wise Friend Mr.

Piozzi has in the World, will advise him not to contest in the Courts of Law for a Life Estate dependent on a Woman whom their Unkindness will help to kill; and at whose Death the Property goes irrevocably to *them*——and my poor Husband be left the Attorney's Bills to pay. Knowing this, they make as if I had been cheating *them* all these Years, and will consider themselves as Merciful whatever be the Terms of Accommodation.

My Master meantime—fertile, inexpedient, and always alive to hope—*swears they cannot hurt us:*——for says he *Veniamo ai Conti* and it will be acknowleged by every honest Man that Streatham is worth very little indeed, when you take off the House and Goods and deduct the Taxes for payment of a Rent Charge—I thought they owed us Arrears, and so they do—*in Justice*, because Crowmarsh brought in only 272£ many Years, and then 366£ but you see they call in Streatham as an Aid——and say we have been *wronging* them.

I have but just Paper enough left to ask you what is meant by a Secret Method of setting Fleets on Fire. Is it the old burning Glass of Archimedes revived or Callinicus's Chymical Process—Medea's Oyl?[4] Adieu ever H: L: P.

Text: Ry. 560.92. *Address:* Rev: Mr: Chappelow / No. 12 Hill Street / Berkeley Square / London.

1. As early as 1778 HLT computed the money which she—as a bride—brought to HT. "Thirty or Forty Thousand Pounds" and glossed her statement thus: "I brought ten Thousand *in hand* . . . My Mother left me 2500, an Aunt—Sophia Cotton—500£ more, this makes thirteen; the Copy holds dropt in Herts to me as heir at Law, which Lady Salusbury forgot—sell for two Thousand, and if my Welch Estate is not worth fifteen more—I am sorry; not reckoning fifteen Thousand Oak Trees on it—for they have all been number'd and marked.—My Aunt Sidney left me 100£ so did Aunt Boycott & Dr B. Wilson 300£ (*Thraliana* 1:320 and n. 6).

2. Sophia Cotton (d. ca. 1763); Sidney Arabella Cotton (d. 1781); Philadelphia Boycott, née Cotton (1699–ca. 1767).

3. The Reverend Bernard Wilson (1689–1772) translated *Monsieur de Thou's History of his Own Time*, 2 vols. (London: E. Say, 1729–30).

4. According to Warton: "Grecian fire, seems to be a composition belonging to the Arabian chemistry. It is frequently mentioned by the Byzantine historians, and was very much used in the wars of the middle ages, both by sea and land. It was a sort of wild-fire, said to be inextinguishable by water, and chiefly used for burning ships, against which it was thrown in pots or phials by the hand. . . . The oriental Greeks pretended that this artificial fire was invented by Callinicus, an architect of Heliopolis, under Constantine; and that Constantine prohibited them from communicating the manner of making it to any foreign people. . . . Procopius, in his history of the Goths, calls it Medea's Oil, as if it had been a preparation used in the sorceries of that enchantress" (1:157).

TO PENELOPE SOPHIA PENNINGTON

Brynbella
1st May 1800.

My dear Mrs. Pennington is *too* apt to be right; You do not I perceive think us safe from this new Attack upon our Property, and we are *not* safe. When drinking our Healths however, a Bumper must be given to Mr. Gillon, *his* Kindness could not be exceeded by that of a Brother.

Thus it stands. If we litigate, such is the dubious Position of Mr. Thrale's Words in my old Marriage Settlement, that Years will roll away, and Empires be overthrown, before the Affair can be decided; and in the mean while Crowmarsh Rents will be retained till the Decision——A Circumstance very unpleasing to *us* for every Reason; the strongest of all—because to Miss Thrale the Estate *must* go at my Death; so that unless my life is prolonged beyond the usual Limits of Humanity—Mr. Piozzi *can hope* for nothing from a Law Dispute—except Attorney's Bills to pay, with a diminished Income.

Of all *this* our fair Enemy *can*not be ignorant; and does not profess to desire anything but Profit from the Contest; So we may be *sure* She will make great Terms for herself. The Parley of Eloquence on Mr. Gillon's Side supported by Butler's Opinion concerning our Case is held today I think:[1] the best Thing is that Mr. Thrale confirmed his Marriage Settlement by his Will, adding the Bequests in that Will to what formerly was provided in the other Instrument: but nothing has been *worded* so as to preclude Discussion among eager Disputants, diligent to catch and cavil, and endowed with Marianne's Powers and Delight in Wrangling.[2] We are in a Wasp's Nest, and must make haste out, and be stung as little as we can——Resistance is vain, and will be impolitic—in my Mind.

I thank you for Beddowes Book, which is the best *Keepsake* and I grieve that you bought me any other, for it never found its way hither; and Trinkets are Things I never wore when young, and to which I should *now* annex no Value in the World but as your Gift——If you booked the parcel I am told Things are recoverable, or their Value.

That People are quiet and the Fires accidental, I would willingly perswade myself, but cannot. That Your Friend Paul Emperor of all the Russias is a true Friend and firm Ally, may now—reasonably enough be doubted.[3] He wants an excuse for falling upon Turkey, and takes that of quarrelling with Great Britain. It is exceedingly offensive to be forced into Submission to his Caprices—but I suppose George the 3d at Close of Life will not find new Enemies a good Thing any more than poor H:L:P does; or will be able any better than H:L:P to find *Supplies* for a new Contest, which like hers *can* terminate in no Advantage, and will be attended with *certain* Loss abroad, Increase of Poverty and of Course Ill humour at home. You may See how spiteful the People are even by their opposition to his private Conveniency in making a new Road to Windsor from London.[4] No want of Spite in this World I'll warrant either to Princes or to People; my Book will have proved that new and wise Remark by this Time next Year: If we go to London with it I shall vote for an Apartment in the Adelphi

Hotel; such a place will do well enough for November and our Income *must* be reduced, and I will not suffer *my* Business or Pleasures to retard my husband's long projected Happiness of not having a Debt in the World;——The very Journey is expence enough. We shall be near Mr. Gillon there,[5] and I shall not have an Acquaintance in London, but Mrs. Siddons and Mrs. Holman—perhaps not the *first* even of those: as the Seasons seem to change so, Everybody makes it Summer till after Christmas, and Winter to July.

There is great Talk of a new Book written by Hannah More, The Progress of Pilgrim Good-Intent thro' the Land of Jacobinism have you read? and is it charming?[6] My Letters contain only Questions and not a Frank can be had here; yours always tell something, and commonly something agreeable——and they come free.

The Rheumatism has caught my Shoulder before Gout seized my Master's Toe this Year. I was to have gone in the Cold Bath this Morning but the Pain prevents me. Our Weather is good at last—not quite Sun enough, fine Spring Rains and a Prospect of Grass if not Corn: we had *neither* last Year. But the Birds sing now, and the Trees come out kindly and—as Mr. Pope says *Hope springs eternal* &c.[7]

Be well dearest Mrs. Pennington, Everything may be endured where Health is; but even this pain in my Shoulder gives all a gloomy Aspect to what it bore Three Days ago.

Farewell! Give my true Regards to your good Husband and service to Mrs. Weston. I dare say She is very sorry for your ever-tormented H: L: Piozzi.

Text: Princeton University Library. *Address:* Mrs. Pennington / Dowry Square / Hot Wells / Bristol. *Postmark:* DENBIGH.

1. Charles Butler (1750–1832), as a Roman Catholic, could not be called to the bar when he began his professional career. He therefore took up conveyancing and helped to edit *Coke upon Littleton*. With the passage of the Enabling Act, he became a barrister in 1791 and king's counsel in 1832.
2. The name was a symbol of the acrimonious debate associated in British as well as French minds with republican institutions as early as the French Revolution. The origin is unknown.
3. Paul or Pavel Petrovich (1754–1801), Czar Paul I from 1796 until his murder 11 March 1801.

HLP alludes ironically to Paul's inconsistency in foreign affairs. In 1798–99 he had joined England, Austria, and Turkey against France. By the spring of 1800, he was taking issue with England's pursuit of the war and he was by the end of the year to adopt a position of armed neutrality against his one-time English ally.

His increasingly erratic, despotic decisions had earned him the sobriquet of "Mad Czar Paul."
4. According to *The Times*, 28 April:

"The Royal Family yesterday morning attended divine service at St. George's Cathedral, Windsor. As the King came out of Church, two Petitions were presented to him from the inhabitants of Colnbrook, Slough, and Salthill, praying his Majesty not to countenance the intended new road to Windsor."
5. Begun in 1768, the Adelphi buildings (in one of which Gillon lived) were erected on the site of Durham House in the Strand. They were designed by the architects Robert and James Adam.
6. *The Progress of Pilgrim Good-Intent, in Jacobinical Times* (London: John Hatchard, 1800).

Published anonymously, it was the work not of Hannah More but of Mary Anne Burges (1763–1813). The allegory traces the descendants of Christian and Christiana—particularly Good-Intent—through a land of republican terrors. Based upon Bunyan's *Pilgrim's Progress*, it is an undisguised attack on domestic and foreign threats to the British establishment.

7. *Essay on Man*, 1.95.

TO THE LADIES OF LLANGOLLEN[1]

2nd May 1800

I thought not to have written to my dear Ladies till I could have told them my pecuniary embarrassments were ended. But Law is tedious, though Life is short, and, though we are now talking the business over by way of accommodating matters thro' the mediation of Friends, decision is at a distance still. Miss Thrale knows perfectly well with what *peculiar* disadvantage my poor Husband must of necessity carry on a defensive suit for the Life Annuity, or Estate of a woman who would in the common Course of Nature dye while that suit was pending; so that she stands on safe ground compared with *us*, and pleads a dubious expression in my old marriage Settlement signed thirty seven years ago. Mr. Thrale's will confirms that Settlement expressly, and if I lose what my Trustees should have taken better care of, I lose it merely by the Testator's earnestness to secure it for me, which appears *Three Times*, yet will perhaps be frustrated at last. I will let you hear when all is over.

What times these are, Dear Madam, and Miss Ponsonby! Meat now in London twenty pence the pound and Butter half a crown. Mr. Chappelow's spirits begin to fail, yet he is rejoicing that the French are beaten in Italy, and to say truth so am I.[2] The Defection of the Czar is dreadful as it is strange.[3] *My* London letters all give hints as if he was not in his right mind. . . . I wish it may turn out so, for sure his Junction with Buonaparte will prove a terrible Alliance to everybody else.

Our dear Mrs. Hannah More is always doing good, so what your Ladyship writes about *her* new 'Pilgrim's Progress' does not in the least surprise me, only sets me all on fire to read the Book. Will the world hold together till mine is finished? I feel almost as if within sight of land now, and shall go to London to launch it if it so pleases God in six months' time. The journey and the embarrassment will eat up all my profits though. It was in an evil hour this Dear Ill-advised Girl was tempted to distress me so, and I think the money if she gains much will not prosper. I brought their Papa more than £20,000 first and last, as the Phrase is, and I now see that if he had not remembered me in his Will these Ladies would have driven me completely on the Pavé. How dreadful is the Retrospect of a Danger I never dreamed of. . . . But I will revert to the vile subject no more. We have friends in London not inattentive to our interests, and Mr. Butler, who possibly your Ladyship may know, as he is Irish and a Roman Catholic, is the man to whom our Cause is confided.

Do the Ministry act wisely in disbanding all the Hunters Corps so?[4] It disobliges the Country Gentlemen who have been at great expense, and it exposes us to Jacobin Fury should the Excitors of a multitude find this scarcity a pretence to enrage them. Let us bless God for the *Prospect* of Plenty. I never saw a more sweet or smiling season;[5] not quite hot enough but the sun will shine now with more power every day and your Ladyship's pretty Cow get grass, and there will be food for Horses, and we must eat the Oats ourselves perhaps. No matter so as we eat them in Peace—Terror never haunts me in any form so fearful as that of an Insurrection.

Have you read Beddowes' Book, Dear Ladies? All about Oxygen, Air and Gas, and how we have Power over our own Lives, and I know not what strange things. It is a curious Performance.

My paper is out, though not my earnest wish for your Ladyship's and Miss Ponsonby's continued Health and Happiness. Accept those of Mr. Piozzi too, and believe that no one can be more truly your obedient Obliged Servant than is your poor tormented / H. L. Piozzi.

Text: The Hamwood Papers of the Ladies of Llangollen and Caroline Hamilton, ed. Mrs. G. H. [Eva Mary] Bell (London, Macmillan, 1930), pp. 313–16.

1. For Lady Eleanor Butler and Sarah Ponsonby, see HLP to Q, 10 March 1796, n. 16.
2. For the war in Italy, see *GM* 70, pt. 1 (1800):
Naples, e.g., was peaceful, awaiting the return of Ferdinando (p. 267). The Austrians had taken the strategic Mount Cenis in the Piedmontese Alps (pp. 378–79).
The last significant French holdout in Italy was centered in the area around Genoa. Reports stated that the Austrians had begun their siege of the fort of Gavi preliminary to their operation against Genoa, "which will be attacked by the Imperialists on one side, and by the British fleet on the other" (p. 266). On 6 March General Melas "invested Savona; the enemy retreating towards Nice" (p. 379).
At the end of its account, however, *GM* provided a caveat, which HLP remembered in her letter to LC, 13 May. According to the journal, "it is proper we should mention, that unofficial accounts appear in some of the Paris journals, stating, that both in this instance [Savona] and in that of Mount Cenis, the French had retrieved their losses, and completely driven back the Austrians to their former positions. These reports, however, had received no confirmation" at this time (p. 379).
3. Rumors of Paul's alliance with France, Spain, and Prussia were beginning to circulate in English newspapers. On 5 May *The Times* reported on the "quadruple alliance . . . said to have been proposed by Dumourier to the Emperor Paul. . . . The kingdom of Poland was to be re-established in favour of the Grand Duke Constantine, the second son of Paul, to whom the Grand Mastership of Malta was to be ceded; the French agreeing to evacuate the Island for that purpose, and also giving up Corsica to the Emperor of Russia, who wishes to have a naval establishment in the Mediterranean."
4. The "Hunters Corps" (officially designated the "Volunteer and Yeoman Cavalry") consisted of gamekeepers and landowners who in November 1796 had been recruited into the provisional cavalry, an arm of the militia. The conscriptions, intended as an emergency measure in the face of growing fears of invasion, were funded only until 24 February 1800. In the Commons debate of 20 February 1799, Dundas as secretary of war had argued that the expense of maintaining the corps could no longer be warranted. In

the spring of 1800, the corps was in the process of being disbanded. See *Parliamentary Register* 8 (1799): 116–19; 10 (1799–1800): 81.

5. HLP's optimism was premature: "two succeeding years had yielded bad crops; that of 1799 being almost the worst ever known, and that of 1800 one fourth below the average." See *AR* 43 (1801): 27; *GM* 70, pt. 2 (1800): 1203–4.

TO THE REVEREND LEONARD CHAPPELOW

Brynbella
13: May 1800.

It is a cruel Tax——far worse than any we lament about—which I impose upon the Friendship of Dear Mr. Chappelow making him pay 8*d*. for a *String* of Questions that if he was not very good natured indeed—he would wish me hanged in.

But I want you to tell me who built the Town of *Pisania* mentioned in Mungo Parke's Book,[1] and why it was called *Pisania* if you can.[2] Who that Dr. Laidler was who lived there so many years, whether Physician or Divine; and what he was doing there?[3] I understand Parke is going out again——sent I trust by the Association for discovering the Interior Parts of Africa, and that's a foolish Thing, for he told us nothing when he came home last.[4] Is it the Society for propagating Christian Knowledge that colonized *Pisania?* And how long has it been a Place such as Parke's Travels show it to be? I remember Philip Beavor colonizing at *Bulam* on the African Coast, but I never asked who set him to work.[5] 'Tis amazing how stupid one is, and what a Dream one is contented to live in.

You will say by and by; that 'tis more amazing by half to see me caring about Dr. Laidler and Mungo Parke rather than about Norris the Attorney and Butler the Chamber Council: but the best Thing Literature can do for one is to drive the Mind out of itself and its own Affairs; which will not be bettered by any Effort of mine, and my Health will be made worse: Let us Think of Africa: we shall not then be fretting about Cumberland Street. There was a Sierra Leone Company but that was a Trading Business I believe.[6] Only tell me what you know, and tell me soon.

The News from Italy seems vague and contradictory and difficult of Belief—— nothing *fixed* but the *Quicksilver;* we are *sure* of that Story I hope. Though 45000 Quarters of Wheat just now is better than any Capture, God send we may get a Snap at it here, for we are almost famishing, indeed we are. If however our Horses have strength to plough the Ground and our Farmers Seed to sow in it, The Weather is good:

Let us hear whether England is happier! I say *not*, for we poor Souls are *used* to hard Living. I fancy an Hotel will suit us best next Winter: nobody we know will be in Town in November and I hope to get away early as I possibly can.

You are very kind about the Dear little Boy; Mr. Gillon say[s] he does not grow tall, but is a stout Fellow, and a true Englishman. The Trees *You* say he is to inherit, grow very fast, and Bachegraig Woods are full of Thrushes and Blackbirds. We will spend what's left of our Money *There* if you please, and not at Streatham Park—we will be *Odnodvortzi*.[7] What's that?

Why my Dear Mr. Chappelow do you mind what *Sweet* Dr. Perney says?[8] We are not coming to live at Streatham assure yourself. Have we not Reason for repenting that we lived there so long? and no Thanks for all we did——Miss Thrale says it was *Optional*. Mr. Piozzi might have let it alone. I suppose Cecilia says so too: They are

tutte Compagne, tutte Compagne indeed.

Adieu Dear Sir and believe me most truly Yours / H: L: P.

Text: Ry. 560.93.

1. Mungo Park (1771–1806), a Scottish-born traveler, had been trained as a surgeon. His book is *Travels in the Interior Districts of Africa: Performed under the Direction and Patronage of the African Association, in the Years 1795, 1796, and 1797* (London: Printed by W. Bulmer and Co. for the Author; and sold by G. and W. Nicol, 1799).

See also HLP to PSP, 27 February 1798, n. 5.

2. According to Park: "Pisania is a small village in the King of Yany's dominions, established by British subjects as a factory for trade, and inhabited solely by them and their black servants. It is situated on the banks of the Gambia, sixteen miles above Jonkakonda" (p. 7).

3. Dr. Laidley is identified by Park only as a trader who was one of three British residents at Pisania; "the greatest part of the trade in slaves, ivory, and gold, was in their hands" (p. 7).

4. At this time Mungo Park hoped to undertake another mission to the Niger. That hope, however, became active only in October 1803 when Lord Hobart, then secretary of state for the colonies, invited him to organize an expedition to Africa. Delayed until 1805, he was killed by natives in the following year.

HLP is harsh in her judgment of Park, whose popular book went to three editions in the first year.

5. "In consequence of the determination of Messrs. Hew Dalrymple and Philip Beaver [in 1791], to attempt a settlement on the island of Bulama, they made known their intentions on that subject to some of their military friends." They and three other men sought to achieve "a settlement upon an eligible spot on the western coast of Africa," which "might lead to the Civilization of the Africans, and eventually put an end to their slavery." See Philip Beaver's *African Memoranda: Relative to an Attempt to Establish a British Settlement on the island of Bulama, on the Western Coast of Africa, in the year 1792* (London: C. and R. Baldwin, 1805), pp. 2–3.

Beaver and a group of colonizers left from England on 14 April 1792 for Bulama at the mouth of the Rio Grande on the west coast of Africa near Sierra Leone. After eighteen months, the Bulama experiment failed and those who had survived left the island in November 1793 and went to Sierra Leone. From there Beaver obtained a passage to England, reaching Plymouth 17 May 1794.

For Captain Beaver (1776–1813), see HLP to DL, 9 February 1796, n. 11.

6. The Sierra Leone Company had been founded in 1791 by William Wilberforce, Granville Sharp, Henry Thornton, and others to form a colony of liberated slaves. Largely through the effort of Zachary Macaulay (1768–1838), the colony achieved a degree of prosperity and order. He had served as governor for nearly a decade. He resigned in 1799 and, once in England, became secretary to the Sierra Leone Company. He held this post until 1808 when the colony was transferred to the Crown.

7. See HLP to LC, [18] May [1800], n. 14.

8. For John Anthony Perny, see HLP to PSP, 15 [December 1793] and n. 3.

TO PENELOPE SOPHIA PENNINGTON

Brynbella Saturday
16 May [1800].[1]

My last Letter was a Wretch—how could you Dearest Friend commend it so; If I remember any thing about it it was low, cold and flat. The usage I had received sunk my Nerves down, they were not irritated. Use of the Cold Bath meant to strengthen them threw me all out in *Nettle Stings*——and *now,* for crowning of all my poor Dear Master's Torment, villainous Gout, has as you once observed of Mr. Pennington's watched the due Time and thrown in *his* assistance to the fair Ladies' Cause. Their Cause is Cold though, and notwithstanding our Defenders cannot bring Matters to Decision yet, they give us Hopes that little will be lost—except the Arrears—worth Mr. Gillon says 1000£. He has behaved divinely to be sure and deserves all your generous Praises of him. Nobody applauds Miss Thrale's proceedings I think: Mrs. Holman and You inveigh *loudest* against her, and it *was* a cruel Thing to fly so upon that Estate which her Father would never have left *her at all;* had I not so requested him because I thought it was unfair that from accumulation of Fortune after they lost *him* his youngest Daughter would be richer than the eldest:[2] but I meant her to have Crowmarsh after my Death and so he meant it too. Well! one has always heard some Nonsense how two Negatives make an Affirmative, so I suppose *in Law* when a Man gives a Thing twice over, it turns out no *Gift at all.* Mr. Thrale tried *Three* Times to secure his Oxfordshire Property for me, and if I miss it at last——no Blame can attach to *him:* The Flaw was in the *Settlement*[3] you see, and the Will confirms the *Settlement*—so God knows how 'twill end at last.[4] The Mr. Butler employed on our Side has a high Character in his Profession as *Chamber Council* &c.: being a Roman Catholic, he cannot reach the honors of his Calling, but rests contented with the Profits.

Dear Keepsake never came, yet cannot sure be lost——for *nothing* comes from Bath: The two great Hampers we packed up and sent before we left that Town—(and Hodgkins booked them)—are not arrived yet. I sent for Books and Pens from London too last Week, but never do *they* come neither. The Law Cases travelled to and fro safe enough—perhaps Brynbella is accessible to nothing but Vexation.

Harriett Lee seems half affronted that I did not write to her, but my heart was really opprest and I *could* not write. There has been Clatter in the Markets there, our Paper tells; and a Gardener hurt—none of *my Friends* I hope.[5] This Rain will soften their hearts sure, it softens every thing, and we have at worst Plenty in *Prospect.* Young Trees prosper most sweetly, and our Cows get Grass and we have *Butter*—more than *Bread,* and if the Master of the House could walk about, and enjoy the Spring I would not suffer other things to kill me, though 'tis a serious Matter to see Expences *grow* thus, while Income diminishes.

Mr. Gray has got a Prebend of Chichester, and his Wife is got well;[6] so his Affairs go better than I looked for—and I love little Mr. Gray. What a Vexation to lose *your* Domestic History and my pretty Candlesticks and all! We are making strict Enquiry though, and I do not yet give the Box up for gone.

Well! here's another Plague, but not so bad as *some*. Cecilia took a Clergyman's Daughter of this Country for her Maid about two Years ago—and here's the Girl Come home *to lye in by her Master*.[7] The old Clergyman *cries,* and interests every body in his favour and purchases Curses for Mostyn—her Mistress is said to have patronized and fondled her, and kept her till the last Minute and till somebody—her Sisters I suppose—cried Shame.

All this you may conclude is *hearsay* Evidence: The last Letter I ever received from any of them, you read in Henrietta Street last February; but *the Facts are so.*

Here's much to do with *Hate* and more with *Love* as Juliet says in Shakespear.[8] A propós to Hatred I am delighted that we know the Author of De Montfort: She must be a fine Creature and will excite no small share of the Hatred She describes.—I *felt* it was a Woman's Writing, No Man makes Female Characters *respectable*——no Man of the present Day I mean, they only make them lovely; We must except *Doctor Moore:* his Mrs. Barnett and his Laura Sedlitz are all that Women ought to *wish* to be.[9]

Don't you admire at my sitting here to criticize Plays and Novels like Miss Seward, while my Husband is *lame*, my Fortune is *crippled*, and my favorite Dog has but *Three Legs.*

Farewell Dear Friend write me one of your sweet long Letters to console me now and then and tell some News or Chit-chat. Once more Farewell! 'Tis five o'clock in the Morning. I was up at *four;* shall call the Men and Maids at six, send away this Scrawl at seven, jump into the Bath at 8. Breakfast at 9. Work at the Book till 1. Walk till 3. Have dined by 4——fret over Gillon's Dispatches[10] and Piozzi's misery all the rest of the Day—a pretty Biographical Sketch of the Life <of your> poor H: L: P.

Mrs. Weston was very kind in being very *sorry,* and Mr. Pennington was very kind in being very *angry,* and you are always very kind, and will give them our best True love.

Text: Princeton University Library. *Address:* Mrs. Pennington / Dowry Square / Hot Wells / Bristol. *Postmark:* DENBIGH.

1. HLP dated her letter "Sat: 16: May Brynbella." Saturday fell on the 17th.
2. The equal legacies to HT's daughters were further complicated by the existence of two Thrale properties in Brighton: a cottage that HT inherited from his father and a house in West Street that HT bought in 1767. The latter had not been "surrendered to the use" of his will and in 1781 it went to his "heir according to the Custom of the Manor," which decreed its descent to the youngest son or, failing sons, to the youngest daughter. CMT inherited the West Street property.

For ten years, however, it had been assumed that the West Street house belonged to all the Thrale daughters. In 1791 they learned that CMT owned it. Although they could have contested the legal disposition of the Brighton property, they did not do so nor did HLP, who was entitled to the possession of the house for her lifetime since that was also the custom of the manor of Brighthelmstone. See Hyde, pp. 258–59.

3. See HLP to RD, 29 March 1800, n. 5.
4. See HLP to [John Gillon, ca. 3 June 1800].

5. From the *Bath Chronicle*, 15 May:
"A most exorbitant price having been demanded for potatoes on [7 May], by certain dealers in that article, who attend our market, much dissatisfaction was shewn by a few women, who cut open some of the sacks, and were proceeding to distribute their contents, (an inferior price having been offered to the proprietors, and refused) when the Mayor's officers interfered, and the greater part was again restored to the owners." The mob regrouped and "demolished the windows in the house of a man accused of monopolizing this necessary root." They then stormed the home of the farmer and seized several sacks of his potatoes. "They were, however, soon interrupted by the arrival of the City Volunteers, who having taken some of the principals into custody, and left a guard on the premises, returned with their prisoners to the city." See also the *Bath Journal*, 12 May.

6. According to *GM* 70, pt. 1 (1800): 583: "Rev. Robert Gray, B.D. rector of Craike, co. Yorke, to be prebendary of Bury, in the church of Chichester." (He received this preferment through the favor of Shute Barrington, bishop of Durham.)

7. But see HLP to Q, 21 December [1796], n. 3, for Mason's father, David, as a farmer.

8. For Romeo's line (1.1.175), see HLP to SL, 22 March 1785, and n. 9.

9. Laura Seidlets, "a Neapolitan by birth," appears in *Zeluco* (1789); Mrs. George Barnet in *Edward* (1796).

10. See particularly his letters of 21 March (Ry. 577.51) and 21 April (Ry. 578.57).
In the earlier letter he had written: "I thought I found [Q] not quite so sanguine in the Business, as she had appeared at my preceding interview. She observed to me, that she had been positively assured that Crowmarsh Estate was hers, and that She had the sole Right to receive the Rent of it. . . . That *her* Fortune was not so great; but that any addition to it, of such Magnitude, would naturally be an Object worth her attention, if it were really her Right: and unless she had been told that it was so, or if it had been an Object of no great amount, she would sooner relinquish it, than make any Stir, or take any Trouble about it."
In the later letter, Gillon reported Butler's opinion that the will altered the "Marriage Settlement" concerning both Crowmarsh and Streatham Park. HLP was bewildered by this opinion and expressed her concern to Gillon. On 28 April (Ry. 578.58) he wrote again, assuring her she owned Streatham Park for life as long as she paid her taxes.

TO THE REVEREND LEONARD CHAPPELOW

Brynbella Sunday Night—
[18] May [1800][1]

True did you say Dear Mr. Chappelow, that the Bullets fired at our dear King would put every thing else out of my Head. That the Man was mad who fired them, is most likely[2]——Mr. Medhurst was mad I dare say who cut his Wife's Throat a Week ago,[3] and Lord Ferrers was mad I am *sure*,[4] because my own near Relation Miss Cotton having married his Brother, I knew more of that Family than I *wished*.[5] Anna Shirley the Sister, was a confined Lunatic many Years—perhaps may be yet alive: when She was well and went to visit her Brother in Prison just before he was *hanged*, he reprimanded her for having solicited Admittance among the *Players;* because it was (he said) a *Disgrace to the Family*.[6]

Mad People are the best possible Instruments in the hands of Traytors; and you see this Mr. Hadfield's hand was steady enough, though they would now make us believe he had been drinking.[7] Those are the maddest among us who abet this Wretch's Escape under pretence of Insanity.⁸ We shall lose our Parent, Prince, and Friend, as his loyal Subject Mr. Sheridan justly calls him:⁹ if Treason is always to be explained away into Accident. The Fellow deserves Death for terrifying the *Company:* and in these *Democratic* Days perhaps *that* will be a Reason for his Punishment—he might have alarmed a pretty Lady to the Danger of her Son and Heir. Who was the *Mad*man that missing his Aim hurt Mr. Ongley I wonder?¹⁰ Those who *stand by* George 3rd in every Sense of the Word, seem to have a Dangerous Post; since Jacobinism has been the Order of the Day.

These Reports make me forget even my own Affairs, but your Friendly and wise Advice shall never be forgotten; We will come to Town upon as cheap Terms as we can:¹¹ Mr. Gillon's Kindness is really surprizing,¹² how to make him Amends I guess not——We are living in hot Water till they inform us how much of our Income they will be content to leave—unclaimed.—The Pretension and the Defence and all will be a heavy Pull upon our Health, our Peace and our Purse, yet God who saves the King will save us too if we trust in him, and surely one is not Tempted to trust in *one's own Wit or Strength;* for all I am Mistress of would never have enabled *me* either to expect or to repel these Assaults.

I will plague you no more with Literary Enquiries, having found my Way to one who can tell me all about it¹³—at least I hope so.

Mr. Piozzi has got the Gout most Severely—most outrageously, but that's no harm: It takes up his Attention from other Things far more disagreeable. The Spring is beautiful and the Newspapers say Cart Loads of Wheat will come to our Share when Ship Loads come to yours in London——but when is That Time to arrive?

The hard Word was Russian for Proprietors of *one House* only; I have already forgotten it.¹⁴

Madame Buonaparte's¹⁵ outshining the Descendant of Charlemagne¹⁶ is perfectly in unison with all one hears and sees——but it will be equally so to hear that her Husband is assassinated, and herself dragged to the Guillotine or thrust into a Dungeon. I think if Buonaparte meant to save Genoa he should have left her fair Side a little sooner, coming too late will bring him to Disgrace and he will tumble down faster than he climbed.¹⁷ "Take Care Children when you come to the Top" is the Instruction of a wise Monitor who stands beside the Flying Coaches now at Whitsuntide (or used to do) in St. George's Fields——*one go up—other go down* says the Cryer.

So farewell Dear Mr. Chappelow! and Heaven keep you from the Gout, for 'tis a dreadful Pest indeed; and I think nobody ever had it as bad as my Master—Hands, Neck, Collar Bone, Arms——you saw him bad once I believe, but now he is all as if nailed down to the Bed.

If I make Terms with Robinson——'tis probable we *must* come to London on that Business, and then living at Streatham would be an out of the way thing; for how should the press be corrected *There?* One might as well stay in Wales: Besides that *making* a *Bargain* to go and live with a *half single* Gentleman and his humble female Friend,¹⁸ seems a very out of the way Thing *indeed* for H:L:Piozzi and her old Bavarian Blood somehow. If we being in a cheap House in Marlbro or Poland Street, or near Bedford Square—or at an Hôtel could get our Business done in those dull Months when nobody is in London and could live there for 100£ the House Rent till [the] Book came out——I should reckon *that* all our Expence for one must eat and drink every where and we should bring no Horses. I think an Hôtel would be cheapest and least embarrassing: but we will call a Council with our true Friends and let them determine for your much obliged &c.

I am willing—mark—to go to Mr. Giles's on Invitation——but not as halving the House with him.

Text: Ry. 560.94. *Address:* Rev: Mr. Chappelow / No. 12 / Hill Street Berkeley Square / London. *Postmark:* DENBIGH.

1. HLP's letter, written Sunday the 18th, responds to one by LC, dated 16 May (Ry. 562.64).
2. On 15 May the Royal Family attended a performance at the Drury Lane of Colley Cibber's *She Would and She Would Not; or, The Kind Impostor,* and *The Humours,* a farce. Just as they entered their box, one James Hadfield rose from his seat in the pit and fired a pistol at the king but missed. "His Majesty shewed the most perfect composure, turned his eye toward the man, and continued standing till the Queen entered, who displayed also the most dignified courage." See the *Morning Chronicle,* 16 May 1800; *GM* 70, pt. 1 (1800): 478–79.
3. In the evening of 4 May Grenvil William Wheeler Medhurst of Kippis Hall, near Pontefract, attacked his wife with a sword, "gave her three stabs in the body, and cut her throat in so dreadful a manner, as nearly to sever her head from her body. . . . As Mr. M. was armed with two or three brace of pistols, besides his sword, [his servants] were obliged to send for a party of Pontefract volunteers, who immediately secured him and carried him off to York castle." Ultimately, he was "acquitted at the York assizes, of the murder of his wife," by virtue of insanity. See *GM* 70, pt. 1 (1800): 490–91; 70, pt. 2: 792.
4. For Lord Ferrers, see HLP to Q [22/23 October 1796], n. 7.
5. In 1754 Catherine Cotton (d. 1786), of Etwall, Derbyshire, married Robert Shirley (1723–87), sixth earl Ferrers (1778). In "Harvard Piozziana" she is identified as a sister-in-law of HLP's uncle, Sir Lynch Salusbury Cotton.
6. Ferrers's half-sister was Anne (d. 1779). According to HLP's "Commonplace Book": "We used to laugh about Lord Ferrers chiding his Sister for Shewing so strong an Inclination to the Stage—because added he——who was *just going to be hanged;* You see 'tis disgracing the Family."
See also HLP's marginalia in the *Spectator* (no. 630, ed. 1789) 8:381: virtually identical comment.
7. From *GM* 70, pt. 1 (1800): 479–80: in the theater "on being questioned by Mr. Sheridan, [Hadfield] said, 'He had no objection to tell who he was—it was not over yet—there was a great deal more and worse to be done. . . . He had served his time to a working silversmith, but had enlisted in the 15th Light Dragoons, and had fought for his King and Country.'"
Hadfield asserted that he had no desire to kill the king but that he wished to die without taking his own life. "He talked in a mysterious way of dreams, and of a great commission he had received in his sleep; that he knew he was to be a martyr, and was to be persecuted like his great master, Jesus Christ."
8. The British legal system was more tolerant of the relatively new plea of insanity than HLP. James Hadfield "was tried at the Court of the King's Bench, Thursday, June 26. The Charge was High Treason. The Trial lasted from nine in the morning till past five in the afternoon. The Jury found a Verdict of *Not Guilty,* it being proved that *the Prisoner was under the influence of Lunacy at the time when the act was committed*" (*Sun,* 27 June).

9. Four times during the evening of 15 May, the audience and players at the Drury Lane sang "God save the King." After the farce was performed, the anthem was sung again with two impromptu verses by Sheridan. The second verse is the one to which HLP refers: "O'er him thine arm extend, / For Britain's sake defend / Our Father, Prince, and Friend, / God save the King." The verses were "received with enthusiastic applause" (*The Times*, 16 May).

10. George III on the morning of 15 May was reviewing the Grenadier battalion of the Foot Guards, "when the shot was fired which unfortunately wounded Mr. Ongley [an official in the Navy Office]. . . . That it was accidental, however, is the opinion of the Government" (*Courier and Evening Gazette*, 16 May).

11. Regarding the Piozzis' visit to London, LC had written: "Mr. Gillon and I agree with him, that you would do well to make my bargain with Mr. Giles—so that you could be at Streatham.—You will pay 1/2 as much at an Hotel, as you will get by your book."

12. John Gillon continued to work on behalf of HLP in her struggle with Q over Crowmarsh. According to LC's letter on 16 May: "I found your good Mediator Mr. Gillon weather bound in a bookseller's shop in Oxford Road.—He said he was going to call on Miss Thrale on Horseback—but the rain obliged him to return to the city when *Omnium* called for him at a given hour.—He desired me to say—he has not yet had Miss Thrale's answer relative to the offer of £50 per Annum:—she intended to consult Cator &c. upon the Subject—You will soon hear from him.—" For an explanation of LC's statement, see HLP to [John Gillon, ca. 3 June 1800].

13. Joseph Cooper Walker.

14. The "hard Word" was *Odnodvortzi*; see HLP to LC, 13 May. Now anachronistic, its political and social implications made the word unacceptable in Russia after the revolution of 1917.

15. HLP's response to LC's comment on 16 May: "Lord Townshend told me . . . that the Court of the Great Consul for magnificence exceeds that of Lewis the 14th—and that no Queen of France ever saw a more brilliant Circle than that which Madame Buonaparte sees every day."

Known as Josèphine, she was born Marie-Josèphe-Rose Tascher de La Pagerie (1763–1814), a creole of Martinique and the widow of Alexandre de Beauharnais (d. by guillotine, 1794). She married Bonaparte in a civil ceremony in 1796. Napoleon was to have the marriage annulled in 1809 because of her alleged sterility.

16. See HLP to LC, 27 December 1795, n. 5. The "Descendant of Charlemagne" was Mme d'Angoulême. Marie-Thérèse-Charlotte de France (1778–1851) married her cousin, Louis-Antoine de Bourbon (1775–1844), duc d'Angoulême, in 1799.

17. HLP refers to the siege of Genoa, 20 April–4 June. Specifically, a force of 18,000, commanded by Generals Masséna and Soult, were driven back by the Austrian, General Melas, into the port and city of Genoa. They were under siege by General Ott's corps and a royal naval force that blockaded the port. Bonaparte thereupon decided to undertake his own offensive. But he could not reach Genoa in time to relieve his compatriots, who agreed to a peace on 4 June. See HLP to LC, 9 June, n. 4.

18. HLP knew of Giles's continuing liaison with Mrs. Ann Jones, his "housekeeper." See his will (P.R.O., Prob. 11/1768/170), signed 25 January 1822 and proved at London, 27 March 1830.

[TO JOHN GILLON][1]

[ca. 3 June 1800][2]

Dear Sir

I am very glad indeed, and so is Mrs. Piozzi, that Miss Thrale changes now her

Opinion of her Guardian and her Attorney, who not only perswaded her to grant a Lease, which was easy—by merely signing a Parchment:—but to write with her own hand a Permission for the Farmer to pay his Rent *to him who married her Father's Widow*.³ The Paper you brought her *yourself*, written clear by Miss Thrale.—Likewise another Letter of which I enclose a Copy that you may see She has changed her Mind now, this being wrote a long Time since She came first of Age, and was under Cator and Norris's immediate Influence.

I much wish her to find they are not so sincerely her Friend as is / Dear Sir / Your much obliged Servant / [Gabriel Piozzi].

Pray is the Map of the Welch Estate among your Papers?

Text: Ry. 533.12.

1. This purportedly legal document was written to John Gillon, HLP's "mediator" in the Crowmarsh affair. It responds to his news in a now missing letter that the "battle" with Q had ended.
2. Although prepared for GP's signature, this letter—a draft—is in the hand of HLP. Q had "given in" on the last day of May. Gillon had sent this information promptly to HLP, who received it about three days later. By 4 June, in her letter to PSP, the armistice was a fait accompli.
3. Upon advice of Gillon, the Piozzis and Q settled their quarrel over Crowmarsh without recourse to further litigation. They agreed to the following: the property was, according to HT's will, Q's but £400 drawn from its rent went to HLP, according to the "marriage settlement." Therefore, HLP was to receive that sum annually. (The rent for Crowmarsh after 1795 was £450, but Q was to retain £50 or any amount beyond the stipulated £400.)

TO PENELOPE SOPHIA PENNINGTON

4: June 1800

Thank you, Thank you, Dear kind Mrs. Pennington: I have got the Box and the Keepsake and the Letters and everything—and with a true heart shall I love them. I lighted up my new Favourites last Night and wrote by their Illumination. The Book goes on——*lamely* perhaps, now my better half has the *Gout*—but it does go.

My Master mends too, and Every thing mends: Miss Thrale *withdraws* (somewhat disgracefully) the Claim She could not *substantiate:* A Tedious Suit against this never-dying Mother would have eaten up all the Profits of her hoped-for-Estate; and nobody would have benefited *but* the Lawyers. *Her* Friends were therefore perswaded by *our* Friends to *give in* as the Boxers say; and so the Battle ends: and on the last day of May She writes to the Oxfordshire Tenant to pay 400£ to us as usual—that very 400£ which on the first of March She wrote the same Man word—*was incontestably her own.*

So much for *our* Affairs; Yours have gone on badly I understand: no wonder with Frank and Lissey, they were sad ones I believe; Mrs. Weston must I think greatly delight in their Departures. *Our* sweet Siddons will have a great Loss of her admirable little Attendant, so long in their Family and who knew their ways so well. What a dreadful Accident! I feel really much concerned. Half Wales will go to see her at Liverpool I doubt not, if She should stay there long.[1] It is a very neat Playhouse and I remember seeing a Farce rehearsed there, I never was at a Rehearsal but that time.

Miss Bayley, a Lady who lives with Mrs. John Hunter,[2] and is related to her; has at length modestly owned herself Author of a Drama that every one would have been most happy to have written: but Mr. Chappelow (no bad Mirror of the fashionable World,) says People think it too *Solemn:*—they *are not amused*.[3] I say they are like old Polonius, See Hamlet's Character of *him* as a Critic.[4]

Kemble is in high favour with the Beau Monde I am told,[5] and his Sister declines: but She will pick up some more Guineas, and then no matter. I reckon her as having only *one* Daughter to portion out; Sally will never marry I suppose, if *half* what I have *heard* of her Ill Health be true.[6]

Mr. Siddons will be a long-lived Man, as sick as he always is said to be; nothing runs on like a Life subject to one Chronic and regular Complaint; Gout, or Rheumatism. Siddons will repeat over to two or three Generations the Lamenting Strains I heard him recite in 1788;[7] and his Daughter will think herself young when every body else sees her grown old—because She has a Father to nurse.[8]

There was a Mrs. Shelley in Sussex—her sneering Neighbours called her Epistle and Gospel, who had two Maiden Daughters—one broke her Leg and died at about 40 Years old; but the other departed not till 5 Years ago: The Doctors informed her *Mama* there was no Hope, and She piously resigned to the Loss—but tell me at least cried She What ails my poor Child—and of what *can* She possibly be dying? *Of Age* Dear Madam answered her Physician. Miss Shelley was never strong, and 76 Years have nearly worne her out. Oh Dear! Is she really? Why I am but 94 myself——and I am not dying of Age. She spoke true, and outlived her little Girl as She called her, Six Years.[9]

Adieu Dear Mrs. Pennington and tell my *old Friend* this Story.

Mr. Whalley's Cottage will just be in order for us to visit, if we can afford ourselves the Diversion next Spring.

Farewell! and love us till we meet again; accepting our Thanks for every Mark of Kindness shewn to my Master and Your H: L: P.

Give our best Regards to your good Husband.

Text: Princeton University Library. *Address:* Mrs. Pennington / Dowry Square / Hot Wells / Bristol. *Postmark:* DENBIGH.

1. Because William Siddons's health was failing, he and his family left London for two months at Broadstairs and two at Brighton. SS's northern provinical tour was cancelled, although she continued to perform in the South.
2. Anne, née Home (1742–1821), had married in 1771 John Hunter (1728–93), the anatomist and surgeon. Before her marriage she had acquired some reputation as a lyrical poet and after 1771 was noted for her literary parties.

3. HLP refers to *De Monfort*, produced at the Drury Lane by Kemble in April. For the scenically magnificent play, "Kemble had 'a very unusual pile of scenery' created in 'seven planes in succession' representing a church of the fourteenth century—'positively a building'" (Manvell, p. 259). Nevertheless, "the incidents were all gloomy, and dark, and deadly" (Boaden 2:330) so that the tragedy had no popular success.

4. *Hamlet*, 2.2.

5. Kemble's favor "with the Beau Monde" was evident as early as his summer tour of 1798 when he was entertained by the earl of Derby near Liverpool, when he acted five nights at the command of the Royal Family in Weymouth, and when he returned to London £1,112 richer. His reputation now and for at least the next two years was to mount, most people believing him to be the *first* English actor, whether in tragedy or comedy, and Garrick's successor. It had become, admits Leigh Hunt, "'a critical religion' to profess oneself a follower of the great Kemble." See Herschel Baker, *John Philip Kemble: The Actor in His Theatre* (Cambridge: Harvard University Press, 1942), pp. 231–35.

6. Through PSP, HLP knew of Sally Siddons's frustrated love for Thomas Lawrence. But Sally was too ill to contemplate marriage, dying of chronic asthma in 1803.

7. William Siddons had become seriously ill of a fever in late autumn 1787 when he was "reduced to a Shaddow and [was] unable to sit upright five minutes." (See SS to Bedina Wynn, 18 September 1787, as cited by Manvell, p. 361.) Once recovered, Siddons recounted details of his illness through most of the following year.

8. William Siddons's crippling lumbago was to prove far more serious than HLP could know. By the autumn of 1804 he had retired permanently to Bath, able to walk only with the aid of two sticks. On 11 March 1808 he died unexpectedly, aged sixty-seven.

9. HLP embroidered the anecdote, but she referred to Eleanor, née Garnier (1702–92), who had married Henry Shelley (1693–1735), originally a mercer in Saint Paul's, Covent Garden, and later a man of wealth. They had six children, only two of their three daughters surviving beyond infancy: Elizabeth (ca. 1726–89) and Eleanor (1729–1813). HLP was distantly related to the family through her cousin Philadelphia Cotton (1738–1819).

TO THE REVEREND LEONARD CHAPPELOW

Brynbella
9: June 1800.

I am sorry Dear Mr. Chappelow that I cannot express my Concern for your Affliction without putting you to Expense of Postage when God knows I can tell you nothing on the Subject which you do not know better than myself. It is however providential that you cannot and must not Indulge Thought of your own Loss, so necessary and even Indispensable are your Consolations to Lady Bradford. She will I hope endure her Share of the Calamity with more Fortitude than her Friends expect from her, and to say Truth—I am sure She will do.[1]

Her Children and Grandchildren will love her, and cling round her; and shew her that there is yet Something worth living for, some People yet left to whom She is deservedly dear. You have *other Friends* who if *They* were to be Separated by a Death-Stroke——would find no such alleviating Circumstances crouding about the Survivor.[2]

Our dear King has 'scaped the Assassin thank God—and seen Affectionate

Subjects, and a fond Family expressing their Gratitude very delightfully: and he seems sensible of the People's Kindness too, and goes into Public without Apprehension.

What will become of Mr. Hadfield? Nobody ever tells me anything.[3]

The News from Italy seems favourable: If Buonaparte gets to Genoa time enough for its Relief, he must be more than Man assuredly: and what shall we think of Massena? He must be less than Man, or he must be starved with hunger before now. I, who you always say eat less than Woman, should famish in a Town besieged so strictly.[4]

We have referred and compromised, and finished with Miss Thrale; Mr. Gillon will tell you a laughable Story (I think it laughable) of her Standing out for *Ten pounds*. We have however made all possible Advances for Peace, and I trust the Negotiation is signed by now.

Robinson has my Title page too, sent him at his own Request; with the *Quantity of Stuff* The *Weight of Metal:* so 'tis the Year of Treaty and Intreaty and will end well at last I hope. Mr. Piozzi's Gout plagues him still, lingering and vexatious, like as he used to have it when we lived in Hanover Square, and dined with You the Day Mr. Ray tumbled down Stairs at pretty Mouse-trap Hall, helping him into the Coach.

Our Spring has been bright, but I see small Prospect of a hot Summer, or plentiful Crops: There was no Grain fit for sowing, how then should we be able to reap? If Potatoes succeed, other Failures may more easily be endured; but you can scarce credit the Sufferings of Poor Cottagers this last Winter——even down to May last. The Barley did not lower till a very short Time ago.

Is the young Lord Bradford in England, and did his Father dye in London?[5] When you have Time and Ease of Mind enough to make Amusement out of writing me a Letter, do pray let me hear from You. I am much Interested in the Fate of a Family which alone has an earlier Claim upon Your Good Wishes than that of Dear Sir / Yours sincerely / H: L: P.

Text: Ry. 560.95. *Address:* Rev.: Mr: Chappelow / No. 12 Hill Street / Berkeley Square / London. *Postmark:* DENBIGH E JU 11.

1. Lord Bradford had died 5 June at his house in Old Burlington Street, London. For Henry Bridgeman, first baron Bradford, and his wife, Elizabeth, see HLP to SL, 11 May 1786, n. 9; to LC, 23 August 1794, no. 4.

2. An unflattering reference to HLP's four daughters.

3. On 26 June James Hadfield was committed to Bedlam and confined until his death in 1841. See Roy Porter, *Mind-Forg'd Manacles: A History of Madness in England from the Restoration to the Regency* (London: Athlone Press, 1987), pp. 116–17.

4. HLP did not yet know that on "the 4th of June, the principal articles for the evacuation of Genoa were agreed on between the French adjutant-general Andreaux, on the one part, and major-general Rest, a staff officer in the imperial service, with the English captain Rivera, on the other."

The French after six weeks of siege found that "the provisions were entirely exhausted; even the last horses and dogs were nearly consumed." See *AR* 42 (1800): 188. For a firsthand account of the siege, see *Journal des Opérations Militaires du Siège et du Blocus de Gênes* (Paris: chez Magimel, an xi–1801), pp. 232–35.

General André Masséna (1758–1817) had become commander of the Army of Italy early in 1800, only to become immobile shortly thereafter in the siege.

5. For Orlando Bridgeman, second baron Bradford, see HLP to Sophia Byron, 2 June [1788], n. 7.

TO THE REVEREND LEONARD CHAPPELOW

Brynbella
10: June 1800.

Dear Mr. Chappelow

Here comes another Letter, but I have a Frank now: The Tenth of June and not a Rose blown, and we shall not have a Peach; no nor an *Apple,* with this horrible North Wind. And here is a Letter from Robinson to say he is grown sick, and old, and going to leave off, and will take no new Engagements: but wishes me Success, and doubts not but many in the Trade,—(those are his Words)—will *give the Money I have asked from him.*[1] It is vexatious enough, but when the World is full as Doctor Johnson Said of *Sin* and *Sorrow*—I must not be talking of *Paper* and *Packthread.*[2]

Write to me at least, and assure me that your Friends' Affliction and your own have not hurt your health.—

The enclosed is for Peny Post. We will come to Town and try the open Market when the Leaves are fallen and No Creature is in London but yourself, and old Mr. Jones, and Dear Mr. Gillon and Mrs. Siddons and Mrs. Holman. If I can put My Stuff to Press so as to bring it out early in 1801 I shall be glad.[3] Who was the Bookseller you named to me as likely to purchase the Copyright if his *Taster approved?*—I am willing to submit it to the *Taster.*[4] Perhaps Robinson is only Coquetting, I have written to him this Evening to quicken his Appetite——but will not starve myself because he is not hungry if it so turns out.

The Bishop of St. Asaph seemed deeply affected by the Death of Lord Bradford[5]—he had not heard of it till I told him——What a Husband! What a Father! is lost to the World.—said he.

My Master is getting better, my fair Daughters The finest at ev'ry fine Show no doubt—will be far removed from London when we arrive there; if Mr. Giles invites us to Streatham Park it will be very nice, but I really hope that the Hotel in Brook Street will be reasonable at such a dead Time of Year, and I wish not to stay an *hour* longer than I'm wanted.[6]

You will I am sure do me all the Good You can; The more my Book is talked of now, the more People will be made to expect it. Silence *once* was a good Thing, but the best for me at present is to have it discussed—at Stockdale's[7] or *any* Dale's.

Dear Sir You understand and will I know be very kind and very useful in giving hints as if *You* had seen and liked it.

Such Approbation is the greatest *honour* at all Times, and may *now* be *real Profit* to / Yours ever / H: L: P.

Text: Ry. 560.96.

1. For George Robinson, now sixty-three and a year from death, see HLP to LC, 21 October 1793, n. 3.
2. SJ would be annoyed by discussions of "airy nothings," once advising a visitor "to study algebra, if you are not an adept already in it: Your head would get less *muddy* and you will leave off tormenting your neighbours about paper and packthread, while we all live together in a world that is bursting with sin and sorrow" (*Anecdotes*, pp. 226–27).
3. On 15 July, HLP wrote: "I have now nearly completed my *Retrospection*. The Difficulty will be to sell it; but we must hope for the best. . . . I think 'tis worth 1000£ I really *think it is*" (*Thraliana* 2:1005). After her struggle for acceptance, the two volumes appeared in January 1801.
4. LC became HLP's "agent," abetted by John Gillon. The latter wrote on 27 June (Ry. 578.64): "I am glad to hear that Mr. Chappelow will so kindly assist about the Sale of your valuable Work. He is 'ipse agmen' in such a Business. . . . If I can be of any use to him, Mr. C, in the Negociation, I hope you believe that it will give me much Pleasure."
Benjamin White II (fl. 1794–1816) was the bookseller mentioned by LC, Gillon assuring HLP that "White is, I verily believe a likely man to act liberally."
5. Lewis Bagot would be affected by Lord Bradford's death because the latter was a vice president of the Welsh Charity.
6. The Piozzis did not stay at Kirkham's Hotel in Brook Street but at Streatham Park.
7. John Stockdale became the publisher of *Retrospection*. See HLP to LC, 1 November 1800, n. 1; "Memorandum of Agreement between HLP and Stockdale, 3 November; HLP to PSP, [5] November.

TO PENELOPE SOPHIA PENNINGTON

Byrnbella
13: June 1800.

My dear Mrs. Pennington is a true Friend, and has acute feelings of Friendship and of Injury: All is over between Me, and my *beautiful* and *deserving* Daughters—*Those* were Mr. Ray's Epithets—Apropós Mr. Ray has got a *deserving* Wife I hope, not very *beautiful* as merry Mr. Davies of Streatham gives hints—and he has also got the Gout.

With regard to *our Cause* mark me!—Mr. Gillon Dear Creature as he is, did not stop its Proceedings by *Perswasion;*—It was carried by *Law* tho' not by *Lit:gation*: Mr. Cator and Mr. Richards on *Miss Thrale's* Part, and Mr. Gillon and Mr. Butler on *our* parts talked the Matter over; and they really *withdrew* the Claim they could not *substantiate*—or make creditable to carry into a Court of Judicature.

Gillon tells a laughable Story of Miss Thrale's standing hard for 10£ which he advanced her—of his own Money—to stop further Absurdity.

And now let's hear no more on't; and do not Sweet Soul! make me in Love with *Resentment* for except in a Friend's Cause like your own; 'tis an unpleasing Quality and productive of nothing but Evil. We must quote our own Book of Knowledge after all, and in the Article—Forgiveness as I *think* you read these Words—A *Wise* Man will make haste to forgive because Anger is a painful Sensation and he wishes to be rid on't. A *great* Man will pardon easily because he finds few things worthy his Resentment, and a *good* Man will never resent at All, knowing how much he has himself to be forgiven.[1] I wrote to the Girls by yesterday's Post, exactly as if no such Transaction had past among us—so long live British Synonymy!——

Well! Robinson refuses my laboured Work. He has been at Bath and Bristol and cannot recover his Health sufficiently to *Enter upon new Engagements;* he is going to leave off Business and cannot prevail upon himself to undertake so large a Book he says——Did *you* see or hear of him? or did he pass any Time at Belvedere House? and does he undertake any *smaller* Works I wonder? *Lesser* is a Word I will not use, but it would gratify me to know.[2]

I sent him a Letter to put him in better Spirits if possible and better Humour, for tho' I despair not of selling my Stuff; I shall hate hawking it about London which will at last be the Case.

Mr. Piozzi's Gout begins to remit, he has had it in his Hands most cruelly: the Feet have escaped pretty well; yet he cannot walk because he cannot lean upon a Stick.

The incomparable Coterie you mention as loving and remembering us with Kindness will make me rich amends in their Society if I can wind up My little Matters and come to Bath in Spring: but here is a Degree of Scarcity and Dearness both present and expected that worries My Master and his House-Book horribly——You and I used to say that Abbess was the best Managing Servant in the World——even tho'——&c. &c. and that Things were always cheapest done under her Care. But I know not how it is, or whether by her Fault or not; Every thing costs double: besides double Taxes, double necessity of Expence and so forth. London will be much my Terror indeed, but I hope our Stay will be a short one.

Oh what would have become of my wretched Nerves had I been in the Theatre that awfully impressive Night!——what would have become of *your* Nerves—or Dear Mrs. DeLuc's?[3] The Tryal would have been *too* great. Susan and Sophy were there, so was Mr. Gillon. It will go hard with the Traytor I am told: If the Jury did not find him guilty—The King's *Guardian Angel* must appear in *Person* to protect him next Time—because it will be such Encouragement for the Jacobins to attempt his Life, that nothing *less* can save him.

Farewell! Dear Mrs. Pennington, and give our truest Love to your good Husband and Mother; and believe me / ever yours / H: L: P.

If you see Dr. and Mrs. Randolph or Miss Case tell them with what Pleasure I recollect the hours spent in their Company and Mrs. <DeLuc's>.

[On the Cover]

Mr. Dobbs from the 2d and 7th Chapter of Daniel proves that the second appearance of Messiah will be in Ireland.[4] Also the 23d Chapter of Jeremiah.[5] He "believes the Word Armaggedon in the Hebrew to mean Armagh."

The Arms of Ireland also being the Harp of David with an Angel in its Front and the Crown being the Apostolic Tradition having long spoken of it as The Land of Saints and above all its exemption from Serpents and all venemous Reptiles proves that Satan the great Serpent is there to receive his deadly <Blow>.—

Ireland he says is no part of Great Britain. England was the last Toe of the Beast <1st> Chapter Isaiah.

Armageddon in the Hebrew Tongue and Armah or Armagh in the Irish means the same.[6]

Text: Princeton University Library. *Address:* Mrs. Pennington / Dowry Square / Hot Wells/ Bristol.

1. See *British Synonymy* 1:244–46. This passage touches on HLP's attitude toward her daughters. Thus, "Complete Forgiveness seems a shade short somehow of free Pardon, which in my notion implies absolute reinstatement in all that we enjoyed before the offence was given." Nevertheless, she acknowledged implicitly her hairsplitting distinction so that before *God*, "*he* will forgive, even our partial Remission of Offences, or how would the affairs of this world go on at all?" For a comparable passage on the nature of anger, see 1:90–91.

2. Belvidere boarding school for girls on Lansdowne Road in Bath belonged to Sophia and Harriet Lee. The association was made between it and George Robinson because he had so far published the first three volumes of *The Canterbury Tales.* See HLP to SL, 17 November 1787, n. 7.

3. In 1785 Margaret Cooper (d. 1806) had married Jean André de Luc (1727–1817), Swiss-born geologist and reader to Queen Charlotte.

4. Francis Dobbs (1750–1811) was an Irish politican who, in a speech delivered on 7 June, attacked the Union bill in the Irish House of Commons. In that speech he argued that the union was forbidden by the texts of Daniel and Revelation. It was then published as *The Genuine Speech, of Francis Dobbs, Esq. . . . in which is predicted the Second Coming of the Messsiah* (Dublin: J. Jones, 1800).

Early in his text, Dobbs set forth three propositions: "The first is, the certainty of the second advent of the Messiah; the next, the signs of the times of his coming, and the manner of it; and the last, that Ireland is to have the glorious preeminence of being the first kingdom that will receive him" (p. 36).

5. To bolster his arguments for the second coming, Dobbs points to Jer. 23 as "one of the plainest and strongest. . . . 'Behold the day is come saith the Lord, that I will raise unto David a righteous branch, and a King shall reign and prosper, and shall execute judgment and justice in the earth—in his days Judah shall be saved and Israel shall dwell safely, and this is his name whereby he shall be called the Lord our Righteousness. . . .' " See especially pp. 39–41.

6. HLP is here summarizing the following passage from Dobbs's *Genuine Speech* (pp. 43–45):

"The army that follows the Messiah . . . amounts to 144,000, and there are a few passages in the Revelations of St. John, that denote the place where they are to be assembled." Dobbs concludes that the place of assembly will be Ireland. "The arms of Ireland is the Harp of David, with an Angel in its front. The Crown of Ireland, is the Apostolic Crown. Tradition has long spoke of it as a Land of Saints, and if what I expect happens, that prediction will be fulfilled. But what I rely on more than all is our miraculous exemption from all the serpents and venemous tribe of reptiles. This appears to me in the highest degree emblematic, that Satan, the great serpent, is here to receive his first deadly blow."

Armagh is etymologically unrelated to Armageddon: *ard magh,* the "high plain," i.e., a flat, open space.

TO JOHN LLOYD

Brynbella
18: June 1800.

Ah Dear Mr. Lloyd that was the last Wednesday and the last Evening: The *Object* of your kind Enquiries has been chained to his Bed since Thursday—unable to have it even *made under him.*

I never saw so rough a Relapse, he has not now a Hand to ring a Bell with; or leisure from his Anguish to reflect on the Disappointment suffered by him and by / Dear Sir / Your ever obliged and Faithful / Servant H: L: Piozzi.

Text: National Library of Wales, MS 12421D. *Address:* J. Lloyd Esq. / Wygfair.

TO LADY WILLIAMS

Brynbella
Longest Day 1800

My dear Lady Williams

Will be sorry to hear Mr. Piozzi has never left his bed——Scarcely, to have it made——Since I wrote last. The law suits have terminated as they commonly do in Compromise and Reference. Sir John Williams was exactly right, the suit which could not be Substantiated was at length withdrawn——and Peace purchased (cheaply I think) with 50£ a Year.—

The news from Italy was what I expected when neighbour Paul deserted so and broke poor Swarroffs heart,[1] who had broken so many Heads. Poor Mr. Piozzi feels so much Agony in his own heel he can Scarce grieve for his wretched Country: tho' the very Place he comes from is now the Theatre of War.[2]

Accept our Truest Respects. My best Intelligence of my Neighbour's Motions is from my Window, and I see Smoke at Llanerch Park now—Dear Madam adieu! and do me the honour to feel perswaded that no Person is more Affectionately / Your Ladyships Obedient Servant than H: L: P.

Text: Ry. 1 (1796–1802).

1. HLP had been following the fortunes of Suvórov during the spring. On 8 April *The Times* reported:

"Marshal *Suworow* is disgraced. The Emperor [Paul] has deprived him of the title of *Italicus*, and prohibited the drums from beating before him according to custom. The colours are no longer displayed as he passes, and his name is omitted in public prayers. He is accused of having caused the misunderstanding between the two Imperial Courts."

On 14 and 15 April *The Times* reported unconfirmed dispatches announcing Suvórov's death, and on the 22d a retraction of them. But on 9 June the same newspaper wrote, "Government has at length received official information [that] Field-Marshal Suworow . . . died at Petersburgh on the 18th of May."

2. On 2 June "Bonaparte entered the city of Milan with an army of 45,000 men, where he proclaimed his intention of restoring the Cisalpine Republic, with the free exercise of the Catholic religion, and appointed a provisional government. Being here joined by General Moncey, from Switzerland, with 20,000 men, the Chief Counsel pushed his army forward, under the command of Berthier; who successively became master of Pavia, Lodi, Cremona, Orsi-Novi, Brescia, Placentia, and Stradella; at which latter place, on the 8th, he collected his forces." See *GM* 70, pt. 1 (1800): 572–73.

TO THE REVEREND LEONARD CHAPPELOW

Brynbella
23: June 1800.

Dear Mr. Chappelow

You are very good to me indeed and your Advice is wise. If my Master is inclined towards taking it I shall not perswade him to the contrary——I never did directly or indirectly try to lead either of my Husbands to a Scheme of Expence in my Life; and that is a very great Thing for any Lady to say, who has lived 16 Years with one Man, and 17 with another. He will probably wish on his *own* Account to have a little London this Year. Mr. Giles is to be settled with, and so I understand is Jacob;—and if they go on together again, Mr. Piozzi talks of taking away some Papers and some Linen left now at Streatham Park; he has besides a little Boy at School there, whom *never to see at all,* is a *Strange* Plan; though seeing too often is a weak and bad one.

Your Kindness however is really beyond Thought, and gives me Spirits to go on with a Book which will I fancy finish with *a King of Italy* like Odoacer in the sixth Century,[1] and then we shall say *Volvitur* &c.[2] I never heard of the Return of the Greatheeds. I never hear any thing but from the public Papers—*They* give me hopes Young Bertie will come Time enough to be Groom's Man to young Siddons when he marries that Miss Scott who is going to bestow on him 10000£ *o'year*.[3]

I have not yet told you that Mr. Piozzi had a furious Relapse of Gout——such as I really never did witness till now—four Days outrageous Agony; and a foot like Philoctetes in Cambrays Telemaque.[4] All will be well however, and all is coming around, but he loses the Summer Season a Bed, and hears his own Complaints poor Soul! instead of those around him. What will become of us next Year God Almighty knows.—*Ipse vides* the Crops so thin, and the hopes of better days so exhausted; You must be kind to the Country Gentlemen *when you come into Power:* and if you don't understand this *last Line now,* you will understand it when you have been in Town a Week.

I am sure you are exceedingly kind to *me*: The Book will not injure those that buy it nor disgrace your Partiality I hope. Everybody—*but me*—will like the second Volume best: You have seen only the first. I wonder who White's Taster is? It will be strange wild Work sending it to and fro and no Copy at home—or none from which prodigious Alterations have not been made: how nervous the poor Author must be methinks with his or her Nonsense on the Road, where if once lost——'Twill be hard to make *it good*. To confess a Truth one *should* be on the Spot for 40 Reasons; but I will suppress them all rather than throw away my Master's Money. The Book has been written under many Disadvantages and may be printed under many more. Never mind! As to my Hand writing it answers no purpose at all. Cadells People made gross Mistakes with a Manuscript much neater written than this will be.[5] And there is a laughable Erratum or two in the Synonymes which ought above all other Things to have been exact.[6] That concerning Agnes and Agues in Johnson's Letters is droll enough too: yet the Compositors knew his Character better than mine.[7]

What will the Expedition of Queberon end in?[8] You must leave Sad Thoughts of the Dead at Weston which I hope will not long be *doleful* and think of our living World. When Lady Bradford finds herself forced upon external Objects, and necessary Cares; and has no one whom She can fright or teize: She will begin minding her Income and her Affairs——will gain Strength of Mind and Body, and live her next 20 Years more happily than *you* hope for, or She dreams of. Mind the Sibyl's Words, and forgive them; *they will come true.* But my truest Word is that I am Dear Sir ever Yours / H: L: Piozzi.

Mr. Gillon interests himself very kindly about the Book, he will tell you what passed between him and the People at Robinson's;——pray speak to him upon the Subject.[9]

Text: Ry. 560.97. *Address:* Rev: Mr. Chappelow / No. 12 Hill Street / Berkeley Square / London. *Postmark:* DENBIGH E <1800>.

1. Odoacer (ca. 433–93) was the first barbarian [i.e., German] king of Italy. He reigned from 476 to 493 and was slain on 15 March by Theodoric the Great (ca. 454–526), Ostrogothic king of Italy. See *Retrospection* 1:143–44, 155.
2. For "volvitur . . . humi," see the *Aeneid*, 11.640.
3. According to *The Times* on 17 June, "Mrs. Siddons's son, who is playing in Scotland, is about to be married to Miss Scott, of Glasgow, with a fortune of 10,000*l*. a year." See also 24 June.
But Henry Siddons (1774–1815) was to marry ca. 22 June 1802 Harriott Murray, who had been an actress at Covent Garden. See the *Morning Herald*, 20 April 1802; *The Times*, 23 June 1802.
4. HLP compares GP's gout-besieged foot to Philoctetes's pierced by an arrow. The incident is dramatized by François de Salignac de la Mothe Fénelon, archbishop of Cambrai, in *Les Avantures de Télémaque* (1699). The wound is described as filled with "black corrupted gore" so that the air was "infected," and "Before its stench the stoutest warriors fall." See *A New Translation of Telemachus in English Verse*, by Gibbons Bagnall, 2 vols. (Hereford, 1790), 2:68–69.

Thomas Cadell, bookseller. Portrait by Sir William Beechey; engraved by Henry Meyer from a drawing by William Evans. (Reproduced by permission of the Trustees of the British Museum, Department of Prints and Drawings.)

5. Cadell published HLP's *Anecdotes, Letters,* and *Observations.*
6. The *Monthly Review* 15 n.s. (September–December 1794): 244, pointed out, e.g., the following errata:
"Vol I, p. 33, 361, &c. we have *adjectivially,* for adjectively. P. 228. 'the *good* Duke of Orleans,' son of the Regent, and grand-father of the *bad,* erroneously said to have died in 1712, was born in 1703, and did not resign his breath . . . till 1752. P. 250, we think our animated authoress wholly mistaken in the idea which she has annexed to the class at present distinguished by the title of *People of Fashion.* The appellation does not imply *fops* and *coxcombs,* and *coquettes,* (as Mrs. P. imagines,) who derive their whole importance from the *fashion* of their dress, but rather means persons of family and fortune, in *fashion* for their taste and the elegance of their manners. . . . P. 319. Though we have lately heard much of *energies,* yet *to energize* is a new verb in our language, first started, we believe, by the writer of the present work. P. 356, Cuzzoni, the celebrated opera singer, is badly described by being called an *actress."*
Similar errors were pointed out for vol. 2.
7. In the first edition of *Letters* (2:203), SJ on 16 April 1781 purportedly wrote "The season for *agues* is now over." The italicized word was meant to be Agnès, for HLT and SJ had a joke of calling a "creeping" woman "Agnes" after Molière's *L'Ecole des femmes.* See SJ's letter to HLT, 25 October 1777 (2:13); Chapman 3:323–24.
8. In the *Morning Post,* 19 June, a report from a French dispatch: "The debarkation the English have effected at Quiberon has been productive of no result in their favour. The enemy are re-embarked, and all is tranquil on the coasts of Finisterre, there are 3000 men at Saint-Renan; and if the enemy present themselves, measures are taken for giving a good reception. . . . The English wished to procure some grain, but did not succeed: they only took away five and twenty cows, which they paid for." See also *The Times,* 19 June.
9. Gillon did not approach Robinson; but RD, who did on 11 June, had written to HLP: "Your Retrospection will be the universal Favourite. I called on Robinson the other day. He shewed me your Letter but said nothing" (Ry. 573.21). Actually he had told RD that he declined the work because he considered it to be too long and because his health was failing. See Gillon to HLP, 22 July 1800 (Ry. 578.66); also HLP to LC, 10 June.

THE REVEREND LEONARD CHAPPELOW TO HESTER LYNCH PIOZZI

Hill Street—
30 June 1800

Dear Madam—
Your last was dated 23 June.—I have not as yet been able to meet good Mr. Gillon, so that I have not Learnt what passed between him and the people at Robinsons.—After all why plague yourself about Robinson if any other Bookseller will give you your price.—White I have seen, He will immediately take the matter into consideration, talk with Brother and *Taster,*[1] but I could not yet persuade him to tell me who his Taster is.—I told him verbatim what Robinson said, namely that Age &c. &c. prevented his entering into any other Engagements, but that he was sure any one in the Trade would give you your price.— Such I told White was £1000. and he seemed not to object to the price.—And said calculations as to the number to be printed must be made.—He said the bookseller's advantage proceeded not from a 2d Edition. Little would be got in the

first Instance, but if the book was such a favourite as to admit of an 8° Edition then came their profits.—It is for you to think about the money business—Whether you must have at first all or ½—Paid as a material consideration. White generally prints books of Natural History and they you know are not for every body's money. Scientific works are not sold in great numbers—but I said your Retrospection would undoubtedly be seen upon every table in the Kingdom.—Printer's work and paper now are at an enormous price. White said some family records in Robinson's House[2] had affected him very much.

I am glad all things will be so arranged, that Mr. Giles or any Master in the world will possess (as Tenant) Streatham Park—as I have all along said 2 Houses would <reruin> you body and soul.—especially as times are.—I never heard any thing Like.—The poor in London are dreadfully suffering—Carter the Fishmonger in the city told me—that he has seen poor people taking from his dunghill—the gutts of fish which used to be eaten by the Hogs.—In the North of England meat is as dear as it is in London.—However we have a fine Hay Harvest, and great crops.—I was 8 days in a mourner's Coach—and never wish to experience again so dreadfully melancholy a scene.[3]—

I have not yet been able to form any opinion of the mysterious phrase in your Last Letter, an explanation of which I was to find before I had been in Town a week.—Do let me know to what you allude, for I hate to be so *puss Led*.—I am determined you see to make you scratch me after having thus plagued my brain to find out your meaning.[4]—

What dreadful news—yet the stocks rise.—and nothing is talked of but a Peace.—

Have *you* not to Miss Scot's £10,000—put the words per annum.—He is, if tis true, a lucky dog indeed—and never did the 2 *money-syllables* make a better match—Scot and Lot—here is stuff for an Epigram.—and Rymes in to the bargain.—

I have put the book about pretty handsomely, and I< > of Little Else.—What you say is already true.—an independent fortune of £3000 per annum:—a new country house at <Stoke> in Derbyshire and a Town House—the consultation of agents &c.—would put some people out of their senses—and others into their senses.—and so it has.—yea verily already I think it has.—but tell it not in Gath nor publish it in the *streets of Askelon*[5] nor Clwyd Vale.—Adieu dear Madam—tell Mr. Piozzi I grieve for the dreadful relapse.—Still I say he has but little mercy upon his poor stomach when he is well—nothing is so difficult of digestion as fat whether animal or vegetable—Two spoonfuls of oil after dinner with crude salad—is end <worth>—The gouty paroxyms are nature's tricks.—

Adieu

Yours ever L. Chappelow

Lord Kirkwall I often see—He is in high spirits—I hear he is going to be wedded.—His Lady will be able to put him into her Pocket and she will be rich.—for he is a good young man.[6]—

P.S. I am afraid to write a word in the news paper as I find so many people have paid forfeit—if tis found out 2*s* is to be paid. How would my master like that?— Will he run the hazard?—

Text: Ry. 562.65.

1. The booksellers Benjamin White II and his brother John.
2. See HLP to LC, 21 October 1793, n. 3.
3. The coach accompanying the body of Lord Bradford, which was being transported from London to Weston, Salop, for burial.
4. See HLP to LC, 7 July, n. 1.
5. 2 Sam. 1:20.
6. LC reported that John Fitzmaurice, Viscount Kirkwall, was to marry Mary Jane Ormsby of Porkington. For Mary Jane Ormsby, see HLP to PSP [ca. 26 July 1800], n. 5; for her wedding to Kirkwall, which did not take place, see HLP to PSP, 30 November 1801, n. 9.

TO THE REVEREND LEONARD CHAPPELOW

Brynbella
30: June 1800.

Dear Mr. Chappelow

You are not half as like Œdipus as I am like Sphinx; for I am ready to throw myself as She did *off the Rock:*——because you *cannot* find out my Riddle, *She* took the Leap as I remember because her Ænigma was understood.[1]

Well! don't you recollect a *Nice* Lady, whom you knew before you knew me; and who is not as many Years younger than you and I are, as you always *persist to say She is:* Now when this *Nice* Lady has taken Possession by *Conquest* or *Treaty*, of Territories now of right belonging to *North Carolina;* You will at least *deserve* to come in power, for having spoken favourably, when others spoke *un*favourably. And——so if it is *still* unintelligible,—
ask Mr. Gillon what I mean.[2]

About the Book, I am willing to be much more explicit; and hope to wind it up pretty tolerably, and to get what it is worth for it; and 1000£ will not be too much: They will make their Money twice over, because of breaking it into four Octavo Volumes for use of Schools, after the Quarto Edition is worked off. The Title page I gave in to Robinson was *this*.

> *Retrospection*—or a Glance backward upon the most Striking and Important Events, Characters, Situations and their Consequences, which the last 1800 Years have presented to the Observation of Mankind by
> Hester Lynch Piozzi.

The Motto is an apt one, and the *Quantity* about equal to Watson's Philip the 2d or perhaps 50 Pages over—not more;[3] tho' his was a full and elaborate Account of about five and forty Years particularly interesting to Europe—my Work a close-clapt Abridgment of what has past in the World since the Christian Æra—a Review of 18 Centuries, and will I really hope, be welcome to it.—

Mr. White will probably wish no Taster but yourself, no Recommendation but yours. If He *does* We will give him The 1st Portion of the 1st Volume and the 1st Portion of the 2d Volume for a Specimen.

If we are alive we shall come to London in October. I am perswaded that we shall:—and if Mr. Giles invites us, we will go to old Streatham Park in our way. Tell Mr. Gillon do Dear Sir—for I forgot—that Mr. Giles seems tardy in his Invitation. Ah Me! how I do wish our poor Labourers here and starving Tenants—poor Souls! had some of the Corn that enriches those full-fed Factors, to put in their little Children's *Estomacs*.[4]

Will Peace make the Poor any happier I wonder! That it will make the Rich more prodigal I doubt not; and that Shoals of Jacobins mad and wise will cross the Seas; and snap their Pistols at our poor King: whilst British Boobies will go over in Flocks to France, and admire to see The Medicæan Venus turned into a Parisian Belle.[5] There used to be an Italian Proverb of a Man who went out and came home with nothing to tell. Questo si chiama andar *a Roma senza vider il Papa.* They may do *that* easily enough now, unless Buonaparte sets up Chiaramonte in the *Old Chair,* which I think Him more likely to send away; and deposit with other Rareties in the Louvre.[6]

I long for the Parliamentary Debates now,[7] and I long for the Expedition to go off if it ever is to go:[8] and I long for some Bill to be past to preserve us from these Madmen's Attempts. Those who take Advantage of their Disordered Intellects by suggesting these strange Things, would be more scrupulous if their innocent Instrument was to suffer perhaps: Something should be done in short, and done quickly. Pray why did not Sheridan appear when called upon? I have no Room but just to say I will be careful of *My Master's ½ Crown,* and that I am Dear Sir Sincerely Yours / H: L: P.

Text: Ry. 560.98. *Address:* Rev.: Mr. Chappelow / No. 12 / Hill Street / Berkeley Square / London. *Postmark:* DENBIGH E JUL 2   <>.

1. For the riddle of the sphinx, see Sophocles's *Oedipus the King.*
2. For a full statement of the riddle, see HLP to LC, 7 July 1800.
3. Robert Watson (ca. 1730–81), *The History of the Reign of Philip the 2d, King of Spain,* 2 vols. (London: W. Strahan and T. Cadell, 1777).
4. HLP also knew that many grain merchants like Peter Giles became rich by price gouging. See, e.g., the trial of a Mr. Rusby "for having purchased, by sample, on the 8th of November last, in the corn-market, Mark-lane 90 quarters of oats, at 41s. per quarter, and sold 30 of them again in the same market, on the same day, at 44s." He was found guilty and the judge praised the verdict as an act of patriotism.

"Several other indictments for the same alleged crimes were tried during this year, which we fear tended to aggravate the evils of scarcity they were meant to obviate, and no doubt contributed to excite popular tumults, by rendering a very useful body of men odious in the eyes of the mob." See *AR,* "Chronicle" 42 (1800): 23.

5. For the Venus di Medici, see HLP to LC, 21 July 1796, n. 7.
6. HLP seemed not to be cognizant of changing French attitudes toward the pope and Roman Catholicism in general.

On 9 July 1800—with or without French approval—Pius VII arrived in Rome to "incredible acclamation. He immediately repaired to St. Peters where a solemn *Te Deum* was performed, at which an immense concourse of people attended. Such a jubilee has not been held at Rome for several centuries. . . . At night the whole city was illuminated, and several triumphal arches." See *AR*, "Chronicle" 42 (1800): 23–24.

7. The most important parliamentary issue of the session was the drawn-out war between France and the Allies. Britain's role was scrutinized by the Opposition and the ministry clung to its position of nonnegotiation.

On 8 May an Opposition member, Thomas Tyrwhitt Jones (1765–1811), led a debate in which he impugned the purpose of the war, denouncing it as a national burden. The speech was anti-Bourbon, anti-Allies, and antiministry. The subsequent motion failed to carry, 8 for to 59 against. On 27 June Sheridan resumed the attack on the same ground as Jones, and again the ministry triumphed over the Opposition, 27 for to 124 against. See *Parliamentary History* 35 (1800–1801): 214–25, 393–401,

8. After the French leaked news of the British expedition to Quiberon, the English presented their side. "A squadron, under the command of sir Edward Pellew, on the 4th of June, attacked the south-west of the peninsula of Quiberon . . . silenced the forts, and cleared the shore of the enemy. A party of soldiers then landed and destroyed the forts. An attack was afterwards made on various posts, and six brigs, sloops, and gun-vessels, were taken, a corvette burned, and a fort dismantled." Despite such successes, "it unfortunately happened, that our gun-boats, in returning, struck upon sand-banks, and above ninety men were made prisoners." See *AR* 42 (1800): 212–13.

TO THE REVEREND LEONARD CHAPPELOW

Brynbella
Monday Morning 7: July 1800

I am glad you have been so *Puss*-led and so *Pur*-plexed; the very Newspapers now give hints as broad as mine about the Loss of Territory to North *Carolina;* and Acquisition of old Grants renewed to Maryland:[1] But I had better mind my own Business. If White will pay 500£ upon delivering the Book on its first Publication, and 250£ six Months after, and 250£ again six Months after *that*—— one full Year from the Work's coming out—My Master will be content he says, and think his Wife deserves a new Gown and a Glass of Bath Water for her Pains. I read a Chapter near the beginning of the 1st Volume and a Chapter near the Conclusion of the 2d Volume to Mr. Lloyd of Wickwor—(Philosopher Lloyd as they call him at Sir Joseph Banks's.)[2] He liked it very much indeed——and says as you do, that it must be a favourite with the Town. I told him I would not as the Horse dealers do——warrant it *free from Blemish;* but I can promise it *A fast and easy Goer.*

Mr. Gillon is our good Ally, and I am really consoled no little by being informed that something is on poor Robinson's Spirits, which I hear from every one——Suspicion had crost my Mind just for a Moment only; that he had been bitten by *Snakes in the Grass*. Have you seen Mr. Gray the Prebendary of Chichester? He has been in Town I believe and is going down to his Bishop——a Living in the North Riding of Yorkshire and a Month's Residence in Sussex is awkward Preferment enough; yet I am glad he is preferred any how——he is an excellent Man——and I have a good Friend in him too.

Mrs. Mostyn and her Sister in Law Miss Mostyn are at Brighthelmstone we are told here: If you know *why* they are there, do tell. Odious Reports are always running about, but they are not true I trust. Lord Kirkwall will not marry a Woman of mean Birth for her Money sure, You mention only that She is tall and rich——but I should like *un peu de Blazon* for old Lleweney Hall. Bachygraig is putting into Tenantable Repair, and I do hope Edward Jones the late Tenant, will be coerced into making good at least some of the Contracts he subscribed to on entering the Premises.[3] Mr. Piozzi was excessively kind to my Caprices in not pulling all down as He was advised, and building a Snug Farm House with the Material——His Reward is coming already; the Tithes let particularly well: he will keep the *near* Fields or Town Ships in his own Hands and yet have an equal Sum to what the whole produced him last Year. Our Fields are parching on these Hills for want of Rain, and what you relate of London Poor pierces one's Heart. I am really very sick to see the Papers giving Accounts of charming Duchesses desirous to *amuse* their charming Daughters with feasts at an enormous Expence while People are perishing at their Doors for Want.[4] It is *so* exactly like the State of Paris in 1788, 1789 and 1790—*that it frights me.* We keep our little Cottagers as comfortable as we can. The Mostyns of Nantwilliam never come near us now—*They are affronted;*[5] and that *is a very good Thing*. My Master mends apace,—He has had the Gout so *very* severely this Time, that I expect him to be quite well for one full Year if not two.

This is a miserable eight-Pennyworth but I thought you would like to hear that Cold Bathing yet keeps me alive to finish my Work of which you give me such good *Anticipation*. Dear Mr. Chappelow Adieu and if you know any thing that Interests either my wiser—or my foolisher Feelings Tell it and be thanked a thousand Times by Your exceedingly obliged H: L: P.—

The *Times* told me that Miss Scott had 10000£ o'Year, and that She was going to give it Harry Siddons. My Fancy represents her a Lady of my eldest Daughters Age whom we used to hear of as a great Fortune many years ago——one of the Girls that *never marry*, or *say* they will never marry.

I *think* so.

Text: Ry. 560.99. Address: Rev.: Mr. Chappelow / No. 13. / Hill Street / Berkeley Square / London. Postmark: DENBIGH; E JUL 9 1800.

1. The riddle was finally deciphered by John Gillon in an undated letter to HLP: "Does not the Ænigma of *North Carolina* and *Mary* Land allude to the P——ss of W and Mrs. F——zh——t and their Christian Names. By the Bye I have heard nothing more of the C——lt——n House Business" (Ry. 579.154).
2. For Sir Joseph Banks, see HLP to LC, 19 March 1799, n. 12.
3. For Edward Jones of Bachygraig, see HLP to LC, 22 May 1799, n. 11.
4. The social season had been notable for masquerades, routs, fêtes, and balls, but none more opulent "than the Ball given on Wednesday night [11 June] by the Duchess of Devonshire. Her Grace had assembled on this occasion the most distinguished families of

the kingdom, at the head of which were the Prince of Wales, with all the Princes of the Blood" (*The Times*, 13 June; see also 14 and 16 June).
  5. For Samuel Mostyn and his wife, see HLP to LC, 30 August 1798, n. 15.

TO PENELOPE SOPHIA PENNINGTON

[ca. 26 July 1800][1]

My Dearest Mrs. Pennington's sweet Letter has lain too long unanswered. I am sorry Mr. and Mrs. Whalley are declining so; their pretty Cottage will be a shady Retreat for them this hot Weather—we are roasting here on the Sunny Side of a high Hill but never was such Hay made before: 40 Acres cut and carried in 12 Days is really curious and without *one* Shower. Did you observe the odd Phænomenon exhibited on Trinity Sunday in the Evening?[2] It alarmed those who *did* observe it, and our Caernarvonshire and Anglesea Neighbours, who understand not how many Tricks Electricity can play; were frighted to see the Sun apparently go *back* when he set, no fewer than Three Diameters of himself.[3]

Mr. Lloyd of Wickwor whom you have heard me mention as an Astronomer, and a Man well known at Sir Joseph Banks's &c. said it was a Surprizing Thing and for what he had observed wholly *new*. He attributed it to the State of the Atmosphere: The Same Appearance was noticed likewise at Shrewsbury. I *saw it not*, I was not looking.

We have Miss Owen with us; She cares not how the Sun rises or Sets so as her Brother keeps his Health[4] and her Niece Miss Ormsby gets a *proper* Husband of sufficient Dignity.[5] What is this Story of Harry Siddons? Is he really to marry Miss Scott the great Fortune of the North?—if he does, The Sun may set in the *East* if it will, without attracting our charming Friend's Attention I suppose; and no Wonder. Miss Lees say nothing, perhaps think the *more*. What a Thing it would be!

My Book must go to the public Market, and take its Chance in October. Buonaparte will possibly finish it for me, and destroy the Empire as he did the Papacy.[6] Our Ministry keep feeding Francis with Money,[7] for which he will sell not his Birthright like Esau, but all *except* his Birthright;[8] and content himself with the old Crowns of Bohemia and Hungary, resigning even the Name of King of the *Romans* to those Gauls who invaded 'em 2000 Years ago, and have never lost Sight of a Hope so late to be accomplished—as poor Rome's utter Destruction.[9] The Sun may well be seen to shew Signs and Wonders, when such Occurrences are coming forward.

Meanwhile what say you to Bishop Horsley's denouncing the *Schools* of Impiety and Sedition?[10] Did even our dear Dr. Randolph think that London was so far advanced in Wickedness?—or even Hannah more! It is truly dreadful. What says my fair Namesake Miss Case? She keeps fat and chearful I hope. Pray tell her how sincerely I am desirous of quick Dispatch in my pecuniary Affairs that we may get to Bath again and see our Friends in our own comfortable Way.

Mr. Piozzi and I have been married now 16 years, and we are used to keep our Anniversary but it happened at a perverse Time of the Week and Month this Year—and so instead of feeding the Rich, We fed the poor; and every one of our 35 Haymakers had a good Noggin of Soup and a Lump of Beef in it and a Suet Dumpling and they were like the People in the Deserter who Sing—Joy Joy to the Duchess wherever She goes.[11] And my Master's Health was *sincerely* drank tho not very *copiously* for Bread and Beer are yet considered as *Luxuries* in our poor Skin and Bone Country while the Lords and Ladies round the Capital are paying five Guineas for a Peach &c. and Daughters of Liverpool spend in one Entertainment, what frighted all France when requested for a Frolick of poor Antoinette—Daughter of the Cæsars.

Well! Mr. Piozzi has gone to a little—not a very little Expence—in repairing old Bachŷgraig for the new Tenant: our Neighbours advised him to tumble the venerable Ruin quite down, and build a snug Farmhouse with the Materials—but he would not—and so poking about we found some very curious Bricks with Stories on them composed in 1500, and one large one with Catherine de Berayne's Arms derived from Charlemagne—Twas She whose husband built the House you know—Sir Richard Clough—See Pennant,[12] and being descended immediately from fair Catherine of France whom Shakespear makes us familiar with, and who married Owen Tudor after her first husbands Death, Heroic Harry the 5th drew her Descent by the Mother's Side from Charlemagne.[13] I have set her Atchievement in Front now—and a Stone to say the Mansion was repaired and beautified by Gabriel Piozzi Esq. in the year 1800. It will last to the World's End now I believe.

The dear little Boy whom you used to love has spent his Vacation Time at Streatham again, he will I hope be wiser in proportion as he is less happy and less spoiled: *safer* he certainly is, and we hear a good Character of his Scholarship. Make a Thousand kind Words from us to your good Husband and Mother and believe me / Dear Friend ever yours / H: L: P.

Text: Princeton University Library. *Address:* Mrs. Pennington / Dowry Square / Hot Wells / Bristol.

1. An answer to PSP's letter of 29 June, HLP's was written shortly after her wedding anniversary on 25 July.
2. Trinity Sunday, the first Sunday after Pentecost, occurred in 1800 on 7 June.
3. See also *Thraliana* 2:1004.
4. For Margaret Owen and her brother John, the latter subject to temporary bouts of insane violence, see HLP to PSW, 18 August 1791, n. 2.
5. The Irish-born Owen Ormsby (1749–1804) had married Margaret (d. 1806), heiress of William Owen of Porkington, Salop. Their only child was Mary Jane (1781–1869), who through her mother was to inherit much of the Godolphin property in Salop. See HLP to PSP, 30 January 1793, n. 7.
6. HLP responds to the news of Austrian defeats in Italy. Thus, on 25 June, *The Times* reported bulletins from French newspapers: "The victory of the French Army was obtained at Marengo. The victory has decided the fate of Italy."
7. Not until 17 July did *The Times* publish the "convention" between England and Austria, which guaranteed the latter £2,000,000 sterling for the continued prosecution of

the war. But by September Thugut resigned; Prince Colloredo as chancellor and Count Cobenzl as vice-chancellor sought terms from Napoleon. By 9 February 1801, Austria was to accept the Peace of Lunéville.

8. Gen. 25:31–34.

9. HLP anticipated by several years the dissolution of the Holy Roman Empire in 1806, when the last of its emperors was acknowledged as Franz I of Austria, king of Hungary and Bohemia.

For HLP's allusion to the Gallic attacks in 57 B.C., see her letter to Q, 27 April 1796, n. 10.

10. In a debate in the Lords, Bishop Horsley maintained that "Schools of Jacobinical Religion, and Jacobinical Politics; that is to say, Schools of Atheism and Disloyalty, abound in this country; schools, in the shape and disguise of Charity-Schools and Sunday-Schools, in which the minds of the children of the very lowest orders are enlightened; that is to say, taught to despise Religion, and the laws, and all subordination." This statement (p. 25) is cited and expanded in *The Charge of Samuel Lord Bishop of Rochester to the Clergy of his Diocese, delivered at his Second General Visitation, in the Year 1800* (London: James Robson, 1800).

11. Charles Dibdin (1745–1814)—dramatist, actor, singer—had adapted a musical interlude from *Le Deserteur*, the popular creation of Michel-Jean Sedaine (1719–97). Dibdin's *The Deserter* was first performed at the Drury Lane theater during the 1773–74 season. The opening "air" in act 1 concludes with the choral line, "Joy and health to the Duchess, wherever she goes!"

12. Katheryn of Berain (1534/5–1591) married in the following order: John Salusbury (d. 1566); Richard Clough (d. 1570), knight of the Holy Sepulchre; Maurice Wynn (d. 1580) of Gwydir; Edward Thelwall (d. 1610). See *Y Cymmrodor* 40 (1929): 1–42.

For Pennant's description of Bachygraig, see HLP to SL, 4 November 1785, n. 1.

13. Catherine of Valois (1401–37), the youngest daughter of Charles VI of France, became the wife of Henry V on 2 June 1420. By 31 August 1422 she was a widow. Within a few years she established a liaison with Owen Tudor (d. 1461), a poor Welsh gentleman who had minimal court connections and whom she eventually married.

She appears in Shakespeare's *Henry V.* For her celebrated descent, see the archbishop of Canterbury's speech in the same play (1.2.32–95), wherein he insinuated that all females of the French royal line may trace their lineage back to "Charlemain." The insinuation is historically dubious.

TO THE REVEREND LEONARD CHAPPELOW

Brynbella
Thursday 14: August [1800].

You are always excessively kind to us Dear Mr. Chappelow. A Visit from Lord and Lady Bradford will be a great honour and if the Weather continues, a plentiful Harvest will add to the Chearfulness of our Scenery; and make a happy Contrast to the rougher Vale of Llangollen.[1]

Who knows but you may tempt the Recluses out to accompany you? Mr. Piozzi anticipates his Share of Happiness in seeing once again at the Forte Piano The charming Lady who used to sing his Musick—at Brussels: where I guess not why I did *not* see her when Lady Torrington shewed me so many Civilities in the Year 1787.[2]

I have written a Note to Stockdale—Kind, with Discretion: as the old Books bid us. There is literary Coquetry enough in the World, and I suppose Booksellers are perfectly well instructed in Author's Wiles——So I used none; but said I scarce thought myself at Liberty to receive Proposals from any other Gentleman, till the Negotiation with Robinson was wholly broken off. This is true, and we must settle it with Some of them in October, and as Hamlet says by his Actors It will be time Then to leave off pulling Faces—and *begin*,[3] or we shall not come out with The Year as I would wish.

Your amiable Adjutant Mr. Gillon, says we must make our first Debut at Streatham Park——which Sir Walter James who left us Yesterday Morning, protests *is a dull Place to this.*[4]

A few refreshing Showers would however greatly add to *our* Beauty; for these Hills are a little too much of a Cote Rotie this burning Summer, which scarce can penetrate the Thick Shades at Weston, where I dare say there is Verdure enough besides roast Meat for the Venison.

A propós Dr. Myddelton will tell you a curious Anecdote of a Buck in his Park which as a Naturalist will strike you forcibly. We spent two Days at his Place very agreeably last Week, they are really charming People.[5] You say nothing of Peace and War—though tis from you we expect all true Intelligence: I am in Love with Marsh's Book, and think it as well timed as well written.[6]

Adieu! we shall begin to count *Hours* not *Days* from the 20th but send a Letter first to say when the Cold Chicken and Sandwiches &c. shall be ready. Mr. Piozzi who joins in a Thousand Respects and Regards, counts on the Pleasure he is to share with Dear Sir Your *now* more than ever Obliged H: L: P.

I put no Compliments into The Envelope——You must make them all for me—I thought that more respectful, tho' Mr. Piozzi half insisted upon *his*.

Text: Ry. 561.163.

1. Lord and Lady Bradford, accompanied by LC, spent three hours at Brynbella on 24 August. See LC to HLP, 28 August (Ry. 563.66).
2. See *Thraliana* 2: 679 and 684; *Observations* 2:380.
3. *Hamlet*, 3.2.251–54.
4. For Sir Walter James, see HLP to PSP, 27 March 1798, n. 2.
5. For the Reverend Robert and May Myddelton of Gwaynynog, see HLP to LC, 15 September 1794, n. 1; 2 July 1799, n. 9.
6. Herbert Marsh (1757–1830) was successively bishop of Llandaff and of Peterborough. The book HLP admired was *The History of the Politicks of Great Britain and France, from the Time of the Conference at Pillnitz to the Declaration of War against Great Britain*. With an appendix, containing a narrative of the attempts made by the British government to restore peace, etc., 2 vols. (London: John Stockdale, 1800). Originally written and published in German (Leipzig: Oykische, 1799).

TO LADY ELEANOR BUTLER

Brynbella
Saturday 16: August [1800].

Lord Henry Petty and Mr. Smyth brought the Dear Letter from the dear Ladies——and dined here; but would not pass the Night, They are very fine Young Men.[1] Your Ladyship and Miss Ponsonby will soon have Lord and Lady Bradford and Mr. Chappelow at lovely Llangollen——They will come on here I hope and trust——Will they perswade you to come with them? Oh yes: I am *sure* they will, and return together; and we will give You a Cold Dinner like last Year's Frolic, and it will do us so much honour, and make Mr. Piozzi such rich Amends for the painful Weeks he passed in Spring—and we will tell your Ladyship and Miss Ponsonby all the News—you know already, about Miss Ormsby's talked-on Marriage with Lord Kirkwall, and how *every*body (for once) seems pleased with the Choice made by two charming Young People who could have found nothing so good as themselves anywhere else.[2]

We shall begin counting Days tomorrow——and on Monday we shall begin counting *Hours* till this fine Weather gives us Opportunity of once more rejoycing in a Visit which confers so much Happiness on the Friends and true Servants which the Dear Ladies possess at Brynbella

Text: Osborn Collection. *Address:* R. H. Lady Eleanor Butler / Llangollen / Denbighshire. *Postmark:* DENBIGH.

1. Henry Petty, later Petty-Fitzmaurice (1780–1863), third marquess of Lansdowne (1809). He had been educated as Lord Henry Petty at Westminster School, at Edinburgh, and at Trinity College, Cambridge, where he received his M.A. in 1801. When only twenty-six, he became chancellor of the exchequer.
Percy Clinton Sydney Smythe (1780–1855), Viscount Strangford (I., 1801), was educated at Trinity College, Dublin, where he took his B.A. in 1800. He was to serve as a notable, if controversial, diplomat, and in 1825 to be created Baron Penshurt of Penshurt, Kent.
For HLP's comments on Lord Henry Petty, as cousin of Viscount Kirkwall, see *Thraliana* 2:1006.
2. By June 1801 Miss Ormsby's "talked-on Marriage with Lord Kirkwall" was over. See HLP to Lady Eleanor Butler, 14 June 1801 and n. 12.

TO LADY ELEANOR BUTLER

Brynbella
Wensday 27: August 1800.

And how did our Dear Ladies get home? Safely I hope—It could not be a more beautiful Evening, and before your Chaise had reached Ruthin——There was an outline of Snowdon discernible. When you do us the honour to write a Line Oh do say how this horrible Conflagration of the Hills has been stopt by Rain which is rather doing harm to our Harvests, and should bring compensation from Radnorshire and Llangollen. It is so far as I know an unprecedented Calamity in our Island: one has read of it in Spain, but till yesterday's Paper arrived, We had formed no Idea of its Extent.[1]

I could not last Sunday express my Concern about the Difficulties with Regard to that dear and celebrated Cottage—which never *never* must slip from the Possession of Ladies which have made its very Name Immortal.

Miss Ponsonby mentioned *Ten Years* as secure I think: In that Time some Method will surely be hit upon for perpetuating the quiet and unalienable Tenure.[2]

Lady Eleanor was very kind in prompting me to write to St. Vallery.[3] I will be more correspondent to Command in future as Ariel says—and do my Spiriting gently.[4]

Adieu dear and lovely Ladies and believe me that no one is more admiringly / Your true and faithful Servant / than is H: L: Piozzi.—

Text: Wicklow MS 4239. National Library of Ireland. *Address:* Right Honourable / Lady Eleanor Butler / Llangollen / Denbighshire. *Postmark:* DENBIGH.

1. See HLP to LC, 27 August, n. 3.
2. In the summer of 1800 the cottage and garden called Plas Newydd had a new landlord, who threatened to curtail the lease held by Lady Eleanor Butler and Sarah Ponsonby for about twenty years.
   The Ladies consulted an attorney from Mold, whom they paid initially three guineas for advice and then five guineas more on 7 July to draw up " 'the Instrument which is to secure us from molestation during the lives of John and Mary Edwards. . . .' " Thus armed, they found that " 'the heart worrying business' " was to be over by late summer. Not until 5 January 1819, however, were they able to buy Plas Newydd. See Elizabeth Mavor, *The Ladies of Llangollen* (London: Michael Joseph, 1971), pp. 133, 179.
3. Joseph Cooper Walker of St. Valeri, near Bray.
4. *The Tempest*, 1.2.297–98.

TO THE REVEREND LEONARD CHAPPELOW

Brynbella
Wensday 27: August 1800.

I *must* write to Thank you dear Mr. Chappelow; because among all the Kindnesses we have received from your active and generous Friendship, this last of making for Mr. Piozzi and me so valuable an Acquaintance as that of Lord and Lady Bradford——is really highest upon the List.

You all got home Safe I hope after seeing a hundred fine Places and fine Things that will put poor little Brynbella out of your Heads: but if you could have staid the Night over, There was a Setting Sun just at the Point which we call the Orm's Head,[1] which would have made you amends——and which no Inland Situation—not Hawkestone itself, can exhibit.[2]

Never was a More beautiful Evening, and I think You had good Light for parting with the Dear Ladies too. We are cutting and carrying as fast as possible, and I am only anxious for these Fires that we read of upon the distant Hills.[3] Will this Rain suffice to quench them? Our Newspaper (silent on the Subject till Yesterday) now gives me serious Alarm, and we have *fancied* a Smell of Burning ever since. Do you know where our amiable Friend Mr. Gray is to be written to? I owe him a long Letter and many Thanks for his pretty little Book[4]——but whether the Prebendary of Chichester is in the South with his Bishop—or in the North at his Living, or at Oxford with his Baronet[5]—No guess can I make.

The Randolphs[6] and Lord Mountjoy[7] come next Saturday; They have been at the Lakes, and have among other pretty Things seen my pretty Daughters, making Drawings there under the Rocks.

Mr. Mostyn and his Sister are come to Llewessog, and Mrs. Wynne (his Mother, whom I think you remember:) is returned to this Country looking like a Girl of 25 years old. We met her at the Bishop's this morning—and could not believe our own Eyes.

Lord Kirkwall is at Porkington——of course.

Adieu dear Mr. Chappelow and say when and where we are to meet. In the Library at old Streatham Park I hope, if You leave Weston before our Journey. Mr. Piozzi is so pleased with himself since Lady Bradford told him he was *not altered* in all these 17 Years, that he looks better than he did on Sunday, and *says* his Voice is more under his own Command. I must take care to keep my Pen under Command tho' and finish this Nonsense, the last you will have this Summer / from H: L: P.

Text: Ry. 560.100.

1. Located northwest of St. Asaph and Bodelwyddan, Little and Great Ormes Head are among the scenic attractions of North Wales on Llandudno Bay. They are notable for their imposing limestone cliffs with caverns formed by sea action.
2. Lord and Lady Bradford and LC planned to visit Hawkstone, the seat of Sir Richard Hill (1732–1808), second baronet, near Hodnet, Derbyshire.
3. According to the *Chester Chronicle,* 22 August:
"A very singular occurrence has lately taken place on the mountains ranging alongside the Vale of Llangollen.—The furze, heath, and fern, at the close of the last week, has been burning for more than eight days, and the flames had spread themselves in different directions to an amazing extent. On Thursday and Friday, the range of fire on that side of the *Vale* adjoining Sir Watkin William Wynn's estate at Wynnstay, was supposed to extend from eight to ten miles, and on the opposite side about four. In the same time, the smoke is seen to ascend in immense volumes to a most amazing height, and the whole country is enveloped as with a thick mist. . . . [At night] a circumference of twenty miles appears like an immense volcano, vomiting forth the most scorching flames, which in their progress have unfortunately communicated themselves to several fields of standing corn." The fire was in fact extinguished by a torrential downpour.
4. *A Catechism, in which the Principal Testimonies in Proof of the Divine Authority of Christianity are Briefly Considered* (Oxford: Hanwell and Parker; J. Cooke, 1800). 36 pp. 12°.
5. RG could have been with Shute Barrington, bishop of Durham, on a holiday in the south of England; he could have been at his rectory in Craike; or he could have been with "his baronet" in Oxford, identified in RG's will as "Sir Henry Browne." See P.R.O., Prob. 11/1839/666.

HLP was aware of RG's whimsical but longstanding description of the Reverend Henry Browne (1760–1838) as a "baronet" because the latter was the fourth in the succession of his family to hold the living of Hoby, Leics. He went there first in 1784 following the death of his uncle, also named Henry Browne.

6. For Francis Randolph and his wife, Mary, see HLP to PSW, 29 August [1791], n. 9; to PSP, 10 March 1799, n. 2.

7. Charles John Gardiner (1782–1829), Viscount Mountjoy [I, 1798]; cr. earl of Blesington [Blessington] (1816). His Irish estates were said to have been worth £14,000 yearly.

TO PENELOPE SOPHIA PENNINGTON

> Brynbella
> Saturday Night
> 6 or 7 of September 1800.

Dear Mrs. Pennington's Eyes yet serve her I find to write the very charmingest Letters in the World; and Doctor Randolph is of the same Opinion: That to the Travellers was admirable, and my own just received—most Excellent. They left Wales Yesterday and have carried ugly Weather home with them; but I hope and *think* that the bright Sun illuminated their last Glimpse of Denbighshire from the Heights round romantic Llangollen. I never saw People so well or so happy or so good humoured on a Journey, where Inconveniencies must necessarily arise, such as would teize many Tempers accustomed to *Home Life*. Every body in our Neighborhood would have adored them had they staid long enough: but Duty called, and you expected them, and they are flown away.

What the meaning can be of *Breadrising* is past my Power to divine: Wheat falls, and Grass grows, and these Rains have put out the Fires which injured the hilly Grounds.[1] Nothing is truer than your Observation of Men's counteracting Providence in all they can—but of late times some Perswasion Seems to have been given them that it *should be* counteracted. Victory bestows Honour on our Arms, but produces no Good to our Nation; Plenty creates no Peace, and Opulence no Wealth among us: I cannot fathom it—We seem upon the Eve of a general Pacification thro' all Europe[2]—but I scarce expect *Quiet* in *any* Country (much less our own) to be the Consequence of such extensive Treaties.

'Tis pleasant to see any body Happy now, and the Dear Randolphs' Company was a Cordial. My amiable Neighbour Lady Orkney's Felicity is too tumultuous, one is fearful of its not lasting. Her Son marries Miss Ormsby, whom perhaps you have seen—and certainly heard of—She will have 10000£ o' Year: a fine form, and unblemished Manners—Gentle withal and young—A Match that pleases all the World I think.

Poor dear Jane Holman complains of the Greatheeds that they were too fine to visit her in London; She is recovering from her severe Lying In, and will I hope be happy tho' the World was all *dis*pleased at her Connexion.

Mrs. Siddons will have a cruel Loss if her husband dies, though he was no professed Wit, nor Beau—nor *Damon:* and tho' I doubt me much if he was even the *very prudent* Man folks take him for.³ Yet will he be a Loss,—and *seldom comes a better's* no bad Proverb. Her Son was expected to make his Fortune among the Fair at one Time, but I now hear no more on't.

Mrs. Wynne, Cecilia's Mother in Law is come home to Wales ten Years Younger than She left it, and infinitely handsomer of Course. I do not think that will be *my Case* when I leave home next; but selling my Book advantageously will I suppose heighten *my Bloom*. We must have *Things as they are*—as Baretti used to say when he threw ill at Back Gammon: My Master's capital Health must keep mine up; I never saw *him* in better Looks, and Mrs. Randolph will tell you how smart he has made old Bachŷgraig—the Name of which they both forgot I'm sure, before Two Miles were past——and Lord Mountjoy only saw Lleweney. Whenever Lady Hesketh crosses your Walks say to her how much I respect her,⁴ and how glad I feel that the sweet little Princess is to be happy in virtuous and wise Attendants on her Infancy, Lady Elgin and Miss Hunt.⁵

"Never harm nor Spell nor Charm will come *that* Faery's
Pillow nigh——while *They* sing her Lullaby."⁶

Brynbella is *the fashion*: We have People coming to take Views from it, and Travellers out of Number—*Tourists* as the silly word is.

Miss Thrales are among the Lakes, I believe there are modish Places now for Summer as for Winter modish *Streets*. Comical enough! yet the general face of Things must be confessed very gloomy: tho' Stocks rise and *that* comforts many who look superficially,—or that never *look at all* beyond Finsbury Square and Hydepark Corner.

My Fear is lest Mr. Pitt should be one of those—if such the Case *He* will be *amazed* whenever the evil Moment comes, which would only grieve, not amaze / Yours / H: L: P.

Kind Words to all you Love.

Text: Princeton University Library. *Address:* Mrs. Pennington / Dowry Square / Hot Wells / Bristol. *Postmark:* DENBIGH.

1. The price of bread rose because that of grain (particularly wheat) and flour rose. At the end of August the "average" price in England and Wales was 96*s*. 2*d*. per quarter. At the end of September it was 107*s*. Flour in the course of that same month had gone from approximately 85*s*. to 100*s*. See *GM* 70, pt. 2 (1800): 807, 911.

2. There was much talk of peace in August but no visible sign of it. For example, an Austrian diplomat in Paris on 28 July signed "Articles of a Preliminary Treaty of Peace," but when he brought it to Vienna, the emperor refused to ratify it. Bonaparte accordingly terminated the armistice that came into being after Marengo and ordered the French armies on the Continent into action.

Moreover, it was rumored that the French would soon offer the British government a naval armistice. See *GM* 70, pt. 2 (1800): 882–83.

3. HLP responds to a statement written by PSP, 3 September 1800 (Ry. 567.92). "Mr. Lysons called upon me the other Day for an hour and gave me a very bad account both of

Mr. Siddons and Sally.—I fear they will verify your *Prophecy*.—He is a confirmed cripple and Mrs. Siddons writes me, 'loses his strength and appetite while Sally's attacks are more frequent than ever.' "

Unlike the classical Damon, Siddons was not remarkable as the faithful friend. He was also unlike the Damon who loved Musidora in James Thomson's "Summer," *The Seasons* (1726–30).

4. PSP had also written to HLP about Miss Hunt, quoting Lady Hesketh as an authority. "That Miss Hunt they esteem so highly in the *Blue Stocking* Circle at Bath, is appointed sub governess to our little Princess. Lady Hesketh and Mrs. Holyroyd who are at Clifton say, 'She is *so well qualified* that it cannot but prove a great National Benefit.' "

5. Martha, née White (1739–1810), had married in 1759 Charles Bruce (1732–71), fifth earl of Elgin and ninth earl of Kincardine. At this time she was governess to Princess Charlotte of Wales and was to remain in that post until 1804. She was regarded as "very little cultivated, but has good principles Religious & moral, & is careful to establish all proper ideas on both subjects in the mind of the Princess" (Farington 6:2028).

Miss Hunt was subgoverness to the young princess from 1800 to 1803 at an annual salary of £300. Succeeding a Miss Garth and probably granted a pension in 1805, she was described as "a Lady who has resided at Bath with her mother. . . . [She] is a very sensible, discreet woman, of plain manners" (ibid. 4:1462; *The Court and City Register*, 1801–3.

6. HLP's variation on the lines of a song in *A Midsummer Night's Dream* (2.2.16–19).

TO THE REVEREND LEONARD CHAPPELOW

Brynbella
19: September 1800.

We will come presently now Dear Mr. Chappelow: our Visitants are gone, and nothing remains but to pack up and away—Those indeed are Ceremonies which will take up no short Time: It is our Intent however to be with you by the Day appointed, 8 or 10th of October.

Shall we get safely thro' Birmingham?——and is it no dangerous Exploit to go into the Environs of London and to a Corn Merchant's Country Seat? Lord bless me! suppose the Rioters should pull down poor old Streatham Park!² Our Ladies would sure enough try to lay all Expences of rebuilding it on *us,* and say we deserved what followed for having *disgraced* their *Family Mansion* by *Letting it.* I am really more than half alarmed, but where we all pay so largely to Government Protection may reasonably be expected sure, and both Landlord and Tenant *ought* to be indemnified when suffering in such a Cause.

"Draw out the Chelsea Cuirassiers,
Where are the Putney Volunteers?
March up to Finsbury in a Trice,
Give our Allies at Bow—advice":²

How you and I remember laughing when Garrick pronounced these Lines in the Rehearsal!—so much worse are the present Moments than those of Charles the 2d and more turbulent——altho' *they* were not calm ones:³ but what was then hyperbolical and ridiculous, now seems more than verified—Tis our best help and hope.

Why are the Poor so little attended to I wonder, and their wants so ill supplied. Here is a lovely Harvest, and one hears of Grain brought in to every Port every day. I thought that was only Newspaper Nonsense, till Accounts from Liverpool assured us there was plenty in *their* Town.

If Justice and Generosity are both dead amongst us, and Humanity to be found only in Kots[e]bue's Plays or Godwin's Novels; Common Prudence should suggest a Consideration for the Poor in Days so dangerous, when they have Teachers innumerable to acquaint them of their own Strength and Capacity (—Ability—I should say—) to help themselves.

The Spirit of Riot and Insurrection has so grown upon us within these last ten Years—no Property can be called safe: and those who are charitable will lose that applause they used to be sure of, when they may be called *Cowards* for merely doing an Indispensable Duty.

The Times are very bad, and when I see Ladies with Jewels about them from Seringapatam, I think of Master Bridgeman's Fable of the Cock and Diamond on a Dunghill——one Grain of Wheat or Barley would be better.[4]

Are all the Dear young People well?[5] I hope so: we shall be better Friends when I have more Time to ingratiate myself. Mean while present us Dear Sir most respectfully to their admirable Parents——most kindly to *them*, and / Believe me ever your more and more obliged / H: L: P.

Mr. Piozzi begs you to present his proper Devoirs—We shall take advantage of this fine Weather and visit Hawkestone.
[In Gabriel Piozzi's hand]:
P.S. I Believe we shall Leave Brynbella Monday 6 of October, and go to Wrexham the first day, the Tuesday to Sir Richard Hill Place, and Wensday to Lord Bradford, ma qualche accidente <può> arrivare, e forse non potremo <essere> a Weston sino le' d'eci d'ottobre—

Text: Ry. 560.101.

1. On Saturday and Sunday (13 and 14 September) efforts were made to induce Londoners to follow provincial towns and "to attend at the Corn market on Monday" in order to bring about lower bread prices. The lord mayor, pledged to secure the peace, gathered together all his civil officers and certain volunteer corps.
On Monday, 15 September, about one thousand persons gathered at the Corn Exchange, where they rioted. On the 18th the king issued "A Proclamation for suppressing Riots and Tumults, and for protecting and encouraging the free Supply of the Markets." Nonetheless, the riots continued in various parts of London, not stopping until almost the end of the month. See *GM* 70, pt. 2 (1800): 894–95.
2. Garrick appeared in the role of Bayes in *The Rehearsal* forty-one times from 1742 to 1772. New lines were constantly interpolated to give the play a sense of contemporaneity. Of the lines quoted by HLP one occurs only in the recitativo of the original act 5. It appears in an exchange between the General ("Draw down the *Chelsey* Curisiers") and the Lieutenant General ("The Band you boast of, *Chelsey* Curisiers, / shall in my *Putney* Pikes, now meet their Peers").

3. *The Rehearsal* was written by George Villiers, second duke of Buckingham, in collaboration with others, such as Samuel Butler, Thomas Sprat, and Martin Clifford. It was first performed in 1671.

4. See fable 1 of Sir Roger L'Estrange's *Fables* [after Aesop] (1717).

> As a Cock on a Dunghill was i' scratching the Litter,
> He happened to spy a Diamond Glitter.
> Had a Jeweller found it, says he to himself,
> It had been of Worth to a Covetous Elfe;
> But as I am a Cock, 'tis to me but a Stone.
> And a Barley Corn's better Forty to One.

5. The children of Lord and Lady Bradford were as follows: George Augustus (1789–1865); Charles Orlando (1791–1860); Orlando Henry (1794–1827); Henry Edmund (1795–1872).

TO LADY WILLIAMS

                                                    Brynbella
                                                    20: September 1800.

My dear Lady Williams must not account herself unlucky in losing Mr. Bianchi——whose Visit gave us nothing but Concern: He passed three Days here——was really quite ill the whole time; never touched an Instrument and could no more have Sung a Note than *I* could. His anxiety to be gone increased his Complaints, and never man was more low spirited.[1]——We likewise are beginning to think of leaving dear pretty Wales and I feel half low spirited about it myself. Let us at least have the Satisfaction to hear that we leave Sir John perfectly recovered, Your Ladyship and Mrs. Williams quite well.

I grieve about these odious Riots more than enough, yet some strange Fate seems really to hang over every Nation, for ours need not be unhappy for anything I can discern:——The Harvests are prosperous, and our Navy every where victorious;[2] Yet nothing seems to produce either Advantage abroad, or Comfort and Quiet at home—but I shall send better—I hope *Chearfuller* Accounts when once arrived within the Vortex of that Grand Mart of Intelligence, that Mass of Good sense and Folly, Misery and Merriment, our famous Capital City.

Let us carry with us Good Wishes from ever kind and ever-friendly Bodylwyddan—where will remain ever much of her Heart who is most sincerely / Your Ladyship's faithful as Obliged / H: L: Piozzi.

Text: Ry. 1 (1796–1802).

1. Francesco Bianchi (ca. 1751–1810) wrote between 1779 and 1794 about fifty operas that were performed at important Italian theaters. In 1795 he came to London as composer to the King's theater. He was also a first-rate harpsichordist and often performed publicly. He was "anxious" to be gone because on 15 November he was to marry Jane Jackson (1776–1858), "whose scientific knowledge of musick, and every part of liberal education,

is only equaled by her resolution and presence of mind" when in October 1794 she saved a near relative of the earl of Stamford from drowning. She was awarded the honorary medal of the Royal Humane Society. See *GM* 70, pt. 2 (1800): 1106.

2. In individual skirmishes with enemy vessels, the English were generally successful. For instance, Lord Keith's fleet captured ninety-six ships in the Mediterranean in two and a half months. (This information was issued by the admirality office on 26 July.)

TO HESTER MARIA THRALE

Brynbella
Equinox [ca. 23 September] 1800

My dear Girl

It was very goodnatured of you to write me the History of a Word eminently well chosen, yet impossible for me to comprehend without Explanation. The Account led me to look over Doctor Johnson's Book again, to see if he gives any Reason for the Name *Icolmkill*——I believe it was *St. Columb's Cill*—meaning *Cell*; and I believe that the Founder was a Religieux devoted to the *Santo Colombo*, the Holy Dove, representing the Third Person of the Blessed Trinity.[1] This may not be new to you perhaps, and I feel as if it was not New to me neither,—Yet I know not where to find the Conjecture tho' by no means sure that it sprung from my own head. Nothing is more difficult than to Settle which are original Ideas, and which are *not*.

When I get to London I will make it a Point to see Mr. Towneley's Musæum and then you shall have more Lights concerning the *Abraxas*:[2] he has two or Three of Them I know, one not fit for *your* Inspection, but Antiquaries never mind *that;* especially Ladies who are themselves become *Antiquities*. The blessed name *IAH* is engraved under the profane Figure, as Report tells me; but I will see before I believe it.

Look at the 17th Verse of the 2d Chapter of St.John's Apocalypse, and you will see the Stone should be pure White, and Plain.[3] *Abrasax* is the right Appellation; Quere if from *that* does not derive *Abrasæ Tabulæ Carte Blanche?* This is *my own* Conjecture.

Dear Mrs. Strickland is nearer to You in Thought than Situation: I had a Letter from her Yesterday dated Standish Hall, with kind Enquiries for your health and happiness—She would have come over here from Lancashire but that we are oyling our own Feathers for Flight, and mean to take Wing for the Environs of London in ten or Twelve days—defying Insurrection and Tumult.

It is an astonishing Consideration, and to me an awful one, that the upper Ranks of Mankind in every Country seem resolved on putting the lower ones *in the right* when they are most outrageous.——Nothing can be truer than that they have suffered much, and suffered patiently; which Merit *they* likewise seem now resolved on cancelling; and Force *must* be used to quell Lamentations in themselves far from unjust or untimely.[4] There is a Fate upon us all for certain, or such Contradictions could not be predicated of any Age as of this—where

Victory confesses no Success, Increasing Riches bring no Opulence, and Plentiful Harvests leave a Scarcity of Grain. Is it that We may remove our Trust from our *own* Sword, our *own* Possessions? and place it on our heavenly Redeemer? May the Effect be hastened! but I see no Sign on't. Man never was so confident of his own Strength or his own Wisdom since Nebuchadnezzar's Time.——Lycanthropy was the Punishment of Pride to that *Individual*;[5] the same Judgement comes now upon the Nations: We are all turning to Wolves and Wild Beasts in the midst of our Self Complacency and Admiration of Civilized Life. Have done, Have done, You're louder than the Weather might we say to the Rioters, as Shakespeare's Mariners cry to each other in the Tempest.[6] It is not easy either, to be more blustering than are the Equinoctial Gales this Autumn, and I see a Flock of Gannets whilst I write—high up in Air, their Faces *from* the Sea, which is a neverfailing Sign of Storms. Your next kind Letter must be directed to Streatham Park however for thitherward we bend our way—stopping awhile at Weston— my Lord Bradford's—where Mr. Chappelow waits for us. When our Neighboring *Nobles* shall be more Settled hereabouts I hope we shall be better off for Franks. Lord and Lady De Blaquiere have resolved to build and fix at little Denbigh of all Places, when the World lay before them for Choice. Their charming Daughter—whom I love because She is so like You, and who every body else loves because She is so amiable and accomplished—caught the Heart of Lord Mountjoy while he was here with the Randolphs; *wondering* that the Heir of Lleweney should have looked further than *her* for a Companion.[7] Our future Lady Kirkwall is an exemplary Character however, and will have Estates to the Amount of no less than 12000£ o'Year; and there is such a Conformity between *her* Situation and her Husband's, that all the World is more than pleased—every body seems struck with delight at their Union——both only Children; both of mixed Blood, English, Irish, and Welsh; both of equal Fortune, and that Fortune detained from them for awhile in the Same Manner.

Lady Orkney is only afraid She says—of feeling too happy—and Mrs. Ormsby, Miss Owen &c. are quite content. So here's a match to every body's Mind. Lady Mansfield's was not such I believe,[8] but the King has appointed *her* Ranger of Richmond Park, and her Husband will have the Advantage;[9] and my Friends the Hamiltons will enjoy the Company of their favourite Niece married to their favourite Nephew always close at hand.[10] Mrs. Holman has been at Birmingham and Liverpool with her Husband, but could not make it suit them to come here; they are now at Edinburgh. *Her* Sufferings in this last Lying In are talked of even in *the Profession* as surpassing credibility: Yet She lives, and hopes for better *Times*, in the Ladies' Sense of the Word. Everybody tells me Mr. Siddons and his eldest Daughter are almost at Point of Death.

What think you of Buonaparte? We shall see him Shine thro' another Campaign, and merit still more completely perhaps, his Name of *Apollione*.——It is at least worth remarking that no conqueror before him ever did *wear* the Name, tho' many have *deserved* the Title of *Destroyer*. The Roman Eagle now scarce able either to fight or fly seems resolved to dye *discrowned* after all, and I respect the Resolution.[11]——There will be fierce Deeds done ere Set of Sun this Year yet, and I expect a Grand Finale of the 18th eventful Century.

Adieu, and enjoy the Environs of Harrowgate; I never was there but have heard much in its Praise. No room to say with how many kind Remembrances from Mr. Piozzi, I remain yours and your Sisters Affectionate H: L: P.

Text: Bowood Collection. *Address:* Miss Thrale / Post Office / Harrowgate / Yorkshire. *Postmark:* DENBIGH.

1. Although SJ discusses the ancient ecclesiastical associations of Icolmkill (one of the small islands of the Inner Hebrides), he does not comment on the etymology of the name.
The Irish-descended missionary saint, Colum (521–97), came to be known as Columba ["dove"] of the church [cell], i.e., Columkill. He left Ireland for Scotland in 563 and established himself on the island known variously as Icolmkill, I, Hy, and Iona. There he spent most of his later years converting the Picts.
See SJ, *A Journey to the Western Islands of Scotland* [1775], ed. Mary Lascelles (New Haven and London: Yale University Press, 1971), pp. 138–53; also *Boswell's Johnson* 5:338.
2. A reference to the significant art collection of Charles Towneley [or Townley]. See HLP to Sophia Byron, 11 August [1788], and n. 15.
For HLP on the abraxas, see her letter to Q, 12 February [1799], n. 8.
3. According to Rev. 2:17:
"He that hath an ear, let him hear what the Spirit saith unto the churches; To him that overcometh will I give to eat of the hidden manna, and will give him a white stone, and in the stone a new name written, which no man knoweth saving he that receiveth it."
4. HLP's attitude echoed the king's "Proclamation" of 18 September, which commanded and required "all the Lieutenants of Our Counties, and all our Justices of the Peace, Sheriffs and Under-Sheriffs, and all Our Civil Officers whatsoever, that they do take the most effectual means for suppressing all riots and tumults." To that end, he invoked an act of Parliament passed in the first year of the reign of George I so that all offenders—those guilty of "riotous and dangerous practices"—might be apprehended and "prosecuted according to law." See *The Times*, 22 September; also 16–20 September.
5. See especially Dan. 4:33, which describes the seven-year madness inflicted upon Nebuchadnezzar: ". . . he was driven from men, and did eat grass as oxen, and his body was wet with the dew of heaven, till his hairs were grown like eagles' *feathers*, and his nails like birds' *claws*."
As late as 1891 Nebuchadnezzar's madness was described as lycanthropy. See Samuel Rolles Driver, *An Introduction to the Literature of the Old Testament* (Edinburgh: T. & T. Clark, 1891).
6. The Boatswain cries, "Down with the topmast! yare! lower, lower! bring her to try with main course. *(A cry within)* A plague upon this howling! they are louder than the weather, or our office" (*The Tempest*, 1.1.34–37).
7. Lord and Lady De Blaquiere had seven children: John (1776–1844); William (1778–1851); George (ca. 1782–1826); Peter Boyle (b. 1783); Anna Maria (1780–1843); Elizabeth (d. 1870); Eleanor (*fl.* 1822).
For the marriage of Anna Maria De Blaquiere, see HLP to LC, 19 March 1799, n. 4.
8. HLP refers to Louisa Cathcart (1758–1843), *suo jure* countess of Mansfield, who had been the second wife of David Murray (1727–96), second earl of Mansfield (1793).
9. The countess of Mansfield married secondly on 19 October 1797 her first cousin, Robert Fulke Greville (1751–1824), third son of Francis, earl of Warwick.
According to the *Morning Post*, 3 January 1801: "The King has presented the Dowager Lady Mansfield with the Deputy Rangership of Richmond Park, which had become vacant by the death of Mr. Smelt, who was Tutor to the Prince of Wales. His Majesty, holding the Rangership in his own hands, makes this gift the more agreeable, as his Steward takes the whole responsibility of the management of the farming concern of it." (The appointment was first reported in *The Times*, 15 September 1800.)

10. Lady Mansfield was related to the Reverend Frederick Hamilton and his wife, Rachel, through her mother. That is, Jean (1726–71), daughter of Lord Archibald Hamilton, had married on 24 July 1753 Charles Cathcart (1721–76), ninth baron Cathcart.

11. HLP refers to Austria's refusal to ratify the "Articles of a Preliminary Treaty of Peace." See HLP to PSP, 6 or 7 September 1800, n. 2.

TO THE REVEREND LEONARD CHAPPELOW

Brynbella
Fryday October [10] 1800[1]

I don't know Dear Mr. Chappelow what Friendship is good for—except to plead Privilege of tormenting those who profess it. We have been such a Hindrance and scourge to you *this* Time, I am afraid of your renouncing us——but when we get to meet, we will ask your pardon prettily.

Something will yet happen before that Day——some *great* Thing I mean; for Buonaparte has not now reigned above a Year, and 'tis hardly possible that a Nation consisting of 20 Millions of Souls should suffer a Man to rule them quietly who obtained not his Seat either by Hereditary Succession, by General Election or by Right of Conquest: besides that his Evil Genius seems to lead him towards Peace as his good Genius pushed him upon War. How does he think to keep in order disbanded Armies hungry tho' pampered, and accustomed to Submission from all the Peasants and Country People round?—Men made eager too by Promises of unbounded Emoluments waiting to receive them and repay their Risques and Trouble. No Rewards ever can satisfy such Expectations, and no decent Comforts will compensate for a Life of Plunder. Peace whoever it ruins, *must* ruin Buonaparte; His Fame, Fortune, and Power depend wholly upon War. Paris endured Robertspierre four Years tis True, but then they saw the Man's disinterestedness; and were obliged to confess that if he murdered his Fellow Citizens they were his Fellow Citizens still, and might murder him if they liked it better. He assumed no State, he took no Rank upon him, he never gained five Shillings by the Revolution; but dictated his Mandates in the same Suit of Grey Clothes, and from the same pityful Lodging which he had punctually paid for, and worne before the King's Death as after it. A Very different Ruler now determines the Destiny of Thousands who will not I am confident suffer a Corsican Soldier to Lord it in their Louvre and Thuilleries *half* as long, as they shrunk and submitted before an Attorney's Clerk of their own Country.[2]

When the Lyon died, the Wolf, a Native Savage bore the Sway; but The Vulture will be considered as un *Etranger*——he will not devour them long.

For England——Peace is Poyson: 'tis shaking hands with an infected Neighbour, and sure contagion follows:—nothing but *Civil* War at home can come of leaving off our *foreign* War with France; The Naval Armistice is fraught with Evils, those that you mention, and a Thousand more; Whoever signs *that*, signs our Ruin.[3]

With regard to the High Price of Provisions I am all of your Mind,[4] and tremble lest by Enquiry, Every Member of Parliament should find it out as well as you and I. Whilst they believe that somebody is in fault who may be punished, or some Cause exists which may be removed, They will be happier——Than when Discovery shall have been forced on them, and 'tis confessed—what we all knew before—that in whatever Place *Money* is plenty *Necessaries* will of *Necessity* be dear. Why else do People give 2 Guineas for A Turkey at Calcutta? or 15^{sh} to see Harlequin at Bengal? why was a Pound of Flesh there at 14*d*. when in Great Britain you might have had it for a Groat? Why—but because Gold was in Plenty there, as now at London Market. Guinea Peaches wanted no Purchasers all the last Winter, and for one pair of Diamond Ear Rings usually seen at the Bath Balls, there were 20 Pair: For one Carriage in the Metropolis forty at least, while the Poor are perishing in Spitalfields by fifties in a Groupe. But do you think this can last long in England because it is endured in East India? No, No; *here* are no different *Castes* of Inhabitants,—no absolute and positive Subordination *here*: no Irremeable Line which one set of human Creatures are divided by—from another Set. Our People are no Cooleys, nor no Foolies; and though Principle and Patience may keep them quiet one Year, and the Terrors of a Troop of Horse may <tear> another Year——John Bull will *roar* when hungry, and *toss* <when> Commerce has overtraded her own Capital, She will pay for her spirit of Speculation by and by: but in the meantime our hapless Husband men are suffering. Down in my own poor Skin and Bone Country the Cottagers actually unthatched their miserable Huts for purpose of keeping Goat or Cow alive last Winter, whilst the Tables of your Taverns in London were groaning under the weight of expensive Dainties. This cannot be borne long—Our Tenant Gittins[5] an Englishman here at old Bachŷgraig—(Hardname House) took his Corn ten Miles off last Week and was near being torne to pieces by the People who said he was carrying it *out of the Country* was their Phrase.

Why what are all these Navigable Canals cut for (says I) if nothing is to go *out of the Country*? We have heard of the Benefits of *Internal Commerce* these last Twenty Years, and now find out that it is a Ruin not a Benefit.

Ah the old Proverb of an Ounce of Salt! *Every* thing is good to Moderation, and *nothing* beyond it. Trade like Time will eat up its own Offspring soon,[6] but the Clergy will be stript first——and the Royal Forests turned to Wheat Fields. Mercury was Patron of Thievery and Traffic I remember in old Classical times[7]——will swallow one another—for Second Course——and I am so true an Aristocrate, I shall think they have their *Dessert*. With one S as well as with two.

Dear Mr. Chappelow Farewell! and believe that between private Disappointments and apprehension of public Evil I am grown very near a Misanthrope. Tho ever Your obliged and / grateful Servant / H: L: P.

My Master mends gradually and sends You his best Regards and *lame* Excuses—Adieu.

Text: Ry. 560.102. *Address*: Rev: Mr. Chappelow / No. 12 / Hill Street/ Berkeley Square / London. *Postmark*: DENBIGH E OCT 11 < >.

1. HLP dated the letter the 9th, but Friday fell on the 10th.
2. HLP, who loathed a dominant Robespierre, loathed him less than she did a dominant Bonaparte. She once assumed Robespierre to be a ruthless dictator. Now she saw him as a misguided but self-sacrificing champion of revolution. She recognized implicitly that he did not make the Terror an instrument of personal ambition, that he confirmed his integrity even in his execution on 28 July 1794.
3. HLP merely restates the opinion of newspapers on the naval armistice. See *The Times*, 29 September, for a moderate statement of rejection of the French proposal.
   The *True Briton* on 9 October splenetically opposed the naval armistice. "It must be obvious to every one, that to open the seas to the French, even for a short time, would be to allow them to victual their Ports, to furnish their Dock Yards, and to receive all the articles of Importation, of which they stand in need; that, which is of no less importance, it would be to enable them to carry supplies to *Malta*, to *Corsica*, and to *Egypt;* that, in short it would be to afford them the means of preparing Combinations and Plans for the moment when they may foresee that the Truce would be broken."
4. That is, both HLP and LC would have agreed that the high cost of provisions and the consequent suffering of the poor were caused not by free-trade economics but by the self-indulgence of the new rich, like the corn factors and speculators. So widespread was this belief that the duke of Portland, on hearing that a riot had been suppressed in Witney, wrote to the lord lieutenant of Oxford county on 29 September. Thus, Portland talked of "the prejudices" that disposed "a very large part of the community to believe that the late Scarcity was artificial, and has been owing to the views and speculations of certain interested and rapacious men, who take advantage of the difficulties and distresses of the times, to enrich themselves at the expence of the publick." See *GM* 70, pt. 2 (1800): 995.
5. John Gittins (1758–1810) had become the Piozzis' tenant at Bachygraig early in the summer of 1800. See Oldfield's letter to GP, 29 July 1800 (Ry. 608.6); "Burial Registers," 1800–1818 (C.R.O., Clwyd).
6. Cf. "Times devours all things." See *Oxford Proverbs*, p. 823 (T 326).
7. Mercurius, the Roman equivalent of Hermes, the god of merchants, thieves, and anyone who frequently took to the roads for gain.

TO JOHN LLOYD

Brynbella
Sunday 12: October *1800*.

I rejoyce to hear that you are returned among us Dear Sir—and hope for the honour of seeing you once more before we Set out for London.

We are told Sir Edward Lloyd is in the Country. How kind it would be in You to negotiate for those Trees behind Brynbella, and if one could get the Fields too in Exchange for some—no less valuable or commodious to Sir Edward—we should consider it as a happy Circumstance and an everlasting Obligation to your friendship.[1]

Think of us some Times Dear Mr. Lloyd and wish me Success on my Cruize against the Critics. My poor Husband has had the Gout again, but is finding his Feet now; and disposing himself to move Southwards. In all Times and Places You are sure of our kindest Respects, and that I am ever with true Esteem / Your faithful and Obliged Servant / H: L: Piozzi.

Text: National Library of Wales MS 12421D. *Address:* John Lloyd Esq. / Wygfair / St. Asaph. *Postmark:* DENBIGH.

1. For Sir Edward Pryce Lloyd, see HLP to Charlotte Lewis, 20 September [17] 89, n. 11.
HLP and Sir Edward conferred often in the next year and a half over the exchange of lands. See, e.g., his letters to her, 6 February 1802 (Ry. 556.130); 2 November (Ry. 556.131); 29 April (Ry. 556.132). In this last letter he virtually wrote off the possibility of any exchange.
"The moment I understood, that Mrs. Piozzi conceived that the Fall of the Trees upon the lower part of the Bryn would in any degree take away from the appearance of Bryn Bella I desired Thomas Foulkes and John Jones (the Purchasers of the Lot in which these Trees were included) I would suffer them to stand, and they might deduct their value out of this sum of money they were to give for the Lot upon referring their value to two Timber Merchants.—" But Foulkes and Jones would not negotiate and Sir Edward declined to suffer any significant financial loss; instead he urged the Piozzis to be more fair-minded in their future offer.

TO THE REVEREND LEONARD CHAPPELOW

Weston
Sunday Night 19: October 1800.

Many a Letter have I received from Dear Mr. Chappelow written at this very Table in the Library at lovely Weston Park——but never had he one from me till now, and they tell me you are but just gone; and here's my Master so well recovered that he even crawled on his hands and Knees thro' Hawkestone Grotto yesterday and I am as tired as Death. Charming Lady Bradford says we must stay till Tuesday, and then I shall have to delay Mr. Piozzi again at Oxford, where our Friend Mr. Gray is resolving to do us the honours, so we shall just get to Streatham Park as You leave Mouse Trap Hall.

Oh pray write to Streatham and tell me you are well and angry, but that you will soon come back well and in good humour.

Dear Sir Adieu—look at the Date only[1] and congratulate Your ever Obliged and faithful / H: L: P.

Text: Ry. 560.103. *Address:* The Revd: L. Chappelow / Hill Streeet / Berkeley Square / London. *Postmark:* OC 21 1800 FREE Bradford.

1. HLP is belatedly recalling the anniversary of her first marriage, 11 October 1763. On 10 October 1800, she wrote, "I pass'd 17 Years & a half with my first Husband . . . & never wished I had remained unmarried, or prefer'd any mortal Man to him: I have now spent 16 Years & a half almost with Mr Piozzi, & every Creature has considered us a Model of Conjugal Felicity" (*Thraliana* 2:1010).

TO HESTER MARIA THRALE

> Streatham Park
> Tuesday 28: October 1800.

I perceive by the obliging Letter found on Mr. Giles's Table that my dear Girl will not be surprized at the Date of this,—but should your Blue Eyes open on reading my Description as my Gray ones did at Sight of the Spot tis written from—I think you will look as you did when Count Grimani picked his Teeth with a large Silver-hafted Knife from the Side Board.[1] Does your nice Memory recollect our Tenant Saying that he would be careful of the Books, but should beg Admission for some *Modern* ones? He *did* Say So, and Sure enough here *are* Modern Books! ! ! To the Amount of *one Thousand Pounds*! I thought myself transported by Magic from the Bodleian Library where Mr. Gray had entertained me for whole Hours and Days, and whence I came to my Maid all covered with Dust—into Edwards's Shop, Pall-Mall[2] which when I last Saw it was Scarce as Splendid as our Library *here*.

> To all their Dated Backs we turn us round
> These Aldus printed—these—Du Sueil has bound.[3]

But never did Aldus and Du Sueil see such Editions—Hotpressed and wire woven Authors.[4] Was it so when your Sisters dined here? And did they tell you? I heard of your health and bene Stare from some Friends who saw you at Ingmere and came to the Vale of Llwydd on a Visit to Doctor Myddelton: The Stricklands too Said You were all well.

Mr. Piozzi had a Touch of the Gout which delayed *our* Journey till the Leaves were rather *too* Yellow; although Hawkestone Woods and Caverns must be always Striking—and Weston Park delightful. Lady Bradford's Good Humour and Hospitality with the agreeable conversation of a travelled Mr. Vernon who had seen the Azores and Greek Islands, and heard High Mass in the Grotta D'Antiparos—detained me a willing Listener Three Nights and Days.[5]

With regard to Newby[6] I can only tell what possibly you know already—that there was a famous Copy from the Medicean Venus made in King Charles's Time by Nicholas *Stone*[7] occasioning many Quibbles how *Stone* was *precious* and copies were become originals and such stuff. I knew not where the Lady lurked who gave Cause for the Nonsense, but by your Letter I gather that She is housed at Newby—If so She is worth Seeing, and will rise in the Value if the Jacobins fire the Tuilleries completely: The last Tryal happily failed.[8]

Your Delicacy in detesting a Table D'Hôtes for such I consider Harrowgate, is very amiable in *una Verginella simile alla Rosa*. For my own Part I like a Table d'Hôtes now and then exceedingly; one is *almost* sure that some of the Company will say Something one never heard before, and *quite* sure that if they are Stupid, Chance may Change them for brighter. The last Time *I* figured at a long Table was at Buxton and Margate—Cecy Mostyn was with us, and I concluded She would be charmed with the whole—as you were at her Age——But She had not the same Reason for being pleased. Why (said I) is not it a pretty Novelty? Any thing but a Novelty (replied She) when 'tis so exactly like *School*. Your Letter had no Date but *Tuesday* and I flung the Frank away; so that 'tis Impossible to guess when twas written. *This* Scrawl is the produce of a dark room, bad Eyes and no Candles: when the light comes in, I shall put up my writing and look at the fine Asiatic Researches; the Herculaneum Antiquities;[9] Cateby's Plants and Animals, and every expensive Rarety in Literature,[10] which can be devised; bound so as to double their Value.—Several Things were purchased at Mr. Concanen's Sale they tell me[11]—a beautiful Shakespear in particular for which Mr. Gillon bid 14 Guineas but it went half as high again. That our old Divinity *Rums* should have given Precedence to these gay Fellows "who tittering pushed the Pedants off the Place"[12] will not astonish you: my scrupulous Care had brought back all the broken Sets I borrowed for my own Work, and now they may go to their humble Brethren in the Garret.—They are however taken Care of: and Mr. Piozzi says if I was to undertake any thing ever again (which I shall not) the best way would be to take a House at Oxford and study in some College Library. So I leave you to laugh and begin turning over Staunton's Chinese Embassy[13] bound worthy of Kien Long himself.[14] We arrived but yesterday and have not half done admiring. Mr. P. begs to add his good Wishes to those of your / ever Affectionate / H: L: P.

Text: Bowood Collection. *Address:* Miss Thrale / Post Office / Harrowgate / Yorkshire. *Postmark:* OC 29 800. PENNY POST NOT PAID.

1. For Filippo Vincenzi Grimani, see HLP to Q, 19 December 1794 and n. 11.
2. James Edwards (ca. 1757–1816) of 77 Pall Mall. In 1784 he and a younger brother became the firm of Edwards and Son under the aegis of their father, William (1720–1808). About 1804 James was rich enough to retire from trade and to live on a country estate near Old Verulam.

According to Dibdin, "no man ever did such wonderful things towards the acquisition of rare, beautiful, and truly classical productions. . . . he was probably born a bibliographical bookseller, and had always a nice feeling and accurate perception of what was tasteful and classical." See Thomas Frognall Dibdin, *Bibliographical Decameron*, 3 vols. (London: Printed for the author by W. Bulmer and Co., Shakespeare Press, 1817), 3:14–16.

3. Pope, *Epistle IV. To Richard Boyle, Earl of Burlington*, lines 135–36.
4. Teobaldo Mannucci, better known as Aldo Manuzio (1450–1515), Venetian printer and founder of the Aldine Press. He was especially interested in preparing Greek and Latin texts in small format at low cost for scholars.

Abbé Augustin Duseuil [also Dusseuil, Du Seuil, De Seuil] (1673–1746), Parisian bookbinder.

5. Probably Francis V. Vernon (fl. 1762–1803), an Irish-born one-time naval officer, who wrote *Voyages and Travels of a Sea Officer* (London: Printed for the author, 1792). As a midshipman he had traveled to America and the West Indies, and he had sailed the Mediterranean, visiting Italy, Greece, Turkey, Smyrna, Egypt, Cyprus, Lernica, Syria, etc.
6. Newby Hall, seat of Baron Grantham (1781–1859).
7. Nicholas Stone (1586–1647), mason, sculptor, and architect, was made master-mason to James I in 1619 and in April 1626 he received a patent from Charles I to be master-mason and architect at Windsor Castle.
8. The Tuilleries was attacked on 10 August 1792, when a Parisian mob stormed the

palace and massacred the Swiss Guards. See HLP to Charlotte Lewis, 18 August 1792, n. 4.

9. The books to which HLP refers are the following:
Asiatic Researches, 5 vols. (London, 1798–99). This was a pirated edition with variations in the title.
John Hayter (1756–1818), *The Herculanean and Pompeian Manuscripts* (London 1800).

10. HLP refers to Mark Catesby (1683–1749) and *The Natural History of Carolina, Florida and the Bahama Islands, containing the Figures of Birds, Beasts, Fishes, Serpents, Insects, and Plants. . . . Together with their Descriptions in English and French,* 2 vols. (London: Printed at the expence of the author, 1731–43).

11. A sale of rare books that belonged to Matthew Concanen, Jr. (fl. 1745–1818), a resident of Southwark. A versifier and antiquary, he had inherited considerable weath and an impressive library from his father, also named Matthew (1701–49).

12. Cf. Goldsmith, *The Deserted Village,* line 28: "While secret laughter tittered round the place."

13. See DL to HLP, 29 January 1796, n. 2.

14. The great emperor of China, Tchien Lung, who had died 5 March 1799, is described in Staunton's *Authentic Account.* The news of Lung's decease "in his 90th year" was reported by *The Times,* 3 January 1800.

TO THE REVEREND LEONARD CHAPPELOW

Streatham Park
1: November 1800.

I found your kind Letters on my Table Dear Sir, and hope that Jacob has—in the Phrase of those I now live with—done the Needful at No. 12.

Robinson and I are Number *Two* now, every thing is over between *us;* and your Friend Stockdale as next Oars, commands my Attendance with the Manuscript; I threw myself on his Daughter's Mercy and his own by the same Post which carries this[1]—and desire a speedy Answer: because let one lose Hopes, Friends or Money——*they* may return, and *will* return in some Shape; but Time will not return; and if my Book does not get early to Press, the Moments of good Appearance and quick Sale in the Spring will be lost.

Little Dear Salusbury loses no Time, he works hard and comes forward as I wish, with that sort of Knowledge which if not engrafted betimes, never takes good Root——and Life is consumed in supplying——The Labours of seven years old.

Mr. Giles's Hospitality and kindness beggar all Description, so does his liberality in Purchasing Books: You never saw any thing so fine as our old Library is grown. I felt as if transported by Magic into Edwards's Shop Pall Mall.

Such Bindings! such Coloured Drawings! &c.!

for Blue Red and Green my Inconstancy burns,
and their Different Beauties subdue Me by Turns.[2]

When will you come to Town and tell of the *Distresses* and partake of the *Splendours* with which I see the Metropolis surrounded. New Houses like Palaces, new Cottages like good Houses; every Table profusely covered, and every Article of Life trebled in Price.

Is my Manuscript the *only* Thing which cannot find a Purchaser? And is every one so happily employed in anticipation of future Felicities that *Retrospect* of past Events is grown uninteresting? Oh pray do Dear Sir wish me Success and believe me ever yours / H: L: P.

Who is Mrs. Hayman?[3] who has made a Friend of mine happy in Anglesey by talking about *You*—for whom that Friend knew *I* had so perfect an Esteem.

Text: Ry. 560.104.

1. Mary R. Stockdale (fl. 1780–1821), a prolific poet and translator, was one of several children of the publisher John Stockdale (ca. 1749–1814) of Jermyn Street. See also HLP to PSP, [5] November 1800, n. 2. Mary Stockdale, John's wife, was the sister of James Ridgway, bookseller and well-known pamphlet publisher, Piccadilly.

2. HLP's adaptation of the concluding air [xxviii] of Gay's *The Beggar's Opera:*

> For black, brown, and fair his Inconstancy burns,
> And the different Beauties subdue him by turns.

3. Susanna, née Cridland (d. 1830), had married 2 April 1771 the Reverend Henry Hayman (1722/3–1809), rector of Lucam and Halstock, Dorset, for over forty years.

MEMORANDUM OF AGREEMENT BETWEEN MRS. HESTER LYNCH PIOZZI AND JOHN STOCKDALE, BOOKSELLER OF PICCADILLY, WESTMINSTER; 3RD NOVEMBER 1800.—

The undersigned mutually agree that the work intituled "Retrospection; or a glance backward upon the most striking and important events, characters, situations, and their consequences, which the last 1800 years have presented to the observation of mankind," be published, at the sole risk of the said John Stockdale, who shall not have it in his power to make any demand there for, on Mrs. H. L. Piozzi for any expense so incurred.—

And it is further agreed that, after the expense so incurred shall be reimbursed to the said John Stockdale, the whole profit shall be divided equally between the two undersigned, and that the property of the copy right in the aforesaid work be the equally divided property of the two undersigned—

Hester Lynch Piozzi
John Stockdale

Given under our hands this third day of November in the year one thousand eight hundred
   Witness John M. Stockdale

Text: The Carl H. Pforzheimer Library. *Envelope:* "Agreement between Mrs. Piozzi and John Stockdale."

TO LADY WILLIAMS

> Streatham Park
> 4: November 1800.

My Dear Lady Williams when tired of being angry that her kind little Note ran before me all the way to London——will be glad to hear that I read it with Grateful Affection when arrived here at old Streatham Park. I little thought indeed that your Ladyship had been behaving so very ill, but Something is always happening to keep my young Friend the only Son of Bodylwyddan.[1] Lady Bradford has no fewer than four Stout Boys and frets for a Daughter. We spent three Days at their Hospitable Mansion and as many at Oxford, and less than two Days were not sufficient to employ upon the Curiosities of Sir Richard Hill's beautiful Grounds at Hawkstone; and its very singular Grotto, through which Mr. Piozzi clambered with more Spirit than Discretion: he was not however *much* the worse for it.

We are Visitors here at our own House—Odly enough; but that our Tenant is likewise admirable in his Character of Landlord, so that We do exceedingly well, and see our nice little Boy every day who really has not been losing any Time, but bids fair to be a good Scholar in A few Years: No child of his own Age is before him *now*, which says very well considering he could not speak or understand a word of English 20 Months ago.

Here is the finest Weather ever seen so late in the Season, but every Article of Life is grown insupportably dear, and whilst all seem enjoying, all seem complaining too: The Environs of London look very gay, and fresh Buildings, Young Plantations and hourly Improvements in Luxury have taken Place since last I witnessed the Bustle of our contradictory Metropolis where every thing one *sees* is Wealth and all one *hears* is about Poverty.

The Bookseller to whom I disposed of My Manuscript this Morning gave a Dinner last Week to his Friends which cost him 52£.4s. at the London Tavern[2] and I saw the Bill.

Mr. Giles with whom we are now living bought a Shakespear some Days back for 20 Guineas, so I think People cannot be starving—he has about 500 living Animals here (of which I am one) eating and drinking at his Expence all Day long, and he says, that encreased Population causes the Bread to run short. Be that as it may Parliament is expected to give vast Bounties on Importation for Present Exigence;[3] and if Country Gentlemen oppose as some People expect they will, any Proposal for taking Commons and Waste Lands, there will be a clamorous Out Cry against *them,* and many illnatured Suggestions will arise as if they valued their sports and Preservation of their Game beyond the feeding of their Fellow Creatures.—I should be sorry such Stuff got once into the low People's Heads.—

Of Fashions and fine Folks nothing can yet be told, The Town is quite at its Thinnest. The Specimen of Haut Ton which your Ladyship so comically describes as exhibited at Holywell Hunt, was I fancy the very Pink of the Present mode.

My hopes are to get to Bath early in the New Year and leave London just as others come crowding into it: Those who know best tell me Miss Thrales are at Brighthelmston, but the last Letters received from them were dated Harrowgate. Adieu Dear Madam! so vile are my Pens and Paper that I find myself glad to end this scratched Letter and Assure lovely Lady Williams and her delightful Family with what affectionate Regard I remain / her Ladyship's Obliged and faithful / H: L: Piozzi.

My Husband says his Compliments *must* be added, Let them be legible or not.

Text: Ry. 1 (1796–1802). *Address:* Lady Williams / Bodylwyddan / St. Asaph. *Postmark:* DENBIGH.

1. Ly W's only son at this time was John, now six.
2. Located at 123 Bishopsgate Street Within, the London Tavern was famous for its dinners, wines, and turtle. It could accommodate as many as 355 people in the spacious dining hall. The Tavern was built in 1765 and closed in 1876.
3. HLP anticipates the immediate action of Parliament to alleviate scarcity. The king in his opening speech on 11 November said that the high price of provisions and the suffering of the poor were the reasons why he had called Parliament together earlier than planned.

The desirability of remedial legislation was quickly referred to select committees of both houses. "The Commons' Committee . . . presented in succession no less than six Reports. They recommended that the King should be empowered to prohibit, by Orders in Council, the export of provisions. They recommended a bounty on certain articles of import. They recommended the prohibition for a limited time of corn in distilling of spirits, or in making of starch. They recommended the prohibition of any bread made solely from the fine flour of wheat. All these proposals, and some others, were passed into law with very slight discussion." See Stanhope 3:250–51; *Parliamentary History* 35:793.

TO PENELOPE SOPHIA PENNINGTON

Streatham Park
[5] November 1800.

Dear Mrs. Pennington will like a Letter with this Date[1] though it tells her nothing except that we are not at home here: It is however exceedingly difficult for us to find that Truth out from our good Tenants behaviour to us or that of his Servants. They are all wonderfully kind and civil and I fancy we shall go on as we *have* done, nothing is as yet finally settled, but we have every pleasing Expectation in *Prospect*.

Retrospect is already disposed of; and you will be pleased that 'tis launched from a good Aristocratic House.[2] How does Colonel Barry excuse himself *to* himself I wonder! for his so long and so wide Deviation from the Train of Opinions he seemed as if well-rooted in when we were first acquainted.[3] An Agreable Talker is a great Loss to the good Cause, and I shall be happier when you tell me that he is tired of the bad one.

We have been but once in Town yet, and that for Two Hours only; one spent with Stockdale and one with Siddons, who is lean and Nerve-shaken, but lovely as ever; and was preparing to shine in Elvira the Evening of our Visit.[4] Her Husband walked in with his two Sticks and chatted chearfully: her eldest Daughter appeared to *me* in high Health and Spirits; and Miss Lee who was there made a good Report of the Youngest. All agreed that poor Mr. Whalley was much broken since we met last, but Mr. and Mrs. Greatheed are grown younger as they tell me.

We live among the Commercial Men here, not the professed Wits: Yet more Love and Esteem for Literature it would be hard to find. Perhaps Familiarity even with *that* lessens Regard. Here has Mr. Giles laid out a Thousand Pounds (no less) in Books for our Library, and Mr. Gillon grieves when a Secondhand Shakespear slips from his hand at an Auction, for want of Courage to give beyond 20 Guineas for it.

Who says Money is not plenty? Truth is England contains more Money than Meat just now. I mean in Proportion—but Corn is coming in, and Rice from every Quarter of the World;[5] and I hope People will forbear to fly out, and encrease their own Distresses. The Coachman will get them through every Bog and safely by every Precipice I think, if they will but let the *Check String* alone and not hinder him from saving them and *himself* who runs *more* than an equal Risque with all of us, and is in haste to find the Carriage clear of Embarrassment as *we* are. If we believe our Eyes all will be well; if our Ears—all will be dismal: Offers of Peace are talked of, and no wonder. France is afraid of being driven from Ægypt, whence She means to fright our East India Company if incapable to injure it.[6]

I hate their insidious Offers; resembling those magical Deceptions we used to talk about, where a friendly hand appeared as if presenting a Nosegay but no sooner was it reached at, than a Dagger started forward in its place. Remember that all our Journey has been thro' loyal Places; Sir Richard Hill's fine Seat, Lord Bradford's, and the old abiding Place of Virtue and Learning Oxford. Two Days the first of these sweet Scenes delayed us, and Mr. Piozzi clambered thro' the Grotto. Three Days were given to the Hospitalities and Comforts of Weston Park; and Mr. Gray was unwilling to let me leave *their* Curiosities unexamined, so kept us three Days more among the Musæums[7] &c. of far famed Rhedycina.[8]

After a fortnight spent upon the Road I found Your kind but not consolatory

Letter. Will it raise your Spirits to hear that I expect release early in January? After Business must come Pleasure, and for that *our* Eyes turn naturally to Bath.

Till then A Hotel and Tavern must be dear Mr. Piozzi's Residence in order to accommodate his Wife by living close to the Bookseller's who assures us that if we will come to Jermyn Street and mind our Book closely—it may be launched with the New Year and 8 Weeks of Confinement finish all.

Wish it Success kind Friend, and make Miss Powell[9] and Mr. Pennington—ay and good Mother too—drink a Glass to the Health of the two Quarto Volumes you saw advertised this Morning[10] under Name of Your / H: L: P.

Mr. Piozzi sends a thousand Regards.

Text: Princeton University Library. *Address:* Mrs. Pennington / Dowry Square / Hot Wells / Bristol. *Postmark:* Penny Post Streatham NO <5> 800.

1. Aware that it was Guy Fawkes day, HLP playfully misdated her letter "6 November." The postmark is "5 November."
2. Stockdale himself was not an aristocrat. He was probably brought up as a blacksmith, becoming valet to John Astley of Dunkinfield, Cheshire, and ca. 1780 porter to John Almon, the publisher. In company he was often eccentric and coarse.
Politically he exhibited contradictory behavior. He first set up in business by opening an opposition shop to John Debrett, whom HLP considered a democrat. But in 1788 he published the Reverend John Logan's *Review of the Charges against Warren Hastings* and was consequently charged with libel against the Commons. Defended by Erskine in 1789, he was acquitted in a decision heralded as a triumph for a free press.
What gave Stockdale particular respectability for HLP was his publication of SJ's *Works* in 1787 and 1788.
3. HLP regarded Barry's politics as suspect when he became Helen Williams's defender. See HLP to PSP, 5 May [1795].
4. Ever since 1794, SS suffered from anxiety and nervousness, exacerbated by recurrent bouts of erysypilas, which infected her mouth.
For SS as Elvira in *Pizarro*, see HLP to LC, 25 September 1799, n. 5. The performance to which HLP alludes occurred on 13 October.
5. For an accounting of the grain being imported into London, see HLP to PSP, [8] December 1800, n. 7.
6. Supporting HLP's belief are various newspaper reports, such as that announcing the surrender of Malta to Britain. As a result, *The Times* on 7 October predicted that "all hopes of maintaining a footing in *Egypt* must now clearly be abandoned by the Chief Consul."
The Times on 24 October admitted further that peace between Great Britain and France would be discussed once "the Preliminaries with the French Republic" were concluded by Austria. By 14 November *The Times* presented the "Papers relative to the Commencement of [English] Negociations for Peace with France."
7. By "Musæums" HLP referred primarily to the Ashmolean, housed in 1800 on the top floor of the present Museum of the History of Science, on the Broad, Oxford. She also had in mind several large boxes or crates, called "musæums," that contained artifacts, antiquities, and curiosities still kept in the above-named museum.
8. For the debate in *GM* 70, pt. 2 (1800) concerning the etymology of Rhedycina, see the statements by "Oxoniensis" and "Academicus," pp. 920, 1136.
Parallel to this debate are HLP's assumptions: "We read of *Rhedycina* for *Oxford* . . . in many local poems. Quere, Was the word borrowed from *Rhedychan* in Welsh? The

Scholars know, I suppose. The *Ford* of *Oxen* is *Rhedychan* in our old Cambrian tongue, that's certain; and I have heard that *Bos-phoros, Bosphoros,* had the same meaning in Greek." See *Retrospection* 2:353n.; also *Thraliana* 2:975; "Minced Meat for Pyes."

9. For Jane Powell, see HLP to PSW, 2 November 1789, n. 2.

10. *The Times* on 4 November advertised *Retrospection* as "In the Press, and speedily will be published, in 2 vols. 4to. / price 2£.2s. in boards."

TO THE REVEREND ROBERT GRAY

Streatham Park
Wednesday [12 November], 1800[1]

Did you drink one good-humour'd glass extraordinary to the health of 'Retrospection,' which will come to light in about a month after your *own* child,[2] and claim some of your superfluous kindness? I hope you did. If it ever should be in the path of those amiable friends you introduced me to at Oxford, they will give it a kick *forward* and drive it along for *your* sake. Stockdale is a good *hoper,* and seems to think well of it upon the *launch.* He is a good aristocrat too; I am pleas'd that it comes out of his loyal shop. We are living here among the wealthy traders,—*merchants like princes* in the strictest sense,—of liberality as of revenue. *One* says how his neighbour such a one has 30,000£. the other 60,000£. a year, and I accordingly do see improvements taking place all about London, which entered not into my thoughts a dozen years ago.

The library *here,* for example, at old Streatham Park has been enriched with new and expensive publications till it looks like Edwards's showy shop in Pall Mall. Our tenant asked leave to purchase some *modern* books as he called them, with permission to displace the old *divines* which you remember standing at the bottom of the room; and so he has indeed! nor has that generous creature spent less than a thousand guineas in literary amusement since he lived here. Meanwhile some frightful hand-bills are in circulation, expressing a dependence upon Parliament for that relief which I doubt they have no power to bestow.[3]

As far as my short sight extends, however, insurrection is completely left without excuse, while such enormous alms are given round this parish as would amaze a native of any kingdom but ours. Whilst they dispense charity with one hand besides, I find them active to defend their property on the other: and if they persist in their present resolution of not being plunder'd, I do think the agitators of evil will see some difficulty in persuading a mob to injure houses whence the poor are so fed, so clothed, so comforted——and in each of which arms are kept to protect those possessions which every man seems trying to deserve.

We were calculating three nights ago that less than one million of pounds sterling was not given away last year in private bounties, besides Poor's Revenues amounting to five times that sum.[4] I question if Sardinia's king ever could boast such a treasure in his coffers.[5] Bread is at eighteen pence the quartern loaf this day, however, and the new Lord Mayor will have a troublesome time of it.[6]

Text: Hayward 2:254-56.

1. At the end of this letter, HLP refers to the new lord mayor of London, who had assumed office on Saturday, 8 November. Her letter is dated Wednesday, therefore, 12 November. See *The Times,* 10 November.
2. Probably John, who was born in Oxford in December 1800 and who died young.
3. The handbill was distributed on 9 November throughout London and various suburbs. It invited "every Journeyman, Artizan, Mechanic, and Tradesman; every Manufacturer, Labourer, &c. to meet . . . on Kennington Common." There they would petition the king and Parliament to pass legislation designed to alleviate the hardships of the poor. See *GM* 70, pt. 2 (1800): 1100.
4. See *Encyclopedia Britannica* (1797), 15:372-75: "Poor's Rate [or Revenue] is the legal assessment for the poor," which began during the reign of Elizabeth I and "hath continued ever since."
5. HLP's cryptic sentence suggests that the money saved by the government in 1799 was greater than the whole of Carlo Emanuele's treasury.
For the king of Sardinia, see HLP to LC, 30 September 1796, n. 4.
6. William Staines (d. 10 September 1807) was a carpenter by trade and a Whig in politics. He had served as alderman from Cripplegate Ward (1793-1807) and as lord mayor (1800-1801). He had been knighted on 26 October 1796, when sheriff of London.
HLP feared that the new lord mayor would be plagued by riots, as his predecessor had been during the month of September. See HLP to LC, 19 September 1800, n. 1; *European Magazine* 52 (1807): 243.

TO THE REVEREND LEONARD CHAPPELOW

Streatham Park
Fryday [14: November 1800].

I was glad to hear from you Dear Mr. Chappelow—my Heart foreboded no good. The kind Apprehensions you feel for *me* will I hope end no worse: Stockdale and I go halves; he franks me thro' all Expences of Paper, Print &c. and then we share the profits. He reserves to himself however the right of buying me *quite out* if such a Measure is upon closer View of Things found likely to suit him; and I keep the Power of Refusal if such a Measure should not on nearer Inspection suit *Us.*

We go to Brunet's Hotel Leicester Square this Morning and shall be happy to dine with Mrs. Clay at your House *this Day sennight:* but the Day after that, *Saturday* Mr. Giles kindly invites us to spend us with him, and stay till Monday Morning when we must all go to Work again, for Stockdale plies me pretty hard with Proofs, and promises to present Retrospection as a New Year's Gift to the Town *very* early in January.[1] Mean while my *best Friends* must make Enquiries about the Work, and desire to be put down for some of the *first Copies* &c. because that will heighten his hopes, and possibly induce him to give me my 1000£ and let me go.

I must not let *you* go Dear Sir, till I have given Two Lines more to Mr. Giles's hospitable Kindness; useful indeed in sharp Times like these, when England is become a sort of Cut-finger-Club,[2] and every body helps himself without thinking on his Neighbour. But I am called, Adieu! keep horrid Gout out of your Stomack, and hasten to desert from that *Cold Stream* Company, which I fear has produced no Good. Come directly a L'Hotel Brunet and receive the Thanks &c. of our good Master and his / H: L: P.

Hotel Brunet
No. 25 Leicester Square

Text: Ry. 560.105.

1. As early as 22 April 1799, the *Oracle* reported: "Mrs. Piozzi, almost forgotten in the Metropolis, besides building a fine house in *Wales*, is busily engaged in adding another *tier* to the Temple of her *Literary* Reputation!"
Once Stockdale bought *Retrospection,* he began advertising it early in November 1800. By the 25th of that month, the *True Briton* ran as a news item that "a new work from the pen of Mrs. Piozzi is announced for publication." Although *Retrospection* was probably circulating by 1 January, the *London Chronicle*, 13–15 January 1801, advertised it as "This Day is Published."
2. "The word [*poltroon*] in old French means Cut Thumb: a Fellow so cowardly, that he cuts off his Thumb to avoid being killed in the Service of his Country" ("Commonplace Book").

TO PENELOPE SOPHIA PENNINGTON

Streatham Park
Monday Morning
[8] December 1800.

I received my Dear Friend your melancholy Letter, and am sorry to agree with you in that croaking Duet which we have long kept up together both by Letter and Conversation. Things do go on very shiningly and even brilliantly; but like the Ice Island you liked so in my Book,[1] There is an unseen Thaw below—and we shall topple over when 'tis least expected. Be perswaded however of England's *comparative* Happiness: Every other Nation suffers more than we do, more than perhaps the deepest Croaker amongst us gives him leave to apprehend: and so singular is the State of Europe just now, that sudden Peace would accelerate the Ruin of France, of Germany, of Russia and of the Britannic Islands.

The First would then be repaid her Ravages over poor dear Italy, by seeing her own hungry and desperate Plunderers come home clamorous for Rewards they never can receive, and Food which the neglected Lands could not produce for them. The second would inevitably split into Divisions productive of certain Annihilation to the *Empire* leaving Francis King only in Hungary, Bohemia &c. while Russia left the Theatre of Paul's caprices, would beat itself into Rebellion soon, and throw the North of Europe into Confusions much worse than those consequent on the present War.[2]

Great Britain would feel herself restrained in her Commerce, cut off from power of adding to that Wealth for which She is now envyed by all Mankind: nor could Cessation of Hostilities benefit any of the belligerent Powers except Rome and Turkey.—And They poor Things! fated to fall, and falling expiate their Predecessor's Crimes and Follies, continue to foment those Troubles to which Whoever conquers—They are sure to be the destined Victims. I think you recollect Mr. Lanzoni, his Accounts of Italian Distress public and private would half break your heart. He is among the few old Acquaintance we have in Town.[3]

Dear Siddons Story is a Tragical one, but the Ending has been happy, She will now I flatter myself be no more tormented. The whole Complaint ended in a Fistula, from which Sir James Earl relieved Her by cutting.[4] Doctor Carrick knows what *She* Suffered—from Experience: and She is now thin as a Lath, and light as Air, but safe as every body thinks,—Her Behaviour—Angelic Creature!—was on *this* Tryal as on *all* her Tryals, exemplary; firm, but unostentatious. Sir James said She was a *real* Heroine and no Actress on the occasion.

Lysons called at the Hotel, and got me a Sight of some Manuscripts kept in the British Musæum which I wanted for my Work, but he is gone to Bath now.

The Work is coming quick to a Conclusion, and will have a Print of the Authour on its first Page:[5] My heart delights not in the Notion of being Book*seller* so, as well as Book*maker;* but one cannot have all as one likes, and I hope People will *buy away.* Those Friends who mean to serve me *in earnest*, write to Stockdale even now, desiring to be "put down for an early Copy." I shall *present* you with one, but do canvass your rich Friends, and get them to purchase for Honour and for Profit's sake and all.

The darling Randolphs have done me all possible Kindness in that Way, so has Mr. Chappelow—and Stockdale shows his numerous *Orders* as Nest Eggs or Decoys.

The Account Mr. Keymer[6] a great Merchant gave me of the Rice coming cross the Atlantic in a fortnight's Time, has given me Spirits;[7] We shall be tried with *Abundance* next Year, but the Ministers will have a Million bounty Money to pay: They should have given the bounties at *home* to him Who sowed most Wheat &c. 'Tis all the fault can be found with Their Management—and had any wise Man suggested that Measure I doubt not but it would have been adopted.

Mean while Miss Thrales drove thro' London to Brighton the Seat of Gayety till Town Revels commence; We dined together and parted at the Lodgings of the Show Woman called a Nyctalope or Albina with red Eyes like a white Rabbet—very curious![8]

But I have written my Paper quite out, and must in the Frank add my true Love to Mr. Pennington <and> your good Mother. I must tell you beside that we have seen Colonel Barry who looks very well indeed—tho' Miss Trefusis seems to have forgotten him.[9] And the Letter must not be sealed till I mention my having met Lady Temple[10] a beautiful American who knew your Friend Anna <Powell>—who died at Detroit[11]——She said her Husband adored her, and was half distracted at her Loss. Farewell and believe me ever Yours / H: L: P.

Text: Princeton University Library. *Address:* [not in Mrs. Piozzi's hand] Mrs.

Pennington / Dowry Square / Hot Wells / Bristol. *Postmark:* DEC 8 1800 FREE; [signed] Free <W. Russell> *1800* / London Dec. Eighth.

1. In *Observations* (2:383), HLP describes "the great ice islands driving down *Rhenus ferox*, as Seneca justly calls it, and threatening to run against and destroy our awkward, ill-contrived boat." It was an adventure that she wanted to recollect "over a winter's fire, some evening in England," not to relive.

2. In December 1799 the commander of a Danish convoying frigate fired upon British boats that were trying to search Danish vessels. Merry, the British *chargé d'affaires* at Copenhagen, demanded an explanation, but the conduct of the Danish officer was defended and the British government was called upon for reparations. This affair was still under negotiation when in July 1800 the *Freya*, a Danish frigate, was taken with six vessels under her convoy in the English Channel.

By 27 August 1800 Czar Paul invited the monarchs of Prussia, Denmark, and Sweden to join with him in the establishment of principles of Armed Neutrality. On 7 November, an embargo was placed on British vessels in Russian ports, to be maintained until such times as the island of Malta should be surrendered to the Order of Saint John.

But more threatening was the rumor (which became fact on 16–18 December) of a series of treaties that would knit together Russia, Sweden, and Denmark in a second Armed Neutrality. See, e.g., *The Times*, 24 January 1801; 26 January; 12 February; etc.

3. Mr. Lanzoni and his Flemish Protestant wife had lived in Perugia, from which they fled when Napoleon overran northern Italy in 1796. They lived in Somers Town, London, at least until 1801. See *Thraliana* 2:1016–17 and n. 1.

4. For James Earle, the surgeon of the Hanover Square Hospital, see HLP to Jacob Weston, 18 December 1798, n. 3.

5. The portrait was painted by the French miniaturist Pierre Violet (1749–1819) and engraved by the Neapolitan Marino Bovi (b. 1758). Both artists had emigrated to London.

6. John Kymer lived in "Wood Lodge," near Saint Leonard's. An affluent landowner in Streatham, he was "a mercantile broker" at 38 Mincing Lane, London. When he died on 8 January 1816, his personal estate was declared at £154,273.

His widow, Mary Anne (d. 1851), and his daughter Elizabeth were to establish and conduct a school in Mitcham Lane, Streatham, for poor girls, known as the "Blue School."

7. By 18 December *The Times* reported: "Foreign Grain is now arriving in large quantities. In the course of the three weeks ending on Saturday last, upwards of 60,000 quarters were entered in the Port of London; and in the last three days, 36,500 quarters. We may therefore reasonably hope for a reduction of price, especially as advice was yesterday received, of the arrival of a very large fleet from the Northward, said to consist of nearly 100 sail of vessels, chiefly laden with corn."

8. The Misses Thrale knew a "Miss Hervey the Nyctalope, an Albinos shown for a Show this Winter, with white Hair & Red Eyes like a Rabbet; yet far from frightful, & even approaching to prettiness" (*Thraliana* 2:1014–15).

9. For Elizabeth Trefusis, see HLP to PSW, 1 September [1789], n. 9.

10. Elizabeth, née Watson (d. 1809), of Boston had married 20 March 1797 Grenville Temple (1768–1829), ninth baronet (1798).

11. Anne, née Powell (1760–92), had married Isaac Winslowe Clarke (d. 1822), deputy commissary general, Montreal. She had died in childbirth.

TO THE REVEREND LEONARD CHAPPELOW

Streatham Park
15: December 1800.

My Dear Sir

As I know how to send you a Letter now without its costing Postage, and at the same Time give myself an Opportunity of making Mr. Piozzi's best Respects and my own to the hospitable Mansion you are inhabiting;[1] I shall not think it necessary to wait for Materials, but begin at the Important Point to *me*, and relate to you charming Mrs. Clay's generous Friendship. She has been herself to Stockdale's, and ordered *Three Copies* of Retrospection. What a pretty Woman She is! says Stockdale. Ay replied I so She is, a *very* pretty Woman sure enough; but such an Errand would have made almost *any* Woman pretty: and he has a particular Pane of Glass to look at Subscribers thro I suppose.

Our Ally Francis has tried his best to end my last Chapter with the taking of Vienna and ultimate Fall of the once holy Roman Empire, but do his *worst*, it will probably last one other Year or two.[2] Paul too is a fine Fellow, the personal Friends of Abbè Edgeworth are under Apprehension that his Louis 18th will be sent to Siberia[3] whither that faithful Adherent will not fail to accompany him—— all this if Buonaparte thinks proper——for Paul is supposed a mere Puppet in the hands of France, while he perhaps means to make them *his* Tools in driving out the Grand Signor from Constantinople.[4]

Meanwhile Mr. Giles tells me that we are *now* before the Arrivals from Ireland, no fewer than 1,500,000—one Million and a half Inhabitants of the Metropolis, which if a Frost comes to block up the River, must absolutely and positively *starve* of Hunger and Cold. He says that Holland has shut her Ports against all Exportation, and that 'tis the Intention of our Enemies to force us to a Peace by Famine: not doubting but the Populace will rise upon a Government which provides against Want, only by recommending Œconomy.[5]

Fine Times! are they not? and getting gradually worse and worse every hour. Dear Lady Bradford was always willing to be of the croaking Party, and if it were not for a few pious and virtuous and exemplary Characters like hers, I think we should come still sooner to an End. For the sake of such People——perhaps we may *yet* be pulled thro' by an all powerful hand; the Embarrassment will however be very serious between this and March. London's present Dependance is on the Carolina Ships loaded with Rice——God send them a fair Wind, and keep the Weather open——'Tis all our Chance so far as human Eyes can see.[6]

Pray give my kindest Compliments to Mr. Dickenson[7] and ask him if he saw the *Fata Morgana* at *Plymouth*. I *think* he said Brest and Plymouth were the Places; but I wish to know exactly.[8] He will recollect the Conversation instantly. The Story Father Angelucci tells is quoted in Swinburne's Travels; but I want good English Evidence—I trust 'twas Summer when he saw the Show.[9]

Adieu dear Mr. Chappelow, write to me soon and say that the little Dears have not forgotten their true Friend / and faithful Servant / H: L: Piozzi.

If the Lady I left at Weston is not gone thence, make her remember me too.

Text: Ry. 560.106. *Address:* Rev: Mr. Chappelow.

1. LC was at Weston, the seat of Lord and Lady Bradford.
2. In this paragraph is HLP's realization that Austria (following the defeat at Hohenlinden) would necessarily yield to superior power, that Naples would soon surrender, that the Peace of Lunéville would be dictated by Bonaparte, and that Great Britain by early 1801 would not have a single significant ally on the Continent.
3. Siberia is called to mind because of a recent event. On 7 November the czar had announced the imposition of an embargo on British vessels in Russian ports. The crews of two such vessels managed their escape. The czar, therefore, ordered the burning of a third vessel, which had remained in the harbor. Many British seamen were marched as prisoners into the interior of Russia, some as far as Siberia.
4. Louis XVIII and his entourage (which included the Abbé Edgeworth) were to be asked by the czar on 14 January 1801 to leave Mittau, Courland. They were to move to Memel in Prussia and then to Warsaw, settling in the latter place until 1804 and returning to Mittau in the following year.
   For the Abbé Edgeworth, see HLP to PSP, 26 April 1793, n. 6.
5. On 23 December (Ry. 563.69), LC dismissed both HLP's fears and information stated in this paragraph.
   "Never mind what Mr. Giles tells you.—The most extravagant Calculator never made the population of *our Island* more than 11 millions.—As to corn—I never mind what a Corn Merchant says,—and the Last Sentence of your Letter—'not doubting but the populace will rise upon a government which provides against want, only by recommending Œconomy'—is a dreadful Idea."
   Despite LC's demurrer, the method of solving scarcity by economy was recommended by the *True Briton* on 10 December, in echo of the king's speech on the opening of Parliament. The newspaper urged "the higher orders of the community" to substitute "some other sort of food" for wheaten products "to the end that bread may become cheaper *to the poorer classes of people.*"
6. Some of the ships that HLP expected arrived at Deal on 1 January 1801. See *The Times*, 3 January 1801: "This morning arrived here and sailed for the River, the Mercury, Tate, from Charlestown; and the Messina, McKinley, from Surinam: parted company from the West India fleet on the 16th of November, in a gale of wind: they were under convoy of the *Hydra* frigate."
   On 5 January *The Times* reported:
   "In addition to [the] supply of wheat and flour, a considerable quantity of rice may be drawn from different parts of the world.
   "From the Southern States of North America, your Committee are informed that a supply may be obtained of 70,000 barrels (each weighing 5 cwt.) of which a part will probably arrive in January, and the remainder successively in the ensuing months."
7. William Dickinson (1771–1837) of Kingweston, Somerset; M.P. Ilchester (1796–1802), Lostwithiel (1802–6), Somerset (1806–31).
8. HLP needed information about "the *Fata Morgana*" in order to conclude *Retrospection* (2:539). The vision appeared off the coast at Falmouth.
9. Henry Swinburne, *Travels in the Two Sicilies . . . in the Years 1777, 1778, 1779, and 1800*, 2 vols. (London: P. Elmsly, 1783–85). In 1:365–67, Swinburne cites Father Angelucci's description of *La Fata Morgana* off the Sicilian shore.

30 December 1800

TO THE REVEREND THOMAS SEDGWICK WHALLEY

No. 25 Leicester Fields
Tuesday 30: December 1800.

My Dear Sir
The kind mention you make of us in the Letter our lovely Siddons shewed us Three Days ago, produces you this Intrusion: chiefly to ask what *can* have Inspired any Countryman of mine to debase his Profession And Birthplace by an Endeavour to traduce that admirable Creature Hannah More?[1]

> I hate when Vice can bolt her Arguments
> And Virtue has no Tongue to check her Pride

says Milton.[2] And they want now to stop the warning Voice which yet should save us, if Men would permit. So valuable a Writer, and Writings so well-timed as *hers* will not be found again: and if their vile Detractions should injure her feeble Health, The Mischief done would be past my Computation.[3]

Let me not detain *you* from supporting her Spirits and her Cause a single Moment; but when a Leisure Hour *does* come give *me* the benefit, by saying a kind Word of Retrospection: which could not quite look over her Merits without a Line;[4] and scarce has that close-clapt Epitome more than a Line to bestow on Characters more prominent tho' not more useful than her own.

We publish on Newyear's Day—and Stockdale seems in high Glee when he looks at his *Order Book*. My own Nerves are not so strong; and I see many a sneering Face, even before anything but the *Attempt,* can have provoked them to sneer.

Adieu my dear Sir! and do me all the Good you can; and believe me ever / Yours and Mrs. Whalley's / Obliged and faithful / Servant / H: L: Piozzi.

Accept 10,000 Respects and Compliments from my good Husband.

Text: Berg Collection +. *Address:* Rev: Thomas Sedgwick Whalley / Longford Cottage near / Bristol. *Postmark:* DE 3<   > 800.

1. An Oxonian with a B.A. from Jesus College (1772), Thomas Bere or Bear (1748–1814), who had been born in Glamorgan, was rector of Butcombe, near Bristol, and curate of Blagdon, Somerset. Having instigated the so-called Blagdon controversy, he often boasted in his charges and countercharges of his "ancient Welsh descent" (Wickham 1:28).
2. *A Mask* ("Comus"), lines 760–61.
3. Implicit in this paragraph is the matter of the Blagdon controversy.
Blagdon School, on the northern slopes of the Mendips, had been financed by Henry Thornton and set up by the More sisters in 1795. Here Hannah More placed one of her most trusted schoolmasters, a Mr. Younge, late of Nailsea and originally from Bath.
The school offered boys of the "superior poor" enough basic skills to become overseers, constables, journeymen, farmers, and tradesmen. The school was first attacked by Bere in 1798 in a sermon at Axbridge. Malicious tales about the school continued. In the autumn

of 1800 Bere wrote a letter to Hannah More wherein he insisted upon the instant dismissal of Younge, whom he accused of being a Methodist.

While much that Bere demanded was satisfied, he continued his attacks and proclaimed his victory over Hannah More, who closed Blagdon School. This is where the controversy stood at the end of December 1800. Lasting until 1803, it revolved about the question of whether the poor should be educated and, if so, by whom.

The phrase "past my computation" is an indirect borrowing from SJ (*Letters* 1: 314) and Richard Cumberland (*The West Indian*, 1771). See HLP to Q, 26 May 1806, n. 6.

4. In *Retrospection* 2:508, HLP makes a comparison between Burke's work on the French Revolution and a treatise by Hannah More on the same subject. She goes on to comment that Hannah More "*strengthened* those eyes, which *his* book did but dazzle."

TO LADY WILLIAMS

No. 25 Leicester Square
London
3rd: January 1801.

That my Dear Lady Williams should not have heard from me is almost as strange as it is vexatious—I wrote a Long letter from old Streatham Park, the very week after we arrived in the Environs of London; enclosing it with another—freed by Lord William Russell[1] and Directed to Mr. Moore of Denbigh, with orders for him to forward it as I thought to save Postage till I had more to tell.

Intelligence does not encrease however——Public matters fly to the remote Provinces so quickly by the Post, that they are known to the most distant before we have done talking of them who live upon the Spot. With regard to Emperor Paul there seems but one Opinion, every one must hear of his Tyrannies with Indignation; and no one can forbear to suspect that half crazy as he certainly is, Buonaparte makes a Tool of him to torment us, while he hopes through French Assistance to drive those wretched Ottomans from Constantinople, who are so hard put to it to keep their Seat.

Upon the other general Subject of Discourse Men's Opinions are less undivided: some Still persisting that there is no Scarcity, Others maintaining the failure of past Crops not only in Great Britain but in those Countries too whence we were used to derive Assistance without Difficulty.[2] But the King of Naples being driven with a prodigious Number of Emigrant Families to Sicily,[3] rendered that Island incapable of exporting Wheat as formerly and dear Mr. Piozzi's Country men tell *him* that the Horses, Oxen &c. in the North of Italy have been so put in requisition that Large Tracts of Land there lie waste for want of Tillage, whilst a civil war of *Opinions* among the Inhabitants, some holding fast by the Old way, some embracing the new notions brought amongst them by the French make that once lovely Country a Theatre of Agony, and produce such Dearness of Provisions that at Genoa a Dog's head was sold for five Shillings English during the Siege; and Friends, Enemies, Soldiers, Traders alike perished more by Hunger than the Sword.[4]—

Here in London the earnest recommendation of Œconomy from the throne has really produced very desirable Effects and tho' Bread does not fall yet, neither does it rise: the Sea is covered with Ships bringing Rice from East and West Indies—all freighted for *Imperial Britain:* The Project of making none *but* Coarse Bread to be Eaten alike in the Palaces and in Workhouses will keep people quiet till those ships come in,[5] and for my own Part, I believe we shall have one more Tryal of Abundance next Summer: Such Immense Orders have been sent out, which once arrived must force the Monopolizers Corn from their Granaries, and shew mankind that there was no Collusion between them and ministry;[6] a Supposition so very dangerous, I know not where its horrible Effects would have stopt.[7] As it is The King went very Peaceably to the House two Days ago, and our new Century was rung in by every Bell of every Church in London.—

My Book is just in the Birth *now,* We wait in London only to see how it is received and then retire to Streatham Park again,—in our way to Bath. Mr. Piozzi has a fashionable Cough and so have I; but Country Air will blow 'em off I hope and never was spring so mild as this merciful Winter. London has been foggy to excess, but the Environs have appeared bright and clear all the Time; and Miss Thrales write word that Brighthelmstone which is a Place of fashionable Resort at Christmas—enjoys a Sunshine like April Weather. Town is dull yet because no Effect has been hitherto produced by the union: Numberless Families from Ireland however are expected, to fill these new Houses among which I really feel quite *lost:* So enormous is the increase of Buildings since our Absence but here is not a bit of Room left for our Compliments and Respects to Dear Sir John and his charming Family.

Text: Ry. 1 (1796–1802). *Address:* Lady Williams / Bodylwyddan / near St. Asaph / Flintshire N.W. *Postmark:* JA 3 .801.

1. For Lord William Russell, see HLP to Q, 13 November 1793, n. 3.
2. An example of such division exists in the First Report of a committee of the Commons on the high price of provisions. "There appears . . . reason to believe, that the general deficiency in the crops of wheat, in England and Wales, below an average crop, *does not amount to quite so much as* One Fourth. . . . It is also probable that, in forming an average . . . where the harvest has been so uncommonly various in different districts, and even in different parts of the same district, greater weight may have been given to instances of deficiency than to those of abundance, and that the produce is more likely to be stated below than above the truth. . . . The accounts of the stock in hand furnished by these returns . . . do not, upon the whole, furnish any ground for doubting the prevailing opinion . . . that the stock of British corn, at the harvest, was reduced far below its usual amount, and was in most places nearly, in many absolutely exhausted." See *GM* 70, pt. 2 (1800): 1203–4; cf. nn. 6, 7.
3. See HLP to Ly W, 10 February 1799, n. 8.
4. For the siege of Genoa, 20 April–4 June 1800, see HLP to LC, 19 May [1800], n. 16.
5. The committee of the Commons in its Fourth Report "recommends an alteration in the dressing of wheat, so as to make only the coarsest bread, which will not only extend the quantity and flour, but also lessen the price. . . . The Committee likewise thinks, that bread made of barley, wheat, rice, rye, and oatmeal mixed, would be good and wholesome bread." See *GM* 70, pt. 2 (1800): 1276. These recommendations were incorporated into the Brown Bread Bill so that by 31 January "the sale of fine wheaten bread" was

prohibited; and "brown bread will consequently be generally used." See *AR*, "Chronicle" 43 (1801): 2.

6. Shortly after the opening of Parliament on 11 November, Wilberforce Bird, an M.P. for Coventry, argued that his constituents suffered "the grievous pressure of an artificial dearth" that could be attributed only to "monopoly and extortion" unchecked by ministry and Parliament. See Stanhope 3:252.

So prevalent were the charges of collusion between corn factors, e.g., and the government that a committee of the Lords examined the evidence and finally vindicated the ministry. See *GM* 70, pt. 2 (1800): 1205.

7. Pitt attributed Bird's "dangerous" charge to "the spirit of Jacobinism, taking advantage of the pressure of hunger, as it does of everything . . . to increase the mischief." As Pitt continued his reply: "I know, too, that there has been a disposition to inculcate the mischievous idea that it was in the power of [government] to make every deficiency disappear—a deficiency arising principally from a succession of unfavourable seasons, whatever other causes may have contributed to it—and at once to produce abundance and cheapness" (Stanhope 3:253).

TO HESTER MARIA THRALE

4: January 1801.
Leicester Square.

"Who has a Mind to teize himself and repent of his Sins (said the Greek Lady I remember) let him travel thro' Transylvania and let *him* miscarry there"—I say who has a Mind to teize herself and repent of her Sins, let *her* write Retrospection! Stockdale advertising the Book for New Years Day has brought in a Crowd of Orders and we have no Copies to send out in any Degree answerable to the Demand.

Mr. Gillon for *private Friends of his own* commanded *fourscore and one*. The Country Booksellers too are quite clamourous, and if it had not been for the Secession of Compositors, Devils &c. who retired to Mons Sacer, and refused to Work; we should have been out of Print during the first Fortnight: such Mortification would have made an Aristocrate of any one.[1]

I hope *Your* Book is arrived—for heav'ns Sake lend it no one.[2] A Fellow Student begged the Loan of a Book from Mr. Gray when he was a Boy at College, and refused—but added as a Sweet'ner—that his Friend might come if he pleased—to his Rooms and *read it*. The Winter was a Cold one, and Gray soon requested his Neighbour's Bellows—Not a Bit on't was the Answer—but he is welcome to come to my Chambers and blow. Seriously however lending a Book ruins its Sale, and you must cry Charming! and keep it at home, if you mean good to the bustling Author. The Copy I dispatched from Piccadilly with a Letter in it to Susette, was packed up *Thursday Evening* for the Brighton Stage—let me hear if 'tis Safely arrived: I fear our Binders must not sleep for three Nights running.

Can you forgive my having utterly forgotten who Mr. Cotton is going to marry.[3] Lady Somebody and there's dear Miss Owen bursting in Ignorance[4] and

I can tell her nothing of what She considers an Event of the 1st Magnitude.—
And so it *is* too in private Life God knows; and so *your* Friend Miss Myddelton
finds it I understand.[5]

Sophia's *lame* Lover haunts me because I am so like her. He is an agreable
Gentlemanlike Man:[6] Mr. Rogers is charming! when will his Play come out, and
what Play will it be?[7] Godwin's Tragedy fell to Ground most mournfully.[8] Mrs.
Siddons's Constance is the nearest Thing to Perfection I ever saw represented on
any Stage, her health seems quite established and She has dressed that antique
Character with Such appropriate and becoming Ornaments, as Garrick's Shade
might gaze on with Delight.[9]

Will Mrs. Wilson be pleased with my 22d Chapter 2d Volume?[10] It would vex
me that *She* should not have one of the earliest Copies, but I guess not to whom
She applies—The 19th is my personal Favourite,[11] and as to the *Tout Ensemble*, I
expect it to be read backwards like a Witch's Prayer; for every one wishes to See
what is said of near Times, rather than remote.

Do tell me what you hear, and Adieu. Mr. Piozzi has got a Cough, and is lazy;
but says the March shall be made out somehow, altho he understands not setting
Music for a Harp—at least tis so I understand him. London fills every Day and
hour, but you must direct if you please to Streatham Park, for thither I shall go—
to hide my Blushes.

Once more farewell! And accept our united Wishes of a happy Year,—a happy
Century. It is not out of *Possibility* to any Child of your / ever Affectionate Mother
/ H: L: P.

I have caught Cold myself at last. We shall spend all our Substance in
Lozenges.—Stick Liquorice is at Double Price now—because of the War.—

Text: Bowood Collection. *Address:* Miss Thrale / Brighthelmstone / Sussex.
Postmark: 5 JA 1801.

1. Not mentioned specifically by name, "Compositors Devils" joined those "conspiracies [which] have been set on foot by Journeymen of various Trades, to enforce an augmentation of wages" (*The Times*, 23 December 1800).
Mont Sacré (Mónte Sacro in Italian), a region near Rome associated in 493 B.C. with an uprising of Roman common people.
2. HLP received ten advance copies of *Retrospection*, which she immediately distributed: one each to RG, Harriet Lee, SS, Lady Eleanor Butler, Jane Holman, RD, PSP, John Gillon. Of the two remaining copies she kept one for herself and sent one to Q as the recipient for the Miss Thrales. See HLP's "Pocket Book" for 1801 (N.L.W., MS 11097 A).
3. On 1 January Lady Anna Maria Pelham-Clinton (1783–1807), eldest daughter of the third duke of Newcastle, had married Stapleton Cotton (1773–1865). An army officer, he was to be elevated to the peerage as Baron Combermere (17 May 1814) for heroism in the Peninsular War; to be further advanced to the dignity of Viscount Combermere (8 February 1827) for the capture of Bhurtpore in the East Indies.
4. Cf. *Hamlet*, 1.4.44–45; frequently quoted by HLP.
5. Charlotte Myddelton (ca. 1768–1843) was to marry on 24 December 1801 Robert Biddulph (d. 1814) of Ledbury, Herefordshire, and Cofton Hall, Worcestershire. See *GM* 71, pt. 2 (1801): 1149.
6. HLP was premature in regarding Samuel Rogers as ST's "lover," even as she had

Samuel Rogers. Portrait by John Hoppner, R. A.; engraved by Henry Meyer. Published in the *New Monthly Magazine* (London, 1 November 1831), by Henry Colburn and Richard Bentley. (Reproduced by permission of the Henry E. Huntington Library and Art Gallery, San Marino, California.)

been in seeing him as CMT's suitor in 1789. See HLP to PSP, 14 January [1794]; *Thraliana* 2:868–69.

7. HLP's daughters had recently met Rogers, who on 19 January wrote from Brighton to his sister Sarah. "Here are also the Miss Thrales. . . . From some accident I have never been acquainted with them, though they accuse me of having shunned them. They are very elegant, sensible women, and are a great addition to the society here" (P. W. Clayden, *The Early Life of Samuel Rogers* [1887], p. 420).

Rogers came close to theatrical composition only in 1795 when he wrote an epilogue for SS, one which she had "spoken . . . 'after a tragedy performed for her benefit at the Theatre Royal, Drury Lane, April 27th, 1795' " (Clayden, p. 292).

8. Godwin's *Antonio; A Tragedy* had opened—and closed—at the Drury Lane on 13 December 1800 with Kemble as Don Antonio and SS as Helena. One critic regarded it "as impotent an attempt . . . as the Stage has exhibited for many years" (Baker, p. 242).

9. SS by royal command first played Constance in Shakespeare's *King John* on 10 December 1783 and frequently thereafter.

In this season *King John* opened at the Drury Lane on 29 November with Kemble in the title role. According to *The Times* on 1 December:

"Mrs. Siddons, who appears to be perfectly recovered from the indisposition which has for some time deprived the stage of her fascinating talent, performed . . . the character of Lady *Constance*, in the Tragedy of *King John*. It has been long considered one of her most finished exhibitions, and her performance on Saturday proved" the judgment correct.

Repeat performances took place on 4, 11, 20, and 30 December, again on 14 January 1801.

10. Mrs. Wilson was Jemima (1777–1823), daughter of Colonel William Belford of Harbletown, Kent, and coheiress, with her sister, of their uncle, Sir Adam Williamson (1736–98), lieutenant general, governor of Jamaica and Santo Domingo. On 8 July 1797 at Gretna Green and again at Saint George's, Hanover Square on 10 March 1798, she married Robert Thomas Wilson (1777–1849), an army officer, knighted (1814), general (1841), governor of Gibraltar (1842).

Retrospection, vol. 2, chap. 22, deals with the history of Europe from 1780 to 1790, ending with portraits of Marie Caroline and her sister Marie Antoinette in 1789.

11. The events described in chap. 19 coincide with the years of HLP's coming of age and maturity. She writes of her father as an early colonist in Nova Scotia, of the growth of British prosperity and culture, naming such writers as Hume, Smith, Gibbon, Robertson, Gray, Beattie, Melmoth, Blair, and SJ.

Chap. 19 (*Retrospection* 2:418–38) is entitled "Great Britain, Ireland, and America, from 1750 to 1780." HLP characterizes the period as one of expanding intellectual discovery and aesthetic refinement.

TO THE REVEREND ROBERT GRAY

Wednesday, 7th Jan. 1801.

For my own part the world has used me to indulgence, so that I feel quite astonished when I meet a little severity.[1]

There has been *very* little yet.[2] One gentleman, in his care for my reputation as to scholarship, sent a friend across the town yesterday to tell me that the quotation in vol. 1st. p. 381 was *quite wrong*, because *Anna*, not *Acca*, was the woman's name there called upon. It was almost painful to me to tell *him* that, tho Dido's sister (like the lady's sister in Bluebeard) was *Anna*, Camilla's companion in flight was Acca, and called sister only from tenderness.[3] Almost *every* Latin quotation and many French ones are wrong printed. . . . Mr. Gillet's rebellion among his compositors was a terrible stroke on poor Stockdale and myself,[4] and I was forced to rout out my dirty manuscript an hour ago to convince a Roman Catholic critick that it was not *my* fault but the *devil's,* that their hymn to St. John was so mangled, 1st vol. p. 251.[5] He made no complaint of any *mistake* in page 304, the same volume.[6]

Dear Mr. Gray, say a good word of the book in general, and let us get out of print, and set forth a more correct edition; and let us never flatter ourselves hereafter that a clean handwriting is any security against typographical errors.

Text: Hayward 2:256–57.

1. Cf. *Anecdotes,* p. 84.
2. HLP was only now aware of the many errors and incomplete statements that plagued *Retrospection*. She therefore prepared an errata sheet (see HLP to Q, 28 January) and corrected copies sent to her by friends for emendation. One such is at the Houghton Library, Harvard. Thus, on 19 June 1802, she wrote: "Mrs. Piozzi has the honour to return to Mr. [Theodore] Broadhead the Book corrected in the best Manner she is able——were the Paper less shocking bad, the Work would not be so difficult, but tis like writing on blotting stuff" (A 1693.5).

In vol. 1, HLP corrected errors on about fifty pages. She did the same for vol. 2, although the errors and additions were less numerous.

3. As HLP cites the *Aeneid* in *Retrospection* (1:381), she introduces the name of Camilla and quotes her dying words to her companion, Acca: see 11.823–24. Quite rightly HLP maintains that Anna (who appears frequently in the fourth book of the *Aeneid*) is Dido's sister.

Blue Beard, an "oriental" tale from the French of Charles Perrault, was translated ca. 1729 by Robert Samber. In the narrative Fatima, who almost becomes one of Blue Beard's sacrificial wives, has an older "Sister Anne."

4. Thomas Gillet (fl. 1778–1810) owned a printing shop (in partnership with a John Ferriday) in Salisbury Square and Hanging Sword Alley, Fleet Street.

5. In *Retrospection* (1:251), HLP cites the first four lines:

> *Ut* queant laxis *re*sonare fabris,
> *Mi*ra gestorum, *fa*mula tuorum,
> *Sol*re polluti *la*bi reatum
> Sancte Johannes!

The Broadhead copy includes the following substantive corrections: fabris >fibris; famula >famuli; Solre >Solve; labi >labiis.

The five-stanza hymn is part of Second Vespers, 24 June, for the *Nativity of Saint John the Baptist*. The music, written by Guido of Arezzo (11th century), "fixes" the hexachord and is a landmark in musical notation.

6. This page centers on Pope Alexander, his power, wisdom, and compassion.

TO HESTER MARIA THRALE

No. 77 Great Pultney Street Bath
Wednesday 28: January 1801.

The kind Letter directed to Brunet's hôtel followed me to Streatham Park and from thence hither. But indeed My Dear Girl does herself and me both much wrong in not Supposing the Praises it contains—exceedingly valuable, and by Me very highly esteemed. Mr. *Gray*'s cordial Commendations run most in the Same Strain with *yours* of all my Correspondents.

Dr. Randolph likes the *Crusading* Chapter and the *last* above all others.[1] Something told me while I was writing the ninth of my 2d Volume that that would be your favourite:[2] The Story of Guido de Montford in the first Volume Page 369 was the likeliest to please Mr. Siddons,[3] and you shall find as Bottom the Weaver says—"It will fall out pat as I told you."[4] Meanwhile the Errors are Intolerable as Innumerable, but instead of Verses I will send you a List of Mistakes; and do for Mercy's Sake correct the Places, or paste in a Copy of these few Errata adding any other you can find. The Words are perpetually transposed—*Yet as*, for *as Yet*,[5] and I am desirous of a new Edition chiefly on Account of these Vexatious *Lapses*—but not of *my Pen*.

Mr. Rogers will not like it I think, but he will give Sophia prettier Verses for her Album than I could.[6]

Those made so long ago on the Library Pictures at Streatham Park are now upon the Sea in their Way to Wales:[7] if none of our numerous Foes catch the Ship they are in with divers other literary Rareties, I will copy them for *you* whose Memory might supply mine perhaps even if they were taken. The *first* would be most difficult for *me* to recollect,—I cannot think on the beginning for my Life, and I have thought of nothing else since your Letter came this Morning.

We have got a nice House: last in Pultney Street, or first in Laura Place, Hannah More at the next Door. There has been a Sad Piece of Work about her and her Sunday Schools, and they have vexed her till She is half dead.[8]

The Duchess of York is coming:[9] all Ex Ministers, all disappointed Lovers, all hissed Actors, all lampooned Ladies, all satirized and mortified Authors are bilious; and try,—whether successfully or not,—to wash away Care with these Waters: Vexation gives the Jaundice always,—don't you remember a Story how Foote Said to Lewcup the Man who had just stood in the Pillory, and been pelted for Forging a Banker's Draft?—Ay Ay I'm come here *to wash the Effs off my Face*.[10] This used to be one of Murphy's best Tales—Susanna should make him tell it her. I hope *her* Friend Mrs. Wilson will be satisfied with what I have Said concerning Lord Chatham and his Son. Here is scarce room to say another Word.[11] No not even kind Words *e*xpressed, of horrible Apprehensions suppressed at the beginning of this *19th* Century. Will any one at the *End* of it write a Retrospection of these Times? and will there by any one alive to read it if they do? Ah Me! what terrifying Fancies fill the Mind of your H: L: P.

Mr. Piozzi sends his best Regards and returns your kind Invitation to Sussex by wishing to see you here.

Text: Bowood Collection.

1. The "Crusading Chapter" is the sixteenth in *Retrospection* 1:271–88: "From the Year 1097, First Crusade, to the Middle of the Twelfth Century, A.D. 1150."
The concluding chapter (2:521–40) is the twenty-fourth: "Last Four Years of the Century, from 1796 to 1800."

2. *Retrospection* 2:181–204: "Portugal, Persia, India, China, Turkey, Africa, and Rome. To 1650."

3. "Simon de Montfort, earl of Leicester . . . had two sons, Simon, and Guy; who after the well known battle of Evesham fled to Italy, and finding at Viterbo young Henry, heir to Richard earl of Cornwall, their's, and their father's enemy of course, being allied to the English throne so closely: they watched him to a church, and killed him undefended at the altar, during the elevation of the host. Edward, returning from Palestine upon his father's death," demanded justice: "but Simon died before sentence could be pronounced, and Guy fled to the Aldobrandini palace for protection." Still the pope drove Guy, like Cain, from society. For Guy's penance, as he stands holding a strangler's cord and a crucifix, "*Retrospection* has but just time to see the culprit tranquillized, and sent to Sicily, where faithful Charles had orders to detain him . . . and the good patriarch of Aquileia was permitted, in his dying moments, to absolve him" (1:369–70).

4. See HLP to Charlotte Lewis, 20 September [17]89, n. 6.

5. HLP had written to John Gillon as her negotiator for the sale of *Retrospection* to Stockdale. In the missing letter she had expressed her anxiety about the errors. Gillon on 26 January assured HLP that she would have "ample Time to correct them" in a second edition. According to the bookseller, "the Sale went on [but] so slowly, that there would be no Necessity for a new Edition for the present" (Ry. 578.71).

6. ST, who had a new album, requested her mother to write a poem for it. HLP wrote twenty-two lines of rhyming couplets, which began: "Alas! dear Sophia what is it you ask? / To write for an album is no easy Task." The hope of the couplets was "That your Life may be as clean as your Album appears." See "Written at the request of Miss S. Thrale for her Album," in "Verses 1," pp. 96–97.

7. "[Twenty-six] Lines written on seeing the Portraits of Burke, Johnson, Garrick, Goldsmith &c in the Library at Streatham Park" (Ry. 656.51). The verses are a tribute to Streatham Park as a "calm retreat / Where Wealth in bounteous Streams was wont to flow / . . . Where long neglected Merit ceas'd to roam / And found an happy hospitable home." In the Rylands draft, the lines are merely roughed out—unsigned, undated, and unpunctuated.

8. For Hannah More and the Blagdon controversy, see HLP to PSP, 5 April, 3 June, 20 July, 28 August, 15 December 1801; to RG, 3 February 1802.

9. The duke and duchess of York resided at Oatlands (he at least on weekends) but not as husband and wife. In coming to Bath—HLP intimates—the duchess would be just one more frustrated person seeking solace there.
For Frederica, duchess of York, see HLP to John Mostyn, 22 June 1795, n. 13.

10. In the preferments list for 1752, Peter Leheup (d. 1777) appears as one of the chief clerks of the treasury. In 1755 he was convicted in the court of the King's Bench for fraud in connection with a lottery. On 9 May 1755, he "just escaped from the pillory" by being fined £1,000 "which he paid immediately in court." See *GM* 22 (1752): 536; 25 (1755): 184, 233.
The anecdote is in *Thraliana* 1:575, dated Bath, 28 October 1783.

11. See *Retrospection* 2:482. "The year 1784 . . . called up Mr. William Pitt, second son to the great Lord Chatham; [who inherited] his talents rather than his animation." As HLP pursued her comparison: the son was "a financier capable of healing Britannia's recent

wounds, soothing her sorrows, conciliating her cruel enemies, and likely, by a series rather than a cluster of endeavours, to seat her high among her struggling competitors; rendering her wealth, her honour, and her happiness, progressive on to times beyond *our* sight; when neighbours unalarmed should let her mount, and touch the pinnacle of earthly perfection."
See also *Retrospection* 2:435.

TO PENELOPE SOPHIA PENNINGTON

31: January 1801

My dear Mrs. Pennington's
is indeed a dismal Letter, and our Master is truly sorry, and so am I.

The Amusement I get at Bath—when without your Conversation—is feeling myself benefited by these darling Waters, and hearing the Circulating Library Men say that the Book sells very well.[1] Stockdale tells me of Praises bestowed on it by the Briton, Times, and Porcupine but I have never seen any.[2]—

Little did I dream that your dear Husband and our amiable Friend Mr. Pennington was suffering such Torture as you describe. Poor Soul! he has our best Wishes for his speedy Recovery, and shall have the finest Turkey ever seen when he can come and eat it.

Miss Jane Powell must be left I think to cut out her own Happiness.[3] She is very sensible and very charming, but you may remember that Doctor Johnson says in his Tale of the Fountains——You may be lovely, but tis not a necessary Consequence that you should therefore be beloved.[4]—We must hope she will not fling so much Merit and Beauty away; but if she does—let us remember She could not have been happy *without* changing her Mode of Life, and those who enter on Family cares no<w> have need of strong Affection on one Side or the other, to support them thro' so rough a journey as what is left of Life's Road is likely to afford them.

The People who are *Indifferent* now, are truly unwise to marry.

We shall look to your *coming home* for much Chat on all Subjects and principally the book which has so long / plagued Your / H: L: P.

If you will bring it with you I will correct *the Typographical Errors myself.*[5]

Text: Princeton University Library. *Address:* Mrs. Pennington / Dowry Square / Hot Wells / Bristol. *Postmark:* BATH.

1. "Mrs. Piozzi told D. Lysons that 25 Copies of her new work *Retrospection,* had been sold in Bath only, which she thought a good sale" (Farington, 3 February, 4:1494). But Stockdale was far less encouraging (see HLP to LC, 14 February, n. 4).
2. Stockdale had placed laudatory advertisements in all three newspapers. See, e.g., the *True Briton,* 25 November; *The Times,* 4 November, 26 December 1800, 8 January 1801.

The *Porcupine* was a short-lived newspaper (October 1800 to November 1801) founded by William Cobbett (1762–1835), politician and essayist. For advertisements, see 20 and 25

November; 4, 11, 18 December; 9, 27 January. A brief extract appears on the 28th: "Mrs. Piozzi, in her entertaining *Retrospect*, observes 'that Bonaparte is the first General, who ever wore, *as a name* the title of Destroyer. This his Christian name, Nappollione, expresses according to Corsican pronunciation.—Turned into Greek it is appollyon which signifies Destroyer.—See 9th chapter of St. John's Apocalypse, 11th verse.' "

Advertisements appeared also in the *Courier and Evening Gazette,* 1 January; the *London Chronicle,* 13–15 January; the *Morning Post,* 19 January.

3. Jane Powell was to marry the Reverend Thomas Warren (1769–1851), vicar of Tolpuddle, Dorset, from 1805 until his death.

4. Lilinet admonishes Floretta: " 'You are not, my dear, to wonder or complain: You may wish for yourself, but your wishes can have no effect upon another. You may become lovely by the efficacy of the fountain, but that you shall be loved is by no means a certain consequence; for you cannot confer upon another either discernment or fidelity; That happiness which you must derive from others, it is not in my power to regulate or bestow.' " See "The Fountains: A Fairy Tale," in Anna Williams, *Miscellanies in Prose and Verse* (London: T. Davies, 1766), p. 126.

5. For HLP's justified anxiety about typographical errors in *Retrospection,* see HLP to RG, 7 January; Gillon to HLP, 26 January (Ry. 578.71); HLP to Q, 21 June.

TO LADY SALUSBURY

No. 25: Leicester Square London
[January] 1801.

Lady Salusbury will with Difficulty recognize in the Portrait accompanying this Letter any Features of the Girl with whom She once was pleased, or of the Woman with whom She once was offended:[1] but since Time's Wing has swept all away that stood between them 40 Years ago; let it—in God's Name—sweep away Offence too: for why when the Figures are removed—should the Cobwebs that clung to them remain?

To the many Manuscript Trifles written by the same hand when *both were Young;* let Lady Salusbury good naturedly add the Acceptance of this Book[2]—— presented by the Author / Hester Lynch Piozzi.

Text: Ry. 533.24; a draft.

1. For several years HT and HLT had been suing the widowed Lady Salusbury. But in 1782 the court ruled that she was entitled to the money her husband had given to John Salusbury to pay off the mortgage on Bachygraig. HLT had assumed that her uncle never meant to be repaid but the court upheld Lady Salusbury's claim for £8,000. Afraid to pursue the matter further, HLT—now widowed—agreed to her opponent's compromise of £7,500. She borrowed from her daughters' inheritance, at interest, and with the mortgage as security. See Hyde, pp. 233–34.

Although the lawsuit was an immediate source of friction, a resentful HLP also held Lady Salusbury responsible for her loss of Offley Place as a rightful inheritance.

See *Thraliana* 1:307; HLP to SL, 23 April [1787], n. 3.

2. Nothing came of HLP's peace offering. Lady Salusbury returned the presentation copy of *Retrospection* by a servant. HLP had been prompted to make the gesture upon the advice of GP, Lady Eleanor Butler, Lord Deerhurst, and John Gillon. When the gesture

failed, HLP wrote: "N'importe!! I deserv'd such Treatment, when I provoked it by such Meanness" (*Thraliana* 2:1014).

TO LADY WILLIAMS

No. 77 Great Pultney Street
Bath
1st: February 1801.

My Dearest Lady Williams
   does me great honour in buying my book and wishing for my Letters——They may perhaps in Some Measure break the uniform Tenor of her Mornings, Nights and Noons:—and by bringing Pictures of more varied Life before her, contribute to Convince her that the shifting Scenes exhibit chiefly a Variety of Wretchedness. Of those Lamentations which principally strike our Ears, that concerning the Dearness of Provision is loudest.—
   Mrs. Powis of Berwick near Shrewsbury[1] and Mother to pretty Lady Denbigh[2]——is now lamenting a Calamity which She shares with Palmer of the Post Office;[3] and another Bath Inhabitant in a Situation much less attractive to the Public Eye.
   Young men from 17 to 27 were never known as madly, so universally dissolved in Vice; nor ever so surprizingly depressed in Consequence of it.
   One of these Boys left Letters behind him to excuse his *last* Error by freely confessing that those which preceded it—had rendered Life absolutely and completely insupportable.—But private Afflictions are nearly swallowed up in the Concern every one now necessarily takes in Public Affairs which have *been so deranged* of late by these odd Rumours from the Northern Courts——*Our* People have been set upon their Heads almost, both at the diplomatic and at the Commercial End of London: where Mr. Rosencrantz's Joke[4]—(if Joke it was) produced *serious* Consequences to Merchants, Under Writers &c. and tumbled the Stocks down in a frightful Manner.[5]
   Meanwhile People *here* dress with an expensive Gaiety beyond what I saw in and about London, and double the Consumption of every Article of which the Price is doubled already. This is strange, but upon my *Honour* (as little Dear says) it is strictly true.
   One Pastry Cook in this Town—Mrs. Bevan by Name,[6] *made and Sold* one Thousand and fourteen Minced Pyes between the 24th of December and 2d of January;—eight Days only—and so many Equipages were never seen at Bath, as since every Horse has cost 26 Shillings o'day, besides the Standing of one's Carriage. Mr. Piozzi has sent Rat and Mole home to Brynbella—They have the honour to carry this Letter for Your Ladyship; with unceasing Remembrances and true Regards to all your charming Family.
   I feel nearer home now than at Streatham Park, which we have *re Let* for a Term of six Years—and quitted without any Regret, to Mr. Giles who seems bent on

Improving the Grounds, Gardens &c. and will be a good Steward for Miss Thrales if I should die within the limited Time.

'Tis the fashion here to say I look fatigued with hard Study; Mr. Piozzi had a Cough in London those foggy Days when one could hardly see across Leicester Square, but he looks very well now, and keeps Gout at a Distance. Our Dear little Boy is exceedingly like him and comes on very nicely indeed.——Considering he had such Disadvantages to struggle with as changing one language for another at five Years old—I think he does Wonders! His joy to see Mrs. Siddons on the Stage, who had called on him two Days before, was beyond all telling: She looks says he like a Peacock with that long Green Tail—and so She did. We hope She will be here soon to see *her* Darling, the same Age of ours, and very lovely—a Girl six Years and half old—and at School with Miss Lees who wrote the Canterbury Tales &c. I shall bring your Ladyship Mrs. West's much admired Novel,[7] and the Memoirs of modern Philosophers which will make you laugh, as the other will make you cry. The Author a Miss Hamilton very comical indeed.[8] The Story of Doctor M[yddelton']s Inoculating with this new fashioned Small pox has reached us *here*. If the Success be what he does not Intend—it will lessen Peoples confidence in Modern Improvements.

We saw nothing of Lady De Blaquiere and heard nothing but from Lord Mountjoy since we came hither: he is nearly related to the Family, but did no[t] know they had quitted our Country and I rather fancy they mean to Return Sometime; most probably late in the Autumn——People now go to the Metropolis in March and stay there till July. My daughters are even yet at Brighthelmstone: I tell them they will scarce *escape* seeing the Flowers bloom and hearing the Birds sing this Year, so forward and fine is the Season.

Lord Kirkwall marries *my* pretty Cousin in May as we are told by the general Talkers on such Subjects;—I have not heard a Word upon the Subject from those who ought to know.[9] Dear Lady Williams does me cruel Wrong to suppose her Letters uninteresting. They are a Proof of that Kindness which is a very great Honour and Delight to hers, and Sir John's and kind Mrs. Williams ever Obliged and faithful / H: L: Piozzi.

Mr. P. sends a Thousand Regards.

Text: Ry. 1 (1796–1802).

1. Lissey Anne Cooper (1753–1832) had on 24 August 1774 married at Saint Mary's, Shrewsbury, Thomas Jelf Powys (1744–1805) of Berwick House, Salop. He had been sheriff of the county in 1776. See the "Burial Records" of Berwick Chapel, C.R.O., Salop.

Mrs. Powys had just endured the death of her son Thomas Henry (1776–1801), educated at Éton and Saint John's, Cambridge.

2. Anne Catherine, née Powis (1772–1852), was the widow of William Robert, styled Viscount Feilding (1760–99), the elder son of Basil Feilding (1719–1800), sixth earl of Denbigh (1755).

After the death of her husband, Lady Feilding (not Lady Denbigh) had the task of bringing up six young children.

3. Born in Bath, John Palmer (1742–1818) was the inventor of the mail coach system and served as comptroller general of the post office from late 1786 to 1792. He had been

elected mayor of Bath in 1796 and was to be reelected in 1809. He sat as an M.P. for Bath (1801, 1802, 1806, 1807) and in 1808 for the Chiltern Hundreds.

Palmer mourned his second son, Thomas, a barrister, who had died in London on 14 December 1800, aged 26. See the *Bath Chronicle*, 18 December.

4. Niels Rosenkrantz (1757–1824), Danish diplomat, ambassador at this time to Russia, and a member "of one of the most ancient noble families of Denmark, which has produced many great statesmen and men of learning." See *GM* 94, pt. 1 (1824): 382.

5. The "Joke," which occupied much space over many days in English newspapers, is summarized in the *Courier and Evening Gazette*, 30 January.

"After the last grand entertainment given by the Czar to the King of Sweden . . . at which Paul himself had figured as a valiant Knight in the Tournament, the conversation of the table turning on the feats of Chivalry," a drunken Paul "got up and harangued the company. He observed, that the blood of nations might be saved, if valorous Monarchs would enter the lists, as Charles the Fifth and Francis the First had proposed to do, and fight out their own quarrels in single combat; and that those Sovereigns who had no stomach for the field, might send their Proxies and Champions to the *tourney.*

"The Danish Minister [Rosenkrantz] . . . took occasion to pique and urge His Majesty to the performance, who thereupon gave him authority to insert the challenge in the German Petersburgh Gazette.—When Paul waked sober in the morning," he found the deed done. Rosenkrantz was subsequently ordered to leave Russia.

See *The Times* for 26, 29, 30 January; the *Courier*, 28 January.

6. Catharine Bevan (d. 31 August 1811) first appears in the Bath directories in 1784 as a pastry cook in Bartlet Street. By 1791 she is listed in the directories as not merely a pastry cook but as bun maker to the queen. Retiring from her shop in 1804, she lived out her remaining years at 1 Belmont Street.

See the "Walcot Parish Poor Rates," Guildhall, Bath; "Walcot Burial Register," C.R.O., Somerset.

7. For Mrs. West's *A Tale of the Times*, see HLP to James Robson, 16 April 1799, n. 2.

8. Elizabeth Hamilton (1758–1816), often a visitor to Bath, wrote *Memoirs of Modern Philosophers*, 3 vols. (London: G. G. and J. Robinson, 1800). This series of humorous sketches was prompted by a conversation with Reverend George Gregory (1754–1808), a diligent parish priest and scholar. *Memoirs* was succeeded by Hamilton's *Letters on the Elementary Principles of Education*, 2 vols. (London: G. G. and J. Robinson, 1801).

9. See HLP to PSP, 30 November 1801, n. 9; *Thraliana* 1006 n. 5. The "pretty Cousin" was Mary Jane Ormsby.

TO LADY ELEANOR BUTLER [AND MISS SARAH PONSONBY]

No. 77. Great Pultney Street Bath
Monday 2d of February 1801.

My dear Ladies
    will receive the Bishop's Book safe,[1] and with it this Letter, to tell the Result of my sending Retrospection to Lady Salusbury——She returned it *back by the Servant*, keeping my Billet; and gave the Man a verbal Message that She had left off Reading now on Account of bad Eyes.

We will think no more about *her.*[2]

I will enclose a List of Errata for the Copy upon Llangollen Table, and only add my hopes that Your Ladyship and Miss Ponsonby will like it no less in Print than when You honoured with your Attention to it in Manuscript. / Your most exceeedingly Obliged / H: L: Piozzi.

Mr. Piozzi begs Permission to add his Respects; The Coachman who travels down to Wales with our Carriage Horses, is entrusted with this Packet.

Text: Hyde Collection. *Address:* Right Honourable Lady Eleanor Butler / Llangollen Cottage / Denbighshire / with a Parcel.

1. Lewis Bagot's book, *Twelve Discourses on the Prophecies concerning the First Establishment and Subsequent History of Christianity. Preached in Lincoln's-Inn-Chapel, at the Lecture of the Right Rev. William Warburton . . . Bishop of Gloucester* (Oxford: J. and J. Fletcher, etc., 1780).
2. See HLP to Lady Salusbury [January 1801], n. 2.

THE REVEREND LEONARD CHAPPELOW TO HESTER LYNCH PIOZZI

London Wednesday
1801. February 4.—

Dear Madam—

The Post comes in so very Late now, that my Letter to Lady Bradford, into which I squeezed your note, was put into the post before I got yours to which this is an answer.—

I have done all I can to drive Retrospection as fast as possible. Stockdale assured me yesterday that the Book went off as fast as almost any Book he ever published. (500 were sold, or at Least sent out of the Shop the first day, and he makes no doubt but the rest will soon go.) He says there are very few typographical errors, but you are perfectly right as to Quotations being falsely printed. In a conversation some Little time ago with Lord Arden[1] &c. &c.—we all agreed that there was but one Newspaper editor, which could print a single Line of Latin orthographically—they mean spell it right.[2]—

I think at Brynbella you once told me if you had any fears about the Book, it was because the Exordium to such a work must inevitably be considered as the dullest part of the Book,[3] and I now verily believe that most people would like the book as well again if they would read the 2d Volume first.—I have this Idea verified from Literary Characters, who will not be perswaded to go on with the book, often having read but ½ the first volume:—Good God Sir! what would you have?—you are quarrelling with the first nine sticks of a beautiful Nest. *Respice finem.*[4]—Does not every Lady begin her beautiful purse with Thrum Threads— and to these Threads are attached the tissued silk.—Who will with too critical nicety find fault with the foundation of a House because the stones are not elegantly sculptured.—Examine the Superstructure, and particularly the elegant Furniture of the Separate apartments, and if you [do], I am sure you will ultimately be richly rewarded for your pains.—

Stockdale did not much seem to approve of the 2d Edition being published in 8°.—But a little time must determine what is to be done. He says all Quartos of the same size are a guinea a volume.[5]

I find by the Reviews (of this month), which I always read and as it were study the taste of the times, that our Friends the Lysons are going on wonderfully with their topographical works.[6]—Why do such works sell better than works of imagination and genius—Vanity finds purchasers. Daniel Lysons has again published an Account of parishes near London omitted in his Last Work.[7]—If you can but tell who the pye-woman's Grandmother was before she changed her maiden name for that of her first Husband who was the famous Richard Appletart in Turnover Lane, at the corner of Pippin Alley, if it is only for the sake of seeing their names in Print, on a <Zundy> at their country House they will give 2 *golden* Guineas for such a book.—Look fader shan't my name be put into the Pettigree—yes my Dear Little non pareil if there is another Hedition.—We will certainly buy it.—The Lysons are now both engaged in a New general Survey of Great Briton.[8]—*Si non unius quaeso miserere duorum.*[9] There's a motto for them.

I can give you no account, being totally at a Loss about a pavillion Dinner.[10]— Your Times of to day tell us Mr. Pitt has got the gout.[11] He, (as Members said) was very much out of spirits in the House of Commons, and made a very moderate speech, but it reads well.[12]—Alas! Alas!—Britannia's Candle is going out—I now fear we are come to the *Save all.* What are we to do?—The Irish say they cannot pay the 10th of *their* Income but are will[ing] to pay half of it, that is a *fifth.*—said one of them. Well if that will content Mr. Pitt we will do it willingly.— But why do we laugh at these blunders—when we all know, that (as one of them said) if an Englishman was to be born in Ireland he would make as many blunders as we do.—One of these poor fellows the other day at the Old Bayley was terribly thrown of[f] his guard.—He was indicted for stealing several articles, and denied all in general Terms. But an unlucky Question suddenly discharged at poor Pat—occasioned him to <discover> both his country and the robbery.

Well fellow—but what did you intend to do with the cake of Chocolate?—Why to *plaise* your Honour My wife and I intended to make *Tea* of it for our breakfast.—

How can you Mr. C.—laugh when all the world should cry.—

Adieu dear Madam / give my best to my Master and H: Lee— / Yours ever. / L. Chappelow.

P.S. I saw that smiling rogue Davis yesterday. He says Picollino is quite well.— but will not do for a Lord Chancellor.—ergo nigrescens igitur industus veste <   > / Sed mihi Furetui non quasi Tutor equos.

You know the Dog ran away with my Horses at Brynbella—they threw him down several times—but for the best of all reasons they could not break his *reserved* neck.

Davis est non oedipus.

Text: Ry. 562.70. *Address:* Mrs. Piozzi / Great Pultney Street / Bath. *Postmark:* FE 4 801.

1. Charles George Perceval (1756–1840) had become Baron Arden of Lohart Castle, co. Cork, upon the death of his mother, Catherine, née Compton (1731–84), who had been created baroness in 1770. She was the second wife of John (1710/11–70), second earl of Egmont (1748). Lord Arden was M.P. for Launceston, 1780–90; for Warwick, 1790–96; for Totnes, 1796–1802. He was a lord of the admiralty and registrar of the admiralty court. In 1802 he was created a peer of the United Kingdom as Baron Arden of Arden, Warwickshire.

Baron Arden's elder brother was Spencer Perceval, the prime minister assassinated in 1812.

2. John Walter II, editor of *The Times.* See HLP to LC, 31 March 1799, n. 11.
3. HLP's preface (1:v–xii) justifies fragmented, simplified history. She proposes "that whilst the deep current of grave history rolls her full tide majestick, to that Ocean where Time and all its wrecks at length are lost; our flashy *Retrospect,* a mere *jet d'eau,* may serve to soothe the heat of an autumnal day with its light-dripping fall, and form a rainbow round" (p. viii).
4. Cf. *Gesta Romanorum,* cap. 103: "Quidquid agas, prudenter agas, et respice finem."
5. The two volumes of *Retrospection* sold for two guineas.
6. During this period, DL had provided the *Views of Hampton Court Palace,* as well as *Account of Hampton Court Palace* [1800], both publications stemming from the work on the Middlesex parishes (n. 7 below). SL was responsible for the illustrations of *Reliquiae Britannico-Romanae, containing figures of Roman Antiquities discovered in England,* 2 vols. (London: Cadell and Davies, 1801; 1817; other eds. 1813–17, 1813–18).
7. *An Historical Account of those Parishes in the County of Middlesex, which are not described in the Environs of London* (London: Cadell and Davies, 1800). Illustrations by SL.
8. DL and SL were collaborating on *Magna Britannia; being a concise topographical account of the several counties of Great Britain,* 6 vols. (London: Cadell and Davies, 1806–22).
9. LC's improvisation, with a borrowing of Ovid's "miserere duarum" (*Metamorphoses,* 9.780).
10. One of the frequent entertainments by the Prince of Wales at Brighton.
11. "We are sorry to announce that the Chancellor of the Exchequer was yesterday indisposed with the gout" (*The Times,* 3 February).
12. Following an address to Parliament by King George on 2 February, Pitt challenged the contention of the Opposition speaker, Charles Grey, that the Ministry was responsible for a "ruinous system of policy, which had been followed with such obstinate perseverance as to place us in our present state of distress and calamity." Grey was alluding to the dangers posed by a coalition of Russia, Denmark, and Sweden. The king had spoken on, among other issues related to national security, the need to effect peaceful negotiations with the Northern powers. Insisting on the futility of such an effort, Grey sought to force an amendment to the king's declaration which would have compromised any possibility of negotiated terms. Pitt, however, denounced the amendment and his majority carried the day. See *AR* 43 (1801): chap. 4; *The Times,* 3 February; for Charles Grey, HLP to Q, 28 January 1795, n. 8.

TO THE REVEREND LEONARD CHAPPELOW

No. 77 Great Pultney Street Bath
Thursday Night [5: February 1801.]¹

And what are you doing in Town—now we have left it—dear Mr. Chappelow? Our *General* really deserted us cruelly, but never man had so active an Aid de Camp.² Pray reproach Stockdale slily with the typographical Errors which are innumerable——and especially in the Quotations. The Rebellion among our Printers was a terrible Blow upon us, and now People wait for a 2d Edition, and resolve to stay till they can get a Correct Copy. There should be a List of Errata run off by all means I think——Do drive the Book along as fast as possible; that we may go to Press again, and that I may get some of those Heaps of Money you kindly promised to my hungry Fancy.

Has not Mr. Gillon been very good and kind?—but I must have done with *my own* private Concerns, and talk of the general Agony which poor Europe is in, and for which I feel truly afflicted.³ How do *you* think all will end? I want some one to contradict my own melancholy Opinion of Matters and Things:

I have not seen the Dowager Lady Bradford, but then we keep quite to our own Set, and so no doubt does *She*. Did you leave all well at Dear charming Weston? And did you find Mrs. Clay as pretty and as kind to *me* as ever? Yes, yes, 'tis poor *Mr.* Clay that is in a Bustle no doubt, with these terrible Combinations against our *Trade*.⁴ Let me have a Letter soon with the *latest* Calamities extant.

All these Horrors originate in Buonaparte's Politics:⁵ He could not bear to see *Europa* confiding herself so classically to the Care of John *Bull* and suffering him to carry her thro' the *Sea* without Molestation; and tis a Mercy now, if they do not drown her amongst them.

I shall try to get this Letter freed by Lord Lansdown who is still smiling and Gentleman-like. Our Reports of Domestic or foreign *Princes* are so contradictory, one can put no faith or Trust in them. People seemed to apprehend a Mourning lately; but be that as it may, you find my Inexplicable Nonsense about the Abandonment of Carolina for Maryland, all turned out *true*. Was there any Dinner made by any Female Triumvirate on Old Ocean's brink lately, for any Dweller in a *Tent* or *Pavillion*? Pray dear Mr. Chappelow pick me up some certain Intelligence for you live among the Ton Folks——from whom Heaven long preserve Your / Unfashionably faithful Servant and / much obliged / H: L: P.

Accept my Master's *best*.

Text: Ry. 560.108.

1. The Piozzis had left London before the end of January and LC wrote from the city on 4 February. Plausibly, HLP wrote the present letter on 5 February, the first Thursday in the month.
2. HLP was premature in her criticism of the general (LC). See his letter to her, 4 February.

John Gillon, the "Aid de Camp," was perhaps more aggressive than LC in pushing forward the notion of *Retrospection*'s second edition and in meeting with Stockdale. See, e.g., his letters to HLP during the first two months of the book's life: on 26 January, 10 and 18 and 16 February (Ry. 578.71, 73, 74, 75).

3. Vol. 43 of *AR* in its opening chapter summarized the precarious situation of Great Britain early in 1801. Most threatening to British interests was the Peace of Lunéville, soon to be signed (8 February) and by which Austria had to admit defeat. "The nations of Europe astonished, terrified, and dazzled by the success of the French republic, seemed to have learnt to respect and admire what, in better moments, they had feared or hated, and to have transferred their homage from justice and public law to fortune" (p. 2).

Continuing its analysis of the effects of the Peace of Lunéville, *AR* pointed out that France claimed and would get "all the territory on the left Bank of the Rhine, making that river, from the place where it leaves Switzerland to that where it enters Holland, the boundary of the republic" (ibid.).

Moreover, "the influence of France in all parts of Italy was unbounded and uncontroulable. The Cisalpine republic, created by France . . . could only be considered a province. The submission of Genoa, Parma, and Tuscany, was implicit and invariable. The Adige was made the boundary of Austria, but to that boundary, the authority of France also extended" (p. 3).

And finally, "Spain, expunged from the list of independent states, was . . . abjectly subjected to the power and views of France" (p. 4).

4. The "Combinations" had to do with the situation created by Czar Paul: specifically, with his embargo on English ships in Russian ports and with Swedish and Danish competition for the freight detained there. See *The Times*, 1, 3, 8 January for attacks on Paul's "combinations with the Northern Powers to arrest the progress of our naval triumphs."

On 24 January, *The Times* reported the possibility "that the King of Prussia had acceded to the Northern League" and so could challenge England's mercantile entry to the Continent.

Finally, *The Times* of 31 January maintained that the Peace of Lunéville "may be expected to shut against the navigation of Great Britain the ports of *Venice*, *Trieste*, and *Ancona*; as it is not to be dissembled in the present circumstances of things, that the weakness of Tuscany and the Pope, and the dependence of the King of the Two Sicilies upon Russia threaten us with exclusion from *Leghorn*, *Civita Vecchia*, and *Naples*."

5. The "Combinations" against British merchants began with France's proposal of a new maritime law based on the following:

"1st. Cruizing shall be abolished in time of war; the sovereignty of a territory is conveyed with all its rights under the flag of those states which do not take part in the contest.

"2d. In times of peace the navigation between nation and nation shall be freed from every prohibitory law: the only exception to be with respect to freight from one port to another belonging to the same state, or from colonies to the mother country." See *AR* 43:8.

TO PENELOPE SOPHIA PENNINGTON

Tuesday 10: February 1801.

My Dear Mrs. Pennington
Mr. Palmer whom I met yesterday at the Pump, told me you were still confined; and I bid him say how truly sorry his evil Intelligence found me.

10 February 1801

To your Enquiries how Things are going here, My Reply is—*never so bad*. Fish, Flesh, and Fowl all at double Price, and tho' we live as retired as 'tis possible, the little red Book you remember of Marketing Expences, goes on worse and worse.

Even Laura Chapel is raised one Third, and the Journey hither cost double what it used to do. These are Facts; It is equally true indeed that the Waters do my Health good, but 'tis a heavy Charge *this same Health*, upon one's husband: though *he* may not *say*, or even *think* so.

Bachelors live at immense Costs however; Mr. Roach or Roche told us yesterday that he and his Son paid 200£ for five Weeks eating and Sleeping at York House, his Servants at Board Wages all the while:[1]

Tea alone stood them in six Shillings o'Day. Fine Times! and Mrs. Mores our next Neighbours tell me Mr. Pitt has already quitted the Helm and old Britannia is left to weather the Storm how She can without Pilot, Rudder, or Compass— and tow a troublesome Sister after her besides.[2]

God send her safe to Port!! He only can. Mr. Boyds[3] Pamphlet seems by its unseasonable Truths—(if Truths they are)—to accelerate, whilst He anticipates our Ruin.[4] My own Book, though much diffused, and rapidly sold; has not yet brought me a *Shilling:* and it was upon *that* I fully depended for our Reimbursement of these few Weeks charges here in Bath. *Six* only of those Weeks yet remain: some of them I still flatter myself we shall pass together, but wherever we pass them I shall ever remain with my good Master's united Regards dear Mrs. Penningtons truly Obliged and faithful / H: L: P.

A Thousand kind Wishes to your Husband and Mother.

Text: Princeton University Library. *Address:* Mrs. Pennington / Dowry Square / Hot Wells / Bristol. *Postmark:* BATH.

---

1. Stephen Roche of Limerick, dying 12 February 1804, was succeeded by his son John (d. 1825), an eminent Dublin merchant.

Founded by Robert St. John Lucas ca. 1775, York House, located at a right angle from Gay Street, was "an excellent Hotel, the only House of Reception which is situated in an open airy Part of the City" (p. 62). So it was described in *The New Prose Bath Guide* (1778). Its reputation had not changed between its opening and 1801.

2. See *The Times*, 9 February:

"Our Readers will have observed for many days past, that we have prepared the public mind to hear of a Change in His Majesty's Councils, which has been in agitation since Wednesday se'nnight, the day when the opening of Parliament was so suddenly adjourned. The interval has been occupied in negociations to reconcile the different opinions of parties on the question of Catholic Emancipation, but without effect, as on Friday Mr. Pitt sent in his resignation to the King, which was accepted; and on Saturday Lord Spencer, Lord Grenville, and Mr. Dundas followed the same course."

3. Walter Boyd (ca. 1754–1837) before the revolution was a banker in Paris. In 1793 he was forced to return to London, where on 15 March he established the house of Boyd and Benfield. A Tory M.P. (1796–1802), he nonetheless concentrated largely on his banking affairs. Although he was able to obtain private help from the government, his firm in 1799 was forced into liquidation.

4. Before Boyd returned to France in 1802 in a futile effort to secure the restoration of his property there, he published *A Letter to the Right Honourable William Pitt, on the Influence*

of the Stoppage of Issues in Specie at the Bank of England; on the Prices of Provisions, and Other Commodities* (London: J. Wright, 1801). The pamphlet, completed on 31 December 1800, was quickly printed and distributed.

It was provoked by the Bank of England's suspension of cash payments in 1797. Boyd argued that "the increase of banknotes is the principal cause of the great rise in the price of commodities and every species of exchangeable value" (p. 7).

TO THE REVEREND LEONARD CHAPPELOW

[Bath]
[14: February 1801.][1]

You were quite right Dear Mr. Chappelow—I *did* say—how can he be laughing so when every body else looks so grave. For even *here* one may now and then see very serious faces: tho this Place is considered as the head Quarters of Pleasure, and one follows a Fiddle Case along the Abbey Church Yard as soon as the Burying is gone by. Bath is a good Epitome of the World, and when Puppets are exhibited in a little Theatre, those who have short Sight or weak Eyes, observe their Motions to more Advantage. I hate Scene-shifting Tricks though in any Drama, and these Changes at home afflict me more than the shutting of every Port against our Shipping. Trade like the Water which Sustains it, *will find its level,* and whilst foreign Nations can afford to buy our Tin Plates, or our Wedgewood Ware, The Sellers feel no Concern. As many Individuals have made Fortunes as have lost Fortunes by the Russian Embargo——and what cares the State?——or what need has it to care whether the Man enriched lives in Pall mall and buys Pictures, or whether he resides in Monmouthshire and sees his Rollers smoothing the Iron for Sale?

My Grief is for the Dissentions at home,[2] and *my* fear of foreign Intelligence all centers in Ægypt: whence if you do not drive the French, your Indian Possessions must inevitably fall: and what Force *can* drive the French when combined with Russia??[3]

I have written on the wrong Side my Paper, and now it will be torne with the Seal. Poor Retrospection is to bring me no Money I find, altho' 30 Copies were sold in the Town in 30 days, which the Booksellers think a famous Occurrence:[4]

Well! The Reviewers will set it going again in March either by Praise or Blame. St. David must protect (as I said to Mr. Gillon) a Native of his own Mountains.[5] Write soon do to yours ever / H: L: P.

Text: Ry. 560.109.

1. Dated by an unknown hand.
2. The most obvious of the "Dissentations" was political; i.e., the factional maneuvering that followed upon the resignation of the Pitt Ministry.
 Almost as explosive was the response to parliamentary efforts in the winter of 1800–1801 to relieve the hardships created by scarcity, efforts that satisfied neither the rich nor poor. Most people believed that monopoly existed and that scarcity was contrived.

3. The French, in concert with the Russians, had a plan for a combined army of seventy thousand men. Paul was to guarantee half these troops at Astrakhan, "who were to embark on the Caspian sea, and await at Astrabad" the arrival of the French. "The combined force then marching by the cities of Herat, Ferah, and Candehar, would, in forty-five days reach the right bank of the Indus. The whole progress was calculated to require 120 days." See *AR* 43 (1801): 290–91.

4. HLP continued to be optimistic about the sale of *Retrospection*. But shortly after 26 February, she was to receive a letter from Gillon. Stockdale, he wrote, " 'cannot state *exactly* the Number sold, but from a rough Estimate believes it to be about 425 and that the Sale goes on very slowly.' At this you will, no Doubt, be surprised, as he said that 500 had been sold, before you left Town. But he hinted once to me, in Conversation, that he had exaggerated the Number, with a View of exciting Purchasers. *Il faut avoir Patience*. The Day of Settlement *will* come, according to what he has allowed to be the usual Term: and if the whole 750 be not *then* sold, the Remainder <must> be found in his Shop. . . . it is altogether *impracticable* to *increase* the Number, as the Types are *distributed*" (Ry. 578.75).

5. Gillon was born in the hilly section of West Lothian.

TO PENELOPE SOPHIA PENNINGTON

Brynbella
5: April 1801.

My dear Mrs. Pennington
  will be delighted to hear that we are got home safe, in spite of my *Nose* which is restored to its original Size, Colour, and Shape; having transmitted all Ill humour to the Shoulder—more fit for Carriage of a Burden so oppressive.

Some Heaviness has reached my heart tho'—and some Weight hangs on my Spirits. The first Intelligence that struck us upon the very Confines of our Principality——smiling as it seemed with hope of future Plenty—was the Death of a Friend—You have I am sure heard me mention as an agreeable Acquaintance and excellent Preacher a Mr. John Mostyn Curate of Denbigh——he *perished* it seems, poor Soul! in the hard Weather which Succeeded that Day on which we dined with Doctor Randolph—walking home from his Father's house to his own:—perished *of Cold!* and was buried in Drifts of Snow[1]——How sunk his Soul! !

> What black Despair! what horrors fill'd his heart
> When round him Night resistless closing fast
> And o'er his inmost Vitals creeping cold
> Layd him on the wild Heath a stiffen'd Corpse
> Far from the Track and blest Abode of Man.
>
> Thomson[2]

These Verses have almost haunted me ever since—so has his Figure chearful and gay, not 38 Years old; but we will change the subject and the Side of Paper. Tell dearest Siddons when you see her, that *her* Picture was the first Thing we unpacked, and *her* Handkerchief the finest Thing I appeared in, while at Bath.—

Hannah More. Silhouette by Augustin Amant Constant Fidèle Edouart (1827). (Reproduced by permission of the National Portrait Gallery.)

—The *only* Thing I shall wear here, till——till what? I can't answer that Question.

Poor Harriet Lee's lowness the Day we dined at Mrs. Stratton's,[3] affected every body present—and She ran home—unable to bear Company. Can you tell whether the Conversation of approving, nay *admiring* Friends has been yet able to reconcile her to past Vexations; for they scarce can be accounted Calamities?[4]

We have Contagion even at St. Asaph, but 'tis occasioned merely by want of wholesome food; when the Plenty I still predict shall once arrive, there will be no Distemper——*but ill Humour.*

Mean while some Cause for *that*, does doubtless exist, when the Ports are filled with Grain, and the Poor perishing of Hunger. Our Bishop detained in London by Illness is much wanted,[5] and we came home too late to save our old favourite Labourer Edward Davies—who expired 8 Hours before our Arrival saying that if we made haste he *yet* should live; because we should send him something *nice* from our own *Plates* as we did when he was sick once before.

When *such* Things present themselves to one's Mind, how vain must be the hope of Reviewers and Critics to draw it on their empty abuse![6] I would there were no worse Afflictions to lament, than those created by Buzzers and Stingers like *Them:* nevertheless *pray* Tell me how Hannah More supports *her* Torrent of

Scurrility;[7] She was a kind Soul, and came to see us for five Minutes before we got into the Chaise at Laura Place, looking very well thank God; apparently not worse for her long Illness and Confinement: her Sister is *too* right tho', concerning the general Distress for *Victuals*.[8]

Mr. Piozzi is come home looking younger and better our folks say than they ever saw him, and the Roads were admirable, and the Weather without a Fault. I carry this Letter with me to St. Asaph Cathedral Easter Sunday—and put it in the Post Office there after Service.

The Ladies at Llangollen enquired much for you, they have more News and more Stories than one could dream of—their *best* however is concerning their own old Maid Mary[9]—from whose Character one would think Sophia Lee had pourtrayed that of Connor in her Tale of the Two Emilys.[10] Mary seeing her Ladies' Eyes fixt one fine Night lately upon the Stars, said to Miss Ponsonby, Ah Madam! you once shewed me a fine Sight in the Heavens. The Belt of *O' Bryan*—but I suppose we shall see it no more since the *Union*. To this nothing sure can be added—I will therefore Give Mr. Piozzi's Shoes' Compliments to those of Mr. Pennington, with best Wishes for the health of their *Inhabitants;* and Adieu. But pray write soon / to yours ever / H: L: P.

Text: Princeton University Library. *Address:* Mrs. Pennington / Dowry Square / Hot Wells / Bristol. *Postmark:* <   >.

1. For the curate of Saint Marcella's, Denbigh, who was the son of John Ellis Mostyn of Holywell, Flintshire, see HLP to Q, 3 April [1795], n. 8; *Thraliana* 2:1023.
2. HLP's somewhat inaccurate and random compilation of lines from "Winter," in *The Seasons*. See lines 289, 293–94, 319–20.
3. Mary Stratton lived at 13 Camden Place, Bath. See the "Walcot Parish Poor Rates," 1800–1823, in the Bath Guildhall. Her M.I. is on the Abbey's south transept wall: "In Memory of Mary Stratton, Widow of Samuel Stratton, who died Nov. 19, 1828, aged 84 Years."
4. Harriet Lee was worried about the reception of *The Canterbury Tales*, vol. 4, soon to be distributed; about her continuing association with William Godwin, who had offered her marriage late in 1798. HLP in *Thraliana* 2:1015 noted that Belvidere House seemed "to have a Cloud hang on it—& there was Talk of a contagious Disorder in their School beside."
5. Bishop Bagot was seriously ill, dying in London two months later.
6. *The Anti-Jacobin Review and Magazine* 8 (March 1801): 241–46 denounced *Retrospection* as "History cooked up in a novel form reduced to light reading for boarding school misses, and loungers at a watering place during the Dog-Days" (p. 241). Gratuitously, the review set forth a series of rhetorical questions: "Does the widow of a respectable merchant make a foolish match? she looks in vain for her former importance in *the arms of impossibility*. Does a weak woman flattered with folly, take up the pen of the historian, and think to add to her reputation and fame? alas she seeks them in the *arms of impossibility;* or should some vain bookseller purchase the precious manuscript, in vain will he seek to find his money again in *the arms of impossibility*" (p. 245). See also the *European Magazine* 39 (January–June, 1801): 188–93, 271–76. The reviewer dismissed *Retrospection* as a "pretty piece of female patch-work" (p. 188).
7. See, e.g., *The Controversy between Mrs. H. More and the Curate of Blagdon, relative to the Conduct of her Teacher of the Sunday School in that Parish, with the Original Letters and Explanatory Notes by Thos. Bere, Rector of Butcombe* (1801); *An Appeal to the Public on the*

Controversy between Hannah More, the Curate of Blagdon, and the Rev. Sir Abraham Elton. By T. B., A. M., Rector of Butcombe (Bath, 1801).

Bere in the above pamphlets referred to Hannah More as the "She-Bishop," a Methodist in disguise who communicated at Jay's Dissenting Chapel, Bath. Moreover, he was convinced that the meetings of her fanatic sectaries would terminate in Jacobin assemblies.

These were early shots in a pamphlet war that was to last for two years. During this time she was accused of being the abettor of fanaticism and sedition, an enemy to liberty and a foe of church and state, a ministerial hireling and tool of government, a warmonger, and an anti-Christian.

See Annette M. B. Meakin, *Hannah More* (London: Smith, Elder, 1911), pp. 326–31; M. G. Jones, *Hannah More* (Cambridge: University Press, 1952), pp. 172 ff.

8. For Martha "Patty" More, see HLP to SL, 5 March [1792], n. 6.

9. Mary Carryll, who began to work for the Ladies of Llangollen at least as early as 1778, was to die in their service in November 1809.

10. HLP refers to Sophia Lee's *The Young Lady's Tale, or the Two Emilys*, in *The Canterbury Tales*. Mrs. Connor was a strict and zealous guardian who had sole authority over the establishment of Lady Emily Lenox.

TO THE REVEREND LEONARD CHAPPELOW

Brynbella
Fryday 17: April 1801.

Dear Mr. Chappelow

I hope Plenty is at hand, for these prudent Fears concerning four Pence or Sixpence poyson all my Enjoyment of Life. Not only we ran home from Bath to meet Snow and Hail and hard Weather, and hear of Friends perishing on a Wild Heath, while dear Siddons was acting Desdemona to a *warm* Audience;[1] but our Newspaper—(its Price *raised*) comes but thrice o'Week now, and our Expectations are *raised* even beyond Thought of Threepence by the Time it arrives. *At this Moment it comes not at all*[2]—and had not Sir John Williams ridden over to tell about some Battle won in the North,[3] and had not Lady Orkney brought us a Letter from her Son with Three Words only

Paul is dead.[4]

We should have remained ignorant of these Wonders till they were well known in Ægypt, and had produced perhaps more than equal Wonders there.

When Your Friend Linnæus celebrates the Felicity of People living out of the World as we do——he considers them as never being Gouty I remember, and never hearing of Quarrels. Oh *felix Lappo!* qui in ultimo Angulo Mundi contentus lates et Innocens. Tu dormis hic sub tua Pelle (Is'nt it?) ab omnibus Curis Contentionibus; rixis liber, &c. Te non obruit nec *Obesitas* nec *Podagra*.[5] The Obesity we shall be sure enough of escaping, at least our poor Labourers; for Barley is at a Price they cannot purchase, and we must feed a few from our own Table, and we must *see the others starve*. Not a Potatoe is come up of all we planted last Year, and by best Computation We *ought* to have had 100 Measures called

Hobbets. Yet those who wish to instigate the Poor for Purpose of commencing a Rebellion, say *there has been no Scarcity:* The ordinary People *know* 'tis otherwise, and bear their Sorrows *very very* gently.

Mean while here comes your kind Letter,[6] which for Love of this same *uncomeatable* Sixpence, was directed to Weston first, and of course brings no News at all: and Intellectual, as well as positive and actual Famine is the Consequence.

Farewell my dear Sir and tell Mr. Gillon how like Hamlet here we *burst in Ignorance:*[7] and ask him—it will only make him laugh; *If he has caught Miss Thrale napping, and got a Pair of Gloves for me?*[8]

Adieu and assure yourself you have not in the World a truer Friend or a more nonsensical Correspondent / than / H: L: Piozzi.

My Master is young and Gay and sends kind Regards to you,—and raves at Stockdale for neglecting to send the Paper.[9]

Text: Ry. 560.110.

1. SS was not at this time performing in *Othello*. From 7 to 21 April she alternated between the Theatres Royal of Bath and Bristol in the following: *Jane Shore, Douglas, The Mourning Bride, The Gamester, Macbeth, King John, The Stranger.*
See the *Bath Journal*, 30 March; 6, 13, and 20 April; *Felix Farley's Bristol Journal*, 28 March; 4, 11, and 18 April.

2. HLP's anxiety for newspapers led LC to write from London on 13 April (Ry. 563.71): "I ordered for you the Evening Mail—tis the best paper—tis the Editor of the Times who writes it—if you remember the Bishop of St. Asaph told you—twas the best Evening paper."

3. On 1 April Nelson took his squadron past Copenhagen to the eastern entrance of the King's Channel. About ten o'clock in the morning of 2 April, the Danes began a heavy fire. Some three hours later, Sir Hyde Parker (1739–1807) signaled to "discontinue the action." Nelson did not obey, claiming that he could not see the signal. The loss of life during the five-hour battle was heavy, particularly among the Danes. About half past two, Nelson, who wanted to end the slaughter, sent ashore a flag of truce, which ended the battle and effected an armistice of fourteen weeks.

For a highly descriptive account of the battle, see the *Courier*, 16 April; and *The Times*, 17 April.

4. See *The Times*, 16 April for a "Copy of the Proclamation / of / The New Emperor of Russia, / On / His Accession to the Throne," which announced the death of Paul "suddenly by an apoplectic stroke, at night between the 11th and 12th day of this month." In fact, he had been assassinated.

The significance of Paul's death was spelled out by the *Courier* on 14 April:

". . . expectations begin already to be formed of his successor's withdrawing from his alliance with France and from the Northern Confederacy."

5. A semicomic, topical imitation of Linné's panegyric on Lapland, "in ultimo Europa angulo latuit." See especially the "Introduction" and the section "Cryptogamia. Algarum" in *Flora Lapponica* (Amsterdam: Salomon Schouten, 1737).

6. LC in his letter of 13 April reported the following news in a postscript:

"The news of the day is curious—Paul has sent over to our Government a triplicate of pass-ports—desiring immediately to see at Petersburgh—Mr. Sharp our Late consul at that place, and with him another Englishman, who used to serve his Court with English Clothes.—What he means no one knows—tis said too that he has quarrelled with Buonaparte.—

"An express arrived this morning—from the Baltic we have passed the Sound and are before Copenhagen—we threw 200 Shells into the castle of Croningen."

7. See HLP to Q, 4 January, n. 4.

8. HLP refers to her new contretemps with CMM over the latter's purchase of gloves in 1793. According to Gillon's letter of 10 April (Ry. 578.79): "As to the article of £3 for 2 Dozen pair of Gloves sent for Miss Thrale, now Mrs. Mostyn, to your House, No. 2, Hanover Square [the shopkeeper] contends that she was at that Time under the Care of you and Mr. P., and that of course they were charged to you as usual. I told him that as Mr. P. had never *paid* that Sum; he never *could* have charged it in his Accounts; and that in Conscience Mrs. M. ought to pay it; and I prevailed on him to make Application *again* to her, for that Purpose; to carry to her the Order for those Gloves, in her own Hand writing, which he is still in Possession of. She would not see him, and sent out word to him that she knew nothing of the Matter, and would not pay it. Mr. M. had already refused, and referred the Man to Mr. Cator, who told him that *you* are the Person to whom to apply." Gillon went on to urge HLP to pay the bill and the matter was dropped. See also Gillon to HLP 21 April (Ry. 578.80).

9. "The Paper" is her slang for money to be paid when the first five hundred copies of *Retrospection* were sold.

TO THE REVEREND THOMAS SEDGWICK WHALLEY

Brynbella
23: April 1801.

Permit me to congratulate you and Mrs. Whalley Dear Sir upon the glorious Accomplishment of your own happy Predictions. At No. 77 Pultney Street Bath did you tell me this Spring, that we should succeed in our Attack on Copenhaguen—an Event I considered as less and less practicable every day, the more I studied its Situation and compared it with that of my Neighbour Lord Uxbridge upon the Banks of Menaï Streight between Caernarvonshire and Anglesey.[1]

God's Judgements however are abroad——and our Enemies will taste of them: This must be a Severe Pang to the Chief Consul who has now but one wise Plan left——He *may* perhaps remonstrate to our Court and say——*I* have endeavoured to possess myself of all the Land in Europe, nor could you hinder me tho' great and powerful——Great Britain has endeavoured to ascertain her Dominion over all the Seas which surround Europe,—nor could *I* tho' great and powerful—prevent her. Let *us* shake hands, and let every other Realm be annihilated.

I should be sorry that he should hold out such a Temptation to Vanity at a such dangerous Moment; because we have been saved——only for having tried to save others—graceless and senseless as they have proved:—and when we desert our Principles of returning Good for Evil &c.—Success will *desert us*.[2]

Now let us see the Event of the Contest in Ægypt——I confess myself like Horace's Dotard who was grown *Spe longus* iners &c.[3] yet the news of Paul's Death will sit *heavy on Menou's Soul in the Battle* if it reaches him before the grand Engagement which tis Sir Ralph Abercrombie's best Plan *not to delay,* so I fear they will not wait for it.[4] Who knows but your Predictions may in such Case prove once more *Anticipated Narrative*. Mrs. Pennington flatters me by saying that you like my big Book: *Do* dear Sir give me Reason to hope She has not—in her flow of Spirits—dreamed it; She is very partial to *it* and to *me*. Her Account of your quelling the Bristol Rioters is charming,[5] but this breaking up of their Northern Confederacy will have wonderful Effects on *every*thing; and our Jacobins must remain under Ground (where they are even now working like Moles) a little longer than they intended.

I hear all Good of our sweet Friend Mrs. Siddons,[6] and feel sorry we could not enjoy her Society or her Performance this Spring; but it was really Time to get home, and we were exceedingly wanted. Next Year Mr. Piozzi promises to make it later, and come home by dear lovely Longford Cottage—The Mendip Lodge of kind Miss Hannah More: who is *one* of your Obliged Servants and Friends but can scarcely be a more faithful or grateful one than Yours and Mrs. Whalleys / ever Obedient / H: L: P.

Write sometimes *do* and think your kind Words well purchased by payment of Costs——No Franks can be hoped for from Country Residences at this Season.

Mr. Piozzi says I have not sent his particular Regards and that they must not be left out.

Text: Berg Collection +. *Address:* Rev. Thomas Sedgwick Whalley / Longford Cottage / Bristol. *Postmark:* DENBIGH.

1. For Henry Paget, third earl of Uxbridge, see HLP to Q, 10 July 1796, n. 2.
2. HLP alluded to the humane behavior of the British. Thus, *The Times* reported on 17 April:
"As soon as the fire of the Danes was silenced, the Hero of Aboukir, with that humanity which is so congenial to true heroism, sent a flag of truce on shore with a letter to the following laconic purport:—
"*The brave English to their brethren the brave Danes.*
"I am now in possession of the batteries; and wishing to stop any farther effusion of blood, I consent to a suspension of hostilities. / Nelson."
3. See *Ars Poetica*, lines 169–74, esp. 172.
4. HLP knew that British forces in Egypt were under the command of General Sir Ralph Abercromby (1734–1801) and that the French were led by Général Jacques-François de Boussay, baron de Menou (1750–1810), who had succeeded Kléber as commander in chief of the Army of Egypt in June 1800.
What HLP did not know was that the second, or night battle of Aboukir had been successfully fought by the British on 2 March and that the campaign would end triumphantly for them six months later.
5. From PSP to HLP, 17 April (Ry. 568.97): "We have had sad Work at Bristol with the Colliers and the Miners all round the Neighborhood and been greatly alarmed.—Mr. Whalley, Sir Abraham Elton, Dr. Randolph and a number of *good* Men have been sent amongst them, with Parties of the Military at their Backs, to Harangue and Reason with them and no Mischief has been done—nor will any, I think and hope, now be attempted."
6. SS had a triumphant visit in Bath. According to the *Bath Journal* on 13 April:
"The incomparable acting of Mrs. Siddons, has afforded the admirers of Dramatic Excellence, a most delicious Banquet: it is certainly a pleasing, not to say a proud Reflection, that the discernment of a Bath audience have brought to maturity many of the brightest Ornaments the British Stage has ever been adorned with . . . and it was the

fostering smiles of a Bath Audience, first gave perfection to the Talents of this Lady, which have so long, and so justly, been the delight and admiration of the Public. Mrs. Siddons, as if animated by a consciousness of this circumstance, has certainly outdone herself. Her Jane Shore, Lady Randolph and Zara, were given in a Stile of excellence, which places her as far beyond the reach of praise as of competition."

TO PENELOPE SOPHIA PENNINGTON

26: April 1801.

What a Letter![1] What a Pleasure to have such a Correspondent. You really can scarce imagine my Dear Friend how completely your kind Frank-full set before my Eyes—the Scenes I was so wishing to have witnessed. Peace and Plenty are coming; and dear Doctor Randolph's first Sermon after the Victory at Copenhaguen must have given a fore Taste of all The Felicities in their Train to his enraptured Auditors I doubt not.

The Effect of National Fervour and National Happiness upon sweet Siddons charmed me,[2] and it was so nicely accompanied too by her maternal Exultation. The Child in your Account has suffered scarce anything from the Alarming Symptoms which so frighted the whole House of Belvedere[3]——May their Cloud be dispersed! I did not as you know, even *seek* to penetrate its Gloom.

The Sharps are interesting Creatures—'Tis seldom I take Fancies, and seldomer still that Parents excite them, if seen in the presence of their Younglings—but my Heart feels nothing but good Wishes towards Mother and Daughter both.[4] Why you have had a nice Holyday time indeed! and *you*, like the Dear King will recover, by dint of good News.[5]

My Rheumatism has mended ever since You said how Mr. Whalley liked Retrospection;[6] and a kind Letter from Mr. Gray saying it was well thought of at Oxford, made me throw off a little fur Tippet which till Today's *Post* I wore to ward off these Easterly Winds.

Ods Blushes and Blooms! the poor Cherry Trees have dropt their pretty Flow'rs in one Night, a sturdy Pear Tree or Two resist all Northern Combinations against *them*, but Peaches and Nectarines we shall have none of this Summer—content to see Wheat falling, Stocks rising, and damaged Rice coming in by Shiploads to feed *those Pigs* which my Friends on the South Parade so talked of.

Meanwhile it was well done of the wise and good Men to go out and harangue the Rioters; they will go under Ground again now, and give their Instigators *fresh* Trouble to find *fresh* Arguments to set them on *fresh* Mischief—*in due Time*.

Well! God save Great George our King! While he lives, many a Laurel Bush will be used to decorate our Doors: I can but think how gay old Master Turner must have made *his* Shop! He is a famous Aristocrate.[7]

By the Time this reaches Your Hot Wells, good Accounts may possibly arrive from Ægypt. The Death of Paul will *sit heavy on the Soul* of Abdallah Menou—like the Ghosts in Shakespear's Richard—and *fall his Edgeless Sword*.[8] May he *but*

26 April 1801

hear That News before the Battle, *I'll* answer for its Success. Great Credit ought really to be given to that amiable creature the Duchess of York for being able to make every body love *her* while they naturally and necessarily abhor her Brother[9]—and it was pretty in her Husband to cry at the Tragedy——They very seldom *do* cry.[10] When you write tell me how Sotherby's Play went off.[11] Our Newspaper never names the Theatre, so Mrs. Siddons's Name reaches me only thro' your Letters. When our Bishop returns I shall get freed Covers and write oftener, for the sake of goading your Pen to an Answer. Meanwhile my heart is happier on *your* Account since I see what inexpressible Comfort Miss Powell's Society affords you.[12]

With Regard to Mr. Pennington he hardly *can* come to any real harm: The Complaints of Gouty Men are sure to end—however they may begin—in a Fit of Gout;—and *better* Assurance of long Life is granted to no living Mortal: he will quarrel with the Man, and vex about the Maid; and they will leave him, and then he will get others——all will lead *uneasy* Lives, but no Lives will be shortened except *your own* by fretting concerning what can neither be helped nor mended.

Adieu Dear Friend! and assure Yourself of our perfect and Affectionate Regard. We call a pale White Spruce very tall and graceful *Mrs. Pennington*: it might be called Miss Jesse by its Growth:[13] we planted it five Years past and 'tis *such* a Heighth already! ! once more Adieu, and love the Master and Mrs. of Brynbella.

Mr. Whalley seems to have been right in all his Predictions if the Tales we hear are true.

Text: Princeton University Library. *Address:* Mrs. Pennington / Dowry Square / Hot Wells / Bristol. *Postmark:* DENBIGH.

1. While visiting SS during the actress's stay in Bath, PSP sent HLP a ten-page letter, dated 17 April, which was a paean to the British victory at Copenhagen. See Ry. 568.97.
2. According to PSP's letter:
"It is such a delight to see [SS] here *within compass* of her charming *natural* Powers, which she feels no occasion, or temptation to *overstretch*.—Dimond, who is not given to praise our Friend too warmly, told me the other Night—'he *never* saw her Play so *chastely* or *so well* as at this time.' . . . Wednesday She sets off for Town. Saturday She is to appear in Mr. Sothebys *New* Play, for which she has been preparing while here, the most magnificent Dress I ever saw and the most ingeniously imagined: *Black Velvet* and *Sables* to wear in the Month of May! !—but then you know the Scene is Winter and amidst the Snows of St. Bernard.
"I really never beheld our Friend *so* lovely, or felt her *so touching* and tender as in Lady Randolph the other Night."
3. HLP believed there had been a "contagious Disorder" at Belvidere School, where Cecilia Siddons was a pupil. But she had not become ill and was able to open a Miss Flemming's ball in the great Assembly Room by dancing a minuet to her mother's delight and amusement. So PSP reported to HLP in her letter.
4. HLP refers to Elizabeth ("Betty") Sharp (1793–1849). As early as the autumn of 1801 she was recognized as a "juvenile singer" of exceptional promise. By 1806 she was a well-known concert performer. In 1812 she advertised herself in the Bath directories as a "professor of music," a title she held until 1826. Thereafter she disappears from the Bath directories.

Her mother was the singer Elizabeth Sharp, née Hopkins (1756–1821), the widow of the oboist Michael (d. 1800); her brother the talented painter Michael William (d. 1840).

5. In the middle of February the king became ill, the symptoms beginning as a feverish cold. But within a few days "his mind was once more deranged." The king's agitation, set in motion by Pitt's resignation and talk of Roman Catholic emancipation, increased and it become "not less acute than in 1788." He was once more under the care of Dr. Thomas Willis. Again there was the possibility of a regency. But on 2 March he fell into a deep sleep from which he arose refreshed and began to improve steadily. See Stanhope 3:292–99.

6. PSP reports TSW's remarks in her letter of 17 April: " 'tho he has not the honour to resemble Dr. Johnson in many points of Character, he has in common with him an invincible reluctance to Reading a *large* Work *throughout;*—That [*Retrospection*] is the only one he ever Read every Word of; that he shall Read it again and again and he believes never Read any other—for it is so rich in anecdote the mind can never weary nor the memory be sufficiently stored.'"

7. According to PSP's letter, "How you would delight to see the City of Bath dressed out in Laurel—every miserable Wretch with a Leaf!—forgetting their Wants and Sorrows in the glory and honor of old England."

The shop to which HLP alludes belonged to Richard Turner, an apothecary and chemist, who practiced in Stall Street as early as 1800 and at 12 New King Street from 1809 to 1813.

8. In *Richard the Third*, the ghosts of Clarence (5.3.134–35) and Lady Anne (5.3.162–63) warn Richard: "To-morrow in the battle think on me, / And fall thy edgeless sword."

9. The duchess of York's brother was Friedrich Wilhelm III (1770–1840), who had become king of Prussia in 1797.

HLP's animus toward the Prussian king was based on the following: Prussia in December 1800 had joined Russia, Sweden, and Denmark in the Second Armed Neutrality, which Bonaparte supported. By March 1801 Prussia abandoned any pretense of neutrality: her troops occupied Hanover and Bremen; the Weser and Ems were closed to British trade. Prussia became part of the Northern League.

10. According to PSP on 17 April, SS was particularly convincing as Lady Randolph. "The little Duchess [of York] is her true Admirer and Auditor each time she Plays.—The Duke was there *that* Night [for SS's performance as Lady Randolph] and altho 'unused to the *melting* mood' wept most abundantly!—So did all the Gentlemen in their Suit!"

11. William Sotheby (1757–1833) wrote only one play that reached the professional stage. Lasting a single night, *Julian and Agnes, or the Monks of the Great St. Bernard* was performed at the Drury Lane on 25 April with SS in the role of Agnes and Kemble in that of Julian. *The Times* on 27 April concluded its tepid review of the play with the remark that "there is nothing in the character of *Agnes* worthy of the power and judgment of Mrs. Siddons."

12. For Jane Powell, see HLP to PSP, 2 November 1789, n. 2.

13. Mary (b. 29 June 1777) was the daughter of the Reverend William Jesse (d. 1815), rector of Hutton Cranswick and descendant of a prominent Somerset family.

TO JOHN LLOYD

12:May 1801.
Brynbella

My dear Sir
 When is our Affair with Sir Edward likely to come on?[1] And how is it likely to end? *That* Fowlkes comes and talks to Mr. Piozzi, and I think between my Husband's Gout, and my Countryman's Awkwardness they are not likely to get thro' the Business without good help from You. Do not let us pay for rotten Trees which are half dead *now*—a Price they would not ask even for sound ones.
 Relying on your kindness I remain Your / troublesome but truly faithful / Servant H: L: P.

Please to send the German Book by the Bearer,[2] and whenever you wish for your Copy of Retrospection to be corrected—Command its Author. Je me tiens sous les Armes.

Text: National Library of Wales MS 12421D. *Address:* John Lloyd Esq. / Wygfair.

1. See HLP's letter to John Lloyd, 12 October 1800, and n. 1.
2. About this time HLP read Christoph Wilhelm von Hufeland (1762–1836), *Die Kunst das menschliche Leben zu verlängern*, 2 vols. in 1 (Vienna and Prague: Franz Haas, 1797). In the same year its translation, *The Art of Prolonging Life*, was published by J. Bell in London.

TO THE REVEREND ROBERT GRAY

Brynbella
13th May 1801.

 I have been *canvassing* Miss Thrales these years, and their votes have a Q before them yet. People skilled in electioneering know *that* letter stands for Query. . . . the steady suffrages have a P for *Promise*. I used to tell the borough folks who kept our books, they must *mind their p's and q's*.[1] So must Buonaparte, if he comes hither on call of our home Jacobins. The wisest people I converse with say he *must* come, or expose himself to danger from vindictive Frenchmen.[2] Things are supposed ripening for revolt in that distracted nation, whence religion and morals are more completely banished—as foreigners have told me—than any living creature in our comparatively quiet land can have a notion.
 The Bishop is just now wholly inaccessible to me indeed, though I did squeeze this frank out of him; because Mr. Chester, one of his nephews, is killed in Egypt,[3] and Mr. Piozzi is in bed with the gout, so that I cannot go and condole . . . but no opportunity shall be lost.
 I printed Hannah More's 'Village Politics' here, and paid near twelve guineas

out of my own pocket-money for its translation and dispersion;[4] but when the good news came and welcomed in this lovely month,[5] the master of our house prevented my wishes, and, forbearing silly expence as to candles, gave all his labourers and cottagers a good mess of soup, a bit of beef in it, and a dumpling,—exactly on your principle of affording them reason to rejoyce, and a pretext for roaring out 'God save the King!'

Text: Hayward 2:253–54.

1. HLT had often supported HT's electioneering efforts, which made him an M.P. for Southwark from 1765 to 1781. See HLP to PSW, 6 August [1791], n. 7.
2. HLP was not alone in her belief that the French would invade Great Britain. According to GM in May 1801:
"The Consul of France, to give employment . . . to the troops which have now almost wholly evacuated Germany, is marching them down to the coasts opposite to our island; against different points of which, it is rumoured, he intends to direct at the same moment the most formidable attack" (71, pt. 1: 474–75).
3. Charles Chester Bagot (1730–93), brother of the bishop, assumed by act of Parliament the surname of Chester (1755). He had married on 5 October 1765 Catherine, née Legge (d. 1819). Their family consisted of three sons and four daughters. See Charles Chester's will, P.R.O., Prob. 11/1232/248, proved at London, 23 May 1793.
The bishop's nephew, killed in the second battle of Aboukir, ca. 8–13 March, was Captain Charles Chester (b. 1772), of the thirteenth Regiment. See *The Times*, 11 May, for casualty lists sent to Downing Street on 9 May by General Abercromby.
4. *Rheolau Llywodraeth ajny Llan, yn Annerch at Holl Grefftwyr, Gweinidogior, A Gweithwyr Fesur y Dydd, Ym Mrhydain Fawr. Y Degfed Argraphiad, Wedi ei gyfieithu ar Ddumuniad Gwraig Fonheddig, Gan Edward Barnes, Athraw-Ysgol, Yng Nghaerwys* (Croesoswallt, 1796).
This copy at the N.L.W. is the tenth impression of More's *Village Politics*, translated by Barnes to comply with the wishes of an unnamed gentlewoman.
5. The "good news" had to do with a note to Sir Hyde Parker from the Russian government "desiring that a suspension of hostilities might take place till a definitive arrangement could be made, which might put an end to the differences subsisting between Great Britain and the Northern Powers." See GM 71, pt. 1 (1801): 473.

TO HESTER MARIA THRALE

[23: May 1801]

I feel much obliged by your Letter my Dearest and am glad to think that my Verses pay Postage so well. It is perhaps a false Taste to be fond of Epigrams—but I delight now in no Reading which leaves not a Strong Flavour behind: like the hard Drinkers who put Red Pepper into their Brandy at Close of a Life spent in irritating the Palate. Turn to Martial L:viii. Ep:68. and as the Preachers say—*You will find these Words.*

> Ut nova dona tibi Cæsar, Nilotica tellus,
>   Miserat hybernas ambitiosa Rosas;
> Navita derisa Pharios Memphiticus hortos
>   Urbis ut intravit limina prima tuæ &c. &c.[1]

23 May 1801

And this old Stuff *in my head* produced the Vulgar Ballad, which Sing to the Tune of Rural Felicity——or I believe they call it Ellen o'Roon.[2]

> From Egypt Old Rome in the Days of Domitian,
>   To make that Tyrannical Emperor Smile;
> Fresh Roses brought over for Winter's Provision
>   To bloom round the Tyber as once round the Nile.
> But bold Abercrombie whom Britons confide in,
>   His Flora sent home with far different Spoil;
> Th'Invincible Standard of Frenchmen deriding,
>   Their Colours he seiz'd on the Banks of the Nile.
> Thus end the Exploits of renown'd Buonaparte
>   Who fell upon Egypt with Force and with Guile;
> Throwing Dust in the Eyes of each Mussulman hearty
>   Dust-pregnant with Plagues on the Banks of the Nile.
> Of Warriors ill-fated if England must tell Soon,
>   Her Losses tho' deep She'll repair in a while;
> With Moore, Smith, and Berry, Ball, Trowbridge, and Nelson[3]
>   A Hero We'll count for each Mouth of the Nile.

You are a wise Child for leaving London in May, and enjoying a little of this very lovely Spring, to the beauties of which nothing but Showers are wanted——though there is an odd Contagion among our Larch Trees—all sick of the same Disease.——God keep us from more serious Afflictions of similar Nature.——I hate all Connections with Turkey.—

You are really doing my Book great honour to read it again, and nothing can speak better for such a Work than to see it give down fresh Beauties on a second Perusal: I have not a Copy at home; but I remember hoping you would be pleased with the Story and Character of Harold the hardy in Vol. 1st[4] and with Blue Tooth the Enchanter in nearer Times.[5] *Nobody* likes the Discovery Chapters I believe; almost every other Part of the Book has some admirers, but *that* is considered (unjustly enough) as a mere Abridgement of Robertson.[6]——Those who live too much out of the World as I do, are apt to think they make *Discovery* of things known to all but Themselves, and that was my Case with Regard to the *Duc de Bronte:*[7] Those who live too much in the World—find a *Hum* in *their Head*[8] after the Noise of clustered Society's loud Approbation, which stuns without Informing;——and I applaud you much for running away and not continuing to live As Intoxicated with the Fume of an empty Cask when the Spirit has been all drawn off.

You are in Sight of Wales——and if you cross the Channel will be marvellously welcome at Brinbella. Mr. Piozzi has fought his Spring Duel with the Gout—which he has repulsed—with little Loss to himself of Good Looks—but He is not yet out of Bed or confident that a Relapse is far off.

If you light on Mrs. Pennington her Conversation will please you, It is often *so very* like your own: *She* sees enough of the World to be sick on't—yet cannot get freed from the Chains which bind her fast to a Ball Room. This is Susette's Birthday.[9] May heaven send her many of them: If you transmit my nonsense to your Sisters pray tell them how little My Lord Courtney[10] or Mrs. Walker of Liverpool[11] can do towards emulating the old Roman Nobleman who for a *January* Entertainment fetched Oysters from England and Roses from Ægypt—to grace it.[12] We are behind hand there even in 1801 But you see Power supplied Contrivance in those Days—and now Contrivance supplies the want of Power: It was beginning to do so when Domitian got Stoves for his Roses

> Ut tu Romanæ jussus jam cedere brumæ
> Mitte tuas messes, *accipe* Nile Rosas.[13]

Adieu, and remember if you please that though We do live near Denbigh, we are not in Denbighshire at all; and that Mistake sends Your Letters sadly roundabout. The sick Lady is lucky in having such a Friend to console her;[14] I know not where Heath House lies, but all those *Conforni* are beautiful, and Mr. Whalley's Cottage most so of all: but I much fear he is dying; and if he does dye, a true and tender and Constant and Steady Well Wisher will be lost to Your Affectionate Mother / H: L: Piozzi.

23: May 1801 My Trunk of Clothes, Books &c. sent *before* me from Bath thro' Bristol, is never arrived——We are at our Wits end for it.

Text: Bowood Collection. *Address:* Miss Thrale / at Mrs. Smyth's / Heath House / near / Bristol. *Postmark:* DENBIGH.

    1. The lines are from Martial, *Epigrammatum,* 2 vols. (Mannheim: Cura & Sumptibus Societatis Literatae, 1782). In this edition the ten-line poem ("Ad Caesarem, de rosis hybernis") appears in bk. 6, as epigram 80.
    2. "Rural Felicity" was also known as "Haste to the Wedding." This well-known jig—of which there are at least twenty-one versions—was introduced 26 December 1767 at Drury Lane in a pantomime, *The Elopement,* as the afterpiece to *The London Merchant.*
"Eileen Aroon" (also "Aileen" and "Eylin a Riuin") is an Irish love song composed by the fourteenth-century harper Cearbhail O'Dalaigh ("When, like the early rose, Eileen Aroon. / Beauty in childhood blows, Eileen Aroon . . ."). It was made into English by Gerald Griffin.
    3. HLP's paraphrase celebrates British glory in Egypt from 1799 to 1801. It singles out not only the name of Abercromby, the hero of the night battle of Aboukir, but also those of the following:
For John Moore, who served with distinction under Abercromby in 1801, see HLP to PSP, 17 October 1799, n. 2.
For Admiral Sir William Sidney Smith, see HLP to LC, 21 April 1800, n. 3.
The next three names were all associated with that of Nelson:
Edward Berry (1768–1831) was knighted for valor in the first battle of Aboukir, cr. baronet in 1806, and promoted to the rank of rear admiral in 1821.
Alexander John Ball (1757–1809), cr. baronet (1801) and promoted to rear admiral in 1805. Similarly, Thomas Troubridge (ca. 1758–1807), cr. baronet (1799); rear admiral (1804).
    4. See *Retrospection* 2:254–55 for a description of "Harold, the hardy brother to Olaus [who] . . . walked out of his own country [Norway] as far as Constantinople" and back again. For his ability to walk vast distances, he became known as Harold the Hardy, a man of "rank so elevated, and prowess so prodigious."
    5. From *Retrospection* 2:192–93, a section dealing with the Sultan Achmet and with the districts of Fez and Morocco. A drought occurred which was "attributed to the powerful sorceries of *Muley Hamet,* whom they averred to have a *blue tooth—blaatant* according to the runick ideas of Denmark and Norway, which seem to have been believed in softer

climates upon this occasion: Achmet commanded the tooth to be drawn; but the enchanter with one hundred men only, defended himself and his tooth so well against two thousand Turkish horse, that the Sultan himself began to fear the wizard; the more, as an express came from Constantinople to tell that a pestilence was begun there according to the words of Muley Hamet. . . . An unexampled tempest now raging in the Mediterranean which destroyed vast quantities of shipping, during which time Muley Hamet dropt down dead by a flash of lightning, confirmed the notion that he was some way connected with the world of spirits, who snatched him thus in whirlwinds from the earth."

6. HLP alludes to the third chapter of *Retrospection*'s second volume: "Containing the Discoveries, &c. from A.D. 1492, down to the Year 1525." Those who considered it merely an abridgment thought of the first volume of William Robertson's *The History of America*, 2 vols. (London: Strahan and Cadell; Edinburgh: J. Balfour, 1777).

7. Horatio Nelson was created duke de Brontë (named after the place in Sicily) by Ferdinando IV in 1799. The dukedom was "worth 3000£. sterling per annum" (*The Times*, 11 October 1799).

8. HLP brings together Milton's "busie humm of men" (*L'Allegro*, line 118) and the "humming in the brain (and head)" associated with overindulgence. See HLP to DL, 5 September 1794, n. 3; to LC, 22 May 1799, n. 5; Howell 2:451, 627–28.

9. SAT was thirty-one.

10. William Courtenay (1768–1835), Viscount Courtenay of Powderham Castle (1788) and de jure earl of Devon (1831).

Q had apparently described Lord Courtenay's concert on 17 May, "one of the grandest in the season either with respect to performances or company" (*Morning Post*, 9 May). She had also anticipated the ball to be given 29 May in honor of his youngest sister's coming of age. A brilliant invitation list was headed by the names of the Prince of Wales and the prince of Orange. See the *Morning Post*, 1 June.

11. Alethea Walker, née James (1769–1805), of Oak Hill, West Derby, near Liverpool, was a celebrated hostess. Her extravagant entertaining was made possible by the wealth of her husband Richard (1749–15 October 1801), a West India merchant (*The Times*, 20 October).

Mrs. Walker's ball was given on 13 May for "two hundred fashionables," among whom were the Prince of Wales, Prince William of Gloucester, the dukes of Cumberland and Orleans, the duchesses of Devonshire, Bolton, Gordon, etc. It was held at the Walker residence on Stanhope Street. One of the attractions of the ball was a "service of new plate . . . made for the Prince [of Wales's] table—the dishes, plates, &c. were of frosted silver, richly chased, except in the concave, where they were gilt."

See the *Morning Post*, 15 and 23 May; for Richard Walker's will, signed 14 October 1800 and proved at London on 22 January 1802, see P.R.O., Prob. 11/1369/73.

For a description of the Walkers' opulence, see Farington 6:2378.

12. HLP's muted horror at the balls was piqued not only by Q's interest in them but also by the description of her own "Rout" at Great Cumberland Street on 27 May. Q's festivities were announced by the *Morning Post*, 25 May.

13. The last two lines of Martial's "Ad Caesarem, de rosis hybernis." See n. 1.

14. Jane Whitchurch (1739–1818) had married on 11 August 1767 Thomas Smyth (1740–1800). For the first part of their married life, they resided at May's Hill, Pucklechurch, where their five children had been born between 1769 and 1778. Later they moved to Heath House, which they had rebuilt on a large scale in 1783–84.

See the "Ashton Court Papers," in the City Record Office, Bristol.

TO PENELOPE SOPHIA PENNINGTON

Brynbella
3: June *1801*.

My Dear Mrs. Pennington
has given me her Direction for the next fortnight,[1] and may count upon its being followed up with a Letter. I do assure you that between your own House and this, no greater Anxiety has been felt for Mr. Whalley;[2] he is our very true Friend and We have Sense enough to know it. He is so much Miss Hannah More's Friend that I am convinced of his fretting at Sir Abraham Elton's Officiousness.[3] Will you have *proof* how wrong those Things are.

I am frequently asked after celebrated Characters when we return home to so remote a Neighbourhood as this is; and to the Questions asked about those exemplary Ladies I made such Replies as a Friend is expected to make.——Some of our Neighbours however within these 3 Months have had a fancy to take in a Bath Newspaper—and Oh says one now, and Ah Ah says another—why you never told *us* Mrs. Piozzi, concerning this *paper War* between Miss More and Mr. What's his Name!——as good as you say they are, those who live in the World see Spots in the Sun we find——&c. &c.——Now would it not have been better far to have left these dear Creatures round Bynbella nothing to talk about but the *going off* of Lord Kirkwalls Marriage with Miss Ormsby—The *coming on* of Mr. Piozzi's Gout just at Laburnum Season?—The Hopes of famous News from Ægypt?—and blessed be God! the near Certainty of immense Crops to feed our Poor, and damaged Rice from India to feed our Pigs. Would it not have been better? But we will talk of something else if you please.

The Trunk is not come but coming, and it was kind in you to let me know how I might look after it; I had no Thought of its taking such a Voyage:[4] The comical Preference shown in your Letter of a Trunk to a Lady, is *more* than Classical; In Homer's Time they preferred a Tripod to the fairest, when the Tripod was chased tho'—and the Damsel a Slave.[5]

I have had a civil Letter from Miss Thrale now. She has retired to a Friend's Country Seat I understand; one Mrs. Smyth of whom I never heard before who lives at Heath House Bristol: The Noise and Racket of London was grown painful to her—and She longed for Sight and Smell of Green fields. I wrote her word that if Chance should bring you and her together, it would be very pleasant to you both who have many Ideas—and many Expressions too—in common. I would the Love of H: L: P lived in *her* heart as in yours,—but of *That* as Sciolto says—"*as of a Gem long lost,—Think we no more.*"[6] Do you recollect that agreeable Morning Dear Mr. Whalley gave us at Laura Place this Spring? And how he talked of the River Euphrates and said it would be one Day *literally* dried up for the Jews' Return? And Do you remember what you said after he was gone upon the Subject? And how I exclaimed Why you are talking just like Miss Thrale? Well! and I begin—since he opened my Mind—to think that it *may* be so, ay and without contradiction of your humorous Asperity against the Talkers and Hearers either. Beg of Mr. Whalley when he is better, and can amuse himself with such Stuff—to look in Plutarch's Life of Lucullus—tis an *early* Life, first Volume I think, and if my Memory fails me not, he will find something like a Confirmation of his own Opinion—and of yours. Now please to observe that I have no Plutarch *here*, nor have seen one since I saw *you:* in such an Act of mere Reminiscence therefore, the Mind may be mistaken: but my Heart tells me that Lucullus perceived some Property in the River Euphrates—some Quality rather: which would, (he observed), make it fordable upon a future Day: altho' so deep when he was wishing to pass over:[7]——All this 70 Years before our Saviour's Appearance in the flesh.[8]

I am always ready you know for a Bit of *old Stilton* as Dr. Johnson called profane History. "Thou dost love (said he) My Dear to play the Part of Swift's Vanessa,

> who nam'd the ancient Heroes round,
> Explain'd for what they were renown'd &c.

and I have *as* steadily resisted that Mode of Conversation——now *pray pray* let's have no more of it."[9]

In obedience to *his Commands* as well remembered sure as Plutarch's Lives; I leave this, and begin saying a good Word of Mr. Murphy's book:[10] and feel delighted that you take an Interest in it too. There was some Danger lest it pleased *me* merely by bringing old Scenes to View, but I will trust *your* Criticism.[11] The Work has the more Merit as Garrick and he certainly never loved each other, and you may see his Praises of the Man he celebrates are dictated by *Duty*[12] while those bestowed on Barry spring from *Fondness*.[13] I had rather he had been kinder to sweet Siddons.[14] What a Thing it is that her Husband cannot at least count, and keep together the Money She gets for him! That Man has I fear some Rage for Speculation—a dangerous Game![15]——The prudent people are for ought I observe no better Calculators than we open-pursed fools, who are cheated out of 20sh. perhaps by Bett Lewis the vagrant; while they lose 200£ sterling in the Management of a Puppet Show *that takes Fire,* or sink Three Times as much in a Canal—*that lets out Water*—or some Nonsense.

We have had an Earthquake here—as they say—for I felt it not; tho' I am confident I was wide awake at two o'Clock Monday Morning; Lady Orkney's Canary birds fell from their Perch however, and some of our Denbigh Friends fancy they heard a Noise—I was thinking about my Master's Bevanda, and he was thinking how thirsty the Gouty Pains made him;[16] so Brynbella was unconscious of the Shock.

Buonaparte is supposed to be all this Time under the Influence of Poyson administered 3 months ago; but I believe *that;* as I do the Earthquake. Poor Selim's Death—of the Continental Apoplexy—is less improbable;[17] so is young Constantine's Hope of restoring the Greek Empire.[18]

No Matter!—Live our own dear King, I care for none of them—Here is his 63d Birthday and the Value of his Life is increased 63 Times at least since it began. But the grand Climacterick past over—I count him safe; and would rather have an Annuity upon *him,* than on the dangerous Dame we fear so justly.

Oh I forgot to tell you—Stockdale sends word we have a wicked Enemy at *Bath*, who injures the Sale of Retrospection by spiteful and Ingenious Censures.—*Who is it I wonder!*[19]

Write soon again.

[indecipherable marginal reading]

Text: Princeton University Library. *Address:* Mrs. Pennington / at Longford Cottage / Seat of / The Rev: Thomas Sedgwick Whalley / near / Bristol.

1. HLP responds to PSP's letter, dated 30 May (Ry. 568.99).
In it, PSP wrote: "You will rejoice to hear Mr. Whalley, who has had a very severe plunge, is recovering his Strength and Spirits again. We are going to the Cottage—Mother, Jane Powell and *all*—a complete Family Party, on Monday for a Fortnight."
2. At this time TSW was suffering from recurrent bouts of ague.
3. PSP had written in her letter: "Have you seen Sir. A. Eltons Reply to Bere's Pamphlet against Mrs. H. More—*I do not like it.* It is not sufficiently *Simple and Concise.*—The Language *inflated* and the Matter confused."
The Reverend Sir Abraham Elton (1755–1842) supported Hannah More with his pamphlet, *A Letter to the Rev. Thomas Bere, Rector of Butcombe, occasioned by his late unwarranted attack on Mrs. H. More, with an Appendix.*
TSW in 1802 joined Hannah More's defenders with his pamphlet, *Animadversions on the Curate of Blagdon's Three Publications, entitled The Controversy between Mrs. Hannah More and the Curate of Blagdon, &c. An Appeal to the Public, and An Address to Mrs. Hannah More.* In it, TSW, while approving the position of Sir Abraham's pamphlet, "disapproved of its extreme politeness, and its superfluous candor" (p. 4).
4. According to PSP, "I have obtained *proof* that [the trunk] went from [Bristol] in the *Polly, Captain Thomas.* The Broker, who takes charge of such things at Bristol, says he has very little doubt but that by this time it is in your possession.—Nothing could prevent your *ultimately* recovering it safe and sound, he says, but the Ships *foundering* at the sea, and they have full assurance that She got safe into Port."
5. The words *tripod, tripod-vase,* or *tripods* appear at least twenty times in Homer's two epics. See, e.g.: "Where high Rewards the vig'rous Youth inflame, / (Some golden Tripod, or some lovely Dame . . ." (*Iliad*, 22.213–14).
6. In Nicholas Rowe's *The Fair Penitent*, Sciolto, a nobleman of Genoa, is disaffected by his daughter Calista, to whom he speaks:

> Hadst thou been honest, thou hadst been a Cherubin;
> But of that Joy, as of a Gem long lost,
> Beyond Redemption gone, think we no more.
>
> (5.74–76)

7. See *Plutarch's Lives*, trans. Bernadotte Perrin, 10 vols. (London and New York: William Heinemann and Macmillan, 1914–26), 2:547.
As Lucullus, according to Plutarch, advanced to the Euphrates, "Here he found the stream swollen and turbid from the winter storms. . . . But at evening the stream began to subside, went on diminishing through the night, and at daybreak the river was running between lofty banks. The natives, observing that sundry small islands in the channel had become visible, and that the current near them was quiet, made obeisance to Lucullus, saying that this had seldom happened before, and that the river had voluntarily made itself tame and gentle for Lucullus, and offered him an easy and speedy passage."

8. The return of the Jews to Palestine was to HLP and many of her friends a prefiguring of the New Jerusalem. See the "Harvard Piozziana," vol. 4.

See also HLP to Q, 19[–20] November 1794, n. 10.

9. This paragraph, including the couplet from Swift's *Cadenus and Vanessa* (lines 350–51), paraphrases HLP's statement in the *Anecdotes* (p. 80): ". . . no kind of conversation pleased him less I think, than when the subject was historical fact or general polity. 'What shall we learn from *that* stuff (said he)? let us not fancy like Swift that we are exalting a woman's character by telling how she 'Could name the ancient heroes round, / Explain for what they were renown'd, &c.' "

The metaphor aptly sums up SJ's distaste for history. Like many Englishmen of the time, he shied away from a cheese—however delicate and expensive—which was believed "brought to the table full of mites or maggots" (*Encyclopedia Britannica*, 3d ed. [1797], 17:800). Cf. *Anecdotes* (p. 41); SJ's *Dictionary* for "profane" (subhead: "Not sacred; secular").

10. Arthur Murphy, *The Life of David Garrick, Esq.*, 2 vols. (London: J. Wright, 1801).

11. According to PSP on 30 May:

"I think the Mores were too severe on Mr. Murphy. To be sure it is rather *flat* work going over the Story of all the old Plays, to those who have been many years well acquainted with them; but he does ample justice to the Character of his Friend, which he winds up very agreeably in the four points of view as an Actor, a Manager, Author and private Man—and took *me* back for a time into Company that I like much better than the present Day will often afford, for which I feel obliged to him.—Perhaps they do not relish his bringing forward in two glaring Instances, Mrs. Garrick's Parsimony and indifference to her Husband's Fame—respecting the *Monument*, and Dr. Johnsons *offer* to *include him* in his Lives of the Poets."

12. Very early in his work on Garrick, Murphy indicates both tone and intention. "He was acquainted with Mr. Garrick so early as the latter end of the year 1752, and from that time lived in great intimacy with him to the hour of his death; and now, being at rest from various labours, he resumes his long-intended purpose, willing to pay his tribute of friendship, and, at the same time, of strict justice, to the memory of David Garrick, in a fair, a just, and true account of his conduct in life, with all the lights and shades of the picture, touched with a firm, and impartial hand" (1:4).

For the tension between Murphy and Garrick and its source, see *Thraliana* 1:152 and n. 1.

13. Throughout the biography, Murphy's comments on Barry are complimentary. In the dedication to Thomas Coutts, Murphy writes: "I knew that you had a just estimate of the genius of Garrick, and was, at the same time, a warm admirer of the wonderful powers of Barry. I hope, Sir, you will find that I have done some degree of justice to the last most excellent performer, who certainly was, in some parts, a formidable rival, if not superior even to Garrick" (1:iii–iv).

14. Murphy's remarks about SS are perfunctory, more suitable to a precocious understudy than the leading actress of the day. See, e.g., 2:94.

15. HLP is responding to PSP's most recent description of SS's activities. The actress, she wrote, "is 'skirring the country round' at Manchester, Birmingham, &c.—Patty Wilkinson writes me (for She has not leisure) She is to play *every* Night for 3 Weeks!!— < > duty I think that She must try to *repair* the Money *so Ill* taken care of by fagging and harrassing herself out to the very last!—I hope however like the Eels she *rather* 'likes it.' "

16. Bevanda, an Italian euphemism here for the wine GP habitually drank to deaden the pains of his illness.

17. For the death of Selim III, see HLP to LC, [25] February 1800, n. 9.

18. Constantine or Konstantin Pavlovich (1779–1831) was the second son of Czar Paul. Although a merely competent soldier, he so distinguished himself at Novi (15 August 1799) that his father named him czarevitch (a title reserved for the royal succession).

From the time of Catherine II, Russia sought to incite Greek Christians to rebel against their Turkish rulers. Thus, Russia had arrived at an arrangement with Austria, known as the "Greek project," for a partition of Turkish territory and the restoration of the Byzantine empire under Constantine, the grandson of Catherine.

19. According to PSP, 14 June 1801 (Ry. 568.100), she and TSW "agree entirely in opinion respecting the *quarter* from whence Stockdale complains of 'Spiteful and Ingenious Censures' on your Book, because our own burning and indignant Ears have heard the same from those very Persons we suspect in the fair City of Bath—but as we dare not give to such 'airy nothings' as Suspicion is made of 'a local Habitation and a Name',—tis better you should not enquire too minutely on the Subject, lest this Enemy should come out in the Form one could least like to make such a discovery."

PSP's reticence was not to last long; the "Enemy" was Harriet Lee.

TO THE LADIES OF LLANGOLLEN

Brynbella
14th June 1801.

I intrude upon Your Ladyship's and Miss Ponsonby's Retirement chiefly to let you see I am still alive notwithstanding the feeble attacks of our Critical Reviewers, meant no doubt to break my Peace and ruin my Reputation for that Learning which I never boasted.[1] They have been hasty in showing me on their parts a degree of Ignorance I should never have suspected them of reaching,— having mistaken the *maritime* City of Laodicea, so named by Seleucus Nicator after his *wife,* to which the Apostle addresses himself, for an Inland Town of the same name, although not only Mons. D'Anville's Compendium of Geography, but even Abbé Marru's edition of old Echard's Gazetteer calls it expressly Laodicea ad mare, and the Turks know it by name of Ladikich.[2] . . . They should not clean Blots with Inky Fingers, as Fuller says.[3]

It *is as* extraordinary to *me* that they should make a wonder at my saying how Polyaenus wrote 900 Stratagems of War in eight Books and dedicated them to Antoninus Pius,[4]—how these Books (the Greek copies) were bought many centuries after by Casaubon and edited at his expense, and how they were Translated and advertised not long ago.[5]

Greek copies!! say the Reviewers, with an insulting sneer.[6] Not knowing, I suppose, that Polyaenus was a native of Macedon and wrote in his own language, and not knowing (which is stranger) that Casaubon was Henri Quatre's Librarian, that he lived much in England, and that James the First employed him to purchase MSS. upon the Continent but 'Ye King having small occasion for *Stratagems of War,* he paid for *those himself*'.[7]

Another scandalous error they commit for the sake of saying: 'Poor Mrs. Piozzi does not know the word Soter means Saviour and was the sacred appellation of Jesus Christ'.[8] I know it well, but I know likewise that it had been the distinguishing appellation of many Princes, Ptolemy Soter, Antiochus Soter, and more beside *them.*[9] Add to this that the appellation *Saviour* had been given by the Pharoah of Egypt to Hebrew Joseph 1715 years before *his* appearance in the flesh of whom that Joseph has been by many learned men supposed a Type and

Representation.[10] These Critics teach their neighbour to walk before they themselves are out of Leading Strings.

With regard to Aventin, who they give out for a writer of the 16th century and call him Aventinus, they are still wider from Truth or Knowledge. The man was a Poor Alehouse Keeper's son at Abensberg born upon *Advent* Sunday 1466 and had no name but what the *Day* bestowed. He made that name famous because he was a good scholar and of Deep Research. One may say of the Residers in distant Towns who buy Books, and read them, as directed by the Critical Reviewers— 'Lo! these are the Gods ye worship!'[11]

I had rather talk of Lord Kirkwall and Miss Ormsby. It is the fashion in these parts, I am told, to blame the Porkington Family for failure of the match. Round Porkington the fault is thrown on Lord Kirkwall. Was there any Fault or Blame at all? Lords and Ladies of such high Fortune and Expectations can never want husbands or wives. Sure 'the world is all before them whence to choose', &c.[12]

What say the charming Ladies of Llangollen to all these stories? Everyone runs with their appeal to them. Witness the intrusive haste of their ever obliged and obedient / H: L: Piozzi.

Text: The Hamwood Papers, pp. 316–19.

1. The *Critical Review* 32 (1801): 28–35 began its attack on *Retrospection* by "confess[ing] . . . disappointment, as the materials are not only, in general, trifling or erroneous, and the arrangement confused, but as the style is often rendered abrupt and quaint, by the pursuit of what the French call *esprit*." It concluded the attack by wishing "for the sake of Mrs. Piozzi's reputation, she had never committed these volumes to the press: nor could her most learned friend have remedied the mischief, as the errors exceed every power of correction. In regard to her sex we are anxious to treat her with all possible lenity; but we should totally fail in our duty if we suffered the minds of youth, or of female readers, to be contaminated by such a flood of idle tattle and innumerable blunders."

Between the opening and closing paragraphs of the review is a detailed examination of HLP's "tattle" and "blunders."

2. In *Retrospection* 1:34n., HLP had written: "'Tis odd enough that Laodicea, like Holland, was a maritime situation—its name means *ad mare*, as scholars tell me."

Her statement is supported by Jean-Baptiste Bourguignon d'Anville in his *Compendium of Ancient Geography* (London: R. Faulder, 1791), pp. 386–87.

"In the description of this maritime part of Syria, we shall take our departure from Laodicea, which was a Phœnician city, before it became a Greek one by renovation under Seleucus Nicator. It then took the name of *Laodicea;* which, distinguished by its maritime situation, was surnamed *ad Mare;* and its name has suffered scarce any alteration in the present form of Ladikieh."

HLP is equally indebted not to an abbé Marru but to the following: *Dictionnaire Géographique-Portatif*. . . . Traduit de l'Anglois, sur la treizième Édition de Laurent Échard, par M. Vosgien, Chanoine de Vaucouleurs, 2 vols. (Paris: chez les Libraires Associés, 1792). "*Laodicea ad mare* . . . . fut bâtie par Seleucus I Nicator, qui lui donna le nom de Laodicée, sa mère" (pp. 354–55).

3. Thomas Fuller (1654–1734), M.D., compiled *Gnomologia* (1732). See particularly no. 1112: "Cleaning a blot with blotted fingers, maketh a greater blur."

4. In *Retrospection* 1:52, HLP had written: ". . . witness Polyenus, the Macedonian, who for eight books, containing an account of nine thousand stratagems employed in the art of war, received a royal present. Casaubon bought the Greek copies many ages after, and I myself saw them advertised in English not seven years ago."

HLP's knowledge of the Macedonian and his work came from *Polyaenus's Stratagems of War, translated from the Original Greek*, by R. Shepherd, F.R.S. (London: G. Nicol, 1793). This, the first English translation of Polyaenus, was dedicated to the Marquis Cornwallis; the original to the emperors Antoninus and Verus.

5. Isaac Casaubon (1559–1614) edited Polyaenus's *Stratagems* in 1589. His edition divides the pages lengthwise. On one half is the Greek; on the other is the Latin.

What Casaubon knowingly bought was not the original manuscript of Polyaenus's *Stratagems* but a transcript made by [Andreas] Darmarius, "one of the last of the calligraphs, a race who had long survived the invention of printing." Casaubon, nonetheless, was able to create an accurate text by borrowing "a MS. Polyaenus which belonged to [Jacques] Bongars," the French envoy at Strasbourg. See Mark Pattison, *Isaac Casaubon 1559–1614*, 2d ed. (Oxford: Clarendon Press, 1892), pp. 37–38.

6. In the statement about Polyaenus, HLP erred when she wrote of "nine thousand" stratagems. The mistake, however, was probably typographical, for in William Augustus Conway's copy of *Retrospection* she penned in "nine hundred."

But the *Critical Review* was wrong when it dismissed HLP's assertion "that Casaubon bought the *Greek copies* of Polyaenus many ages after he wrote," arguing instead that "it would be complete waste of time to offer any remarks on ignorance as gross as the darkness of Egypt."

7. Generally recognized as the consummate Greek scholar, Casaubon was in November 1604 appointed by Henri IV to be sublibrarian of the royal library in Paris. In 1610 he came to England and soon enjoyed the patronage of James I, through whose efforts he was collated to a prebendal stall in Canterbury and an annual pension of £300.

8. In its array of HLP's errata, the *Critical Review* cited "this note of profound erudition!" about Antiochus Soter, who "was called *Theos*, God, for his wise judgment, but took in modesty the anagram *Sothe,* corrupted to *Soter,* as I have read and heard" (2:508n.). The reviewer then defined *soter,* related the term to Jesus in the sentence that HLP quotes in her letter.

9. Ptolemy I Soter (ca. 367/6–283 or 282 B.C.), a Macedonian, who declared himself king of Egypt early in 304, conquered Palestine, Cyprus, and many possessions in the Aegean Sea and Asia Minor (ca. 301–285).

Antiochus I Soter (ca. 324–262 or 261 B.C.), of the Seleucid dynasty, assumed the name Soter about 275 when he was victorious over the Celts in Asia Minor.

10. For HLP's free adaptation of *soter* to Joseph, see Gen. 41:38–43.

The analogies between Joseph and Christ are significant: they were both the chosen objects of a father's love, were hated by their brothers, who denied their superiority and conspired to slay them. Each became a blessing among the Gentiles and gained a bride, etc.

11. The struggle over Aventinus or Aventine indicates that neither the *Critical Review* nor HLP relied wholly on facts.

It was the name assumed by Johann Turmair (1477–1534), born in Abensberg (Lat. Aventinum) and the author of *Annales Boiorum* or, *Annals of Bavaria*—written between 1517 and 1521. An abridged version was first printed in 1554 but a fuller edition was printed at Basel in 1580 by Nicholas Cisner.

Far from being a writer whose "testimony [was] of no weight" (according to the *Critical Review*), he is often called the "Bavarian Herodotus."

For HLP's reference to Aventine, see *Retrospection* 1:20.

12. HLP's adaptation of *Paradise Lost,* 12.646. For HLP's account of the failure of the Kirkwall-Ormsby engagement, see her letter to PSP, 30 November 1801 and n. 9.

TO THE REVEREND LEONARD CHAPPELOW

Brynbella
18: June 1801.

My Dear Mr. Chappelow
 is really very kind to be so angry——but it would not be worth while to quarrel if every one could judge fairly as *you* can.[1] 'Tis for the Sake of Readers in distant Provinces—and People abroad too—that form a Judgment of Books from what The Critical Reviewers say of them, that I feel interested in repelling their Charge of Ignorance. Many Female Friends too, and demi Sçavans will catch at this Publication, and consider the Imputation as unanswerable, if I answer it not.
 Another Reason. If we sit down tamely, and sit down *long*, the Reply will be worth less, as supposed to be more studied; and People will care less who gains or loses in the Controversy. Besides that these Rejoinders &c. contribute to Selling A Work about which some bustle has been made——If we sit still we sink quietly to nothing: The Book is light, and so is a Shuttle Cock; beating it forth and back *keeps it up*.[2]
 Let them see that they made false Charges, and shew the World as Daniel did the Eastern King whose Dragon he got Leave to poyson; that they are not Immortal or Invulnerable——and now said he when the Creature burst in sunder—*Lo these be the Gods ye worship*.[3] Perhaps indeed the Critical Reviewers never heard the Story; *such* Ignorance would be more pardonable than never to have heard of Regnard the French Poet[4]—of whom Their Friend Voltaire speaks largely,[5] and says Boileau broke his Heart by writing against him——Did they never read Boileau neither?[6] If French is out of their Way——some of Regnard's Adventures may be found in the Universal Musæum 1765—I forget what Month.[7]
 Looking over my manuscript I found the Words concerning the Lyon and the Slave written thus.

> "Aulus Gellius relates the Story of the Lyon whose grateful Recollection spar'd the Slave, observing that they had often been met in the Streets together during the Reigns of Caligula and Claudius collecting Money from Children and Passers by."[8]

Errors of the Press are certainly numerous but it is cruel to take advantage of them so; Gillet has printed Lewis the fourth for Lewis the 14th and Joseph *the fifteenth* in Letters, when the Manuscript had Joseph 1st in *Figures:* unaccountably enough to be sure. Shew Mr. Gillon this Letter Dear Sir, and make me up a little Pamphlet of Refutation. Non c'è Tempo da perdere. I have written Robson of Bond Street—who sent me the Review—an Answer to their principal Charges,—to lye about his Shop and shew People my own Defence in my own Hand Writing. Look at it yourself, I dare say Mr. Gillon has already showed you my Epistle to him. The Story of Hyder's Ali's[9] Tumour on his Back was told me by Mrs. Light,[10] and She *knew* it for a *Fact:* you remember Mrs. Light at

Streatham Park, She married Captain Anstey afterwards.—Mr. Gillon's Brother knew the Fact too,[11] and helped her Escape from Hyder who would have catched her if he could for his Seraglio—at least his Agents—but her Husband and his Friend sent her safe to Ceylon, where She stole the Cinnamon Tree and brought it (when out of Danger) back to our Settlements in India. Mr. Gillon and Mrs. Anstey are both dead, and I can get no written Evidence of the Fact.—They called him Herod Ali—because he killed the Babies to make a Poultice of their Liver in consequence of a Quack's recommendation.[12]

The Story of Caroline and Adelaide Broyard I have the power of Authenticating when called upon.[13]

And now Adieu! Dear Mr. Chappelow and forgive all this Trouble from Yours ever / H: L: P.

I am most anxious to see the *British Critic*——The *Monthly* Review will abuse the Book I doubt not, but they will do it better I am afraid: *These* Men are no formidable Foes: let us kill *them* first.[14]

Mr. Piozzi has had his Fit of Gout and is mending—how is your own Health? Pray accept all our best Regards and Thanks.

Mr. Gillon has written again and I am more convinced, and my Spirits quieter, since I hear the Book's Sale has not suffered: but I rejoyce that the Critic *himself* at least sees my Defence——it is a very polite one; and cannot offend.

Adieu, and do the best for me you can, and get a Purchaser for our fine Horses among your fine folks—Mr. Gillon will tell you all. Adieu and thank you kindly.

Text: Ry. 560.111. *Address:* Rev: Mr. Chappelow / No. 12 or 13 / Hill Street / Berkeley Square / London. *Postmark:* DENBIGH; E JUN 19 1801.

1. LC's letter is missing. But see a similar letter from TSW, dated 1 October (Ry. 564.8), to which HLP responds on 9 October 1801.
2. HLP had already answered the *Critical Review*er on 12 June. See her letter to Mr. Urban, dated Brynbella, 12 June. It was published in the July issue of *GM* 71, pt. 2: 602–3. Her response begins: "What makes our Critical Reviewers so outrageous? I expected more candour from *these* enemies, and censure better founded." The attack continues with her list of errors made by the reviewer and so the attack becomes a form of self-defense. Cf. *Boswell's Johnson,* 5:400.

She berates him for an inability to distinguish between typographical and factual errors. She justifies her statements about Aventin, Laodicea, Polyaenus and Casaubon, the derivation of Napoleon from Apollion, etc.

3. See "The History of the Destruction of Bel and the Dragon from the End of Daniel" in Apocrypha.
4. HLP mentions the French dramatist Jean-François Regnard (ca. 1655–1709) early in *Retrospection* (1:17): "When Regnard and his companions had made many voyages, had seen three continents, and wintered in three different zones, they came at last to a point in Lapland, beyond the Arctic Circle. There with no small labour erecting a rustic column, they engraved on it their names, and the names of some places they had visited, ending the inscription with this impressive line—'Hic tandem stetimus, ubi nobis toto defuit orbis.'" In short, HLP discussed Regnard not as a dramatist but anecdotally as an adventurer. See n. 7, *Thraliana* 1:69; Seward, *Anecdotes* 2:166–67.

The *Critical Review* wrote: "Of Regnard we know nothing, nor can we find him mentioned in the catalogue of voyages by Dufresnoy."

5. Voltaire wrote about Regnard in several places: *Du Siècle de Louis XIV,* 14:120–21, 419; *Théâtre-Tome Deuxième,* 3:444; *Dictionnnaire Philosophique,* 17:418–19; *Mélanges/Conseils à un Journaliste,* 22:247; to M. LeComte Woronzoff, 26 February 1769 in *Correspondence* 46:265, all in *Oeuvres Complètes de Voltaire.*

Voltaire was aware of Boileau's unflattering view of Regnard and countered it in *Du Siècle de Louis XIV* (14:120–21).

6. In 1694 Regnard and Boileau engaged in a literary skirmish. Boileau published a satire against women. Regnard counterattacked with a satire against husbands. Boileau sneered at Regnard in *Epistle 10;* Regnard responded with *Tombeau de M. Boileau-Despréaux.* The two men, however, were reconciled, Boileau removing Regnard's name from *Epistle 10* and substituting for it that of another poet, then deceased.

See Boileau-Despréaux, *Epistres,* Édition Critique avec Commentaire, par Albert Cahen (Paris: Librairie E. Droz, 1937), pp. 86–87, n. 36.

7. See *"The History of Regnard, the French Comic Poet," Universal Museum and Complete Magazine,* 1 (May 1765): 245–47. The article, whose facts are dubious, tells of Regnard's elopement with Zulima, of their imprisonment by Algerian pirates, and of their enslavement. Eventually they were released and about to be wed when Zulima died. In despair, Regnard fled to Lapland. In time he returned to Paris, made a fortune, lived in a mansion but could not forget Zulima. He therefore committed suicide.

8. HLP's narration of Androclus and the lion (*Retrospection* 1:23) is not accurate but the *Critical Review* compounds the inexactness by misreading it. Thus the reviewer comments: "We leave it to herself, for instance, to explain . . . how Aulus Gellius, who lived in the time of Antoninus Pious, could have walked the streets in the reign of Claudius, who died 100 years before."

For the anecdote by Aulus Gellius, see the *Noctes Atticae,* trans. John C. Rolfe, 3 vols. (London and New York: William Heinemann and G. P. Putnam's Sons, 1928), 5.14.5–26.

9. Haidar Ali Khan (ca. 1722–82) began life as a soldier of fortune and eventually assumed the throne of Mysore. Betrayed by the English in 1772, he hated them, and from 1779 to the end of his life fought them, although he had long been suffering from cancer. He died in the middle of the war against the English, leaving Tippoo—his only son—as successor.

In *Retrospection* 2:483 HLP had written: "To hear the cry against [Hastings], one would have thought that he had nightly killed a child, to make a poultice for a pimple on his back out of the baby's liver. *This* Hyder Ali did for many weeks. A lady who lived long in Hindostan assured me, that *she knew* of sixteen infants which, when the tyrant had a tumour on his shoulder, were all devoted to this dreadful purpose, and our horror-stricken English called him Herod."

10. For Lucretia Light, née Luders, who married Robert Anstey, see HLP to Charlotte Lewis, 9 May 1791, n. 2.

11. William Gillon was a merchant-member of the East India Company, whose records show that he was buried on 17 October 1798 in Saint Mary's Parish, Fort Saint George, Madras.

12. The story about Haidar Ali was probably suggested by Herod's behavior in Matt. 2:16.

13. See *Retrospection* 2:465–66, wherein HLP describes an edict of Mustapha III upon beginning his war against Russia "in 1769 or 1770." The edict prohibited Christians on certain martial occasions from appearing in the streets or in windows. "Two flippant females, French women of course, defied the united prejudices of nations, and took their dangerous stand at a balcony." They almost were put to death, but eventually spared on the grounds " 'that females having no souls, ought not to lose their sole existence for their senseless faults; and that what could be done by Christians of that sex, should be forgotten by wise servants of the prophet.' "

14. The *Monthly Review* did not review *Retrospection* but the *British Critic* did in April 1802 (19:355–58). The latter's review was over all favorable.

"We have suffered time to proceed, till it becomes a work of *Retrospection* to examine this publication. It must not, however, be allowed to go out of sight, which it may perhaps, if we delay much longer. But how shall we characterize a work so perfectly singular? An universal history from the Christian æra, translated into chit-chat language; the result of much, very much reading, containing facts and characters put together certainly as they were never put before; a string of reflections chronologically arranged, full of good sentiments, but so expressed,—as what, shall we say?—as the Anecdotes, Letters, Travels, and Synonymes of Mrs. Piozzi!"

Of factual errors in *Retrospection*, the *British Critic* concluded: "It will be a good exercise for those who, for any reason, suspect such failings, to compare our lively lady with more elaborate historians; and instruct themselves, without telling tales of her."

TO HESTER MARIA THRALE

Brynbella Solstice 1801.
[21 June]

I receive your Letter Dearest Girl with double Pleasure—it tells me you are well and among my Friend's Friends—and it gives me an Opportunity of amusing you by confessing my Country's Irascible Disposition quickened by the Critical Reviewers. You *said* good naturedly when I told the Story of Acca and Anna, that you hoped all those who criticised my Book would be as *hasty* as that Man was—to shew their Ignorance,—These Gentlemen have been *slow,* but they are *Sure:* and think themselves witty to hoot me for Saying that Laodicea—stood on the Sea or took its Name thence—they confound it with an Island Town of Asia Minor now Jouski—formerly Laodicea Libani, and want to be told that the City spoken of in the first Chapter (I think) of Retrospection, was a Phoenician Port, before it was a Greek one; that Seleucus Nicator rebuilt and named it after his Wife—or Mother Laodicea because She was born at Sea—The Romans knew it by Appellation of Laodicea *ad Mare,* and Monsr. D'Anville calls it so *still.*

That Polyenus should write in Greek they consider likewise as a *laughable* Mistake, having reflected that he dedicated his Book to Antoninus Pius: and *not* having reflected that he was a Macedonian and wrote as Plutarch did in his own Language. Of Casaubon—they seem to know as little, though he lies buried I am pretty confident in Westminster Abbey,—was Librarian to Henri quatre, and refuged in England on Account of the Protestants being not suffered to remain in quiet on the Continent and James the 1st often employed him to buy Books—But as *that* Monarch had small Taste to purchase *Ruses de Guerre,*—he paid for them out of his own Purse to the Ambrosian Library at Milan.

As to Aventine They have the Assurance to Say his Authority is good for nothing, and that I *can* know nothing about him, and if [I did should call him by the Latin Pronunciation Aventi*nus*. I wrote them word that had he *not* been a Writer of good Authority, he would never have obtained a Latin Termination to his Name *at all;* for that he was a poor Alehouse keeper's Son at Abersperg—and had his nominal Distinction bestowed on him merely because he was born on an *Advent* Sunday—No uncommon reason on the Continent.

But The Critical Reviewers say tis a Shame for Mrs. Piozzi not to know that the Greek Word Soter Means Saviour and belongs exclusively to Jesus Christ; I could not help telling them that I knew the Word meant Saviour, but I knew likewise that it was an Appellation of many Eastern Kings, Ptolemy, Antiochus, and some others: the Custom having been borrowed from Ægypt, where Hebrew Joseph was called Saviour 1715 Years before *his* Appearance in the flesh, of whom that Joseph was a Type and Representative.—One might aptly quote *another* passage from Scripture and say of such Critics when People look up to them for Characters of Books:—*Lo these be the Gods Ye worship.*

They are however capable of finding out a Printer's Mistake of *Lusit*ania for *Lith*uania, and laying it to my Charge, but happily I have called Poland Lithuania once if not oftener, in Course of the Work; so I suppose they will perswade no one that I *can* be Ignorant to *such* a Degree. If Mr. Piozzi had not kept their Ill humoured Nonsense in his Pocket Two Days for Fear of its vexing me, I had sooner vindicated myself from their Charges:—did I do right in sending them a Refutation or no? I hope you will say *Yes.*

As to Errata they are truly numberless; pray do rectify this which had escaped us all so often, of *Lusitania* tis in the 2d. Vol. p: 491. There is a Passage too in the 1st Vol. *213* stark Nonsense as it stands now; You must be so good to scratch out the Word *Though* before the Words King Offa. With regard to Buonaparte—I never imagined he was *baptized* Apollyon:[1] It is not unusual for Italian Ladies to put their Baby under Protection of some Saint to whom they addressed themselves during Gestation: If they were troubled with Weak Sight—The Tutelar Patroness is Santa Lucia,[2] who had her Eyes blinded before Martyrdom—if Tooth Ach was their Complaint, recourse is had to Santa Appollonia, who suffered all her beautiful teeth to be torne out by the Executioner—and then was burned at a Stake.[3] The Sons—if Sons—are named in Consequence of such Devotion *Lucien* or *Appollonio*—and Corsican Pronunciation has I trust accidentally produced the Affinity between the Word *Destroyer* and this Hero; who alone ever, and who above all Mortals has deserved it—but *hinc illae Lachrymae,*[4] the Reviewers are Democrates; and I will say no more about them.

Here are fine Prospects of Hay and Corn, but *I* am of Opinion the Crops will be very Light; Potatoes thrive however, and as there was something of an artificial Scarcity *last* year, there will be something like an artificial Plenty this.—
—But I like not the Appearance of ought I see. Have you read Mr. King's new Publication! ! ! ! ![5]

Well! Poor Rat and Mole are gone to London to be Sold, and tho' the Agony I suffered from Terror when the last named Hero flung up both his Legs between the Wheel and Splinter Bar twelve Days ago, was too great to bear; and tho' Mr. Piozzi was forced by this Frolic to walk down St. Asaph Street when he had not set a foot to Ground for six Weeks at least——I cried at parting——but go they must; where more Work and less Meat will keep such fancies out of their heads.——

There was no kicking Time with *us* last Christmas between Streatham and London and all the Way to Bath——but Prosperity is hard for Man or Beast to bear, and Dear Dr. Johnson always said you know—that Indulgence naturally and necessarily ended in Severity.[6]

I have written this Letter by Owl-Light, and tis so interlined you will scarce read it, yet I'll not copy it over again, because if I slip this Post, you will be returning to London; and it will have to follow you all over the World——like my Trunk——which returned home *last Night*—just two Months, No, just *Three* Months has it been on the Road.

Miss Williams said She had carried you something, or carried something for you, and now I understand her: and will convey your Acknowledgments. The *dear* Blackbirds have I fear cause to curse *me* and the Attention you paid while writing that kind Letter—You might have saved the Next else. I once saw a Pair of Ravens actually *beat* old Jacob for tearing down their House and Family: till between them and Mr. Piozzi and myself we forced him to restore his Prize. The young ones were well fledged and suffered little or nothing. The old Birds sate on Lyon's Kennel and scolded us all so comically, and quarreled with each other as if reproaches of Neglect were passing between them; that I remember nothing better than the Scene—and our earnestness to quiet their Distraction.

Adieu! and accept our best Wishes, and do not sit too long in the same Room, There is nothing worse for Health or Spirits; and *you* have not, as Mr. Piozzi says *I* have *Salute de vendere*.

Once more farewell, and say where you are sometimes; and *do* say something about my Battle with these odious Reviewers.—Tis a Manuscript Battle merely on my Side, but I could not bear to be called such a Blockhead.

I am ever my dearest Soul Your truly Affectionate / H: L: P.

My dear Mr. Whalley gets better, his poor Lady is a sad Invalide; but always clever and lively and comical.[7]

Text: Bowood Collection. *Address:* Miss Thrale / at Mrs. Smyth's / Heath House / near / Bristol.

1. In *Retrospection* 2:523–24, HLP had written: "And Carnot, to keep turbulent spirits quiet at home, sent to the fighting field his trusted friend Buonaparte. This general, the first who ever wore *as a name* the title of *Destroyer*; Apollyon Buonaparte burst on Italy." The passage continues with HLP noting that the Corsican pronunciation of Apollyon is Nàpollione.
See also HLP to LC, [25] February 1800; to PSP, 31 January 1801, n. 2.

2. "Possibly on account of her name, which is suggestive of light or lucidity," Lucia or Lucy died at Syracuse in 304 during the persecution of Diocletian. She "was invoked during the middle ages by those who suffered from eye-trouble, and various legends grew up, *e.g.*, that her eyes were put out by the tyrant, or that she herself tore them out to present them to an unwelcome suitor who was smitten by their beauty. In either case they were miraculously restored to her, more beautiful than before." See *[Alban] Butler's Lives of the Saints,* ed. Herbert Thurston and Donald Attwater, 4 vols. (London: Burns and Oates, 1956), 4:549.

3. Saint Apollonia, who was martyred by the heathen populace of Alexandria in 249, was an aged deaconess whose teeth were knocked out by a mob. When threatened with death by fire unless she spoke impiety, she herself leaped into the flames. "She is invoked against toothache and all dental diseases" (ibid. 1:286).

4. A proverbial phrase, it appears, e.g., in Terence's *Andria,* 1.1.126, and Horace's *Epistles,* 1.19.41.

5. HLP refers to vol. 3, 2d ed. of *Morsels of Criticism.* . . . To which is now added, by the Author, A Second and Supplemental Part, Designed to shew, still more fully, the perfect Consistency of Philosophical Discoveries, and of Historical Facts, with the Revealed Word of God (London: J. Davis, 1800).

For Edward King, see HLP to PSP, 22 October 1798, n. 4.

6. See HLP to RG, 7 January, n. 1.

7. HLP had last received a long letter from TSW, dated 6 June (Ry. 564.7), in which he explained the Blagdon controversy, his work on behalf of Hannah More, "who approves of my poor efforts, in her righteous Cause."

Elizabeth Whalley had been an invalid since 1789 when her carriage overturned and she suffered a spinal injury. As a consequence, her body was much disfigured. She was to die on 8 December.

TO PENELOPE SOPHIA PENNINGTON

[ca. 20 July 1801][1]

Doctor Randolph is a wise Man for not caring what these foolish Fellows say, and Mrs. Randolph is a sweet Lady for caring.[2] On the like principle H: L: P is a Dunce for being *angry,* and Dear Pennington is a kind Friend for being enraged at these odious Critical Reviewers. Those who say my Book is merely good for nothing cannot be answered.—The Book says some thing like that—of itself; but its worthlessness consists in telling People what they knew before, not in telling what *is false;* for that is the Charge that offends me. Much of this Obloquy might have been avoided certainly by quoting Authorities, but they would add more to the Work's Weight, than its Value, were the Deed done tomorrow: and I thought it a mere Insult on the Public sitting gravely to *inform* them of what they may read in the seventh period of the 3d. Chapter of the *first Part* of Mosheim's Ecclesiastical History[3] edited by our Friend *Macleane,* who in a Note *confirms* the Fact of Tiberius desiring the Roman Senate to deify our Saviour.[4]——One would really wonder at a Man's Assurance who like our Critical Reviewer boldly asserts "That this is an exploded Fiction."[5] It stood on the Testimony of Eusebius and Tertullian for 16 Centuries before it was disputed——And Monsieur Iselin with Hase the Hebraist and numbers since the Year 1700 have proved its Truth beyond all Power of Denial.[6]

I saw Miss Case[7] with Macleane's Mosheim in her hand when I last visited her——*She* need not be deceived, *She* can enquire and *see* the Truth of my Position. When I wrote to Mr. Gillon expressing my Uneasiness under a Charge of Ignorance ill-deserved, he said my Antagonist was a Man of Immense Abilities, and I had better *let him alone:*—but Robson the Bookseller who sent me down the Review, liked my Refutation so well that he requested Leave to print my angry Letter *to him* on the Occasion, (I suppose it resembles that I wrote to you) and you will see it in the Gentleman's Magazine for July [71, pt. 2: 602–3; 688].

I am sorry about Hannah More: These Things are upon the whole very mortifying, and injure the Cause of Religion, Virtue, and sound Literature *too much* at a Moment when Enemies to all three are ready and keen to take every possible Advantage.[8]

I have a cold and reproachful Letter brought me just now from Harriett Lee: accusing my Heart of Alienation because I made no enquiry conerning *her* State of Mind altho' I saw (She says) that it was an uneasy one.[9] How unreasonable the People all are! I thought myself acting delicately to make no Enquiries, where nothing was *avowed* as capable of being construed into more than a past Vexation about the Children's Sickness—on which Subject We were all enjoined Secrecy beside.[10] Nothing would be less pleasing to me, than the Thought of having offended any of the House of Belvedere. Never did I say a slight Word, or write a peevish one about *Them*—never did I fail to express my just Admiration of their Talents, or even suffer myself to be provoked to more than Sorrow,—not Anger; when I had Reason for believing that Robinson was better disposed to the purchase of my Book before his Visit to Bath, than he was afterwards.

I hope She will write Kindly and make all up——I am ready——If She does not——We must sing Ralph's Song in the Maid of the Mill I think

> Nothing's tough enough to bind her,
> Then agog when once you find her
> Let her, Let her go, Let her go, never mind her
> &c.[11]

Poor dear pretty Siddons! What has she been doing to her Mouth?[12] Picking it my Master says, as I do my fingers; which he Threatens me are one day to resemble poor Mr. Pennington's Toes. But in earnest and true Sadness what can be the Matter with her Lips? Lips that never were equalled in Enunciation of Tenderness or Sublimity!—Lips that spoke so kindly *to* me, and *of* me! Dear Soul! what can ail them! She dreamed once that all her Teeth came out upon the Stage I remember; I told her She would go on acting till Age had bereft her of them:—but God forbid She should lose them *now*. Her Husband will mend at Bath; they have saturated that wretched Man with Mercury till nothing but those Waters could restore him. You *know* they are a certain Cure for the poor Men who work in the Quicksilver Mines, Throwing them into the Hot Springs has an almost immediate Operation like the Dog in Italy plunged into Lake Agnano after he has been poysoned by foul Air in the Grotto. Sally's Death will be no *Loss* to her dear Mother, altho' a very poignant Affliction without doubt; and Cecilia will be her Delight I dare say: but Sally and her Father both will yet last Many Years I am confident.—Shall we have a Bath Winter all together and comfortable? Or will they pay her and lure her back to Drury Lane? You must get her Mouth in good Order, that She may look like my *little* Miniature of the *greatest* and *only unrivalled* Female, this Century last expired, has pretended to produce——When her Lips close, what good will our Ears do open? Yes, Yes, they will hear Randolph preach, Piozzi sing, and Pennington converse. Comfort the charming Creature all you can tho, and get her into her accustomed Beauty; and tell her how She is beloved at pretty Brynbella.

Miss Lees say there is a Volume of Tales—new ones—lying for me at Robinson's.[13] God bless you all and write me a long Letter.

P.S. I find a Little Room in Mrs. P. Letter and so I will say I Love you and Dear Mr. Pennington and Mrs. Weston. Well! I think it Time to forget the Critical Review, and Mrs. P. she is persuaded to do so—, the writer is a very miserable wretch wanting Bread, and so *sufficit*. Belvidere people they can write but they can never understand *Retrospection*. Next Week Little John we expect him at Brynbella—and next January we shall have the pleasure our best friend as usual at Bath, and we hope to stay there Longer than last time. Addieu when we shall have the pleasure to see you at Brynbella. My best respects to Mr. Pennington and Mrs. Weston, believe me always / your best friend G. P.

Text. Princeton University Library. *Address:* Mrs. Pennington / Dowry Square / Hot Wells / Bristol. Postmark: DENBIGH 224.

1. HLP's letter responds to two written by PSP and dated 14 and 15 July (Ry. 568.100, 101).
2. HLP responds to PSP's description of Francis Randolph's brush with opprobrious critics. Thus on 15 July PSP had written:
"Poor Randolph at last, I *hear*, has come in for *his* share . . . but I am told that there is a tremendous Letter written to the Editors of the Anti Jacobin, cutting up their *unqualified* Panegyric of his Sermons most famously. Mrs. Randolph always said *this* would be the consequence of their *overdone* Praise. . . .
"The Doctor does not seem to care about it—but *he knows* the value of the *first* Report having gone forth so strongly in his Favor.—It settles the opinions of many who cannot think for themselves, and who, perhaps, never see what is further said on the Subject.—"
3. John Lawrence Mosheim (ca. 1694–1755), *An Ecclesiastical History, Antient and Modern, from the Birth of Christ, to the Beginning of the Present Century* . . . translated from the original, and accompanied with notes and chronological tables, by Archibald Maclaine, 2 vols. (London: A. Millar, 1765).
4. According to Mosheim: "And so illustrious was the fame of Christ's power grown, after his resurrection from the dead, and the miraculous gifts shed from on high upon his apostles, that the emperor Tiberius is said to have proposed his being enrolled among the gods of *Rome*, which the opposition of the senate hindered from taking effect. Many have doubted of the truth of this story: there are, however, several authors of the first note who have declared, that the reasons alleged for the truth of this fact are such as have removed their doubts, and appeared to them satisfactory and conclusive" (1:26).
5. In *Retrospection* (1:19), HLP had written: "Tiberius . . . moved the Senate to deify our Saviour, while he refused divine honours to his own person, polluted by a long course of far beyond brutal depravity. In this *one* instance the Patricians manifested their ill-deserved independence; in this *one* instance their dissembling master shewed himself sincere. He never would be worshipped."
6. To his statement on Tiberius, Maclaine appended a note. "See Theod. Hasæus, *De decreto Tiberii, quo Christum referre voluit in numerum Deorum;* as also a very learned letter written, in defence of the truth of this fact, by the celebrated Christopher Iselius, and published in the *Bibliothèque Germanique*, tom. xxxii, p. 147 and tom. xxxiii, p. 12." See also Maclaine's further contribution to the argument (1:26n–27n).
7. For Hester Case, see HLP to PSP [ca. 12 December 1799], n. 2.
8. Still plagued by the Blagdon controversy, PSP wrote on 15 July, Hannah More "will be sadly worried and galled by her coarse Antagonist, who, tho he is most disgustingly Vulgar in his retort on Sir Abraham, has tipped his Shafts with a sort of Ridicule that will

render them much more irritating; and discovered some *Shades* that, with all my partiality to the Parties, I cannot help feeling will produce their effect on the Public Mind;—which the Mores, and their Allies, must be conscious have *some* foundation in *Truth*, and therefore should have prudently guarded against their being laid open.—Some of the Friends concerned too cut a most paltry figure in the Business, having egregiously *changed* sides. That is, they acted at *first*, most certainly, without a proper comprehension, and clear understanding of the Business,—or, they *now* act against their Judgement from mere Influence.—A Number of Clergy have taken it up very warmly, and where it will end God knows!—Bere has closely, and plainly challenged his Accusers;—even the Bishop of the Diocese to stand forth, and convict, or acquit him. . . . The *Fanaticism* of the School master appears plain enough, and indeed the *same taint* is discovered in *all* the People employed by H. More in her Schools;—but Nothing I think is brought *Home* to the *Curate* either against his Morals, or *orthodoxy* that can merit so severe a punishment as expulsion from his Curacy.—"

9. Harriet Lee's letter is missing, but the tension between her and HLP was probably exacerbated by PSP's letter of 29 July (Ry. 568.102). ". . . yet, I cannot help saying that both Mr. Whalley and myself *know,* tho we should not much like to be brought to our *proof* and purgation in this matter, that H[arriet] L[ee] has not a just, or proper appreciation of either your Virtues, or Talents;—nor does She always *mention* them with the estimation that would well become her Taste and discernment—putting *Gratitude* and *partial* attachment out of the Question."

10. See HLP to PSP, 5 April 1801, and n. 4.

11. See the comic opera by Isaac Bickerstaffe, *The Maid of the Mill* (1765), 3.3.

12. PSP had written on 15 July: "I have seen nothing of the Siddons's—It has not been in my power to go over, and Sally has been too Ill to come to me.—I hear a very bad Report of *her general* Health, and fear our precious Friend will be the most unfortunate of Mothers in her Daughters.—I am uneasy also at hearing *She* has an ugly complaint in her *Mouth*, which broke out on her Lips when I was with her at Bath, and has, I fear, continued rather encreasing than giving way ever since. She is to join her Family at Bath in about three weeks."

13. Vol. 4 of *The Canterbury Tales*, recently published.

TO THE REVEREND LEONARD CHAPPELOW

Brynbella
Wensday 22d July 1801.

Dear Mr. Chappelow

This is your Side of the Letter, the other is for Mr. Gillon; but I am weary of making him pay so for Trouble incessantly repeated under different Forms, and never compensated by any Intelligence——for of what can I inform him but that we remain—daily more and more obliged. Our Newspaper brings down Torrents of private Wickednesses in the Law Reports which overwhelm the Guilt charged on Mr. Cator Twentyfold. Fraud and Avarice are the *natural* Crimes of a cold Climate, but we are now adding to them the gross Vices long confined to more Southern Regions, and it appears to me as if the relaxation of Morals among high and low would in a short Time be likely to produce some very dreadful Consequence. Meanwhile the French appear to have small Chance in Egypt[1]—They must depend upon Citizen Duroc's Management of Duke Constantine:[2] without Success *there*, even what they have gained in Italy will much of it be lost——and as for the Armament at Brest,[3] our gallant Commander will give a good Account of *that*.[4] Nothing would surprize me less than Buonaparte's refuging here after all, and few Things would be less beneficial to this Realm, where so many Secret-Society-Men are working like Moles under Ground, and only watch the Moment when they can rise unperceived, and crumble our Government and Religion round us into Dust.

Even *these* remote parts of the Kingdom are strangely tormented by them, and consequent Migrations to America prevail most wonderfully——but such Matters are little thought on by Londoners, who consider Wales as of no Importance whether full or empty;—and to say true, if Population is discovered to be an *Evil* instead of a Good——Those who lure our poor Folks away and make Slaves of them, are the best Patriots—next to Mr. *White*[5]——who hinders People from ever being born at all. Mercy on us! What is this Country coming to? Its Health under Protection of Mr. White—its Literature in Care of Mr.*Mortimer*. How little do the Reading Clubs——and indeed many hundreds of Readers—out of Clubs—imagine when they take our Critical Review in hand, that they are losing their Time in perusing Productions of a wretched Man who writes for Bread?—in the most literal Sense of the Word—and who would say the direct contrary of what he *does* say——for a half Guinea.[6] The Libraries *abroad* too, and the *Librarians*, consider that Pamphlet as the Nation's Sense of its own Literature; I know they do: but surely Matters are ill managed where such People are left to conduct them. I only grieve for having treated him too civilly.

Rat and Mole you see are beautiful Creatures still, and will not I hope *be given away;* they are Horses of very great Value. We expect our little Boy down upon the 1st of August, if you send me a long Letter full of good Chat and true Intelligence Abbè Davies will convey it hither in the Pocket of Salusbury's Preceptor who comes with him.[7] I took the Liberty to send this to Weston with Compliments and Enquiries, but do not mean the Continuation of such Irregular Practice. What a good and a wise, and a happy Family *that is*? And how few follow their Example!

Lord Kirkwall's Match with Miss Ormsby broke off unluckily for both Parties, if the World's good Word is the best Thing in a Marriage; never were Nuptials so generally approved: but the Arrangements of such immense Expectancies were difficult and

> A Knife Dear Girl cuts Love they say,
> Mere Modern Love perhaps it may;
> For any Tool of any Kind
> Can separate what was never joined &c.[8]

But here is scarce Room for my Master's true Regards which he will *not* separate from my Letter to Dear Mr. Chappelow who must tear the Paper, and give t'other half of our Hearts to Mr. Gillon whom God bless as well as yourself so Farewell——and as you taught our Parrot to say Hang Buonaparte!

How comical you are Dear Mr. Chappelow! and what droll Anecdotes you do pick up of Stockdale and his Correspondents.⁹ So Rat and Mole are gone, and have by what I hear got a good Mistress once again. Ignorant as you take me to be in Horse Flesh, I knew upon what *Footing* they would stand with Connoisseurs well enough; and however other branches of Science may decay, there are Twenty Men who understand the Dealer's Art now for one who knew it forty years ago. It is all pretty much as it *must* be between us and our Stable Business; If Alexander of Russia can accommodate the Affairs of Europe with no more proportionate Loss, he shall be Alexander the *Great* with My Consent.¹⁰ Buonaparte will need no Blistering if a Northern Coalition is put in force against him, Rough Exercise will cure his Rheumatism, and France will sink under a *Colliquative* Fever; yet I see no Good coming forward one Whit the more.

Mr. Piozzi has bright Visions of Italy's Restoration; *I* think that on the same Day his Country shall be restored to Happiness and Tranquillity——will be restored to Youth and the Brilliancy of 25 Years old his faded Wife; and Dear Mr. / Chappelow's most Obliged Servant / H: L: P.

Text: Ry. 560.112/113. *Address:* Rev: Mr. Chappelow / No. 12 Hill Street / Berkeley Square. *Postmark:* Two-Penny Post 46 Strand; 2 o'Clock 24 JY 1801 A < >.

1. Behind HLP's statement are the following facts: On 9 May General Hutchinson's attack upon the French at Rhamanich drove 3,000 infantry and 800 cavalry into the fortress. This, however, "they evacuated the following night, and retired towards Cairo, leaving only a small garrison of 110 men . . . who . . . surrendered to the English on the 10th." On the 14th the English captured "several heavy guns, great quantities of cloathing, wine, spirits, 500*l*. in specie, and 150 prisoners." Two days later, "600 of the best French troops in Egypt, together with 550 camels, were taken."

The Turks defeated the French at Reibeis on 16 May.

"The Mamalukes, under the orders of Osman Bey (successor of Murad Bey), have also joined the British army, with 1500 of the best cavalry in the world; and a Bombay detachment has arrived at Coffire, in the Red Sea, expecting daily to be joined by General Baird, with the main body of auxiliaries, to be debarked at Suez, for cooperation with the allied British and Turkish forces."

See *GM* 71, pt. 2 (1801): 657; also *The Times*, 2 May, 16 and 22 July, for optimistic reports of British prowess in Egypt.

2. Géraud-Christophe-Michel Duroc or du Roc (1772–1813), cr. duc de Frioul (1808); général de division (1803).

As a young army officer he had in 1798–99 fought at Salahieh in Egypt, at Jaffa, and at Acre. Returning to France with Bonaparte, he took part in the coup d'etat of Brumaire and became the first consul's chief aide. As much a diplomatist as a soldier, he was in the late spring of 1801 minister to the Court of Saint Petersburgh. Apparently, he was able to work with Lord St. Helens to help end difficulties between the northern powers and Great Britain—or at least he did nothing to hinder the signing of the Convention of 17 June between the Russian ministry and St. Helens. See *GM* 71, pt. 1 (1801): 562.

3. The Brest Armament had been in the news since January. But specifically, HLP refers to an extract of a letter, dated off Alexandria, 23 April, in *The Times*, 10 July 1801:

"On the 4th of March last we sailed from Mahon Roads with four sail of the line . . . in quest of Gantheaume's squadron of seven sail of the line. . . . We were proceeding off Toulon, when on the 25th, in the morning, we fell in with the *Salamine* brig, which informed us that the French had sailed from Toulon on the 19th, and were supposed to be bound for Egypt. . . .

"We joined Lord Keith next morning, (April 20) and found him standing off and on

Alexandria with seven sail of the line, frigates, &c.; and Petowna Bey, the Turkish Vice-Admiral, with two sail of the line, sloops, &c. The Captain Pacha is laying in Aboukir Bay, in a three-decker, with two sail of the line."

On the 21st of July, *The Times* admittedly reported rumor about Gantheaume's squadron, this time that he and his men "had disembarked at Derna, in the kingdom of Barca, on the African coast. . . . Derna is said to be only five days march to Cairo."

4. George Keith Elphinstone, cr. 16 March 1797 a peer of Ireland by the title of Baron Keith of Stonehaven Marischal. At this time he was commander in chief of the Mediterranean fleet and would be advanced to the rank of admiral of the Blue and enrolled 15 December among the peers of the United Kingdom with the same title and rank as he bore in Ireland.

See also HLP to Q, 7 November 1796, n. 6.

5. Charles White (1728–1813) of Manchester, F.R.S., and a member of the Royal College of Surgeons. He is best known for revolutionizing the practice of midwifery.

6. By implication the reviewer was Thomas Mortimer (1730–1810), a prolific writer. His longest work was *The British Plutarch* in six volumes (1762); revised and enlarged (1774). It was translated by Mme de Vasse, 1785–86, and published in Paris in twelve volumes.

7. During his summer recess JSPS was to be tutored by "Professor" Henry Wood (b. 1768), formerly of Milton Abbas, Dorset, who had earned a B.A. from Oxford in 1791.

According to RD, writing from "Streatham University" on 30 July: "The Professor is to me a Jewel inestimable. The pains he has taken with Salusbury *I know,* but you will not believe. . . . *I* will pay him the six guineas. You may, if you please, tell him so. He already knows it" (Ry. 573.31).

8. While visiting Garrick's widow at Hampton in 1777, HLT saw "a sweet pretty little Copy of Verses from a Gentleman to his Wife on the Subject of his giving her an elegant Penknife as a Present—I was not permitted to write it out, & I can remember the two first Lines only." Shortly thereafter she discovered the entire poem in the *Public Advertiser* and transcribed it in part. It begins:

> A Knife Dear Girl cuts love they say,
> Mere modish Love—perhaps it may

and concludes:

> All cutting here would be in vain,
> Except to cut—and come again.

A few years later (1781) GP saw the lines and asked HLT to explain them. She obliged and added a hasty translation into Italian. She assumed the original was by Garrick; GP had heard they were by William Locke, the elder (1732–1810). See *Thraliana* 1:125, 131–32, and 493.

9. Not to be confused with John Stockdale, publisher of *Retrospection*, the Reverend Percival Stockdale (1736–1811) as successor to William Guthrie (1708–1770) was editor of the *Critical Review*. One of his "Correspondents," thus, was Mortimer, the "wretched [reviewer] who writes for Bread." For Stockdale's Johnsonian associations, see *Boswell's Johnson* 1.337, n.1; 2.113, 203, n.3, 435, n.7.

10. The "question which so lately agitated the Northern Powers of Europe (on the subject of the right of search, in the case of neutral vessels steering for belligerent ports)" had been settled between Great Britain and Russia (Sweden and Denmark had also been invited to accept the settlement.)

The new czar had been friendly to British requests. "In less than 20 days after his arrival at St. Petersburg, had Lord St. Helen's so ably cultivated the friendship and good dispositions of the Emperor Alexander, as to effect the termination of a dispute that had occasioned the most serious alarm in the commercial, as well as the political world; and thus enabled the British fleet of 25 sail of the line, which had been sent to the Baltic, to return at a most critical hour to defend its own shores from the threatened invasion." See *GM* 71, pt. 2: 656–57.

TO THE REVEREND ROBERT GRAY

Brynbella
2nd August 1801.

Lord bless me! what an expence they do put us to with their frivolous and vexatious menaces! Those vile agents who buy up even the standing corn to make artificial scarcity, and irritate our lower ranks to rebellion, are more hateful pests than even the French themselves. 'Tis confidently asserted here that men live in the great towns of London and Liverpool by throwing corn into the sea by night, or into the river, and that their pay is a guinea for every six hours' work. How dreadful![1]

Text: Hayward 2:257.

1. See HLP to PSP [ca. 4 August 1801], n. 10.

TO PENELOPE SOPHIA PENNINGTON

[ca. 4 August 1801][1]

You are a Dear Friend and a wise Lady and——Conscience (says I) you counsel ill——Pennington (says I) you counsel well[2]——see the learned Launcelot Gobbo.[3]——But my heart tells me that the Gentleman's Magazine will exhibit a Letter of more Anger than Good Sense—at least being written on the Spur of the Moment—the very day I read my Antagonist's spiteful Accusation—*'tis most likely;* for it never entered my head that Robson would print what came straight to him in form of Complaint just as I wrote to you. Yet when he asked leave to shew it up before the public, and said several Friends in his Shop advised the Measure: I would not shrink from it.

Harriet Lee has sent me a making-up Epistle,——so we make up——but it is a cold and flat Paste, we make on't at last: and as little George Siddons said of his Brother's friends whom he *had* been half afraid of—"*I know what they are now.*"[4] I know what She is too; and worded my Answer accordingly.

She lamented the Ill Nature of the Critical Review to me with due and proper Pathos—I replied lightly, that they were not half as ill natured as they were ill informed—and that if charming Hannah More valued such Abuse as little as H: L: P did, She would live long a *Champion* of Religion's Cause, and not dye as they wished her to do—*A Martyr* to't.

The Truth is, her Controversy gets very stale now, and like her Torment *Beer Bere*,

Though stale not ripe, tho' thin yet never *clear*.[5] I will hasten to expose *my* Gentlemen's Ignorance, and then release People to think and care about Matters more worth their Attention.

The Loss of those two fine Ships was vexatious enough, but we must have a few Knocks. *Hannibal* lost one Eye early in Life you know—so these fellows came on the *blind* Side of him *that's all:*[6] Our cutting the Corvette from Camaret Bay was an Exploit worthy to be preserved in History till Time shall be no more, but nothing ever equalled the Hardihood of Naval Officers shown in Course of this War——it is a Tissue of Heroism;[7] and to attempt Shores so guarded, would seem Frenzy;[8] had one not to recollect apparent Impossibilities conquered by Buonaparte: particularly his passing Mount St. Gothard in Winter never relaxed—which however *did* yield, (God only knows how)—to the French Artillery: suffered to cross that Mountain for the Sake of gaining a decisive Battle at Marengo.[9]

We must have more Sense if they *do* land, than fight any Battle at all with such Troops—Our Business is to harrass them, and thin their Numbers not easily repaired and attacking them only by *Night* assure to ourselves the Advantages accrueing from our own Knowledge and their Ignorance of the Country.

Mr. Pennington will tell you I am *quite right;* and it was for want of knowing as much in old Times, that Harold foolishly set his Island on the Hazard of one grand Battle which he lost at Hastings.[10]

Our secret-Society Men[11] who buy up the Corn and fling by Night into the Rivers or Sea, are far more dangerous Enemies; and will if Matters ripen into Reality of Bustle, be less afraid of acting openly: their present Intentions towards irritating our lower Ranks, and making them willing to rebel, are happily counteracted by the enormous Quantity of Corn in The Field and Ports and Harbours.[12] *They too are known*—and People see into their Machinations pretty clearly.

Bath is a well-judged Place for the King during Times of apprehended Turbulence, and the Waters may do him good as they do me; by washing away Care and Bile, and giving Tone to the Stomach and Bowels. 'Tis a nice Place beside for a Man of his open Character and Manners to attack Individuals and delight common Folks with his familiar Way.[13] I am glad he will see *Captain* Dimond play Lothario at Threescore Years old to our lovely Friend's inimitable Calista.[14]

She and Mr. Whalley and yourself are *true* Friends indeed; so I believe is Doctor Randolph, so I am *sure* is *little, great* Mr. Gray—nor will the public in general delight in seeing Knowledge hissed out of Doors by Snakes—or *blown* out by *Emptiness*.

Picking one's Fingers, Face &c. is as I begin to find, no good Joke after all: pray warn sweet Siddons against it. I had laid bare the Nerve some how to'ther Day, and then by an Accidental *manœuvre* hurt my Hand terribly. Writing is not yet an easy Operation to me; and a Black Ribbon is still necessary to the *Wrist*, tho' I hoped only the Finger was injured.

Adieu therefore and God bless you——We have got a Dear Member of Parliament now close by us in Denbigh Town.[15] So Heaven have Mercy on the Correspondents of Your / H: L: P.

Text: Princeton University Library.

1. HLP's response to PSP, 29 July (Ry. 568.102).
2. PSP approved HLP's response to the *Critical Review* that had appeared in the July issue of *GM*.
"It is very well for good Mr. Gillon to shrink from such Sort of Controversy [with the *Critical Review*]. He may not feel equal to the combat; but 'The *Scholar* arm'd at all points', like yourself, need not fear to take the Field on such *fair* Ground, and must come off victorious. . . . To *liberal* Criticism one may feel Respectful deference—but an impudent, or ignorant misrepresentation, and contradiction of *Facts* demands to be exposed, and refuted;—it is a Respect due to ourselves."
3. The clown, servant to Shylock in *The Merchant of Venice*, has a debate with his conscience (2.2.1–32).
4. George John Siddons (b. 1785) and Henry Siddons (b. 1774), SS's sons.
5.
> Flow, Welsted, flow! like thine inspirer, Beer,
> 'Tho stale, not ripe; 'tho thin, yet never clear.
>
> *Dunciad*, 3.169–70.

6. HLP's reference to the Carthaginian general Hannibal (247–ca. 182 B.C.) was prompted by the loss of a "fine Ship." According to *The Times*, 23 July:
"Yesterday we received by express *Paris Journals* to the 19th instant inclusive. They contain . . . the relation of an event so very unfortunate and extraordinary, as to be incredible. Upon the evening of the 18th, a Paper was read at all the Theatres, by order of the Government, and signed by the Minister for the Marine, importing that the English ship of War the *Hannibal*, of 74 guns, commanded by Captain Ferris, had been captured by a French Squadron in the Bay of *Algeziras*, off Gibraltar, in the course of an engagement, in which the British had twice the force of the Republicans." The French were commanded by Rear Admiral Linois in a battle that lasted more than three hours. "The *Hannibal* is reported to have had three hundred killed [of a crew of six hundred] before she struck her colours."

On 27 July, *The Times* reported the loss of the *Swiftsure* of seventy-four guns to Admiral Gantheaume.

7. Under the dateline of 26 July, Plymouth, the *Courier* on 28 July announced: "Arrived this morning . . . La Chevrette, French national corvette, of 22 guns, which ship was on Wednesday night last cut out from under the Batteries in Camaret Bay, near Brest . . . after a conflict of two hours and a half, all which time the batteries on shore kept up a tremendous fire of round and grape shot, and shells; but she was at last carried by the persevering courage of British seamen, after as warm a contest as, perhaps, has not been exceeded during the war." The loss of life on both sides was high.

8. Preparations were under way to counter alleged French attempts to invade England. Under date of 31 July, *GM* reported:
"A very large fleet of bombs and gun-brigs are assembling in the Downs; they are under sailing orders, and expected very shortly to proceed off the coast of France: supposed, either to destroy the gun-boats now fitting out in the ports of Calais, Dunkirk, and Boulogne, or to bombard those places. Admiral Dickson's squadron remains in Yarmouth-roads. Adm. Greaves's squadron is cruizing off Goree" (71, pt. 2: 662).

9. Bonaparte had led his army across several Alpine passes in May before the snow

had melted. Despite this tactical difficulty and preliminary military encounters, he went on to win the battle for Marengo on 14 June 1800.

See HLP to PSP [ca. 26 July 1800], n. 6.

10. HLP refers to the famous battle of Hastings on 14 October 1066 between Harold, king of England, and William, duke of Normandy. The gamble involved Harold's bold advance with about seven thousand ill-trained men against William. Harold's troops, eager to push the invaders into the sea, were no match against William's archers and cavalry. By nightfall, after the death of Harold, the English line broke and scattered to leave William the victor.

11. HLP's belief in the conspiracies of "secret-Society Men" was upheld by parliamentary measures for restraining sedition and rebellion. The restrictive measures were varied: an Irish martial law bill; a suspension of the Habeas Corpus bill; and a bill for preventing seditious meetings. Despite opposition, all were passed into law on the assumption that "secret-Society Men" sought to overturn church and state. See *AR* 43 (1801): 195–235.

HLP's view of what caused grain shortages underwent several changes: e.g., deficient harvests; the greed of corn factors and merchants who created artificial shortages. In this letter, she attributed scarcity to republican conspirators.

12. Under date of 31 July: "it is with sincere satisfaction we learn that large supplies of grain may be shortly expected from Russia and Canada. The agents of government at Quebec had by the last accounts from that place, purchased 60,000 quarters of wheat, which were to be shipped for this country with all possible dispatch." See *GM* 71, pt. 2: 662.

13. On 29 July, PSP reported: "What the Kings particular object is at Bath I cannot conceive.—I hope no ill advised Plan respecting the Waters draws him there: to meddle with them must, I should imagine, be fatal to him."

The *Bath Herald* on 4 and 15 August announced a visit of the king and queen, who had been on holiday at Weymouth. But by 5 September, the same newspaper wrote: "The loyal inhabitants of this city have experienced a serious disappointment, it having been announced that his Majesty has, for the present year at least, given up his intention of visiting this city."

14. HLP fantasizes a performance of Rowe's *The Fair Penitent* with William Dimond (now about fifty) as Lothario and SS (now forty-six) as Calista.

15. Baron De Blaquiere or Miles Peter Andrews.

TO HESTER MARIA THRALE

Brynbella
23: August 1801.

I have followed your Example my Dear Girl, and enclosed this Letter to our common Friend Andrews;[1] who will forward it either to Lowestoff whence you date your last, or to Scarborough whither Mr. Gillon told me long ago, that you were all gone together.

Lowestoff is a Place not to be found by Me in Map or Gazetteer, yet I recollect nothing better than your pleasing Account of an old Man in or near that Town, who Showed you the rare Gem called *Abraxas;* and you Sealed your Letter thence to me with the Stone.[2] My Care of that Seal has defeated its own Purpose, I have so hid it that I cannot find [it]: would it be too much to request such another favour? There was a Cock and a Sheep and I think an armed Head upon it: but my Eyes were never calculated for small Objects, and when they were—I spoiled them by writing and cutting Watch Papers, working open-Work as it was called—by *Threads;* and such silly Practices.—This Seal however I doated upon, and having missed the Examination of Mr. Towneley's *Drawers* last Winter, it was to me doubly valuable.[3] Constantius Chlorus you told me was the original Possessor,[4] and I told you *as strange* and curious a Circumstance; namely that the great Scholar Doctor Burney so celebrated for his Skill in the Greek Language and considered as so very eminent among the Learned Men, really knew no more about either the *Name* or the *Thing* than Sophia's Maid Mrs. Primrose would have known, had I asked *her.*[5]

Well! but if you will look at the 17: Verse of the 2d: Chapter of St. John's Apocalypse you will wonder less at the veneration of the early Christians for *Abrasax* or the *White Stone* by a Corrupt Mixture of Persic and Latin Languages.[6]

Why do you make no Answer to what I said of the Critical Reviewers and their Abuse of Retrospection? Do you think it a Sore Place? *Not it indeed.* They are grossly malignant and merit Abhorrence, but they are so Ignorant that one's Aversion evaporates in Pity and Contempt.

I like the *other* People best—('Tis not the Anti Jacobins)[7]—that say Mrs. Piozzi is so fond of *Latin* and *Latin* Idiom, that She uses the Word *Ephemeron* perpetually, when speaking of *Modern Wits.* Oh Dear! Oh Dear! What Blockheads there are in the World! and what Fools are those who trust to them! *Ephemeron* is a Word of Greek, not Latin Derivation; these Fellows should know the *Almanack* at least before they Set up for Critics.—Is it not called *Ephemerides confessedly* from the Greek?[8]

Enough of this Nonsense.

I rejoyce you have left London, where the Heat and and Thickness of the Atmosphere excited that Hæmorrhage from your Nose which Cupping so judiciously removed. Should you ever be alarmed by its return, remember that to stop it is always in your Power, by a Cold Spunge and *Bason* of fresh Water, or rather *Bidet,* on which *sit;* and *wash,—but not your Nose:* you understand me. It is however very injudicious to stop any Hæmorrhage except by turning the Current of Blood another way; and the means I mention should be used only if you feel weakened by such an Evacuation, or by way of gaining Time till other Assistance can be got.

Our upper Servant Samuel Hodgkins whom you remember [as] Footman, and who has been Butler and Valet Seven Years to Mr. Piozzi; lay in a Lethargy and Coma here this last Week for forty Hours that we could not guess whether he would live or die:[9] All is safe notwithstanding, *et nous sommes quittes pour la Peur cette Fois.* He is to us a very valuable Servant. The Weather affects Sanguineous People greatly. We have not yet left off talking about a Seaside Expedition for our own Benefit—but as the painting this House will keep us completely out of it next Summer, 'tis possible we may defer such a Measure till *then.*

My Lord Nelson found the Invaders fastened to their own Homes I See,[10] and an odd Cause of Triumph it is to *them,* that our Gulliver could not bring their whole Fleet of Gunboats away with him like the little People of *Blefuscù.*[11]

He will doubtless be much mortified.

Dear Mr. Nicholls is one of my very earliest Acquaintance, we were Children together at East Hyde in Bedfordshire—Years ago, and are I believe *just of an Age*. He has given me many a kind Invitation to Blundestone,[12] but we lie quite East and West somehow; The whole Island between us: I have a Notion you are near my pretty Cousin Mrs. Mackay too.[13] Give our truest Regards to your Sisters: If Cecilia is with you and you go on Northward, She will remember Scarborough.[14]

The Harvest is truly abundant, and The Weather has been *scorching hot* for Great Britain; Peace seems at present further off than Plenty, but I hope both are within a *distant Ken*. If Buonaparte can sit fast himself or set up those who have a Right to Sit—all may yet be well; and Mr. Piozzi has bright Visions—never realized—of *Italy's* Restoration under *Scythian* Auspices.[15]—Well! *Every*thing is *possible*, and *one* Thing is *certain*—That I am / Your Affectionate Mother / H: L: P.

Come now—try to write more often than a quarter of a year.

Text: Bowood Collection. *Address:* Miss Thrale / Lowestoff / Norfolk. *Postmark:* Free Aug 27 1801. "Portsmouth August Twenty Sixth 1801 M. P. Andrews."

1. Miles Peter Andrews, as M.P. for Bewdley, franked HLP's letter.
2. See HLP to Q, 12 February [1799], and n. 4.
3. As part of his "museum" of classical antiquities, Charles Towneley had a large collection of drawings. John Thomas Smith (1766–1833), e.g., and other young students of the Royal Academy were paid by Towneley to make such drawings for his portfolios.
    For Charles Towneley, see HLP to Sophia Byron, 11 August 1788, and n. 15.
4. For Constantius Chlorus, see HLP to Q, 12 February [1799], n. 12.
5. For Charles Burney, Jr.'s dislike of the term *abraxas*, see HLP to Q, 12 February [1799].
    In his own lifetime, Charles Burney, Jr., along with Samuel Parr and Richard Porson, were recognized as England's most distinguished classicists. If Burney's excellence as a Greek scholar has since diminished, he did make at least two significant contributions: his edition *Appendix ad Lexicon Graeco-Latinum, a Joanne Scapula constructum, et ad alia Lexica Graeca, e Codice Manuscripto, olim Askeviano, in lucem nunc primum vindicato* (1789); and the more ambitious *Tentamen de Metris, ab Aeschylo, in choricis cantibus, adhibitis* (1809).
6. See HLP to Q [ca. 23 September 1800], n. 3.
7. For the punishing statement of the *Anti-Jacobin Review and Magazine*, see HLP to PSP, 5 April 1801, n. 6.
8. The charge was not made by a reviewer. On the contrary, "it was Harriet Lee (I am sure it was) that censured my Affectation of Classic Knowledge and said I was so fond of bringing in *Latin* Words that I called the Wits of the Day *Ephemeral* Writers. Such a remark no *Man* would make most surely." See "Minced Meat for Pyes."
9. For the butler at Brynbella, see HLP to Q, 1 August 1793, n. 8.
10. HLP's summary of Nelson's failed attacks on the ships in Boulogne harbor, ships allegedly massed for an invasion of England. See, especially, *The Times*, 18 August. "The action commenced early in the night of Saturday by the boats and launches of the squadron, which attacked and carried with irresistible resolution the line of gun-boats which the enemy had stationed in front of the pier. . . . It was found, however, after taking possession of them, that these boats could not be brought away, owing to their being grappled with strong mooring chains, not only to each other, but to the shore." (This attack had been made on the night of 15 August.)
11. See the concluding chapter of the "Voyage to Lilliput" in *Gulliver's Travels*.

12. The Reverend Norton Nicholls of Blundeston, Suffolk, owned a large farm and house that included books, prints, pictures, manuscripts, maps, etc. See HLP to PSP, 11 May 1795, n. 2.

13. HLP was reminded of the Mackays because they too lived in Suffolk, about eight miles northeast of Bury.

14. CMT had been with the Piozzis in Scarborough in June 1789.

15. GP had jesting visions of the ancient Scythians—nomadic conquerors and skilled horsemen (fl. eighth to fourth centuries B.C.)—miraculously resurrected to effect "Italy's Restoration."

TO PENELOPE SOPHIA PENNINGTON

Brynbella
[ca. 28] August 1801.[1]

Be in better Spirits Dear Friend, or at least be in the best Spirits that you *can:* Things will draw cross sometimes—We *know* they will;

> We know that all must Fortune try,
> And bear our Evils wet or dry.[2]

My Masters Misfortunes are few—but *dry* ones. He has now a Chalk Stone in his *Ear,* but Siddons's *Mouth* is a more important Ailment by half. My Heart tells me from your Letter that 'tis of a Strumous Nature; they would not send her to the Sea else: and if so, *I am truly Sorry.*[3]

What is the meaning of Hannah More's Marriage being thus *gravely* announced in every Newspaper, and resounding here in North Wales from every Mouth, while you say not one Word upon the Subject?[4] When after long Silence I saw your beautiful Handwriting to day, I made sure of Certain Intelligence—but no Syllable concerning it seems to have reached the Spot where it was said to have taken Place——Give me an Answer to the Thousand Enquiries buzzing round me, and give it quickly, that the Talk may end.

Our Harvest is beyond all Hope and all Calculation; The Wheat got in without a Shower, The Oats hurrying home for fear of a Shower; The Barley begging to be cut before the Rains fall, and the Grass crying Pray make haste for we are *very dry.*

Out little Boy is as blithe as a Bird, almost as wild, A Model of Gayety and Good humour: with

> Smiling Cheeks and roving Eyes
> Causeless Mirth and Vain Surprise.

As Hawkesworth describes Childhood[5] such is He—may he get safely thro' *the next Stage!*

I have not yet seen Harriet's Tale, and without your Information should never have heard about Belinda.[6] These soft'ning Books greatly encrease the Dissolution of Manners, tho' each unexceptionable in itself, cannot be complained of. The Youth of our present Day however *read nothing else,* and how they should escape such melting Relaxers, added to their own Feelings in the warm Season of Life—I guess not. Literary Arrogance and early Ambition are the only Antidotes which *this* World will supply.

Education is a mere Word now for a Theme or Subject on which to display the Eloquence of Teachers; and the Teachers themselves—Miss More perhaps excepted—are drawing Boys and Girls into Love's Labyrinth with one Hand, while they are pointing to distant Wisdom and Virtue with the other.[7]

The Curate and Barber who burned Don Quixote's Library of large Romances[8] would have been frighted to see them thus epitomized into the Power of a School Boy to purchase, as India's fragrance is happily compressed into a Guinea Phial of Odour of Roses.

Our Novel Writers have a Right to hate *me* who set my face so against Fiction, and who have endeavoured (tho' fruitlessly) to make Truth palatable: but when they boast that *my Book* is liked only by the Old Heads of Houses at Oxford and Cambridge, and chained up in the *Bodleian or all Souls:* 'tis such a Vaunt as the French make when they chain their Ships a'shore.

It is in the meantime very Surprising that Nelson should try again, after seeing that he attempts Impossibilities.—I think he has played double or Quits too often, and tempts good Fortune too far.[9]

Egypt is our own at last, and will bring its *Plagues* with it; for how should *we* garrison such distant Possessions, which the French may disturb whenever they are disposed to rid themselves of a Troublesome General and forty Thousand open Mouths? I wish the East Indians for whose Sake we drove these Fellows out, would be pleased to keep them away now they are gone.[10]

So my Lord De Blaquiere is run away to make Drawings beyond Snowdonia—and the Bishop is in Anglesey and no Frank for Love or Money can I get. Miss Thrale wrote to me from Lowestoffe but Mr. Gillon says they are gone on to Scarboro'. I hear Mrs. Mostyn has a Son *Arthur;*[11] He will I hope fill his Round Table with Knights, and revive the Spirit of Chivalry. M—— L—— is the great Dragon which devours us all, and 'tis said there is a Train laid to rid the Kingdom of a Combination so strong, that relying upon its Force a Gentleman offered yesterday to bet a Wager that Corn would be as high prized next November as it was last January—but this is croaking worse than Mrs. Pennington, and I believe that the Gentleman *will lose.*[12]

Well! Sorrow in every State; and we have lost poor *Reechard* as your little Sweet Heart called him, but he is preferred to be Mrs. Clough's Butler, and her Son's Valet.[13]

The Day Labourers Wages are raised *triple* what they were, and our Folks whom we keep and feed all Winter—run from us *now* for higher Salaries, and My Master *wonders* at their Ingratitude; but I think I have seen worse behaviour in better Situations.

Adieu kind Friend—but not for long. Write often and divert the Time till we meet again: assuring yourself that you are *valued*——not to your Worth perhaps, because that's difficult;——but valued very *very* highly indeed by many whose

Good Opinion is worth having.—The Randolphs, the Mores, Lady Hesketh, Mrs. DeLuc and your Faithful / H: L: P.

All these besides your own immediate Household—mind! to whom our best Regards,—and sweet Mrs. Siddons—and my Master says I have not named *him*.

Text: Princeton University Library. *Address:* Mrs. Pennington / Dowry Square / Hot Wells / Bristol. *Postmark:* DENBIGH 224.

 1. HLP's letter responds to PSP's, dated 25 August from Bristol Hotwells (Ry. 568.103).
 2. Matthew Prior, *Alma; or the Progress of the Mind*, 3.584–85.
 3. PSP had reported: "Dear Mrs. Siddons has been some time at Bath.—I have not yet seen her, but have taken Lodgings in Bristol for the time of her performance there, which commences Monday Senight, the 31st.—Unless the weather is cooler I know not who will be able to endure the Theatre;—even her Powers will not I believe very often, draw me there.—I am very sorry to find She still complains of her *Mouth.*—Very alarming in my opinion and shewing something very much amiss in the System! . . . She writes me, that she is 'advised to the Sea and shall leave Bath before the King and Family arrive there, which will not be till the beginning of October.'"
 4. *The Times* on 25 August had announced as fact: "Married: Dr. Crossman, to the celebrated Miss Hannah More, of Bristol." On 2 September *The Times* produced "An Epigram on the Recent Marriage of Miss Hannah More."

> Spotless she liv'd till past three score;
> But now poor Hannah is *no* More!

"The report of Hannah More's marriage is, we believe, 'a weak invention of the enemy.' She has, indeed, got into a controversy about *Sunday Schools* and *Methodism*, in which two Bishops and a dozen Clergymen are involved, and which is carried on with great perseverance, and a wonderful contempt for the price of paper" (*The Times*, 10 September; see also 12 September).
 5. See John Hawkesworth, "Life. *An Ode*," in *GM* 17 (1747): 337.
 6. That is, Harriet Lee's *Kruitzner: or the German Tale*, in vol. 4 of *The Canterbury Tales* (1801).
 Maria Edgeworth's *Belinda*, 3 vols. (London: J. Johnson, 1801).
 7. HLP's attack on modern novelists and writers on education was prompted by PSP's statement. "Have you seen Harriet Lees last Volume of Canterbury Tales? That sort of Stuff is always in such constant demand in these sort of Places that I have not been able to get at it, without more trouble than I felt it worth while to take. Mrs. Carrick likes the *first* Tale very much.—Miss Edgeworth's Belinda is in great vogue and Miss Hamiltons 'Letters on *Education.*' I have seen none of them and cannot think what Miss Hamilton could find to say on the latter subject, after charming Hannah More."
 8. See chap. 6 of bk. 1.
 9. HLP's allusion to Nelson's efforts to bring away the French flotilla in the harbor of Boulogne on 15–16 August. See *The Times*, 18 August, in HLP to Q, 23 August 1801, n. 10.
 10. "It appears, that, on the 21st of June, the allied armies commanded by Gen. Hutchinson, the Grand Vizier, and the Captain Pacha, had advanced within cannon-shot of Cairo, and made the necessary dispositions for assaulting the place. On the next day, the French Commander sent out a flag of truce, informing Gen. Hutchinson, that he wished to treat for the evacuation of Cairo. After a long negociation, the conditions of the surrender were signed and agreed to on the 27th [of July]; and on the 28th the British troops and allies took possession of two of the gates; and the whole was to be evacuated in 12 days." See *GM* 71, pt. 2: 756–57.

After the victory at Cairo, many English newspapers anticipated the surrender of Alexandria and the retreat of the French Army of the East from all of Egypt.

11. Thomas Arthur *Bertie* Mostyn (d. 1876), CMM's third son, had been born in July.

12. An allusion to HLP's consistent fear that scarcity and the high price of provisions served the aims of revolutionaries, the "secret-Society Men."

In Mark Lane, between Fenchurch and Great Tower Streets, was London's great corn market where the price of grain was established.

13. Richard Clough (1753–1814) of Glan y Wern and Plas Clough, Denbighshire, had married ca. 1780 Patty, née Butler (1761–1838). At this time they had three sons: Richard Butler (1781–1844); Hugh Powell (1783–1804); James Henry (1784–1841).

TO PENELOPE SOPHIA PENNINGTON

                        Brynbella
                        [6]: September 1801.[1]

My Dear Friend

The Heavy Rain which accompanied Your last Letter is far too violent to be lasting; and our folks comfort us by saying that it will do more good to the Grass than harm to the Barley—which being in large Shocks ready for carrying, can—I hope—be hardly set o'swimming even by these Mountain Torrents—fierce as they fall, but unaccompanied by Thunder, Thank God, or Lightning; and the Weather quite soft and warm.—

—Our Barometer begins rising whilst I write, and the Plantations drink their fill from the Horn of future Plenty.—Ploughing and preparing Ground for next year's Crop will *now* be all done by Michaelmass, and the Dwellers in *Mark Lane* may pray for their own *Safety;* it is in more Danger than our Purses and Stomachs. God Almighty will send *Victuals*—and He——may take Care of the *Cooks.* I know not how you gathered from my Letter that *I* believed in Hannah More's Change of Condition, tho' my Neighbour's did: yet never having heard that Dr. Crossman was a married or a single Man, and seeing no Jokes accompany the Intelligence, which came in the regular List of Weddings for the Week; I own myself staggered:—and now the Papers are filling with Epigrammatic Nonsense which will confirm People in their Credence if no Contradiction is given.

With regard to our Dear charming Friend *her* Tormentors *must* be private ones: The *Public* would not suffer their truly deserving Favourite to be insulted: and She should run *to,* not from the *Theatre* for Protection—I guess not what *Character* it was, in which you say She will appear no more—*tell* me; and tell me what She thinks of the enclosed.[2] Oh How you and I must for ever hold abhorred of our whole Souls, the Human Creature who can thus delight in torturing a Heart like hers! Have I ever *seen* him think you! Has he made Advances to her, and been refused? Or does he protect a rival Actress rising into Fame? Or *what* inspires such horrible Malignity?

I pretend not to trace as Fanny Burney and as Harriet Lee can do—vile

Passions to their Source; but such Characters prove the Play of Hatred, and Feelings of du Montfor<t> not out of Nature.³

Mr. Siddons had to set out with a very strong Constitution no doubt and he will resist violent Remedies and cruel Diseases till the very Principle of Life is *Bit by Bit* destroyed——*Your* Headach assure yourself dear Friend—has nothing in common with *his*: I am sorry for what both of you are suffering.⁴ Mr. and Mrs. Twiss are very clever People, and greatly delighted in at Belvedere House of Course.⁵ I suppose the Author of that German Tale, had a Mind to shew Godwin She understood *his* Walk in Literature as well, and could tread the Path as firmly as himself.⁶

My Packet of Macaroni came down without the Book in it, so I still remain ignorant of all but what you tell me: Mr. Gillon was out of Town to whom I had written for purpose of getting it from Robinson's to the Hay Market.⁷

Well! I shall read it sometime; and will learn (even without its Assistance) to give my Esteem where Confidence would be ill bestowed; I wish all the Lees very well notwithstanding what has passed in my own Mind concerning their Conduct towards *me*. We must take People as they are, and *such* People are at any rate, extremely difficult to meet with——

Our little Boy left us Yesterday, and for Mr. Davies's Credit and his own—left us chearfully. A sweeter tempered Creature lives not, nor one better disposed to smooth down Life's Asperities before him, either by well-applied Strength—or by a Power happier still of rolling over them, and suffering little hurt.

Miss Thrale has written to me very civilly from Lowestoffe,—we have the whole Island between us: for Mr. Piozzi promises me a Dip in our Irish Channel next Week, and we go on Thursday next to a Bathing Place called Prestatyn about 14 Miles off.—Now do not exclaim, What are you 14 Miles from the *Sea?* because We are scarcely *four* Miles; but from any Conveniencies we are at least fourteen. The Invasion seems to keep nobody InL*and* and by the King's giving up Bath entirely, I gather that the Ministry no longer feel apprehensions. If French Chicanery cannot raise a Famine or a Sedition among *us*, and if "Evenhanded Justice does indeed return th' Ingredients of that poysoned Chalice—to themselves,"⁸ and set on Foot a Mutiny among their own Soldiers:——*Peace must follow*—I told you it was coming, and Plenty too;—*and what I told you then, my heart adheres to still.*

Adieu and give our Compliments and kind Wishes to your whole Household, and give the enclosed Letter to sweet Siddons,⁹ and take her Attention up with your own Silver Tongue, and don't let her be thoughtful and pick her Mouth.

One word more—If the Lip swells and cracks in the middle—changing Colour; even though it should heal up—*'Tis Struma*—if the Corners only are affected and little Ulcers there come and go—*it's not so:* but one is *alarmed* for her *health* only in either Case: Life is in no Danger—nor is a Cancer in my Thoughts.¹⁰

God bless you—The Weather clears—the Cloudy Curtain draws up *even now*, disclosing our rich and extensive Prospect once more gilt by the Golden Sun, and promising renewed Greenness to console our Cattle——Ships cover the Coast going to and from Liverpool, and every thing cries out *Carpe Diem*—Catch the Hour of Enjoyment. Once more Farewell! says / Yours ever / H: L: P.

Text: Princeton University Library. Address: [in another hand] Mrs. Pennington / Dowry Square / Hot Wells / Bristol. *Postmark:* DENBIGH 224. Franked by De Blaquiere and dated Denbigh September six 1801.

1. HLP's letter responds to one by PSP, dated 2 September (Ry. 568.104).
2. According to PSP, SS "received a Letter *(extremely well written)* upbraiding her with the *inhumanity* with which She Sports with the *last* Sufferings of expiring Nature.—saying they understood 'it was her custom to attend, with *unfeeling apathy*, *Death Bed* Scenes, in order to render the Impression on her audience more strikingly shocking and affecting, and that She had taken her *last* Lesson from *that* of her *Daughter*—which she was supposed to represent with the nicest Accuracy.' . . . The Effect on the Feeling of our sweet Friend was painful in the extreme.—Such Floods of bitter Tears! such Nervous Agony as we had the greatest difficulty to soothe!!—I really question whether She can ever go through the Character again.—It is the Idea that has been present in her Mind ever since the Death of Maria and that she has always been fighting against.—How cruel to lacerate such a Heart and to open such half healed Wounds!!!"

The character SS thought she would never play again was that of Jane Shore, but she quickly changed her mind. See HLP to PSP, 9 October.

3. HLP's response to PSP's statement: "I have Read Harriet Lees German Tale—It displays a *wonderful* power of *artful* discrimination of Character and the most *subtle* of Knowledge of all the *dark* shadings and Tints that form the strange mass of Human purposes and Passions."
4. PSP reported that William Siddons "appears to me, much better in his Limbs. He can Walk very tolerably and to some distance without Crutches, but his *Neck* is *contracted* and he has constant Rheumatic Pain and Agony in that and the back part of his Head."
5. For Frances and Francis Twiss, see HLP to PSP, [29 April] 1798, n. 4.
6. HLP alludes to William Godwin's pragmatic attraction to Harriet Lee, also to their possible rivalry in turning out popular fiction. Godwin had succeeded with *Caleb Williams* in 1794 and with *St. Leon* in 1799.
7. Gillon informed HLP on 24 August that he had sent her a copy of *Kruitzner* (Ry. 577.20).
8. HLP's adaptation of the lines from *Macbeth* (1.7.10–12).
9. The letter is missing.
10. SS was exhausted and had been tormented for more than two months by clusters of sores about her mouth. As she described her ailment to her friend Mrs. Fitzhugh on 14 July, "My mouth is not yet well, though somewhat less exquisitely painful. I have become a frightful object with it for some time, and, I believe, this complaint has robbed me of those poor remains of beauty once admired, at least, which, in your partial eyes, I once possessed" (Campbell 2:263).

SS aggravated her condition by nervous anxiety. According to PSP: "The Complaint in her *Mouth* has, I really think, nothing *alarming* in it if her Fingers could be kept from perpetually irritating the part; but as she persists in tearing off the scarf Skin, even at the moment when you are talking to her and warning her on the Subject, one cannot say *what* the consequences may be; and the Habit is so inveterate that nothing but tying her Hands can prevent the practice."

TO PENELOPE SOPHIA PENNINGTON

[ca. 12–21 September 1801][1]

My Dear Mrs. Pennington
Since I received your last kind Letter, Harriet Lee's truly Impressive Tale has reached my Hands, and although the Novel Writers accuse me of Insensibility to all Works of mere Imagination, I will confess myself not only filled with admiring Esteem of the Authour's penetrating Keenness, and strange Intimacy with every Turn in that perplexing Labyrinth—Man's heart;—but also will avow that whilst I read the History of Kruitzner—his Story seized upon my Mind so strongly—*That Matter of Fact* flew all away before it, and faded from a Fancy wholly occupied by his Adventures and by his Distress.

In Proof however that *Home Scenes*—can supply Incident and even Character worth the relating—had Chance but sent one of these Writers where a Pain in the left Shoulder sent *me* for Purposes of Seabathing ten to Twelve Days ago——"*I will a round unvarnished Tale deliver*" which you may call the *Cambrian Story* if you please, and read it to dear Siddons.[2]

Will you come out *now* Miss Caroline and hear the young Clergyman Sing? said Kitty Sharp her Maid officiously. It is not much past eleven o'Clock, and a sweet Night—and here's nobody to know, and nobody to tell if they did know—for not a Word's spoken but in Welsh unless by one Person or two thro' the whole wretched Village. Miss Caroline Ma'am will you come? No, Sharp, I shall go to Bed directly. My Papa sent us all Three here for my youngest Sister's Health as you know perfectly well, because 'tis a busy Time at home, and because he thought himself quite sure that there was ne'er a Man in the Neighbourhood—no not for Miles—except the poor Clowns and Cottagers. He committed Gertrude and Fanny both to my Care and I shall not walk out at Midnight to hear young Fellows sing upon Dysart Rock in order to attract our Notice because they have heard already that we are *English* Girls of large Fortune: I can give my Guinea and hear the best Music thats to be had for Money—at Liverpool.—Leave the Room. Kitty obeyed and on the Stairs met with the Daughter of the Farm House they lodged at, trying but vainly to open a Window that looked back towards the Mountain. Failing in their Attempt from the old Casements accumulated Rust—they resolved to go out together and they did go—in search of the singing, but no singing could they hear. It was a sweet Night as Kitty had observed—Obedient to the Moon the refluent Tide which had six hours before left a broad Margin to our Irish Channel and tempted out the Babies of the Village to look for Shells, now—creeping over the soft Sand wave after wave—paused not till all the little Bay was filled which Nature had scooped out with her own hands, between projecting Hills roughened by Milk White Spar.

Rhydland's tall Castle rising to the Eye and beetling heavily over a Basis still firm and durable, which mocked the human Toil it bore aloft—lost every now and then some Time-dropt Pieces that awkwardly broken off left what remained to assume various and ill formed Shapes when viewed by Moonlight——The

two Girls sate down and listened for awhile, but hearing no Noise except the gentle rushing and retiring of a near Sea they were familiar with, began to think their Silence melancholy, and Ah Mrs. Sharp said her Companion what a fine Thing it is to see that Monstrous Body of Water all so quiet——You never was here in a rough Season such as My Mother said it was when I was born: the few People of Quality that come to our little Place here always make choice of Summer and they are very right—'Tis better for Bathing to be sure; has it done your young Ladies good. I think it *has* Miss Helen replied Kitty, but I don't much care about them to say true—for tho' good Ladies enough and tolerable generous, they are exceeding proud and keep every body—Lovers and Servants—and even my Master himself somehow at a great Distance tho' to be sure he having no Sons they will be prodigious Fortunes especially Miss Caroline, whom my Master's Partner has in a Manner adopted—not being able to find any Relation of his own and he is 84 Years of Age, hearty as he looks: but you were saying what a Storm there was once—tell about it—tis such a Comfort to get a little Chat in one's own Mother Tongue. Why English is as agreeable in my Ears as Welsh Mrs. Sharp; for my Father came from Oxfordshire himself but marrying my Mother who had a little Property here has improved it by living on the Spot, and Farmers have had very good Times lately—tho he never did fancy the Place, and when we are rich enough he says we shall go to what He calls *Home* for since She died he never took kindly to our Neighbours here—Poor Creatures! How could they help her dying! It was a Mercy She lived so long after it I think—After *what* says Kitty.—After that horrid Storm I spoke of. Ah Mrs. Sharp figure to yourself what a Night it must have been—In dark December——The Sea running Mountains high; a Dublin Packet shipwrecked on the Shore—a Lady's dying Shrieks piercing the thick Air, and drawing Attention even from these ill provided Cottagers—Every one *ran,* and even the Old Woman who was attending on my Mother as a Midwife to bring me into the World——I have heard indeed that they *called* her to save the Lady's Life, but be it as it will—Father never would speak with her again—nor look at her—because She left his Wife in such a Minute for the sake of making her Fortune as *he* said, tho She argued it was Compassion, for She thought my Mother safe enough. Howsoever here I am born, but to be sure the neglect, or the Labour or something did lie so hard upon my poor Parent, that I lost her before I knew her——ten Months after the Accident, and no good came to the Midwife: for the Parish being poor, refused to be burdened with the Boy that She got from the dead Lady, and so She had to nurse him herself——and did She nurse him? poor Thing? enquired Sharp. Yet that She did sick and well for seven Years, and A great Plague he was to her. I remember the boy perfectly. A melancholy Lad, and hated by his Playmates in the Street for that odd pensiveness that never let him join in Children's Sports—
—Tho he was very pretty in his ragged Coat, and I used to be sorry (when I knew no better) to see Father have such an Antipathy to him. However we were all quit of him when least expecting. An elderly Lady that lodged at our House for Bathing—There was no Inn in the Village then—took a Fancy to the Child because he gathered up some Apples that the other Boys had flung down to plague a Poor blind Woman who could not find or pick them up again, and She

carried him away with her, and said She would put him to School, so we never heard any more about him——I just recollect his bidding me good bye in Welsh and saying Farewell Ellen, but I dared not look sorry.

Is the Midwife alive now and here?

Oh no, She died soon after the Child was gone I believe, a Sister of hers from the Hill lives in her Cottage now.——Well we must go back—cries Kitty—If my Ladies should know I had been out tho' but with you, they would be very angry; and Miss Caroline is particularly stern, since her eldest Sister is on the Point of Marriage and She will be all in all at home: especially when old Mr. Lewis dies and leaves her *his* Fortune in addition to that my Master can give her himself—— Indeed She looks down upon *that* already, and half despises it, and the Servants *do* say that She will give it to Miss Gertrude her favourite—as soon as Mr. Lewis's Death puts her in Possession of his immense Estate.

Mr. Lewis did you say? replies Helen—Well but tis no Matter, we must go to Bed. Good Night Mrs. Sharp, sure I heard your Ladies' Bell ring.

And so it did.

Miss Fanny had eat Muscles for Supper and felt an Indigestion for which her Sister had sent off to St. Asaph to get the nearest help. When Kitty answered the Bell her Lady was of Course excessively angry, and tho' The Child—for She was but 14 Years old was recovered and asleep—so was not her Sister's just Resentment against their Maid whom She taxed with being out o'Sweetheart hunting: and loudly exclaimed against the vexatious Responsibility attached to overgrown fortunes—adding that all the Trumpery Girls who had not scarce 10000£ in the World, were happier than She; who if She was not eternally upon the Watch, might see (for ought She knew) one of the Miss Smiths stolen away by a Singing Parson, if no other Fellow could be found.

Sharp's Protestations that they had never seen or heard or named any such person, with the Grooms Return to say Mr. Pugh would wait on them in the Morning, and some Repose after the little Bustle, filled up the Time till next day when the Apothecary arrived and pronounced pretty Fanny, well to the no small Consolation of Miss Caroline who half gave, half *threw* her Couple of Guineas in a Paper to the Village Doctor; who felt in the Gift a Solidity which made him ample amends for the haughtiness of her who gave it; and in the best Good Humour possible he sate him down to chat, while his Horse hung at the rails.

And so Ladies says he I heard how you dined at the Dean's o' Tuesday, and saw the handsome young Clergyman that bathes here. In his next Drawing of these Rocks and Sands, I warrant we shall have the Three Miss Smiths all in White——observing a Frown gath'ring on the Brow of his chief Auditress—nay nay says Pugh—I'm sure he is not one of those that thinks more on himself than on the *Ladies;* and tho' the Dean cannot but own that he is a good Scholar, and we all hear how he sings and plays—he has an *humble* Heart I'll be sworn for him—Ay, and an Empty Purse no doubt, interrupted Miss Caroline. Why Yes, *poor* enough I conclude he is, *poor enough,* and always poking into mean Cottages and the like. Lady Lucy says 'tis to find Subjects for Painting, but he might see prettier Faces at fine Tables in my Mind.

Well good Mr. Pugh let's hear no more about it. Whenever the Man seriously wants Money You may call upon me. I am willing to give to People that *know their Places* as I call it—but when miserable Wretches will put themselves on a foot with People of Fortune—I really cannot bear it—Who is the Lady Lucy you mentioned? A Scotch Lady of Quality Ma'am—a Widow as I understand by my Wife who loves gossiping Stories. But I know *She*'s poor and lodges at St. Asaph for cheapness—and very pretty She is too, and so's her baby—and my Girls *do* say——but then they are always reading Novels and filling their Heads with Stuff—that She casts a Sheep's Eye now and then at the young Divine.

Ha ha! cries Miss Smith colouring yet titteringly to her Sisters, The best Novel would be if they were to marry *one* another: and we would call it The Beggar's Wedding——While Caroline looked off to enjoy her Joke—Pugh had thrown up the Sash and How d'ye do How d'ye do Mr. Griffith bawls he out to the Clergyman who was going down to the Sea.

This vulgar Fellow will call the other in says the Lady whispering between her Teeth: Go to the other Room dear Gertrude and finish that bit I left undone at the Tambour.

There was no Danger; Griffith waved his hat and walked forward. Mr. Pugh laughing out——he won't venture, he won't venture—took a hasty Leave promising to see Miss Fanny on the morrow, mounted his Nag and rode after.

Text: Ry. 568.152; an incomplete draft.

1. The Piozzis were at Prestatyn from ca. 12–21 September. HLP's letter to PSP could have been written any time during their stay there. What follows is an incomplete draft of a homespun adaptation of Harriet Lee's *Kruitzner.*
2. HLP's satirical attempt at fiction is provoked by her attitude toward the reader and writer of the genre. Thus, in "Harvard Piozziana," vol. 5, she wrote: "The Novel Reader lives in a Dream, till waked by positive and Ill prepared for—Anguish.——But Novels have another ruinous Tendency, they destroy all Taste for other Writing; and as the profligate Man of the World thinks every woman *vicious* in the Way he is accustomed to; so the Mind saturated and debauched by perpetual Fiction, ends in believing every Fact a Falsehood."
"I will a round unvarnish'd tale deliver," *Othello,* 1.3.90.

TO THE REVEREND REYNOLD DAVIES

> Brynbella
> [ca. 15 September 1801][1]

Dear Mr. Davies—

We have been strangely disappointed somehow by your not writing——what could have hindered you? Everything goes well in the Country, God be praised.——And Wales will exhibit a new Phænomenon this Year, and shew every bit of Harvest safe home before Michaelmas Day. The Crops are beyond Hope or Calculation in our Valley, which does of a Truth laugh and sing; as Mr. Wood can witness.

I have every possible Reason to be pleased with Mr. Wood, and flatter myself that between him and you and I; our little Black Eyed Salusbury will be a fine fellow——such he *shall* be, if ought in my Power or Wish can avail. Mean while let Parkinson look to his Mouth directly,[2] for it is so constructed he shews his Teeth every Time he speaks—and there *are those* who regard *them* more than the *Words* you know, which will *at any Rate,* come with a better Grace from between Two Clean Rows of Fencibles in fair Uniform, than from an illformed and masked Battery of black Fascines. Take Care of his Mouth therefore, and let nothing odious either go in or come out.

He seems to do his Writing and Geography *con Amore,* and Mr. Wood and I think he will shine at the Multiplication Table: We must drive the Nails that will *go;* yet not relax from setting those forward that are backward. When Reading comes familiar to him, good Taste will help him to love good Learning; and till *then,* the Plumb Cake and the New Machine must do their Duty——allure and impel. A sweeter-tempered Thing lives not; You may torment, but cannot possibly affront him; and he goes chearfully about his Business——tho' apt to drone over it while doing.

Reading English is what he does worst: I have begged of Mr. Wood with your Leave to buy that oldfashioned but very valuable and too-much-neglected Book, Watts's Art of Reading for his Use; likewise the same Author's First Principles of Geography and Astronomy, and Watts's Improvement of the Mind.[3]

In due Time we will go on to *all* That Author's Works: none better have been ever composed for youthful Students—and these empty Tales of Titty Mouse and Tatty Mouse, and Miss Polly and Master Tommy, are but thin Food if the Children *did* remember and digest them;—which I think they never do. When you and I learned there were no *Amis des Enfans* nor no Baby Stories;[4] and we studied in the Testament, and took up the Seven Champions,[5] or London 'Prentice for our *Pleasure,*[6]—and we did very well—with help of Robinson Crusoe.[7] One thing which perswades me strongly of the pernicious Tendency of Novels, is that I see plainly they never please—till Appetite and Passion lends them Poignancy: but those who write them are already sufficiently disposed to throw Stones at my Head; so I will say no more about the Matter.

Now Dear Mr. Davies write sometimes for pity *do;* or make the Child write, or coax Mr. Wood to write: for it does seem so long always between Letter and Letter to your ever troublesome but apprehensive humble Servant / H: L: P.

Text: Harvard University Library: Houghton Autograph File. *Address:* Rev: Mr. Davies / Streatham / Surrey.

1. JSPS, accompanied by "Professor" Wood, had been at Brynbella for his summer holidays (ca. 1 August–5 September). HLP's letter was written sufficiently before Michaelmas Day (29 September) to allow her to anticipate the harvest but after JSPS's return to school in Surrey.
2. John Parkinson, Sr. (fl. 1749–1802), surgeon-dentist, who appears in the "Streatham Land Tax" from 1793 to 1802 (C.R.O., Surrey).
3. HLP refers to the following works by Isaac Watts: *The Art of Reading and Writing English* (1721); *The Knowledge of the Heavens and the Earth made easy: or, The First Principles of*

Astronomy and Geography, etc. (1726); *The Improvement of the Mind; or, A Supplement to the Art of Logick* (1741).

4. For Berquin's eight-volumed *L'Ami des Enfans,* see HLP to LC, 28 August 1792, n. 11.

5. *The Famous Historie of the Seven Champions of Christendom* (ca. 1596), by Richard Johnson (1573–ca. 1659), a compilation of the legends of Saint George of England, Saint Denis of France, Saint James of Spain, Saint Anthony of Italy, Saint Andrew of Scotland, Saint David of Wales, Saint Patrick of Ireland.

6. *The Famous History of the Valiant London 'Prentice* (ca. 1750), a 24-page chapbook with woodcuts.

7. *The Life and Strange Surprizing Adventures of Robinson Crusoe, of York, Mariner* (1719).

TO THE REVEREND LEONARD CHAPPELOW

Prestatyn
17: September 1801.

I am very sorry indeed Dear Mr. Chappelow—and very little desirous of adding to your present state of Uneasiness by silly Condolance which can do no good: but when you have seen Lord and Lady Bradford somewhat tranquillized, if you will come to Brynbella and by change of Scene contribute to *your own* Tranquillity, it will be a good Deed and a wise Measure, and *do* come: and see how the Trees are grown, and make yourself a little temporary Interest in *our* Affairs, and hear Mr. Piozzi tell you what he has done to the Farm, and let me shew you how neat old Bachŷgraig looks, and let Lord Kirkwall tell you his *Escape* from a fall to which that you saw him make, was tumbling on a Down Bed.[1]

At any Rate do not stay too long at Weston: yet before you leave it, try to make our most respectful and even anxious Enquiries acceptable. Charming Lady Bradford will recover from her Shock twice as fast as any of the Dissipated Dames would do. *She* knows, and meditates upon, and is in constant preparation for that *only* Event, which tho' common to all, and certain to all; is by most of us ever unlooked for, and when it happens is *surprizing.*[2] Poor Kitty Beavor too——Lady Lucy's admiring Friend—in the same Newspaper:——by Name of Mrs. Gillies.[3] Very sad indeed, and very melancholy.

Yet perhaps I am even now lamenting the Living——as since our silly News-papers announced with so much Gravity the Marriage of Hannah More with Dr. Crossman, who has had a Wife these Dozen Years;[4] small Reliance can be made on *them:* and where *we* are,—(a little Bathing Place under Dysart Rock)——no other Intelligence can be obtained.

Never were such copious Harvests in *this* Country—to You who are an Agri-colist, one may talk *in Terms:*——Even the coldest Provinces of North Wales; Caernarvonshire and Anglesea, have had Returns of six and Twenty for one; and the Weather now mild as May, the Sea smoother than I ever saw it in July, although the Equinox gives Symptoms of Approach by the tide's retiring in such a Manner one may drive Miles upon a firm Sand; and when I dipt to Day, the Guide said we were quite far out in the Irish Channel.

A Thousand beautiful Birds attract my Notice here which seem banished from populous Ports, and Bathing Places visited by Society. The Gannets here following a Leader Chief, fly over one's head all Day; while Auks and Guillemots and screaming Gulls seem to feel no Fears of Disturbance, and fish close up to our Machine,—I know not their Success indeed; for Fish except Salmon and a Fluke or two, never come to Table.

'Tis pleasant however to contemplate this friendly Ocean which gives renewed health and protects from Buonaparte those who inhabit this hitherto highly favoured Island. Altho' the Stocks droop I see, since 'tis supposed all Negotiation is breaking off.[5]

Adieu dear Sir, write when you can, come when you will; the Letters and Company of Mr. Chappelow are ever most welcome to My Master and to Your ever faithful and Obliged / H: L: Piozzi.

Are all the dear Children well at Weston? especially sweet little Henry,—I hope so.[6] We have had our *Boldface* home this Summer, and a fine Fellow he is; and can construe Deus Creavit Terram.——

We go home to Brynbella tomorrow.

Text: Ry. 561.114. *Address:* Rev. Mr. Chappelow.

1. On 7 July, Lord Kirkwall had a nearly fatal accident. "Exercising his troop of volunteer cavalry, together with his corps of infantry, on the lawn before his house in Denbighshire, in making a charge at the head of the former upon the latter, his horse reared and fell back with him, with such violence that his helmet was completely crushed, but fortunately prevented him sustaining any more material injury, than a severe contusion on his neck and back." See the *Bath Herald*, 11 July.

2. One of Lord Bradford's brothers was the Reverend George Bridgeman (1765–1832), rector of Wigan, Lancs., and Weston, who had in 1792 married Lady Lucy Isabella, née Boyle, daughter of the seventh earl of Corke and Orrery and maternal cousin of Lady Bradford. On 7 September Lady Lucy had died at Weston.

3. Catherine Gillies, née Beaver (1763–1801), had died 7 September.

4. George Crossman (1754–1803), rector of Blagdon and West Monkton since 1780, was originally from Plymouth, Devon. A student at Christ Church, Oxford, he received his B.A. in 1775, his M.A. in 1778, and his D.C.L. (Doctor of Canon Law) in 1787.

On 8 January 1784, Crossman married Elizabeth Brickdale (1766–1805), at West Monkton. They had four children: Elizabeth (b. 4 October 1784); Lucy (b. 30 November 1785); Francis Geach (b. 6 February 1788); George Brickdale (b. 18 July 1791).

See the West Monkton parish records—baptisms, marriages, and burials—in C.R.O., Somerset; also John Collinson, *The History and Antiquities of Somerset*, 3 vols. (Bath: R. Cruttwell, 1791), 3:454–55.

5. In an extensive article setting forth reasons for the failure of the peace negotiations between Great Britain and France, *The Times* on 11 September began with the following:

"The long delay and known indisposition of the French Government towards a Peace with this Country have so effectually prepared the public mind for the rupture of the Negociation, that whenever Government shall announce that event, it will occasion not the smallest astonishment."

6. Henry Edmund Bridgeman (1795–1872), the youngest son of Lord and Lady Bradford.

TO THE LADIES OF LLANGOLLEN

> Brynbella
> 23: September 1801.

The charming Ladies of Llangollen Vale bid Doctor Myddelton tell me I am indebted for *two* Letters thence, since I wrote last.[1] This Paper brings my Acknowledgments for *One* worth *Two* of any other Correspondent's; it was franked, but I forget the *out*side in kind and grateful Recollection of what was *within*.

Sweet Words all, and most obliging Acceptance they expressed, of our desire to Detain longer at Brynbella Friends that were flying forwards to a Cottage all the World wishes to arrive at; especially such who like Lady Downe and Miss Dawney have claims on the Friendship of its dear Inhabitants.[2]

I hope we shall live to receive their Civilities in London next Year, though Death is so busy among People one knows, and People one knows through Intimate Acquaintance, that I catch myself wondering very often that we have so long been spared.

Mr. Chappelow is doubtless in cruel Affliction for that charming Lady Lucy he had so much regard for, I have written to the House of Mourning—Weston Park—but no Answer as yet has come to hand.

Our amiable Dean of St. Asaph has been ill too, very ill—but the danger past quickly away. We were Seabathing this last Week or ten Days under <Dysart> Rock, at a rueful Place called Prestatyn not far from where the Dean lives, but Miss Yonge could not see us he was so bad.[3] Mr. Piozzi said it was fine Scenery for the Novel Writers;[4] and I do think with a Storm and a Shipwreck and a Lady in Distress &c.——one might form one of those new fashioned Tales that at a Moment such as We live in, when every body seeks to be agitated, and nobody to be instructed might serve to gain Attention for an Hour—Then—dully take its Turn and be forgotten. Apropòs have Your Ladyship and Miss Ponsonby read Harriet Lee's last Work? a *German Tale* very impressive and in some Respects a Performance of no small Merit. The Abbé Edgeworth's Sister has written a Story called Belinda. Very much liked, but I have not yet seen it.

My Genius certainly does *not* lead me to Works of Imagination: and You would rather employ my Pen in True History——if Prior's Verses did not stare me in the face so, I really should long to make a *first* Vol: to Retrospection and like the Lady in the Second Canto of Alma, just—*Take the Romans in the Close*.[5] But I have had Stones enough thrown at me, and will provoke no more. Life is not sufficiently long, nor Health sufficiently firm to battle thro' any more Literary Contests, and there is no Sense in chusing to dye in the Arena.

Our Newspapers of late seem wondrous dull: no Facts of any Consequence, no Reflexions producing any Entertainment. One is tired out with Talk of an Invasion which everybody prepares for, and nobody expects. Yet Peace vanishes from before our Eyes——and they do say—that Plenty will vanish from our Grasp too—but that I hope is in its very Nature Impossible.[6] Our rudest and coldest Counties here in North Wales have had returns of 26 for *one*.

Is pretty Miss Ormsby going to be married to Sir Watkin's Brother as the People here say She is?—That would be an abrupt Change indeed from Black to White.[7] We think that Lord Kirkwall will be called to Town soon on the Marquis of Thomond's Account who is suffering at 80 years old by a mere Accident of putting out his Arm.[8]

But all this Stuff your Ladyship and Miss Ponsonby have heard from twenty People. Let me hasten to tell you what nobody knows so well as Mr. Piozzi and myself, with how Sincere and respectful an Admiration I have the honour to remain dear Ladies / Your true and faithful Servant / H: L: P.

Text: Wicklow MS 4239. National Library of Ireland. *Address:* Rt. Hon. Lady Elinor Butler / Llangollen (franked De Blaquiere). *Postmark:* DENBIGH 2 <180> 1.

1. For the Reverend Robert Myddelton of Gwaynynog, see HLP to LC, 2 July 1799, n. 9.
2. Laura or Lora, née Burton (1740–1812), had married in 1763 John Dawnay (1728–80), fourth viscount Downe (I, 1760). Their only daughter was Catherine (d. 1821). See P.R.O., Prob. 11/1533/215.
3. For the Reverend William Shipley and his sister-in-law Barbara Yonge, see HLP to LC, 30 September 1796, nn. 9 and 10.
4. For HLP's comments on "melancholy . . . very romantic" Prestatyn, see *Thraliana* 2:1028.
5. For Prior's wry description of the Lady's ability "To cut Things short," to move in five lines from Adam to Babel "Thro' Syria, Persia, Greece" and to "take the Romans in the Close," see *Alma*, 2.374–78.
6. HLP had not kept up with newspaper accounts of the peace negotiations between England and France. By 18 September *The Times* reported a new flurry of diplomatic activity, concluding "that some new propositions have been made on the part of the Chief Consul, as we have reason to believe that the negotiation was on the point of terminating unsuccessfully not ten days since."
7. Sir Watkin's brother was Charles Watkin Williams-Wynn (1775–1850), an M.P. since 1797 and destined to become an important Tory figure. On 9 April 1806, he was to marry Mary, née Cunliffe (d. 1838).
8. HLP's jest about Lord Kirkwall's grandfather Murrough O'Bryen, marquess of Thomond, who on 15 September was created Baron Thomond of Taplow Court, co. Buckingham. See *GM* 71, pt. 2 (1801): 954.
For Murrough O'Bryen, see HLP to LC, 5 March 1792, n. 5.

TO THE REVEREND LEONARD CHAPPELOW

Brynbella
30: September 1801.

Nothing so true dear Mr. Chappelow as that you and I have often Agreed upon——that those who make their *Retrospect* of our present Times will be most at a Loss to express their Admiration. Everyone preparing for what no One expects—Invasion——and preparing too with an Expense and Care and Inconvenience to Individuals, which proves them in positive and serious Earnest.

Every one celebrating the Abundance of our Crops, yet contentedly paying enormous Price for Cattle; and attributing that Price justly enough too to the Quantity of Pasture and increase of the Circulating Medium. Our Neighbour Sir John Williams is said to have sold an Estate of his in Cheshire for Thirty one Thousand Pounds which never had brought him in more than a neat Rent—not nominal 500£ o'Year——putting the Money in our Stocks *now* the Profit will be prodigious.[1]

I believe Your Establishments in Norfolk are particular with regard to Poor's Rates, but the Quantity of Corn ought to reduce them; and when The Ships loaded with Rice arrive from India—as arrive they must and will,—our Pigs will live merrily on the Damaged Stuff that will be spoiled by lying long under Water.[2]

It would grieve me You should be forced to part from your Native Soil which believe me will grow dearer and dearer every Day, whilst the Joys of London fade imperceptibly before your fatigued Eyes. A little of both is best. If Bath Water and Idleness get me into tolerable Spirits, Mr. Piozzi proposes that we should see what you are about in Town next Spring while this House is new painting; I hope many Verses of the great Work will be written by then, and not only Stones brought from the Quarry——but some Cement used too, that one may better judge of its Form and its Extent.[3]

A long Visit to Brynbella will be necessary to compensate such Absence: our Scotch Gardener asks often when Mr. Chappelow comes to admire his Operations, and I must confess the Planting does succeed to a Wonder.

Did you observe the Maculæ upon the Sun's Disk? they were visible almost without any Glasses, but are now nearly lost to even a Telescopic Eye.[4] 46000 Miles of Opacity!! Apropos when comes out Mr. King's new Book? A very learned Performance I am told and full of recondite knowlege we shall find it.[5] Is Stockdale's his Shop? or has *he* had enough of *Quartos*.[6]

The Enemies have left off worrying me and are fallen upon Hannah More you may observe: as they consider Marriage the greatest Crime a Woman who knows how to read and write can possibly commit—They accuse *her* of it with a Man who has had a Wife of his own many Years. It is however good for us all that the Controversy is at an End—

> Which flow'd and flow'd like its Inspirer *Beer*—Bere:
> Tho' stale not ripe; tho' thin yet never clear:
> So sweetly mawkish, and so smoothly dull,
> Heady not strong—o'erflowing tho' not full.

You tell me nothing of the Rheumatism nor of the Urticaria, but of your new Curate for whom I care not a Pin. *We* likewise have a new Curate; not like that Mr. Jones you hated so because he pulled off his Hat at the wrong Time—or rather My Master says—did not pull it off at any Time——but a well bred genteel Man who has lived in an Officer's Mess room since the Day he was a Tuft hunter at College, and knows all the Forms of Life to Perfection.[7] I am so sorry he is *deplacè* here! and I suppose he is so sorry too! The Lysonses called at Brynbella in a Tour they have been making thro' these Counties for purpose I trust of adorning their new Work[8] which will make Campden's Britannia cheap,[9] and themselves *dear* to old England: They are diligent creatures, that they are; and merit Encouragement from Small and Great. Did I tell you that one of the principal Peaks of Snowdon is discovered to be——a Rock of Copper[10]——or that an Immense Piece of Penmanmawr fell from the Top upon the high Road, and impeded the Passage to Ireland for some Days before its Removal could be effected.[11]

Are you very far from Lowestoffe in Suffolk? I had a Letter from Miss Thrale saying that She and her Sisters are bathing there—not Cecilia, who is alone somewhere——Mr. Mostyn is said to be in Wales.

So here's a long Letter litterally made out of nothing, but that Friendship and those good Wishes which is felt for Dear Mr. Chappelow by my Master and by Yours faithfully / H: L: Piozzi.

Have you read Harriet Lees new Canterbury Tale? I never remember whether Moydon or Roydon is the name of your Place, and by the hand-writing—(Pardon me)—it is impossible to decide.

Text: Ry. 561.115.

1. The estate came to Sir John indirectly through his great-grandfather John Williams of Chester, a barrister.
2. As early as 5 January 1801, *The Times* reported the findings of the Sixth Report of the parliamentary committee appointed to consider the high price of provisions: "From India, a much larger quantity [of rice] may ultimately be expected [than from the Southern States of North America].... It seems therefore not unreasonable to expect from that quarter, in the months of August and September, about 35,000 barrels; which, added to the importation from America, will amount to 105,000 barrels. Each barrel may be considered as more than equal, in point of weight, to the Flour of all descriptions, extracted from 12 bushels of Wheat, but in point of nutriment to a much larger quantity."
3. LC was slow in answering HLP's "hope" but on 9 November (Ry. 563.72) he picked up her imagery. "... you want to see some of my Stones brought from the Quarry, and I can literally indulge you with the sight of one not finished, but you will wonder primâ facie, by what kind of Cement, that is with what propriety, I can introduce a piece of Sculpture into my poems which I have made you believe, were intended only as vehicles for various descriptions in natural History." Then LC provides a comic account of his arguments for the book as a whole and thirty-two lines dealing with a "Stone." LC concludes his metrical performance, complete with pseudo-emendations, by urging HLP to throw it into the fire.
4. "Capel Lofft, an ingenious Astronomer, states, that there are now several clusters of spots on the sun. One of these, as measured on the 28th ult. by a micrometer, spread over nearly an eleventh of the sun's diameter in length. Another measurement, taken rather roughly, of a spot on the 27th, was six seconds, or very nearly, in passing by the edge of the telescope, and consequently was the 20th or 22d of the sun's diameter, about thirty-five or forty thousand miles in length" (*The Times*, 14 September).
5. Edward King, *Munimenta Antiqua; or, Observations on antient castles*, etc., 4 vols. (London: G. and W. Nicol, 1799–1805).

6. A wry allusion to the poor sale of *Retrospection*.

7. The man disliked by LC was "John Jones, minister" of Tremeirchion Church for 1797–98. He probably continued until 1800, when he was succeeded by "John Stodart [b. 1731], Curate." He in his turn was succeeded by Griffith Griffith, who was originally from Dines, co. Merioneth. He was an Oxonian who took his B.A. in 1780 and M.A. in 1783. His name appears in the Tremeirchion parish registers frequently from January 1800 to January 1802. See "Tremeirchion Churchwardens accounts: (P/65/1/17) and "Overseers accounts: (P/65/1/25), in C.R.O., Clwyd.

8. The book that was to make DL and SL rich was *Magna Britannia*.

9. William Camden, *Britannia. Sive florentissimorum regnorum, Angliae, Scotiae, Hiberniae, et Insularum adiacentium ex intima antiquitate chorographica descriptio,* etc. (London: Per Radulphum Newbery, 1586).

10. Although HLP's description is probably exaggerated, Snowdon has been noted for an abundance of copper in certain areas of the mountain, such as Cwm Llan and Llyn Du'r, and has given the volcanic rocks where it is to be found a distinctive purple color. See Howel Williams, "The Geology of Snowdon (North Wales)," *Quarterly Journal of the Geological Society of London,* 83 (1927): 346–431, esp. 408, 425.

11. Penmaenwaur rises thirteen hundred feet almost perpendicularly from the sea and forms the termination of the Snowdon range on the north coast of Carnarvonshire. The rockfall described by HLP could have impeded passage to Ireland since the main road of Bangor and thence to Holywell—the point of embarkation—was at the foot of Penmaenwaur.

TO PENELOPE SOPHIA PENNINGTON

Brynbella
Fryday 9: October 1801.

Well my dear tardy Friend! Your Letter is come at last, and a nice Letter it is.[1] I have one too this post from Mr. Whalley—*so* kind! He has had enough to do with his Lady Writers; but he loves both Hannah More and myself and the least we can do in return is to be *merry;*—Love our Friends, forgive our Enemies—forget Offenders and Offences, and light up our Windows for the Peace.[2]

The Terms are certainly in no sense disgraceful——and since we have all been saying so repeatedly "Let us heal our own Wounds, limit our own Expences, and care no longer for Allies who 'tis sure care not for *us:*" I pronounce our Ministers fully justified to *this* Country for quitting their Post and leaving every *other* Country to the Fate they would none of them resist. While France having enlarged her own Territory beyond the proudest hope of their own proudest Monarch——has prudently bought us off from fighting Europe's Battles with two eminently rich, useful and valuable Islands: well knowing that an Englishman will always be quiet, while his Palate is pleased and his Pockets full.[3]

The Gold and Silver and Rubies and Rice from Ceylon, sweetened by sugar from Trinidad will keep Great Britain in perfect Good humour——and the Commercial Treaty will keep her Employed;[4] and in the Mean Time Alexander and Buonaparte mean to divide the Globe. Such is apparently their Project for 1801—how—and by what Means God Almighty will render it abortive remains to be Seen. The internal Politics of our united Kingdom here at home offer a *fair Shew* certainly, for if People are not pleased with seeing their Ports filled with foreign Corn and their Stack yards groaning under the Weight of our own harvests—What *will* please them? Not the Price of Mutton in the Markets I trow, for between the Inclosing Commons, and *Improving* the Breed of Sheep in Counties where such large Animals cannot find Pasture; with many other Reasons—Their Flesh will sell for *6d. an Ounce* next Year, and we shall have more Mouths to feed after the War is over—unless this Mortality at Liverpool goes on.

Ah Dear Friend! I *told* you how it would be, and true did I tell you, but no matter.

> For other Thoughts mild Heav'n a Time ordains,
> And disapproves that Care tho' wise in Show,
> That with superfluous Burden loads the Day:
> And when God sends a chearful hour refrains.[5]

Let us light up our Windows and be merry. Mr. Piozzi will not just now lend a Voice to huzza with, for he has got the Gout; but charming Lady Hesketh's Voice being restored is a delightful Circumstance,[6] and most encouraging to People plagued with Maladies upon the Nerves——They leave the patient free when least expected.

I suppose Sally Moore will recover her Voice too.[7]

Dear Siddons has written me a long and kind Letter.[8]—She hopes Sea Bathing does her Mouth good—it is a vexatious Complaint for *her* to labour under. Is She engaged anywhere for the Winter? I hoped your Letter when it came, would say that Dimond had secured her for *us*. Her acting Jane Shore in defiance of the Tormentors was sweetly done and like a Friend of Mr. Whalleys. What a Cordial his Letters bring with them! We ought all to be happy and try to deserve *such* Praises, so exprest! I hope we shall meet at his place next summer somehow, for tho' sound Health is certainly not of our Coterie, Death will knock down many Rank and file Folks, perhaps before our Turn comes.

Little did I dream seven Years ago of seeing Peace proclaimed between Great Britain and the *Consular State* of France—Little could I *ever* have dreamed that I should see Venice annihilated,[9] Genoa forgotten:[10] Piedmont's Alpine Barrier insufficient to keep out Invasion even in the Depth of Winter[11]——and old Rome divided against herself—dropping into her Enemies' Mouth almost without Invitation.[12]

The World as it appears consenting to all this, and even happy to think Things have gone no worse.

We shall see more yet——but shall not see *all—all!*—no nor *half*.

I am ashamed to hear the Name of Mrs. Hamilton[13]—but her Letters from me are doomed to be directed Bath—even as it seems if I give them to be franked. They cost her a fine Penny by the Time they reached Richmond——and Holman gone home I suppose.

His Wife seems exceedingly happy, and for an odd Reason—because they are *borrowing* Money; *my* Felicity is to think that *we* are *paying* Money, and shall shortly have no more to pay.[14]

I wrote Harriet Lee word how much her Tale impressed me; Tis a Characteristic of this Age I think to shew what forcible Impression may be made by setting only our *mean* Passions to work—Avarice, Fraud and Fear——instead of Generosity, Love and Valour. What she has done however is very striking; and every one I lend the Book to, is amazed to find Conrade the Murderer of *Stralenheim*.[15]

Dear Friend Adieu! This is a good for nothing Letter, but then it costs nothing: and it tells you all I know, which is that my Master has the Gout; and I have the Rheumatism in my Shoulder, (like Mrs. Weston if you will, but not at *all* like Mr. Siddons)—that we have already written to Mrs. Garrat about the House,[16] and that I hope to hear Dear Dr. Randolph's Christmas Day—no no, his *New Years* Day Sermon at Laura. / Farewell! and love Your Affectionate / H: L: Piozzi.

Text: Princeton University Library.

    1. PSP's letter is missing.
    2. The "Preliminaries of Peace between His Majesty and the French Republic were signed [on 1 October] at Lord Hawkesbury's Office, in Downing-street, by the Right Hon. Lord Hawkesbury, one of His Majesty's Principal Secretaries of State, on the part of His Majesty, and by M. Otto, on the part of the French Government." See *The London Gazette Extraordinary*, 2 October 1801.
    3. Among the terms of the "Preliminaries," the British would withdraw from Malta within three months and the island would be turned over to the Knights of Malta. The rights and territories of the Ottoman Empire and Portugal would be honored except that France would retain Portuguese Guiana. There would be an exchange of prisoners of war; peace and friendship were to be maintained between Great Britain and the French Republic. See also n. 5.
    4. In its discussion of the "Preliminaries of Peace," *The Times* on 3 October emphasized the commercial advantages that would accrue to Great Britain:
"[England] will retain the invaluable Island of *Ceylon*. . . .
"She will also, as some indemnification and security in the West Indies, preserve the full Sovereignty of *St*. Trinidada. . . .
"The *Cape of Good Hope*, which, considering the connection of France and Holland, involved the greatest difficulties, but which can never otherwise be considered as desirable to England than from the danger of its belonging to a Power hostile to that country, will be declared a free Port, (which, to all commercial purposes, has long been the object of this country,) under what guarantee and colours its neutrality and privileges are to be maintained, is not yet decided."
    5. See Milton's sonnet (no. 21) "On Cyriack Skinner," lines 11–14.
    6. For Harriet, Lady Hesketh, see HLP to PSP, 20 December [1799] and n. 1.
    7. Sarah and Clementina Moore were sisters whom HLP had met in the spring of 1795. See HLP to Q, 3 April [1795], n. 1.
    8. SS's letter is missing.
    9. Eager to control the Venetian state, Bonaparte declared as a pretext that Venice was hostile to him and a threat to his possible line of retreat during the Austrian campaign of 1797. The Peace of Leoban left Venice without an ally and saw her last doge deposed. A provisional democratic municipality was set up in place of the republican government, but later in the same year Venice was turned over to Austria. Between 1798 and 1814 Venice was handed back and forth between Austria and France.
    10. Despite Masséna's capitulation at Genoa in early June 1800, Austrian control lasted only until 24 June, when the French arrived under the command of General Louis-Gabriel Suchet (1770–1826). The Austrians, along with their British naval allies, then abandoned

Genoa. Under French domination, the city (suffering from the siege and Austro-British reprisals) was "forgotten" until 1805, when it was formally annexed to France. See Jean Borel, *Gênes sous Napoléon 1er* (Paris: Attinger, 1929).

11. In May 1800, before the snows had melted, Bonaparte led his army across several Alpine passes. He moved his troops through Piedmont and went on to win the battle of Marengo on 14 June, to triumph over virtually the whole of Italy. See HLP to PSP [ca. 26 July 1800].

12. With the signing of the Peace of Tolentino (February 1797), Pius VI saved Rome only by surrendering a large part of the papal states. By February 1798 Rome was occupied by the troops of General Louis Berthier. Pius VI was exiled and the republic was governed by an executive of seven consuls. See HLP to LC, 21 February 1797.

In November 1798, Ferdinando IV reentered the war against France. The Neapolitan army led by General Karl von Mack entered Rome on 29 November, but the French returned in December after General Championnet's victory over Mack at Civita Castellana. The reestablished republic lasted only until 1799, when the French were again driven out.

With Bonaparte's second conquest of Italy in 1800, Pius VII in July was allowed to reenter the city, to maintain a nominal hold on Rome and certain of the papal states. See Pastor 40:344–47.

13. For Rachel Hamilton, see HLP to Ann Greatheed, 2 April [1788][b], n. 4.

14. For Jane Hamilton's marriage to Joseph George Holman, see HLP to LC, 9 February 1798, n. 2.

15. HLP's surprise emerges from the complex plot of *Kruitzner*. At odds with his self-indulgent son, the elderly Count Siegendorf threatens to make over the honors of the family to the collateral branch headed by Baron Stralenheim. The count's son impetuously leaves Bohemia, assumes an alias (Kruitzner), wanders through middle Europe, marries Josephine, and has a son Conrad who, at the age of eight, is turned over to his grandfather.

Twelve years pass during which Stralenheim pursues Kruitzner. Both men recognize each other as enemies, their goal being the possession of the Siegendorf estates.

Conrad, now a man, returns to his parents. Soon thereafter, Stralenheim is murdered by an unknown hand. Kruitzner (now Count Siegendorf since the death of his father) is suspected of the crime and forced to flee, only to return to his inherited estate. Actually Conrad, given to "savage and ferocious pleasures," slew Stralenheim, sought to implicate his father, and so gain the Siegendorf wealth. In time Conrad is killed in a military skirmish. His father dies, recognizing in his son the same moral weakness as in himself.

16. Elizabeth Garrett (1741–1832) is listed as the owner of houses at 7 Laura Place, at 40 and 77 Pulteney Street (the latter rented by the Piozzis during their last visit to Bath) from about 1800 to 1823. See the Bath directories, 1800 to 1819; "Poor Rate Book," Bathwick, 1818–23, in the Guildhall, Bath; "St. James's Burial Register," C.R.O., Somerset.

TO THE REVEREND THOMAS SEDGWICK WHALLEY

Brynbella
9: October 1801

Such a Letter my Dear Sir is well worth waiting for;[1] Your Praises would overbalance better Criticism—and severer Censures, than any I have yet heard answered and forgotten.[2] Keep up our valuable Friend Hannah's Spirits; and I will promise you mine shall not droop, while they can boast such a Supporter.[3]

9 October 1801

> The World is sick of the long Controversy which
> —flows and flows like its Inspirer *Beer* Bere—
> Tho' stale not ripe, tho' thin yet never clear—

It may now be handsomely dropt, and lost among the Heaps of Sense and Nonsense, Spite, and Panegyric which this newer and more interesting Subject Peace will bury in Oblivion.

Did you hope, or could either you or I dear Sir have dreamed, of living to see the Wonders hourly exhibiting? A French Republic! consolidating under *that* Name an Empire beyond the Grasp, beyond the Expectation I believe of Louis quatorze himself.

That Buonaparte is Author of their Greatness I am not confident, but that he has contributed to it is certain; and strangely retributive must that Justice appear in *his* Eyes, which dooms the Men who have annihilated the Independence of Italy—to shrink and tremble under the Command of an Italian.

The Fable recited by Jotham in the 9th Chapter of Judges would suit one of the Bourbon Princes now exactly——and if Fire does *not* come out of Abimelech to devour the Men of Shechem, and if Fire does *not* come out of Shechem to devour Abimelech I shall be much disappointed.[4]

Mean while we have done wisely tho' perhaps not kindly in forbearing to fight Europe's Battles any more—against a Power She was willing to set over herself——but the Day we signed those Preliminaries was in my Mind a fatal Day for all the World, France, Russia, and ourselves excepted.

Our Commercial Gentlemen have every Reason to be pleased. The Aldermen will eat Turtle and their Wives will wear Gems from our new Acquisition. The Taprobana of the Ancients—The terrestrial Paradise Ceylon—whence only, Swallows never migrate; who are contented to stay no where else.[5]

Nous autres Campagnards will find our Estates rise in Value every hour, and Provisions——I hope——sink in Price. The Money bought in at 57 for Mr. Thrale's Daughters at *his* Death, will at *my* Death be nearly doubled to them; and pay them for waiting so long.

I shall not surely eat Goose at 99 Years old like lovely Mrs. Whalley;[6] one slice of it would make me even now so ill, Bath Water alone could restore me. How happy that my Husband has a Stomach as strong as mine is weak! The Gout always in my Mother's Family—never in *his*——would if it once attacked *me* fly to the feeble Part at once, and dispatch a Life that has been comparatively an exceeding happy one.

Our Dear Siddons complains sadly of her Mouth. A strumous swelling in the Lip if I understand Mrs. Pennington perfectly; it will hurt her Enunciation, and plague her cruelly besides: but hers is the real unpretending Virtue that bears and forbears all for conscience sake——The longer one knows that incomparable Creature, the more Reasons spring up to love, and to esteem her—it is to you and Mrs. Whalley that I owe the Happiness of her Friendship and Acquaintance. Mrs. Whalley's tender and fragile Frame will outlast *this*, and perhaps many a Winter: let us only look back and we shall observe those who have been overset upon the Ocean of Life, and left us paddling on;—to have been the Robust and vigorous, not the delicate and slight Vessels:—They are *so* careful, and excite in others such unremitted Care to keep *them* safe, their Misery is often the out living their healthier Friends.

God keep us all together to meet happy at Longford Cottage next Spring. We shall have enough to chat about. La Conversation des Amis ne tarit pas, and those wicked French Fellows whose Language I love almost as much as I hate their Philosophy will give us Subjects of Admiration—sometimes without their own Consent. Witness their being obliged to leave Egypt that basest of Nations— —to Slavery—whilst they have set free all the World beside: under the Yoke too of those wretched Turks! who having resisted an armed Constraint in former Days, now fall themselves without a Blow.

Adieu to them, I have long been sick of all Alliance with such dull Souls who have done nothing as I find but *sit cross-legged* to bring us *good Luck.*[7] Let us see what results from their Quarrel with Passowan Ogli;[8] and learn if possible what the Quarrel is *about.*[9]

Old England has nothing to do but to look on. You should pay forfeit for not telling me the Anecdote of Buonaparte.

Do now kindest Mr. Whalley write again when a Moment's Time to throw away offers; You cannot bestow it upon anyone more sensible of the Honour done them in such a Correspondence, and I feel quite eager to learn that *he hates* a Jacobin, there can be no doubt but he fears them.

The Epigram about Cerberus and your delightful Drollery concerning these Cynics and Snarlers, is pleasant beyond Measure:[10] Let us join all our Forces to keep up the Spirits of our precious Friend in Pultney Street [Hannah More], which will be best done by changing the whole Course of her Ideas and making her Think of Something else till She feels ashamed to go back and look her Head over for *Rubbish.*

Our dear and inestimable Sovereign too whom You and She and I unite to venerate, will be made happy by this Peace, and his Paternal Estate safe to please him. I cannot but feel for those sort of Prejudices, remembering how Miss Thrale's Guardians advised me to sell or *Give away* my little Property here in Wales as beneath the Notice of their Mother whose Papa had provided for me so amply was their Phrase. And my Woods too said I. *Woods!* replied Mr. Crutcheley with a loud Laugh——Oh Yes, I *do* recollect an Old Plum Tree.

I fear they talked something like this to George the 3d. *I fear so*——about Hanover.[11]

But what is left of my Paper will not let me say with how many Thanks and Regards / I remain Dear Mr. and Mrs. Whalley's / ever Obliged and faithful / H: L: Piozzi.

Text: Hyde Collection. *Address:* Revd. Tho. Sedk. Whalley / Longford Cottage / Bristol. *Postmark:* DENBIGH 224; franked by De Blaquiere, Denbigh October nine 1801.

    1. HLP's letter responds to one by TSW, 1 October (Ry. 564.8).
    2. In his letter TSW had fulminated: "The abominable Strictures of the Critical Re-

viewers, on your *Retrospection*, have *not* excited *my* Rage. *They are not worth it. Disgust* and Contempt are the strongest Emotions they have awakened in my Bosom. But I am heartily glad they goaded *you*, to vent *your just* and *chastening* Anger in an Answer,—currente Calamo—'to your' Publisher. For had it not been *Currente Calamo*, on *the very Spur* of the *Moment*, your Anger would soon have run to waste, and left only such Dregs behind it, as none of their Black Arts would have had power to work up unto an efficient *fermentation*, to their *utter discomfiture;* as the *sooty* Alchemyst is sometimes scorched by the Flames, or disfigured, and put to shame by the overflowings of his *own* alembic."

3. TSW had written: "As our excellent Friend, Hannah More, resembles you in genius, and virtue, so I wish she partook of your quick and elastic animal Spirits, which soon rise buoyant above the base attacks of Malice and Envy. But with all her wisdom and her goodness, she cannot say to her Friend 'sta firma' against Malevolence, which cannot sully her bright Frame, or the despicable arts of falsehood and Envy to distort her Piety and misrepresent her conduct. . . . She has promised me that she would never cast her Eye over any thing that either [Bere] or his Presbyterian and Socinian, Partizans may publish in future; and *wisely determined* never to degrade her fair frame by answering them herself; she has, also, adjured her Friends to pass over their scurrilous publications in silence. Indeed, *this* is all who love and honor her must desire for her precious Life is *seriously at stake."*

4. Judg. 9:16–21.

5. For the Greek name of Ceylon, see HLP to LC, 13 [January 1796], n. 3.

6. For Mary Whalley, see HLP to PSW 15 October [1791], n. 9.

7. Like many of her contemporaries, HLP regarded Turkey's military efforts with suspicion. This distrust was to grow within the next few years; cf. *The Times* for 29 January 1803, which was to editorialize on Turkish incompetence and ingratitude.

8. According to *The Times*, 12 August, Pasvan Oglu had won a major victory over the Turks at Vidin.

The same newspaper on 10 September reported further that "in the beginning of last month the Janissaries at Belgrade mutinied, and compelled the *Pacha* of that place to throw himself into the citadel, with a small number of officers and men who remained faithful to him. The rebels, on this occasion, declared themselves in favour of *Paswan Oglou*." The report went on to say that "A corps of *Paswan Oglou*'s troops was then on its march to join the rebels."

9. Pasvan Oglu or Pazvantoglu (1758–1807) is associated with the hostility engendered by Turkish rule in Bulgaria, a rule that began in 1396 and ended in 1878.

He was one of the feudal lords of the Krjalis. Moved by ambition, brigandry, and a hatred of the Turks, he defeated in 1794 three large Turkish armies dispatched against him. Even as he continued his fight against the Turks, he set himself up as an independent sovereign at Vidin, where he erected handsome buildings, maintained order, levied taxes, and issued a separate coinage. In time he was to be defeated by the Turks, who nonetheless restored him to his sovereignty in and about Vidin.

10. TSW, in commenting on the *Critical Review*'s judgment of *Retrospection*, went on: "I remember an Epigram on a Mr. Rice, with a huge head, who wrote Lampoons, some years since, on the Ladies of Bath;

> 'Old Cerberus, so fierce and fell,
> Snarl'd with his three Great Heads in Hell;
> But was not half so *fell* as thee,
> Who snarl'st with *one*, as big as three.'

"So can *I fancy* these fell Hypercritics, snarling with *three venomous Tongues* each of the true *Hell Hound breed*, against your incomparable Publication.—But old Cerberus *knew his Duty*, and whom to attack or spare; but these *Puppy* Cerberus's, bark and growl, and rend, and tear away, right or wrong, without discretion or discrimination, when the *Fit* is upon them . . . and [deserve] *That* disgrace your recriminating Letter in the Gentleman's Magazine has justly covered them with, by proving their *Ignorance equal* to their Malice."

11. Newspapers in late September reported the almost immediate evacuation of Hanover by the Prussian troops. The removal had been effected by "some remonstrance of the Emperor of Russia's Minister at the Court of Berlin." See *GM* 71, pt. 2 (1801): 849.

TO PENELOPE SOPHIA PENNINGTON

Brynbella
30: November 1801.

No; thank You my Dear anxious Friend; we are pretty well, and pretty happy as Health and Happiness in this World go.[1] I have had *more* than my Share of both, blessed be God. My Master has an addition to *his* Torments—St. Anthony's Fire in and out, but much less afflicting than troublesome. It keeps him from going to Neighbour's Houses, and without *that,* there is no hope of Autumnal Society at Brynbella: it will keep him from going to *yours,* and then he must learn to swear of Dear Mr. Pennington.

Lord De Blaquiere who used to free my Covers is gone to London, and my Prudence—for the first Time in my Life:—overbalanced my Tenderness, and so I made you uneasy—and so I am glad you *were* uneasy, and there's an End. We have written about the House to Mrs. Garrart and to Harriet Lee both—They say My Lord Kinmare is in now, and will be out on the 12: January.[2] That Time will do nicely, and the poor Folks round here are glad he does not quit sooner, tho' Mr. Piozzi has given a Dozen of them good warm Winter Jackets, and a Petticoat each to the Wife—and Barley which last Year was at 32*s.* They may have now at 18*s.* and good Wheat at a Guinea, so I shall leave them with less regret this Year than last, for all those Reasons; and we employ a vast many hands in Planting.

We were at the Bishop of St. Asaph's to Dinner last Week. Hannah More's Books lay on the Drawing Room Table—he laughed at the Nonsense talked about her Marriage &c and when I seemed to fear that they would vex her—Oh No; replied he She has too much Sense not to disregard such Stuff, and too much Wit not to know how to repel it——Tell Lady Hesketh what I say,[3] and tell her in Addition that you and she and all Friends who half perswade, and half help her to be *grieved,* do her less good than will H:L:P when She protests that although Seventeen Years engaged in the *Beer Business,* none was ever found so Sour, *Stale, flat and unprofitable* as this Bristol Controversy.[4]

Mrs. Randolph has more good Understanding than any of us, but since She could not hold her dear warm-hearted Husband quite *in,* the best way now is to let him quite *out:*[5] and if he uses the Argument his Antagonist best deserves, and will best comprehend, we shall hear but little more of him: and something either Tragical or Comical *must* be done I see plainly, or poor Hannah will be wedded to his *Bier* in good earnest. My Comfortings will divert her at least, and She knows I am a Sister in Affliction; but My Countenance—unlike old Hamlets

Ghost, was *more, much* more, in Anger than in Sorrow⁶——As Dromio says to his Master in the Comedy of Errors,

—I think these Witches be afraid of Swords.

Mine are laid safe in the Red Sea you may perceive.⁷

Something is the matter at Belvedere House, I do *think;* Harriett says She has the *Black Dog* upon her Back, and writes as if wishing to be courted out of the Secret: instead of doing which, I wrote her a Rhodomontading Letter all Mirth and no Matter (as Beatrice says,)⁸ to turn the Course of her Ideas: for I wish not Confidence where real Kindness has ceased to reside: and If these Novel writing Ladies fancy that they, and they alone can read the human Mind—'tis a Mistake——Your Imagination is *bound* by the Juggler who rattles and talks while he ties a Knot in your Pocket Handkerchief—as *surely* as by the sly Thief that steals it, only the Intention is more honorable.

We shall get too late to Laura for the New year's Sermon, but I hope to stay with you till May day or very late in April—The house here is to be done up, so we are all unroosted by Painters, Whitewashers &c. for the Summer: because beautiful as dear Mrs. Randolph found it in her kind partial Fancy—nothing has ever been done to the Walls, except building them; and Cracks will be the Consequence of longer neglect.

Oh do tell the Doctor that Lord Kirkwall did *not* marry Miss Ormsby, and that everybody says—it was because he felt that he liked Miss Blaquiere better; certain it is the first Match went off——and if this second does not come on; I shall wonder.⁹

You were always more sangwine about the Benefits of Peace than I was; but Tranquillity is the best Consequence it *can* have, let's not therefore disturb that by putting Monopoly in Peoples heads or in their Mouths; Such Talk leads to nothing but Riot. If there is no Scarcity there will be no Monopoly; The People *can* monopolize nothing that is not already scarce. A Peace which leaves unresisted France Mistress of more Territory than was ever hoped for by her proudest Monarch in his proudest day; which annihilates before her Grasp, Principalities and Powers: and leaves her tributary Republics secured to her Services by the cheap Garrison, *Opinion:*—can not be viewed without horror by the mere Writer of Retrospection: tho' such were the Miseries of War, and such the acquisitions by Treaty to Great Britain; that Peace has a right not only to please, but to console and even *delight* a true English Subject / and dear Mrs. Pennington's Affectionate friend / H: L: P.

Text: Princeton University Library. *Address:* Mrs. Pennington / Dowry Square / Hot Wells / Bristol. *Postmark:* DENBIGH 224.

1. HLP responds to PSP's letter of 25 November (Ry. 568.105).
2. Valentine Browne (1754–1812) was created 14 February 1798 baron of Castlerosse and Viscount Kenmare [I]. He had married firstly in 1777 Charlotte, née Dillon (1755–82), and secondly in 1785 Mary, née Aylmer (d. 1806).
3. According to PSP's letter: "Lady Hesketh, who is still at Clifton, and myself when we

meet, for half an Hour, do nothing but deplore this most unlucky business" (i.e., More's involvement in the Blagdon controversy).

4. Even a Hamlet soliloquy can serve an HLP pun. See 1.2.133.

5. PSP wrote: "Dr. Randolph, notwithstanding his dear little wifes most vigilant precautions to keep him out of the Scrape, is at last come in for a cut from the *Mohawk*." For Randolph's oblique involvement in the Blagdon controversy, see HLP to RG, 3 February 1802.

6. Hamlet describes his father's ghost as having "A countenance more / In sorrow than in anger" (1.2.231–32).

7. Antipholus of Syracuse says to his servant Dromio: "I see these witches are afraid of swords" (4.4.147).

8. *Much Ado About Nothing*, 2.1.330.

9. For Anna Maria De Blaquiere, see HLP to LC, 19 March 1799, n. 4.

The story of Lord Kirkwall's intended nuptials is told by Farington on 1 October 1804 (6:2420).

"Miss Ormsby is the Heiress of much of the *Godolphin* fortune, may claim the *Barony* of that name. She has a good figure, is modest and amiable, & will possess £8000 a year. Such a match wd. have been a great acquisition to Lord K[irkwall]. & every preparation was made for the marriage when his attention was drawn to Miss De B[laquiere] whose Father had taken a House in the neighberhoud with a view it was believed, to bring on a Union with his Lordship. It succeeded, & Miss Ormsby was pointedly neglected for Miss De B—at a ball, which took place a week or two before Lord K was to have been married to Miss Ormsby.—The consequence of this union has been a great disappointment and unhappiness" to Lord Thomond (Kirkwall's grandfather), to his mother, and friends.

TO THE REVEREND ROBERT GRAY

Brynbella
2nd December 1801.

My learning, that the people laugh at so much more justly than they *think* they do, comes chiefly from the Spectators and Tattlers, but is not sufficient to inform me what was meant a hundred years ago in common colloquial chat by *vowelling* a man. Some of those charming papers has this phrase: 'Such a one, says he, has been vowell'd by the Count, and resolves to demand satisfaction.'[1]

I should like to know what it means. Was there a quibble intended? Had some fine fellow lost money at play to some other fine fellow, and was he forced to say I O U? When we were at Vienna our cicerone showed us these letters over the Arsenal, and asked all the gentlemen in our party if we could explain them: A. E. I. O. U. After everybody had confessed ignorance, he said 'Austriacorum Est Imperare Orbi Universo' was the device intended,[2] and I remember some of the company,—a Frenchman, I think,—objected. Buonaparte has vowelled them pretty well since then.

If this phrase means picking one's name to pieces, how terribly has poor H—nn—h M—r— been treated during this Bristol controversy! Her health, always feeble, has given way to their ill-usage, and those who are near intimates tremble for the consequence. We shall go to Bath next month, and then I will try to comfort her.[3] A sister in affliction may have peculiar chance for success; but, I don't know how it is, I never was in affliction. *My* countenance, unlike that of old Hamlet's ghost, was more, much more in anger than in sorrow, and so grew less like a ghost, I do believe in proportion as my critics charged me with loss of youth and beauty.[4] They had need be very young and handsome themselves to make such nonsense tolerated.

Text: Hayward 2:257–8.

1. In *Tatler* 12 (7 May 1709) by Steele, there is a comic dialogue among Pip, Trimmer, and Acorn. The first admits to being "voweled by the count." But the other two companions are ashamed to admit they are ignorant of the contemporary slang term for "to pay a creditor with an IOU."
2. *Menagiana* 1:403–4.
3. All during the controversy Hannah More suffered from violent headaches, which even before 1801 were severe. Once the Blagdon controversy was over, she collapsed completely. For two years she was afflicted by her self-designated "great illness." And yet after she mended, as she wrote to Wilberforce, "in that long affliction, though at one time I very seldom closed my eyes in sleep for forty days and nights, I never had one hour's great discomposure of mind, or one moment's failure of reason, though in health very liable to agitation."

But Hannah More was often ill. She "believed that God sent her poor health to turn her thoughts toward Him. When she was depressed, she thought about God, while cheerfulness attended her practical activities. She served the Lord with joy; she worshipped Him in gloom." See Mary Alden Hopkins, *Hannah More and Her Circle* (New York and Toronto: Longmans, Green, 1947), pp. 195, 198.

4. The *Critical Review* had written:
"In attempting to read the work itself, we were so disgusted with its infinitude of puerile errors, of all kinds, that we must pronounce our firm opinion, that it is ill adapted to any class of readers. To the learned, it must appear as a series of dreams by an old lady."

TO PENELOPE SOPHIA PENNINGTON

Brynbella Tuesday Night
15: December 1801.

I write to Dear Mrs. Pennington with my Glove on the right Hand, having picked the best Finger quite to Agony[1]—and almost to Danger——because of my Master getting a new and sharp Fit of Gout again in this Cold Winter Weather—which makes my finger worse as well as his Foot. Well!—Time passes away, and so do Torments; and poor Mrs. Whalley will have no more in this World. I shall have that of telling you that there will not be any *habitable Brynbella this Summer,* that is coming.——We shall be thrown on the wide World ourselves; and mean to pass the early Part of it at Streatham Park on a Visit, the latter End in Caernarvonshire, where my Lease of a little Estate is out,[2] and then call here for a Month or two in our Way back to *Winter Quarters:*——*Whence,* in the Spring

1803 It is, and has been long our fixed Intention to bring our kind partial Friend; and hold *her fast* from April to November.

On this hope of real Comfort, let us live till then and pass some chearful Hours together at Dear Bath where I would I were this Moment! Mr. Piozzi playing on the Piano e forte to Mrs. DeLuc—you and I listening, and hoarding up Chat for the half Hour after he and his Auditress are a Bed and asleep. I suppose when We are *quite alone*——You who so seldom are mysterious—will be pleased to speak *quite plain*, and tell me in so many Words what it is that this Man charges Hannah More with.[3]

"Come to the Point (says I like Escalus) and tell me what was *done* to Elbow's Wife: Make short on't I say, and *tell me* what was *done* to her."[4] This Controversy will outlast a Night in Russia when Nights are longest there. Observe that I am wholly in the Dark as to the Accusation—but Letters never convey Hints, and I never understand hints.

The Bishop of St. Asaph is no *Man of firm Nerves:*[5] 7 Years ago Hannah More could have blown him away like her Thread Paper—but now She stands still it seems, as Dr. Goldsmith said he saw a strong Fellow do at an Ale House; while some little Fellow for a Wager knocked him down with oft repeated, and well-laid-in Blows of a *Farthing Candle.*[6]

Write to me once more before we meet, and tell me that charming Lady Hesketh—(for so She will ever be;) kindly accepts my Compliments.

Mrs. Leo died three Days ago, and the Disposal of her Estate occasions much Chat among us Neighbours, but nothing is yet decided.[7]

I cannot yet rid myself of this Bristol Quarrel—If the Mores are and have been always Sectaries—why do they deny it? Where's the Harm done? I had rather they were good High-Church Folks like you and like myself, but the Religion that was good enough for Isaac Watts need not be shrunk from: What are they afraid of?[8]

Mr. Piozzi leaves his Bed today; next Monday sennight we will pack and run—*slide* rather I suppose, for there will be Ice enough.

Mrs. Hamilton tells me sweet Siddons is *alive,* but I fancy She is on no Stage now[9]—poor Mrs. Whalley's Death will grieve *her* unaffectedly: I was never intimate enough to *feel* her Loss, but She was no common Character that's certain:[10] Half a Dozen Gentlemen who lived much together abroad, were so sincerely vexed when She left presiding at their public Table, that they quitted the House——a surprizing Testimony to the Conversation Talents of one so wanting in Youth or Beauty.

Mrs. Randolph and the Doctor will not be half as glad to see me at Laura Chapel as I shall be to find myself in my *old Place:* God send us Safe among you, and make us thankful for continued Ability to move *at all:* Mr. Piozzi's hands and feet ossify as poor Mrs. Lewis's did for 20 Years together. He will soon be carried up and down in the same Manner She was.

Adieu! and tell Mr. Pennington I am sorry for his Sensibility—*His Heart* never *Ossifies.* God bless you and continue your partial kindness for all belonging to Your / H: L: P.

Text: Princeton University Library. *Address:* Mrs. Pennington / Dowry Square / Hot Wells / Bristol. *Postmark:* DENBIGH 224.

1. HLP replies to PSP's letter of 11 December (Ry. 568.106), which is unusually petulant; it assumes that HLP's attitude toward the Blagdon controversy is flippant.
2. For HLP's property in the parishes of Llangwadl and Tydweiliog, Carnarvonshire, see HLP to Hugh Griffith, 20 October 1792, n. 2.
3. PSP had written on 11 December:
" 'The Blagdon Controversy',—I am sorry to say, is any thing but *flat* and *stale*. On the contrary it seems here to be revived with fresh Spirit. . . .
"Lady Hesketh and myself, tho in the number of the sincerely *afflicted* on this Subject, are not amongst those who, in your *comical* way, you say 'help poor H. More to be *grieved*' on the occasion; for we are neither of us fortunate enough to have any immediate Intercourse with her. . . . But tho we do not *help* her to *grieve*, we are far from thinking, with the Bishop of St. Asaphs, that it is a Subject to exercise her *Wit* upon—or that *Wit* is at all a proper Engine to repel this attack—H. More is entirely of the same opinion and I understand, with true Christian Humility, is much more disposed to lay it at the *Foot of the Cross*." PSP complains that Bere has directed "the keenest of his Shafts where the *Female Bosom* only is vulnerable."
For the charges leveled by Bere against Hannah More, see HLP to PSP, 5 April, n. 7.
4. *Measure for Measure*, 2.1.115–118.
5. Macbeth (3.4.101) thinks of himself as having "firm nerves."
6. See *British Synonymy* 1:172–74, under "Dubious, Doubtful, Uncertain."
"Adverbs, or adverbial adjectives, very nearly synonymous, of which the first was most used in conversation till about twenty-five or thirty years ago, when a popular though paltry drama, by putting it ill pronounced into a clown's mouth, rendered it ridiculous; and people grew afraid of uttering the word. . . . Johnson relates a similar accident to have been the theatrical death of Thomson's Sophinisba. Slight causes will operate on the mere taste of pleasure; yet we may not unreasonably pity the author who is pommeled down thus with a farthing candle, as I have heard Dr. Goldsmith say he once saw a man eminent in strength treated at an alehouse for a wager. The manner [of] playing the trick I have forgotten; but the strong fellow was made to submit, though his antagonist had no other weapon—and therein consisted the joke. Bentley suffered much in the same way from Pope's tormenting him; but 'twas a mere temporary suffering."
7. Letitia Leo had died 12 December. For her will distributing her large property holdings in three counties of North Wales, see N.L.W., Gwysaney MSS, GR II/167.
What was remarkable about her will was that Henry Leo was the principal beneficiary. He was "now aged two years or thereabouts the natural or illegitimate Son of my said husband Daniel Leo by Mary Shepard of Usk." Indeed, the will generously provides for not only Henry Leo but for all of Daniel Leo's children should he marry again.
To her husband Daniel she left only £100 "as a small token of my remembrance" because "of his being so amply provided for in and by my said marriage settlement."
8. PSP admitted that Bere "has likewise torn away the Veil and discovered to all, what was but partially known, that H. More *has* always favored *Sectarianism* and this with every aggravation that the most consummate Malice could add to the charge."
9. SS was in London during the 1801–2 season, performing over forty times at the Drury Lane.
10. PSP had reported that Elizabeth Whalley's death on 8 December at Longford Cottage "with respect to the Time, was sudden and unexpected, tho she has been gradually sinking under such a state of Debility and encreasing Infirmities that it is more afflicting than surprizing and to herself poor Soul! a most happy exchange.—He is, as you may suppose, violently affected and strictly and earnestly prohibits all Letters and Visits of Condolence which he says his Mind cannot bear in its present and perturbed state—so that I am unacquainted with any particulars."

TO LADY WILLIAMS

No. 77 Pultney Street Bath[1]
30: January 1802

My Dear Lady Williams
   will now be recovered sufficiently[2]—or I hope so,—to be diverted with a Letter from Friends to whom her whole family is so kindly partial. The Letter would be better if I went more into public, but Mr. Piozzi's health is still so little mended, that I feel as if deserting my Post when ever I stir out in Search of Information or Amusement. The Fate of Governor Wall seems a universal Topic of Discourse just now, tho' Heaven knows the world affords Novelties sufficient to *claim* attention from wise People and *force* it even from dull ones—without the *Retrospect* of his Crimes, being added to the Catalogue of present Rareties.[3]

A Black Republic established, and as the Phrase is—*organized* in those very West Indies where they have so long been *Slaves*, is perhaps *first* on the List of Wonders; If the French subdue them (which they will *not*) I shall consider that as *Second*.[4]

Mean while here reigns perfect Liberty at home, that's certain; altho' one can say little concerning Equality: as no two People dress alike, or talk alike, or think alike and Still less do they *sing* alike. Mara delighted in displaying her unrivalled Power of running rapid Divisions with a Voice which for Strength and Clearness has no Equal at 60 Years Old and while Billington's beauty and sweetness carries away The passionate Love of her Auditors,—rests her Triumph on the Admiration of the Orchestra—which has applauded her so many Years, and which never applauds from Passion—but from Conviction of true Merit.[5]—

The Theatre I have not yet attended but am earnest to go. It exhibits Infernal Agencies as we are told, instead of Tragedy; and such low Farce in the Room of once genteel Comedy that no Tongue can express——I speak only as far as Reading goes.—Of Literary Productions those written by the women are I think best Approved; Miss Hamilton who diverted the Town with her Memoirs of Modern Philosophers, has written upon Education, and Hannah Mores admirers are flying fast away to the newer Favourite.[6] Dear Hannah More is not quite Philosopher enough to endure the Scurrility with which she has been treated by some neighbouring Enemies who persecute her almost to *Death* in the most literal sense of the Word; and their Cruelty, added to some neglects from the Public seem to go very close to her Heart.

The dashing Dames who let *nothing* go near their Hearts—or who have no Hearts I believe; are endeavouring (but vainly) to attract Attention by other Methods. I saw one upon a Dicky Box learning to drive an Empty Chariot round Laura Place Yesterday of an experienced Whip;—But tho' pretty, Young and *Confident* nobody looked, or stared, or took any Notice at all. The Lady who Tyed a Pair of Bath Garters round her head at the Ball Succeeded better, People spoke of *that* Exploit for 24 Hours at least.

Miss Williams will be sorry to know that poor Clementina Mayhew is in Danger of a Consumption and Carried to Devonshire not to the Continent that reason.[7]—Wicked and wild as Society seems to become every day there is a *little Dread* of Paris as a worse Place than either Bath or London.—

A Lady high in Rank had a Letter from a Friend in Lord Cornwallis's Suite:[8] he tells her——"how he dined at a very great Man's table—how the Company consisted of Men and Women——The latter, Naked *usque ad Umbilicum*.[9] Sir John must translate it for me. Your Ladyship and Mrs. Williams will be sufficiently shocked with the rest, when I have the honour to assure you that they sate down Indiscriminately Wives and Kept Mistresses—*all together* in perfect Freedom and Equality, after the Repast—*was shocking*." This letter is handed about.

In spite of all this however, there exists a Spirit I do not comprehend, of Admiration towards France and its Grand Monarque Buonaparte for tho' everybody is well apprized that he did not actually poyson his own sick Frenchmen in Egypt because he would not be plagued with carrying them to a Safe Place:[10] and tho' every one can tell that he massacred 1400 wretched Turks in Cold Blood one morning while he remained in the East[11]——Yet a Picture of Buonaparte is to be seen on all the Queen's Ware, Mugs &c.—all the ordinary Peoples Pocket Handkerchiefs &c. whilst Puppet shows exhibiting the Hero of Italy, and Figures imitating the Battle of Marengo are among the favourite shows of the Place—— All Printshops set out the first Consul as a Decoy to passers by and tho' the Populace in general speaks ill of him—he seems more wondered after—than abhorred at last.

Now dearest Madam have I not wearied your Ladyship's Patience? and filled my Paper completely? Have I room? No nor half Room to insert my Regards and Thanks to Sir John for his friendly and obliging Letter. Make Mr. Piozzi's truest Respects with mine acceptable to him and Mrs. Williams[12]——Does She know that Sir Walter James has been confined these Many Months with *the Same* Apprehensions of *the Same Complaint*, as her own?[13] It is situated *in his Lip*. I hope her Spirits have been raised by caressing my Sweet Godson. To him and all the Dear ones my best Wishes always flow spontaneously—receive them lovely Lady Williams from the truest of your Servants / H: L: Piozzi.

Text: Ry. 1 (1796–1802). *Address:* Lady Williams / Bodylwyddan / St. Asaph / Flintshire / N: Wales. *Postmark:* BATH.

    1. On 4 January HLP and GP "left Brynbella at 11 o'clock in the Morning." They spent successive nights at Wrexham, Shrewsbury, Iron Bridge, Worcester, Rodborough. On Saturday, 9 January they "Arrived at Bath at 2 o'clock at the House No. 21 Henrietta Street. Seven Guineas per Week, very cold House, and disagreeable Situation." By Friday, 22 January they "went in the House of Mr. Garrett, No. 77 Pultney Street at £8 per week." See HLP's "Pocket Books," 1802 (Ry. 616.2).
    2. Lady Williams's second son, Hugh (HLP's godson), was born on 8 January 1802. Becoming third baronet of Bodelwyddan (1859), he was to die in 1876.
    3. The Irish-born Joseph Wall (1737–1802) entered the army as a cadet, took part in the capture of Havana, and was elevated to the rank of captain. He served in the East India Company, where he became notorious for his duels and love affairs. In 1779 he became lieutenant governor of Goree (i.e., Senegal). A cruel disciplinarian, he had a sergeant named Benjamin Armstrong charged with mutiny and flogged to death. In England Wall was court-martialed (1782) but escaped to the Continent, where he thrived

socially. In January 1802, however, he was tried for Armstrong's murder, found guilty, and executed.

4. Toussaint l'Ouverture (1743–1803) had been born a slave in what was then the French colony of Saint Dominique. When in 1791 the slaves in the northern part of the colony revolted, Toussaint became one of their leaders. Changing sides upon need and supporting one European power and then another, he commanded four thousand men who served only him.

By 1798 or shortly thereafter, he was able to expel all foreign forces and in 1800 defeated General André Rigaud, who had created a mulatto state in the southern provinces. Toussaint was now the ruler of all Saint Dominique. Early in 1801 he took over the Spanish colony of Santo Domingo at the eastern end of the island. In the same year he took the title of governor general for life with the right to name his own successor.

What HLP did not know was that Toussaint L'Ouverture was soon to be betrayed, dying as a prisoner in France.

5. For Gertrud Elisabeth Mara, see DL to HLP, 2–10 October [1796], n. 21.

Elizabeth Billington, née Weichsel (1765 or 1768–1818), was born in London into a musical family. A child prodigy, she performed on the harpsichord and wrote sonatas before she was twelve. On 13 February 1786, she sang by royal request the part of Rosetta in Bickerstaffe's *Love in a Village*. In 1802 she was the recognized prima donna of Italian opera.

6. Elizabeth Hamilton, *Letters on the Elementary Principles of Education*, 2 vols. (Bath: G. and J. Robinson, London, 1801). For her earlier work, see HLP to Ly W, 1 February 1801.

7. Clementina Mary was the daughter of a wealthy Bath apothecary, Richard Mayhew of 1 Vineyards, a niece of William Lutwyche, and the sister of Sophia, later Lady Bayntun (d. 1830).

Clementina Mary began at this time to suffer from a "long and debilitating illness" from which she died at Sidmouth on 14 October 1816. See *GM* 86, pt. 2:569.

8. In October 1801, Lord Cornwallis had been appointed British plenipotentiary to negotiate peace with Bonaparte. He left Dover on 3 November and after an interview with the First Consul at Paris, he went on to Amiens to work out a treaty with his French counterpart, Joseph Bonaparte. After many blunders from the English party and much wrangling, a treaty was signed on 27 March 1802.

9. Cf. Horace, *Epode*, 14.8.

10. After the defeat at Acre, Bonaparte had to move twenty-three hundred sick and wounded soldiers whom Admiral Perrée refused to take on board the Jaffa flotilla. Apparently Bonaparte suggested the killing of the hopeless cases. (While this suggestion was momentarily aborted by Desgenettes, there is little doubt that these casualties were not long transported during the French retreat from Acre to Jaffa and finally to Katia.) See Chandler, p. 241; Farington 6:2100.

11. HLP refers to an incident in March 1799, when three thousand Turks in the citadel of Jaffa accepted the word of a French officer that they would be granted quarter if they surrendered. "Bonaparte ordered the execution of every man and of a further 1,400 prisoners." See Chandler, p. 236.

12. For Eleanor Williams, see HLP to the Ladies of the Williams Family, 3 May 1797, n. 1.

13. For Sir Walter James, see HLP to PSP, 27 March 1798, n. 2.

TO THE REVEREND ROBERT GRAY

Bath
Wednesday, 3rd February 1802

One always hopes that true friends are happy,—one always believes them happier than they are. You have been thinking that I was speculating on character while I was fretting over Mr. Piozzi's health, till at last I have half frighted him about my own. All will, however, be well *by and by*——and our plagues have been small compared with those of our next door neighbour, Hannah More, who has been hunted to a sick bed with strange success indeed. I flattered myself she would better have withstood the torrent of scurrility which ceases not to drive her down, as poor Hawkesworth was driven long ago.[1] Whether our friend Randolph mixed in the controversy I know not, certain it is included in the abuse;[2] but these distresses of sentiment are after all like *stage sorrow* compared to what your brother-in-law is suffering; and 'tis a serious mercy that Mrs. Gray has borne with such resignation the loss of such a daughter.[3]

When the Negroes have learned to be scholars, as they have already learned to be soldiers, a history of St. Domingo Republic will be published in *black letter*, I suppose. Oh dear! what a strange thing that is, and how observable that the very island where slavery first was instituted among Christians, should be the very first where African freedom hoists her horrible standard, a white infant on the point of pikes brandished by men of colour.[4]

Can the French subjugate this rebellious island? The West Indians with whom I have conversed say it is impossible. Meanwhile here at Bath it certainly does appear that Buonaparte is the idol of an English populace, which I consider as another novelty, but cannot possibly deny the fact, because every puppet-show exhibits the hero of Marengo on his horse, every print-shop calls in customers by an exact likeness of the great First Consul, and every linendraper tempts passengers by a bust of Buonaparte in their pocket handkerchiefs——sure that is equally new and strange, when so many of their warrior countrymen rest unadmired, while Moreau[5] is prefer'd to General Moore, and Berthier[6] set out at the windows before Abercrombie. Surely whatever *else* we can wish, novelty is no longer a thing to be cry'd for.

Text: Hayward 2:259–60.

1. Upon Garrick's recommendation in 1771, John Hawkesworth was chosen by Lord Sandwich, then first lord of the admiralty, to rework and publish an account (by several commanders and Joseph Banks) of the late voyages to the South Seas. The manuscript being handed over to him, Hawkesworth left it virtually untouched and sold it to Cadell and Strahan for £6,000. The work appeared in 1773 as *An Account of the Voyages undertaken by order of his present Majesty for making Discoveries in the Southern Hemisphere*, etc., 3 vols. Hawkesworth listed himself as the author.
   The work was attacked for inaccuracies and indecencies, for an antireligious position. Thurlow, e.g., in his speech on the copyright question on 24 March 1774 condemned Hawkesworth's book as "a mere composition of trash."
2. The Reverend Francis Randolph did not take part overtly in the Blagdon contro-

versy, but as a prebendary of Bristol he would have been an object of abuse, even if unnamed, along with Dr. Moss, bishop of Bath and Wells. The primary targets of Bere and his supporters were Beilby Porteus, bishop of London; Lord Loughborough; Sir Abraham Elton; Samuel Horsley, bishop of Rochester; George Pretyman, bishop of Winchester; William Wilberforce. See particularly Edward Spencer, *Truths respecting Mrs. Hannah More's Meeting-Houses, and the Conduct of Her Followers; Addressed to the Curate of Blagdon* (Bath, 1802), pp. 9–10.

3. On 1 February (Ry. 571.23), RG wrote to HLP: "You must employ your Talents . . . in writing to console me, who with all my Family here have for some Weeks been in very great Affliction for the loss of a very Dear and admirable Sister whom I believe you have seen, and whom if you did see I am sure you must have admired as a very amiable Woman. I speak of my youngest Sister who was married to a very worthy man and settled in Somersetshire. . . . She has left two very interesting daughters, and a most distressed Husband who has not yet recovered the least composure, or consented to leave the scene of his Affliction."

On 27 December 1801 died Anne, wife of Samuel Norman of Taunton.

4. HLP knew that slavery had flourished in a Christian Rome until at least the fourth century. But in this letter she alludes to its practice in the Caribbean. Slave labor had been introduced into America by the Spanish colonists of Santo Domingo in the late fifteenth and early sixteenth centuries. See HLP to Q, 19 December 1794, n. 8.

5. For Jean-Victor Moreau, see HLP to LC, 2 July 1799, n. 12.

6. Louis-Alexandre Berthier (1753–1815), maréchal de France, prince de Neufchâtel et de Wagram, was commissioned in 1766, rising in rank so that in March 1795 he was promoted to général de brigade and sent as chief of staff to the Army of the Alps and Italy. Involved in the First Italian Campaign and later in the expedition to Egypt and Syria, he commanded the Army of Reserve for the Second Italian Campaign. From October 1800 until 1807 he was minister of war.

For General Sir Ralph Abercromby, see HLP to TSW, 23 April 1801, n. 4.

TO PENELOPE SOPHIA PENNINGTON

Wensday 10: [February 1802][1]

Will you not be very sorry Dear Mrs. Pennington to Hear that our Darling Doctor has got the Complaint himself?[2] A Sore Throat and Hoarseness such as mine exactly, with Pain in the Chest and Gout upon him too! Poor Fellow! I thought the Day so raw last Monday, there was no trusting it; altho' I had gained Permission; but Yesterday Pultney Street and Sydney Place witnessed my wond'rous Exertions.

At four o'clock while we were dining, entered Parry; but could scarce hold a Conversation, and to day I trotted off to the Circus and enquired after *him*.[3]

The Maid gave a bad report, but he was gone out after these *Guineas* for which so many Men in so many Modes risque Ease and Health and Life. Pretty Mrs. Carrick gave me an interesting Account of *her* Husband's Illness last Year. Hannah More is mending; She will live to speak the epilogue of this wretched Drama, after *itself* has been *hissed* I hope: and you will come home o'Fryday, and we will be merrier than we have been, and see the *Jew* and have done with the Doctor.[4]—The Bristol *Folks* have much of my Esteem for Driving off the Phantoms:⁵ let us have solid Foolery at worst. Oh come home and save me from reading any more modern Plays—among which The new Opera Chains for the heart must have the Pre Eminence—It is foolish beyond all Folly; past, present and to come.⁶

Mr. Pennington will be a most welcome Visitant whenever he finds it not inconvenient to come and be thanked for the true Pleasure with which his Wife's valuable Company is always received by her Obliged and Affectionate / H: L: P.

Present us kindly to all your Inmates, my Master sits on the Sopha, and hears the Ladies say how well he looks.

Text: Princeton University Library. *Address:* Mrs. Pennington / Dowry Square / Hot Wells / Bristol. *Postmark:* BATH.

1. This letter may be dated February 1802, when the 10th was a Wednesday. See also n. 6.
2. For Caleb Hillier Parry, see HLP to PSW, 1 September [1789], n. 7.
3. Dr. Parry's surgery was at 27 Circus, Bath.
4. HLP's wordplay was based on a popular farce—*The Jew and the Doctor* (1798)—by Thomas John Dibdin (1771–1841).
5. Bristol Hotwells was largely frequented by the mortally ill, particularly those suffering from tuberculosis and other respiratory ailments. Yet during periods of remission they participated in the usual social activities of a spa, "Driving off the Phantoms."
6. Prince Hoare (1755–1834) wrote the libretto for *Chains of the Heart,* first performed at Covent Garden, 9 December 1801, and often thereafter for the next few months.
    It was published as *Chains of the Heart; or, The Slave by Choice.* Music composed by Joseph Mazzinghi and William Reeve. 3 Acts. (London: Barker and Son [etc.], 1802).

TO THE REVEREND ROBERT GRAY

No. 77, Pultney Street,
Tuesday, 17th March 1802

Has it been in your way to look at a Miss Baillie's Dramas written, not for the stage, but for purpose of tracing the progress of the passions? Her *Tragedy* on *Hatred* was deservedly admired three years ago——and called De Montfort. She has now published a *Comedy* on *Hatred* very striking indeed, and possessing, in my mind, wonderful merit.¹ Miss Hamilton wins all hearts in this town, which is full of showy talkers——I get more conversation here than in London. Our modern Plurality of Worlds is much admired,² and justly——my worst fear is lest, in these daring days of bold and unauthorized conjecture, some one should start out, and go as far *below,* as Mr. Nares has gone *above,* the old standard.³ We might then see printed George Psalmanazar's speculative ideas concerning the souls of brutes, and have old Cicero rummaged for quotations.⁴ Mr. Piozzi's notion of modern music helps me to illustrate my own meaning. "*Variations* are very entertaining," says he, "but I like a quick return to the *subject*, which never should be too far forsaken."

Text: Hayward 2:260–61.

1. Early in 1802, Joanna Baillie issued the second series of *Plays on the Passions*, which included a comedy on hatred called *The Election*. Along with it were *Ethwald* (on ambition), a tragedy in two parts, and *The Second Marriage*, a comedy on ambition.
For an analysis and judgment of *The Election*, see Allardyce Nicoll, *A History of English Drama, 1660–1900*, vol. 4, *Early Nineteenth Century Drama, 1800–1850* (Cambridge: Cambridge University Press, 1955), pp. 208, 257–58.
The Election, to which music had been added, was performed in June 1817.

2. Edward Nares, ἙΙΣ ΘΕΟΣ, ἙΙΣ ΜΕΣΙΤΗΣ; *or, an Attempt to Shew How Far the Philosophical Notion of A Plurality of Worlds Is consistent, or not so, with the Language of Holy Scriptures* (London: Printed for F. and C. Rivington [etc.], by R. Rickaby, 1801).

3. Edward Nares (1762–1841). An Oxonian, he graduated B.A. from Christ Church in 1783 and M.A. in 1789. From 2 August 1788 to his marriage in 1797, he was a fellow of Christ Church.
In 1797 he had married Lady Georgina Charlotte, a daughter of George Churchill Spencer, duke of Marlborough. She had died at Bath 15 January 1802, at the age of thirty-one.

4. In *An Historical and Geographical Description of Formosa, an Island subject to the Emperor of Japan* (1704), Psalmanazar writes about "the souls of brutes" in a section covering pp. 206–9. For Cicero on the same subject see, e.g., his *Tusculan Disputations*, 4.14–32, and the commentary by Bayle 4:552n.

TO LADY WILLIAMS

Bath Thursday
18: March 1802

My Dear Lady Williams sends me somewhat a melancholy but a truly welcome Letter: I thank you for it a thousand Times, and feel Sorry on every Side my Head and Heart, that I cannot in return—send a more cheerful one than this will be to amuse the partial Friends at Bodylwyddan—but Mr. Piozzi is laid up with the Gout again, and has not quitted his Bed for ½ an hour these last 8 or 10 Days. In the mean Time I must not complain of my own Confinement, where numberless agreeable Acquaintance are dropping in all Day, and soothing my Anxiety with their pleasing Conversation. Mrs. Pennington—of whom your Ladyship has heard me speak in Terms of high Esteem, has kindly remained with me all the while, and if the News of every passing Hour fails to bring in *Forage* for Chat; We read to one another by Turns.

Do you remember the Tragedy on Hatred which pleased you all so much two Years ago? The Author has published a Comedy on the same Subject—*so pretty!* I have bought the Book, and hope to divert the same dear Interesting Amiable Party with *that*—this next Autumn——Heaven and the Gout permitting.

My Godson will be well then, and short Coated; and very charming——sweet

Emma must recover tho', and her eldest Sister keep up her Dignity of Appearance to make us all happy.[1] I shall try to see the Princess who is of the same Age when I get to London, and give you an Account which holds the little Head highest.[2]

Mrs. Williams will receive Consolation in hearing that there is good hope of Sir Walter James.[3] Although this Age is I think pregnant with more Evils than any I have read or heard about, there are in it more Efforts made for Alleviation of Ill than ever yet were attempted. It is boldly and perhaps truly asserted that Oyl will *cure*—and stop Infection of the Plague——my Heart assures me that it is good in every *Schirrhous Tumour*. Your dear Mamma has certainly found Benefit from the Lancashire Application—was [it] not the *Oyl* which was useful? And would not *any* Oyl do? There is a Talk now of trying it on Gout. I will find out Walmesley and do your Commission with Pleasure concerning the *Views*;[4] Mr. Leo has no Mercy upon *ours* from Brynbella: If he cuts those Trees 'twere better to dispark the Place at once and make Enclosures—I should like that better than a bare *Knoll*.[5] People here seem to fancy if once the Peace gets signed, no Man will ever want Money more, and no Woman want Amusement: No Estates will be sold nor no Sorrows known. How *can* they think so? Buonaparte will scarce *indulge* us I suppose, without securing Malta for himself; and then our East India Gentlemen may look to their possessions, for the Danger will be great.[6]

The West seems getting into Black and Tawny Hands as fast as possible, and one Excuse for our haste to make Friends with the first Consul is a Desire of seeing Europeans at least our Neighbours at Jamaica rather than Africa's Woolly-headed Sons:[7] In fine The existing World is hard *pressed* somehow—I think by an unseen tho' strongly felt—and irresistible Power.

Some witty Person said the other Day that England resembled Issachar in the Bible—"an Ass between two Burthens;" The Burden of *War* said he—and the Burden of *Peace*.[8]

There are all manner of Inventions at the same Time getting ready on both Sides to make the next War most dreadful and decisive: Colonel Blaquiere has exhibited a very important Improvement in our Artillery,[9] and 'tis well known that our Enemies are learning to go under Water and by a new Contrivance—— (not yet exhibited)——blow up our best Ships unobserved.[10]

But I will relate no more conjectures, rather finish with a well known certainty, that every Part of Your Ladyships Household is dear to us; that every good Wish on our Part awaits you all: and that I have the Honour to be ever / Your Ladyships and Sir John / Williams's Affectionate as Obliged / H: L: Piozzi.

A Thousand Compliments to Miss Williams, True Regards to Mr. W: Williams[11] when you see him.

Text: Ry. 2 (1802–6).

---

1. Ly W now had four children: John, aged eight; Harriet, five; Emma, almost four; Hugh, three months.

2. For Princess Charlotte Augusta, born in 1796, see HLP to LC, 13 January 1796, n. 2; to PSP, 6 or 7 September 1800 and n. 5.

3. See HLP to PSP, 27 March 1798, n. 2.

4. Thomas Walmsley (1763–1805), a landscape painter, lived in Bath. He was noted for his series of views, capably reproduced in aquatints by others: e.g., views of the Dee and North Wales (1792–94); larger views of North Wales (1800); etc.

5. For Daniel Leo and his tree cutting at Llannerch Park, see HLP's letter to him [ca. 1 March 1795].

6. HLP recognized that Malta was a bargaining point at Amiens. According to the treaty, "The 4th Germinal, in the year 10 (March 25, 1802)," the islands of Malta, Gazo, and Camino "shall be restored to the Order of St. John of Jerusalem. . . . They will there form a general Chapter, and proceed to the election of a Grand Master, chosen from among the natives of the nations which preserve their language [i.e., Maltese]." To guarantee the independence of Malta, the British agreed to evacuate their forces within three months and to join with France, Austria, Spain, Russia, and Prussia, in pledging the neutrality of the island. See *GM* 72, pt. 1 (1802): 453.

7. HLP admired the courage of Toussaint L'Ouverture in fighting French rule in Santo Domingo even as she admired his effort to frustrate the practice of slavery. Nevertheless, she feared the spread of a black rebellion into places like Jamaica, which had been claimed by Great Britain in 1670.

8. Gen. 49:14.

9. William De Blaquiere (1778–1851), who was to become a general in the army (1841) and third baron De Blaquiere (1844).

10. The first practical submarine is attributed to Cornelis J. Drebbel, ca. 1620. The first such vessel used in combat was invented by the American David Bushnell in 1776. Its principles were later developed by Robert Fulton for the construction of the *Nautilus*, a submarine successfully operated (1800–1801) on the Seine and at Le Havre.

11. HLP refers to Sir John Williams's unmarried sister, MW, and to his brother William Williams (1774–1829), rector of Saint George's, Denbigh. See the "Burial Register," Llanynys (C.R.O., Clwyd); HLP to Ly W, 18 December 1798, n. 1.

TO THE REVEREND LEONARD CHAPPELOW

Bath
1: May 1802

Dear Mr. Chappelow

You are very kind indeed to let us know how happy you are all at charming Weston, which will daily become more beautiful, and its Environs more chearful under the Auspices of its lovely Mistress, who I rejoyce to hear reaps *some* of her Reward in this Life.[1]

Lord Torrington is likely to spend an Old Age of great Felicity. There *are* People in high and low Stations particularly fortunate in their Children. Our Old Acquaintance Mr. Este is of the Number——You recollect Mr. Este——He was no *rich* Man I believe when we knew him, but was caring (among all his Flights) how to bring forward a handsome Boy, an ugly Boy, and an awkward little Girl he had. Well! they are all grown up now: The Lady is very elegant indeed; and tho' not quite a Beauty, justly admired for her Person and Conduct.[2] She has married a West India Merchant with 10000£ per Annum and 40000£ in the Stocks[3]——and they have bought *Persfield near Chepstow.* The handsome Boy turns out a capital Scholar, and is bred to Practice of Physick[4]——The ugly Boy has married Sir Robert Smith's Daughter with an immense Fortune, and has established himself as a Banker at Paris, in the most superb Style possible—all this in ten Years.[5]

We shall see some of their Flash in London soon I suppose; mean while coax Lord Bradford to free the enclosed to our fair Recluses, who hear of all these Events without participating of any. In the Peace however we are all alike concerned, and truly delighted am I to be at a Distance from the Noise of rejoycing: Every body is delighted at feeling themselves freed from the Income Tax, and nobody cares how miserable Europe is now, or how much more miserable She *will* be—when a Division of the old Turkish Empire takes Place, and brings on a fresh War.[6] To be sure we *may* not live to see the Occurrence; and the first Consul *may* be blown up before it happens, or he *may* be entertained with the Tragedy of *Toussaints* abroad,[7] or his own *Comedie de la Religion* at home; and be delayed in his Project.[8]

So we must heal our Wounds and be happy, and Adieu Dear Mr. Chappelow; when we meet next it will be at No. 5 George Street Manchester Square.

Accept our united Regards and / believe me ever yours / faithfully / H: L: P.

Text: Ry. 561.116.

1. The "Mistress" at Weston was Lucy Elizabeth, Lady Bradford, daughter of the widowed fourth viscount Torrington. See HLP to Sophia Byron, 2 June [1788], n. 7.

2. At St. George's, Hanover Square, on 9 June 1801, were married Nathaniel Wells, of St. James, Westminster, and Harriet Este of the parish of St. George. A minor, she was married by license and with paternal consent.

3. Nathaniel Wells (d. 1852) bought the Piercefield estate near Chepstow in 1802. The purchase price for the mansion house along with several farms and lands in various parishes as well as the manor of Saint Kinsmark (or Kingsmark) was £90,000. An offer of £110,000 for the entire estate was made in 1825 but the offer was rejected. Wells occupied Piercefield until 1845. He was in London two years later and spent his remaining years in Bath. See P.R.O., Prob. 11/2157/606.

According to Farington, he was "a West Indian of large fortune, a man of very gentlemanly manners, but so much a man *of Colour* as to be but little removed from a Negro" (6:2017).

4. For the "handsome" Michael Lambton Este and his brothers, see HLP to Sophia Byron, 3 August [1798], n. 3.

5. Charles Lambton, later Baron Este, had recently married "at Lord Whitworth's chapel at Paris . . . [the] daughter of the late" Sir Robert Smith, baronet. See *GM* 73, pt. 1 (1803): 380.

Sir Robert, who had died in Paris 12 April 1802 (but was buried at Berechurch, near Colchester), had married 10 September 1776 Charlotte Sophia Delaval, née Blake (d. 4 February 1823; buried at Versailles). They had one son, George Henry (b. 1784), who became sixth baronet, and two daughters, Louisa Caroline (alive in 1838) and Charlotte Sophie (ca. 1778–1857). The latter married Charles Lambton Este, who had served in her father's banking firm in Paris; Louisa married his brother Thomas Este. See Prob. 11/1377/500, proved (London) 26 June 1802, for Sir Robert's will.

For the death of Charlotte Este, see *The Times,* 7 March 1857; also C.R.O., Essex.

6. HLP saw Turkey as eager to appease France and yet weakened internally by the insurrection of Pasvan Oglu. Thus, *GM* in February pointed out that "Citizen Sebastiani, arrived from Constantinople, was presented yesterday to the First Consul, to whom he delivered a letter from the Sultan Selim. Citizen Sebastiani informed the First Consul of the distinguished manner in which he was received by the Sultan, and the principal officers of the Porte" (72, pt. 1: 170).

Moreover in European Turkey—as HLP interpreted the situation—the revolt of the Janissaries and their murder of the Pacha of Belgrade, Mustapha, on 27 December, further weakened the Porte. By March, *GM* reported that "the Grand Signior is much affected by the assassination of the Pacha of Belgrade," and resolved to send "60,000 men against Passwan Oglu" (72, pt. 1: 263).

7. Dated 9 February 1802, dispatches from General Leclerc and Admiral Villaret indicated the need "to use force against Toussaint, notwithstanding the supposed understanding between the French Government and the Negro Chief." Early in the fighting, however, conciliatory gestures were made toward Toussaint. Still, the struggle continued at least through May with the French meeting "great and numerous" obstacles in fighting "of the most bloody and obstinate description." See *GM* 72, pt. 1 (1802): 266, 466.

8. HLP refers to the concordat of 15 July 1801, approved by the Corps législatif on 8 April 1802. Its seventeen articles represented the essentials of a working agreement between the republic and the papacy. The so-called Organic Articles, tacked on to the concordat, were intended to abort any fraternization between the French bishops and the pope, to subordinate the church to the state. See the "Convention *Between the French Republick and his Holiness Pius VII.* exchanged *Sept. 10, 1801*" as cited in the April issue of *GM* 72, pt. 1:360–61.

On Easter Sunday (18 April) Bonaparte rode in state from the Tuileries to Nôtre Dame, accompanied by a procession of generals, officials, and diplomatic representatives. There he heard a pontifical high mass with a Te Deum in honor of the pacification of Europe and of the Catholic Church. See *GM* 72, pt. 1:362–63; J. M. Thompson, *Napoleon* (New York: Oxford University Press, 1952), pp. 188–89.

TO PENELOPE SOPHIA PENNINGTON

Saturday 22: May 1802
George Street
Manchester Square
London. No. 5

My Dear Mrs. Pennington

will begin to expect *Accounts,*—and I think the first Thing to give *Account* of—is our House; wherein was no Bed, no Fire, and no Spit—upon our first arrival:[1] *here* therefore none save a Negative Inventory of Felicities can be given—but we hire, and we croud, and we dine out; and we endure the Inconveniencies with the more Philosophy as neither House nor Lodgings nor Room even in a Hôtel can be got—nearer to Christian Dwellings than Cecil Street in the Strand where Governor Bruce has housed himself.[2] So much for *Residence.*

The Cards of Visitors and Inviters however cover our little Table and we have already passed Three Pleasant Evenings enough.—The first at Dear Siddons's where Lady Percival,[3] Mrs. Barrington,[4] Mrs. FitzHugh,[5] and Mr. Whalley, all met us—and we talked of you: and everyone talked as you would have wished to hear, but Mrs. Siddons disclaims Letterwriting and Says her *Friends* must be contented without being her *Correspondents*. Among them they perswaded us to push for Places at the Theatre *next Night,* where Hermione's Statue was exhibited for the last Time.[6] I never did see anything so admirable, or so much like a *Statue* of our lovely Actress, for it really did *Seem Stone:* and the whole was got up with such Taste and Splendour that I wished for Garrick to witness the Magnificence of modern Drury Lane.[7] He would have wondered tho' what was become of his old Florizel and Perdita[8]—Barry[9] and Mrs. Cibber. Kemble played Leontes better than I ever saw him do anything since the *Regent;*[10] Apropòs to which, here is the *Author* looking as well as ever, handsome, gay, and brilliant. Mrs. Greatheed alters, and becomes very fat; their Habitation is said to be fixed at Guy's Cliffe, though they are hastening to Paris as I understand, where Helen Maria Williams and the famous Polish hero *Koskiusko* attract general Notice.[11] Buonaparte is considered as tottering on an illfixed Seat of Power;—if he can once convert it to a *Throne,* it will perhaps stand firmer.

We dined with Miss Thrales yesterday, the Party particularly agreeable, and very good *talkers* in it. We Women retired to Coffee as the Clock struck *nine.* The Men followed in less than an hour, and when Tea was taken away at 11 o'clock, we came home to sleep, and the rest went out to various Parties for the *Evening.*

Fryday was passed at Streatham; little Salusbury seems much improved—I heard his whole Class say their Lesson, and made Observations like those of Mrs. Quickly in the *Merry Wives of Windsor.*[12] It was in those Characters Susanna and Sophia shone it seems, at the last Masquerade—dressed exactly alike for Mrs. Ford and Mrs. Page.[13] I wish my rich Tenant Mr. Giles would get a Wife that one might with better Grace accept his kind Invitations to Streatham Park which never was so fine before,[14]—Braave Alteraations!! Maister Whalley! *Chickens to peck*—above all. They have 160 feeding, and we pay three half Crowns a Couple here in London Every thing double the Bath Price, and Lady Orkney says 'tis no better, but rather worse in Wales.

Miss Blaquiere is supposed to mend; our dear Countess protests there is no danger but from her own Giddiness of Spirit—and her Mother's anxiety of Care.

Mr. Piozzi bids me not shut up my Letter till I have added his Surprize that no one has yet applied concerning some Money which you wrote about before we left Bath.

The Weather is warm today and I am glad, because all the World raved so while it was Cold—and sure enough I felt quite *starving* in a crouded Theatre where one should have expected Suffocation: My Nose has been blown half off ever since that Night at the Play—Yours is quite well I hope. My Master is all alive and completely / Yours, as is his / H: L: P.

Give our truest Regards to your Household, and accept every Kind Wish and write soon, and remember that all this Stuff was written in the Dark—how you will read it I know not.

Text: Princeton University Library. *Address:* Mrs. Pennington / Dowry Square / Hot Wells / Bristol. *Postmark:* MA 22 802.

1. On 13 May the Piozzis left Bath and traveled to London, arriving at 5 George Street on the 17th. For this house they paid six guineas a week. See HLP's "Pocket Book," 1802 (Ry. 616.2).
2. Charles Andrew Bruce (1768–1810), the third son of Charles (1732–71), fifth earl of Elgin, was governor of Prince of Wales's Island. HLP knew Bruce from her last visit to Bath. She notes in her "Pocket Book" that she and GP dined at his house on 20 April.
3. On 10 March 1792, Bridget Wynn (d. 1826) married John Perceval (1767–1835), styled Viscount Perceval until 1822; fourth earl of Egmont (1822).
4. Jane, née Guise (d. 1807), was the second wife of Shute Barrington, bishop of Durham.
5. Charlotte Hamilton (1767–1855) had in July 1792 married William Fitzhugh (1757–1842). Earlier he had gone to China as a factor of the East India Company and made a fortune. He bought the Bannister Estate in Millbrook parish near Southampton shortly before his marriage. He was M.P. for Tiverton; a friend of SS, who named him executor. See C.R.O., Hampshire.
6. According to the "Pocket Book," HLP and GP saw *The Winter's Tale* on 19 May, with *The Anatomist* as the afterpiece. See the *Morning Chronicle*'s advertisement on 11 May.
For SS, Hermione was a new part in which she opened on 25 March. She chose the role deliberately, recognizing that she was no longer slim. When, therefore, she stood on the pedestal, carefully draped from the waist down in order to conceal her stoutness, she focused the attention of her audience on the perfection of her head and shoulders. After she came to life and embraced Perdita, " 'the heart of everyone who saw her,' " wrote Campbell, " 'must throb and glow at the recollection.' " See Yvonne Ffrench, *Mrs. Siddons, Tragic Actress* (1954), p. 218.
7. An allusion to John Philip Kemble's emphasis on the physical appearance of his important productions at Drury Lane, particularly on scenery and costuming. His efforts in this direction allowed Boaden to write: " 'All the truth, all the uniformity, all the splendor and the retinue of the stage came in, but did not die, with Mr. Kemble' " (Herschel Baker, *John Philip Kemble* (1942), p. 268.
8. Garrick's successful *Florizel and Perdita*, "A Dramatic Pastoral in three Acts. Altered from the Winter's Tale of Shakespear," was first performed 21 January 1756 with Garrick as Leontes and Cibber as Perdita, and published in 1758.
Garrick's play is built primarily on the acts 4 and 5 of *The Winter's Tale*, with the early action of the original compressed into a 150-line prologue narrative.
9. There is no record of Spranger Barry (1719–77) playing Florizel. But HLP would have associated him with Susannah Maria Cibber, née Arne (1714–66), because they were friends, protégés of Garrick, and fellow performers, whether at the Drury Lane or Covent Garden.
10. Despite several eighteenth-century adaptations of *The Winter's Tale*, Kemble on 25 March produced a version that was nearly complete Shakespeare. (He omitted only the speech of Time as Chorus and used Garrick's ending.) In the spring of 1802, Kemble was a greatly admired Leontes.
11. Thaddeus Kosciusko (1746–1817) was very visible as a visitor—among many foreigners—to the salon of Helen Williams during the Peace of Amiens. They were politically close; they shared the same friends and ideas of government, the same suspicion of Napoleon. For HLP on the Polish revolutionary, see *Retrospection* 2:507.
12. See *The Merry Wives of Windsor*, 4.1, during which Evans examines William's knowledge of Latin. Mistress Quickly, standing by, is scandalized by what seem to be the bawdy syllables uttered by the boy while she herself habitually falls into unconscious obscenities.
13. Characters in *The Merry Wives of Windsor*, who worked together to make a laughingstock of Falstaff when they learned that he courted both of them.
14. See HLP to LC, [18] May [1800], n. 18.

25 May 1802

TO LADY WILLIAMS

> London George Street
> Manchester Square No. 5
> 25: May 1802

Your Ladyship—my dearest Madam—shall now have a long Letter with a new Date from the *great* City of London—because so much greater since I saw it last, that upon my honour I can hardly believe my own Eyes, or find my own Way up and down. The Truth is, that last Year having set up our Temporary Residence in Leicester Square, and visiting *these* Parts only in a Carriage I was not aware of the Town's Increase, which amounts almost to Immensity. All Marybone, Paddington, Pancras—once neighbouring Villages: now form part of our enormous Whole; and when I was in Beautiful Fitzroy Square Yester morning—*on Foot*—asking what Church that was over against me, and a Person replied—*Islington;* my Astonishment was indeed prodigious.

Mr. Piozzi has not been Idle concerning Your Ladyship's Commission for a Grand Piano e forte: He fell in Love with one at Bath which we paid Hire for whilst we lived in Pultney Street, and which I often heard him say he did not expect to find greatly excelled by any that London could produce, having a peculiarly fine *Touch,* with the additional Keys beside, and its Appearance (tho' not quite new out of the Maker's hand,)—exceedingly elegant. Having examined Numbers *here,* and observing them to be much more costly than admirable; Mr. Piozzi has upon mature Deliberation *fixed on that,* and we shall see and renew our Acquaintance with it at Dear Bodylwyddan.—One Reason of his Preference is the Happiness he felt in his Experience of its peculiar Virtue for *keeping in Tune.*

'Tis now Time to tell the Price, which is only *40 Guineas,* to which some additional expense *must* be added for the Cover &c. The Instrument will be brought hither, and from hence take its Journey to Chester.

We are here in a pretty little House, far inferior to that we commonly occupy at Bath, but 'tis a favour we can have any House at all; so full is the Town, and so high prized every Place of Residence——Show and Balls and Theatres were never so crouded. I was among 4 or 5 Thousand who got into Drury Lane to see charming Siddons stand for the Statue of Hermione in Shakespear's Winters Tale: and what perhaps surprized me most—was that I felt perishing with *Cold,* but it happened just before this violent and sudden Change in the Weather. Every one has a Friend sick and many are in Mourning for dead ones; yet Gayety goes on with a Rage unknown before——More Equipages, and those more ugly and awkward than ever London exhibited. The Carriages do all *but* Drag upon the Ground they are hung so low; and People call them Bond Street Muddies.

Magnificence and Meanness may be seen every Day in Perfection about this great Metropolis, and to say Truth 'tis *not* quite easy to separate them. If you go to a grand Dinner—it is Odds but the Cook was *hired* to dress it, and the Plate to send it up upon.—The Chairs are all hired except just a few which nobody sits upon; and I am told that a Young Man often *hires* a Lady for a Week—with Furniture and Lodging, besides hiring Birds to Sing to her—and Flowers to perfume her Apartments. In 8 or 9 Days the Lady and the Roses fade upon his

Eye——and another fortnight sees the same farce played in another Street by the same Gentleman, who drives his Muddy to another Quarter of the Town upon the same Business of Hiring.

Now Ladies, ask Dear Sir John, how this system would suit *his* good Sense, and steady Principle? But I must tell your Ladyship how much more costly every living Article is in London than in pretty Bath, which I now prefer upon Experience to this Place of Confusion——besides that the Meat is so much worse here than there, and Poultry too: I feel quite disgusted.

Let me have a Letter to say your dear Household is all well, and write *soon*, for nothing shall keep us here long——but 'tis silly to go before the [King's] Birthday.

The little Princess is out of Town—I wanted to compare her with your eldest darling—but here's my Paper all gone and no Room to tell how Truly I am your Ladyship's ever faithful / H: L: P.

Text: Ry. 2 (1802–6). *Address:* Lady Williams / at Bodylwyddan / near St. Asaph / Flintshire / N. Wales. *Postmark:* MA 25 802.

TO PENELOPE SOPHIA PENNINGTON

No. 5 George Street
Manchester Square
Wensday 2: June 1802

My dear Mrs. Pennington's beautiful Letter is the Picture of her Mind,[1] a Mind which only this vast Town can fill—and She starves at pretty *Bristol* as I call it, like a large Fish put in a small pond pining for more Space, and more of Something to occupy that Space. My Taste is different: I really feel more confounded than amused at every public Place, more Stunned than Informed by every Conversation, and more generally perplexed than pleased with the Multitude of Faces, Voices, and Caprices that surround me.

Banti[2] and Billington sung three Nights ago at Viganoni's Benefit,—we heard them; not a Duet, Two separate Songs of the same Class; Italian airs and both of them Bravura.[3] When they had done—I am a *Bantist* says one Critic, Ah! long live Billington exclaims another, *hers* is the only strait Road to Fortune and to Fame.—*All* appeared quite *distracted* with the Delight they had enjoyed yet none seemed *satisfied:* for scarce a Female in the Room except myself went home to Bed at Midnight—but some at Ranelagh, some at my Lady Pomfret's[4] disposed of the Hours *once* consecrate to Sleep: while many filled the back Rooms of Fancy Dress Makers, who this Year keep Houses open all Night for *various Purposes:* the ostensible one (and that rational enough too,) is that the Women may chuse Habits unobserved by each other, for these Innumerable Masquerades, where two or three different Characters are supported every Evening by Ladies of the Haut Ton; increasing Expence, and facilitating Intrigue, in a Manner hitherto unexampled. *One* Consequence of all this is our paying ½ a Guinea for Chickens—the *Couple* I mean—and 9d. o'Pound for what I should have termed *Soup Meat* at Bath Market. *Another,* happier Consequence to Country Rustics like *us,* will be Reconcilement to quieter Scenes and far more tranquil Pleasures.

I grow very much to resemble the Ill bred Fellow You and I used to laugh about, who when Lord Mount Edgecumbe shewed him the Glories of our grandest Sea View from our most cultivated Spot of Earth in Devonshire, commanding the Exits and Entrances of Fleets, Armies, Commerce &c. from Plymouth Sound and Dock;[5]—declared that he had been exceeding happy at the *Leasowes,* for that he liked *Inland* Prospects (for his Part,) and *River Fish.*

In no unsimilar ill humour, do I vaunt the Comforts of Bath Society and a Sedan Chair—when the Pole of some gay Carriage runs into our Pannel; or when to avoid *that,* I take a run in the Rain and wet my Feet upon their wide Trottoirs.

Apropòs to Bath Conquests made, it appears I have retained but one. General Smith is *faithless,* and has so completely forgotten us he never has left a Card.[6] Mr. Simmons is a fav'rite among the Great, and we humble Lodgers are not likely to be remembered, while Suites of splendid Apartments in every grand Street and Square, are open to Talents—of whatever kind.[7]

Edmund Charlton alone *is true.*[8] I have a Letter from *him* signed my very *Dutyful and Affectionate friend;* and saying he is *less unhappy* now, than when he wrote his Mama word he was *miserable.* Mr. Davies read the Epistle with me, and we agreed he would turn out a fine fellow. Our own Titmouse bids fair to possess Abilities for Bustle, and by the Time he comes into the World—it will be a Mad World enough.

Well! I can yet make *new* Conquests—Lord Stanhope professes himself my admirer and the Admirer of *my Books.*[9] Lady Corke called *him* and about 300 People much round her last Night—on the Spur of a Moment, because Mr. Piozzi who had met her in Cumberland Street, had promised to sing at a *very private* party for her Ladyships Amusement:[10] and there was H: L: P caressed by all the *Liberty Lovers*[11]—Sweet Lady Derby more lovely than them all, and protesting that my Husband never looked younger nor sung better. There was a Mr. Moore,[12] a new Favourite with the Public—who makes his own Music and Poetry, and pleases People very much—a Sort of English Improvisatore—and there were the Abrahams[13]—and there were everybody—and all our Talk was the Terrors and Riots of a Masked Ball held the Night before at Cumberland House—now the Union Club.[14] Many Women were hurt, and many frighted—
—my Susan Thrale came off with a black Eye but her Fingers were well, and she played on the Harp at Lady Cork and Orrery's—Sophia went for a Comic Muse but said the End was very nearly Tragical: Those who fainted from Fear were trode upon——Lady Derby stood still and *cried,* and succeeded better in obtaining Compassion.—The Men's Brutality Mr. Andrews protests, was quite unexampled in a Civilized Country—but Mrs. Greatheed a jocund young Sheperddess, went thro' the whole unhurt; under the Protection of such a Husband and such a Son as are rarely seen; and both striving which shall most *pet* and most adore *Her.* They are now all of them repairing their Charms for Mrs. Drummond Smith's Assembly,[15] and Boodle's grand Ranelagh Fête to be held next Fryday.[16]

So much for Flash Intelligence.

The Weather is dreadful; continued East Winds remind our Nabob Acquaintance of the *Monsoons* in Bengal—We had none but Western Breezes or Western Hurricanes the Last Half Year if you recollect—so equal a Division was never before experienced in the North Temperate Zone.

Political Matters do not run quite so *even*. Buonaparte tho' is likely as we hear to be made all he wishes; and if he lives to coin the Money—Apollion Buonaparte *Dei Gratia Imperator Gallorum* it will be very curious indeed.[17] In our furnished House here, we have his Bust over the Chimney.

Adieu and God bless you and since you are to pay so for Letters, here is at least a long one from / Yours Sincerely / H: L: P.

Dear Siddons went off to Ireland without saying a Word.[18] <Present> our proper Regards to all your Household and Farewell.

Text: Princeton University Library. *Address:* Mrs. Pennington / Dowry Square / Hot Wells / Bristol. *Postmark:* JU 2 802.

    1. HLP responds to PSP, who on 26 May (Ry. 568.108) lamented the narrowness of Bath and Bristol society, extolled the vitality of London's sophisticated conversation and its *"Public* Exhibitions and Amusements." Indeed, "All else is Jejune and *second* Hand at best—with so little Variety and so much *alike* that as the Man said by the Pictures, one would not give Sixpence to choose."

    2. Brigitta Zaccaria Banti, née Giorgi (ca. 1756–1806), operatic soprano, taught in turn by Sacchini, Piozzi, and Abel. By 1795 she was engaged as "principal woman" at King's for reputedly 2,000 guineas a season.

    3. Giuseppe Viganoni (1754–1823 or 1825), a Brescian, recognized as one of the great operatic tenors in Europe.

According to the advertisement in the *True Briton,* 28 May, a benefit concert for Viganoni was performed that day in the Great Concert Room of King's. In the first part Mme Banti sang an aria by Bianchi. In the second, Mrs. Billington sang two selections, an aria by Friedrich Heinrich Himmel and a recitativo and rondo by Giovanni Paiesiello.

    4. Mary Browne (with a fortune of over £90,000) had in 1793 married George Fermor (1768–1830), third earl of Pomfret (1785). They soon separated. She was to die in 1839 at Richmond.

    5. Richard Edgcumbe (1764–1839), second earl of Mount Edgcumbe (1795). His seat, Mount Edgcumbe in Cornwall, was on the peninsula between Plymouth Sound and the Hamoaze.

    6. Either Edward Smith (d. 1808) or Richard Smith (1734–1803).

In 1804, Edward Smith (who had attained the rank of general on 1 January 1801) was commander—and had been so since 26 April 1792—of the forty-third, or the Monmouthshire Regiment of Foot. He retained this command until his succession by Sir John Cradock, Knight of the Bath, on 7 January 1809.

In December 1752 Richard Smith became an ensign in the Bengal army, a lieutenant by 1753, a captain in 1761. Despite a brief period of retirement in this last year, he rejoined the army and as a colonel in 1764 he accompanied Clive to India. Within four years he was a brigadier general, who had amassed a large fortune by lending money to the Nawab of Arcot. Returning to England, he became an M.P. from 1774 to 1796. Originally from Wiltshire, he and his family since 1784 lived either in Harley Street, London, or at Chiltern Lodge, near Hungerford. He died in 1803.

    7. The surgeon John Symons (fl. 1750–1811) was often a member of the Bath Com-

mon-Council, and mayor in 1795 and 1803. Much interested in the architectural development of Bath, he was associated with Caleb Hillier Parry in an unfinished project to build a great crescent with wings, forming Upper Camden Place. Even in its truncated state, it is one of the city's landmarks. Symons was also "named in the 33d. of George III. 1793, for *Paving, Cleaning, Lighting, Watching,* and *regulating* the Squares, Streets, &c. within such Part of the Parish of Walcot, not within the Jurisdiction of the City of Bath" (*Robbins's Bath Directory* for 1800, p. 134).

8. Edmund Lechmere Charlton (1789–1845) was to matriculate at Christ Church, Oxford, in 1807, becoming M.A. in 1810. Settling in Ludford, co. Hereford, he began to practice as a barrister in 1829 and served as M.P. for Ludlow, 1835–37.

9. Charles Stanhope (1753–1816), third earl Stanhope (1786).

10. Mary Monckton (d. 1840), the daughter of John, first viscount Galway, had been the second wife of Edmund Boyle (1742–98), seventh earl of Corke and Orrery (1764).

11. HLP's ironical term for those members of the Opposition who had long sought peace between England and France.

12. The poet-musician Thomas Moore (1779–1852), whose playing and singing about this time had opened the houses of the English aristocracy to him.

13. William Abrahams (or Abraham) was one of the governors of the Bath General Hospital and a partner in the Bladud Bank. He resided at 19 Bathwick Street, Bath, until his death, ca. 1804. His wife, Eliza, continued to live there until 1813.

14. See the *Courier,* 2 June: "Another disadvantage which attended the vastness of the assembly [at the Cumberland House Ball], was also the necessary compression by which the characters were rendered unable to exert their powers. They were consequently locked up like militia men. . . . While the troops were distributed over the whole field of action, the want of sufficient room to manoeuvre was not so perceptible. But when the hour of supper arrived, and the charge was made upon the tables, the whole body was thrown into confusion. There were two staircases, but the company were in general only aware of one, and there consequently prevailed a severe struggle for precedence. . . . Those who were upon the stairs, finding it impossible to fall back, rushed with increased eagerness forward, and forced into the supper-rooms already crowded to suffocation. . . . Twenty Ladies might be seen fainting at the same moment in the same room. In this state some of them were placed upon the table among other forbidden fruits and flowers. Others were laid out in the balcony to recover among the bow-pots."

The ball did not end until 10:00 A.M. Some guests, all of whom came by paid subscription, did not even get a glimpse of the supper table.

For further information about the ball, see HLP to Ly W, 4 June.

15. Mary, née Cunliffe (d. 1804), was the first wife of Drummond Smith (d. 1816), cr. baronet 11 June 1804.

According to *The Times,* 31 May, "Mrs. Drummond Smith's Rout, Hyde Park Corner," would take place 4 June.

16. See the *Courier,* 3 June, which gave over more than a column to a description of the fête held by members of Boodle's Subscription Club on Wednesday, 2 June, in Ranelagh House and the Rotunda Gardens to celebrate the peace. See also HLP to Ly W, 4 June.

17. In gratitude for the Peace of Amiens, the French senate proposed on 8 May Bonaparte's reelection as First Consul for ten years. But a group of legislators wished to do more for him and proposed a plebiscite, that Bonaparte become consul for life with the right to choose his successor. Finally, "A person of the name of Bonneville Ayral, stiling himself a Chef de Battalion in the 14th regiment of the line, lately stuck up a bill at Paris; in which, after extolling the service of Bonaparte, and comparing him to Titus, he says, 'My wish is, that the French people may proclaim Napoleon Bonaparte First Emperor of the Gauls, and fix in his family the hereditary power, upon re-establishing the Salic law.' " See *GM* 72, pt. 1: 465–66.

18. SS was in Ireland from May 1802 to early April 1803. For details of her stay there, see HLP to PSP, 21 December 1802.

TO LADY WILLIAMS

No. 5: George Street
Manchester Square
4: June 1802

Your Ladyship's very kind Letter my Dear Madam gave me much Pleasure; We are here in the midst of Engagements and Amusements which really amount almost to Frenzy. Nobody has a Notion of lying down to Sleep till after Sunrise— but as I cannot bear to be cheated of my Morning Hours—those of *this* Morning shall be consecrated to Friendship and Bodylwyddan. Mr. Piozzi says Sir John Williams must not wed his Prejudices to a *Name;* The new Piano e forte is made by *Houston Tomkinson* and Co. and my Husband praises their Work above every one's.[1] The World is mad for Music, and new favourites start up among the Makers, as well as among the Performers. I was ready to cry last Night for poor dear charming Mara, though She was said to clear a *Thousand Pounds* Profit—We were at her Benefit where the Applause given to *her* was doubled upon Billington whose Powers are *prodigious* and assisted by the Possession of Beauty, besides a Degree of Good Humour very uncommon and very sweet indeed: as She sings for her Rivals without pay or Reward—visibly contented with her own marked Superiority—Banti alone shares the public Attention with this new Wonder, and *She* obtains Notice chiefly by singing the *Men's* Songs to Billington's female Voice and gentler Graces.

Sir John Williams would I think be greatly shocked at the odd frequency—now so common—of the Sex's changing *Character:* Half the Gentlemen at every Masquerade are in Women's Clothes, while our London Belles delight to disguise themselves as *Waggoners* and *Stage Coachmen*. A Groupe of insolent young Men of Fashion imitating Boarding School Misses and their Governess were the Scourge of the *fine Union Ball* which cost such Treasures in decoration of a Festival very few ever arrived at partaking; many having passed the whole Night in their Carriages wholly unable to get up at all: many were frighted into Fits and *trodden* when they *fell down*—so brutal was the Conduct of those who used to protect Ladies, not insult them.

To remedy these Grievances, Boodle's Club[2]—for which and the Union together[3]—Three Thousand Chickens were killed: gave their Friends a Dress Ball, and Things were carried on more decently——The Plates of Pease at 15s. each, were eaten, not *devoured* as at the other Place, where all the Glasses broken, seemed an incalculable Expense; The Managers after subscribing Six Thousand Pounds having gained no Thanks from any one. Private Theatres[4] beside the Pic Nic[5] are preparing in all great Houses, and there are more great Houses than one can Count——If I outlive the Squeeze at Mrs. Drummond Smith's tonight, more shall be told; but 'tis *expected* that Bones will be broken in such a Croud as her magnificent Preparations must necessarily collect. One Sees the Workmen throwing up temporary buildings in her Garden as one drives along Hyde Park: and those who have no Cards of Invitation make a Mob at the Door, to see People pass in and out; which is exceedingly dangerous.[6] Meanwhile nobody is contented with *one* of these Bustles in the Course of a Night. I was at Viganoni's Benefit where *every* one was—even the Princess of Wales—but tho' it was Morning when we separated, I was almost the only Female in the room who came away to bed——Lady Pomfret's Assembly and Ranelagh Gardens received those who however *distracted* with Delight as they pretended—were certainly *unsatisfied* or they would not have Sought for more—but the fancy Dress Shops were open, as they are now all Night, where changes of Habits are Supplied for these Masquerades that Ladies may *never be* known except for their Skill in maintaining two or three Opposite Characters with Spirit—and these Shops increase the Expences, and facilitate Intrigue in a Degree hitherto unexampled. At all these Diversions Mrs. Fitzherbert is received and entertained with every honourable Distinction——an ornamented Box prepared for the Prince and *Her* &c.[7]

When the Duke of Brunswic's Daughter appears in Public, She generally comes in a Hat, with two or Three Ladies and one or two Gentlemen——Sits in a retired Part of the Room, and is noticed by nobody except as a *remarkably pretty Woman*, a Praise which cannot be refused her.[8] What a World this is!——fit for a Corsican adventurer to rule—*and he does rule it:* I have always observed that Slaves fit themselves to their Tyrant, and Europe hastens to accommodate her Morals to the Taste of Buonaparte.

5 o'clock Fryday. I return home to Dinner and to dress after a vain Attempt to see the Court Finery——no Powers of mine could battle thro' the Throng and dangerous Press of carriages—so we saw nothing but went with our Friends the Greatheeds to choose a Grand Piano e Forte for their Country Seat. Among Numbers and Numbers that Mr. Piozzi touched this Day, none did he like *half* as well as that he has secured for your Ladyship——none have we seen or heard of under 75 or 80 Guineas——but Mrs. Greatheed would purchase no Work but Broadwood's to which Name *She* is wedded,[9] and he had nothing worth her Money as he almost confest.

Now if Sir John is really serious in his equal Passion for Stodart[10]——Mr. Piozzi begs to hear once more from him upon the Subject, and he will keep the Houston and Tomkinson for ourselves at Bath——but then he should have a Letter *soon* because it is already in this Town on its way to Wales. It comes to forty Guineas—The *Instrument;* Packing Case and Porterage one Guinea more—— Carriage Expences out of Question, the saving in *them* by a *Water* Journey would be little indeed compared with the Risque of sending such a Thing by Sea. The Money to be paid either to Hugh Lloyd Grocer at Denbigh, or to Hammersley's bank in London as Sir John likes best.

I shall now give Our best Regards to all of the Dear Household, and particularly my sweet Godson——his elder Brother must really prepare for School now—his friend and Playfellow our little Nephew, is got into Latin Testament. Mr. Davies does bring those Children forward surprizingly. I can never thrust the Account of tonight's Gala in this Paper.—It would be squeezed as we were last Night. Dearest Madam Adieu, says / Your H: L: P.

Text: Ry. 2 (1802–6). *Address:* Lady Williams / Bodylwyddan / near St. Asaph / Flintshire N:W. *Postmark:* JU 5 802.

1. Thomas Tomkison, associated with one Houston in the manufacture of grand and square pianofortes, at 55 Dean Street, Soho (1798–1851).

2. "The gentlemen of Boodle's Club gave a grand entertainment [on 2 June] at Ranelagh; and though it was not equal in point of splendour to that of the Union Club, yet of the two it was preferable, as there was more space and consequently better accommodation for the numerous company which attended. At ten o'clock the lottery began drawing as the ladies presented their tickets. All prizes and no blanks. . . . The miniature opera performances began about eleven. The ball began about half-past eleven, and about thirty couples danced. The prince entered alone at half-past eleven, dressed in scarlet regimentals, the uniform of a field marshal; and Sir Willoughby Aston immediately attended his highness round the room. The Duke of Cumberland entered arm in arm with Sir Sidney Smith. Some persons came in masks, but they were refused admittance. The business was well conducted by several gentlemen of the club; and the supper consisted of every rariety."

See *AR*, "Chronicle," 44 (1802): 49; *Courier,* 3 June.

3. Despite the mob scene at the Union Ball, its intention was to celebrate the peace. According to the *Courier,* 2 June, "This magnificent *Fete* was given on Monday night [31 May], under the patronage of the *Union Club,* and management of the Earls Moira, Llandaff, and Cunningham, and Lord Cahir. The history of our amusements presents no period that abounds so much in this species of *Spectacle* as the present. For weeks past we have had to notice a series of them, vying with each other in splendour and variety.— That, however, of which we are now speaking, appears to have been a *chef d'œuvre,* produced by the delirium of the day, leaving us little hope of ever finding an equal."

4. A Society for Private Theatricals was created, with a membership, with rules and regulations prescribed. There were to be twelve patronesses: duchesses of Devonshire, and of Gordon; the marchioness of Salisbury; Countesses Cholmondeley, Buckinghamshire, Mount Edgcumbe; Viscountesses Melbourne and Dungannon; Lady Templeton, Lady Campbell; the Honorable Mrs. Damer, Mrs. Crewe. There were also six managers, with Henry Francis Greville "Director for the whole Establishment."

According to the rules and regulations of the Society, "The Evening Amusements shall commence at half past 8: After the Plays or Proverbs, the Theatre will be converted into a Ball-Room, and Apartments made ready for such of the Company as chuse Cards; at half past 12 there shall be a Pic-Nic Supper, succeeded by Catches and Glees.—The first representation to be on Monday, March 1, and to be continued once in every alternate week, till future notice." See *The Times,* 23 February 1802.

5. According to *The Times,* 27 March:

"As the expression of a Pic-Nic Supper is become so fashionable, though it is much oftener used than understood, it may be necessary to explain it for the information of our Readers:—

"A *Pic-Nic* Supper consists of a variety of dishes. The Subscribers to the Entertainment have a bill of fare presented to them, with a number against each dish. The lot which he draws obliges him to furnish the dish marked against it, which he either takes with him in his carriage, or sends by a servant. The proper variety is preserved by the talents of the *Maitre d'Hotel,* who forms the bill of fare," which "can boast of the refinement of the art."

6. *The Times,* 31 May, had announced "Mrs. Drummond Smith's Rout, Hyde Park Corner" for 4 June. Until her death on 27 February 1804, Mary Smith, née Cunliffe, was a leader of London society. Described as Ly W's "amiable cousin," she entertained lavishly at both the Hyde Park residence and at "Old Colman's elegant Richmond Villa . . . [recently] purchased by Mr. Drummond Smith, whose accomplished Lady will undoubtedly render it a fashionable resort."

See the *Oracle and Public Advertiser,* 22 March 1796; HLP to Ly W [16]–18 March 1804, n. 2; to Mrs. Pemberton [ca. 24 December 1814], n. 4.

7. In March 1800, after a separation of five years, Maria Fitzherbert and the Prince of Wales were once more united. Having earlier appealed to the Vatican for advice, she received a brief from Rome that declared her the only true wife of the prince. To provide official acknowledgment of the renewed relationship, she gave a large formal breakfast on 16 June 1800, with the Prince as the guest of honor. For the next eight years theirs was a comfortable association, sanctioned by the Royal Family as preferable to the Prince's involvement with other women, such as Lady Jersey.

8. HLP's sympathy for Princess Caroline as the woman scorned is not wholly realistic. In 1802 the princess had an extravagant establishment at Montague House. Her conduct was eccentric. Although her conversation was "'uncommonly lively, odd and clever,'" she had not—according to some—"'a grain of *common* sense' . . . she had a 'coarse mind without any degree of moral taste.'" Others were offended by her "'low nonsense, and sometimes gross ribaldry.'" A few even thought her "insane." See Christopher Hibbert, *George IV Prince of Wales, 1762–1811* (1972), pp. 206–7.

9. John Broadwood (1732–1812), innovative pianoforte manufacturer, whose work was recognized throughout Europe.

10. A firm of piano makers, founded by Robert Stodart in 1775 in Wardour Street, carried on by his son William and his grandson Malcolm. It ceased production in 1861.

TO THE LADIES OF THE WILLIAMS FAMILY

London
18th: June 1802

Well! Dearest Ladies the Instrument is on the Road, Mr. Piozzi will bring the Set of Strings himself. Instead of telling London News—I am all on Tip toe to enquire for Flintshire Intelligence; how does Miss Blaquiere in the first place? The Report here is that She does not mend—at least not rapidly; but I give little Credit to Report.

The Promotion of a man so celebrated for Loyalty and Learning as Doctor Horsley occasions much Talk in literary circles *here;* his Promotion to St. *Asaph* must I should suppose, engage Attention Round our little Valley in a still greater Degree. His well known Hospitality and open Manners will be very pleasant; and I hope he will love us, and take to us, and wish to go no further.[1]

Doctor Vincent's able Defence of public Education has stood him in good Stead, after so long waiting; I feel quite glad always Literary Characters are in *favour* with those who have *Favours* to bestow; and doubt not but the best Scholars among our Clergy, will bid fairest to be well with our new Bishop.[2]

We have been to Streatham Park since I wrote last; our Tenant there buys Books with a Liberality almost unexampled: Miss Thrales and Mrs. Mostyn and ourselves have had the turning his fine Library about for a whole Week together——he is a good humoured friendly Soul, and we have not failed to profit of his kindness. Since our Return we visited the Opera, where Mr. Piozzi lamented the Decay of Italian Music as much as I did the Changes visible in English Manners.

Population however certainly does increase surprizingly, the War and Scarcity and All Things considered: London appears to me to be as much *fuller* than it was—as *larger*. Every Street thronged like Cheapside on a busy Day: and in these parts of the Town too, where formerly one walked as quietly at Noon as I now do before Breakfast, when nobody seems alive but Soldiers exercising, or Servants selling old Clothes, Kitchen Stuff &c. before the Master and Mistress are Stirring after last Night's Gala.

But Your Ladyship and Dear Mrs. Williams will be wearied with all these Reflections or else I would tell you about the famous Doctor Philipstaal who after a hundred Tricks played on the Continent exhibits his Mechanic Powers *here*, professing to *detect Imposture* and show how easy 'tis to counterfeit supernatural Appearances, for purpose of deceiving; a Contrivance No man can understand better than Himself: It is made an extremely entertaining Show, and I do think that Mechanism was never brought to half the Perfection we find it in the Year 1802.[3]

With Regard to Fashions, I remain quite dazzled with the Changes of Toys, Trinkets &c. The women have a *Topaz Fever* on them as it should seem, and these bright Yellow Stones or Imitations of them, cover so many Necks and Arms that I am confident *Mines* cannot supply *half*— -They must be artificial. It was the same when feathers were worn: No seven Ostriches could have dressed all the Heads I have seen feathered on one night in London. Yet did I never arrive at knowing how the Shopkeepers obtained them, or *whence*.

But Mr. Piozzi cries out that I have not said half enough of him, or of his Hopes that the Piano e forte will please dear Lady Williams, or of his Thanks for your kind disposition to be pleased with his best Pains to promote your Ladyships Pleasure. A Word too should be said about Corn when Mouths do so multiply— Will the Harvest be prosperous? God send it, and may all his Blessings light on sweet Bodylwyddan, every Inhabitant of which claims the truest good Wishes of dearest Ladies / ever Yours / H: L: P.

The Piano e Forte is directed to Gabriel Piozzi to be left at Chester till called for; Sir John Williams's People who fetch it, must therefore *use his Name*.

Text: Ry. 2 (1802–6). *Address:* Lady Williams / Bodylwyddan / near St. Asaph / N: Wales. *Postmark:* JU 19 802.

1. For Samuel Horsley, see HLP to Q, 7 November 1796, n. 12. The announcement regarding him was made only on 26 June: "Right Rev. Samuel Horsley, D.D. Bishop of Rochester, translated to the see of St. Asaph, *vice* Dr. Bagot, dec." See *GM* 72, pt. 1 (1802): 578.

2. William Vincent (1739–1815), D.D., headmaster of Westminster School (1788–1802); dean of Westminster (1802–15).

He emphasized religious education for his pupils, a fact that allowed him to answer the attacks of Thomas Rennell, master of the Temple, and Thomas Lewis O'Beirne, bishop of Meath, who had charged headmasters with neglecting this branch of their duties. His defense of public education secured for him the deanery of Westminster, which Addington said was "a public reward for public service," a reference to Vincent's *A Defence of Public Education, Addressed to the Most Reverend The Lord Bishop of Meath* (London: A. Strahan, 1802).

3. According to the advertisements:

"*Under the Patronage of their Royal Highnesses the Duke and Duchess* of York.—Upper Theatre, Lyceum. The Public are respectfully informed, that the Amusements of this place consist of many beautiful Experiments in Hydraulics, Acoustics, and Aerostation, the like of which has never been attempted in this kingdom.—The Mechanical Ingenuities and original Phantasmagoria, by Mr. De Philipstal. . . . Admittance, Boxes 4s. Pit 2s. Gall. 1s." The performance began at eight.

He used his "Spectrographia" to do Milton's *L'Allegro,* scenes from the *Mysteries of Udolpho,* etc. See the *True Briton,* 12 April; the *Morning Herald,* 15 April; *The Times,* 17 April 1802; the [Sunday] *Observer,* 13 February 1803.

TO LADY WILLIAMS

> No. 5 George Street,
> Manchester Square
> 2: July 1802.

My dear Lady Williams will be easily perswaded to believe that her kind letter put me in a fright; so we set out and drove all over the City in Chace of our Forte e Piano. A wise Quaker—Master of Blossoms Inn, Lawrence Lane[1] assures me that on the 18th of June last; it left London for the Wool Hall, Chester; at which place your Ladyship will doubtless find it by the time this reaches you. I wrote this Morning—to the Woolhall, to charge the Bookkeeper to keep it safely till it should be sent for to Bodylwyddan. The Man of the Swan, Holborn Bridge says he has Wakeman's Receipt——so I am confident it left our Town in *good Health.*

Miss Blaquiere must make haste and get well, and be married; and put a Stop to Conjectures: I think she cannot be exceedingly bad for we saw Lady Orkney in Town three days ago.

People in London are all talking of the Air Balloon, which I saw flying over Portland Place in the highest Wind possible, and losing itself in Clouds at an astonishing altitude indeed.

Monsieur Garnerin goes up again to morrow with an Umbrella Thing to hinder his *Fall,* he calls it for that Reason a Para*chûte.*[2] We shall see how it answers—taking so much Money at such a Risk of breaking all his Bones. People are going fast into the Country. We have almost done eating *Breakfasts* whence we return at 8 in the Evening, and *Dinners* which break up at 12 at Night: Electioneering Matters fill every Mouth, that is not discoursing about Garnerin, who travels 67 Miles an Hour in the Air.—Such Expedition on such Errands would be useful; but neither He nor the Candidates seem to know where they are going.[3]

I am sorry sweet Miss Williams wants a Collar and Backboard, but so it is, if She will grow up and be sweet *Miss Williams.* When She was pretty *little Harriet* She bridled and looked as *proud* as Princess Charlotte of Wales:[4] but I have long observed that the Life of Man goes by *Septenaries.*[5] The Baby becomes a Boy or Girl at seven Years old, the Teeth change, and a manifest Alteration takes Place in

Body and in *Mind*—which our English Law being well aware of, makes the Evidence of a Child *past* that Age sufficient to hang a Man in Criminal Cases—— which before they arrive at it—is disregarded. Where Things are left to *Nature,* the Smallpox regularly and of *itself* comes at Seven Years old, and assists the Change *She* is making. At 14 a new Character is taken up by Male and Female:— The Youth learns Courage, and the Virgin—Modesty. Whilst almost every Nation agrees to consider People as *complete* at the Years of 21. Dropping and stooping of Head and Shoulders is only a temporary Symptom that the *first-*Change is past——and I should be inclined to put some more Bones into *Wide* Stays, and leave Nature her own Work to do; only giving some support to the Ribs and Sides, while growing somewhat too fast for Strength. Another Letter shall find me obedient to your *Ladyship's Command* however, and not obtrusive of my *own Advice.* You will tell me that the Instrument is come, and order the Collar and Backboard *irrevocably* if such be *your Pleasure.* They make those Things (as every thing else) very nicely now, and to a great expence.——

My dear little Godson is a fine fellow to promise so fairly; I consider my Responsibility as an Honour—not a Burden—and I hope he will be glad to see us.

To no one living out of Bodylwyddan House can Stories of the lovely Children there be half as Interesting as to Sir John's, and Mrs. Williams', and Your Ladyship's / truly affectionate and / Obliged Servant / H: L: P.

Mr. Piozzi sends 1000 Regards: he is in Agony about the Piano e forte till he hears it is got home.

Text: Ry. 2 (1802–6). *Address:* Lady Williams / Bodylwyddan / near St. Asaph / Flintshire / N: Wales. *Postmark:* JY 2 802.

1. Located in Lawrence, or St. Lawrence Lane, Cheapside, Blossom Inn Yard was a depot for dispatching goods by wagon to various parts of Great Britain.
2. The *Morning Chronicle* of 13 May announced the exhibition at the Pantheon of "An immense Parachute of the invention of the celebrated Aëronaut Garnerin" who had recently arrived in England "together with a Baloon of 10,000 cubic feet."
See the same newspaper, 21 May. "Ascension in a Baloon and Descent in a Parachute. On the 2d of June next . . . Garnerin will ascend from Marlborough-gardens between the King's-road and Blackland's-lane, Chelsea, into the upper regions of the Air, and when at the height of 10,000 feet, separate from his Baloon, and Descend without any other assistance than that of his Parachute."
Paris-born André-Jacques Garnerin (1769–1823) designed the parachute and made his first descent with it in 1797. For further accounts of his flights in the summer of 1802 in England, see the *Courier,* 6 and 22 July; the *Bath Herald,* 4 September; *GM* 72, pt. 2 (1802): 663–68.
3. Parliament after six years had been dissolved by the king on 28 June, and a general election was held during July. The struggle was once more between ministerial forces, whether led by Pitt or Addington, and the Opposition, or HLP's "Liberty Lovers." The new Commons would not differ materially from the old. The new parliament did not meet until 16 November.
4. According to Farington (6:2028), the eight-year-old princess "is perhaps early impressed with a sense of Her own importance, and indicates pride."
5. For HLP's assumption that seven is a significant, even "perfect," number, see her letter to Clement Francis, 13 November 1810, n. 10.

TO LADY WILLIAMS

London
13: July 1802

My Dearest Lady Williams's kind Letter set my Mind free from much Anxiety. We should have been half wild had any harm come to that charming Instrument.—Mr. Piozzi says there is no Maker to be compared with Tomkinson:[1] he has his Hands full of work now for 8 Months to come, and not a Grand Piano e forte to be *seen* without a marked Price of 75, 80 and 85 Guineas. We consider ourselves on this Occasion as in *very high Luck*, and being confident such an Accident will happen no more; are delighted to find you all pleased with the Bargain. Mr. Piozzi will teach your Ladyship how to manage the Pedals &c.

We set out for the *Principality* next Monday Morning thro' Oxford and Cheltenham which delay us a week, and I have begged a Dozen good Dips in Cardigan Bay to wash off the London Dust and Dirt and Smoke, before I present myself at dear Bodylwyddan; and present my sweet Godson with a Town Toy which he will soon—by your Ladyship's Account be big enough to make use of. His Sister would be more benefited and less injured by *Sea Bathing* which strengthens the Habit during *all changes* of Human Life;—and promotes a free and graceful Carriage more than those cruel Collars; which *necessarily* cut the Neck and Throat up terribly, and give the Wrinkles early power to ruin Beauty long before their time. When I was but 36 years old I could not wear Necklaces like other Ladies, but always prefered *Ruffs* and *Collets montez* because of the Yellow Streak left by a long worne Collar. Your Ladyship's kind resolution to reprieve *your* Daughter is in my Mind a very wise one——Strong Health, and frequent Admonition will do all that *can* be wanting in such a Symmetric form as hers was by Nature.

The Town is getting dull now, no more Talk of anything but Electioneering. Sir Francis Burdett is very ill thought on for his perverse Interference, and desire of a Bustle when every body—speaking popularly—are in their own Hearts—content.[2] I hope these Democrates will lose Ground by shewing so plainly that nothing will please them but Mischief.[3] Mr. Travers has plaid the same Trick in the *City:* He was for abolishing all Test Acts,—and now he presents a Test to the Electors; he piqued himself on never having drank to the Health of *any King;* and now he professes to stand on the Brunswick Interest.[4] Such contradictions are really very offensive, and I must hope the People will resent it—by electing none of their Society. I have seen a Gentleman just come from visiting France whose Account of that Nation and its Metropolis would put one compleatly out of Humour with *State Quackery* and its dreadful Consequences.

Not one old Country Seat or Palace standing from Calais to Paris—all pulled down!! Not one Place of public Worship in any of the Country Towns—till they have cleared that which was once a Church, of Temporary Shops and Stalls; or else of Stores and Merchandise;—Buonaparte however has declared his Resolution to hear a *Military Mass* four times a'year—and one Church is set apart for this Act of Courtly devotion.[5] Some Fanatical Preachers *do* get into a Pulpit now and then he says, and harangue the People—but that's all; and Marriage has been so completely forgotten among them that the present Rulers believing such Licentiousness hurts population—mean to enforce it by Law and Arms after the 14th.[6] Meanwhile Beggars from 2 to 300 at once surrounded his Carriage at every *Inn*, where Extortionate Prices are demanded for miserable Dinners: and this Gentleman's Word I find myself obliged to take, as he knew France perfectly well in its old original Days; and is a Man of *keen Intelligence,* without *quick Feeling*.

Such tales reconcile one to old England and even to London; which though wicked enough, wants not opportunities of being better: *our* Places of Worship being very numerous, and so crouded there is no Chance for a Seat except among the *Sectaries;* which enjoy full Toleration and build Chapels every hour of the day. There is an odd Reason for many fine People's dislike of attending a Parish Church here——They will not sit to hear 68 Couples asked on a Sunday Noon as my Maid did at St. George's. The good effects are discernible however in *our* Population. When Garnerin went up in his Balloon last Time the Throng of People was so prodigious one might have walked upon their Heads I think—and yet I am told that at the Southwark Election that very Day *nobody was missing; that End* of our Metropolis seemed [as] full as *this End*.[7] But my paper is full too; and without one Word of the Compliments and best Regards Mr. Piozzi bids me send from him to your Ladyship and Your Dear Mama; and Sir John and Mrs. Williams who I rejoyce to find are all pretty well, and good natured enough always to remember him and her who is ever / your Ladyship's obliged and ever faithful Servant / H: L: P.

Direct to Tenby, Pembrokeshire S. Wales.

Text: Ry. 2 (1802–6). *Address:* Lady Williams / Bodylwyddan / St. Asaph / N: Wales. *Postmark:* JY 13 802.

1. For Tomkison, see HL to Ly W, 4 June, n. 1.
2. For Sir Francis Burdett, see HLP to LC, 10 April 1799, n. 4.

On 13 July the Middlesex election began with George Byng, the Whig candidate; Sir Francis; and William Mainwaring, a banker and chairman of the Middlesex Bench of magistrates. Byng and Mainwaring had represented Middlesex in the preceding parliament. "Byng's election was a certainty, and the real contest lay between Mainwaring and Burdett." See M. W. Patterson, *Sir Francis Burdett and His Times (1770–1844)*, 2 vols. (London: Macmillan, 1931). 1:135–36.

3. Sir Francis attacked his opponent, Mainwaring, for having supported the "gagging" acts of Pitt and for having defended Aris, the jailer of Cold Bath Fields prison. Even before the election began, Burnett had announced that he would fight it chiefly on the question of the atrocities committed at the Cold Bath Fields prison and on his view of Mainwaring as the abettor of the cruelties there. For HLP such arguments were merely democratic "Mischief." To Mainwaring, Burdett and his supporters were guilty of "treasonable practices" (Patterson, 1: 137).

4. Benjamin Travers, an alderman and a fishmonger, was one of seven contestants for a parliamentary seat for the City of London. At a meeting of the Livery of London in the Guildhall, Travers set forth what he believed to be the qualifications for a "British Senator." He had to be "a man of large and liberal mind who understood the principles of the British Constitution"; loyal to the House of Brunswick; supportive of peace and a lower national debt; committed to principles of justice; opposed to slavery and the income

tax; "illustrious for his wisdom and virtue." See *The Times*, 6 July. By the 16th the same newspaper announced the winners: Harvey Richard Combe; Charles Price; William Curtis; Sir J. W. Anderson.

5. HLP picked up this rumor from a returning English visitor to Paris. While newspapers like *The Times* and the *Courier* do not confirm it, Bonaparte himself would have supported such an act as necessary for his rapprochement with Rome.

French newspapers during June and July were filled with information concerning the "restoration" of religion in France. The pope, e.g., verified it in an "extraordinary Consistory at Rome upon the 24th of May, upon which occasion he published all the objects relative to the Church of France, as also the nomination of all the Bishops. Upon the 27th, Ascension-day, he pronounced an allocution upon the subject of the restoration of religion in France, and the present state of the church" (*Courier*, 11 June). According to the same paper on 22 June, "the most useful persons to Bonaparte upon the subject of the consulship for life, have been the priests and the returned emigrants."

6. Marriage was emphasized as part of the new regime in France. On 13 July, "the 12 Mayors of Paris conducted to the Prefecture 12 young maidens portioned by the Commune, and intended to be married the next day. They were accompanied by their future husbands and relations." The contracts having been signed, "The ceremony concluded with a banquet given to the young people, their families, and the 12 Mayors, by the Prefect.

"On the 14th, the marriages were solemnized before each Mayor; and the new couples were conducted with pomp to the parish-church, where their marriage was blessed by the Rector."

See *GM* 72, pt. 2 (1802): 669.

7. According to *The Times* on 1 July, "The Borough of Southwark promises to be the scene of as smart and active a contest as the approaching state of the country will produce." The campaigners were Sir Thomas Turton; George Tierney (the Whig incumbent); and H. Thornton. After several recounts, the vote was: Thornton, 1667; Tierney, 1341; Turton, 1183. See also *The Times*, 12 July.

TO PENELOPE SOPHIA PENNINGTON

Tenby Fryday
6: August 1802

This is indeed a dismal End to the long Silence of poor dear Mrs. Pennington; Your Letter kept us both awake last Night——yet I have fixed on no mode of Consolation to be offered you in the Morning. Should it please God that you were to become once more a *Single Woman,* I hope *we* should always be able and willing to afford you Shelter: In the mean Time it is Your Duty to be careful of your Health, your Husband, and your *Mother;* who of the Three is really most to be pitied. There is always some brighter Part than the *rest*, of every cloudy Sky; and that Part gets more luminous as one fixes one's Eyes upon it.[1]

Mr. Pennington's Situation will mend—and by some Accident equally unlooked for as this last *evil* one, he will drop into a Down Bed (I'm confident he will) before he dies.

Be perswaded to anticipate possible tho' distant *Good;* you *will not* believe in

Ills till they are near *indeed:* my Croaking with regard to public Matters you rejected as disturbing your Rejoycing in the Peace and the Plenty and the taking away of The Income Tax: but what I said *then,* might *now* be *seen,* if we were not *blind:* and will shortly be *felt,* for feeling is a sense that will remain long after the others are blunted.

If the Parliament by finding Sir Francis Burdett's Votes illegal make the Westminster Election void,[2] who will stand forward to oppose him? Mainwaring? And if he does, will that be very advantageous (Think you) towards the Peace of the county and our Sovereign Lord the King?——or will his *next* Opponent if Mr. Mainwaring be weary, have any better Success?[3] And will you give The Democrates a fresh Triumph, because this last is not sufficient?——If he is *outed* at Stroke, and Mr. Mainwaring called *in:* The Consequent Violence will be great indeed, and the Uproar deafening;[4] it was an Ill-managed Business, I know many Free holders——cool, not *warm* friends to Decency and good Order,—who were never asked for their Votes or Interest; and who would have thrown *both* into the right Scale, had they been properly canvassed.

What *you* have lost, could not I suppose have been saved; What Government loses, they do not much struggle to keep. Every Thing is done in a new Way, and we who lived in former Times do not much like it. But as Barretti said when losing at Back Gammon: These are bad Dice, but we must play them as they are.

I wrote you a long Letter from Cheltenham which may help to divert Care, after you have beaten every Bush, and found out that *Care* is of no Use; and can but add to the Weight of Affliction——but I mistake, 'twas *not* from Cheltenham, it was from here my Nonsense went——all about Helen Williams and Koschieffsky.[5]

We board in this Place at the same Table with a Lady who knows Miss Lee, and is a Sort of Aunt or Cousin to her pretty Protegée Miss Tickell.[6] The Lady knows Mr. Whalley too, and says how agreeable he made himself to our tiny Society at Tenby. It seems to me as I look over the Bay, that his Cottage commands just that part of the Ocean which faces upon our View—as it sometimes extends quite to King's Road.

Hannah More is wise to have done fretting—The Abuse thrown at *her* like *other* Poysons will work itself off, leaving only a Languor, and Indisposition to write again and provoke more. I shall be glad when you are got back to the Wells, where every one will endeavour to console you: Miss Powell's Company and Conversation will prove Soothers likewise, but I know not from *what* Source, (except the best,) poor Mrs. Weston *can* hope Comfort. Let her believe at least that I grieve for her.

Sea Bathing is beautifully pleasant in this little Place—fertile in Fish beside, but seeing no Fruit makes one feel as if Summer was quite over, and we have had but two warm Days.

Mr. Piozzi waits here very good humouredly till Brynbella has made her Toilette: What a Mercy 'tis that Gout has not yet laid hold on him! Doctor Crawford said at Cheltenham that he never saw him look so well.[7] He sends true Sorrow and Tender Regards, and *I* am ever Yours / H: L: Piozzi.

6 August 1802

Text: Princeton University Library. *Address:* Mrs. Pennington / Dowry Square / Hot Wells / Bristol.

1. PSP's letter has to do with her financially irresponsible brother, Gilbert, whom she had once kept from insolvency by lending him £1,000. On 3 August (Ry. 568.110), she had written from London. ". . . my unfortunate, and I am compelled to say, with respect to us, *unworthy* Brother—is *dismissed from his office* in conjunction with two others, one above, the other below him in the same department;—for some *irregularity* of proceeding, not approved by the Treasury Board; but *clear* of any *criminal* charges.—His *total* Ruin is the consequence. . . . He has *disappeared* and a few Lines he thought proper to Write us declares him 'on the point of leaving the Kingdom.'—So there goes for the present £130 per year out of our little wretched Income, and my *Thousand* Pound, lost for *ever*!!! The only little Independence I had to support me against the Casualties of Life!"

2. The Middlesex election continued from 13 to 28 July. During the first thirteen days of the poll, Burdett was losing to Mainwaring by some 400 or 500 votes. But by the fourteenth day, he trailed by only 14 votes, and by the next day he was ahead, the final tally being Byng—3,848; Burdett—3,207; Mainwaring—2,936.

Mainwaring challenged Burdett's election, but only on 9 July 1804 did a select committee of the Commons void the Burdett victory in favor of Mainwaring.

A new election was ordered by the Commons. The candidates for the election (23 July to 6 August 1804) were Burdett and G. B. Mainwaring, the son of William Mainwaring. Again the results were contested. Only on 10 February 1806 did the select committee report in favor of Mainwaring. See Patterson 1:137–38, 146–47; also the *Morning Chronicle*, 30 July 1802 for the results of the original election and Mainwaring's decision to contest it; *The Middlesex Election* (London, 1803); Thomas Tegg, *Memoirs of Sir F. Burdett*, 8th ed. (London, 1804).

3. William Mainwaring (1735–1821) of Hanover Square, London; M.P. for Middlesex (1784–1802). He was a Pitt advocate who spoke frequently but never on any significant political issue during his tenure; e.g., parliamentary reform, India, or the Regency Bill.

4. HLP regarded Burdett as politically dangerous but she was equally aware that setting aside his election would perhaps be even more dangerous. See, e.g., an editorial in the conservative *Morning Post and Gazetteer* 3 August, which pointed out that "Sir Francis Burdett and his party have obtained a triumph, is a fact, which cannot be disputed." The article went on to stress the popular outrage that would follow upon reversing Burdett's victory.

5. Her English designation for General Thaddeus Koskiusko (1746–1817), the Polish champion of independence for his country and America. See *Retrospection* 2:507.

6. For Elizabeth Tickell, see HLP to LC, 7 or 8 May 1799, n. 9.

7. Irish-born Stewart Crawford (1772–1847) received his M.D. from the University of Edinburgh, 24 June 1795, and was admitted as a licentiate of the College of Physicians, 16 February 1796. After serving as a medical officer in the army from 1799 to June 1802 and from July 1803 to June 1805, he would set up a Bath practice in 1805 and two years later be appointed physician to the Bath United Hospital, a post to be held until 1819. In *Guy's Bath Directory* (1819), he is listed as surgeon to the Bath Infirmary and Dispensary. See also the "Burial Register," Weston (C.R.O., Somerset).

TO THE REVEREND LEONARD CHAPPELOW

Tenby in South Wales
Monday 16: August 1802

It was very kind of you to write at last Dear Mr. Chappelow,—I thought we were making *Mum.*

Coax my Lord Torington—or *any* Lord, to free and direct the enclosed to The Rev: *Doctor* Robert Gray at Craicke near Easingwold Yorkshire. Though his Academic *honours* are come at last, and late enough I think;[1] he is much less able than he ought to be to pay Eighteen pence for a Letter.

I have not yet seen our new Bishop [Horsley]. The Old Bishop died as poor as those of the primitive Church:[2]—but Buonaparte will be able in ten Years I trust, to tell how Family Connexions keep a Man's Purse from filling, and his Heart from enjoying the Riches or Dignities heaped upon *himself.* I have often thought, and somewhere *said* that Life is a large Plumb Cake where if exposed—to a hot Sun, the Wasps fight and quarrel and massacre one another, and die in Agony——for what! Why for the Sake of depositing their Eggs in it—which are to be happily provided for—next Summer. Will the French endure *his* planting a new Family in their old Seat of Power?[3] (I can't believe it—), *his,* who has not even the Claim of original Fraternity——your Anecdote concerning Le Croix de Saint Louis is very likely to keep Hope alive in the Heart of the Bourbons: They will perhaps come Home as Charles 2nd did after the Usurper's Death——yet it were Policy in them to drink his Health *meanwhile,* as his *early* Extinction would only bring on fresh Convulsions. Let France groan under a heavy Military Yoke and hard Discipline for *a Dozen Years,* let their Tyrant fill every Department of Honour and Profit with his own Ignorant or worthless Relations, and let him lead a gloomy Life shut up in his own Camp—not Court—at Mont Martre[4]——and they will call in Le Duc D'Angoulesme of their own accord.[5]

Well! but our Fools never find the Example of their Neighbours a Warning: We sing Ca Ira, and plant Trees of Liberty at Nottingham and Brentford, as if we had a longing Desire of Ruin;[6] and as if we *envied,* not *pitied* the present State of Brussells or of Italy.

Vainly did Pilatre de Rosier break his Neck from an Air Balloon——all our Blockheads sigh to break theirs never a whit the less.[7] Whoever preaches therefore against Revolutionary Principles is surely in the modern Phrase—deserving well of their Country;—and dear Doctor *Randolph* who I fancy is the Man you mean, when you write Dr. *Ratcliffe* does that with sensible Impression.

I am glad all your noble Friends are so happy. Nell Gwynne's House is an Interesting Spot, but why does the King wish to sleep at Windsor?[8] He must not desert his Post even in Death; We must have him in Westminster Abbey. Richard the 4th——as you call *Edward,* was very well preserved as I remember hearing; but I think they have left off embalming royal Bodies now.[9] Perhaps among the many Wonders brought from Egypt they may have learned that old Device over again. It is pretty and curious to have the decree for deifying old Ptolomy lying at

16 August 1802 373

our Somerset House for Inspection of Antiquarians.[10]—Will nothing cure People of expecting Stability from ought in this World?

Your beautiful Poem will take Advantage of this bright Sky, and polish itself to perfection. What a Resource will you find it when the Gout *really* confines you in *earnest*. I suppose this *last first Fit* was more than half a Joke, but it will at least cure the *Urticaria*.

We came here from London thro' Oxford, Cheltenham, <Ross,> Monmouth &c.——a beautiful Drive, and here I have bathed in the Sea and am refreshed; and we are going home across the Principality 125 Miles more, over Mountains and Moor Lands.

Adieu Dear Mr. Chappelow. Direct your next to Brynbella; You will always have Franks at Command, and if not; the Letters are truly welcome to our good Master and your faithful Servant / H: L: Piozzi.

Text: Ry. 561.117. *Address:* The Revd. Mr. Chappelow / Hill Street / Berkley Square / London. *Postmark:* Free Torrington; WINDSOR; Windsor August Nineteenth; FREE AUG 20 1802.

1. RG had recently received his D.D. from Oxford.
2. Lewis Bagot had died in London, 4 June, and was buried 18 June "in the Cathedral Church Yard." See the "St. Asaph Burial Register," C.R.O., Clwyd. His will, proved 10 June, itemized a total of £3,630 in bequests (P.R.O., Prob. 11/1377/494).
3. Having been made first consul on 9 November 1799 and consul for life on 2 August, Bonaparte began to advance several of his brothers through the ranks of French officialdom: Joseph (1768–1844), Bonaparte's eldest brother, elected a French senator, made grand officer of the Légion d'Honneur, 4 August 1802; Lucien (1775–1840), minister of the interior, 25 December 1799; ambassador to Spain, 7 November 1800; French senator and grand officer of the Légion d'Honneur, 4 August 1802; Louis (1778–1846), married on Bonaparte's order to *Hortense*-Eugénie-Cecile (1783–1837), only daughter of *Alexandre*-François-Marie (guillotined, 1794), vicomte de Beauharnais; Jerôme (1784–1860), a close associate of Bonaparte from 1800 onward.

Bonaparte had three sisters: Marie-Anne-*Elisa* (1777–1820); Marie-*Pauline* (1780–1825); Marie-Annonciade-*Caroline* (1782–1839). All had to wait until their brother became emperor of France to receive their royal titles.

See Frédéric Masson, *Napoléon et sa Famille* (Paris: P. Ollendorf, 1897–1919).

4. HLP alludes to the military pomp of Bonaparte's court, tracing his absolute power to a dubious etymological interpretation of Montmartre as *Mont de Mars*.

The Times on 9 August (under the dateline of Paris, 3 August) wrote: "Yesterday the Members of the Senate went in grand procession to the Thuilleries to present their *Senatus Consultum* [by which Bonaparte was made Consul for life with the right to name his successor] to the Chief Consul. At the moment of their arrival [he] was giving audience to the Foreigners of Distinction recently arrived at Paris, who were witnesses of this august ceremony, which had been purposely fixed to take place when the Court was expected to be most crowded."

5. For Louis-Antoine de Bourbon, duc d'Angoulême, see HLP to LC, 4 September 1795, n. 4.

6. The incumbent Parker Coke withdrawing from the election on the sixth day of polling, "Mr. Birch was then declared *duly* elected, and conducted to the *Deputy* Sheriff's house, where he addressed [his followers], *reminding* them it was the 14*th of July, the day* when *France shook off the happiness of monarchy*." He was then chaired triumphantly through

the town, flags in the procession being the French tricolor and tree of liberty as well as a representation of the French Goddess of Liberty. Revolutionary songs and the "Marseillaise" were sung. See *The Times*, 13, 16, 20 July 1802.

In the Middlesex election [or Brentford] Byng and Burdett were chaired. The "Ça Ira" was "sung in front of the King's Palace at Kew; the horses were removed from the carriages, and . . . the populace drew them the whole way to London. . . . The day ended with a dinner at the 'Crown and Anchor' attended by some 600 people." See Patterson 1:138.

7. Jean-François Pilâtre de Rozier (1756–85), a chemist born in Metz, was early inspired by the work of the Montgolfier brothers and devoted himself to the science of aerial navigation. He died 15 June when he (along with a companion) lost control of their balloon, which hurtled to the ground in the vicinity of Boulogne-sur-Mer.

8. That is, Burford House in Windsor. For details of the house, see Robert Richard Tight, Esq., and James Edward Davis, Esq., *Annals of Windsor*, 2 vols. (London: Longman, Brown, Green, Longmans, and Roberts, 1858), especially 2:327, 441–42.

Because LC's letter is missing, it is difficult to determine the relationship between Burford House and the king's desire to be interred at Windsor. He was in fact buried there in Saint George's Chapel on 16 February 1820.

9. LC had confused the names of the two sons of Richard, duke of York, by his wife, Cecily Neville, daughter of the first earl of Westmorland: i.e., Edward IV (1442–83); Richard III (1452–85).

That Edward IV was well embalmed is indicated by the fact that when his coffin was opened at Saint George's Chapel, Windsor, in 1789, his skeleton measured no less than six feet three inches in length. See *GM* 59, pt. 2 (1789): 271–72.

10. A decree inscribed on the Rosetta Stone, brought to England from Egypt in February 1802. It was promulgated by a number of Egyptian priests gathered at Memphis "to celebrate the first commemoration of the accession of Ptolemy V Epiphanes to the throne of Egypt (197–196 B.C.)." The "deification decree" eulogizes the ruler, rewarded by the deities, as a great benefactor of the Egyptian people.

For further information on HLP's attitude toward the Egyptian antiquities brought to England, see her letter to DL, 3 September 1802. See also Sir E. A. Wallis Budge, *The Rosetta Stone in the British Museum* [1929] (New York: AMS Press, 1976), pp. 41–46.

TO THE REVEREND ROBERT GRAY

Monday, 16th August 1802

I fancy Bagot died poor, as Buonaparte will die poor—his nephews eat him up.[1] Family fondness is the common ground on which wise and foolish, brave and meek, all meet at last; and of three hundred Roman sovereigns since celibacy was required, only *three* I think escaped censure of *nepotism*, and one of them was a foundling.

Buonaparte's rapid advancement of a family which can have no claims upon the country he governs, will at last undo him: he would be a happier man, and so would his uncle, the Archbishop of Lyons,[2] if they were looking over their farms at Craicke and at Brynbella, like you and Mr. Piozzi.

Text: Hayward 2:261.

1. HLP's joke, associated in her mind with papal nepotism. Bonaparte at this time had no nephews.
2. Joseph Fesch (1763–1839), a Corsican, was half brother to Napoleon's mother and, after the death of her husband in 1785, became protective of the young Bonapartes. In 1789 he served as archdeacon of Ajaccio. During the Terror, he entered civil life and worked in various capacities until the appointment of Napoleon Bonaparte as commander of the Army of Italy. At that time he became a commissary attached to it. When the first consul began to think of a Catholic restoration, Fesch became a cleric once more and was active in the negotiations for the concordat. In August 1802, he was elevated to the archbishopric of Lyons.

TO PENELOPE SOPHIA PENNINGTON

Brynbella
30: August 1802.

Sick or well, sorry or glad; nobody Sure does write such Letters as our dear Mrs. Pennington—it is because nobody else writes from the Heart.—I suppose.[1] Let not a Heart so sensible so sincere want that Support from within which *we are told* the Consciousness of Rectitude will always bestow; and let no ill Thoughts steal in to destroy the Operation of virtuous Talents and Conduct.

Mr. Pennington was always an *honourable* Character, and since you are to be a dependant Wife, be thankful your Dependance is upon a *Gentleman* who while he deems himself such—will never desert you. Be Thankful too that you have no young Family—you *cannot now* I think, be Parent of two Children and live to see the one rob the other, and run away.—These are Sins against Nature! My Heart recoils from Thought of them. Poor Mrs. Weston!! I who am a Mother must feel for *Her*.

After long wanderings, and washings like the Lady in Hannah More's Village Politics, with Hot Water and Cold Water, and Salt Water and Fresh Water;[2] here am I returned to Brynbella and if I thought it would divert you for a Moment, I would tell you how sublime and beautiful a Journey we had across this Principality from South to North. Fine Alpine Scenery between Machynlleth and Bala, varying at every Step; and presenting now a rough high uncultivated Rock, and now clusters of small Corn Fields round a tiny Village—that for ought I see *need* not be so poor, because the Grass and Grain are really plentiful. Small Lakes among Volcanic fragments are perpetually occurring, and our Guide shewed us one which had *literally no bottom*. From Bala Pool indeed the River Dee takes its Source, and winds about with very elegant bends, till it reaches Chester; but Kader Idris is the Chief Feature of the whole Country, and tho' far smaller than Snowdon, is much more impressive. Our Weather likewise on that Day was gloomy

> The Winds were high, the Clouds low-hung,
> And drag'd their sweepy Trains along
>   The shaggy Mountain's Side.[3]

Apropos to *Verses*—you must read the British Critic for last April, and what he says of Retrospection:[4] it has entertained me exceedingly, and will amuse General Smith and Doctor Randolph. I hope those two Friends will join to console you; what Talents and Literature can do *they* are above all Men I know, capable of administering. But it is a grievous thing to think how very little can be done by *either* Talents or Literature.

Piety and Business will effect in a Month what the other Two could not perform in a Year:—Fly to *those* dear Sophia; and be not solitary or idle for an Instant.[5] Your Situation is happy in that too, it forces You on Company: nor is it wise at any Time to be fastidious—You may receive from *very plain People* very good hints—and one comes away having learned something where 'tis least to be expected, much oftener in your Life than you would think for.

Mr. Siddons's is I fancy quite a *Nice and Montpelier Case;* and as every Man likes his own Son's Company best if he can get it: George and Papa may find their Journey a wise Undertaking.[6]

Our Master has no serious Attack of Gout yet, the Feet indeed are exquisitely tender &c. but he looks very well, and is truly afflicted for your Sufferings.

We have not seen dear Lady Orkney or her Children—for my Lord *is* married, as I suppose the Newspapers have announced,[7] but they are all gone to bathe in the Sea, while Lleweney makes herself fine to receive the sweet little young Mistress, provided for her by Heaven, which directs all Events, and has perhaps (and I *think* so too,) set down for your good Husband Some happy Harbour into which these apparently cross Winds will blow him, while we toil to keep him off the Rocks—for such they may appear to *us*—unknowing of what Shore he should be steering to.

Have a good Heart; Virtue and Honour made more visible by the Reflector—Talent:—will not be left to perish in this Country.

So says our wise Master and so prays Your / H: L: P.

Your Letter followed me < > ——We received it but last night.—I wrote directly.

Text: Princeton University Library. *Address:* Mrs. Pennington / Dowry Square / Hot Wells / Bristol. *Postmark:* DENBIGH 234; franked by Kirkwall, Denbigh August Thirty 1802.

1. HLP's response to PSP's letter of 17 August (Ry. 568.111), in which the latter details her sufferings and fears of insolvency, fears shared neither by her husband nor her mother.
2. One of the characters in *Village Politics* comments on Sir John's wife, the Lady of the Castle. "Now in this village; what shou'd we do without the Castle? Tho' my Lady is too rantipolish, and flies about all summer to hot water and cold water, and fresh water and salt water, when she ought to stay at home with Sir John; yet when she does come down, she brings such a deal of gentry that I have more horses than I can shoe, and my wife more linen than she can wash. Then all our grown children are servants in the family, and rare wages they have got. Our little boys get something every day by weeding their gardens, and the girls learn to sew and knit at Sir John's expence; who sends them all to school of a Sunday." The allegorical Lady, who is attracted to new places and new ideas,

eventually returns to the Castle, the tried and true way—the British monarchy. See the 2d ed. (London: F. and C. Rivington, 1792), pp. 15–16.

3. The beginning of a seven-stanza poem, dated "Brecknock," 16 October 1749 and attributed to William Markham by Horace Walpole in MS notes found in *A Collection of Poems in Three Volumes. By several hands* [edited by Robert Dodsley], 2d ed., 6 vols. (London: R. Dodsley, 1748–58), 4:310. See British Library copy, c. 117.aa.16.

4. For the review of the *British Critic* 19 (April 1802): 355–58, see HLP to LC, 18 June 1801, n. 14.

5. When HLP was grieving for her son Harry, SJ urged: "Remember the great precept, *Be not solitary; be not idle*" (*Letters* 1:310 [30 March 1776]). Cf. *Letters* 1:243; a frequent sentiment in *Idler* and *Rambler*; *Rasselas*, chap. 21. See also, Burton, *Anatomy of Melancholy*, conclusion.

6. With SS in Ireland, William Siddons was responsible for an ailing Sally and the seventeen-year-old George, Henry having married Harriott Murray on 22 June.

From PSP's letter, which reported rumor, HLP read that William Siddons "means to pass the winter at Nice with his son George." But in fact the latter was planning to travel to India for employment in the Bengal Civil Service. See Campbell 2:284.

7. For Lord Kirkwall's marriage, see HLP to LC, 19 March 1799, n. 4.

TO THE REVEREND DANIEL LYSONS

Brynbella
3: September 1802

And now we are come home at last after an 8 Month's Absence, and a 500 Miles Tour,—'tis high Time to congratulate dear Mr. and Mrs. Lysons on the happy Event of which the News Papers informed us—whilst in a *far Country*[1]—— though none more pleasing than Gloucestershire.

We passed a fortnight or three Weeks at Cheltenham, where I remembered the pretty planted Walk finishing with a tall Spire when I was there a *Child* in Company of my Mother and my Aunts; and I *think* I remember the *Smith's* Epitaph in the Church yard;[2] because when reading Camden's Remains many years after, it came in my head how much cleverer *that* is, which *he* preserves—— and in the same Style.[3]

John English's Inscription on his Monument was however *too deep* for me then to be struck with; 'tis almost *too deep now*:—The marking Capitals to denote the Name of Jesus in that Strange way—neither Anagram nor Acrostic, is exceedingly curious;[4] I warrant you have a true Copy of it, and perhaps will give me one.

Write to me Dear Mr. Lysons and *tell* me something: Tell me particularly about the new Comer to Rodmarton's—Health, Strength, and Beauty. The Excellence of *so* new a Comer will be comprized in those Three Words; and if the Truth were well known——The first implies the other two completely.

Here am I without any thing to feed on but my own Thoughts[5]—Our House is painting and ornamenting, and they have thrust the few Books I possess, all into One closet on a heap. My Thoughts are fuller than they were tho'; by the Addition of Your Brother's Kindness in Shewing me the Stone at Somerset

Daniel Lysons. Pencil drawing by George Dance (14 December 1793). (Reproduced by permission of the Trustees of the British Museum, Department of Prints and Drawings.)

House,[6] from which if I could *learn* but little for want of more Skill in Languages; I can please my busy Fancy well enough, perhaps better than if sullen Truth intruded and catched Imagination by the Bridle.

For Example my Recollection says that among the Hieroglyphicks I saw a *Crow* perpetually,[7] and I *do* think, that this same *Crow* came originally out of the same Nest as Old Odin's *Reafan*[8] that King Regner Lodbrog's 3 Weird Sisters[9] worked for Hialmar:—a Standard—of Victory[10]——(Ladies *still* present consecrated *Colours* to the Troops you know)——and a Raven then was the lucky Impress in *every* part of the World, which had not perhaps wholly forgotten its being dismissed from the Ark as a Bird chosen for purpose of fixing future Nations in permanent Happiness.[11] The Ægyptians least of *all* forgot that great Event,—— and when I see in the Library at Somerset House a Vase brought from the *Musquito* Shore adorned with *Grecian* Fretwork,[12] I cannot wonder at any Marks of Affinity between old Coptic and Scandinavian Ideas.

Samuel Lysons. Pencil drawing by Sir Thomas Lawrence (1790's). (Reproduced by permission of the National Portrait Gallery.)

Besides does not *Justin* say?[13]——I told you *true* that I could not get at a Book;—does not *some one* say how Ptolomy that finished the Cut from Nile to the Red Sea[14]—and whose *Deification Act* is said to be now in our Antiquarians Room in the Strand;—joined with Gallo Greeks and Galatians against Antigonus?[15] The *Gauls* wherever planted, considered a Crow as their Coat Armour,[16] if we may call it so; and lost all Courage for that very Reason, when the fatal Bird perched on a Roman's helmet—called *Corvinus*[17] from that Day by his own Countrymen, who readily adopted *all* neighb'ring Superstitions. I do believe the croaking Raven meant Victory in Hieroglyphic Language,[18] and am impatient now till clear Translation shews the Analogy, and makes some Explanation.

If the *British Critic* was to see *this* Stuff, he would say my Letters were in *Rhyme* I suppose, as he says Retrospection is written in blank Verse. Lord bless the People! what Things do come into their Heads! *Mine* is at present very full of Kader Idris——I never saw it till this Summer, and a Grand Sight it is.

We crossed South Wales, and bathed in the Sea at Tenby; Mr. Piozzi kept clear of Confinement at least, tho' he complains of being very Tender footed. He unites with me in true Regards and *Compliments;* or more properly in Sincere *un*complimentary good Wishes to you and Yours; and bears me Witness that I am always very /truly Dear Mr. Lyson's / faithful Servant / H: L: P.

Pray write me a long Letter.

Text: Hyde Collection. *Address:* Rev: Daniel Lysons / Rodmarton / Gloucestershire. *Postmark:* DENBIGH.

---

1. DL had married Sarah, née Hardy (d. 1808), at Bath on 12 May 1801. They became parents of a daughter, Sarah, 23 July 1802. See *GM* 72, pt. 2 (1802): 684.

2. A guidebook to the Cheltenham Parish Church (Saint Mary's) gives the following inscription from the tombs in the churchyard:

"To the memory of John Paine, blacksmith, died 1796"

> My sledge and hammer lies reclined,
> My bellows pipe have lost its wind,
> My fire's extinct, my forge decayed,
> And in the dust my vice is layed.
> My coal is spent, my iron's gone,
> My nails are drove, my work is done.

3. "Vpon a Puritanicall Lock-Smith"

> *A zealous Lock-Smith dyed of late,*
> *And did arive at heaven gate,*
> *He stood without and would not knocke,*
> *Because he meant to picke the locke.*

"Epitaphes" (pp. 360–420), in *Remaines concerning Britaine . . . Written by William Camden, Esquire. . . .* (London: John Waterson, St. Paul's Church-yard, 1636), p. 408.

4. On the east wall near the altar is the following inscription:

3 September 1802 381

The sad Memoriall of John English, Doctor in Divinitye, to Jane his most deare Wife, Daughter to the Honourable Elizabeth Lady Sandys, Baronese de la Vine Comit. Southton; from whom he was divorced by 18 Weekes close Imprisonment, which soone after caused her Death on August 8, 1643. To Mary his second Daughter, who deceased Oct. 25 following.

> Sic cecinit lugens, et dissolvi cupiens,
> Pius conjux, ac moestus parens.   I. E.
> Qui mundo, suspirans, et coelum aspirans,
>   Indesinenter clamat
>   Bone Jesu, esto meus Jesus!
> Sis meus o Jesu! sis Jesus (Christe) meorum!
>   Sweet Saviour of mankind,
>   The Saviour of mee and mine.
>   Spirans oravit
> Sic   Expirans exoravit,
>   Respirans perorabit,
>
> John English { Sacri / Sanctae / Sempiterne } Verbi { Veritas / Vitae } studiosus
> Obiit anno Christi   Amen.

See [Ralph Bigland], *Historical, Monumental and Genealogical Collections, Relative to the County of Gloucester; printed from the original papers of the late Ralph Bigland* . . . 2 vols. (London: Printed by John Nichols, for Richard Bigland, 1791–92), 1:314; John Lee, *The New Guide to Cheltenham and its Environs* (Cheltenham [ca. 1845]), p. 120. For the death date of Dr. English in 1647, see *Notes and Queries* 8, 5th series (1877): 67, 179, 359.

5. Cf. Milton, *Paradise Lost*, 3.37–38: "Then feed on thoughts, that voluntarie move / Harmonious numbers; . . ."

6. The famous Rosetta Stone had been found by the French in August 1799 near the small Egyptian town of Rashîd (Rosetta), some thirty miles from Alexandria. They removed it to the Institut National in Cairo, but after the fall of Alexandria (17–27 August 1801) were obliged to cede it to the English under the terms of article 16, "Articles of Capitulation" (30 August). It arrived in England February 1802, aboard *H.M.S. Egyptienne*, under the custodianship of General H. Turner. Before transference to the British Museum for permanent display, it was exhibited in the library of the Society of Antiquaries at Somerset House, as were several massive companion pieces.

7. HLP attempted to interpret a sign language that would not become accessible until the publication of the French Egyptologist, Jean-François Champollion (1790–1832): *De l'écriture Hiératique des Anciens Égyptiens* (Grenoble, 1821). In this work, which established the principle of deciphering Egyptian hieroglyphics, HLP would not have discovered crows, but an abundance of other birds: vultures, buzzards, falcons, owls, cormorants; even geese, ducks, and sparrows. Sir Alan Gardiner, *Egyptian Grammar*, 3d ed. (London and Oxford: Griffith Institute; Ashmolean Museum; Oxford University Press, 1957); Edwyn R. Bevan, *The House of Ptolemy: A History of Egypt under the Ptolemaic Dynasty* (Chicago: Argonaut, 1968).

8. There is a physical affinity between ravens and crows, insofar as both are glossy and black and belong to the genus *Corvus*.

Two ravens are associated with Odin, the Norse god of war; *Hugin* is representative of reflection or thought; *Munin* of memory. Legend has it they would perch on Odin's shoulders and whisper their knowledge in his ears. He was known as *Rafnagud* (raven-god). See n. 17.

9. Ragnar [Regner] Lodbrok was a legendary Danish king whose heroic deeds have been celebrated in *The Saga of Ragnar Lodbrok* (a sequel to the *Volsung Saga*) and in his death song, *The Lay of Kraka* (the *Krakamal*). His daughters (here lightly compared with the Fates of classical mythology) are said to have woven and embroidered a raven on the Danish

war standard. The raven is frequently invoked as a warlike bird in the *Saga* and *Lay* of the king. See the translation of this material by Margaret Schlauch, published in 1930.

10. HLP alludes to *Histoire d'Hialmar, roi de Biarmlandiæ, et souverain de l'île Thulemarkie, composée avant le viiie Siècle, par un anonyme, fils de Hrandur:* a translation of the supposed Runic MS, containing "Hialmars och Ramers saga," written by Lucas Halpap, 1799. The work first appeared as: *Fragmentum m^{ser} runici (Hialmars och Ramers Saga), cum interpretatione vernacula nec non aphorismi selecti quae . . . eruditorium examini subjicit Lucas Halpap,* etc. (Upsulae: J. Bilberg, [1690]).

11. In superstitious lore, the raven is treated as a bird of ill omen, endowed with powers of augury (nn. 8 and 17). As a Judaeo-Christian symbol, however, the raven may be a harbinger of good fortune. See Gen. 8:7: Noah "sent forth a raven, which went forth to and fro, until the waters were dried up from off the earth."

12. The Mosquito Coast defines an area on the eastern borders of Nicaragua and Honduras. The name was derived from the Miskito Indians.

13. *Iustini historici politissimi Epitoma in Trogi Pōpeii historias pemiũ incipit* ([Rome]: Udalricus Gallus, [1470]). See especially bk. 25, chap. 2–4.

Justin was Marcus Junianus Justinus (ca. third century A.D.). The best edition of this work available to HLP was by A. Gronovius (1719).

14. A canal was constructed from the Nile to the Red Sea in the reign of Ptolemy II for commercial traffic (Bevan, *The House of Ptolemy,* pp. 154–55).

15. HLP's allusion is obscured by duplication of famous kings and their wars: Ptolemy I (see her letter to the Ladies of Llangollen, 14 June 1801, n. 9); Ptolemy II (Philadelphus, ca. 308–246 B.C.); Antigonus I (Cyclops, ca. 382–301 B.C.); Antigonus II (Gonatas, ca. 320–239 B.C.).

16. The Roman eagle had become a part of the French coat of arms in the reign of Charles IX (1560–74); and it was embossed on the standard of the French republic.

17. See nn. 8 and 11. Since ancient times, the emblematic bird of the Roman militia and legions had been the eagle rather than the "fatal" crow or raven *(Corvus).*

18. HLP mistook the falcon, which was a symbol of victory in the Egyptian royal arms, for a raven.

TO PENELOPE SOPHIA PENNINGTON

Brynbella Thursday
7: October 1802.

When a Member of Parliament says to me Shall I give you a Frank?—Oh Yes I always reply—for *Mrs. Pennington.* Lord Kirkwall's Generosity is the Cause of *this* Letter, because in these hard Times one likes you see, to get a little Chat gratis. The next Thing to be considered is——What shall I ask, and what shall I tell?

That my Master has had a Smart Fit of Gout in his Hands, and that I expect him to have one in his feet may be told with Truth—That the Countess of Cork and Orrery drove up to our Door while he was confined, may be told with some Degree of Vexation; because I knew not how on Earth to amuse her, but She was goodhumoured, and gave little Trouble——and after a fortnight's Visit—went away.[1]

What She related of her adventures among the Crags of Kader Idris, her Admiration of that wild Mountain Scenery, and the Contrast *our* gay Prospect afforded her—will I suppose be Served up at many a London Assembly next May.

Ladies appear now to travel all Autumn upon a foraging Plan of gleaning Talk for their Spring Parties——They who spend June and July in London, can never perswade me that they are really in Search of rural Pleasures the remaining Part of the Year in *our* Cold Climate, or that rural Pleasure is really to be found where Deformity is sought;——Miss Thrales have been looking for *both* as I understand among the *Western Islands,* described by every Traveller as barren, bleak, and dangerous.

Had Mr. Piozzi and I known, that they were navigating the Stormy Sound of Mull when we heard the Wind roar so a fortnight ago irritated by Equinoxial Gales;—we should have been in pain for *them,* not for the Furniture, expected from Mayhew and Ince[2] to decorate pretty Brynbella.

All is safe however. Mrs. Bagot used to say it was superfluous to wish any body a good Journey, because said She—*every* body has a good Journey.——"Ah Dear Friend! (I hear you exclaim) Many have a good Journey thro' Life too; yet is it not Superfluous to wish their Neighbours one likewise——for surely mine has been a very bad one." Come Courage.—The next Stages will be smoother, for you shall not predict of your own Fortune with that unlucky Acuteness you show in discerning the future Lot of others.

Poor Tommy—our simple Footman goes the precise Road which you marked out for him, 'spite of the more pleasing Prognostics drawn by the Bath Physicians—Harington and Parry:[3] It is a melancholy Sight, but I will hope no *unimproving* one——Whither he goes, We must follow;[4] and he may yet outlive us his more healthy Friends.—Poor Lad! I really feel exceeding sorry.

A Chain of Thoughts *you* will but too easily detect—leads me to sweet Siddons: She writes me word from Belfast that She will call here in her hurrying Journey back to our Metropolis.

Jane Holman's Letters are full of her Praises, *as* full as they can be, while an Event still more interesting fills her heart with *Hope,* and with all those airy Delights that can be contained in a Bubble so brilliant.[5] *She* is expecting,—not Money, She is contented without *that:* not Friends, She has left them on t'other Side the Water; and will never see them more. Not Health—for *that* She willingly risques the Loss of; but She expects a *Child.* The last was mangled and herself left for dead Three Hours—Never Mind—She is looking forward as her Artless Letter says with *Pleasure void of Fear* to an Event, which will *ensure her Happiness.* Dear Soul! I shall be anxious till her moment comes. Mr. and Mrs. Hamilton I fancy have found that having Children does not in an absolute sense *ensure one's Happiness.*—I never saw Creature so altered and broken up as that Lady, partly no doubt by Absence of a Daughter so passionately beloved; and Thoughts of *her* approaching danger will contribute nothing to restore the Looks of such a Parent.

Lady Orkney is a happy Mother however, and a true Friend; and remembers you and your Afflictions in her Prosperity. If She ever *can* serve you she will, and so will Lady Corke too, to whom I told something and She said it was a Shame, and that Government would one Day make you amends by bestowing on you a

Place if properly applied to——and we will talk seriously upon that Subject when we meet.

                                                            7 October 2—

It will be best to come early this year to Bath and get home early—for after all we are *not* putting up our Furniture which lies warm in our Barn and Stable and *shall* lye there all Winter and set Matters to rights in Spring. Meanwhile here is an End of Paper for this Time, and I hope it will produce me a long Letter from you. Put Harriet Lee's Epistle in your Post Office.—She says Mr. Garratt has left our favourite House to his Wife—and we have the same Chance of it as last Year.[6]

Give our true Regards to Mr. Pennington, and Compliments to Miss Powell and Your Mother and believe me ever equally Yours / H: L: Piozzi.

Text: Princeton University Library.

    1. For Mary, countess of Corke and Orrery, see HLP to PSP, 2 June 1802, n. 10.
    2. The London upholsterers; see HLP to LC, 17 June 1798.
    3. For Henry Harington, see HLP to SL, 15 November 1788, n. 6; for Caleb Hillier Parry, see HLP to PSW, 1 September [1789], n. 7.
    4. John 13:36; Rev. 14:4.
    5. Jane Holman was now living in Dublin, where her husband had gone shortly after a quarrel between the proprietors of the Covent Garden and eight of the principal actors (of whom Holman was one) during the 1799–1800 season. The issues of the quarrel had been submitted to the lord chamberlain, who had decided for the proprietors. Seven actors accepted the decision and continued at the Covent Garden. Holman either resigned or was fired. In Dublin he was successful enough to take a share in the Theatre Royal.
    6. According to the *Bath Herald,* 7 August, William Garrett (1733–1802) had died on 1 August "at his house in Laura-place." The house he had bequeathed to his wife was at 77 Pulteney Street, Bath.

TO MR. JOHN LLOYD

                                               Fryday 26: November 1802
                                                        Brynbella

My dear Sir

    Do me the honour to accept a very neatly corrected Copy of Retrospection in exchange for Your own. It may perhaps *some* Day, be of *some* Value if only for the Notes' Sake.

    Send me at the same Time Lysons's Letter if you have done with it.[1]

    We go on Tuesday; and Mr. Piozzi is so lame, he is afraid of being catched on the Road if we do not make haste. He is forced to deny himself even the Pleasure of calling on Mrs. W: Evans, a Visit we always thought upon with Pleasure.[2] For your Part, I hope we shall see you at Bath.

    'Tis a nice Place, and forms an agreable Contrast to our own Vale—apropos how very beautifully must Wygfair have shewed off on Monday last! It was a heavenly day.

Yet I long to be nearer the Centre of Intelligence in these Interesting and busy Times, when every News Paper teems with fresh Wonders, fresh Horrors.

Well! Adieu! and love my poor Book—the better because it was my own private Copy with Verses &c. in it, meant for no one's perusal but / that of Dear Sir / Yours faithfully / H: L: P.

Mr. Piozzi['s] best Regards attend you ever.

Text: National Library of Wales MS 12421D. *Address:* John Lloyd Esq. / Wygfair. "with a Parcel and for a Parcel."

1. DL's—now missing—letter, which described the Rosetta Stone and to which HLP replied on 3 September.
2. The widow of William Evans of Parc y Twll, who had been buried 28 May 1802. See "Henllan Parish Registers," C.R.O., Clwyd.

TO JOHN EWEN

Brynbella
November 1802

It was most exceedingly good natured in our valuable Friend to depute dear Mr. Ewen as the Answerer of my long Letter, and a nice Acquisition for me to gain so agreeable a Correspondence.[1] You could scarce have learned more even had You staid longer——as to *General* Matters—in France; and for *particulars*, more Months than you remained days there would have been necessary.

I long to be told however somewhat concerning the Churches; You know how splendid and how numerous they were in *my Time:* Are they destroyed? or only deserted; or are they converted to other Uses? No one has yet given me any Satisfactory Account. I do not expect the Silver to have been spared, but the fine Perspective *inside* St. Rocque—a Masterpiece of Art:[2] and the Façade of St. Genevieve, the Sculpture of which boasts—if I remember rightly the Hand of Bernini, may perhaps yet remain.[3] L'Hôpital des Invalides likewise once so much my Envy, when comparing it with our Chelsea;[4] Is it still standing? *Vit il encore?* Under this truly warlike Usurper *such* Things should be cherished, tho' the Transfiguration of Rafaelle endures French Varnish on its Characters.[5]

Well! I am of their Mind completely, that *any* Despot suits Parisians of modern Times better than Freedom does: and Buonaparte has my full Consent to rule them with a Rod of Iron. If he lays that *Rod* by——even for a Moment, it will like Aaron's of old——turn to a *Serpent* and *affright* him:[6] for it does not appear upon Investigation that this Corsican Warrior is a *Hero at his Heart*. Sir Sydney Smith always averred he had no Pretensions to such a Character——and your Account of his personal Manners is like that Dr. Crawford gave me——who said he looked *anxious and bilious*.⁷ These as you know are no more the Diseases of a Hero, than a System of Espionage is the Mode of Rule which a Hero would adopt. One sees plain by all rational Narratives of his Conduct, that the Man invites Assassination;——but that Carnot who wanted to tan his own Countrymen's Hides for use, in Days of the Guillotine: has no fancy for a Pair of Gloves *a la Buonaparte*.⁸

Mr. and Mrs. Fox will do well to stay a while in Paris——*why* was not the Lady *presented?*⁹ I understand not such *half* etiquette, such *Demi* Caractere:——Les Sœurs de la Liberté are as good as les Freres in my Mind.

Mr. Giles will not feel as pleased with his own or his Neighbour's Paintings now,¹⁰ as he was before going abroad——and as for all Casts and Imitations of the sublime Apollo, they always *did* make me sick.¹¹ Never having read Homer in the Original, Pope's beautiful Iliad and Odyssey fill up all my Ideas of Poetry in Perfection——but I *have* seen the Apollo, and 'tis cruel to present me a *Bronze* of him. Such a Speech would seem pedantic to many a one, but Dear Mr. Ewen *deserved* a Sight of the Apollo; *he* praises him con vero Amore.

How goes the French Idea now of Modern Politics? Will they absolutely devour poor little Switzerland?¹² I am sorry. Our last Newspaper tells of two *Roman* Ravens pursuing an Eagle on the Grampian hills; I rather fear the Roman Eagle is pursued—by *Gaulish* Ravens;——The Author of the Paragraph understood little of *Augury*.

'Tis monstrous that these marauding Fellows have robbed every body's Library thro' all Europe, and yet have no Regard to their own common Stock of Literature. Once I possessed a *Marvilliana* but now wish to buy it again. It consists of 3 small Volumes collected by Noel D'Argonne a Carthusian Fryar under the name of *Vigneul Marville*¹³——If you ever see such a Thing Dear Sir do me the honor to inform me——such Reading just suits now with Your Idle, but / ever faithful Servant / H: L: Piozzi

Text: Hyde Collection. *Address:* J: Ewen Esq.

    1. John Ewen (fl. 1750–1813) is associated with HLP's tenant, Peter Giles, who "changed [Streatham Park] rather for the better than the worse—Books of enormous Value drove my old *Rums* behind them, & for Collections of curious engravings—Oriental Landshapes, Chinese Dresses & Customs, fine Holbein Heads & exquisite Specimens of Natural History: we must I think go to Peter Giles the Cornfactor, & his Friend Mr Ewen—a broken Apothecary as I understand; who purchases & arranges Things for him, with very solid Judgement & very excellent Taste" (*Thraliana* 2:1012).
John Ewen did in fact own an apothecary shop in Leadenhall Street in 1779 and was a member of the Society of Apothecaries at that time. After that year his name disappears from the society's membership lists. His name, however, is carried on the "Streatham Land Tax Assessments" as late as 1813. See C.R.O., Surrey.
    2. That is, the church of St-Sulpice, whose classical building was begun in 1646 and was regarded as one of the noblest structures in Paris.
Of the five chapels encircling the church, the fifth contains the tomb of the curé Languet de Gergy (1675–1750), founder of the Enfants Malades. The tomb was sculpted in 1747 by Michelangelo Slodtz, influenced by Giovanni Lorenzo Bernini (1598–1680).

For a description of HLT's experiences at St-Sulpice, see the *French Journals*, pp. 96–97, 144–46, 197.

3. On the east side of the Place Ste-Geneviève is the Church of St-Étienne-du-Mont, which had been in almost continuous construction from 1495 (to 1586 and later). The church exemplifies the architectural transition from the Gothic to the Renaissance style. We can find no evidence of Bernini's work in this church.

4. The Hôtel des Invalides was founded by Louis XIV in 1671 as a home for disabled soldiers, the first of its kind. HLP correctly compares it to Chelsea Hospital, whose structure was conceived by Sir Christopher Wren and whose first stone was laid by Charles II in 1682.

5. See HLP to Joseph Cooper Walker, [30] November or [1 December] 1799, n. 6.

6. See HLP to Q, 19 December 1794, n. 7.

7. Many English visitors to Paris in 1802 believed Bonaparte's appearance was either ghostlike or unhealthy. According to J. B. Trotter, e.g., who had accompanied Charles James Fox to France, one night "when Bonaparte entered his box in the theatre the light from the stage fell upon his face 'so as to give an unfavourable and ghastly effect.' " See John W. Derry, *Charles James Fox* (New York: St. Martin's Press, 1972), p. 395.

8. Lazare-Nicolas-Marguerite Carnot (1753–1823). Having trained as an engineer, he had become politically active during the revolution as the elected deputy for the Pas-de-Calais. Reputed to be a stern republican, he served as a member of the committee of Public Safety, thus becoming identifiable with the violence of the Reign of Terror.

Years later HLP wrote of him in the "Commonplace Book": "The Man who suggested in some of the French Assemblees Nationales a Notion of tanning human Hides to make Breeches for les Sans Culottes is still alive I hear *1814*. I remember [an English] Lady telling me that Madame Carnot was the last Friend she embraced at Paris—whither her Husband hasted—I forget how many Miles—for the pleasure of seeing Louis seize Guillotined——Il faut avouer continued She, que c'etoit un beau Jour pour la Liberté— . . . Carnot wrote pretty Verses . . . will poor Lewis the 18th make *him* Poet Laureate? What a Den of Tygers is he gone amongst! ! Poor Man! How will he conduct himself?"

See also HLP to LC, 18 June 1804.

Carnot in 1802 "fut le seul membre de cette assemblée [tribunat] qui osa voter contre le consulat à vie. Il combattit avec plus de force encore l'élévation de Bonaparte à l'empire, et refusa de signer le registre d'adhésion." See Décembre-Alonnier 1:434.

9. About 1783 Elizabeth Armistead became the mistress of Charles James Fox. On 28 September 1795, they were secretly married, she signing the register as Elizabeth B. Cane (ca. 1750–1842). The identity of Mr. Armistead has never been established or even his existence. But only in 1802, just before their French journey, did the Foxes admit they were legally married.

On 29 July, the Foxes left for France and returned to England on 17 November. "There was no doubt that Fox was well received in Paris, nor was this limited to demonstrations of popular respect." He received visits from Talleyrand, Lafayette, Sieyès. "But the most dramatic event was the meeting with Bonaparte . . ." (Derry, pp. 122–24, 293–97).

10. The rich merchant John Kymer; see HLP to PSP, [8] December 1800, n. 6.

11. HLP's paragraph moves in two directions at once. The "sublime Apollo" refers to the marble statue, which prior to its confiscation on "the 27th Thermidor, 4th Year of the French republic," stood in the Belvedere of the Vatican. As far as HLP was concerned, its presence in Paris stemmed from an act of piracy.

But her statement also refers to the debate that concentrated on the originality of the marble statue. From the last two decades of the eighteenth century some art historians believed that the Apollo Belvedere was a copy (as indeed it was) of a bronze, now ascribed by some to Leochares, who flourished mid–fourth century B.C.

HLP would have little to do with the "Casts" used to prove the earlier existence of a bronze Apollo. See Farington 1:442–43.

12. A counterrevolutionary movement had developed in the Helvetic Republic, culminating in a rebellion in Vaud and disturbances in the Aargau and in Bern. Bonaparte

intervened, sending in General Ney with some thirty thousand troops and orders to crush all dissent.

According to the British press, "it is . . . no longer doubtful, that the Cantons of Switzerland, have found it most prudent to submit to the dictates of the Chief Consul." So *GM* had written in October; a month later it confirmed its opinion (72, pt. 2: 963, 1056).

13. Vigneul-Marville was the pseudonym for Noël Bonaventure D'Argonne (1634–1704). The work to which HLP refers can be found in vols. 5 and 6 of Charles-Georges-Thomas Garnier (1746–95), ed. *Ana* (Amsterdam and Paris, 1789–99). In another edition the work is called *Vigneul-Marvilliana,* 2 vols. (1789).

TO PENELOPE SOPHIA PENNINGTON

Gloucester, Saturday Night
4: December 1802

And so I lose Hannah More,[1] and so I lose Mrs. Siddons,[2] and so I lose Dear Mrs. Pennington;[3] and so I lose my favrite House at Bath——

Still drops *some* Joy from with'ring Life away![4]——but 'tis all *for their Good* as the Children say, and I resign to my fate. Let us hope at least that increase of Health and Fortune may make *them* happy. My Master comes better from Brynbella this Year, than I scarce ever saw him——so we may stand in the Street for ought I care, when he's in no Danger of catching cold——

And now let's talk of something else. You cautioned me Dear Friend not to tell of your Arrangements. Assure yourself I am incapable of any such Breach of trust; if one lets the Maid comb one's *own* Secrets out of one's *Head*—(and I have none in,)—Those *confided* to me are in a safer Place; lodged in my *Heart.* I hope your new Projects will answer, and that you will tell me so on New Year's day after Dinner.

We have left dear old Lleweney and pretty young Brynbella as happy and smiling as possible: Shall we bring back News of War or Peace I wonder?[5] My Voice is seldom for *Change*——Let us be quiet now we are quiet: says H: L: P. Colonel *Desperado* was not of that Mind but Botany Bay—or worse—may change his Opinions.[6]

The People in this Town are enraged against Ridgeway; his Book is considered as a very cruel and infamous Libel.[7] But I would rather be talking of our old Acquaintance Jane Holman——of whom I now think more seriously than when I wrote last: Mrs. Siddons's Letters have opened my Eyes upon that Subject and I see there was no Sense nor no Wit in laughing at her Want of Children or Difficulty in bringing them—more of this when we meet: only 'tis in the Case with me as in many more——I think Things comical with a first Glance which turn out even solemn at a second.

Adieu! and never put down Penetration among the few good Qualities of your / H: L: P.

Direct Post Office Bath——We have there neither House nor Home I find.

Text: Princeton University Library. *Address:* Mrs. Pennington / Dowry Square / Hot Wells / Bristol. *Postmark:* GLOCESTER.

1. PSP had written 19 October (Ry. 568.113): "You will miss one Pleasure at Bath this Winter. Mrs. H. More finds her health [plagued by recurrent bouts of 'ague'] so much benefitted by her new Residence at *Barley Hill* that She intends, with her Sisters, to remain there the Winter, and to let their House in Pulteney Street; therefore should you be disappointed of Mrs. Garratts, or disposed to take one with *fewer* apartments you may have theirs."
2. HLP had hoped to see SS in Bath. But under financial pressure from her husband, SS had to continue acting. He allowed her to choose between Liverpool and Dublin. "She preferred the far more lucrative speculation of continuing in the Irish capital" where "her popularity, both personal and professional, was unabated," and where she stayed through the winter until 10 March. See Campbell 2:284–85.
3. On 21 November (Ry. 568.114), PSP told HLP that they would not be able to meet often in Bath. "The *altered* state of my affairs will compel me to stay at home and look after my 'Mops and my Money.' . . . *Another* tye upon me will be the company of a Lady, a Protegee of Dr. Randolphs, the Dutchess of Devonshire, and Lady Baths,—the *Marchioness* I mean, who seeks an Assylum, from some unpleasant Circumstances in Life, in my Family, and whose residence with us will, *now*, be necessary to enable me to support our accustomed Establishment."
4. SJ's *Vanity of Human Wishes*, line 306.
5. England was to renew the war with France 16 May 1803.
6. Irish-born Edward Marcus Despard (1751–1803) had been unjustly dismissed from his military post in Jamaica ca. 1790 and returned to England, where he could find no employment. When he persistently demanded restitution, he was in 1798 sent to Coldbath Fields prison without any charge directed against him. In that same year, he was again imprisoned. When he was released in 1800, he began to form a plot against the government: to seize the Tower and the Bank of England, to assassinate the king, and to stop the mails from leaving London. The government arrested Despard and forty others—laborers and soldiers—who were mostly Irish, at the Oakley Arms, Lambeth, on 16 November 1802. See Stanhope 3:398–99.
For his trial and subsequent execution, see HLP to Q, 2 March 1803.
7. The barrister William Ridgeway (d. 1817) wrote *A Report of the Proceedings in Cases of High Treason, at a Special Commission of Oyer and Terminer, Held in and for the County and City of Dublin, in the month of July 1798* (Dublin: John Exshaw, 1798).
It reports the trial of Henry and John Sheares for high treason committed in Dublin on 20 May 1798. According to the charge they enlisted the aid of John Warneford Armstrong and planned to seize the king's militia, his artillery, and the city of Dublin, and to depose George III. When the brothers were brought to trial, the case against them depended on the evidence of Armstrong, who served as an informer and whose evidence was described by Henry Sheares as "one of the most ingenious, and malicious fabricated stories . . . I ever heard of" (p. 168).
The presiding judge, Lord Carleton, in his charge to the jury, virtually found the defendants guilty. The jury deliberated for seventeen minutes before handing in a guilty verdict (p. 176). The brothers were executed on 14 July.
The assumption that Ridgeway's book was a libel arose from the fact that the defendants emerge as morally strong figures, that they were convicted without sufficient evidence and too speedily executed. Actually Ridgeway, a trial reporter as well as barrister, recorded only what was said.

TO MRS. PENNINGTON

No. 5 Henrietta Street
Thursday 16: December 1802

Dear Mrs. Pennington
is always right——The Letter was *a mere nothing:* Such will I hope prove the more rationally alarming Report of Constantinople's Sudden and unlooked for Destruction.[1] Be that as it may, our charming Doctor Randolph took occasion to draw thence a most beautiful and Impressive Sermon last Sunday, when he preached better than ever I heard him, to a Heterogeneous Congregation which attracted my Notice as much as the Discourse did: Mr. Pitt,[2] Dr. Maclean, the Duchess of York and Bishop of West Meath.[3]

Tell me Dear friend if we are to expect *you* in that odious Room close to the prison——next Saturday or *when?*

Mr. Whalley and I had some pretty cool Chat two Days ago, but *nothing worth repeating*—his Health I perceive is very furiously bad now.

Miss Case dined with us once.[4] She is a good bit of Talk as can be; but Harriet Bowdler is a sad Loss to me,[5] and so are the Moores.[6]

Bath is scarce Bath this year somehow, were it not for Laura Chapel and Pump, I should regret leaving Solitude and Brynbella—but then Laura and Pump are two good Things for Soul and Body——and what is all the rest?

Write at least if you don't come; and say how Matters stand with the ever partial, the ever kind friend of your / H: L: Piozzi.

Text: Princeton University Library.

---

1. According to *GM* 72, pt. 2 (1802): 1153:
"A very violent earthquake was experienced, with greater or lesser effect, on and about the 26th of October, in Constantinople and in all Syrmium. It extended as far as Servia, Bosnia, and the other Turkish provinces on the Black Sea. At Constantinople, we find, a number of houses and mosques in the suburb of Galata were destroyed. The shocks lasted more than 30 minutes, and followed each other with the greatest rapidity. The Seraglio was much shaken. The Grand Seignior fled into the principal mosque, formerly the Church of St. Sophia, where the people collected in a mass; that mosque being reputed indestructible."

2. Toward the end of October, Pitt honored his promise to Sir Walter Farquhar and went to Bath where he showed "no symptoms of illness; very slight traces of it in his looks, and none whatever in his appetite and spirits." He remained in Bath until 27 December. See Stanhope 3:400–29.

3. Thomas Lewis O'Beirne (ca. 1748–1823) was born an Irish Catholic who became a Protestant, was ordained a priest (1773), and served as chaplain to Lord Howe's fleet in 1776. He became involved in English politics as a strong Whig and pamphleteer. His political friends rewarded his fidelity by appointing him first to the bishopric of Ossory (1795) and then to that of Meath (1798–1823).

Snidely the *Morning Herald,* 8 January 1799, reported "Mr. O'Beirne has been translated from the See of *Ossory* to that of Meath, in Ireland, through the interest of the Duke of Portland [whom he had once served as secretary and chaplain], and not his own well-known zeal in defence of the *Catholic Faith!*"

4. For Hester Case, see HLP to PSP [ca. 12 December 1799], n. 2.
5. Harriet Bowdler was visiting her brother Thomas at Saint Boniface, Isle of Wight.
6. Hannah More and her sisters.

TO PENELOPE SOPHIA PENNINGTON

[Bath] Tuesday
21: December 1802.

Well, Well! as Sir George Colebrooke says,[1] If we must not meet we may write I suppose; and I really will *try* to rejoyce if my absent Friends are happy.

Dear Siddons's Letter was of more real value than you seem to think it.——All our News Papers and News Talkers have been telling how She was hissed in Dublin, and how Ill it had made her; with long and vexatious Et Cæteras of their own devising:[2] but all is well, and so that wise Man Mr. Twiss, with his clear straightforward Understanding said it would be;[3] and February will bring her home with all her Money safe I hope; and a good Account if so please God of poor Mrs. Holman, whose Situation I knew only through Mrs. Siddons's Information.

Little Cecy has been in Marlbro' Street for *Months.*[4]

The Bishop of West Meath preached our Hospital Sermon at pretty Laura yesterday, and we had a great Collection. The Irish are famous for Eloquence in Praise of Almsgiving.—There are you know marvellous Tales told of a Mr. or Doctor Kirwan who preaches the People's Money out of their Pockets at Dublin.[5]

But there is other Talk too. A Letter has been handed about from an Ecclesiastic at Paris to one of his own Profession here at Bath, expressive of strange Confidence that a Short Time will produce no small Burst among the Frenchmen——and then, who will be sorry? No one. And who will be benefited? No one.

Our Weather here is wondrous mild and Soft—good for Brynbella Planting, and very good for the *very poor* People, who cannot keep themselves and their one Cow alive in hard Frosts. It is however bad for the Ground I think, and not favourable to Health: besides that as Cold sharp Winds *must* come, it will vex me to get them all setting in keenly to meet us on the Welsh Mountains.

Here is ne'er a Room to be had for Love or Money, and Miss Sharp's Fame increasing daily, She has 8 Lessons to give o'Day we hear;[6] So that is a good Thing—and another of your favourite Misses is going to be rich in another Way——Miss Honour Gubbins. She marries a gay Mr. Dutton who is much with her Protectress the Duchess of York.[7] This is Mrs. Randolph's news,[8] and I suppose *She* knows, and *you* care: and therefore and therefore only does it find a Place in this Letter.

Mrs. Stratton is not well[9]——but She gives Tea, Cake and Music——and then——We all say Oh She is well enough, and so She is poor Soul! for *our* purpose. Such is Bath and London Friendship.

God bless you Dear Friend—and continue to be good humoured, and take what Heaven sends with Chearfulness: and Make all your *Inmates* love the < > Name of your / faithful H: L: Piozzi.

Did you see the Lightning on Sunday Night?

Text: Princeton University Library. *Address:* Mrs. Pennington / Dowry Square / Hot Wells / Bristol. *Postmark:* BATH.

1. For Sir George Colebrook, see HLP to SL, 28 November 1789, n. 6.
2. In the summer of 1802 the manager of the Theatre Royal in Dublin asked SS to perform for a local charity. This she agreed to do, leaving the choice of charity to the lord lieutenant's wife. The lying-in hospital was proposed but nothing more was done about the matter. The newspapers subsequently announced that the actress refused to play a benefit for the hospital. But in time its trustees printed a statement to the effect that SS had never refused to perform for the hospital and that in fact she had never been asked to do so. See Ffrench, pp. 223–24; Campbell 2:286–87.
3. For Francis Twiss, SS's brother-in-law, see HLP to PSP [29 April] 1798, n. 4.
4. Cecilia Siddons had been withdrawn from Belvidere School prior to its closing, in 1803.
5. Irish-born Walter Blake Kirwan (1754–1805) was by 1778 made chaplain to the Neapolitan ambassador at the British court and was already known for the popular eloquence of his sermons. In 1787 he left the Roman Catholic Church and in June of the same year preached his first sermon in Anglican Saint Peter's Church, Dublin. His oratory brought in so many worshippers that Sunday collections were sometimes as much as £1,200. He rose steadily in the Anglican hierarchy, becoming in 1800 dean of Killala.
6. For Elizabeth Sharp, see HLP to PSP, 26 April 1801, n. 4.
7. Honoria Gubbins was in 1803 to marry Ralph Dutton (1755–1804), of Billingford, Norfolk, a younger brother of James, first lord Sherborne. Dutton, a steward of the Jockey Club, was a well-known racing man to whom the duke of York was indebted for large sums of money. When Dutton died, the duke still owed him £6,060. In 1805 Dutton's widow was to accept an annuity of £606 in place of the principal.
8. For Mary Randolph, see HLP to PSP, 10 March 1799, n. 2.
9. For Mary Stratton, see HLP to PSP, 5 April 1801, n. 3.

TO PENELOPE SOPHIA PENNINGTON

[ca. 24: December 1802.][1]

My dear Mrs. Pennington's Friends will learn to *hate* poor H: L: P's Name, and that of her *Family* I fear; when I have told her——how my little John Salusbury and his Preceptor Mr. Davies are coming for ten Days in the *Middle of January* to occupy our *only Apartment*——and that as you know, a bad one.

The Time is past when he was *Piccolino* and slept with Allen, and played with the Men and Maids; he is a great Boy now, and I would not trust him out of my own Sight except with his Tutor for all the Territory of Venice. And now let us talk of sweet Siddons, who next to immediate Home Concerns, is dear to you and me. Here is her Letter back, and truly sorry am I for her.[2] Be perswaded now, and remain convinced that neither Fame nor Fortune can make Happiness. Jane Holman's Husband wrote me word that *his* poor Wife was safe: and her Child dead—God send her better Luck another Day; I am now anxious for the Event—Will even *that* bestow Felicity? I fancy *not*, unless it please Heaven to give a Blessing with it—Lady Kirkwall's pregnancy is announced; if Children convey Comfort, 'tis to *that* Old House they will bring it.

How People *do* study to prolong their own Existence *in* this World, and their own Enjoyment *of* this World, thro' their Offspring; may be learned by the strange Tale now revived of Hugh Capet's being told by an Astrologer that his descendants should reign over France *not quite* 800 Years. Will it (said he) add to their Time of sitting on this Throne if I do not reign at all? Oh yes, replies the Man, Your Dynasty will then continue *806* years——Hugh Capet was for that Reason never crowned; and if you will add those 806 Years to AD: 987 when he asked the Question, they will make 1793 when his last Descendant was deposed and murdered.[3]

This Story now comes in People's heads because of the Surprizing Labrador Stone dug up in Russia, and containing Lewis the 16th's Profile delineated upon it by the *Hand of Nature*. Miss Thrale has seen it, and there is a Fac Simile handed about this Town: Yet many think it an Imposition, and those who think otherwise are ashamed to say they think so.[4] I wish to look at it in Your Company, which always adds to every Intellectual gratification bestowed / on Yours truly / H: L: P.

Accept our Christmas Wishes and hope of a happy New Year.

Text: Princeton University Library. *Address:* Mrs. Pennington / Dowry Square / Hot Wells / Bristol. *Postmark:* BATH.

1. The year of this letter can be determined from the fact of Jane Holman's pregnancy and the exchange between PSP and HLP of SS's letter. The month and day are derived from HLP's last paragraph.

2. In a letter now missing SS in all likelihood wrote about the death of her father, Roger Kemble, aged eighty-two; the imminent departure of her son George for India; the uncertain health of Sally; and her husband's frequent cries for money.

3. The apocryphal anecdote was provoked by events of the French Revolution and a contemporary interest in prophecy. The facts, however, to which HLP alludes are accurate. Hugh the Great (d. 956), duke of the Franks and count of Paris, waived his right to kingship. In 987 his son Hugh Capet (938–96) became king of France. His descendants remained on the throne until the death of Charles IV in 1328, when the crown passed to the collateral House of Valois, then to that of Valois-Orléans and next to the branch of Valois-Orléans-Angoulême, and finally in 1589 to the Capetians of Bourbon.

HLP added the anecdote as marginalia in her copy of *Retrospection* (1:239); and in a presentation copy to William Augustus Conway (11 April 1819), she updated the prophecy to account for the restoration of Louis XVIII in 1814. Thus, the original figure of 806 was altered in the margin to 810. See Merritt, pp. 156–57.

4. The Labrador Stone belonged to a Count Rombassomé, who allowed it to surface periodically. Occasionally—as at this time—he "sold facsimiles of it for one guinea each," HLP buying one for Lady Williams (see Mangin, p. 195). Several years later, he offered to dispose of the copies through a lottery. A young friend, Marianne Francis, on 19 May

[1808] reviewed the story of the stone for HLP. Rombassomé says, "when he was in Russia, he bought of a Jew, a large lump of Labrador, which he took to shew to a Friend: *Baron Monkhausen*, I think, or some such name, who kept it for some time, and at last entreated the Count to sell it him. This he refused, but told him he would be welcome to it as a present if he liked. Well, said the Baron, as you *are* so kind, I'll confess to you, I have broken the Stone. 'Never mind, said Rombassomé: give me the pieces and we shall be quits.' These were returned, and taken to a Jeweller to be polished. The Count assisted at the work, and discovering an extraordinary appearance one day in a broken piece, polished it himself, and purified it—and there *he* says was this extraordinary head" (Ry. 582.18). The head, as HLP describes it, bore a "Resemblance" to "poor Louis seize"—his crown dropping off and spots of blood visible about his neck.

The stone turned out to be a ruse although in 1802–3 its authenticity was claimed by the jewelers Gray and Rundell and by the chemist Richard Chenevix.

TO THE REVEREND REYNOLD DAVIES

Bath Tuesday
4: January 1803

Dear Mr. Davies

My Master must have gone out of his Room if you *had* come, and I must have made many new Arrangements——So we will give up the Pleasure for this Time and depend upon it for another if you please——Thus decrees Gabriel Piozzi and his Wife finds him always right.

Men with Two Thumbs have two Sons at a Time I see[1]——and Women without their old Husband and Companion had better be dead than alive—*that*, I am perswaded of[2]——So much for the Stanleys and Macs.

Our little Boy begins his New Year happily I hope, pray do not disappoint him by saying the Wonders he should have done or seen *here*[3]——for we are engaged every hour, and he will be better able to taste the Pleasures of Bath in the Spring of 1804 when Sydney Gardens will be open,[4] and his own Mind more disclosed to the Enjoyment of such Amusement as I could procure him.

Did Miss Thrale and Mr. Gillon talk to *you* about the Lusus Naturæ resembling Louis seize? and have you seen it? No I dare say: You see no Marvels but those recorded in Ovid's Metamorphoses; unless you have got a new *Professor* whom you and I shall like as well as Dear Mr. *Wood*: and *that would* be a Marvel.[5]

Well! God bless you and be glad to see us when we come to London and Streatham, and love my *Son Salusbury* and tell him he has a very *Affectionate* Aunt in his Friend / Mr. Davies's faithful and Obedient / H: L: Piozzi.

Mr. Piozzi lets the Wine and the Affidavit both alone.

Text: Hyde Collection. *Address:* Rev: Reynold Davies / Streatham / Surrey. *Postmark:* 1803.

1. The cryptic allusion is to Edward Smith-Stanley (1775–1851), thirteenth earl of Derby (1834), who with his wife Charlotte Margaret, née Hornby, were the parents of Edward George Geoffrey (1799–1869), fourteenth earl, and Henry Thomas (1803–75).
2. Widowed for three years and missing the companionship of her husband's niece Margaret O'Brien, Catherine Macnamara died 2 January, aged eighty-two.
For Margaret O'Brien, see HLP to Robert Ray, 23 July 1798, n. 5.
3. For some reason the plan to have JSPS spend his midwinter holiday in Bath with the Piozzis was canceled. See HLP to PSP [ca. 24 December 1802].
4. Laid out by Charles Harcourt Masters in 1795, Sydney Gardens are "beautifully situated East of Bath, facing Great Pulteney Street. . . . The amusements of these gardens begin early in the Spring with public breakfasts, Evening Promenades, and temporary Illuminations, enlivened with music." The pleasure gardens spanned "about 16 acres, laid out in Serpentine Walks, Water-falls, Pavillions, Alcoves, Grotto, Labyrynth, Bowling-Green . . . & every requisite that can be conducive to health & pleasure." There was a fee for walking in Sydney Gardens. See *Robbins's Bath Directory,* 1800; *The New Bath Guide,* 1801.
5. For Henry Wood, see HLP to LC, 22 July 1801, n. 8.

TO THE REVEREND LEONARD CHAPPELOW

Bath
25: January 1803.

My dear Mr. Chappelow
 must recollect when he no more believed in the Stone that fell from heaven, than he now believes in that which was dug out of the Earth. I keep your Letters carefully; and can turn to that in which You scorned my Intelligence of A strange Volcanic Mass which dropt in Topham's Garden[1]—a Tale corroborated by some Irish Gentleman's Account of a Similar Accident in *his* Country——but that Letter struck me more as a *Word Catcher* than a Naturalist——The Man said he sent a *Garzoon* to pick the Stone up, and I forgot the thing itself in my Wonder to observe French Words used so near us as our Sister Kingdom quite familiarly——What does Sir William Hamilton think of these bursting Meteors?[2] I should lay no small Stress on *his* Opinion in such Cases. He attests the Labrador Stone bearing poor Louis seize's Resemblance to be *genuine:* Gray[3] and Rundell[4] make Affidavit that no Art has been used, and Chenevix the Chymist[5] says no Human Power could have produced the Effect.

Human Power however produces Effects new and strange every day—it sets Buonaparte on an Imperial Throne, And it now professes by Galvanism to reanimate the Dead[6]——let the Emperor of the Gauls take Care lest Robertspierre should revive: if all those Wretches murdered in Egypt were to come back, I think he would be sorry to see them——Why we shall be like the Characters in Voltaire's Candide anon; hanged to day, and well again tomorrow:[7] Mr. Greatheed is perfecting his Son in these Things I trust,[8] Lord and Lady Bradford were right enough to come home; The Cloud is gath'ring over Paris apparently, and *prudent* Mortals will leave the Inhabitants of that City to *conduct* the Electric

Matter as they may.⁹ I was glad when Miss Thrales gave up their once-entertained Intentions of passing a Winter in France, after a Summer spent in Skie, Mull and Staffa. What a Contrast it must have been!

We are hearing Chat and Music at Bath in a quiet confined Way; but the Hours suit us Invalides, and les Plaisirs bruyans no longer suit / Dear Mr. Chappelow's / ever Faithful and Obliged / H: L: Piozzi.

Text: Ry. 561.118.

1. See HLP to Q, 10 July 1796, n. 3.
2. HLP was aware of Sir William's scientific activity, especially his research on volcanic phenomena. Elected a fellow of the Royal Society in 1766, he published his findings in the *Philosophical Transactions,* 1766–80. His chief work on the volcanoes of the Two Sicilies was *Campi Phelgraei,* 1776, with a supplement in 1779. See also his *Observations on Mount Vesuvius* (1772) and *An Account of the Earthquakes in Calabria, Sicily* (1783).
  For Sir William's other interests, see HLP to Q [ca. 25 March 1796], n. 7.
3. HLP refers to William Gray, goldsmith and jeweler, who from 1792 to 1825 headed the firm, which he inherited from his father, Robert (d. 1788), located at 13 New Bond Street. (William was RG's brother.)
4. Rundell and Bridge, goldsmiths and jewelers to their Majesties, 32 Ludgate Hill.
5. Irish-born Richard Chenevix (1774–1830) was a sometime dramatist, a chemist, and mineralogist who began to publish in his scientific fields as early as 1798. In 1801 he had been elected a fellow of the Royal Society, publishing frequently in the *Philosophical Transactions.*
6. See, e.g., the *Courier,* 21 January, headed "Galvinism":
"The body of *Forster,* who was executed on Monday last [the 17th] for murder, was conveyed to a house not far distant, where it was subjected to the *Galvanic* Process, by Professor Aldini, under the inspection of . . . several . . . Professional Gentlemen. M. Aldini, who is the nephew of the discoverer of this most interesting science, shewed the eminent and superior powers of *Galvinism* to be far beyond any other stimulant in nature. On the first application of that process to the face, the jaw of the deceased criminal began to quiver, and the adjoining muscles were horribly contorted, and one eye was actually opened. In the subsequent part of the process, the right hand was raised and clenched, and the legs and thighs were set in motion. It appeared to the uninformed part of the by-standers as if the wretched man was on the eve of being restored to life.—"
7. Dr. Pangloss, who is hanged in chap. 6 of *Candide,* returns in chap. 28 to explain his remarkable survival.
8. In December 1802 Bertie Greatheed, his wife, and son left England for an expected six months in Paris. They went in part for the same reasons that attracted many Britons to France after the Peace of Amiens. But they also wished young Bertie, who had recently exhibited for the first time at the Royal Academy, to study the works at the Louvre.
9. HLP had read several times during the month that an intention had been declared at Paris of creating Bonaparte *"Emperor of the Gauls"* and that resistance might be anticipated. See *GM* 73, pt. 1 (1803): 73.

TO THE REVEREND LEONARD CHAPPELOW

Bath Wednesday
2: March 1803.

Tell Mrs. Clay my Dear Sir that I *do* know how to pity her;[1] as her Husband was brought home to *her,* so was my Father to *me*——I was looking out of the Window for him and he came home a Corpse.[2] It is indeed somewhat difficult for an Acquaintance of *mine* to suffer what I have not myself in some Measure, in some Degree, *endured.* But Mrs. Clay is happy in a true Friend——When I found myself a Widow, I was surrounded by Interested and unfeeling People, who watched and sneered, and plundered: but never tried to console or assist me.

Dear Mr. Piozzi has I think had la Grippe; and the Treacherous Gout always lieing in wait to do one a Mischief, was ready to leap upon the weakened Parts—Throat, Lungs, Larynx—every dangerous Situation. It is a fortnight since he was seized, *exactly;* and he is *now* pronounced out of all Danger——but greatly weakened: It was Dr. Parry saved his Life. I will perswade him when recovering, to go from *this* and every *other* Town immediately: to Clifton Hill in our Way home if possible; for going into London's infected Air just now would surely be quite too ridiculous: I wonder at Mr. Gillons staying there, and Miss Thrales——but People will follow their own Funerals rather than not be at *every Show.* Lord! Lord! what a Set of Fools we all are——pretending to resuscitate the Dead too! till God sends Mortality among us, that we may learn in *whose* Hands are the Issues of Life and Death.[3]

The Ladies at Llangollen are like George the Third; they know what is going on in every Place and among all Sorts of People: their Intelligence concerning our Musical Party was perfectly correct.[4] Mr. Gillon shall have a Letter from me by this post, pressing him to sleep at least out of London for a while.

Have you read the favourite Novel Delphine? I never saw any Book so voraciously devoured——but it has every Stimulant to awake the Literary Appetite, and every Power to corrode the Constitution of those who swallow it.[5] There are strange new Remedies in the World, strange new Diseases, strange new Books——Have you heard of the Man who finding the Gout in his Head, wrapped it up in a cold wet Towel? Angina Pectoris is *not* new, but very dreadful; and quick in its Effects—upon strong and sanguineous Subjects—for 'tis the *Well* people who die always—not the sick ones.

Dear Mr. Chappelow keep *yourself* well and comfort your Friends. Mrs. Clay's Children are happy in having you to see over *their* future Welfare.[6] Let us hope they will be good to their amiable Mother. Make her my *truest* Regards, and Farewell! I hope her Uncle or Cousin Wilmot the Master in Chancery[7] will be kinder to *her* than he was to *hers* and your faithful se<rvant> / H: L: P.

Not a Frank to be had here for Love or Money.

Text: Ry. 561.119.

1. The merchant William Clay had died in February. While his death was sudden, it was not unexpected, for as early as 22 July 1797 he had drafted his will. See HLP to LC, 18 September [1797], n. 8.
2. At 9:00 A.M. on 21 December 1762 John Salusbury went to visit his brother-in-law Sir Lynch Salusbury Cotton, who lived nearby. He "was brought . . . home a Corpse—before the Dining Hour." See Hayward 2:21; Clifford, p. 38.
3. See Ps. 68:20.
4. When the Piozzis visited Bath, they usually gave at least one "Musical Party" at home—a concert performed by singers and instrumentalists—for about a hundred people. This year, because of the influenza epidemic, the Piozzis first postponed the party and then gave it up altogether. See her note to PSP [ca. 12 March]:
"Paris is too near us Dear Mrs. Pennington; we are always catching what comes from the Skirt of some black Cloud hanging over Frenchmen: and now we share slightly—in the Epidemic Disease. *Every* body has Cough and Cold, Doctor Parry was called to eleven new Patients on Thursday when I fetched him to my Master, whose Catarrh aided and excited by Gout torments him beyond all telling.—I sent Mr. Whalley a Card of Put-Off: and we must give up our Musical Party at home for this Day sennight. . . . So while we are making the Dead Ox roar by Galvanic Process,—God shews us that in him and him *alone* are the Spurs of Life and Death" (Princeton University Library).
5. Anne-Louise-Germaine de Staël-Holstein, née Necker (1766–1817), wrote *Delphine,* which was translated into English and published in six volumes (London: J. Mawman, 1803).
Lady Orkney on 26 February (Ry. 580.5) wrote to HLP: "You mentioned that Lord Lansdown was up at six every morning reading Delphine—This Book Lord de B[laquiere] sent to Lady de B. and during my illness I read it—What an infamous, wicked Book! and it concludes more in character than I should have thought Madame de Stael would have wished—An Atheist and a Deist could not end otherwise, circumstanced as they were."
6. For Mrs. Clay's two children, see HLP to LC, 18 September [1797], n. 8.
7. For John Eardley Wilmot, master in chancery, see HLP to Arthur Murphy, 31 July 1797. For a summation of his report against the Piozzis and for Cator and the Mostyns, see *Thraliana* 2:983 and n. 2.

TO THE REVEREND REYNOLD DAVIES

Bath, Wednesday,
2nd March, 1803.

Dear Mr. Davies,

Write me word that you are well, and the Child well, and that no Contagion is come to Streatham University. We heard Reports of London's great Unhealthiness; and I know *you* are famous for catching horrible Colds.[1] Mr. Piozzi has had this Influenza very badly indeed, and the Gout fell on him beside, and he has not moved *out* of his Bed—nor scarcely *in* it—for this Fortnight.

A Side Wind blows us ill news of Mr. Gillon too, and tho' I write to him I get no Answer. Send me some Words of Comfort, as Baretti used to say, and write seriously, for 'tis no joke to see one's best Friends ill so. I heard from Cumberland Street to-day, and am surprized Miss Thrales do not go out of Town a while till la Grippe is gone by. God bless you, Dear Mr. Davies, and do pacify the anxious Heart of Salusbury's and yours ever.

Mr. Chappelow has lost an old intimate, Mr. Clay; and is very melancholy upon it. / H: L: Piozzi.

Text: Broadley, p. 51. *Address:* Rev. Reynold Davies, / Streatham, Surrey.

1. So widespread was "the Influenza, or Catarrhal Fever . . . in the Metropolis" that physicians wrote to Mr. Urban offering palliatives or cures. See, e.g., the letter of Dr. E. Peart in *GM* 73, pt. 1 (1803): 203–4.

TO HESTER MARIA THRALE

> Bath Wednesday
> 2: March 1803.

My dearest Girl will believe me when I say that at the Time I wrote my little Note by Mr. Whalley, I knew not what—or how much ailed Mr. Piozzi——I only saw Cold and Catarrh, and began to hear the most outrageous Cough that could torment a human Creature—But Gout—which always lyes in wait to fall on a weak Place, soon striking at his Throat and Breast, lifted the Pulse up to 112; while it chained him to an *immoveable* Position on his Bed. From that horrible State Dear Doctor Parry has at length released him, and *this* Day takes his Leave of him as *a Patient*. The Instant we are able to write TTL I shall endeavour to get him home, into some uninfected Atmosphere;——not London——where I am Sorry to think you are Staying while such Reports are current *de la Grippe*. Mr. Chappelow writes me Word Mr. Gillon is in ill Health; every Letter brings account of some Death I think, or some Danger——and all the Wonders our Metropolis exhibits will not tempt me to enter it—till Matters mend. Among those Wonders Mammoth is in every Sense the *greatest*.[1] I used to wonder what those huge Deer were made for, Whose Horns are every now and then dug up from Irish Bogs or North American Swamps——but I suppose they were for Mammoth's Dinner: like the old Story in the Jest Books——What Sir could be the use of such a Copper? Oh Sir—to boyl your Turnep in,—no doubt.[2]

Lord bless us—! What surprizing Days do we live in! when Satan tries every Engine true and false to sap and batter and drive down Christianity. This AnteDiluvian, is by *les Esprits forts* as you well know—called a *PreAdamite Creature;* and is brought forward to overturn the Mosaic Account of Creation, and while such Studies occupy the *Learned,*——*Essence* of Infidelity is administered to the *Lady* Readers in Delphine;—sweet as the Otto of Roses from the East, soliciting every Sense. Lord Lansdowne put that Work into my Hands six or eight Weeks ago; said he rose at 5 o'Clock in a Morning to get thro' with it; and "purchase it at once (says he) Mrs. Piozzi, carry it into Wales, and lend it your Neighbours there—I know you keep a little Circulating Library." Well Well! The Black Statues always clatter and threaten loudest when they are nearest being destroyed; and though they *do* by their Enchantments move the Muscles of the

Dead, and bring even *literally* Fire from Heaven by Electricity &c. reforming Signs and Wonders capable of deceiving[3]——if it were possible——even the Elect——I yet trust in Heaven that they shall be taken in their own Toils, and that all their Resistance will at length tend to God's Glory.[4]

To be less serious.—Delphine is delightfully written;—the End of the first and beginning of the fifth Volume unrivalled for ought I ever read in passionate and Picturesque Scenes—The Reflexions wonderfully acute beside, and a Knowledge of the human heart *so Perfect* that it really *ought not* to be produced in open Day so. Her combating the Christian Precept Love your Enemies,[5] has been done with such insidious neatness, such artful ingenuity; I think it must obtain her ever lasting Renown as Lucifer's must useful Agent:—and whoever has the *Tabouret* in *Tartarus* at present,[6] will I think yield it to Madame Staal when She arrives there. Au reste there are and must be little Faults in every Composition. The Heroine submits but once to Public Opinion—and then undoes herself.[7] The Hero however shaking the Convent Gate is so grand an Idea; so natural, so striking, one forgives every Lapsus to such a Writer.[8] I could not keep Delphine out of my head sleeping or waking for many days, nor could avoid admiring at her much misused Powers of agitating the Human Mind. Buonaparte and I are both angry with this great Author, and tis *one* of the odd Things that we should so well agree.[9]

His Treatment of our Ambassadress does not displease me *au fonds*.[10]—— There was neither Good Sense nor Good Breeding in making such a Dinner and such a Man wait;[11] and it was dangerous exposing herself and her Nation to the Contempt he shewed them: but "Les Dames n'ont pas toujours Raison." The Choice of Envoys to a foreign court, is in such Times as these, Matter of no small Moment; a rough Sailor should not be sent to a semibarbarous Country for Example, where the Grandees pride and quite pique themselves on shewing to the World how they are *Civilized*——and fluttering Women of Fashion are in my Opinion better calculated to gain Attention in a Bath Ball Room than at an Entertainment given by Veteran Officers in a Palace——which still bears some Resemblance to a Camp.[12] Denon's Book is one that lays very fast hold of one,— tho' written with such a partial Spirit one abhors it[13]—I prescribe Sir Robert Wilson's Pamphlet—to be taken immediately after—and form a *Neutral Draught*.[14] Of Colonel Despard's Exit his best Friends seem to think it best to say nothing as far as I observe, but that the Societies should continue seducing the King's Soldiers under his very Gallows, *is too bad*.[15] Oh Where and Oh When will these Things end! We have caught too much of the Paris Contagion Medical and Political;[16] Do you hear of People hasting home from France? Or do they stay there as you do in London, unimpressed by the Danger? Dear *Dear* Girls take Care and do not catch *la Grippe*. Accept my best Thanks for your sweet Letter— —Mr. Piozzi sits up today only one ½ Hour, and that for the first Time the Fortnight. Adieu and God bless You all prays your / Affectionate Mother H: L: P.—

Text: Bowood Collection. Address: Miss Thrale / Great Cumberland Street / London. Postmark: BATH F MAR 3 1803.

1. According to an advertisement in, e.g., the [Sunday] *Observer,* 13 February:
"*Mammoth,*—A stupendous Monument of the *Antediluvian World,*—hitherto unknown only by a few Teeth and Bones, similar to those which have been seen since 1740 [sic], in the British Museum, and other Collections in Europe and America.—Nearly a complete Skeleton is now exhibiting at Mr. Christie's Room, No. 118, Pall-Mall, near Carlton-House, by Mr. Peale, under whose direction this Extraordinary Skeleton was dug up from a Morass in the State of New York, in America.—Admittance One Shilling, from Ten in the Morning till Five in the Evening."

For an expression of wonder evoked by the sight of Mammoth—"11 feet high—17½ long,—and 5 feet 8 inches wide.—The weight of the whole about 1000 pounds"—see Farington 6:2049–50.

2. According to Anthony Copley's 1614 edition of *Wits, Fits, & Fancies:*
"A Traveler affirming that he saw a Colewart so monstrous huge that five hundred men on horseback might stand in her shade, another answered, 'And I for my part did once see a Cauldron so wide that three hundred men wrought therein, every one distant twenty yards from other.' Then the Colewart liar asked him to what use the Cauldron was made. He answered, 'To seethe your Colewart in.'" As reproduced by Paul M. Zall, *A Nest of Ninnies and other English Jestbooks of the Seventeenth Century* (Lincoln: University of Nebraska Press, 1970), p. 6.

3. Matt. 24:24.

4. 1 Cor. 10:31.

5. Matt. 5:44; Luke 6:35.

6. HLP's play on Aeneas's descent into hell and Virgil's description of Tartarus as a region of Hades where the most impious and wicked of mankind are punished. See *Aeneid,* bk. 6.

7. Delphine d'Albemar's defiance of public opinion provides the tragic conflict of the novel and reveals her as Mme de Staël's prototype of the free woman, responsible only to the commands of inner faith and virtuous instincts. The contrasting ways in which Delphine and her would-be lover, Leonce de Mondeville, respond to social form determine the tensions throughout most of the six volumes. See, e.g., letter 19 (1:146–47) from Delphine to her sister.

She finally submits to public opinion, but only as directed by her own conscience, by a retreat to her Swiss nunnery ("Paradise Abbey"). Thus she hopes to avoid tainting the marriage of Leonce and Matilda and to quiet the gossip about herself and Leonce. But Delphine is indeed "undone," because she cannot escape physical love even in religion. Matilda's death comes too late to effect a resolution for the lovers; Leonce's patriotic fervor compounds matters when he finds "life . . . insupportable without honour" (6:115). He is executed by a firing squad; Delphine poisons herself.

8. See *Delphine* 6:591–61, a letter from M. de Lebensei to Mlle Albemar.

"As Leonce entered the [Abbey] parlour, Delphine appeared shrouded in her black veil behind the fatal grate. At the sight Leonce was seized with a convulsive tremor. . . . 'Is she then a nun? has she taken the veil?' exclaimed he. At the sound of his voice, Delphine recognized Leonce. . . . 'Matilda is dead, Delphine; can you not be mine?;— 'No,' said she; 'but I am willing to die:'—and down she fell motionless on the ground."

9. When Mme de Staël first met Bonaparte, she admired what seemed to be his sincere republicanism and selflessness. But within a short period of time, they became mutually defiant. By 1798 Mme de Staël's liaison with Benjamin Constant further irritated Bonaparte, who suspected the political maneuvers of those visitors to her salon in the faubourg Saint Germain. When he learned that she enticed to her "foyer des mécontents" some of his own family (Louis), his ministers, and military advisers, he decided to rid himself of "cette canaille de Constant" by imposing on them periodic terms of exile.

Bonaparte found *Delphine* particularly offensive and for three reasons: England was praised; Protestantism was exalted when he was reestablishing Catholicism; the novel further upheld the right to love and divorce when he was rehabilitating marriage.

10. Charles Whitworth (1752–1825), Baron Whitworth of Newport Pratt, co. Galway (I.)

in April 1800; Viscount Whitworth of Albaston, co. Stafford (1813); Baron Albaston and Earl Whitworth (1815). He had married 7 April 1801 Arabella Diana (Sackville), née Cope (1767–1825). Upon the death of the duke of Dorset (1799), she inherited £13,000 a year, besides the borough of East Grinstead, and in time Dorset House and Knole Park. In September 1802 Whitworth was made ambassador to Paris and in November he and his wife traveled to the French capital.

11. The dinner to which HLP alludes was given by Talleyrand, the minister for foreign affairs. This was "a great *diplomatique* dinner, and of course no person admitted but such as the Duchess of Dorset [could] meet with propriety." Bonaparte was present, but the duchess was late, delaying the dinner and guests. See *England and Napoleon in 1803, being the Despatches of Lord Whitworth and Others*, ed. Oscar Browning (London: Longmans, Green, 1887), pp. 26–27.

12. HLP regarded Bonaparte's court as a military establishment. See her letter to LC, 16 August 1802, n. 4.

13. On 1 November 1802 was published a translation of the work of Baron Dominique-Vivant Denon (1747–1825). The original had earlier been published in Paris in 1802 as the three-volumed *Voyage dans la Basse et la Haute Égypte, pendant les campagnes du général Bonaparte*. The translator, working from the original folio edition, was Francis Blagdon. Entitled *Denon's Travels*, it appeared in two volumes and sold for 14s.

What irritated HLP about Denon's book were its loyalties. Not only did the author dedicate it to Bonaparte but in acquiring his information he allowed himself to become part of the French military machine in Egypt.

14. Sir Robert Thomas Wilson (1777–1849), *A Narrative of the Expedition to Egypt under Sir Ralph Abercrombie; containing an Exposition of the Principles and Conduct of Napoleone Buonaparte. Abridged from the History of that Campaigne, by Sir R. T. Wilson.* . . . (London: R. Dutton [etc.] . . . [1803]); or Comte Jean Louis Ebenezer Reynier (1771–1814), *Campaign between the French Army of the East and the British and Turkish Forces in Egypt, by General Reynier. Translated from the French. To which are added, Observations and Corrections. By an English Officer* [Sir R. T. W.], *of Hompesch's Dragoons* (London: 1802).

15. Despard and twelve others were tried before a special commission, which opened at the new Sessions' House, Borough, on 20 January. He was found guilty of high treason and condemned to death. On 21 February, he was drawn on a hurdle to the county jail at Newington with six of his associates. He gave a long speech from the scaffold that was loudly cheered. He was then hanged and decapitated. See *GM* 73, pt. 1 (1803): 80, 173–77, 275, 377.

16. HLP assumed an undefined plague from such as the following:

"A letter from Paris, dated Feb. 12, says, 'The mortality by which Paris is desolated, may be said almost to exceed the bounds of credibility. Within the last ten days, I have been assured . . . the number of interments has amounted to 400 *per diem* on the average, or 4000 in the whole of that term.'" See *GM* 73, pt. 1: 180.

TO PENELOPE SOPHIA PENNINGTON

Monday 7 March [1803]

Mrs. Holroyd Said She was going to Clifton—and asked me kindly for Commands:[1] so I give her this Letter to let my dear Mrs. Pennington know that my Invalid and his *faithful* Servant H:L:P dine together in your Bed Chamber today upon Roast Chicken.

Such are the Occurrences which stand prominent upon the Annals of Gout,

Catarrh and Years drawn longer than gay Lookers-on like to think of——a propos to Sir Robert Burton etc.[2] Miss Honoria Gubbins gave her White Hand to Mr. Dutton's lame one this Morning—but the *Parchments* will I hope make ample Compensation.[3]

Here is Frost and Snow again, and I hope it will kill the Contagion which you say *exists not*. Lady Orkney got safe to London, I wish her well *out* of it for my own Part; and I begged her to buy *Wife and Mistress* to illuminate our Welsh Friends, and shew them that *truest* Picture I have yet seen of modern Ton and Town Manners.[4]

The Writer mistakes Arachne for Ariadne indeed in Course of the Work; but *that's nothing* as her Character *good* Mrs. Couden says at every word: She *never* mistakes a Knave for a Fool, or an artful Hypocrite for an honourable Person. 'Tis quite my favourite Novel.

Adieu, We shall wait quietly I see till you return, and then go *to London*, where Influenza and la Grippe are waiting I suppose to have a Snatch at Yours ever truly / H:L:P.

I only wish Miss Thrales would go out of Town and Mr. Gillon.

Text: Princeton University Library. *Address:* Mrs. Pennington / Dowry Square / Hot Wells / Bristol. *Postmark:* By Favour of Mrs. Holroyd.

1. Sarah Martha Holroyd (1739–1820), sister of the first earl of Sheffield, lived as early as 1800 at 3 Queen's Parade, Bath. Fluent in German and French, she translated Christoph Christian Sturm's *Betrachtungen über die Werke Gottes im Reiche der Natur und der Vorsehung auf alle Tage des Jahres*. It was published anonymously in 1788 in Edinburgh as *Reflections on the Works of God and of his Providence, throughout all Nature, for every Day in the Year* (3 vols.). The translation went through at least ten editions in her lifetime.
See "Walcot Parish Records," C.R.O. Somerset at Taunton.
2. A political crony of the Prince of Wales, Sir Robert Burton (ca. 1738–1810) had been M.P. for Wendover, owing his seat to Lord Verney, a Rockingham Whig. In December 1788 he worked hard to promote "the sole Regency of the P. of W." Arthur Aspinall, ed., *The Correspondence of George IV, King of Great Britain, 1762–1830*, 8 vols. (New York: Oxford University Press, 1963–71), 1: 396–97. Burton was knighted in 1800.
3. Honoria Gubbins and Ralph Dutton were married in Bath on 7 March by special license.
4. Mary Charlton (fl. 1794–1830), *The Wife and the Mistress. A Novel*, 4 vols. (London: Lane and Newman, 1802). The novel deals with the relationship of "a clever husband-hunting, marriage-making mamma" to her children (1:11) so that they turn into a "smiling cemetery of departed equity and virtue" (4:326).

TO PENELOPE SOPHIA PENNINGTON

[Bath] Thursday
14: April 1803.

I promised Dear Mrs. Pennington that I would write you word after I had been *out*.[1]

Doctor Parry and Mr. Bowen[2] both Called Yesterday, *to bid* me go out at Noon this memorable Thursday——so I *went;* but found no Enjoyment except in returning without any apparent Harm, or fresh Access of Fever, which they had all so imbued my Mind with——That I felt nothing while from home, but *Fears of a Relapse.*

It does not appear however that such an Accident has happened to *me* as yet: and perhaps God Almighty will permit us to see Brynbella once again. A Drive into the Country tomorrow Morning will help season me for the Journey, and I will then make a Point of walking a little every Day till we go——If any thing should arise to stop us from Setting out on the 25: as we *intend:* you shall hear it.

Mean while See what an Egotist Sickness has made of your H: L: P. who used to ask and tell of any thing *but* herself, altho' the Subject was never so truly disagreeable as *now.*

Let us hear how Dr. Randolph is,[3] and *who* succeeds the lamented Dean of Bristol.[4] Let us hear that Your Family continues to brave the Epidemy:

As for Gout, Mr. Pennington will suffer no Injury from that. I know nothing of Music Meetings or Theatres, or of *anything* but how much Acid is to be squeezed into my Lemonade.

Poor Dr. Maclean has been as Ill as I, we met in the Crescent Fields (in our Chairs,) and chatted of our mutual Afflictions:[5] giving one another those *good Hopes,* which tho' neither *felt* I suppose, both had in their Power to *communicate.* Adieu.

Text: Princeton University Library. *Address:* Mrs. Pennington / Dowry Square / Hot Wells / Bristol. *Postmark:* BATH.

1. The influenza epidemic spread from London to regions as disparate as Somerset and North Wales. Eager to nurse GP, who had caught the disease, HLP became a victim about the middle of March and ailed for a month.
See the letters of De Blaquiere, 23 January, and of William Bradford, 24 January 1803, both of Lleweni (Ry. 580.4, 52).
2. William Bowen (1761–1815) at the time of his death was identified as "an eminent physician, and one of the members of the [Bath] corporation." See *GM* 85, pt. 1 (1815): 378. On the south wall of the Bath Abbey there is an M.I. for him, "a member of the Body Corporate and by his Will a liberal benefactor to the General Hospital and other charitable institutions."
3. According to PSP, 22 April 1803 (Ry. 568.115):
"Poor Dr. Randolph is reduced by the potent Medicines they have obliged to give him, to dislodge this morbid Bile that has been seated between his Stomach and Bowels, to nearly the *same* Complexion.—However they think him out of present Danger. . . . Dr. Lovell says *had* the Influenza really seized him in *that* state, nothing could have saved him!"

4. According to *The Times*, 8 January 1800, "The King has been pleased to grant to the Rev. Charles Peter Layard, D.D. the place and dignity of a Dean of his Majesty's Cathedral Church of Bristol."

Layard (1748–1803) received his D.D. in 1787, becoming chaplain in ordinary to the king (1790–1800), rector of Uffington (1798–1803), and dean of Bristol (1800–1803). It was thought that Layard's preferments were secured through the interest of his sister Mary Anne (1743–1804), originally a governess to a sister of Brownlow Bertie (1729–1809), fifth duke of Ancaster and Kesteven, whom she married. He was succeeded at Bristol by Bowyer Edward Sparke (1759 [or 60]–1836), later bishop of Chester (1809) and Ely (1812).

5. For Archibald Maclaine, see HLP to PSP, 9 March 1800, n. 2.

TO THE REVEREND REYNOLD DAVIES

Bath
15: April *1803*.

What a nice Child is our Salusbury! thus to work *hard* and keep *well*, and give one no Pain but all Pleasure.

I thought *you* would scarce escape this horrid Influenza, and how weak and how low it does leave one! My first Attempt at going out of the House was Yesterday in a *Sedan Chair,* by Leave of Doctor Parry and Mr. Bowen——our good *Countrymen both:* and at the Head here of a Profession which this Spring will be found but *too Lucrative* God knows.

May *we* but get safe back to Wales! The Change of Air will set all up again: and if it might suit Mr. Wood to come once more to Brynbella with little Dear it would be a choice Delight for his *Aunt:* who will not suffer him to come there *alone*, and spend his Time in Stables and with Servants in Danger not only of forgetting all he now *thinks* he knows, but in Danger of *every possible Mischief.* A Boy of 10 Years old being much less safe than one of 5 under Miss Allen's Protection.[1]

We must think how to manage all this—and Oh that Dear Mr. Wood were the Man!

Well! as to Whitelock[2] Mr. Piozzi must as Dr. Johnson advised in a Similar Case once, "If the Fellow is refractory Sir—send a rough Attorney to him, and all will be well."[3]

When next Michaelmas comes—let you and I *begin* our long *Carrière* de Vingt-sept Ans—and may we finish it happily—in 'Spite of Influenza.[4]

Pray be so good as [to] receive our £12:10 of Ray due at last Lady Day,[5] and *Vale* Dear Mr. Davies. *Jubeo te bene valere.* / H: L: Piozzi.

Text: Arthur G. Rippey Collection. *Address:* Rev: Mr. Davies / Streatham / Surrey. *Postmark:* 10 o'Clock AP 16 1803 BATH.

1. For Elener Allen, see HLP to PSW, 29 August 1791, n. 8.
2. John Whitelock (fl. 1770–1805) rented land from the Piozzis at Streatham, ca. 1800–1803. In all likelihood Whitelock objected to the expansion of RD's school onto his rented land. See "Streatham Land Tax Assessments," C.R.O., Surrey.

Samuel Johnson ("Blinking Sam"). Portrait by Sir Joshua Reynolds (ca. 1775). (Reproduced by permission of Mr. Loren Rothschild, Beverly Hills, California.) Johnson complained that " 'he would not be known by posterity for his *defects* only, let Sir Joshua do his worst'. [Mrs. Piozzi] said in reply, that Reynolds had no such difficulties about himself, and that he might observe the picture which hung up in the room where we were talking, represented Sir Joshua holding his ear in his hand to catch the sound. 'He may paint himself as deaf if he chuses (replied Johnson); but I will not be *blinking* Sam.' " *Anecdotes*, p. 248; *Boswell's Johnson* 4:449–50.

3. HLP repeats an oral statement of SJ that synthesizes his attitude toward some practitioners of the law. See, e.g., an episode recorded by HLP: ". . . a gentleman leaving the company, somebody who sate next Dr. Johnson, asked him, who he was? 'I cannot exactly tell you Sir (replied he), and I would be loth to speak ill of any person who I do not know deserves it, but I am afraid he is an *attorney*'" (*Anecdotes*, p. 272; *Thraliana* 1:176. In *Boswell's Johnson* 2:126, the same witticism improves in the telling.)

4. RD became curate of Saint Leonard's in 1777.

5. The £12.10 was a partial payment for land that Sarah Ray (Robert Ray's mother) rented from the Piozzis. See "Streatham Land Tax Assessments," 1796–1800, in C.R.O., Surrey. HLP sent this money on to RD to help defray the annual cost of JSPS's schooling, which came to £220.3.12, payable at Christmas and midsummer.

TO PENELOPE SOPHIA PENNINGTON

[Bath] Sunday
17: April 1803.

My Dear Mrs. Pennington has too much Good Sense to *risque* a charge of Impertinence; and I have too much Common Sense not to know that other Ills attack Life Impetuously, carrying it by a *Coup de Main;* while Gout turns the Siege into a *Blockade*,¹ during which many Accidents arrive, and which is often lengthened till the Enemy itself grows feeble and even tired.²

Mean while *die we must,* of one Thing or another; and at one Place or another: I hope to live long and end my Days at Brynbella, and be buried there with my Fathers and my Husband.

We shall set out if it please God tomorrow Sennight, and sleep at Fleece Inn Rodborough. Allen wrote to say her Sister was not to be married till Tuesday next; so I lengthened her Furlough, out of a Desire to make her happy——She had been miserable long enough.

Mr. Chappelow has been ill, so has everybody, but I am glad Dr. Randolph will recover:—*His* Life is of real Consequence.

My airing in the Carriage did me good; and the *knocking Knees* took a Walk with me yesterday—up Pultney Street and down again,—no more: Today I will go *twice* up and down, and so season myself by degrees.

Mr. Pennington must do so too, and we shall be brisk Folks again sometime; so will Mr. Piozzi I doubt not,—'spite of your heavy Denunciations, and melancholy Predictions for us all.

Why *now* you croak worse than ever croaked Your / faithful Servant / H: L: Piozzi.

Text: Princeton University Library.

1. See *The Vanity of Human Wishes,* lines 283–84:

>Unnumber'd maladies his joints invade,
>Lay siege to life and press the dire blockade.

2. The PSP letter [ca. 15 or 16 April] to which HLP is responding is missing but its substance is repeated in another, dated 22 April (Ry. 568.115). What provoked the tension between them was HLP's dismissal on 14 April of Pennington's gout as anything serious.

Thus PSP did *"risque* a [second] charge of Impertinence" when she began her letter with "dear *inflexible* Friend. . . . How can you then persist in saying my dear Friend 'Mr. Pennington will suffer *no* Injury from the Gout?' He suffers *every* Injury possible from it—but one [death], from which he is by no means so secure as you and Mr. Whalley fancy him."

TO THE REVEREND LEONARD CHAPPELOW

Bath Sunday
17: April 1803.

My dear Mr. Chappelow's Hand writing was very welcome to us indeed—I *thought* how Matters stood; and begged of our *common*——our *un*common Friend Mr. Gillon, to let me know; but nothing transpired till your Letter of today. Mr. Piozzi and I have both had the Influenza most *terribly; his* Share of it—combined with Gout——was dangerous and dreadful: Dr. Parry has however pulled us both Through. My Strength is just beginning to recover, and my Hand does not *now* shake *very* bad——The poor Knees totter under me Still. But Change of Air (the Moment I can move with Safety) will give me Spirits and Courage——There never, no *never* was so depressing a Disorder, I tremble at going out, or staying *in,* am afraid of Pestilence in the Air, and of *decline* from hovering over Beds and Fires at home, while Summer drives Spring away in such an unexampled manner—We have the Heats of August in April. How does Mrs. Clay bear these additional Torments? I hope the Influenza has not touched her Darlings. Children have suffered from it here at Bath beyond all telling: a Medical Man told me that he was afraid one of his Baby Patients would have actually *burst* in his *Hand.*

Make haste and get out into the fields——another Week will give *us* Liberty; for tomorrow sennight if it please God we shall sleep at the Fleece Inn Rodborough on our Way to Wales.

Look you, no People have a better Right to a Rasher of *Dunmow Bacon* than my poor Master and myself;[1] who have reciprocally nursed and cryed over each other, and who are now happy in the hope of going on together—10 or 20 Years more——till *another Influenza.*

A propos Miss Thrales wrote with great Politeness and Attention when they first heard I was seized with Illness: but soon as Mr. Piozzi said the *Danger was over,* and invited them to come and see their *Chere Mere* in good Time! not another Scrap did we ever see under their fair Hands.

The War and the Peace are both unpleasing to *me*——almost *alike* unpleasing. Some one said the other Day——(Doctor McLean I believe) that the Birth of Buonaparte had been fatal to Europe, I agreed with him, and with Millions who must needs think so too: yet will the Day of his *Death* be no happy Day for Europe in my Mind.

A blazing Torch is a frightful Thing——A blown-out Torch is a stinking Thing.

Adieu Dear Mr. Chappelow! direct your next to Brynbella where soon will reside Your ever obliged and truly faithful / H: L: P.

Text: Ry. 561.120.

1. An ancient ceremonial reward for fidelity. It was originated by Robert Fitzwalter, lord of the manor, who offered a flitch of bacon to any man who affirmed that he had not repented of his marriage vows for a year and a day. The ceremony, which took place in the Augustinian monastery of Little Dunmow, Essex, was still recorded in the eighteenth century.

TO LADY WILLIAMS

Bath
17: April 1803.

After so long a Silence What am I to tell My dear Lady Williams?—That the Silence was occasioned by Illness and Influenza,[1] which Mr. Piozzi and I have both been scourged with, to a very terrible Degree. He who is exceedingly strong, shook off a frightful Attack indeed, which being combined with the Gout, added greatly to the Danger and Distress.

Fever however is a new Thing to me And a new Thing is always a *bad* Thing: it has left such Weakness behind it——I can hardly hold my Pen, and they will not suffer me to try at walking out, for fear of Relapses which are for the most part *Fatal*. I hope your Ladyship and your charming Family have escaped all these Mischiefs; and that Dear Bodylwyddan still boasts healthy and happy Inhabitants.

We long to see home again and our kind Neighbours: The Air will refresh, and send away all that remains of the Cough and that odious Catarrh so offensive and afflicting——and my pale lean Face will plump up with Country Living on my native Soil.

A Sea Breeze from Rhyddlan (Rhuddlan) or Prestatyn,[2] is at present considered as the greatest possible luxury by Dear Madam Your Ladyship's and Mrs. Williams's Ever Obliged &c./ H: L: Piozzi.

My Husband joins me in best Regards to Sir John.

Text: Ry. 2 (1802–6).

1. The Piozzis reached Bath ca. 4 December, lodging once again in Pulteney Street in the parish of Bathwick. By March they were both immobilized by the "scourge" of influenza, which had broken out in January and continued until July 1803. Recovering enough to travel, they left for Brynbella on 25 April 1803. See HLP to PSP, 14 April 1803, n. 1, for the nature of the widespread contagion.

2. HLP thought of seabathing as pleasurable therapy for many maladies. She and GP had visited Rhuddlan on the banks of the Clwyd and Prestatyn, a seaside resort north of Offa's Dyke in early April 1801. (Both towns were in Flintshire.) They went again to Prestatyn in July 1804, returning to Brynbella slightly before 23 September. See *Thraliana* 2: 1057; HLP to Ly W, 29 September 1804.

TO THE REVEREND REYNOLD DAVIES

Brynbella
5: May 1803.

Dear Mr. Davies—

Your Letter followed us on, and I think we read it at Worcester. Mr. Piozzi is sorry and so am I that you have been exposed to any Incivilities on our Account. We will Send People to Mr. Whitelock whose Manners he will better understand perhaps, and who will care little about *his*.

Mean while you are fortunate Folks at Streatham; it is lucky that you keep such Advantages *Secret*, or I think all the World would come and Share them: No Place *else* except a Village called Rodborough in Gloucestershire, has 'scaped this odd Pestilential Cough and Fever; *Little Dear* must tell his Parents how good the Air is at Mr. Davies's, and how sick poor Uncle and Aunt have been: How *they* were afraid of coming to London this Spring, because of the reported Contagion, but that (Deo volente) they will come to the great Metropolis before this Year closes, and Salusbury shall sit for his Picture to Mr. Barber of Southampton Street, and then they will *see* what a fine Fellow their Son is.[1]

A propos are his Teeth beautiful?

Mr. Gillon does not seem to think you reported *marvellous Progress* of his Namesake *Johnney* when he enquired last Week concerning him: but I have lived long enough to count little on *premature Fruits:* Some Storm always rises and blows 'em away. Let our Little Boy be well grounded in Grammar, and learn his Rudiments perfectly——when a good Foundation is laid, *any* Structure may be built upon it——I hate the modern Method, 'tis like Gulliver's Premium offered in Laputa for them who could raise a fine House by beginning at the Upper Story.[2]

Here is a Second Winter very unfavourable to the Recovery of Invalides, yet I have lost all my Complaints thank God, and get better Appetite than usual. My Master mends less rapidly, but the Gout keeps him in such perpetual Torment, 'tis no wonder that any Disorder super-added to one so constant and so cruel, is less easily removed——he *did* lose the Influenza *once*, but contrived Somehow to catch it again.

You never tell me about War or Peace, or Pache or Buonaparte;[3] nor You never tell me about Lord and Lady Deerhurst——nor how Mr. Giles goes on, nor how the Trees look in old Streatham Park——no, nor how pretty Lady William Russell looks,[4] nor how young Lambton shines at his Book[5]—and Ker——and Coventry——and all the Lilliputian Squadron.⁶ Sir Henry Calder I suppose is at the Top of the Tree of Science by now.⁷

Farewell Dear Mr. Davies, give my / kind Services to Mr. Wood: and believe me ever / Yours truly / H: L: P.

Text: Hyde Collection. *Address:* Rev. Reynold Davies / Streatham / Surrey. *Postmark:* MY 7 <   >.

1. For John Thomas Barber, see HLP to the Proprietors of the *Monthly Mirror,* 17 June 1798, n. 1.
2. In the "Grand Academy of Lagado," one of the projectors "was a most ingenious architect who had contrived a new method for building houses, by beginning at the roof, and working downwards to the foundation; which he justified to me by the like practice of those two prudent insects the bee and the spider." See *Gulliver's Travels,* chap. 5 of "A Voyage to Laputa, etc."
3. HLP is here talking about opposites: peace or war, a retired Jean-Nicolas Pache or an aggressively active Bonaparte. For Pache, see HLP to LC, 29 June 1796, n. 13.
4. All residents of Streatham.
5. John George (1792–1840), later Viscount Lambton and first earl of Durham (1833) was the son of the late William Henry Lambton (1764–97) and Lady Anne Barbara Frances, née Villiers (d. 1832), daughter of the fourth earl of Jersey.
6. For William Kerr and John Coventry, see HLP to RD, 9 November 1799, nn. 6, 9.
7. The eldest of the "Lilliputian Squadron," Henry Roddam Calder (1790–1868), fifth baronet (1792), was the son of the late Sir Henry (ca. 1740–92) and his second wife, Louisa, née Osborne. The boy's father had been lieutenant governor of Gibraltar and colonel of the Thirtieth Regiment of Foot.

TO THE REVEREND LEONARD CHAPPELOW

Brynbella Monday
9: May 1803.

My dear Mr. Chappelow's very good natured Scrap found us just come home, but scarcely well recovered from the Depression left by this odious Influenza. I think it was somewhat in the Air. The Birds have been affected by it: We have scarce any Swallows, and fewer Crows than I ever remarked in Spring; when a Cuckoo is heard, we all go out to listen as if it were a Wonder: and the poor Thrushes are sensibly diminished. Sharp Frosts every Night will purify, and rough Winds will ventilate however; and if there are not Oak Leaves enough to shade a King upon the 29th of this cold May, 'tis better than losing his Subjects by Ill Health.¹ Physicians conceal many Deaths, and People are fearful of being called *Alarmists,* but there has been a very uncommon Mortality since the Year 1803 *set in.*² How will it *end* I wonder! We are waiting Buonaparte's Convenience as it appears; when *He* is ready, *we* go to War:³ and the other *Courts* of Europe, (one cannot call them *Powers;*) will go to the Windows to see which beats the other——*France* which they *fear,* or *England* which they *hate.*

The Forgery of Lord Hawkesbury's hand and Seal was a Masterly piece of

Rascality:[4] It surpasses all I ever witnessed, and will have *one* Effect more than it intended—it will nip Credulity in the Bud; We shall believe nothing now, till we see Buonaparte riding thro Guilford towards London.

Lady Orkney comes in and reads this Letter, and says 'tis so good a one She will carry it home for her Son to free / So Adieu Dear Sir / H: L: P.

Text: Ry. 561.121.

1. HLP looks ahead to Oak-apple Day, or Royal Oak Day, 29 May, the anniversary of Charles II's restoration. On that day oak-apples or oak leaves are worn in commemoration of his hiding in the oak at Boscobel on 6 September 1651. See John Brand, *Observations on Popular Antiquities,* ed. Henry Ellis, 2 vols. (London: F. C. & J. Rivington, 1813), 1: 273.

2. There was a high degree of mortality in England from January through April 1803. Almost ten thousand people died, more in March than in any month before or after that four-month period.

3. The Peace of Amiens, despite the croaking of HLP, was popular. On 1 June there had been "a General Thanksgiving for the return of Peace" with a service at Westminster Abbey and at Saint Margaret's, London (*Courier,* 2 June 1802).

In less than a year the tensions between England and France were so apparent that Lord Whitworth's recall was rumored (*Courier,* 2 May 1803). On 7 May, the same newspaper reported that the French ambassador to England, General Andréossi, would return to France and Lord Whitworth to England. By 10 May, the *Courier* admitted that peace between the two countries could not be preserved and on the next day that war was inevitable. On Monday, 16 May, the *Courier* announced the "official" declaration, stating, "The die is cast; and, at the moment we are writing, Great Britain may be considered at war with France."

4. See *The Times,* 6 May:

On 5 May, a man who seemed to be a traveler came to the Mansion House, "enquired for the Lord Mayor, declared himself a Messenger belonging to the Foreign Office, and said he was charged with a letter to his Lordship." Although the lord mayor was away, the letter was left. On his return the lord mayor found the letter, "sealed with Lord Hawkesbury's Official Seal. . . .

" 'Lord Hawkesbury presents his compliments to the Lord Mayor, and is happy to inform him, that the Negotiation between this Country and the French Republic has been amicably adjusted.' "

The lord mayor was delighted. "He accordingly took a copy of [the letter] with his own hand, which was instantly affixed in a conspicuous part outside of the Mansion House. His Lordship took a second copy to Lloyd's, and went immediately afterwards to the Stock Exchange with the original."

Very soon thereafter, the lord mayor learned that the letter was a fraud, its detection causing the rapid fall of the Funds. "In consequence, a Committee of the Gentlemen of the Stock Exchange was appointed; after a very full and animated discussion, all bargains done on that day, both for money and time, were declared to be null and void."

TO JAMES ROBSON

> Fryday Night
> 17: June 1803

Your Letter dear Mr. Robson[1] was exceedingly good natured and like yourself,—mindful of an Old Friend. It will be very pleasing to me to see your Son here in Wales, but he must learn the Language if he means to reside much and do Duty.[2] How glad am I that Lady Mary Wortley had the kind Word in Retrospection which She so well deserves.[3] Be so good as send her Works to Mayhew and Ince directed for me at Brynbella and they will come safe.[4]

The Democrates Foreign and Domestic have brought all Europe into a miserable Condition and poor old England *must* take Share with the rest.

Like Polypheme, the Gyant of *our* Day will fling a Rock after us, I doubt it not: had we kept Peace with him——*he* would perhaps have kept Polypheme's Promise to Ulysses:

> When all thy Company have felt my Pow'r
> No man shall be the *last* that I'll devour.[5]

These were the *best* Terms we could have hoped for, and open War is surely better than they.

Pitt and Addington have very high Characters—both of them—as Men of Integrity and Honour. They will not sacrifice a Nation to private Pique, and gain that Nation's Curses—I won't think it.[6]

Mean while Your Son has chosen a Profession which all Parties seem uniting to degrade:[7] Two Bishops and one Dean dead lately have left their Families piteously provided for[8]—yet are these Democrats never contented till Tythes shall be no more.

Where will such Evils stop? And who shall live to see the End of them? Not I believe Your Faithful Servant and Old Acquaintance / H: L: P.

Mr. Piozzi is a'Bed with Gout in Hands and Feet: but joins with me in best Wishes, and warm Invitations to Brynbella.

Send me some *good* Pens, and Paper with the books for *very Pity:* The Paper like this, but *larger* 4to Size if you please. I can get nothing here.

Text: Boston Public Library MS Eng. 308.

1. For the bookseller James Robson, see HLP to SL, 26 February 1785, n. 8.
2. The Reverend George Robson (1773–1851) had been a student at Queen's College, Oxford, receiving his M.A. in 1798. He was preferred by Dr. Horsley, when bishop of Saint Asaph, to a prebend of that church in 1803; the vicarage of Chirk in 1804; and the rectory of Erbistock in 1805.
3. See *Retrospection* 2:394: "Lady Mary Wortley brought from Constantinople, where the small-pox first began, its happy mitigant (if I may call it so) the practice of innoculation.... A woman of gaiety, and carriage lighter by far than was the mind which animated her motions, saved by the introduction of this happy art, numberless valuable

members to society, and taught a power of specifying the dreadful disease even when caught by infection."

HLP admired Lady Mary's letters, which "are sparkling Things indeed—I wonder the world is not fonder of them" ("Harvard Piozziana," vol. 4).

4. *The Works of the Right Hon. Lady Mary Wortley Montagu*. . . . Published, by permission, from her genuine papers. Edited with a memoir of the author, by I. Dallaway, 5 vols. (London: R. Phillips, 1803).

5. Pope's *Odyssey*, 9.435–39. HLP substituted "Company" for "wretched crew."

6. Friction between Pitt and Addington began as early as November 1802, when Canning devised a scheme for urging Addington to resign in favor of Pitt. Although Pitt requested that the plan be dropped, he followed his friends' advice that he give no support to the ministry.

Shortly before a renewal of hostilities with France in May 1803, Addington recommended a substantial increase in naval strength and a call-up of the militia. Because both measures were unpopular, he sought to strengthen his ministry's position with the help of Pitt. He suggested that they both serve under a first minister whose power would be nominal. When this failed, Addington proposed that Pitt become first minister and that he serve in a subordinate capacity. Pitt, however, insisted on the virtual dissolution of the cabinet and the introduction of certain members of the "New Opposition," who had opposed the Addington ministry. Negotiations ceased and so did the friendship of Addington and Pitt—at least for a time.

7. Parliament was trying to enact (across party lines) a measure that would enforce the residence of beneficed clergy and so insure their performance of duty. Implicit in the measure is criticism of large-scale absenteeism by clergymen and their neglect of parishioners' needs.

8. The dean who had died on 10 April was Charles Peter Layard; one bishop was Lewis Bagot of Saint Asaph (d. 4 June 1802). The other was Charles Moss (d. 13 April 1802) of Bath and Wells. The first two men were hard pressed for money, but Moss at his death left £140,000.

TO PENELOPE SOPHIA PENNINGTON

Brynbella
19: June 1803.

Assure yourself Dear Mrs. Pennington that my Thoughts towards You are in no wise changed—and if I *always* thought you the best Letter-Writer in our Kings Dominions (before *they* were curtailed by Loss of Hanover) how much more do I think so since your last arrived—full as it is of pungent and tender Reproaches.[1]

When the Throws went badly with poor Baretti as we played together at BackGammon—or when Matters went ill with his Game by his own fault: These, would he say are cursed Dice, but we must play them *as they are*. I can find nothing better to say when Life and the Occurrences of which it is composed, displease me.

There are two Bishops and one Dean dead you see, and their Families left low in the World; yet the Democrates keep on stripping Clergymen of every Reason for becoming such; and tear away Tythes &c. without Money.

You may put down all our Names for the Layards, Lady Orkney, Lady K.,

Lady de Blaquiere and Myself. Mr. Piozzi has been in his Bed just 20 Days,—he is in it still; but the Violence of his Disorder is beginning to remit now.

Dear Doctor Randolph's Powers of breaking one's heart by Eloquence I doubt not—God grant he may never afflict his Friends but with his own Intention.[2]— Sweet Siddons is at Cheltenham healing *her* honourable Heart I hope, and washing away its Cares.[3] Mr. Whalley is happy, it is a Cordial to hear of *Somebody* being happy[4]—You are too Nervous—as the Phrase is; meaning that Your Nerves are too irritable to be placidly content: and that is the best State to be in. No Danger however can attach to your late Illness, and I will be *Sworn—on Your Last Letter;*—that the Dear *Head* has had no Harm come to it.[5]

Lady Hesketh is *so* good to remember. *The Mouse with quick Motions.* Make my Compliments as acceptable to her as you can, and to Miss Case and all who recollect with Kindness *Their* very Obedient, and *your* very Faithful Servant / H: L: P.

There is a Talk of Mr. and Mrs. Mostyn having Sown their Wild Oats, and intending to return home here; but perhaps *this* is too good News to be true.

Are you sorry for Mrs. Greatheed?[6]

Text: Princeton University Library. *Address:* Mrs. / Pennington / Dowry Square / Hot Wells / Bristol. *Postmark:* DENBIGH 22<4>.

1. PSP wrote an apologetic letter to HLP on 12 May (Ry. 568.116). HLP's reply, now missing, was found by PSP, 10 June, to be "a little *Chill,* some thing correspondent with the Season, I think I perceive in your *Style* which the Truth and warmth of my Friendship *will* and *shall* chace away, as, I trust, the blessed Sun must shortly do all these Vapours which have lately hung so heavily around and almost deluged us. . . . I will, for the time to come, look close into my little Bag of Faults and Foibles that I may trespass as little on your Indulgence as possible, and with the tenderness and fidelity of an *old* and proved Friend, be cautious to present to you all the agreeable parts of a *new* Acquaintance only" (Ry. 568.117). This letter of HLP's on 19 June thaws some but not all of the chill.
2. HLP responds to a section of PSP's letter:
"To see such a robust Creature [as Dr. Randolph] reduced to feebleness, inspired me with a sort of Tenderness I never had any Idea of feeling for *him* before;—and the Condition in which he stood forth to preach his Sermon on the Death of our ever lamented Dean, nearly broke all our Hearts!—There was not a dry Eye I verily believe in the Cathedral!! As for poor Mrs. Randolph I was obliged to set open the Door of the Pew to give her Air,—I really thought she would have been suffocated by the violence of her Emotions!—A Volume of the Deans Sermons are going to be published for the relief of his *almost* destitute family by Subscription.—Mr. Whalley and Dr. Randolph interest themselves in getting as many Names as possible; and have desired me to mention it every where.—Perhaps you would speak of it to Lady Orkney and Lady Kirkwall?—The Subscription is only 12s. and my Heart swells within me while I say, you cannot contribute to an act of more real *Charity.*"
3. Suffering from chronic asthma, Sally Siddons had died 31 March in Great Marlborough Street before SS could return from Ireland. It was not until May that the actress, her companion Patty Wilkinson, and young Cecilia went to a farm near Cheltenham, where they stayed until July.
4. In May 1803 TSW married Augusta Utica Heathcote (1742–1807).
5. PSP described her unexpected ailment in the letter of 10 June. While talking to Hester Case, PSP was "interrupted by an attack in my *Head* which *surprized* me, and

greatly *alarmed* my kind Friends—It was like a sudden *Bolt* of Electricity shot through it, which threw me off my Seat and tho it did not absolutely take away my Senses, rendered me very Ill and languid for some Days. It has made an *aweful* and, I trust, not *unuseful* Impression in my Mind,—without depressing my Spirits. . . . I bless God I do not feel *afraid* to Die.—"

6. See HLP to LC, 7 July 1803, n. 9.

TO JOHN LLOYD

Fryday 29: June [1803].
Brynbella

You must my Dear Sir give us a favourable Answer to the enclosed Card and at the same Time be kind enough to promise us Your Company for next *Monday sennight* 9th of July, to meet the Bishop of St. Asaph and the Family of Bodylwyddan at Dinner.

This Letter is likewise an Acknowledgement that I have—in Loan—the 1st Volume of your Abbé Raynal, and that I will beg the 2d to keep it Company for two or three Weeks only.[1]

Accept our most faithful and united Regards; and do me the honour to believe that I am with the greatest possible Esteem / Dear Sir / Your Obliged Servant / H: L: Piozzi.

Text: National Library of Wales MS 12421D. *Address:* John Lloyd Esq. / M:P: Wygfair.

1. Guillaume-Thomas-François Raynal (1713–96), *Anecdotes Littéraires*, 2 vols. (Paris: chez Durand, Pissot, 1750).

TO THE REVEREND LEONARD CHAPPELOW

Brynbella
July 7th 1803.

It is very charming in you Dear Mr. Chappelow to remember old Friends wherever you are; and the Place you are now in is a magnificent one.[1] Our own little Plaything improves surprizingly; and as you liked it very well four or five Years ago, I think it would amuse you to see the growth of those Plantations put in by the Man who had *once* seen *Wandsworth*.[2] Well! Heaven preserve our Property to us, and us to our Property[3]——*The Foe vaunts in the Field*[4]——but in *another* Book——older than Shakespeare——tho' not so much *read;*—We may as you Preachers say, *find these Words.* "Let not him who buckleth on his Armour, boast himself like him that putteth it off."[5]

I hope we shall all of us pay our Taxes chearfully, and give a great Example to Europe of one Nation not contented to sell her Sons for Slaves to Buonaparte.[6]

Two Years from this Hour will decide our Fate; and for Two Years, scarce any Effort will undo us.[7] Dear Mr. Piozzi can neither fight nor fly, but he must make his Purse his Substitute; and no Man is more loyally attached to the Throne and Government of England——Don't you remember how he entered his Income higher than there was any need to do, once before? and would not appeal when advised to it.[8]

For my own part I am glad we are come at last to a State of Decision: We shall now have a *lasting* Peace, when Peace is made again. France will convince herself that Britain possesses an unyielding Spirit—and will torment her no more if upon this Occasion She proves true to her own Honour.

Mrs. Greatheed was offered Leave to come home, but resolved to remain—as I am told the Story—with her Husband and Son at Fontainebleau.[9]

My Friend Lady de Blaquiere has got one of her Young Men home safe at last:[10] The same you remember here when Lord Kirkwall tumbled out of the Post Chaise on Denbigh Green[11]——Her Daughter married our young Heir of Lleweney you know, and we expect a little Boy there every Day: Had Miss Ormsby been an Angel we need not regret her, and 'tis impossible to find a happier Family, or a Mother more contented, than our charming Countess of Orkney.[12]

Summer seems just beginning; the Grass grows, and the Flowers spring like May:—not like *July*—but the Seasons seem to me keeping Pace with the Fashions, and getting later and later every Year——We may perhaps have some Fruit ripe *in October*.

Well! Dear Sir—now *do* write sometimes—not Blank Verse about Animated Nature, and the green Millions of the peopled Ground: but about Sir Sydney Smith[13] and Lieutenant Temple,[14] and a kind Word occasionally about my good Husband who loves you sincerely, and about my Daughters—who love neither You nor him I believe, nor Your truly / Faithful Servant / H: L: P.

In short, let us have Letters oftener.

Text: Ry. 561.122.

1. LC was with the marquess of Bath at Longleat. HLP's letter was written in response to LC's of 20 June (Ry. 563.75), in which he announced his impending visit to Longleat.

2. Wandsworth, as implied by HLP's pleasantry, was not a typical English community. Situated near London, it was small and quiet; but many of its residents—apart from the gentry—were descendants of Dutch and French settlers who sought religious toleration. See *The Victoria History of the County of Surrey,* ed. H. E. Malden, 4 vols. (London: Constable, 1912), 4:108–20.

3. Implicit in HLP's statement was the possibility of a French invasion. Bonaparte had since the renewal of the war made several threats to different groups of a descent upon England. Charles Yorke, as secretary at war, dared Bonaparte to cross the channel. More concretely, he had proposed to the Commons on 20 June that a reserve army, consisting of fifty thousand men, should be created by ballot to serve for four years. See Stanhope 4:62.

4. *Richard the Third*, 5.3.288.

5. 1 Kings 20:11.

6. By June 1803 the Addington ministry, hoping to raise £12 million, introduced such new taxes as those on *"West India* produce" and, more importantly, on income or "Property." The "many Murmurs" were so instantaneous that *The Times* on 28 June retorted with a defense of the income tax as moderate and just.

7. Yet in *Thraliana*, under date of July, HLP altered the time necessary to determine England's fate, writing: "Well! I am really better contented with our Public Affairs than *I have* been,—just because now in a Twlevemonth's Time we shall know our Fate—bad or good" (2:1039).

8. HLP's paragraph is a response to the opening of LC's letter of 20 June and a mild reprimand for his lament over taxes. After writing that he could not pay them, he continues: "What worries me is, that twas said the war would make Buonaparte more unpopular than ever in France, but I fear the Countenance he meets with from the Northern powers, will have a contrary Effect.—Yesterday at Stockdale's privy Council, many and various opinions were delivered, as to the possibility of our Enemies making a serious impression against [us] by invasion.—I hope he will not come—but if he does we must all Fight—even our good master [GP] must Fight, and stoutly too, with might in his bottom pocket, his guineas must *march* though he cannot.—In short we are got into a dreadful scrape."

9. There were many rumors about the Greatheeds. On 20 June, LC had written: "So our Friends the Greatheeds are amongst the English Prisoners in France—I am not sorry for them, Why could they not have staid in good old England.—The Grand Consul I understand affronted Mr. Greatheed, at a Levy when Englishmen to their disgrace were kicking Shins for an introduction—are you a German—No I am an Englishman—and Buonaparte turned away in a passion."

In his journal Bertie Greatheed described an interview that he and his son were granted by General Junot. "We were let in directly and immediately received our permission in the handsomest manner from the General to remain at Paris on our Parole." *An Englishman in Paris, 1803*, ed. J.P.T. Bury and J.C. Barry (London: Geoffrey Bles, 1953), p. 155.

10. John De Blaquiere (1776–1844), who would in 1812 become second baron.

11. HLP's recollection of Lord Kirkwall's accident on 7 July 1801 was inaccurate. See her letter to LC, 17 September 1801, n. 1.

12. According to Farington, Lady Orkney was unhappy about her son's marriage to Anna Maria De Blaquiere and within a year was "obliged to quit His Lordship's House, where with His aunt she was on a visit, & this by the rude behaviour of the Young Wife, whose fortune is to be only £600" (6:2420).

13. In 1803 Sir William Sidney Smith served under Lord Keith while in command of a squadron of small craft off the coast of Flanders and Holland. To many Englishmen, he was a hero, the equal of Wellesley and Nelson. In *GM* for 1803, he is described as "the day-star of [English] safety . . . the instrument of the deliverance of his country," specially chosen by heaven (73, pt. 2: 804).

14. Henry John Temple (1784–1865), third viscount Palmerston (I., 1802). Having been extensively educated abroad, at Harrow, and with Dugald Stewart (1753–1828), professor of mathematics at the University of Edinburgh, he was admitted to Saint John's, Cambridge, on 4 April 1803. But instead of matriculating, he joined the Johnian corps of volunteers and early revealed his interest in national defense. Not until 27 January 1806 did he matriculate in the university, the same day on which he proceeded master of arts without examination, *jure natalium*.

TO THE REVEREND LEONARD CHAPPELOW

Brynbella
30: July 1803.

I had your kind Letter two Days ago Dear Mr. Chappelow,[1] and hasten to tell you how welcome a Week's Visit from You will be both to my Master and myself. We shall have much Chat, but I think the Subjects very mournful.[2]

That any Warrior of the 19th Century should advertise the Pillage of a Conquered Country, is strange and horrible: He must look to mere Barbarians for a Precedent; and will find none nearer than the Gothic Wars—unless he means to emulate the Savages of North America. I have not seen the Newspaper where the marked Houses are enumerated.[3] I have however read both in History and Drama, of the French sending to Harry Monmouth for his Ransom——and Lord Mountjoy's Ancestor was the Herald[4]——before the Battle of Agincourt was fought—the gaining of which gave our King the City of Paris and Crown of France——His Princess married Owen Tudor afterwards[5]—and while any remain of *her* Race, they will defend *this* Principality from Usurping Cruelty and *such* Scenes—as are now exhibiting in Ireland.[6]

Poor Lady Kirkwall's Relations and Friends are all murdering and massacring——I mean *Passive Voice,* being Murdered and Massacred in Dublin Streets: She and Lady Bath[7] should make haste, if they hope to be delivered before the French set out; for all agree that they will come in *Harvest Time.*

> If so methinks fair Rosalind
> May take the Cart to sheaf and bind.[8]

Women must get the Harvest in, if men are employed in Arms; and I should think it were no bad Policy to lay up Depôts of Corn in your Inland Counties, Warwick particularly: lest Detachments of Marauders might do us Coasters more Damage than is prudent to permit.

Ireland will take off some of the Numbers you boast,[9] and to say true 'tis not in *Numbers* we must put our Trust——rather in the old Adage of one Englishman beating Three Frenchmen; We are not to France as one even to Three:[10] yet they [are] People willing to defend our tight Little Island against Invasion, tho' I have no Notion of doing more than *that* for Amusement of Foreign Powers.[11] Were we to put a Bourbon on the Throne of France tomorrow, he would fly in our Faces that Day sennight if strong enough; and you see Louis dix Huit half *thanks* Buonaparte for the Aggrandisement he has been cause of to the *Great* Nation.[12] A good Peace and keep Malta is all I wish, after having baffled and disgraced our Enemy.[13]——

The Dinner you speak of, where Mr. Twiss shone away so, was at dear Siddons's House, he married her Sister. And the Miss Mostyn you mean who married Sir Robert Salusbury Vaughan t'other day,[14] is a Sister to Mrs. Champneys a Lady who makes Masquerades 16 Miles from Bath, whose Husband will be Sir Thomas Champneys, and who is now spending about 15000£ o'Year.[15]——

—She is a Flintshire Woman, and Sir Roger Mostyn's Daughter. Cæcilia Thrale that was married [to] *their Cousin:* She seems to have finished sowing Wild Oats now, and talks of returning to their proper home. Our Neighbourhood has undergone some Changes. The Bishop and his Lady gone, Leo and his Wife both gone; pretty Madox gone, and the very agreeable Bishop of Killala come to the House they lived at.[16]

Nothing Immortal save the Lovely Ladies of Llangollen. Lord Kirkwall *will* be a good Father I hope, and *soon:* His charming Mother is in Town the while, watching the old Marquis of Thomond's last Moments——She is an exemplary Character,—always preferring Duty to Inclination tho' She does not write Sermons.[17] I fancy Harriet Bowdler *publishes,*——rather than *composes* these Preachments you tell me of[18]——but Lady Eleanor and Miss Ponsonby must know more of the matter than I do. Present me to them and to Lady Bradford with all possible respect——I hope the little Dears at Weston keep well, and beautiful, and amiable as when we saw them last. You are very good to remember Salusbury. Make haste now, and don't stay away till the Leaves are falling, and the Place looks frightful: but come and tell My Master how pretty he has made it——for so thinks the partial Eye of yours truly / H: L: P.

Text: Ry. 561.123. *Address:* Rev: Mr. Chappelow.

1. HLP responds to LC's letter, dated Longleat, 23 July 1803 (Ry. 563.76).
2. LC had written: ". . . to morrow I go to Bath [from Longleat]—and from thence to Weston—and about the middle of September—I may probably go to Llangollen for a day or two, and from thence to Brynbella for a week—and then into Norfolk, to Lord Bradford's new estate. . . . What a dreadful thing it would be to have all these delightful *Sejours* in the possessions of nasty, *spitting,* snuff-taking Frenchmen.—Poor Brynbella too would go—I know not whether Madame Buonaparte, would not condescend to like it—its very name has its attractions—She is very fond of music, and my Master and the French Lady might soon contrive to send you off the stage."
3. According to LC: "I think if the French get to the Capital, mouse trap hall will escape plundering—all the fine Houses in England as you see by the paper are marked down in Paris—that are likely to produce good booty.—I hope Brynbella will escape." Although there was a good deal of such scare talk about, we suspect that LC was jesting in order to frighten HLP "wonderfully about the invasion." See n. 1 of HLP to LC, 2 November 1803.
4. Just prior to the decisive English victory at Agincourt (25 October 1415), the French Charles VI (1368–1422) sent to Henry V (1387–1422) an emissary charged with delivering arrogant threats and demands. The messenger, identified in Shakespeare's *Henry the Fifth* (3.6.119–78) only as "Montjoy," bore that title as chief herald of France. See the Arden edition, ed. J. H. Walter (London: Methuen, 1960), p. 80n.

HLP thus confused the titular French office "Montjoie-Saint-Denis" with an English pedigree: with the family of Blount, whose last member, Charles (ca. 1562–1606), became eighth baron Mountjoy (1594) and first earl of Devonshire (1603); with John Stuart (1744–1814), fourth earl of Bute (1792), cr. Viscount Mountjoy of the Isle of Wight (1796); with the Mountjoys of co. Tyrone, whose last member was Charles John Gardiner, Viscount Mountjoy (HLP to LC, 27 August 1800, n. 7).

5. The battle of Agincourt, among other military actions of the invading forces, culminated in the Treaty of Troyes (1420). The subsequent marriage of Princess Catherine of Valois and Henry established the latter as a potential claimant to the French throne,

although—having overrun Normandy and entered Paris in 1420—he did not live to complete the conquest of the entire country.

For the marriage of Owen Tudor and Katheryn of Berain, see HLP to PSP [ca. 26 July 1800], n. 13; also *Thraliana* 2:1040–41.

6. HLP refers to an Irish rebellion planned by Robert Emmet to coincide with England's renewed war with France. The rising was fixed for the people of Dublin on 23 July. About four hundred assembled but then separated into groups, one of which killed Lord Kilwarden, chief justice of the King's Bench. "It is stated, that his Lordship was in his carriage, accompanied by his nephew and two daughters, when he was attacked by the assassins. His nephew, it is said, shared his fate; but the young Ladies escaped" (*The Times*, 28 July). By the time the various bands in Dublin regrouped, they were met by the military and dispersed.

Emmet and nineteen other prisoners, who had taken part in the Dublin conspiracy, were tried in August and September. Eighteen were executed. See Stanhope 4:71–75; *The Times*, 29 and 30 July; *GM* 73, pt. 2 (1803): 686–87.

7. Isabella Elizabeth, née Byng (d. 1830), third daughter of the fourth viscount Torrington (and hence sister of Lady Bradford) had married on 24 April 1794 Thomas Thynne (1765–1837), second marquess of Bath (1796). They were to have a large family of seven sons and three daughters. Their fourth son, William, was born 17 October 1803.

8. HLP telescopes a song by Touchstone in Shakespeare's *As You Like It*, 3.2.104–8.

9. LC had written: "I am very glad Mr. Pitts plan of arming the people [against a French invasion] meets with such universal approbation.—400,000 men in arms besides our Regular Army—Militia, and army of reserve that is 200,000d more—why Bobadil his self could not kill them all."

10. The adage went back to the time of Agincourt. Shakespeare altered it in *Henry the Fifth*, 3.6.148–50: "When they were in health . . . I thought upon one pair of English legs / Did March three Frenchmen." But the adage could be reversed to French advantage as in Walpole's letter to George Montagu, 13 July 1745 (*Walpole Correspondence* 9:17).

11. See, e.g., the declaration of the inhabitants of Lambeth on 27 July " 'That it appears to this Meeting, the First Consul of France . . . is now determined on the invasion of this United Kingdom, and is making the most formidable preparations for that purpose. . . . That this Meeting, in thus calling upon its Fellow Citizens to arm, hope they shall be excused for reminding them, they are invited to come forward in defence of the happiest and wisest Constitution ever known to the world—in defence of a Sovereign, who . . . has shewn himself to be the Father of all those who have the happiness to live under the British Government'" (*GM* 73, pt. 2: 686).

12. HLP alludes to the proclamation of Louis XVIII rejecting Bonaparte's suggestion that he renounce the throne of France. The first paragraph of Louis's declaration irritated HLP. Thus:

"I am far from being inclined to confound M. Bonaparte with those who have preceded him. I think highly of his valour, and of his military talents. Neither do I feel ungrateful for many acts of his admiration; for whatever is done for the benefit of my people, shall always be dear to my heart. He is deceived, however, if he imagines that he can induce me to forego my claims; for in fact he himself would confirm and establish them, could they be called in question, by the very step he has now taken." See *GM* 73, pt. 2: 680.

13. In *Thraliana* 2:1039, HLP insisted that "without [Malta] we *cannot* have a lasting Peace, because Malta is the Security for Aegypt & *the East*."

14. Anna Maria (1777–1858), daughter of Sir Roger Mostyn (ca. 1735–96), fifth baronet of Mostyn (1758), and Margaret, née Wynn (d. 1792), had married in September 1801 Sir Robert Williams Vaughan (1768–1843), second baronet of Nannau, co. Merioneth. An Oxonian, he was M.P. for Merioneth (1792–1836).

15. On 21 April 1792 Thomas Swymmers Champneys (1769–1839), second baronet (1821), had married at Saint George's, Hanover Square, Charlotte Margaret (1767–1845), daughter of Sir Roger Mostyn.

One masquerade for which Mrs. Champneys acquired renown occurred in December

1796 and set the standard for her subsequent masquerades. It was "a most elegant Masquerade Ball . . . at Orchardly House near Frome, at which near 200 Persons were present, who dressed in various characters and supported them with great spirit and correctness.—The supper was sumptuous, and in great plenty.—The rooms were elegantly decorated with laurel, roses, &c. . . . The company departed at 6 o'clock the next morning, highly delighted with their convivial entertainment" (*Bath Herald*, 19 December 1796).

16. Lewis Bagot had died 4 June 1802 in London, his wife, Mary, on 17 August 1799 at Saint Asaph. Daniel Leo had died at Llannerch Park, Flintshire, in July 1803, and his wife Letitia on 12 December 1801. Elizabeth Madocks had died 3 January 1799 at Bath.

The bishop of Killala was Joseph Stock (1740–1813). See HLP to John Roberts, 2 March 1807; to Q, 11 August 1807.

For Bagot, see HLP to LC, 15 September 1794, n. 9, and P.R.O., Prob. 11/1377/494 (proved 10 June 1802); for the Leos, HLP to Q, 23 February 1794, n. 3; for Elizabeth Madocks, HLP to Margaret Owen [ca. 12 February 1799], nn. 2 and 6.

17. On 1 July, Farington visited Lord Thomond, with whom he had a dinner appointment. When he arrived there, "the Servant told me His Lordship was very *seriously* ill, worse than the Butler had ever seen him.—He went to Taplow on Tuesday, & on Wednesday rode out there, & returned home very unwell. On Thursday (yesterday) he was brought to town so weak as to require support. Sir F. Milman had been with him.—The Servant seemed very apprehensive and said His Lordship had used too much exercise" (6:2071). He suffered from a debilitating fever and loss of weight, but by 17 July he had begun to rally and by 1 August sent out "a Card of thanks . . . announcing *his* Recovery" (6:2078, 2083, 2093).

18. LC had written: "I saw Mrs. Bowdler at Bath—the divine Mrs. Bowdler—literally so for she has written sermons which have fascinated, all Bishops and priests and Deacons—Ladies into the bargain—are in Love with her doctrine."

The work to which LC alludes is *Sermons on the Doctrines and Duties of Christianity* (1803), which by 1836 had reached its forty-fourth edition.

TO PENELOPE SOPHIA PENNINGTON

Brynbella
31: July 1803.

Such is the present Situation of Everybody and of Every Thing——that even *your* lovely Description of Nature and her Beauties in some Place which you Dear Mrs. Pennington call Bower Ashton[1]—but of which I never heard in my Life before—fail to detain my Mind from Events in Prospect, and near Prospect *now*, of enormous Importance indeed.

Poor Jane Holman, cy devant Honourable Miss Hamilton is running hither for Refuge from Murder and Massacre,—She has written today to bid us expect her every Moment[2]—and though the Ground *is* covered with wavy Corn, and the Trees are loaded with Apples, Pears, all useful Fruitage;—my heart at this Instant feels more Bent on their Defence than on their Admiration.

I deferred writing till the Time that your Letter gives me Leave to suppose you are under the half-Sacred Roof of a Lady, to whom if we direct in *Europe* it will find the destined Way.[3] Present me with truly respectful Attention where I wish

31 July 1803

so sincerely never to be forgotten; and in return I will enclose you some Impromptu Verses which I threw across the Table to Mr. Piozzi last Monday. We had no Company—his Health tho' mended could not admit of any, only one Friend from Denbigh, and the Parson of the Parish who translates Miss Moore's admirable Stories into Welsh for Benefit of his poor and Ignorant Parishioners[4]—but here are the Lines to Gabriel Piozzi 25 July 1803.

>   Accept my Love this Honest Lay
>   Upon your Twentieth Wedding Day.
>   I little hop'd that Life would stay
>   To hail the twentieth Wedding Day.
>   If you're grown Gouty, I grown Gray
>   Upon our Twentieth Wedding Day,
>   'Tis no great Wonder; Friends must Say
>   Why 'twas their Twentieth Wedding Day.
>   Perhaps there's few feel less Decay
>   Upon a Twentieth Wedding Day:
>   And many of those who used to pay
>   Their Court upon our Wedding Day;
>   Have melted off and died away
>   Before the Twentieth Wedding day.
>   Those Places too which once so gay
>   Bore Witness to our Wedding Day,
>   Florence and Milan blythe as May
>   Marauding French have made their Prey.
>   If then of Gratitude one Ray
>   Illuminates our Wedding Day,
>   Think, midst the Wars and Wild Affray
>   That rage around this Wedding Day;
>   What Mercy 'tis, we are spar'd to say
>   We have seen our Twentieth Wedding Day.[5]

If Helen Williams—ever lovely, and once *so* beloved! is looking towards England now in Preference of France, it is a great Testimony to our Island's Felicity and Honour[6]—for such Suffrage is not mean, and Helena has had experience of *both Nations,* since She published that little Book in which She charged our Londoners with Harshness, Avarice, and Want of Feeling, because they suffered Some Monsieur de Fossée to wear Straw Boots.[7] The Londoners behaviour *now* does them vast Credit in the Opinion of all Thinking People, and Mr. Bosanquet's Speech will doubtless be handed down to Posterity as giving great Example.[8]—Should not You be struck with The Sight of a Metropolis you lived so long in,—*Fortified* against *hostile force?* It would to *me* bear an extremely awful Appearance.

Dear Mr. Whalley's Acquisitions are come to him in a lucky Time; for the Character I hear of his Lady, She will *Strengthen his Hands* to every Act of Generosity, Public and Private.

Miss Thrale has written to me an obliging Letter, She is somewhere in your Neighbourhood—Heath House—I know not its Situation. Mrs. Mostyn is said to meditate *her* Return to the Rustics of N. Wales, who will receive her as if She came to confer on us both Benefit and Honour.

Such is the Consequence of that lofty Conduct which forces People into their *Places* as The Ton Ladies call treating their humble Servants with Distant and scarce lukewarm Civility——Well! Those who take the *other* way are worse used in *this* World, and I suppose will stand no better in the *next* for directing to Miss White, instead of plain *Sarah:*[9] I cure every day of some Prejudice or other.

Ask Miss Hannah More if She has seen a Sermon on the Obligations to a Religious Life? preached by a Mr. Roberts before the University of Oxford, and displaying much Virtue and Learning? He is our Curate here at Brynbella newly so appointed.[10]

Farewell: My Master's Foot mends: He goes out now in the rolling chair we bought when living at 77 Pultney Street Bath; and looks as well as he is remembered *ever* to have looked by his / H: L: Piozzi.

Lady K[irkwall] is yet undelivere[d.] Her Friends <are murdered> in the streets of Dublin. Lady Orkney in London attending a sick Father.

Text: Princeton University Library. *Address:* Mrs. Pennington / Hotwells / near / Bristol. *Postmark:* BRISTOL AUG.

    1. HLP's letter responds to that of PSP, dated Bower Ashton, 17 July 1803 (Ry. 568.118). Bower Ashton is a hamlet in Somerset, near Bristol.
    2. Jane Holman and her husband had fled the uprising in Dublin to return to London, stopping for a while at Brynbella.
    3. The letter had been originally directed to "Mrs. Pennington / at Miss Hannah More's House / Barley Hill." But there the letter was redirected and sent on to "Hotwells / near / Bristol."
    4. Denbighshire-born John Roberts (1775–1829) received his B.A. from Jesus College, Oxford, in 1796. He remained for a while at Oxford as a proofreader of the Society for the Preservation of Christian Knowledge's Welsh Bible and Prayer Book (1799). Although he had been made curate of two parishes in Oxfordshire, he wanted to return to North Wales. He therefore served as curate to the vicar of Tremeirchion in 1803, succeeding to the vicarate only in 1807. Fluent in Welsh, he was to edit—among other works—a Welsh translation of the *Book of Homilies* and a hymnary for use in the Welsh Church.
    5. HLP wanted a permanent record of her celebratory poem, transcribing it in "Verses 1" (pp. 20–21) "To Mr. Piozzi; 25th July 1803."
HLP saw her twentieth wedding anniversary as an answer to the "Vipers." Thus, it was spent "in our new House—elegantly furnish'd; our hills clothed with unhoped for Woods, the Debts, all but a few Bills, paid off; the Church repairing & beautifying—by this *formidable* Foreigner, whom my Daughters & my Friends said was to ruin my Fortune, & change my Religion, and use me I know not how ill besides. He certainly has been a faithful & tender Husband to me notwithstanding their Denunciations now for 19 Years" (*Thraliana* 2:1039–40). See also *British Synonymy* 1:52.
    6. HLP's reaction to PSP's receipt of "a long Letter, three Sheets of Paper, from Helen Maria Williams, in reply to one I had written to her (as an Introduction) by Mr. Palmer, considerably more than 12 Months since.—She does not touch at all on *Public* Affairs but enters largely into her private *Concerns,* and from the dignified Principle of desiring to prove herself *worthy* of the Esteem she seems still tenderly and generously to Value, appears anxious to clear herself from the gross Calumnies which Party prejudice has

delighted to heap upon her, and to misrepresent her Conduct, in every point of view in this Country.

"To *me* the exculpation was unnecessary as I never, for a moment, in my own Mind laid any thing to her Account, beyond *Political Error*.—She says She has seen much of the Greatheeds, and enquires after her former Friends, on this side the Water, with a warmth of Interest and Tenderness of Heart, that always formed so fascinating a part of her Character. . . . On the Subject of her own *Personal Purity*—poor Thing! She says 'Her Witness is in Heaven,' and that She has the prospect before her of being shortly called to that Account, from which no Subterfuge can shield us.—The Complaint She was always subject to in her Chest, being so much aggravated by the many Sorrows She has experienced, and particularly by the last dreadful Blow, the Death of her beloved Sister, that She feels hastening towards the Tomb.—"

7. *Letters Written in France, in the Summer 1790, to a Friend in England; Containing Various Anecdotes relative to the French Revolution; and Memoirs of Mons. and Madame Du F——* (London: T. Cadell, 1790).

From p. 123 (letter 16) to p. 214 (end of letter 25), Helen Williams described the suffering of Augustin-François-Thomas du Fossé (1750–1833) and his wife, Monique, née Coquerel, both in England and France.

The allusion to which HLP refers occurs on pp. 183–84 (letter 21). After being reunited with his wife, "Mons. Du——went to London the next day, and hired a little garret: there, with a few books, a rushout, and some straw in which he wrapped his legs to supply the want of fire, he recollected not the splendour to which he had once been accustomed, but the dungeon from which he had escaped. . . . His clothes being too shabby to admit of his appearing in the day, he issued from his little shed when it was dark, and endeavoured to warm himself by the exercise of walking."

8. *Address of Jacob Bosanquet, Esq. on Tuesday the 26th of July, 1803, at the Royal Exchange, as Chairman of a numerous and respectable Meeting of Merchants, &c. of the City of London . . .* (London: Booth, Duke-Street, Portland-Place; Hatchard, No. 190, and Ginger, No. 169 Piccadilly, 1803). Price 6d., per dozen. This was a rhetorical "Address"—printed as a broadside—urging merchants in all parts of Great Britain to make sacrifices so that an energetic, aggressive military action might be taken against France.

9. For Vitalba's sister-in-law, Sarah White, see HLP to PSP, 27 March 1798, n. 5.

10. *A Discourse on the Necessity of a Religious Life; comprehending the Substance of a Sermon preached before the University of Oxford, at St. Mary's, on Sunday, the 22d of May, 1803* (Oxford: At the University Press for the Author, 1803). The thirty-two page sermon is now catalogued as Bodleian 8°. BS. M.248. No. 6.

TO ELIZABETH [DE] BLAQUIERE

[July 1803][1]

I wish my dearest Miss Blaquiere[2] that my Lord had brought better News *from Ireland:* his Presence will however be a Consolation to Lady de B[laquier]e—and to yourselves.

Lord Thomond will yet live to see many Things new and strange, to one who like myself lived in former Days. You Say nothing of your Sweet Sister——I think it would be prudent to keep *her* from Alarms: Lady Orkney will now hasten homeward to comfort the Dears She must have been long wishing to see again.

God will preserve your Brother Peter;[3] I suppose 'tis for *him* you are agonizing: but your Papa will tell you that we must all expect 'Bustle, and be prepared.

In this Moment I *turn* your kind Note, and find Lady Kirkwall keeping quite Well. While that is the Case, we *must* not *look* uneasy. She will bring a Young Hero[4] for future Times to love as She herself is loved and respected—by her's and Dear Madam / *Your* H: L: Piozzi.

Present me respectfully to both my dear Lords.

Text: Harvard University Library. *Address:* Hon: Miss Blaquiere / Lleweney Hall.

1. This letter was written during Lord Thomond's illness in July and just before the birth of the Kirkwall heir; see n. 4.
2. Elizabeth De Blaquiere (1786–1870), Lady Kirkwall's younger sister, was in 1807 to marry the London banker John Barnard Hankey (1784–1868), whose estate was in Fetcham Park. See "Burial Register," Fetcham, C.R.O., Surrey.
3. Peter Boyle De Blaquiere (1784–1860) was an officer in the Royal Navy, having served as a midshipman under Captain Bligh of the *Bounty,* and was present at Camperdown in 1797. He was now part of the reactivated Channel Fleet. It was not Peter about whom the De Blaquieres were concerned but their eldest son, John (1776–1844), who was a prisoner in France and would remain so until 1813. See *Journals and Letters* 7:173. At the time of his father's death in 1812, John—while still a prisoner—succeeded to the title as second baron De Blaquiere of Ardkill [I.].
4. The "Young Hero," Thomas John Hamilton FitzMaurice, was to be born 8 August at Lleweni Hall.

TO THE REVEREND LEONARD CHAPPELOW

Brynbella Sunday
28: August 1803.

Dear Mr. Chappelow
must always be welcome to *our* House, full or Empty. We shall have some Refugees from Ireland to give you the Meeting at an Evening Commerce Pool.

Cy devant Miss Hamilton and her Husband Mr. Holman—a very pleasing Man, are runaway from Murder and Massacre; and little Brynbella new tricked up, cannot refuse old Streatham Friends——but we have one Bed Chamber more than *you* remember, *in* o'Doors: and Mr. Piozzi has fitted up and furnished an Apartment one might almost call *elegant* over your old *Bathing Room* the Brewhouse: so you see there is no Excuse for staying away——Let me only have a Scrap Letter first.[1]

By next Fryday Sennight we *may* hear something to our Satisfaction of this fierce Fellow across the Water: He longs for *Peace* now, and has sent a beautiful Dame spirituelle to coax Alexander of Russia to mediate for him[2]——but I confess my own Unwillingness to lay down our bright and shining, and *doubly-Gilt* Sword, till it has terrified him into better Manners, and secured us the Stable Possession of Malta, besides the newly-taken Sugar Islands;[3] for I suppose Guardalupe is ours by now.[4]

With less than *that* our Ministry ought not to be contented, and our truly patriot King deserves Hanover for his honourable Preference of England's Interest to his own.[5] Another smart Attack upon the French Coast may obtain us *these* Terms surely;[6] and I should like to see the Bourbon Standard luring *all* Emigrant Frenchmen out of Great Britain——Conde[7] and Pichegru[8] and Dumouriez[9] will do *us* no good, unless by carrying their Countrymen away with them; and willingly would I send them off together, with every Cook and Taylor belonging to the *Great Nation*.

Adieu Dear Mr. Chappelow, and believe my Master—tho' he expresses himself *lamely* when he sends You sincerest Compliments by the Hand of Your truly Faithful and Obedient Servant / H: L: Piozzi.

Text: Ry. 561.124.

1. HLP replies to LC's letter of 24 August (Ry. 562.77), wherein he begins: "Many thanks for your charming letter which was dated 30. July.—If you are not engaged—you will see me in the first week of next month—about the Latter end of it—I shall go by Llangollen and stay there a day or two, Let me know how your engagements stand—for tis possible your house may be occupied."
2. When a Russian messenger or courier arrived in London, provoking rumors, HLP took note of his presence. Newspapers toward the end of May began to read meaning into his arrival. See, e.g., the *Morning Chronicle*, 28 May 1803.
"We seldom have felt greater pleasure in reporting the proceedings in the House of Commons than last night. The motion of Mr. Fox respecting the mediation of Russia has been productive of explanations highly important. . . . Mr. Pitt was among the first to applaud and to compliment Mr. Fox's views."
The mediation effort dragged on for about three months, only to fail. HLP would have been more censorious of the effort (as many conservative newspapers were) except for the fact that it apparently had the support of Pitt.
3. HLP refers specifically to the capture of Sta. Lucia and the Tobago Islands in the Caribbean. See, e.g., the *Morning Chronicle*, 1 August; also 16 August.
4. Despite the promise of many English newspapers that the French islands in the Caribbean would soon fall to Great Britain, Guadaloupe remained French until 1810. (The British returned it in 1816.)
5. HLP insisted that Hanover be returned to George III before Great Britain sign a lasting peace with the French. But her insistence was unsupported by the events of the last three months.
The *Morning Chronicle* of 13 June had cited Paris newspapers to the effect that French troops had (as of 28 May) been at the frontiers of Hanover without attempting to proceed farther. On 15 June the same newspaper announced (as it had the previous day) that "the French troops are now completely in possession of Hanover and its dependencies. They are in possession, as General Mortier says, of the mouths of the Elbe and Weser. This is evidently the consequence of their seizing the Hanoverian dominions. . . . the trade of this country to the North of Europe by these channels is therefore put off for the present, unless by some interference, of which we see not the slightest chance, the just neutrality of the North of Europe should be restored."
For continuing French efforts to seal their possession of Hanover, see *GM* 73, pt. 2 (1803): 676, 775.
6. Since the resumption of hostilities, the English fleet had made only exploratory moves against the French coast. In August some "cruizers lately looked into Dunkirk," where they found that the alleged invasion fleet was limited to a few privateers. "The

troops had suddenly been withdrawn from the coast, and were, it was reported, concentrating in the neighbourhood of Paris."

Another report during the month maintained that "the blockade of Toulon is strictly continued. The French force is 10 sail of the line and five frigates; Lord Nelson's force blockading that port is nine sail of the line, including the Victory and 3 frigates" (*GM* 73, pt. 2: 774).

7. Louis-Henri-Joseph de Bourbon (1756–1830), last prince de Condé, had been sent to England 3 September 1795 in order to prepare for the arrival of the comte d'Artois and to renew the war of the Vendée. His expedition, however, failed and he assumed no further military responsibilities. He set himself up in London, where he achieved a certain notoriety. He returned to France only in 1814 with the Bourbons.

8. For Pichegru, see HLP to Q, 28 January 1795. He had been elected in 1797 to the Council of Five Hundred and made its president, but he was proscribed at the coup d'état of Fructidor. Subsequently deported to Guiana, he escaped in 1798 and reached London, where he remained until ca. September 1803.

9. According to the *Morning Herald*, 19 August, "the famous General Dumourier is just arrived in England, and has been so well received by Government, that there is great reason to believe he will have a principal, if not the chief command of the expedition" against France. Instead he took up residence in Clarges Street, Piccadilly (ibid., 26 August). See also HLP to PSP, 7 February and 21 April 1793, 5 April 1799 and n. 8; to LC, 2 July 1799; "Verses 2," pp. 14–15.

TO HESTER MARIA THRALE

Tuesday 20: September 1803.

Your Letter was doubly dear to me this Morning because the same Post brought one from Sophia—who scarce ever writes—saying you had a return of the Old Cramp in your Stomach. For Mercy's Sake neglect it not; and since you will not come to *us*, go to Dr. Parry at Bath; and put off Seabathing till all is well within.

I never meant (Dieu me pardonne) inviting your *Sisters* hither. Such is the State of Mr. Piozzi's Health, and such my accumulated *Kitchen Griefs* I could not have made my House pleasant to *Them*: but had *you* rode over in the friendly Way you mention, it would have been a dear Delight indeed.

The Approbation you shew of my Ballad is very flattering, and I shall like of all Things to see it printed and dispersed.[1] Being merely *local* my Notion was that the Thing was *a veritable Rien* except 20 Miles round our own House—Sophy praises one, Lady Tuite Has written,[2]—and tis right for us *all*, to do *all* we can.

Mr. Chappelow called here and says Dumouriez's Tableau de L'Europe has been translated already;[3] I live out of the World,—and resemble the Recluse who asked if *Jealousy* would not be a *new* and admirable Subject for Dramatic Composition? *You* should have stopt me from touching it.

Butter *is* at an enormous Price—more than enormous I think it—We *sold* all Summer, and had 17d. for every Pound; but, now the Country is dry, and the Cows are dry, and we are forced to break up our Winter Store in Autumn. Salt Butter such as you wish, will be 14d. per pound at least; and Carriage beside—to

London without doubt—must make it costly. Tell me my Dear in your next Letter, and write quick, where you would have it sent, and how soon; for the Markets *may* fall by these coming Rains, and I hope they *will:* unless Foreign Troops fastening on the Island tho' forever so short a Time, create high Prices for Provision of every Sort. Our Cattle will after all our hopes sell for just nothing I suppose; because nobody has a blade of Grass upon their Park or Lawn——even pretty Wickwor is burnt up. I shew it Mrs. Holman tomorrow.

Mr. Piozzi is very thankful for your kind Letter to *him*, and as a Proof he deserves it, walked out this Morning two or three Hundred Yards I believe, altho all Night he was in violent Pain indeed—with his *Side* which ought to be quite easy while the Foot is in such a Condition: but he really does bear more *Torment* with less alteration of Temper than any one I ever saw, and I should have liked you to *witness* what is certainly difficult enough to believe.

Have you read a new Book called Animal Biography? and is it worth reading? or only a Collection of the *Bons Mots* as I used to call them of Crop, Tinker, Flo— and Company.[4] I have no Dog now that I care a Pin for, but a great Grayhound, Mona; and they have lamed *that* poor Beast. Mr. Piozzi has repaired and beautified Old Bachygraig and Gilt the Lyon at Top, and 'tis inhabited by comfortable Tenants and the Curate lodges with them in old Catherine de Berayne's Apartment with the Fleur de Lys[5]——and we are now putting little Dymerchion Church in order; paving, glazing, slating, painting it &c. and we give them a new Pulpit, Desk, and Cloths besides—with a brass Chandelier.—

It *was* a Place like a Stable you know; and we have made a Vault for ourselves and my poor Ancestors, whose Bones were found by digging under the Altar; Dear Grandmama's Skull had a black Ribband pinned tight round it with Two Brass Pins—Old Lucy Salusbury[6]—A Brass Plate over her, and one or two of her Sons. There was no Flannel Act then, so I suppose they buried her in the Cap and Knot She wore.[7] My Uncle Thomas lies at Offley Place.[8]——Apropos Sir Robert Salusbury who will possess it,[9] wrote to Lord Kirkwall soliciting an Exchange for Lleweney Hall—was not that curious?

So here's a long Letter and no Frank, because Lord Kirkwall is gone o'Shooting, and Lord de B—— is in Ireland, and I want to know about the Butter, and to tell how cordially we drank your Health last Saturday, and hailed the Hour— "when those blue Eyes first opened on the Sphere."

Keep them bright and blue as our Sea dear Hester, they are just the Colour now, as I see it from my Chamber Window.

> Then do what Parry's Wisdom will advise
> To keep such Talents—and preserve such Eyes.

Mean while the World is in a strange Way. Our Nation defending the Ministry, instead of a Ministry defending the Nation.[10] And Europe carrying a lighted Torch to set herself on Fire, and calling *that* Illumination!! Oh Wondrous Times! I hope Mrs. Smith and I shall live to see the Drama's End more clearly unravelled than *now*—or we shall surely die croaking:[11]

Give her our respectful Compliments and believe me ever / Your Affectionate Mother / H: L: Piozzi.

Text: Bowood Collection. *Address:* Miss Thrale / Queen Square / Bath. *Postmark:* 23 Sep 1803. [With a postscript in Italian by GP.]

1. In "Verses 1," pp. 29–30, is "A Ballad written in July 1803 when threatn'd with Invasion." It consists of five seven-line stanzas, beginning

>   Our Ancestors ever were famous in Story
>   To Valour well train'd and a terror to France
>   Yet Frenchmen forgetfull of all our past Glory
>   To plunder and plague us are making advance
>   But let them come near
>   We'll make it appear
>   Each bold Cambio Briton's a Stranger to Fear, etc.

2. For Elizabeth, Lady Tuite, see HLP to Q, 8 September 1795, n. 2.

3. Dumouriez's *Tableau spéculatif de l'Europe* (1798) appeared in London in the same year as *A Speculative Sketch of Europe, translated from the French of Monsieur D.*, to which are prefixed Strictures upon the chapter relative to Great Britain.

According to LC's letter, 29 September (Ry. 563.79):
"I asked young Stockdale, whether I was mistaken in an Idea, the Dumouriers Tableau &c.—was translated into English? It certainly was, said he, for I translated it myself.—and he has again published with a Map &c.—that part of Dumouriers Tableau which relates to an Invasion of England.—I would have got it, but though I had it in my hand I could not take it away—because it was the Last copy which a Gentleman had just purchased.—it is reprinting, and as soon as it is reprinted, which will be in 2 or 3 days—I have desired him, as you have an Account with him to send it."

4. HLP referred to a work by the Reverend W. Bingley (1774–1823), fellow of the Linnaean Society and late of Saint Peter's College, Cambridge: i.e., *Animal Biography; or, Anecdotes of the Lives, Manners, and Economy of the Animal Creation, arranged according to the System of Linnaeus*, 3 vols. (London: R. Phillips, 1803). Printed in octavo, it sold for £1.7s. For a favorable review of what was regarded as a "ground-breaking" work, see the *Monthly Review* 42 (1803): 178–87.

5. John Gittins and his wife, who rented Bachygraig in the summer of 1800, accepted John Roberts as a lodger.

6. Lucy, née Salusbury (ca. 1667–1745), HLS's grandmother, had married her cousin Thomas Salusbury (d. 1714), of Bachygraig.

7. During the reign of Charles II, Parliament passed three acts "For Burying in Woolen" (in 1666, 1678, 1680). Purportedly these acts stimulated the sale of the British staple—wool—and discouraged the purchase of foreign silks, etc. When Lucy Salusbury died in 1745, there was a Flannel Act but it was loosely enforced.

8. For Sir Thomas Salusbury, see HLP to SL, 23 April [1787], n. 2; to the *Monthly Mirror*, 17 June 1798, n. 15.

9. Sir Thomas in his will (P.R.O., Prob. 11/992/447) provided that "after the decease of my said Wife [Dame Sarah Salusbury] I give and devise my said Real Estates unto Robert Salusbury oldest Son of Robert Salusbury of Cotton Hall in the County of Denbigh."

Robert Salusbury (1756–1817), cr. baronet (4 May 1795) had married on 16 May 1780 at Saint Margaret's Church, Westminster, Catherine Van, or Vann (d. 1836), of Llanwern. Of their large family, two sons and three daughters survived.

10. The Addington ministry was successful shortly after the resumption of the war with a bill for the armament of the nation. Before long, however, his war preparations were regarded as inadequate. His rules with regard to the volunteers were read as a

means to discourage the movement and to limit its efficiency. The naval administration under Lord St. Vincent was found deplorable (see the *Morning Chronicle*, as early as 4 April). Ministerial friends, therefore, mounted their attack upon the opposition by beginning a pamphlet war. Without the prime minister's knowledge or consent, a Mr. Bentley published *A Few Cursory Remarks*, which attacked Pitt. The war of words—pro and con—continued.

11. Penelope (Cooke) Smith, née Bowyer (d. 1821), lived in Clifton with her second husband, General Edward Smith (d. 1809), uncle of Admiral Sir William Sidney Smith. See HLP to Q, 10 July 1796, n. 5.

TO THE REVEREND LEONARD CHAPPELOW

Brynbella Thursday
2: November 1803.

My dear Mr. Chappelow's

Letter is encouraging—though I guess not why Lord Deerhurst should think *me* so particularly cast down. He and Davies live in a Joke; but I never increased their Mirth with Expressions of Fear. *It is the way* here in Wales, to say there never was any Intention of Invading us;[1] and that all the Preparations on the Continent are feints to amuse our Government whilst Buonaparte devours Portugal,[2] puts Egypt in one Pocket;[3]——and I suppose holds Malta fast between his Teeth. May one at least hope for an End to our Suspense by the 1st of January 1804? I shall really be very glad.

In the mean Time can you tell where an *honest Man* is to be found? or do any of Lord Bradford's upper Servants know? or would you Dear Sir kindly call any day at Bourgeois in the Hay Market—and ask *him* for such a Commodity?[4]

Poor Hodgkins has broken a Blood Vessel, and has been *shelfed* now four weeks——Had Mr. Piozzi been taken with one of his Agonizing Fits of Gout during those Weeks—I should have *wished* for Buonaparte, to *hang* me.

He has however kept quite well; and I do believe now that his Quondam Valet *may* recover, but we must have a *Third Man:*——who can shave, and dress and wait on Mr. Piozzi——yet will wear a Livery and submit to Hodgkins during his *Life*—in hopes of *Post Obit* Preferment. Such a Mortal would be of more value to me than you can Imagine——he must be English or a Swiss Protestant——for fear of Vexations.

And now We have dispatched Public and private Afflictions—tell me (as a naturalist) what think you of this *novel* Distress? a Want of *Water*—and cry for *Rain* the first Week of November.[5] We have not in our Principality a Man old enough to remember *such* a Grievance. The Green Corn is all curling and twisting up like fried Parsley round London or Bath Soles; The Gravel Walks loosened by Drought as in some very, *very* hot Summers one may have seen 'em by Chance, and many Wells are dried that never used to fail. I long for a Letter full of Information, The last was a sweet one.

Miss Lees are going to London: you will meet somewhere and talk about *us*.

Lleweney Hall suspends Festivity now for awhile; We have had gay Days sure enough, and expect more when the Hon. Elizabeth Blaquiere gives her hand to The Rev. George Henry Glasse, Son of the Doctor, and Father to seven Children[6]—The Eldest a very pretty Woman indeed.[7] *You* know him of course; he is Rector of Hanwell in Middlesex—is full of Talents, full of Talk, and full—of Money: preaches divinely, and makes beautiful Verses. You know Bessy Blaquiere too—next Sister, but five Years younger than Lady Kirkwall: they are to be married in 3 or 4 Weeks, and then we shall sing and Dance again I suppose.[8]

Write soon Dear, kind Mr. Chappelow, and say more than I could cram into this little Paper. We are ever Yours and in that believe / H: L: P.

I liked your Text so that it vexes me I could not hear or even see the Sermon.

Text: Ry. 561.125. *Address:* Rev: Mr. Chappelow / Hill Street / Berkeley Square / No. 12 or 13 / London. *Postmark:* Two-Penny POST <Denbigh>; < > o'clock NO 11 1803 NT.

1. HLP responds with mild irritation to the jocular opening of LC's letter, dated 26 October (Ry. 563.80):
"I am just now returned from Hyde Park—it has been unluckily a very foggy day for the Review, so that out of 15,000 Men I could only see 2 or 3000d—The King and Queen were highly delighted and received with shouts of applause—I suppose there were 59000d spectators.—Had Bonaparte been there, he would have been in a sad passion—Lord Deerhurst desires his compliments to you—he says, that in consequence of what he had said to Davis, you had been frightened wonderfully about the invasion.—We are however in the highest spirits. The sooner he comes the better. . . . [Mr. Gillon] says at all events, The Tyrant has ruined himself—he is pledged to come, if he does he will inevitably [be] thrashed, if he does not come—he loses all in France. The <Gentleman> at Stockdales told us, he had been to day at a house in Hyde Park to see The Review. Lady Harrington &c. &c. were of the Party—so was Pichegru—He says That this country will most undoubtedly be invaded, and that Bonaparte will certainly come himself.—Government has this morning received an express from Ireland which says that it is reported that the French have landed at Sligo Bay—but it is hardly credible. . . . but all are in high spirits in Ireland."

2. According to reports General Augereau had joined an army assembled at the foot of the Pyrenees. From this position he could watch Spain and menace Portugal. Negotiations were going on between France and Portugal based on the following conditions laid down by the first consul: "1. An adequate satisfaction for the hostile transactions which have lately taken place in and near Lisbon.—2. Admission of a corps of French troops into Portugal, to remain there till peace be restored between France and Great Britain, and to be maintained at the expence of the Portuguese Government.—3. Expulsion of all Englishmen from Portugal and confiscation of their property. Unless these conditions be complied with on the part of Portugal, war is to be immediately declared against that country." See *GM* 73, pt. 2 (1803): 967.

3. There were several uprisings in Egypt—in Cairo and Alexandria—against Turkish rule. According to a report dated "Constantinople, Aug. 20," the rebellious Arnauts "have formed a close connexion with the Mamelukes, and, with their combined forces, have entirely defeated the army of the Turkish Pacha; several thousand of his troops were left dead in the field, and the rest are dispersed" (*GM* 73, pt. 2: 967). For HLP, any threat to Turkish rule in Egypt left the country open to French invasion.

4. The firm of perfumers was founded by Lewis and David Bourgeois at [32] Saint James, Haymarket, as early as 1776. Thereafter Bourgeois was the identifying name but

associated with several others: Amick, Huguenin, Therenot, and Delcroix. In 1803 the perfumers were Bourgeois and Huguenin, with Sir Francis Bourgeois as the head of the company. After 1819 the Bourgeois name, and undoubtedly the business establishment, disappear from the London directories.

5. According to the [Sunday] *Observer,* 16 October:
"The want of rain has been productive of considerable inconvenience in many parts of England, the springs having been generally dried up, and persons not only obliged to send their cattle, in many instances some miles to water, but compelled to draw it the like distance for domestic purposes. Vegetation has consequently been suspended, and the dairy farmers in particular, have been obliged to fodder, which has already added to the price of hay."

6. George Henry Glasse (1761–1809), the son of Dr. Samuel Glasse (d. 1812), was an Oxonian who received his B.A. in 1779 and his M.A. in 1782. He took holy orders and in 1785 became rector of Saint Mary's, Hanwell, Middlesex. He also served as chaplain to the earl of Radnor, the duke of Cambridge, and the earl of Sefton, successively. Prodigal with money, he became embroiled in such financial difficulties that he hanged himself on 30 October 1809 at the Bull and Mouth Inn, Saint Martin's-le-Grand, London.

He had married Anne Fletcher (d. 1802) of Ealing.

7. His eldest daughter was Caroline, who on 11 May 1805 was to marry Dr. Thomas Hume (b. 1774) in a double ceremony at Hanwell, which witnessed the wedding of her father to Harriet Wheeler.

8. HLP often heard wedding bells when none sounded. This time, however, she had the word of Glasse himself in an undated letter (Ry. 555.83):

"Well, my dearest Lady—Let me repeat, *well*—and all well, thank God! But that happiness to which I now may aspire, was never absolutely *confirmed* to me till last Saturday. Then for the first time I received my Fair-one's solemn, irrevocable promise!

"My present situation will I hope plead my excuse for not coming to dear Brynbella as often as my wishes would [have] had me. . . . I am permitted to walk and read tête a tête with Miss [Elizabeth] Blaquiere—and after so many melancholy months of deprivation and despondency, can you blame the miser, if he considers the sight of his eyes as well nigh useless, but when they are fastened on his treasure? Every hour, every minute has its employment—with every hour, with every minute, my Elizabeth is identified."

Glasse did not marry Elizabeth De Blaquiere (d. 1870), who in 1807 became the wife of John Bernard Hankey (1784–1868) of Fetcham Park, Surrey. See HLP to Margaret Williams, 28 May [1807] and n. 4.

TO PENELOPE SOPHIA PENNINGTON

Saturday
5: November 1803.

Our Correspondence has languished miserably of late Dear Mrs. Pennington, but tho' your Letters may be unacknowledged,[1] they cannot be forgotten, and so I told Mr. Layard[2] by whom I sent you many a pretty Speech. God knows he delivered them,—for he was looking very Ill when we met at the Bishop's great Dinner.

I have heard from more People than from *him* or from *You* how much Notice you attracted from the Duke of Cumberland,[3] while he was remaining in or near

Bristol—and heard it with a great deal of Pleasure.[4] Indeed *I* ever thought it a consolatory Circumstance to live where a Royal Family is established, and possessing a large Stake in the Country one Inhabits; They are the most likely People to be active in protecting it, and the present Situation of Affairs in England, added to the exemplary Conduct of our British Princes makes me cling closer to my old Opinions. We have had the Duke of Gloucester's Son in *this* Country;[5] he spent some Time at Lleweney Hall, and Lady Orkney came here herself to insist on my dining with him there: but Mrs. Holman was just come from Ireland—and I would not leave an old Friend for a Young Prince You may be sure. His Behaviour was much admired wherever he appeared.

The Festivities that have *since* taken Place on Account of Lord Kirkwalls Birthday, and his Baby's Christening had *us* for sincere Admirers.[6] It was a pretty Sight to see The four Generations of an ancient and Noble Family all in one Room so——The Marquis of Thomond kissing his Great Grandson, and dancing himself at the Ball.

I hope Buonaparte will not disturb our Happiness in *this* Country, which never looked more beautiful; but here is no Rain—which some grieve at, and all wonder; because the Season is really now very far advanced.

Mean while I have had domestic Vexations more Serious than such as Weather brings or takes away.

Poor Hodgkins broke a Blood Vessel some Weeks since; and has long lain between Possibility of Recovery and Probability of Departure; a Burden to himself and to us. We have now *some Hope* that he *may* tye up again——Dear Mr. Moore is *such* a Skilful Practitioner and such a valuable Friend, as few Places remote like this from the Capital can boast—and we have got a Clergyman to our Mind besides: and Mr. Piozzi has permitted me to pick up all my poor old Ancestor's Bones, and place them in a new Vault under the Church; which he kindly repairs and floors, and beautifies at no small Expence.

So here is fair Account given of my long Silence——and now Adieu! give my best Compliments to Mrs. Weston and Mr. Pennington and Miss Powell and believe me ever Yours sincerely / H: L: Piozzi.

When you See dear Doctor and Mrs. Randolph make them my truest Regards. His Friend Mr. Glasse is to marry Lady Kirkwall's Sister—*as we hear.*

Text: Princeton University Library. *Address:* [in Lord Kirkwall's hand] Mrs. Pennington / Hot Wells / Bristol. *Postmark:* DENBIGH 224 [signed] Kirkwall / Denbigh November five 1803.

1. HLP replies to two letters of PSP, dated 21 August and 3 November (Ry. 568.119, 120). In the latter PSP bemoans HLP's unexplained and long silence.
2. The eldest son of the late dean of Bristol, the Reverend Brownlow Villiers Layard (1779–1861) had been ordained deacon and priest at Saint Asaph in September and on 6 October had married Louisa Port of Ilam, Staffs.
3. Ernest Augustus (1771–1851), duke of Cumberland (1799) and king of Hanover, fifth son of George III and Queen Charlotte. At this time, Cumberland was a lieutenant

general in the English service (1798). He was present in Bristol as commander of the Severn District.

4. According to PSP on 3 November:

"His Royal Highness, the Duke of Cumberland, was here several Weeks, and honored both Mr. Pennington and myself with the most distinguished marks of his Favor and kindness.—My Husband Dined frequently with him, and he still more frequently Visited me, with the most gracious Condescention.—His notice of us was indeed the most flattering possible, both in Public and private;—but to our excessive Regret, he is removed from this Command to one that, I suppose, is considered as more important, and we are left to feel the Effects of that *Envy* which his obliging Attentions excited. . . . The Evening previous to his departure he did us the Honor of passing at our House with a Party, where he staid, in the utmost good Humor and good Spirits till 2 o'Clock in the Morning.—He is a most excellent *Judge* of Music, and *would* sing well, if his Chest was not too weak.—Had H.R.H. stayed the Winter, as was expected, he would have been much at Bath, and I had promised him the Pleasure of hearing our dear Master, of whose fine and *matchless* Taste he had heard much."

5. William Henry (1743–1805) was the first duke of Gloucester; his only son was William Frederick (1776–1834), styled Prince William until his father's death, when he succeeded to the dukedom of Gloucester and Edinburgh, and the earldom of Connaught. He was trained in the military, advancing to the rank of field marshal in 1816.

6. Lleweni celebrated the christening of Thomas John Hamilton and, particularly, Lord Kirkwall's "*coming of age to receive his estate* being now 25 years old [on 9 October]." See Farington 6:2138.

TO THE REVEREND LEONARD CHAPPELOW

Brynbella
17: November 1803.

Your Account of that Dear Boy and the Specimen of his Intellectual Powers delighted and pained me exceedingly—*Flosculus Eheu! quam subito ricisus!*[1] It is however the Season for *Precocity*. We have a Preacher in this Country—an Itinerant Performer of Course; who when 15 Years old, drew Multitudes of Auditors from the Established Church: and Ireland has produced a Theatrical Prodigy who at *eleven* Years of Age acts Osman, Romeo and Jaffier with more Effect than has been produced since Barry's Time: I should not mind other People saying so——but Mr. Holman's Testimony may be taken.[2] His Lady left us long ago——and 'tis much my Sorrow that they are not at Richmond.[3] Surely Surely Ton *might* give Way to Tenderness at the *Close of Life:* must Fashion and fashionable Airs and Care for what Men will *think*, and Women will *say*, devour our dying Moments?—Suck my last Breath, and catch my flying Soul!?![4]—Well! as I am neither Preacher nor Player it is no Part of my Business to condemn, or ridicule People for knowing their own Affairs best. Meanwhile Hodgkins gets better, and will I hope be all he ever was. It is a great Mercy his Master is not Ill while he is laid up.

You tell me nothing of this horrid Plague at Newcastle,[5] I like that less than Buonaparte's Conscripts: Give us at least good Lord such Enemies as Human

Skill can elude, and human Courage controul. The Dean of St. Asaph had little to talk on, when he made Old England's Address to her Daughters the Subject of Conversation: It is one of the 500 Stimulating Sheets which were dispersed about this Autumn—Somebody told me that Faulder printed it——If any one knows the Author, *he* does.[6]

But say the brave Men and the wise Men what they will, Great Britain is in a State of *Siege;* and in a very distressing Situation——I am tired on't: and Ministers will find France exciting all the World against us—*America* the most easily———because West India Riches lye so near *her* hand, She only waits for an Opportunity to seize her *old Mother's Jewels,* while *She* is quarreling with a *Troublesome Neighbour* at her next door.[7] The Ministers besides seem not to know how to conciliate Country Gentlemen and obtain their Support. I hear a great many Murmurs, which are tho' unintelligible,—unpleasant too: and the new Taxes offend all Mankind.[8]

Some late Newspapers told us that Bertie Greatheed—whether Father or Son I know not; has obtained Leave to quit France——but upon Parole to reside in Germany and never come to England more—This can be no great punishment to them who always appeared to like home least of any Place.[9]

Lord and Lady de Blaquiere are moving Heaven and Earth to get *their* Son safe away.—They will have a new Son soon; Mr. Glasse.

Here's a long Letter, pray *pray* for News Dear Mr. Chappelow as the Children say pray pray for a Biscuit: You *must* know some Tattle, and any Tattle will be Information *here.* Lady Mary Wortley's Letters confirm your Doctrine of the Gazelle or Antelope; the Turkish Love-Verses She printed, have this Burden.——

> Your large Stag Eyes where Thousand Beauties play,
> As bright, as lively, but as wild as They.[10]

I suppose all timid Animals have *open Eyes* to watch their Danger——Hares have particularly such——and Sheep have the Pupil drawn Horizontally to catch (as I conceive) Objects which coming *beside* them, might take the poor Creature unawares else.

Adieu—ever faithfully &c. / H: L: P.——

Here is a Snow Thank God; it will stop the Progress of Infectious Fever better than Vaccination.

Text: Ry. 561.126. *Address:* Revd. Mr. Chappelow / 13 Hill Street / Berkeley Square / London [in De Blaquiere's hand]. *Postmark:* DENBIGH 224; FREE NOV 21 1803; [franked by] De Blaquiere / Denbigh Novr. nineteen 1803.

1. In a letter now missing, LC described his visit to JSPS at RD's school in Streatham. There he heard the boy speak the sentence, "Flosculus eheu! quam subito ricisus." In a letter of 5 November (Ry. 563.81) LC noted that *ricisus* should be *recisum.*
2. William Henry West Betty (1791–1874) was to become known as *Young Roscius.* Apparently motivated by a performance of SS as Elvira in *Pizarro,* the boy decided to become an actor. He made his debut at Belfast on 19 August 1803 in the role of Osman in

Aaron Hill's *Zara*. He achieved immediate success before a crowded theater. He then performed in Belfast for four nights. In November he was at Dublin, where he played for nine nights and then moved on to Cork and Waterford.

HLP was to follow Betty's career for many years and usually with admiration.

3. Living in Richmond, the Reverend Frederick Hamilton and his wife, Rachel, were for vague reasons estranged from their daughter Jane. See HLP to LC, 10 December 1803.

4. Pope, *Eloisa to Abelard*, line 324.

5. Newspapers began to print reports of the "plague" by 8 November. A summary of its progress during the plague's first week appeared in the *Evening Mail*, 9–11 November: "During the last week, the number of victims to the dreadful malady which prevails [at Newcastle upon Tyne], has been greatly increased, and the disease is no longer confined to the lower part of the town, but has spread to some of the most elevated and airy situations. . . . During the last week, there were upwards of 30 funerals at the Ballast Hill, the burying-ground of the dissenters."

By 15 November *The Times* indicated that the plague was in fact typhus fever and that it had begun to abate. On 22 November the newspaper was "happy in being able to state, that the fever at Newcastle has entirely subsided."

6. HLP is coy, hiding the fact that she was the author of *Old England to Her Daughters. Address to the Females of Great Britain* (London: Printed for R. Faulder, New Bond Street . . . [by] J. Brettell, Printer, 1803). This folio broadside, consisting of two columns, sold for 1d. or 9d. per dozen. See No. 1506 of *Bibliotheca Lindesiana. Catalogue of English Broadsides 1505–1897* (1898); or the Houghton's *A Marvellous Collection of 121 contemporary English Broadsides concerning Napoleon Buonaparte's Threatened Invasion of England* (*pFB8/N1627/Z803n/f.94).

7. Implicitly HLP recognized that the riches of the West Indies had been and continued to be a ready prey for the European powers—particularly France, Spain, and England. To HLP, proud of Britain's recent conquests in the area, a "rebellious" America had the advantage of geographical proximity. Moreover, she was aware that the latter's suspicions of France were being lulled by the Louisiana Purchase (2 May, backdated to 30 April) and that American quarrels with nearby Spain (which controlled access to the strategic Gulf of Mexico) were being arbitrated diplomatically.

8. At the outset of his ministry Addington was particularly popular with the landed gentry. But his popularity was eroded by the renewal of hostilities with France and the consequent imposition of heavy new taxes, which hit the squirearchy hard. Moreover, he became suspect for negotiating an "indefinitive" peace treaty and for inadequate military preparations. "Country Gentlemen" were now looking forward to the formation of a new government under Pitt, who would become first lord of the treasury and chancellor of the exchequer on 10 May 1804.

For attacks on Addington, see *The Times*, 11 and 13 October 1803; 10 February 1804.

9. *The Evening Mail*, 7–9 November 1803, reported that "Mr. Bertie Greatheed has received the permission of the French Government to remove from Paris to Germany, upon condition that he does not attempt to visit England."

10. In his letter of 12 May (Ry. 563.82), LC had written that "the sacred writers took their similes from such objects as were" recognizable to "the people" and he cited as an example biblical references to the antelope, its fleetness and beautiful eyes.

HLP thereupon remembered a translation of verses by Ibrahim Bassa [i.e., Pasha] to his "contracted Wife" in part because—as Lady Mary wrote—they are "most wonderfully ressembling the Song of Solomon, which was also address'd to a Royal Bride." What HLP alluded to particularly were the following lines: "Your Eyes are black and Lovely / But wild and disdainfull as those of a Stag." See Montagu, *Complete Letters* (Lady Mary to Pope, 1 April 1717), 1:333–34.

TO JAMES ROBSON

Brynbella Fryday Morning
25: November 1803.

Dear Mr. Robson
when he has rejoyced over his truly amiable and accomplished Son,[1] will perhaps recollect and make some friendly Enquiries after his old Acquaintance.

The Truth is, we have seen too little of one another: but the Bishop's Lady was so ill at the Palace,[2] and my Husband so very much confined by Gout at his own Habitation We could not find a Day to make one Dinner for Neighbours new or old—till the long Nights came in:—and then—our upper Servant The Butler and Valet, broke a Blood-Vessel and kept his Room five Weeks without *Hope of Recovery.*

He is getting well however, and proves to me that no Disorder should be despaired of. Mr. Robson says you are lowspirited about *your own* Health, but take Comfort, we will yet have a Chat or Two in the little Parlour before many Months expire, and we will rejoyce together in the Defeat and Disgrace of Buonaparte before we dye. Have we not already outlived the Monarch of France, the Aristocracy of Venice, the Independence of Switzerland?[3] And shall we not see the End of Buonaparte? The Crisis must be Soon; and if there is any thing going forward to make one believe his Projects are gathering to a Head——take Pity on a distant Friend, and if Writing is Inconvenient, coax your good natured Son to give me a Line: It will be less Trouble than Dancing down 15 Couple with his Father's Contemporary—and he offered me his hand *for that Purpose* a few Weeks back at old Lleweney Hall—the Seat of my Ancestors; now possessed by Lord Kirkwall, only child to Mr. Fitzmaurice who bought it of my Uncle.

Genealogy and Farming divide Conversation in this Country, and the last of the two Subjects never afforded so little Room for Lamentation. Our Weather has been excellent, and though it does Thunder and lighten this Evening the Air is not cold, or unfavourable to any Purposes of Agriculture. And now Dear Sir accept our joint Regards and Compliments and best Wishes of speedy Recovery / from yours ever very faithfully / H: L: Piozzi.

Mr. Piozzi says *Bath* is the True Place for you to recover in: and *I* say tis the *very Place* I could best help you to make agreeable. Come and lodge near us, and dine with us every day, and we will tell old Stories and sing old Songs, and make it out very cleverly. Send word when you will come, and set me about finding Apartments; we shall be going soon *now* / Adieu.

Text: Peyraud Collection. *Address*: [in De Blaquiere's hand] James Robson Esqr. / Bond Street / London. *Postmark:* Franked by De Blaquiere, Denbigh Nov. < > 1803.

1. The Reverend George Robson (1773–1851), an Oxonian, was in 1803 preferred by Bishop Horsley of St. Asaph to a prebend at that church.

2. Samuel Horsley's second wife Sarah, née Wright (1752–1805), suffered from a debilitating heart condition. She died ultimately of dropsy.

3. The fall of the French monarchy preceded the execution of Louis on 21 January 1793. Girondin deputies in the National Convention had argued that the monarch's abdication was implied in his flight to Varennes (June 1791) and subsequent capture.

For the dissolution of the Venetian "Aristocracy," see HLP to PSP, 9 October 1801, n. 10.

For the defeat of Switzerland as an independent country, see HLP to LC, 25 September 1799, n. 8; to PSP, 17 October 1799, n. 1; to John Ewen, November 1802, n. 12.

TO PENELOPE SOPHIA PENNINGTON

Brynbella
3: December 1803.

When other Things go pretty well, let us not Dear Mrs. Pennington despair of the Commonwealth.[1] If the Ministry cannot or will not take Care of us, we must take Care of the Ministry: and sure I am that hitherto History affords no Example of a Nation enslaved, whose Inhabitants resolved to be free.[2]

For the rest I am ready enough to confess that unprecedented Occurrences are in these strange Times, to be witnessed every Day—and God only knows what may happen; Yet I do surely hope and trust Old England will never disgrace herself.

Mr. Piozzi has for some Days been confined with Shrieking Pain—a cretaceous Abscess in the Heel, such as he is too often tortured with—and tho' it freely discharged at last—There has been a Gouty Cough—somewhat like but not so bad as the Bath Influenza. It is all getting better now however, and since the Cold was caught at dear old Lleweney Hall we say but little of the Matter. Is Doctor Randolph *very* lowspirited about public affairs? He was always one of us Croakers, but Mr. Whalley used [to] have a better Heart of Things. This famous Armada however—and its *Xerxes*, do not seem in haste to try the Courage of their *only* Opponents; tho' backed with the Assistance of our old Allies, and gilt with the Trappings torne from our Sovereign's immediate Family and Possessions.[3]—He will be right to say as Macduff does "*Within my Sword's length set him*" &c.[4]

Meanwhile I understand little Harry Jackson who used to say God save the King and my own dear Mamma has been but a Plague to her after all—and She will be a Miss Trainer—with Marianne for a Pattern.[5] Comical enough! Mrs. Holman staid with us 8 Weeks exactly, no more;—She has been gone away 8 *other* Weeks—Her Husband is writing for the Stage.

I fancy the Greatheeds are got safe away from the Land of Bondage;[6] Lord and Lady de Blaquiere have a Son there still. Mr. Layard looked when I saw him at the Bishop of St. Asaph's dinner as if he had *nearer Concerns* to be thinking on— Poor Soul![7] than my Speeches pretty or kind. Hodgkins will Soon recover to be— *As stout a Man as he*; and as strong as Your amiable Cousin Mrs. Lechmere Charlton who had the Same Misfortune as I recollect[8]——and something tells me that we read her Mother in Law's death in a late Newspaper.⁹ The Colonel's old Papa seems likely to outlive all he ever heard of in his Youth I think:

The Monarch of France, the Haughtiness of Spain; the Papacy of Rome, the Riches of Holland—The Independance of Switzerland—*and the Prosperity of Great Britain.* While *one* general Pulse however keeps beating, my Hopes will live, and beat too: Buonaparte's Fate draws towards a dreadful Crisis, let him *but come out;* and our Admirals will give good Account of him. Miss Thrales are at Broad Stairs¹⁰ under Lord Keith's Protection who fears them not;¹¹ they row out to Sea for Purpose of looking at the *Wolves over the Water* and say it is an enormous Preparation sure enough, but our Sailors have no doubts of the Event: and Mr. Gillon's Letters are encouraging. *He* likes what has been doing in West India very well. Oh! how it must provoke the Tyrant of Europe to think he cannot likewise tyrranise in America!¹²

The Seizure of Alexandria too proves the Active Secrecy of our Government and I remember Ministers who would have much praised for such a Step.¹³ Once more Adieu and do not despair of the Commonwealth.

Our Plans must wait permission from above. If these Marauders come, home is the proper Place to be found in: besides that my Master must see some Weeks over before *he becomes portable,* and in those Weeks!!! Oh Heavens! What is there dreadful in this World that may not happen before the 1st January 1804?

God preserve *you* dear Mrs. Pennington and have Mercy on the anxious Heart of your / H: L: P.

Make our proper Compliments to all: You say nothing now of Mrs. Tryon.¹⁴

Text: Princeton University Library.

1. HLP replies to PSP's letter, dated 26 November 1803 (Ry. 568.121).
2. The Penningtons, like most conservatives, had initially supported the Addington ministry and then turned against it. Thus, PSP had written: "The frightful Crisis seems at Hand and I tremble at the View!—More, *much more,* as Mr. Wyndham says, 'at the *marked Imbecility* and *decided* Incompetency of our Ministers to steer and conduct the Vessel, than even from the *Danger* of the Storm' altho such a one never threatened these happy shores until now—for the Spanish Armada was *nothing* to it.—Mr. Whalley, who used to be the most sanguine of all Politicians, is dejected with dismay on this Subject, and for the same reason:—viz a want of Confidence in the Abilities and Talents of the ruling Powers.—and Mr. Pennington, who has had too much experience in these matters, firmly believes that our *boasted* Navy is not sufficient to protect us from *so many* points of attack as we are exposed to and that a large part of our Force *ought* to have been recalled from the West Indies, a *secondary* object, and not even *that,* under such Circumstances as the present terrific Face of things exhibits at Home, if it had only been to supply Men—the *absolute want* of which, it is a known Fact, prevents many of the Ships that we have from being sent out;—while every one is anxious for the *small* Fleet we have off the *Texel,* whence a powerful Force is expected daily to issue under a great Commander."
3. According to newspaper speculations, Bonaparte planned a naval flotilla at Boulogne to invade England, an army at Brest to threaten Ireland, and another at Bayonne to intimidate Portugal.

Xerxes was the metaphor for Jan Willem de Winter (1750–1812), comte de Huessen (1811), the Dutch admiral who revealed a steadfast loyalty not only to the French but to the Bonapartes. In England he was best known for his defeat by Duncan at Camperdown. See HLP to LC, 20 October 1797 and n. 5

4. Said by Macduff on learning of the murder of his wife, children, and servants. See *Macbeth*, 4.3.234.

5. HLP responds to PSP's statement of 26 November: "Will it interest you to hear, that Mrs. Jackson, injured in her Circumstances by, possibly, the too profuse Liberality of her own Spirit, and the Vices of her Children, has engaged in a sort of Seminary, something *between* Mrs. Beavers Plan and that of a *School,* for the reception and Instruction of about 20, or 30 young Ladies?—and what is more strange that She is just as much *delighted* with this undertaking, as *I* should be with an *Independence* of £2000 per year."

HLP relates her image of E. E. Jackson as governess to the "growing up" novel of Pierre Carlet de Chamberlain de Marivaux, *La Vie de Marianne,* 3 vols. (ca. 1731–42). It was translated into English as *The Life of Marianne: or, The Adventures of the Countess of ***,* 3 vols. (London: Charles Davies and Paul Vaillant, 1736–42).

6. "Travelling via Meaux, Epernay, Chalons, St. Dizier, Vitry, Nancy, and Sarrebourg [the three Greatheeds] reached Strasbourg on the 18th and finally crossed the Rhine into Germany on Saturday 22 Oct. 'on a poor bridge of boats'. We felt extreme pleasure in crossing it . . . it seemd as if a load of dependance was taken off our shoulders; we are no longer liable to the caprices of a wayward despot, nor the obsequious moroseness of his creatures in office, both civil and military. We have now been for 5 months without claim or right in a state of uncertainty and exposed to every insult. I hope never to experience a similar situation. . . ." See *An Englishman in Paris: 1803,* p. 187.

7. Brownlow Villiers Layard looked sickly because in July (according to PSP's letter of 17 July) he had "burst a Blood Vessel" and lay "at the point of Death." Nevertheless, he recovered sufficiently to be ordained in September and married in October.

8. Susanna, née Case, of Powick, Worcestershire, had married Nicholas Lechmere (1733–1807) of Hanley Castle, Worcs., and Ludford, Salop, colonel of the Worcestershire militia, who had assumed the additional surname of Charlton on succeeding to the estates of his uncle Sir Francis Charlton (d. 1784).

9. Nicholas Lechmere Charlton's stepmother was Elizabeth, née Whitmore (d. 1803), who in 1765 had become the second wife of Edmund Lechmere (1710–1805).

10. Broadstairs is near Ramsgate, Kent.

11. When war between England and France broke out again in May 1803, Lord Keith was appointed commander in chief of the North Sea fleet. For the next few years and especially in 1803 he was occupied with preparations for the defense of the coast, eventually reaching into the channel as far west as Selsey Bill (Sussex). He held this command until the spring of 1807.

12. John Gillon's letters on the West Indies were written in November. But in the large collection of his correspondence to HLP and GP there is a hiatus between October 1803 and 9 June 1804. But in November he undoubtedly pointed to British victories against the Dutch Guiana settlements of Demerara and Essequibo and against the French islands of Sta. Lucia and Tobago. He would also point to the French loss of St. Domingo to the black population assisted by a British squadron.

13. HLP was responding optimistically to uncertain reports from Constantinople and perplexity by the British press.

According to *The Times,* 2 November, all of Egypt was in the hands of the Beys, who had revolted against Turkish rule. But on the 24th the same newspaper asserted "that Alexandria is not lost to the Porte." *The Times* went on to comment:

"Accounts from Venice of the 28th of October state, that several vessels have arrived there, as well as at Trieste, from the Levant, which mention that an English flotilla has been dispatched from Malta, and appeared before Alexandria, where it landed several thousand troops, who, with consent of the Beys, had taken possession of the forts and vicinity of that city.—"

The Times could not believe the report, however attractive it was, insisting that "further and more authentic information seems to be absolutely necessary to elucidate the real state of that interesting corner of Egypt."

14. For Margaret Tryon, see HLP to PSW, 21 [November 1792], n. 10.

According to PSP on 18 December (Ry. 568.122), "Mrs. Tryon is, thank God! very well—but has lately had a very narrow escape from a *Fall*, down a flight of Steps leading to her Garden—. She struck her *Head*, violently, and had it not been composed of the very best materials, I think it must have been fatal."

TO THE REVEREND LEONARD CHAPPELOW

Brynbella Saturday Morning
10: December 1803.

I *did* my dear Sir receive the Packet from Stockdale's, but your kind and agreable Letters are ten Times more pleasing, and more Instructive.[1] I will have no more Packets:—but Letters as many as you can spare. We are all on Tip-toe here now with Expectation of some great News, and few imagine the old Year will expire without very Strong Convulsions. You comfort me concerning the Endemial Disease in the North; Such an Enemy is worse than Buonaparte.[2] Mr. Piozzi is in *the Gout*—and that vile Tormentor now regularly brings an Ally with him, so that if Pain would suffer him—(or his Attendants)—to sleep; This horrid Cough wakes and irritates and shakes his Frame to Pieces.

I think Cecy does well to forget us all for my Part, yet it *must* be *Ton*—all *that* must; and I suppose wins the Hearts of other Ladies, if it failed with Mrs. Lowndes or Lowther; for I could not read the Name:[3]

Mrs. Holman is lying perdue in some cheap Place while Her Husband—who has joined her——writes for the Stage and presents his Piece for acceptation.[4] What now *but* Ton can keep her Father's door shut? We all know the fondness he *used* to feel for all She said and did——but now there's his Nephew Mr. _____ who married his Niece my Lady _____ close to him at Richmond, and what would *they* think? and what would *they* say? Poor wretched Soul! I am truly sorry for her.[5]

Meanwhile our little Church grows very neat and smart,[6] and we plant Trees, and see those that were planted, grow: and if Gout did not disturb us we would defy Buonaparte——with the Help of Lleweney Foresters, Denbigh Volunteers, and Doctor Myddelton's Infant Regiment, headed by his sweet little Son six years old; who parades about very comically with all the Baby Boys after him in *marvellous good Order too*——and with a steadiness that would amaze you—pretty Creature![7] Lady Kirkwall has vaccinated *her* Nursery, he will be big enough to join the Corps soon. Lady Williams gave us a little Girl last Week.

Come now *do* write, and tell me Something of more Consequence than this Stuff. In your variety of Knowledge Dear Mr. Chappelow—you must needs be Sensible how Dulness spreads round a sick Room, and quenches every Spark of mental Fire. The dear Folio Sheet of News true or false, just blows up our Embers for an Instant, with hope of *some* Event that may change the Current of

Things abroad,—and of *Talk* at home: nor suffer us to dwell upon the dismal Subject of Limbs lost, and Life blockaded.

Farewell! and do not *you* like Cecy forget the Existence of poor / H:L:P.

Text: Ry. 561.127.

1. LC had Stockdale send HLP several political pamphlets and Dumouriez's *Tableau*.
2. LC had written inaccurately on 5 November (Ry. 563.81): "There never was any plague at Newcastle. People are always more harried, and worry themselves about imaginary than real miseries."
3. LC had written on 5 November:
"Yesterday I went to Kensington to baptize a little infant—I believe the 15 or 16 Child of Col: Lowther—They have men in the Army 2 or 3 and twenty years old.—What a Rabbit is the Lady.—to say nothing of the old Buck.—Mrs. Lowther Last Summer saw a great deal of your Daughter[s], and your 3 Grand Children at Tunbridge.—Cis said [she] had a Letter from her Husband—how rejoiced you must be?—not at all—I have not known where he is, nor any thing about him for many months.—Mrs. L. all astonishment. Yet Cis is in Spirits.—her boys not bright.—nor handsome.—Mrs. L. was very intimate with Cis, who never mentioned you or her Husband."
4. For Holman's effort at play writing, see HLP to PSP, 6 March 1804.
5. Parodying the printing niceties of English "ton" fiction, HLP also referred to the Reverend Frederick Hamilton's sister Elizabeth (1720–1800), who on 15 May 1742 had married Francis Greville (1719–73), first earl Brooke of Warwick Castle (1746). One of their daughters—and hence Hamilton's niece—Lady Louisa Augusta, had married in 1770 William Churchill and lived in Richmond.
In her own mind HLP had long associated Richmond with the artificialities of ton life. See her satire, "A Party to Richmond," in "Verses 2," pp. 120–23.
6. With the repairs and improvements made, Tremeirchion church was to be reopened in January 1804. The event was celebrated by HLP's two-stanza "Hymn for the opening of Dymerchion Church." GP provided "the Notes of a little Air which Rauzzini & he, & Miss Sharp used to sing Collins's Verses to at Bath last Year." See *Thraliana* 2:1048 and n. 1.; "Verses 1," p. 99.
7. For the Reverend Robert Myddelton, see HLP to LC, 2 July 1799, n. 9. His son was Robert (1795–1870).

TO ELEANOR WILLIAMS

Saturday Night
10: December 1803.

My Dearest Mrs. Williams

is a sympathizing Friend; You have been sitting at *your* Beloved's Bedside[1]—and so have I.

Mr. Piozzi is not up yet, but I think tomorrow he will be more willing to rise: The Weather is so Cold indeed, that there are few Temptations offered towards going down Stairs; and *my* Master has such an untoward and continual Cough, that one shall consider his first Flight however short—to be dangerous.

There has certainly been somewhat of an Infectious Fever *about*: but the Frost will check it effectually. I am more afraid of such Things than I am of Buonaparte, and it is now the Fashion to say *he* is in Danger from his own People—if we may so Call the French Nation——The Soldiers however are so desirous of being brought to England, where all the great Houses have been marked down for Plunder; that *they* are Mutinous at being restrained I believe: whilst the Parisians are crying out for Bread,[2] and Peace to eat it in.[3] Sure it is, that Country does exceed in Wretchedness as in Guilt every Thing we can Imagine; and those who come from thence bear Testimony to the Distresses of Individuals under their Foreign Tyrant——so as to make it not unlikely that they should after a very few more strong Convulsions—come to their right Senses, and call home their much injured King.

May we Dear Madam live to see that happy Day, so truly desired by our tranquil Firesides; and so comfortable even in Idea to Sir John and Lady Williams, and to theirs and Your ever Obliged and faithful / H: L: P.

True Love to all your Darlings——and principally to my own sweet Godson. Lady Kirkwall is said to have given *her* Baby the Cow Pox, but I have never seen her since that Day we were going home to the Gout from Pontriffeth—and met Mr. William Williams on Horseback. Mr. Piozzi has lain on his Back in Misery ever since *then*.

Text: Ry. 2 (1802–6).

1. In the first week of December Ly W gave birth to her fourth daughter, baptized Mary Elizabeth (d. 1890).
2. HLP was aware that the war between England and France was as much economic as military. She therefore looked for any sign of financial distress within France. The *Courier*, e.g., on 28 November provided a news report that would allow HLP to believe the French were crying for food. "Some despatches from the First Consul to Gen. Rochambeau, who commands the remnant of the French force in St. Domingo, had been lately intercepted by one of our cruisers. In these despatches Bonaparte is said to have informed General Rochambeau that the French Treasury was quite inadequate to 'furnish him with any further pecuniary supplies.' "
The Times on 2 December pointed to "the miserable hordes of Bonaparte" who had "to endure the severity of winter, exposed on [their] native shores." Artisans were sacrificed to the war effort so that Bonaparte "by the point of the bayonet, presses the wretched carpenters of France and Holland into his service, and requites them by bills drawn payable when he has accomplished his conquest!!!"
The notion of French poverty had become a staple of English journalism throughout the war years. Paris, even during times of military victory, "was converted into the appearance of universal poverty; no evidence of the existence of trade or manufacture remaining; and every class of a community which once demonstrated the possession of affluence and independence, exhibited the deprivation of every comfort, and the effects of oppression" (*Courier*, 14 February 1806).
3. HLP builds upon at least two items in *The Times*: e.g., on 12 October it printed a report from Paris, dated 24 September, implying the French senate's hope for peace negotiations with England. On 9 November an editorial in the newspaper stated, "The public may depend upon it, that the rumours of Peace said to be propagated on the Continent, originated from Bonaparte himself, and from no other source. There are two reasons for this conduct; the first is, that a large proportion of the French nation are

adverse to the war, and another part are at a loss to account for his delay in putting the projected invasion in execution."

TO THE REVEREND LEONARD CHAPPELOW

Thursday
29: December 1803.

I thank you very sincerely dear Mr. Chappelow for your *prudent* and entertaining Letter. What I write now is *inter nos* completely. Mr. P. has been in very serious Danger with Internal Gout—either in the Lungs or on some of those Parts which you Naturalists have names for, that hinder the Valves from opening, shutting &c. Orthopnæa with a tremendous Cough and low Pulse. Dr. Thackeray when called gave him strong Madera.[1] All is safe over now, and he will read your Answer to this Letter; so pray speak in general Terms only. When he—and poor wretched Hodgkins are once become portable, I will take them thro' Chester where Dr. Thackeray lives, to London; and then to Bath in the Spring for *my own* Sake, who am half destroyed with anxiety, Watching, and Fatigue. Eleven Days and Nights without taking my Clothes off; and all my poor Maids worne out with *Tiredness*. Is not that a *new* Word?——it is a *very true* one.

Our reports here are, that the French have been already seen covering the Sea——which I hope will soon be seen covering *them*.[2]

Mean while it was Somebody else that raved against Vaccination—not *me*: *I* say, that if that Process cures the *Plague,* The Cow will once more be adored in *Egypt,*[3] where *Isis* first was sacred.[4] Contagious Distempers to me appear more dreadful, than Death in any other Form. All Sickness is afflicting, and very dismal truly; but Infectious Diseases terrify my Spirits above all things.

Thank God the Gout is not catching!! My Health has had enough to contend with during the *last 11 Days* of Mr. Piozzi's five Weeks Confinement——my Clothes were *off but once*——The Hill is turned however, and we dined today in the little Balcony Room where the Organ is, as a Prelude to going down Stairs. Our next Uproar will be about this long-delayed Invasion I suppose, The modern Xerxes must throw a Chain over the Winds——and lash the Ocean like his less crazy, and less proud Predecessor;[5] but I do not think he will enslave *English* men, or any Men indeed who do in earnest resolve to be free. Small Time will now decide, and here is beautiful Weather.

Earth, Heaven, and faithless Europe judge the Combat. Your *Sharp Shooters* may employ their guns against Frenchmen instead of Pheasants. I have not seen one this Year, and there are fewer Growse upon our Hills than ever. Mrs. Myddelton the Doctors Wife—a pretty Woman if you remember, is very Ill indeed: but of no catching Disorder——If She should die tho' in this Lying In it would be a cruel Event, and four young Babies left Motherless.[6] Mostyn of Segroid has been Ill too, and in Danger——Dr. Thackeray attended him at Chester; says he never saw a Man so much alarmed at Thoughts of leaving *his* beautiful Wife and children: the eldest is gone to School with Mr. Davies at Streatham.⁷

Write to me Dear Sir, and tell me *true* News; I shall get false Intelligence enough in the Papers. Oh what Lyes will be bandied about whence once this *new Sporting Season* commences! Your Landing Place is well guarded I trust, Buonaparte has given us Time and Warning enough: and the sooner the duel is fought the better: says Your ever faithful &c. / H: L: P.

Text: Ry. 561.128. *Address*: Rev: Mr. Chappelow.

  1. For William Makepeace Thackeray, see HLP to LC, 23 August 1794, n. 7.
  2. Newspapers so frequently warned of invasions that many people confused the words for the reality. According to "a late Paris paper . . . it is now reported, that both the armaments at Brest and in the Texel are destined to invade Ireland, should they be able to escape the British cruizers. . . . The armaments in Flushing are, however, if possible, to make a diversion on the Eastern coast of England, to create confusion, and to prevent reinforcements being sent to Ireland." See *GM* 73, pt. 2 (December 1803): 1175.
  3. A sky-deity, Hathor was given the shape of a cow-goddess. Her cult was centered in Dandarah and she seems to have been a primitive mother-goddess.
  4. In Egyptian religious mythology Isis, the wife of Osiris and the mother of Horus, was the nature goddess. In the Hellenistic age she was ranked as a leading deity of the Mediterranean world.
  5. HLP's image was drawn from *The Vanity of Human Wishes*, line 232: "The waves he lashes, and enchains the wind."
  6. May Myddelton had already produced two sons, Robert and Ogilvie John (who died in 1799 as an infant). She also had three daughters: Caroline May, Maria Dorothea, and Mary Anne Charlotte. Her next child was also a girl, Louisa Dorothea.
  7. John *Salusbury* Mostyn was to spend the next six years at RD's school, after which he attended Westminster for four. Then upon the advice of Lord Keith, he moved on to Edinburgh to complete his studies (Ry. 587. 223).

TO LADY WILLIAMS

Brynbella
1: January 1804.

My dear Lady Williams
shall be the first Friend to whom I wish a happy—a *very* happy New Year. The sweet Children will contribute to that Felicity by their continued Health and annual Improvement: What is the Stranger's Name?

Mr. Piozzi is come out of his Room at last—not down Stairs tho', but in the little Apartment where is the Organ and Balcony. Doctor Thackeray was well sent for; and did *us all Good*: for next to the Sick Person, those are true Sufferers who delay fetching in a Physician: Mrs. Williams alone *could* have out-coughed my Master on Christmas day, but they recover; and your Ladyship and I must Thank God for it, and get forward how we *can* with them.

Buonaparte's Armament will be immense no doubt but we were never better prepared to meet the Danger, and by what I hear from Chester—our Volunteers will make work for themselves, if the French make none for them.

Your Ladyship is well however, and your dear Mama brisk, and a sure Friend to talk to. Such a Friend had I *once* and She left me not till I was in my 10th pregnancy—and her Loss was Irreparable even *then*——nor have I ever recovered it.[1] What Doctor Thackeray told me of Mrs. Williams, comforted my heart; He says She has a most admirable Constitution. The Babies are all stout and we trust stand the Brunt of whatever is to happen; I am of Sir John's Mind that Home is the proper Place to be found in, should anything serious befall the Country——altho' it would be curious to be in London too, and see the great *Ant Hill in Motion*.

God send us safely through; I feel but little Fear upon my own Account. Mrs. Horseley will be a sad Burthen on the Bishop neither sick nor well so: but the Sight of London revived her no doubt, and having lived long in the Front of Life She felt *lethargic here* as well as Dropsical I suppose.[2]

Farewell dearest Lady / and forget not / your / H: L: P.

Text: Ry. 2 (1802–6). *Address*: Lady Williams / Bodylwyddan / near / St. Asaph. *Postmark:* DENBIGH 22<4>.

1. Hester Maria Salusbury died on 18 June 1773, five months before the birth of Ralph, the second son and ninth child, on 8 November.
2. Samuel Horsley took as his second wife, Sarah Wright (1752–1805), who had lived much of her life in or near London.

TO PENELOPE SOPHIA PENNINGTON

Brynbella Thursday
5: January 1804

Enjoy your Ball Dear Mrs. Pennington[1] and be assured that all is at *least* as well with Your particular Friendships as with that one great public Family, to which we all belong.—Both will yet stand many Storms; and receive little Damage, I hope.

Mr. Piozzi has weathered this Fit, and is come down Stairs once again——It was a very long Confinement certainly, and poor Hodgkins being wholly incapable of bearing any Share of the Fatigue, it lay the heavier on *us*: besides that *his Danger*—Hodgkins's:—threw an additional Burthen upon every Shoulder. He is still alive and Mr. Moore who never despairs of any one; rather feels some hope or *possibility* at least, that he may recover.

My own Health will do all that is wanted from it, and as to wishing myself at Bath *I do not*. Doctor Thackeray galloped over from Chester; and what he did, afforded more immediate and visible Relief than anything I could hope; *more* than any thing I ever saw done either by London or Bath Physicians.

There is besides one Comfort in a Country Doctor, one never can have from a Town one; they stay, and sleep at your House, and have Time to observe the Progress of your Complaint, and the Power of their own Medicines over it: and the Years 1803 and 1804 have convinced me that Brynbella is just as good a Place to be ill in, as a crouded Metropolis; where one has no Business but to be merry, and mingle with the Talkers, Singers &c.

Shew Doctor Gray this Letter, and Share my Thanks for his and Mrs. Gray's and your own kind Anxiety: I am all of his mind that England *can* be no better prepared for Defence, or France for Attack—'Tis a grand Tournament,[2] on the Decision of which the World waits as composedly, as it did 2000 Years ago when the Plains of Pharsalia determined the *Names* of their Sovereigns; The Issue of *this* Contest will settle what *Nation* the others are to serve.[3]

Meanwhile I am glad Mr. Whalley's Spirits rise, when *his* droop, Things go low with *me* always; and I do really wish the Crisis was come now;[4] for after the dinner is once ready you know, be it little or much, it gets worse for waiting: Our Volunteers will make *themselves* work, if Buonaparte finds them none of the right sort: Let *him once appear* and we know who to turn our Swords upon.

Adieu! and accept the best Acknowledgements / of Yours faithfully / H: L: Piozzi.

A Happy New Year to all—and *20* more at least to *Mrs. Weston*.

Text: Princeton University Library. *Address*: [not in H:L:P.'s hand] Mrs. Pennington / Dowry Square / Hot Wells / Bristol. *Postmark*: DENBIGH 224; franked Kirkwall / Denbigh January five 1804.

1. HLP replies to two of PSP's letters: 18 December 1803 and 1 January 1804 (Ry. 568.122, 123). PSP had talked of being favored by the duchess of Devonshire and of her "promising to come over [from Bath] and bring a large Party of Fashionables with her, to Mr. Penningtons Ball at Clifton on the 3d of *next* month [i.e., January]."
2. Newspapers continued to report rumors of the French invasion, led by Bonaparte. Thus, the Hamburg mails reported the first consul "to be continually employed in consultation respecting the means of carrying into effect his menaces against England. He at one time immures himself in the Cabinet, consulting with Engineers, with Generals and Counsellors of State, and for his amusement he practises his guard in manoeuvering gun boats upon the Seine at St. Cloud! On the ponds and canals of his gardens this dreadful tragedy is daily rehearsed!" See the *Morning Chronicle*, 1 November 1803. Variations on the rumor were repeated 3 November, 26 December 1803, and 2 January 1804.
3. The battle of Pharsalus (48 B.C.) was the decisive engagement between Julius Caesar and Pompey for the rule of Rome, establishing the former as victor.
4. HLP responds to PSP's commentary on the times which—the latter wrote—"are *aweful* undoubtedly and the *Crisis* seems at Hand—but the Country is full of Loyalty and bright with Hope—and, with Gods help, I trust we shall get *nobly* through the Struggle, and live to see *far better* Days than we have lately known.—Dr. Gray and all the wise People are of this Opinion—and even Mr. Whalleys languid Spirits are reviving, and he seems getting into better Heart.—In short every one seems so full on *Confidence*, which I hope is *well founded*, that I feel half ashamed of my *own Cowardice*—for I own *my* Fit of Terror, in the prospect before us, is too apt to return" (Ry. 568.123).

TO THE REVEREND ROBERT GRAY

Brynbella
9: January 1804.

I am of your opinion that Bristol and its opulent environs are not as safe as the metropolis, though I hope dear Hannah More is premature with her packages.[1] When the lists are drawn, however, and preparations for this grand tournament are made in the face of all Europe so, *something* must in honour be done by the challenger, who, if he does *any*thing, must do some *great* thing, or endure that disgrace which it seems his sole endeavour to shun. *The stage waits,* as they say to Mrs. Siddons when she is slow in changing her dress where characters require more toilettes than one. Well, if they come now, we shall be invaded by men with snow upon their helmets, as Nixon the Cheshire ideot predicted long ago.[2]

Text: Hayward 2:262.

1. RG on 2 January (Ry. 571.28) spelled out his fears that Bristol was particularly vulnerable to invasion. "I wish that [Mr. Piozzi] may be able to bear a Journey to London or Bath—<Rent and enjoy> Mrs. Hannah More's House. She is about to let it and to live awhile at Barley-Wood House. I hear that she has every Thing packed up Now, to be prepared against any of Buonaparte's Banditti. She is the only wise Person in the Neighbourhood. The Inhabitants of this City are infatuated. . . . They conceive that because the Bristol Channel is of dangerous Navigation they are secure. Yet [it] is certain that there are two Places at which the French might land—and from one of them they might if they landed in the Night be at Bristol in the Morning."
2. Robert Nixon (fl. 1620) was the alleged author of certain predictions well known in Cheshire. Presumably, he was mentally delinquent and supported by the Cholmondeley family of Vale Royal. At intervals he made predictions, both national and local. His prophecies were first published by John Oldmixon ca. 1714 and in another form by W. E. in 1716. The story asserts that Nixon was called to the royal court, where he starved to death because he forgot to eat—as he had anticipated.

TO THE REVEREND LEONARD CHAPPELOW

Brynbella Wensday
25: January 1804.

You are very good to us indeed my dear Mr. Chappelow,[1] and I hope we shall meet soon in London and Thank you for all your Friendship and Kindness. I do not with you think the greatest Town the safest Place; but I think Danger, and Decision both, further from us than many People do. Perhaps the *form* of our Danger may be somewhat changed: for my own Part, that which presents itself in Shape of a Foreign Foe displeases me least. I am not of King David's mind who chose Pestilence rather than War[2]——Tho' his Horror was of Disgrace, which we have no Reason to dread. Old England and her Sons will not shame their Ancestors, nor give bad Example to their Posterity I dare say——Yet is my Heart low spirited about Public Matters, and so I dare say is Lady Bradford's.[3]

The Season is forwarder than any I ever remember; even in *this* cold Climate, Thrushes are Singing most sweetly, and Vegetable Life keeps pace with the Animals.[4] Our Weeping Willows have a Green Tint on them already, and Pear Trees are pushing in a Surprizing Manner. How must it be about London? I shall expect to see Almonds in Blossom very soon——A Tree in Streatham Pleasure Grounds *once* had pale Flowers on it in February, but it might be an early Thorn perhaps; I only recollect its Appearance as striking but have forgotten what Year the Thing happened.

Mrs. Holman is at Cheltenham, and her Husband plays *primo Uomo* on Glocester Theatre. The Hamiltons have not been *very* happy in any of their Children, tho' one of them is Rich and great and Gay[5]——and few Parents wish more for their Progeny, unless it is like our friend's Mother who charged her Son whatever befel him *to make good Acquaintance.*

I told you that Lady Kirkwalls Sister would be married soon, but one never tells Truths when one talks of a Wedding:

Like Things of greater Consequence *tis melted into Air,* (as Shakespear says—) *into Thin Air*[6]——and has lessened our Neighbourly Stock of Conversation, in which These Nuptials have for a long Time held the first Place.

Mr. and Mrs. Mostyn are flourishing away at Bath as we hear, and their eldest Son settled with Mr. Davies at Streatham University—but all this may be no truer than Mr. Glasse's handing Miss Blaquiere away from us to his Living at Hanwell in Middlesex.[7]

Adieu dear Sir, and find us out in London if you care for us, as is hoped by yours truly / H: L: P.

Text: Ry. 561.129. *Address*: Rev: Mr. Chappelow.

1. HLP replies to LC's letter, 11 January (Ry. 563.83).
2. Chron. 21:11–14. See HLP to LC, 7 or 8 May 1799, n. 8.
3. HLP was "low spirited" in reaction to LC's description of "Public Matters." He reported a rumor "that the French from Holland were Landed on our Coast.—Pray God they may not come . . . for thousands of our Brave volunteers would fall in the dreadful conflict, and many a widows tears would flow—the weather has been favourable for some days, but particular reasons, which we know not of, have operated against the Dutch Fleets—for no other do we hear, nor them much, though their forces are very formidable. Besides Line of Battle ships and gun boats, tis said they have 300 transports filled with men.—The paper of this morning says—the French soldiers captured in the Last engagement their gun boats had with The boats of *immortality,* most mortally abuse the government of France for forcing them on board such miserable craft.—I think now Bony is out crafted, he must be sick of his expedition scheme against England—and if, (as is said) the invasion is deferred till the spring, I make no doubt but that before next April the first he will find what a fool he has made of himself."
4. See *GM* 74, pt. 1 (31 January 1804): 83:
"As a proof of the unprecedented openness of the season, the polyanthus, the crocus, and the garden daisy, are in full bloom; the lilac has spread its foliage, and the complexion of the grass-fields is that of May. The Robin is sweetly in song, and the rooks and daws

begin to rob the farmers of their dry sticks, while the loquacious sparrows round his cow-crib would persuade us, that 'January is the Father of Love!' "

5. For the three children of the Reverend Frederick Hamilton, see HLP to Sophia Byron, 2 June [1788], n. 5. The Hamiltons' elder daughter, Elizabeth, was "rich and great and Gay" as the wife of the third earl of Aldborough.

6. *The Tempest*, 4.1.150.

7. HLP is discreet in her explanation of the failed nuptials. "Mr Glasse is, or affects to be—ignorant why he is at last rejected by the Blaquieres: And They are,—or affect to be,—influenced by some suppos'd Stains in his Character: *had his Fortune* however, answer'd his own Description & their Hopes; I know not when we should have heard Talk of the *other* Scruples." See *Thraliana* 2:1047 n. 4.

For another version of Glasse's dismissal by the De Blaquieres, see Farington, who had been filled in by Lord Thomond (6:2420).

TO LADY WILLIAMS

No. 11 Holles St.
Cavendish Square London
Thursday 16: February 1804.

My dear Lady Williams

will like to have her long Letter early, and yet, such is the State of Suspense concerning every Circumstance worth writing about, that I almost wish to defer it. Well! whilst I wait the result of Events much more important, you shall hear what I have been able to pick up concerning this unaccountable Mrs. L[ee] whose *free will* has certainly been violated, and as for the silly Dream, People tell me 'tis a mere fabrication of those merry Gentlemen to render her Applications for Justice ridiculous.[1] They will however have to pay for their Frolic—altho' fashionable Folk say it *was*, and *could* be, nothing *but* a Frolic. Because her Fortune is 4000£ o'year Annuity paid Quarterly—and into her own Hands only, so that Robbery is scarcely possible,—and for the rest—*The Parties are Old Acquaintance.* To the Man therefore who ran away with his own Wife—I forget *when*, and to the Man who ran away with his own Father—I forget *why*, we may now add the man who ran away with his own Mistress in 1804.

But a worse frolic was committed the other day by a merry Fellow, who giving in a respectable Name, and wearing the proper Clerical Dress, called on an old Valetudinary Minister of a small Church near London—offering to serve it for him Gratis on Sunday Morning. The offer was accepted, and *such* a Discourse pronounced, as first diverted, and then enraged the Congregation, till leaving the Preacher alone (who soon disappeared) some ran with Complaints to the Rector, some to the Bishop; Accounts of which being suddenly carried to the Sick old Minister, Violent Spasms seized his Stomach and killed him in Six hours.

Such are the *Amusements* of many young Fellows here, who Lament the Insipidity of common Pleasures grown tasteless by too frequent Repetition and such the Madness of this Town's Inhabitants, whilst a Menacing Foe threatens its

The Prince of Wales (King George IV). Portrait by Richard Cosway (1792). (Reproduced by permission of the National Portrait Gallery.)

annihilation, and the Sad state of its dear Sovereign's Health terrifies all *thinking Beings*—far more than any foreign Invaders *can* do;[2] although we dined at a friend's House yesterday, who *knows* that the House we dined in is marked for Pillage: an Occurrence which its Mistress swears she will prevent by firing it, when once the expected danger shall approach. Meanwhile dear Sir John will like the following Epigram——'Tis *in his own way*

>Says Boni to Johni, I am coming to Dover
>Says Johni to Boni, That's doubted by some;
>Says Boni but what if *I really come over?*
>Why *really* says Johni, You'll be over come.[3]

So here is some little Shadow of Consolation—for all the true *Substance is Sorrow;*—and I would rather ask after my very precious Neighbours at Bodylwyddan than tell them my thoughts of what is passing here—*upon paper*; we shall have Subjects of Chat when we meet, and in the mean while may God bless my pretty Godson and his Brother and Sisters and may your Ladyship and dear Mrs. Williams never cease to / Love their truly Affectionate and Obedient and Faithful / H: L: P.

Mr. Piozzi is very lame but pretty well, and is looking for Valets &c.
I am now putting up my Letter, and all *grows worse and worse.*[4] Good Lord! deliver us!
The Prince of Wales very ill too!!!![5]

Text: Ry. 2 (1802–6). *Address*: Lady Williams / at Bodylwyddan / near St. Asaph / Flintshire / N: Wales. *Postmark*: FE 16 80<4>.

1. "Mrs. Rachael-Fanny-Antonina Lee, *soi-disant* Baroness le Despencer . . . we believe to have been a natural daughter of Sir Francis Dashwood, Bart. Lord le Despencer. She was married about 1794 to Matthew-Allen Lee, Esq. but separated in 1796, with the settlement of 1,000*l.* a year. In 1804 she became highly notorious by an alleged abduction from her house in Bolton-row, by two brothers, the Rev. Lockhart and Mr. Loudoun Gordon, cousins to the Earl of Aboyne. . . . The gentlemen were tried at the Oxford Assizes, when Judge Lawrence presided; and on Mrs. Lee admitting . . . that on the Uxbridge-road she drew from her bosom a gold locket containing a camphor-bag, exclaiming, 'This has hitherto preserved my virtue!' threw it away, and added, 'Now welcome pleasure!' his Lordship stopped the trial, and directed the jury to acquit the prisoners, at the same time censuring their conduct as disgraceful in the extreme." See *GM* 74, pt. 1 (1804): 81; 99, pt. 1 (1829): 649–50.
2. According to Lord Malmesbury's diary: " 'On the 12th or 13th [of January] the King (after having taken cold by remaining in wet clothes longer than should be) had symptoms of the gout. He could not attend on the Queen's birthday, though he appeared in the evening at an assembly at the Queen's House; he was too lame to walk without a cane; and his manner struck me as so unusual and incoherent, that I could not help remarking it to Lord Pelham, who, the next day . . . told me . . . that it was too plain the King was beginning to be unwell' " (Stanhope 4:119).
Attended by Sir Francis Milman, Sir Lucas Pepys, Dr. Henry Revell Reynolds, and Dr. William Heberden, the king evinced symptoms similar to those of 1788 and 1801. A new doctor, Samuel Foart Simmons, physician to St. Luke's Hospital for Lunatics, was

The Prince of Wales (King George IV). "A Voluptuary under the horrors of Digestion." Caricature by James Gillray; engraved by H. Humphrey (21 July 1792). (Reproduced by permission of the National Portrait Gallery.)

called in. Once again the king was restrained in a straightcoat. And again there was talk of a regency bill.

But by 26 February, London churches could offer a hopeful "Prayer and Thanksgiving . . . upon the Prospect of his Majesty the King's Recovery from his dangerous Sickness." See *GM* 71, pt. 1: 177; also Jesse 3:341–46.

3. Such political humor was typical of Sir John Williams through most of his life. Thus, during a birthday party and ball in honor of his son on 10 January 1814, "that most loyal and hospitable Bart. gave a toast after dinner, 'A Head to France, and Bonaparte without one.' " See the *Morning Post*, 17 January 1814.

4. See Spenser, *The Faerie Queene*, bk. 5, "Introduction," st. 1.

5. On 2 February *The Times* announced: "We are much concerned to state that his Royal Highness the Prince of Wales is much indisposed at Brighton: and early yesterday morning Sir Walter Farquhar and Mr. Walker set off to attend his Royal Highness." Bulletins continued almost daily, seesawing with the Prince's recoveries and relapses.

According to Farington, "the Prince of Wales has had an inflammation on His Stomach for which Sir Walter Farquhar & Mr. Walker, apothecary were suddenly called to Brighton. The Duke of Clarence says it was the effect of drinking hard three days successively" (6:2231).

TO LADY WILLIAMS

Monday 20: February 1804
No. 11 Holles Street
Cavendish Square

I had just dispatched your Ladyship my promised Letter when your own was brought me by Betty. Allen says that the Girl enquired for is so certainly honest and Sober,—She may be taken upon Tryal without any hazard whatever; as to her Merits as a House Maid they were too few in Number to warrant Recommendation, nor would She even strive to make herself useful at *our House* without perpetual urging forward—or what the Servants call *following her up*.

We are harrassed with the Sight of Valets, Butlers, Cooks and Footmen by which our very Doors are besieged: yet though every Third Person one meets in the Streets is a Servant out of Place, and every fourth Dwelling as one drives along, is a House to be Lett:—never were Lodgings or Attendants seen, much less *offered* at such enormous Prices. 8d ½ for the coarsest pieces of Beef to put in Soup is a frightful addition to London expences; but the Fish is cheaper and better by far than at Bath——Such Dear Madam is the state of *private* Affairs, the *Public* ones clear up a little thank God; but St. James's Street *did* exhibit such a Scene of Affliction when the King was at worst, as could only have been equalled at Rome when the Emperor Antoninus Pius was on his death Bed.[1]

We went last Night to the Play—The *English Fleet* was acted and every loyal Song, every patriotic Expression was applauded with an enthusiasm *so affecting*; the Performers catched and Echoed all our Sentiments, till tears accompanied the Acclamations——Those who frequent Oratorios say it was the same *there*.[2]

We have been hourly expecting the French to take advantage of the internal

Distress, but our Sailors double their Diligence, and Lord St. Vincent says they cannot come out but during a *Calm*, which is favorable to *their* Vessels, and hinders all Resistance from ours:[3] They must for *that* Reason wait till settled Spring Weather——and by *then,* Buonaparte *may be* blown up or destroyed by his own People—not by the Soldiers, who love him, and mean to add the Plunder of London to their past Exploits: *They,* the *Army* are mad to come over; and keep up the Spirits of their Consul, who 'tis said feels sometimes, some what anxious; but still resolved on the Tryal—and some hard Blows will certainly be struck on both Sides.

General Boyer is said to have been much surprised that our Common Herd manifest aversion to his Country Men——He thought we were likely to *welcome* our Destroyers, as they do in other Countries, but I trust no such Fools will be found in Great Britain.[4]—

I am agreeably Interrupted;—the King *sleeps,* he *mends,* and we shall—(if such tremendous Illness does not leave a great Debility indeed;)——We *shall have him again* and *deafen* him at this Return to Life and its Enjoyments with a Thunder of Applause. Oh! What Transporting Consolation will he receive the first night he meets his Subjects on any Public Occasion!! I shall not venture to make *one*—— The Crowds even of Enquirers were not encountered without Danger.

I shall make no excuse for sending my Letter unfranked—such News will I am sure pay its Postage to dear lovely Loyal Bodylwyddan; whose truest and faithfullest / Servant now in London is / my dear Lady Williams's own / H: L: P.

Text: Ry. 2 (1802–6). *Address*: Lady Williams / Bodylwyddan near / St. Asaph / Flintshire / N. Wales. *Postmark*: FE. 20 <.804>.

1. Titus Aurelius Fulvus Boionius Arrius Antoninus (86–161), Roman emperor (138–161). He died of fever at Lorium in Etruria, about twelve miles from Rome. Allegedly, he summarized the values of his life in the last word he spoke—*aequanimitas*. His biographer was Julius Capitolinus, *Historia Augusta*.
2. According to advertisements the Covent Garden offered "A new Historical Comic Opera call'd The English Fleet in 1342, of which Mr. Dibdin, jun. is the reputed Author." It was first performed on 13 December 1803.
The opera deals with the subject of a French civil war in 1341–42, occasioned by a disagreement between Charles of Blois and John de Mountfort over the rightful ruler of Brittany. The *Morning Post* for 14 December 1803 stated that the audience was enthusiastic and admitted that the opera was meant to evoke "the idea of British naval glory, which was repeatedly cheered, in 'Rule Britannia,' and a grand finale."
3. The first lord of the admiralty made several statements designed to assuage English fears of an invasion. Yet the statements were not convincing, certainly not to *The Times*, 18 February: "Every thing, indeed, confirms the opinion . . . that it was in the contemplation of the enemy (should our blockading squadrons be still enabled to keep their stations) to make one vast effort to cover the ocean . . . with his ships, in the hope that though many of them should perish, still a portion of them, at least, may be able to effect a landing."
4. Pierre-François-Xavier de Boyer (1772–1851) entered the army in 1792 and rose to the rank of général de brigade, ca. 1800. He fought at Saint Dominique in 1801. And two years later, while returning to France, he was taken prisoner, his ship having been boarded by the English. His "surprise" took place on English soil, where he remained until almost 1809.

6 March 1804 457

TO PENELOPE SOPHIA PENNINGTON

No. 11 Holles Street
Tuesday 6: March 1804.

So many Things have occured since I received your last Letter dear Mrs. Pennington, that this will of Course be a long one: The Kings Illness and Recovery, the continued Talk of Invasion, the Widowhood of your Fair Friend cŷ devant Honoria Gubbins.[1] The Correspondence of those French Noblemen so fête and so admired in Bath and Bristol;[2] and these present Conjectures concerning Sir Sydney Smith, fill every Mouth;[3] and render me still more enraged when Toothach hinders my listening to such interesting Circumstances. Never was there a Moment more favourable for Rusticated Folks like myself to pick up opinions, Facts &c. *and fill my little Bag*: but Lord St. Vincent's ill Timed Ill Health, is among the Things I should wish to fling out of it.[4]

Dear Mrs. Siddons is in great Beauty this Year, her Zara was never more passionately admired;[5] The Kembles look happy too, and so do Miss Lees: but when I was introduced to Mr. Cumberland at Lord Deerhurst's Dinner yesterday I did not know *him,* nor he *Me.* The public will not however fail to recognize him I suppose, he tries them in a New Play very soon.[6] Poor Holman is—Poor Holman!!! and every body seems grieved at his *double* Disappointment.[7]

Miss Thrales are well and gay—Mrs. Mostyn plump and pretty—so are her sturdy little Boys: Of Mr. Mostyn no good Accounts are transmitted by the Bulletin *his* Physicians send up from Chester, Bath or Oxford;[8] whither Mr. Bouchier Smyth[9] told me he was gone after his Case had baffled many Men of Science, to consult this new favourite of Mankind, Mr. Grosvenor;[10] concerning A sore Hand he has. Oxford will be rendered a fine Amusing Place for the gay Fellows by Mrs. Lee's accusation of the Gordons:[11] it was always a good Place for those who liked looking over Books, conversing with Scholars &c. We staid two Days there on our Journey to London for me to make my Respects to the Eleusinian Ceres;[12] but She Alas! was gone to *the other House* as the Players say; Lord Elgin who sent her over being a Cambridge Man.[13]

The Weather has been very odd this Year, we enjoyed Spring at Brynbella where Birds were singing and Trees coming out every Day before we came to Town *for the Winter*: It has snowed and *blowed* and hailed and rained ever since I think, and The Thames looked all in a Storm today from dear Lady Orkney's beautiful Apartments at Chelsea.

Adieu! and present us properly to all enquiring Friends: believing me with every good Wish Your good Mother's and Husband's and your own much obliged and Faithful Servant / H: L: P.

Text: Princeton University Library. *Address*: Mrs. Pennington / Dowry Square / Hot Wells / Bristol. *Postmark*: MR 6 1804; Wimpole < >.

1. Ralph Dutton had died suddenly in "Grenier's hotel in Albemarle-str." See *GM* 74, pt. 1 (1804): 281; HLP to PSP, 17 July 1799, n. 6, and 7 March 1803, n. 3.

2. HLP referred to certain distinguished Frenchmen, now English prisoners of war. Thus, General Rochambeau "(captured at St. Domingo) gave an elegant dinner at his lodgings, in the market-place [at Ashburne]: at which were present Generals Boyer and Puget . . . and several other officers. This has been followed by similar complimentary parties by the other generals, who frequently walk with their general en chef. . . . Gen. Rochambeau has solicited to be indulged with a horse, fearing, by the deprivation of the accustomed exercise, to add to the injuries his health has already received by his fatigues and hardships while in St. Domingo." According to his account, he and his men escaped from "'enraged negroes,'" only to be "'taken by the English *pirates.*' These are the captured general's words, the last of which seems to be a most ungracious term of acknowledgment to the brave commanders of those vessels, who, though as prisoners, bore him and his suite with full swelled sails from the fury of the most terrible and powerful of enemies!" See *AR,* "Chronicle" 46 (1804): 369–70. For a more sympathetic depiction of Rochambeau, see Farington 6:2264.

3. On 24 February 1804 *The Times* reported: ". . . the public is informed, that dispatches were received in the course of yesterday from Sir Sydney Smith, off the Dutch coast, which are said to communicate some important information relative to the enemy's motions."

4. The first lord of the admiralty had been indisposed but by 4 February *The Times* announced, "The country will rejoice to hear, that the Earl of St. Vincent . . . is happily in a great measure recovered. The report that Dr. Baird was called in upon the occasion, is without foundation."

5. This was SS's first season at the Covent Garden. From September 1803 to May 1804 she performed sixty nights, two of them given over to the role of Zara in Congreve's *The Mourning Bride* (*The Times,* 24 February, lamenting the waste of her talent on a worthless role). It was a favorite of SS, which she had played intermittently since 1783 until she retired from the stage. See HLP to PSW, 5 March [1792], n. 4.

6. Cumberland's new play, *The Sailor's Daughter,* was to open 7 April 1804. See HLP to PSP, 16 April 1804.

7. Holman and his wife, Jane, were childless, her several pregnancies ending in miscarriages. Moreover, his new comedy, *Love Gives the Alarm,* was performed only once—23 February—at Covent Garden and never printed.

8. John Meredith Mostyn had begun to ail as early as 1803. He was self-indulgent, playing, eating, and drinking too much. According to Gillon (Ry. 578.107), "Mostyn's Complaint is of the Stomach, with Palpitation &c. I understand from my Physician, *inter nos,* who attends him; that he makes too sure of himself and eats too much, and of too great a Variety. . . . He is advised to go to Bath; but does not follow the Advice."

9. The son of a doctor, Joseph Bourchier Smith (1759–post 1813) was born in Oxford and grew up there. He had matriculated at Queen's College in 1775 but left without a degree. To HLP he was a Bath resident, not always agreeable, but with whom she could be friendly whenever she lived in the city.

10. John Grosvenor (1742–1823) was a surgeon born in Oxford and educated at Worcester and London hospitals. A noted practical surgeon in Oxford, he specialized in the treatment of diseased and stiff joints.

11. Rachel Lee's alleged abductors, Loudoun Gordon and his brother Lockhart, were tried at the Oxford assizes.

12. "The Colossal statue of the Eleusinian Ceres, the work of Phidias, given by Pericles to her temple at Eleusis, has been removed thence by two gentlemen of Jesus College, Cambridge, on their travels in Greece; and is sent to England, as a present to their University." See *GM* 72, pt. 1 (1802): 270.

13. HLP had assumed that the Ceres was part of the marbles and other antiquities (now known as the Elgin marbles in the British Museum) being sent from Athens by Thomas Bruce (1766–1841), seventh earl of Elgin and eleventh earl of Kincardine (1771).

Lord Elgin had not attended Cambridge, having been educated at Harrow, Westminster, and St. Andrews, and in Paris.

TO THE REVEREND JOHN ROBERTS

Fryday Evening
16: March 1804.

Dear [Mr. Roberts]

We were happy to see your handwriting tho' the Contents of Your very kind Letter are nothing less than exhilarating. Poor H[odgkins]! I am Sincerely grieved at his Sufferings—and have no doubt but he will afford to those who are near him an Example of Christian Courage supported by faith and Hope.[1]—

The Account Mr. M[oore] gave of his wasted strength made us fear things went worse with him than when We parted—and the Difficulty Man finds to die in many Complaints, evinces that Death is contrary to Nature, and shows that we were meant to live for ever. This is however by no means the Doctrine of the present Day; One must be deaf and blind not to see how swift is the progress of Materialism among our London Talkers, and Your very amiable Friends who were so good to me at Oxford, on Your Account; Said that Infidelity made large Strides towards that last Refuge of Orthodoxy, Loyalty and Learning.[2]

The Ceres I looked for there was sent to Cambridge after all, because Lord Elgin was of their University: God knows whether that luckless Nobleman will ever get safe home now;[3] for since this Conspiracy has been talked of in France[4]—Our Poor Countrymen have been Considered as in a perilous Situation—and if one was to escape they say, it would serve as Excuse to destroy all the rest. Mean while assure yourself that British Ministers never, no never mingled in any Plots for assassinating any Tyrant of latter Times:—The Virtue of Old England as an Aggregate stands yet on the very highest Ground, and I am Confident no dishonourable advantages will be taken, of the Present Disturbances in Paris which the Emigrants here are on Tip-toe to learn the Issue of.[5]

I was shown this morning at the house of one among them, The wonderful Labrador Stone bearing the exact Resemblance of their murdered Monarch, traced by the Hand of Nature; and concealed—as strangely—as it has been discovered.—O'Beirne Bishop of Meath looks on it I believe as the thing pointed out by the Prophet Habbakuk and mentioned again by fictitious Esdras. It is at least a very wonderful Curiosity.[6]

I make my Pleasure out of seeing what Wales Cannot Show me, of Nature and of Art: We are going now to view the Wet Docks; Considered as an immense work and I am Told Surprizingly elegant.[7] Allen and I have each of us one Eye a little inflamed, but I believe 'tis only with seeing Sights as I tell her——When we have given our Little Boy his Easter Holydays, The Prettiest Sight will be B[rynbella] and the best Pleasure of telling our Friends and Dear [Mr. Roberts] how many kind words Mr. Piozzi wishes to send him by the hand of his Obliged Servant.

Text: Victoria and Albert Museum Library; a copy.

1. When the Piozzis returned to Brynbella in mid-May, HLP was to comment: "Poor Hodgkins! *He* died whilst we were absent—so we bring back Three new Serv^{ts} . . . it lowers my Spirits tho' to see all new Faces about us so" (*Thraliana* 2:1049). See HLP to Q, 1 August 1793, n. 8.

2. HLP echoed a fear voiced by many Oxford faculty during the last fifteen or so years. During most of the eighteenth century the university seemed a stronghold of loyalty to church and state. Its theology, in liturgy and sermons, was founded on the work of Tudor apologists and Caroline clergy, on the opinions of patristic philosophy leavened by latitudinarianism. Most of the university scholars were conservative, politically and intellectually.

Behind this solid front a few questioned the demands made on students at the time of matriculation and even the necessity of subscribing to the Thirty-nine Articles. Such questioning became the new radicalism, which the defenders of the status quo feared would erode the university's position as an adjunct of the Church of England and turn "that last Refuge" into a melee of ecclesiastical schism. Not only were the Methodists and Evangelicals suspected of conspiracy, but "Infidelity," the product of the French Revolution, threatened the academic whole.

See the following sermons, which gave credence to HLP's fear: Edward Tatham, *A Sermon* [on Ps. 72, 76, 77] *preached before the University of Oxford, on the 5th of November 1791*; R. Churton, *A Sermon preached before the University of Oxford, at St. Mary's on Friday, April 19, 1793, being the day appointed for a General Fast*; Samuel Parr, *A Spital Sermon* [on Gal. 6:10], *preached . . . upon Easter Tuesday, April 15, 1800*; also J. M., "On the Proposed Regulations in the University of Oxford," in the *British Magazine* 1 (January–June 1800): 425–27.

3. Lord Elgin, en route from Turkey (where he had been British ambassador) to England, was "detained" until 1806 in France after the failure of the Peace of Amiens.

4. HLP refers to an anti-Bonaparte conspiracy planned by a young Chouan, Georges Cadoudal, and Pichegru. "It appears that 150 men were to assemble in the uniform of guards, to seize Buonaparte at Malmaison while he was hunting, or wherever else he might be found, and to carry him off." The French police arrested Pichegru on 28 February and Cadoudal soon thereafter. (Pichegru was found strangled in his cell on 5 April 1804.) See *GM* 71, pt. 1 (1804): 265–67.

5. While HLP doubted an English plot against Bonaparte, it was known that the British government, which wanted him deposed or assassinated, even provided subsidies to French royalists for that purpose. Certainly French newspapers broadcast their view of British complicity.

See, e.g., *The Times*, 8 March:

"The following article appears in the *Moniteur* of the 23d ult. in the form of a note, upon an extract from the *Morning Chronicle*, relative to a posting-bill which was stuck up in different parts of London, stating the probability of the speedy assassination of Bonaparte, and the speedy restoration of Louis XVIII.

" 'In our paper of Monday last we inserted an extract from another London paper (*Courier de Londres*), in which the assassination of the First Consul was openly stated as likely to take place in a short period. Persons who have arrived from England inform us, that, for the last fortnight, it was every morning announced on the Exchange at London, that the First Consul had just been assassinated; and on those occasions the names of *Georges, Pichegru*, and *Moreau*, were publicly mentioned.' " See also *The Times*, 14, 15, and especially 21 March.

6. See HLP to PSP [ca. 24 December 1802], n. 4.

7. HLP refers to the following:

"The WEST INDIA DOCKS, occupying a surface of 30 acres for unloading *all* vessels coming from the West India Islands and Colonies, have been completed some time since, and there is now sufficient accommodation in the substantial and extensive stacks of warehouses for such merchants as wish to bond or to house their commodities within the walls. . . .

"The LONDON DOCKS, forming in Wapping, for the accommodation of shipping, bringing wines, spirits, rice, and tobacco, and for the *whole trade* of the port (West and East

India shipping excepted) of such as choose to avail themselves thereof, are in a very advanced state of forwardness. . . .

"The EAST INDIA DOCK, for the use of the East India shipping exclusively, is as yet in a state of infancy. The Dock Company have purchased Mess. Perry's and Well's Wet Dock, for the purpose of forming part of the Dock for loading outwards; and the Dock for unloading is excavating with all possible dispatch, on a site or marsh above, and is to occupy a surface of about 18 acres, and is likely to be completed in the Spring of next year."

See *AR*, "Chronicle" 46 (1804): 353–54.

TO LADY WILLIAMS

London Monday
[19] March 1804.

When your Ladyship Dear Madam! looks at the enclosed You will say 'tis a Play thing for your Daughter not for you.—Yet these are the modish Needle books, and one of my own Girls made me *this*: Let Sir John admire how we are prepared for Invasion—but some Crane-Neck turn always has saved us hitherto, and at this Moment every body is expecting a Burst in Paris that will produce some excellent Effects——In the mean Time a project is setting forward to sink immense Masses of *Wale* and *Cement* in our old Superannuated Vessels, sealing up the Harbour of Boulogne so that no Ships can come out, and Spoiling the Place completely in such a Manner that they will have Amusement enough in clearing all away, without trying any more to annoy us.[1]

So much for foreign Affairs. Among the Domestic Occurrences, poor Mrs. Drummond Smith's Death is deeply regretted[2]—and we all *say*—I hope not truly, that Lady Cunliffe's Life is worth but little, so dreadfully have these disasters hurried Her.[3] Nothing consoles me so certainly for passing nine months in Wales, as the seeing how Ignorant of every thing one wishes to know—are those who live in London. They only hear the same Silly Reports Three Days sooner than they are heard at Bodylwyddan or Brynbella, where Contradiction arrives *later*,—that's all. And your Ladyship may *guess* as easily as I can *relate* the reigning Joke when female Reputation is represented as tarnishing,—how Mrs. Such a one has lost her *Camphire Bag*.[4] I think the nonsensical Romance of those Gordons and their Ideot Companion could not have ended better——They are all three Universally hissed out of Society and Lockhart loses the hope of 600£ o'Year designed for him in the Church.[5] Their Mother only is to be pitied: She is a very unhappy and very respectable Lady of ancient Family and broken Fortunes.[6]

The Dear King mends every day and won two Games at Chess yesterday from a distinguished Player. Lord Camelford is not supposed to be any loss to any body: he was a hot-headed dangerous Man; avoided by the wise, and only compassionated, not loved or esteemed by his nearest Connections.[7] Of the new Publications I seem best pleased with Lewis the 16th's Letters; They are wonderfully interesting as they contain his private thoughts and opinions written in such trying Moments as few have ever passed thro' since time began; and such as no Man *could* pass thro' with a Mind so unstained by Passion, unwarped by Prejudice—and unembittered by Vexation, without God's special Grace——He was a wonderful Creature, and comes out such upon full Proof.[8]——The Emigrant Nobles here in London——starving in Garrets,——some serving as footmen, some acting the happier Part of busy and thriving Shop-keepers; *are all alive* just now with hope of Restoration to the Bourbon Family in consequence of these Ups and Downs at Paris; but God only knows how they will end.

Here is beautiful Weather truly, and soon as we have had our little Boy home for the Easter Holydays, and passed another Week after that, with our agreeable Tenant at Streatham Park—it will be Time to think of Home where I trust the little Birds are singing sweetly.

On Examination the Needle Book cannot be enclosed; it would over weight this Letter—which being begun two days ago, does not speak with Emphasis sufficient concerning a Plot which *may* set Europe in a Flame—or give Peace to all four Continents according to the close of the Catastrophe. It is a moment of immense Importance; and must at any rate relieve dear Mrs. Williams from all present Terrors of *Invasion*—They have other Affairs in hand. To her, and to Sir John we beg that our best wishes may be presented by the hand of Your Ladyship's ever Obliged and faithful / H: L: P.——

Text: Ry. 2 (1802–6). *Address*: Lady Williams / Bodylwyddan / near St. Asaph. *Postmark*: DENBIGH.

1. See *The Times*, 10 March:
"At home a secret expedition is spoken of to block up, or rather wall up, the enemy's ports, by sinking old vessels in the roads loaden with stones and rubbish. To this we are as little disposed to give our assent, as to the preceding [a French invasion of Denmark]. It would be impossible to shut up Brest, and the more important harbours, in this manner."
2. At his house at Hyde-park-corner, [Mary] the wife of Drummond Smith, esq. Her death was occasioned by grief for the death of her sister, which brought on a violent fever. Lady Cunliffe is inconsoleable for the very recent loss of her two daughters."
Mrs. Smith's death occurred on 26 February. See *GM* 74, pt. 1 (1804): 281.
Her sister was Margaret Elizabeth (d. 18 December 1803), who had married William Gosling (d. 1835) of Roehampton Grove, a banker in London.
3. Mary, née Bennet (d. 1814), of Moston, Cheshire, had in 1760 married Ellis Cunliffe (1717–67), of Liverpool, cr. baronet (1759).
4. An allusion to Rachel Lee's abandoned safeguard of chastity. See HLP to Ly W, 16 February, n. 1.
5. The Gordons—Loudon and Lockhart—were tried on 6 March at the Oxford assizes for the abduction of Rachel Lee. During the trial "Mr. Justice Lawrence said to jury 'it did not appear that any force had been used to bring Mrs. Lee into the county of Oxford, and observed to them that Mrs. Lee might have had assistance at the different turnpikes through which she passed on the road to Tetsworth, as well as at the inns where the horses were changed; you must therefore acquit the prisoners.' The jury immediately pronounced the prisoners 'not guilty.'
"Mr. Justice Lawrence addressing himself to the prisoners said 'their acquittal was no cause of triumph to them, as their conduct had been disgraceful. . . .'"
See Loudon Harcourt Gordon, *An Apology for the Conduct of the Gordons; containing the*

whole of their correspondence, conversation, &c. with Mrs. Lee: to which is annexed, an accurate account of their examination at Bow Street, and their trial at Oxford (London: John Ginger, 169, Piccadilly; and Thomas Hurst, Paternoster-Row, 1804), pp. 142–43.

6. The Honorable Lockhart Gordon (d. Calcutta, 1788) was the third son of the third earl of Aboyne. He had studied for the law but entered the army, becoming a lieutenant colonel. He was appointed judge advocate general of Bengal in 1787. In 1770 he had taken as his second wife Catherine Wallop (d. 1812), sister of John (1742–97), second earl of Portsmouth.

7. Thomas Pitt (1775–1804), second baron Camelford (1793), was a quarrelsome naval officer. Promoted, nevertheless, to commander on 12 December 1797, he decided almost a year later to acquire a set of French charts for his new ship and new command. Armed with a letter to Barras, he hired some boatmen to take him to France. The admiralty, when he was apprehended, relieved him of his command. In his turn, he asked that his name be removed from the list of commanders.

From this time onward he lived in London. On 9 March he provoked a duel with a former friend. During the duel on the 10th Camelford was mortally wounded. The night before, he had written his will, "appointing His Sister, Lady Grenville, His Executrix & leaving to Her disposal £150,000. He also directed that His body should be buried in an Island in the Lake of Vevay in Switzerland between 3 trees which He specified, adding 'that there nature might smile on His Bones after the world had forgotten Him'" (Farington 5:2270, 2272–73).

8. A spurious collection of Louis XVI's letters was edited by Helen Maria Williams: *The Political and Confidential Correspondence of Lewis the Sixteenth* [in French and English]. *With Observations on each Letter*, 3 vols. (London: G. and J. Robinson, 1803). In 1804 appeared A. F. de Bertrand de Moleville, *A Refutation of the Libel on the Memory of the late King of France*, published by H. M. Williams under the title of Political and Confidential Correspondence of Lewis the Sixteenth.

TO LADY WILLIAMS

Holles Street Thursday
12: April 1804.

My dearest Lady Williams's agreeable Commands have been obeyed—soon as they came to hand. The Books will go by an early Waggon, and comical enough it is, that the Same Conveyance should bring to my lovely Godson—Prayer Book from me, and Hobby Horse from a Bishop; He will laugh when grown up, at the odd Recollection of it. My Needle Case and Ring shall not be trusted to any Carriage however, for those I will bring myself: unless my Mind alters and Circumstances change, which they *may* do, even before Night.

Three Days ago Colonel Stanley himself told me that the Proclamation was prepared for putting us all under Martial Law;[1] on the instant when Telegraphs and Beacons should give notice of an Enemy's Approach;——and Government most certainly did expect the French to have taken advantage of this *very high Tide* accompanied as it is, with a gentle Sea and light Breeze particularly favourable for the Descent. There are however, those who *think* or *who say* they think Buonaparte will find Business at home, and that his late atrocious Conduct will arm indignant Europe against such Tyranny.[2] I am not of their Mind; my Heart trembles for our acquaintance Mr. Drake, who will probably be seized and shot:[3] so will the King of France: his Emigrant Nobles here, have scarce a hope He can escape the Snare; and as for Prussia's Protection I would give little for it; he must run hither *to be safe,* if safety is a word lawful to use in such Moments, and on such occasions.[4]

I am glad your Ladyship is so happy in your own Connections. A good Husband, a fond Mother, and six promising Babies are such Blessings: one can only pray for *Continuance* of your Felicity, not for Addition to it. God keep dear Mr[s]. Williams from growing worse, and all will do well enough: nor can any thing be less prudent than to worry your own heart with Anticipation of uncertain Evils. Mr. Piozzi says I contradict my own Position daily, but it is only upon Subjects where Supineness is worse than Anxiety.

We shall be coming home soon now; The Business we came up for, that of getting Servants, seeing our little Boy, and shewing Mr. Piozzi's foot to Sir James Earle, is all done;[5] and the projected 3 Month's Absence nearly at an end. It is a shame to think how much Money one spends in so short a Time; I buy no fine Clothes Heaven's my Witness, yet the absolute Necessity of *Some* Change in one's Dress, and the going out every, every day so——costs incredible Sums: not a Hat or Bonnet of any decent Appearance can be had under 2 or 3 Guineas—and *young* Women *do* go in their Hair only, for that Reason—but the Hair is filled with Combs and Trinkets which take the money to the Jewellers Shop instead of the Milliners, and I see nothing gained by the Exchange. Ribbon Bonnets are worne, and very pretty of their Kind—Shag Hats, and Straw, and Beaver, and Velvet, fill the Streets: and Playhouse Expences are higher now than ever. Those who have not private Boxes feel quite in the Back Ground, at close of a Season which has cost them 20 or 30 Guineas dropt at Door of the Theatres.

At Bath amusements are far less expensive, and one has a better house and better Table Provision for one's Money——The Card-players too, tell me that even *their* outgoings are greater in the Metropolis, but of that I can be no Judge—We shall be willing to get safe home again and hear the Thrushes sing in our young Plantation.

Buonaparte would not be true to his Assignation, so I only see the Army preparing to receive him, and see myself preparing for Wales where I shall have the Pleasure to say how truly I have the honour and happiness / to be Your Ladyship's ever faithful / H: L: P.—

Text: Ry. 2 (1802–6).

1. Thomas Stanley (1749–1818) of Cross Hall, Lancs., had been commissioned in the First Regiment of Royal Lancashire militia on 28 October 1783. As commanding officer, he was named colonel on 14 March 1794, a rank which he held at least through 1807. He was also a Member of Parliament for Lancashire from 1780 to 1812.

Cross Hall, a small estate within the manor of Latham, was the patrimonial property of the elder branch of the house of Derby. It was bequeathed to Colonel Stanley's branch of the family by James, tenth earl of Derby.

2. HLP alludes to Louis-Antoine-Henri de Bourbon-Condé (1772–1804), duc d'Enghien, the only son of the last prince de Condé. The duc d'Enghien, seized in the neutral

territory of Baden, was tried without counsel by a military tribunal on 20 March for treason and was executed on the 23rd in the forest of Vincennes by order of Bonaparte. See *GM* 74, pt. 1 (1804): 366–67.

The Times on 11 April wrote of Bonaparte's "tyranny," or "This cruel murder, for we cannot give the execution of the duke D'Enghien a more appropriate name. . . . Its injustice is of the most glaring kind, and the whole proceeding must be lamented and execrated by every enlightened mind in Europe. It seems, in our contemplation of it, to be dictated by a capricious or desperate spirit of resentment against the royal Family of France. . . . his conduct betrays every symptom of a mind agitated by fears and suspicions."

3. For Francis Drake, see HLP to James Robson, 16 April 1799, n. 5.

In order to exacerbate prejudice against England, Bonaparte accused Drake and Spencer Smith, British envoys at Munich and Stuttgart, of conspiring with the ringleaders, Georges, Cadoudal, Pichegru, and Moreau. As a result the envoys were expelled by the courts of Bavaria and Württemberg. See *AR* 46 (1804): 162–63.

4. For the travels of Louis XVIII, see HLP to LC, 15 December 1800, n. 4.

5. For James Earle, see HLP to Jacob Weston, 18 December 1798, n. 3.

TO PENELOPE SOPHIA PENNINGTON

Holles Street
Monday
16: April *1804.*

Dear Mrs. Pennington's beautiful Letters shall lie no longer unacknowledged: Mr. Parsons brought me the first, and I thought by his Looks that Bath and *Bristol* (as we call Clifton and the Hot Wells,) had done him no Good.

Doctor Gray came to see us since that, for the first Time; but *his* Appearance spoke Happiness, and his *Conversation*—unaltered Friendship to you and to ourselves: he is a good Man, and he liked our little Boy, who was at home just then for Easter Holydays.

Of the Layards I was not in haste to hear; Mr. Whalley had better lay down the Money for *me* and write to Lord Kirkwall concerning the other Subscribers,[1] for I hate to be answerable for charity not my own: As to dear Lady Orkney She takes her Lodgings on a Milestone I believe for there is no catching *her* Town or Country.—I understand the Ladies of *that* interesting Family The *Layards* are not as easily induced to the Miss-training Art as poor Mrs. Jackson has been: We were told one of them refused a very great Situation *in that way* as beneath her Acceptance.[2]

Lady Hesketh will be amused to hear that the People who have seen her Cousin Cooper's Snuffbox, or the Seat his favourite Mary sate in; cry "Touch me, Touch me, that you may Say you have touched the Person who sate in Mrs. Unwin's Chair, or handled Cooper's Snuffbox."[2] This is all good is it not? for Mr. Hayley.[4]

Cumberland's Play keeps the Stage, in Spite of younger Wits who wanted People to laugh at the Author instead of the Comedy;[5] but Mrs. Abingdon and

Sophia Lee. Drawing by Sir Thomas Lawrence; engraved by Ridley. In George Colman (1762–1836), ed. *Posthumous Letters, from Various Celebrated Men* (London: Cadell and Davies, 1820); extra-illustrated, facing p. 224. (Reproduced by permission of the Henry E. Huntington Library and Art Gallery, San Marino, California.)

I—Veterans like himself—are glad that he succeeds; for as She expresses it "He has a graceful Mind."[6]

Miss Lees and us have met Twice or Thrice, but either the Life of a Lover— Sophia's new Novel, is not out;[7] or I have not seen it—Holcroft's Paris[8] and Miss Edgeworth's Popular Tales are the only Books found in Windows, on Toilettes &c. No tales of Wonder, and such are *not* hers[9]—can equal the Death of Le Duc D'Enghien or the Apprehensions seriously entertained at present for Mr. Drake British Ambassador in Bavaria, and our good Friend as you remember; who used to meet him visiting us at Mrs. Garret's: he married Miss Mackworth—and now we expect him to be *hanged* as he surely will be poor Fellow![10] If Buonaparte catches hold of him. These are Novelties at least tho' not Novels—yet few Romances would have ventured such an Incident.

Mrs. General Smith is charming; but her Husband has most of my Heart. Will the Air and Water in your part of the World do him good? We cannot any of us spare dear General Smith.[11]

Mr. Piozzi *does* look remarkably well; We have dined out very often indeed in Parties, and he never gave up but one at Sir Walter James's—*he* has Daughters whom I think very highly of indeed,—unsophisticated modest Maidens, such as I remember in Days of yore, and very pleasing mannered.[12]

My own Girls have remained in Confinement on Sophy's Account some Weeks now. She has been plagued with St. Anthony's Fire [erysipelas] in and out; and I think few Complaints more troublesome. Mrs. Mostyn is full in Feather, and high in Song, as the Folks say who keep Canary Birds, and her immense Aviary put me in Mind of the Phrase: She has three very sturdy Boys beside.

De Blaquieres, Kirkwalls, all Holles Street I believe, dined with her Yesterday: and among the rest my gay Master, and his and your H: L: P.

Present me kindly to your Husband and Mother. The Siddons Eye and bright and kind as ever.

Text: Princeton University Library.

1. On 19 June 1803 in her letter to PSP, HLP agreed to contribute to a subscription on behalf of the Layards following the sudden death of the dean of Bristol. Apparently the money was slow in coming in, including HLP's.

2. The Reverend Charles Peter Layard had three sons: Brownlow Villiers (1779–1861); Henry Peter John (1783–1834) in the Bengal Civil Service; Charles Edward (1786–1852), also in the Bengal Civil Service.

The late dean had five surviving daughters: Charlotte Susanna (1780–1858); Marianne (1781–1840); Henrietta Margaret (1782–1855); Caroline Bethia (1787–1827); Louisa Frances (1789–1851). The daughter who "refused a very great Situation" was Charlotte Susanna; she was to marry on 18 November 1809 (as his second wife) General Albemarle Bertie (1744–1818), ninth earl of Lindsey (1809), and secondly on 14 April 1821 the Reverend Peter William Pegus (d. 1860).

3. For two years William Cowper had resided in Huntingdon with the Reverend Morley Unwin, master of the free school there, and his wife Mary, née Cawthorne (1724– 96). Following Unwin's death in 1767, the poet continued under the guardianship of Mrs.

Unwin at Olney, except for a year's interval when he was looked after by the Reverend John Newton (1725–1807). From 1774 until her own disabling illness (1791–94), Mary Unwin provided Cowper with a home and encouragement. For Lady Hesketh, see HLP to PSP, 20 December [1799], n. 1.

4. While projecting a translation of Milton's Latin and Italian poetry—to be illustrated by Henry Fuseli and published by Joseph Johnson—Cowper met William Hayley, biographer for a new edition of Milton's works (1794–96). Learning about Cowper's proposal, Hayley reassured him that he need not fear competition. Thereafter, until the former's death in 1800 and beyond, Hayley proved to be a good friend.

Between 1803 and 1812, he wrote extensive biographical accounts of Cowper. In addition he wrote the preface for the posthumous Milton translations (1808) and subsequently (1810) added his own *Life of Milton*.

See *The Letters and Prose Writings of William Cowper*, ed. James King and Charles Ryskamp, 5 vols. (Oxford: Clarendon Press, 1979–86), 4:28–29 and n. 1; Norma Russell, *A Bibliography of William Cowper to 1827* (Oxford: Clarendon Press, 1963), pp. 175–83, 244–56. For HLP's dislike of Hayley, see her letter to Q, 10 March 1796, nn. 1–5; *Thraliana* 2:795–96.

5. *The Sailor's Daughter* was first performed on 7 April at the Drury Lane and played every night from the 9th to the 13th. On 14 April Cumberland's most popular play, *The Wheel of Fortune* (1795), was presented at the Covent Garden.

The Sailor's Daughter received mixed reviews. The *Courier* on 9 April thought "that the piece may for a few nights form an agreeable variety in the amusement of the town, although, for the sake of Mr. Cumberland, we should have been happy that it had never been written, or brought on the stage." See also the *Observer*, 8 April; *The Times*, 9 April.

6. For Frances Abington, see HLP to SL, 1 March 1786, n. 12.

7. Sophia Lee, *The Life of a Lover, In a Series of Letters*, 6 vols. (London: G and J. Robinson, 1804).

8. *Travels from Hamburg through Westphalia, Holland, and the Netherlands*, 2 vols.; (London: R. Phillips 1804). The whole of the second volume deals with Paris.

9. Maria Edgeworth, *Popular Tales* (with a preface by Richard Lovell Edgeworth; London: J. Johnson, 1804); Matthew Gregory Lewis wrote and collected *Tales of Wonder* (1801).

10. On 31 March 1795 Francis Drake was married to Elizabeth Anne (1774–1838), daughter of Herbert Mackworth (1736/37–91), first baronet (1776).

11. For General Edward Smith, see HLP to PSP, 2 June 1802, n. 6; and his wife, Penelope, see HLP to Q, 20 September 1803, n. 11.

12. Sir Walter James had six children: Francis, who was killed at Badajos in April 1812; John (d. 1818); Jane; Mary–Anne (d. 1845); Frances (d. post 1823); Charlotte–Elizabeth (d. 1820).

TO THE REVEREND LEONARD CHAPPELOW

Brynbella
18: June 1804.

I was certainly wishing for a Letter when yours came Dear Sir,[1]—It brought me the first Intelligence of the Tax which Sweet Siddons has been paying for her Superior Charms of Person and of Talents[2]——I had a Present from her of a Veil She had been netting for me, with Two or Three Lines lamenting her Husband's long continued Absence, but not a Syllable concerning the Adventure which another Woman *in her Situation* would be vain of: but She is as the man says an adorable Creature——and puts even Buonaparte out of one's head for a while. You ask me what I think of The French: I think no Play ever exhibited such true Poetical Justice as the winding up of their long Romance has done. Carnot—— who proposed tanning human Hides,——and Garat—who carried the Sentence of Death to Louis seize, both sent into Banishment[3] by the new Emperor;[4] who with more Truth than Policy perhaps, openly censures the Princes for deserting what he justly calls the *Constitutional* Throne—Though he chuses to usurp it: are really such Strokes of retributory Payment as I could not have hoped for Life to admire at. Your Sunday Observer makes very good Observations too: but Buonaparte is not like Sylla of an old Patrician House; or like him a reading Man, and such a Lover of Literature as to prefer Books and Solitude at last to every thing the busy World could offer.[5] This founder of a new Dynasty actuated by the true Selfish Spirit of a novus Homo, means to concentrate Power, Pomp and Riches all in his own Person and Family; and truly glad am I to see the French, who followed up their native Prince who loved them—with Curses, because he was *L'Homme a vingt Cinq Millions* they said: stopping the mouth of this devouring Despot and his Dame with Millions, and Millions, and Millions. He is Emperor over the *Gulls* as you call them, indeed: let him have no Interest among *Sea Gulls* to waft him *hither,* and in every Act of Oppression in this new home I wish him Success.

So let's have done with the *Vulture,* and think about the Swallows; they are very few in number this Year—or do I dream so: and one scarce hears a Cuckoo tho' our Weather is well enough for *Greenland,* where you always say we <live.>

It *is* curious as you observe that *my* Thoughts should run chiefly on the Business of Men and Manners—who pass the greatest part of my Life among the mute Objects of a brilliant Landschape; while you are spending whole Mornings in *Bow Street,* whole Evenings in Describing the *Innocence* of *Lambkins,* and Sweet Singing of dear Philomela.[6]

Well! the Concordia Discors does best for both I suppose;[7] our Friends at Llangollen who know not the Existence of Discord but by Book; will have too close a Study near them if this Cotton Mill takes Place——but these are no Days in which to expect that Commerce will keep her *Clack* quiet for purpose of indulging fair and noble Ladies in their Scheme of Retirement.[8]

Do you read Malthus upon Population? It is a very great Performance, and so full of *your own Notions* I expected You to be an Admirer of the Work. Mandeville saw long ago with Spectacles from *the same Shop*——but People in his Day were frighted lest Philosophy should see *too far*: our Times enlarge the *Powers* of her Telescope without Fear——or Discretion.[9]

Acerbi's Travels has amused me very much, and there is an Anecdote of Linnæus in it that would divert *you*.[10] The Critical Reviewers said they never heard of *Regnard,* and supposed his Existence to be only in the Imagination of a *Female* Geographer:[11] They may learn better *now*; Acerbi takes him for the Motto of a Journey to Lapland full of entertainment as I trust *they will find*.[12]

The Disputes in Parliament keep all Frankers in London,[13] and you must pay Nine Pence or 18d: I know not which; for hearing that Mr. Piozzi unites his truest Regards to Those of Dear Sir Yours ever / H: L: P.

The Rt. Hon. Lady Eleanor Butler and Miss [Sarah] Ponsonby, the "Ladies of Llangollen." Drawn on stone by J. H. Lynch. In Elizabeth Stone, *Chronicles of Fashion*, 2 vols. in 14 (London: Richard Bentley, 1845); extra-illustrated, 11/247-1. (Reproduced by permission of the Henry E. Huntington Library and Art Gallery, San Marino, California.)

18 June 1804

Plas Newydd, near Llangollen. The Seat of the late Lady Eleanor Butler and Miss [Sarah] Ponsonby. Drawn on stone by W. Walton from a picture by the publisher, Edwin W. Jacques. Printed by C. Hullmandel in Elizabeth Stone, *Chronicles of Fashion*, 2 vols. in 14 (London: Richard Bentley, 1845); extra-illustrated, 11/247-7. (Reproduced by permission of the Henry E. Huntington Library and Art Gallery, San Marino, California.)

Do you remember Doctor Thackeray? Oh yes, you knew his Mama I remember;[14] Well, he is happily married to an Agreeable Widow with a very good Fortune: and we are all exceedingly glad of it.[15]

Text: Ry. 561.130. *Address*: Rev: Mr. Chappelow / Hill Street Berkeley Square / London / No. 13. *Postmark*: DENBIGH 224; E JUN 22 1804.

1. HLP replies to LC's long-awaited letter, dated 13 June (Ry. 563.84).
2. According to LC's letter:
"In this mornings paper there is a long account of a young Irish student [aged 23] in the Temple, who has (as I suppose you have heard) lately persecuted your friend Mrs. Siddons with his amorous Importunities,—after continually repeated visits, without success even as to a personal conference, and after having written innumerable Letters— she was advised by the Bow-Street Magistrates—to consent to a proposed Interview, but on the appointed day and hour—The Runners of Bow Street—instead of the said Lady received the sighing visitant—and conducted him to the Magistrates—who after a long recrimination &c. dismissed the Gentleman under certain promises to be no more troublesome—Mr. Kemble managed the Business—The Hero must have fallen desperately in Love—with her Calista.—but Mrs. Siddons never intends to act the fair Penitent."
For another version, see Farington 6:2374; also the *Monthly Mirror* 17 (1804): 426–27.

3. Lazare-Nicolas-Marguerite Carnot (1753–1823) and Dominique-Joseph Garat (1749–1833) were discussed in an article in *The Times,* 13 June.

"It seems to be a principle with the French Emperor to remove, by one way or other, all his former Revolutionary friends. The Republican spirit is certainly not suited to a man who has just dissolved a Republic. Bonaparte, therefore, has . . . very consistently ordered Carnot, Sieyès, Garat, Coulon, Gregoire, and Lanjaunais to reside on their respective estates in the country, until further orders; which will probably remove them altogether out of the country."

Carnot had been living in retirement since 1801, fighting Bonaparte's increasing monarchism. (See HLP to John Ewen, November 1802, n. 8.) Garat had been in 1793 the minister of justice and in that capacity brought Louis XVI notice of his death sentence. He was always an ardent admirer of Bonaparte, who named him a member of the Institut (1803) and elevated him to the peerage as a comte.

4. As early as 11 February 1804, *The Times* reported: "Accounts from Paris mention, with some degree of confidence, that Bonaparte is very seriously occupied in completing his project of being declared Sovereign of France, under the title of King or Emperor, which he proposes to render hereditary in his family. In short, it is his object to form a new dynasty."

According to *AR* 46 (1804): 166, "The first decided step towards the accomplishment of this long-meditated measure, was an address to the first consul, on the part of the senate, dated the 27th March, proposing to constitute him hereditary emperor of France."

On 18 May Bonaparte became emperor of the French.

5. HLP refers to an article in the *Observer,* 10 June:

"Buonaparte in character, and many acts of his life, offers a strong resemblance to Sylla:—like the dictator, he is devoid of religion, faith, honesty, or mercy. Sylla murdered 5,000 Praenestines who had surrendered to him under capitulation, and the most positive assurances of safety;—Buonaparte in Syria did the same. Sylla murdered 9,000 of his own followers, no longer useful to him;—Buonaparte poisoned his sick. Sylla in one list proscribed 80,000 people, and, as Seneca observes, made a slaughter-house of Italy;—Buonaparte has proscribed all Europe, and made a slaughter-house of the universe. The Roman and the Corsican were both raised from poverty and obscurity by the favour of prostitutes; they appear equally fortunate, ambitious, tyrannical, and enterprizing. Sylla embarked in the invasion of Greece and Persia, regardless of the discord which he left behind him in Rome;—it remains to be seen whether Buonaparte will engage in the project of invasion, without consideration to the myriads of enemies which his conduct has created at home."

6. A reference to LC who, while living in London, rose at five in the morning to versify his love for the animal kingdom. See HLP to LC, 3 June 1796, n. 11. His unpublished manuscript, entitled "The Sentimental Naturalist," is now at the Cambridge University Library.

7. The main tenet of Empedocles' philosophy. See, e.g., Horace, *Epistles,* 1.12.19; Ovid, *Metamorphoses,* 1.433; Lucan, *De Bello Civili,* 1.98.

8. See the *Courier,* 28 January 1804:

"The two Ladies of Llangollen Vale are, it is said, determined to quit the beautiful and elegant residence, because a silk manufactory is about to be established in the village which they inhabit. We do not, however, comprehend the reason why the sylphs, the fairies, and the genii of the place, should be disturbed at such a circumstance unless they should be alarmed at the approach of so many *spinning Jennies.*"

9. Thomas Robert Malthus (1766–1834), *An Essay on the Principle of Population* (1798). A new edition, very much enlarged (London: J. Johnson, 1803). Bernard Mandeville (ca. 1670–1733), *The Fable of the Bees; or, Private Vices, Publick Benefits* (1714). The 2d edition, enlarged with many additions. As also *An Essay on Charity and Charity-schools.* And *A Search into the Nature of Society* (London: E. Parker, 1723).

Only a superficial similarity exists between the economist Malthus and the satirist-philosopher Mandeville in that both visualized a grim society, with human beings, motivated by selfishness and poverty, competing for survival.

10. Joseph Acerbi, *Travels through Sweden, Finland, and Lapland, to the North Cape, in the Years 1798 and 1799,* 2 vols. (London: Joseph Mawman, 1802).

Acerbi cites two or three anecdotes that Linnaeus in his "extreme vanity . . . carried to the most disgusting length." Thus, on one occasion, the botanist was showing his museum to a lady, who said *"I no longer wonder that Linnaeus is so well known over the whole province of Upsala!* Linnaeus, who instead of *the province of Upsala* expected to hear *the whole universe,* was so shocked, that he would shew her nothing more of the museum, and sent the lady away quite confounded at the change of his humour" (1:243).

11. See HLP to LC, 18 June 1801, n. 4.

12. The reference to Regnard comes in the "Conclusion" to Acerbi's *Travels.*

" 'Thus ends a course,' says Reignard, in conclusion of his Journey to Lapland, 'which I would not but have made for all the gold in the world, and which I would not for all the gold in the world make over again.' The French traveller could not, in my mind, have drawn a juster picture of his character, and the spirit in which he undertook his distant travels, than is exhibited in this enigmatical mode of expression" (2:127).

13. The disputes confronting the new Pitt ministry were so numerous that *The Times* on 18 June commented:

"The state and conduct of the present political Parties not only occupy, but, in a great measure, appear to absorb the public attention. The general subjects of foreign politics seem to be almost forgotten, and even the invasion itself is suspended to consider the progress of Parliamentary contest; while the spirit of prediction leaves the Emperor of the French to his fate, and directs its views to the establishment of Mr. Pitt in the government of the country, or his speedy resignation of it."

14. For William Makepeace Thackeray, see HLP to LC, 23 August 1794, n. 7.

15. Thackeray had recently married Eliza, née Wilson (d. 1833), of Liverpool and the widow of John Jones of Gelly-Gynan, Flintshire. They met while he was on a walking trip through North Wales. See Jane Townley Pryme and Alicia Bayne, *Memorials of the Thackeray Family* (London: For Private Distribution, 1879), pp. 89–93. See also HLP to LC, 23 August 1794.

TO JOHN SALUSBURY PIOZZI SALUSBURY

Brynbella
1: July 1804.

My dearest little Boy

It was very good natured in Mr. Davies to carry you half a Crown, and *exceedingly* good natured in him to make you write that bit of a Letter, which was worth Two Half Crowns to *me;* because I wanted Comfort very much, Your Uncle is so bad of the Gout, and cries out terribly:

When you write to your Papa and Mama,[1] give my Love and Compliments; and say that Mr. Piozzi has no hand he can write with, or else he would have sent them a Letter long since.

I have lost an Aunt——an Uncle's Wife at least,[2] as I am to you; and She did love me once, and so I am Sorry, as I dare say you think you shall be when you lose / Your Affectionate Aunt / H: L: Piozzi.

Mr. Davies should write sometimes, because he hears all the News, living near London; and I hear none——If it had not been for the Public Paper I should never have been told of Lady Salusbury's Death.

Text: Hyde Collection. *Address*: The Revd. / Mr. Davies / Streatham / Surrey. [franked by] Kirkwall, Denbigh, July Two 1804. *Postmark*: 10 o'Clock JY 4 18<04>.

    1. For JSPS's parents, see HLP to Jacob Weston, 18 December 1798, n. 2.
    2. Lady Salusbury had died on 24 June, "In Harley Street, aged 83." See *AR*, "Chronicle" 46 (1804): 489.

TO LADY WILLIAMS

14 July 1804

I see my dear Lady Williams does not know that a smart and painful Fit of the Gout has visited Brynbella since *she* did—Mr. Piozzi's Hands have been put to uncommon torture—Yet He is once more out of Bed and hopes to see Friends on the 25: of July, completing 20 Years.[1]

After that we will talk of the Christening, which ought to follow a wedding your Ladyship knows. We have asked Mrs. Mostyn of Segroid, who has not seen Brynbella now several Years. No sore eyes yet, but Easterly Winds always *did* bring Plagues;[2] They will now bring the Invaders—if not afraid—we see plainly at present—that it is not The Elements which keep them away: as no Encouragement on *their* Parts had been wanting since last Monday Morning, and I guess not how Buonaparte means to content his Army without the long-promised Plunder of London——less still can I figure to myself his ability to keep France in Awe, when Royalists and Republicans must alike feel hurt I think; one by the guillotining of that gallant Creature Georges; the other by driving out a successful General in Banishment.[3]

How is dear Mrs. Williams[4] and *all* the Dears?[5] My own Hugh in particular.[6] Let me have another line before you leave them; promising to honour on Wednesday Sennight by your Ladyship's and Sir John's company *at four o'clock* my good Husband and Lady Williams's ever Faithful/ Servant/ H: L: Piozzi.

Text: Ry. 2 (1802–6).

    1. HLP wrote that she "put on a white Gown . . . upon the 25th of July, & celebrated the Anniversary of my Wedding in company of my Husband & his Friends, sitting down 17 to a beautiful Dinner; & Mr Piozzi able to Sing a Song *too:*—& Lord Kirkwall drank bumpers to our Felicity.—& Mrs Mostyn bore Witness to it: *She dined wth us!* The little Boys & girls beside, Children of our poor Folks; with their Tutors &c came & sung to us in hon^r of the Day" (*Thraliana* 2:1055).
    2. "Easterly winds and rain bring cockels [disease-carrying weeds] here by Spain" (*Oxford Proverbs*, p. 213).

3. HLP alludes to the aftermath of the anti-Bonaparte conspiracy, specifically to Georges Cadoudal, Jean-Charles Pichegru, and Jean-Victor Moreau.

On 25 June "at noon, Georges and 11 of the conspirators against the Consular Government were executed in the Place de Greve. . . . most of them, as they submitted their heads to the guillotine, exclaimed *'Vive le Roi!' 'Vive Louis XVIII!'* "

Of Pichegru it was believed that he "was *racked to death* in the Temple, in order to make him confess; and that the body which was exhibited at the Hotel de Ville was not his." (A suicide, he was found strangled in his cell, 6 April.) See *GM* 74, pt. 1 (1804):367.

The republican Moreau had his "sentence of imprisonment . . . commuted for exile; and he, with his family, have arrived at a Spanish port to embark for America" (*GM* 74, pt. 2 [1804]: 678.

4. Eleanor Williams (d. 1810) was suffering from a slowly developing malignancy. See the *North Wales Gazette,* 17 May 1810.

5. In 1804 Ly W had two sons: John (b. 1794) and Hugh (b. 1802); she also had four daughters: Harriet (b. 1797), Emma (b. 1798), Margaret (b. 1799), Mary Elizabeth (b. 1803).

6. Born on 8 January, 1802, Hugh Williams was HLP's godson.

TO PENELOPE SOPHIA PENNINGTON

Brynbella
Sunday Morning
19: August 1804.

I am the wretchedest Quarreller on Earth dear Mrs. Pennington, and not the most ingenious Reconciler.[1] Like mine Hostess Quickly,—I am the *worse* when one *says*—quarrel.[2] Nor did ever the Country Gentleman in Ben Jonson need London Instructions in the Art of angry Reciprocation more than I do.[3]

Let us leave a Subject I really understand so little, and lament that the universal Quarreller—Death—has been So busy among our common Acquaintance since we parted.

How Senseless!—not to say offensive, must yours and my Master's mutual Complaint appear in the Eyes of poor dear Mrs. Dimond just now![4] Such a Son! The Parents just Pride and Joy—so snatched! and that unhappy Mrs. Adams who you may remember said She had heard the Bell ring for her own Execution: She has lost the Daughter She alone desired to live for.[5]

Few People find the Way of being happy, and those who throw little Hedgehogs in one another's Paths,—like the Rioters—to make them stumble and roll about—have none of my Approbation. It is a Cordial to hear that good Mr. Whalley is so happy, and you will find Hannah More so, and that will be a sweet Comfort; She has had Nervous Complaints enough sure, and shewn in the Subjugation of them, (for I suppose Conquest is impossible)—a truly Invincible Constitution.[6]

Dear Siddons was not happy when She and I last parted,[7] and all you told of the Randolphs was rather bad too; but *her* Health mends no doubt or I should have heard before now.

You will not be talked to (you say) of the Cat and the Dog, and the times and the Weather——Tho' really the *first* of these Subjects is not amiss for you quarreling Disciples—and I will not like Grumio talk to *you* of how bad my poor Master was when your Letter came to *him*, and in what a Shocking Situation his Fingers have been placed by the last Fit of Gout; no, nor what a Loss we have sustained in poor Hodgkins——nor what a Successor we picked up for him; but all these wonders as old Shakespeare says shall now be buried in Oblivion, as shall all my true Expressions of Admiration at your Letters, which still exceed every-one the last received.[8]

Farewell then, and be merry; and believe me with every possible good Wish / Your ancient Jigg-maker / H: L: P.

Text: Princeton University Library. *Address*: Mrs. Pennington / Dowry Square / Hot Wells / Bristol. *Postmark*: DENBIGH 224.

1. On 10 July 1804, PSP wrote and admitted that she had heard through a third party—"a side wind"—that HLP was annoyed with her. Over six pages she apologized for an unknown offense, which she could attribute only to "petulence" or "indiscretion." HLP did not reply. On 15 August PSP tried again: "If however you are weary of being kind, be at least *candid*, and inform me what this mortal offence has been." (In the course of this letter PSP hints that GP wishes the friendship of the two women to be ended but does not elaborate upon the hint.) PSP continues: "yet let me frankly tell you I do not wish to receive Letters without *kindness*, or *Interest*, about the cat, or the Dog;—the Times, or the Weather.—" HLP responded to this letter with a nonanswer and wrote no more to PSP until July 1819. PSP had tried again on 2 April 1805, 23 March 1806, 23 April 1809 but evoked no known reply from HLP. See Ry. 568.125–29.

2. HLP's reference to Mistress Quickly might provide some clue to the misunderstanding that now existed between the two women. In *The Second Part of Henry the Fourth*, 2.4.104–5, 109, Hostess Quickly says, "I am the worse when one says swagger" and then adds, "I cannot abide swagg'rers." In several letters over the past few months PSP had quietly swaggered over her associations with dukes and duchesses: e.g., the duke of Cumberland and the duchess of Devonshire.

3. HLP refers to Kastrill, the angry boy, in Jonson's *The Alchemist*, and specifically to the dialogue between Kastrill and Face (3.3.14–37).

4. See *The Times*, 15 August 1804: "Mr. Dimond, son of the Manager of the Theatre at Bath, and Author of several dramatic Pieces, died on Friday [10 August] on his road to that City from London." Of him HLP wrote: "A Strange Thing! Young Dimond is turned Roman Catholic" ("Minced Meat for Pyes").

5. Susan Adams (ca. 1786–1804), daughter of Tobias Adams (d. 1805), rector of Britway and Aherne (1796–1805). HLP was asked to write an epitaph by the girl's mother, Jane, née Owen (fl. 1758–1810), who in 1798 in Ireland heard the bell "toll for her own execution" (*Thraliana* 2:993, 1054). See the "Biographical Succession List of the Clergy of Dublin Diocese," by the Reverend Canon J. B. Leslie, in the library of the Representative Church Body, Dublin; the "Testamentary Index," P.R.O., Ireland.

The epitaph, which HLP wrote, is as much concerned with Susan as with "her Afflicted Mother." See Ry. 629.23.

6. For the nature of Hannah More's complaint, see HLP to RG, 2 December 1801, n. 2.

7. In July HLP had learned that "Siddons & his Wife are going to part seriously & eternally, after living 35 Years together;—can that be worth their While?" (*Thraliana* 2:1055, n. 5).

But SL had learned of the friendly break-up of the Siddons's marriage earlier. On 20 June he told Farington (6:2356): "Mr. & Mrs. Siddons have acquired £40,000, that Mr. Siddons has lately settled upon Her £20,000, which He will also leave and all the rest *at*

Her disposal.—Her £20,000 brings in £1000 a yr. Lysons recommended the settlement and is a Trustee along with Kemble & a Mr. Morris. Mr. & Mrs. Siddons are not suited to each other. While the daughters lived they went on tolerably.—There is much wicked allusion—abt. Lawrence & Her in public papers."

The allusions were to be made explicit about SS and the artist in the newspapers on 1 December. At that time William Siddons returned from Bath and publicly rose to SS's defense. See the *Morning Herald*, 1 December.

8. Again HLP uses Shakespeare to imply a meaning. Thus Grumio, Petruchio's servant, says to Curtis: "But hadst thou not cross'd me, thou shouldst have heard" the news. However, these "many things of worthy memory, which now shall die in oblivion, and thou return unexperienc'd to thy grave" (*The Taming of the Shrew*, 4.1.72–84).

See also *All's Well that Ends Well*, 5.3.23–25.

TO LADY WILLIAMS

Brynbella
Fryday 7 September 1804

How kind is my Dear Lady Williams! with her charitable and friendly enquiries. Mr. Piozzi is once more down Stairs and in his usual Dress. He recovers faster than I do, though he has been so much worse: but we are going to the Sea on Monday, and I hope to have a few Dips in this bright blue Irish Channel—while it is yet *our own*.[1] There is no doubt of there being a Contest for it sooner or later, and God send the Event favourable.

Make our best Regards to Sir Thomas Clarges,[2] and beg of Dear Mrs. Williams to accept my truest Wishes:

Tho' not as the Bird Fanciers express it, *full in Feather and high in Song*, we remain

Your Ladyship's and Sir John's ever faithful as Obliged Friends, Neighbours, Servants, etc.

Text: Ry. 2 (1802–6).

1. With the disruption of the peace of Amiens on 18 May 1803, many English, suspicious of Irish loyalties, feared a French invasion through Ireland, the "Achilles' heel" of British home defense. For example, even before the peace of Amiens became a fact, Hoche in December 1796 tried to get ashore at Bantry Bay but failed. During the following autumn, a second expedition sailing to Ireland was delayed by Duncan's victory at Camperdown. Without waiting for promised French support, Ireland in May 1798 erupted into violence against the British. The short but ferocious campaign ended with the defeat of the Irish at the battle of Vinegar Hill. In July a French force under General Humbert landed on Irish soil but was defeated at Killala.

With Ireland an uncertain quantity and with Napoleon's promise to his troops of their right to plunder London, HLP divided her fears between a rebellious Ireland and the French prepared to use Irish discontent for an invasion of England.

2. Sir Thomas Clarges (ca. 1780–1834) was the fourth (1782) and last baronet of Aston, near Stevenage, Hertfordshire. He was to outlive his entire family: his father, Sir Thomas (d. 1782); his mother, Louisa, née Skrine (d. 1809), and his younger brother, William (d.

TO LADY WILLIAMS

Brynbella
29: September 1804.

My Dear Lady Williams

will like to hear that we are come home much amended by our Visit to Prestatagne;[1] I hope all is well at the House I have so much Reason to love. The dear Children thriving &c.——and heavenly Weather for us all: A fair Wind too for our Bombardment of Calais.[2] My eldest Daughter says that our own old and excellent King was never in higher health or in more composed and perfect Spirits; She has been seeing and hearing him every Day for these last six weeks he goes out o'Pleasuring Miles and *Miles* from the Shore in full Security;[3] while Buonaparte keeps skulking under his own Batteries——so far, so good.[4]

God send us no worse Intelligence before I have the honour to say personally how much I am Your Ladyship's true and faithful Servant / H: L: P.

Text: Ry. 2 (1802–6).

1. The Piozzis arrived at Prestatyn on 31 July, remaining there for almost two months.
2. Calais had been blockaded as early as 9 August and HLP expected the admiralty to take the next aggressive step: the bombardment of the port.
3. George III and the Royal Family left Windsor on 24 August for Weymouth, where they arrived the next day. According to reports, the king's health and spirits were visibly improved by the seaside holiday. See *GM* 74, pt. 2 (1804):1233–34.
4. HLP had learned as early as April that the French were repelled by the execution of the duc d'Enghien. In *GM* 74, pt. 1 (1804):367, she read of "the disgust and indignation of the [French] at the late inhuman murder of the Duc d'Enghien. Bonaparte has appeared once since at the theatre; but the moment he entered, half the audience withdrew." This account probably enabled HLP to think of Bonaparte "as skulking under his own Batteries."

TO THE REVEREND ROBERT GRAY

Brynbella Saturday
13: October 1804.

When will the French be weary of their dangerous playthings, and call home their old Bourbon House? Perhaps this last attempt at burning the flotilla may have *some* good effect;[1] it may sicken Buonaparte of his project, or fright his sailors from following him; or it may provoke him to put his threats into execution and bring on a crisis *some* way; *any*thing better than this vile suspense. Mr. Piozzi says peace must be made if contagion spreads upon the Continent, and *that* for love of general safety. Gustavus[2] seems a true descendant of Frotho the Fierce, and Harold the Hardy[3]——but the *poor* traveller always sung safely even in company of thieves;[4] and he knows Monsieur Napoleon, as he calls himself, can get nothing but snow-balls at Stockholm, where winter barricades the realms of frost.[5]

Abbé Maury's mean acknowledgment of a usurper over the kingdom *his* courage adorned a dozen years ago,[6] grieves me more by half than Braschi's forced submissions to a man who placed him there only to submit;[7] and the poor Stadtholder cringing to him for an annuity is a wretched sight too.[8]

Text: Hayward 2:262–63.

1. "On Tuesday night [2 October] . . . a little before midnight a most tremendous cannonade was heard in the direction of Boulogne, which was continued without intermission for some hours. . . . Three distinct explosions were heard during the cannonade, which were supposed to proceed from the blowing up of the same number of fire-ships sent in among the French flotilla, an operation for which the direction of the wind was particularly favourable."
There were variable estimates of French losses, which ran from forty-eight gun brigs and boats destroyed to numbers as high as 150.
"The plan of attack . . . [was] suggested by Sir Home Popham, who superintended the execution of it in person; and it is said that boats or machines of a particular kind . . . were employed on this occasion. Those machines were represented as capable of being floated under water and towed along by a small boat. Each machine is reported to have contained four tons of stones and several barrels of gunpowder; and having, under the darkness of the night, been previously placed as near to the flotilla that was anchored in Boulogne roads as possible, exploded after a certain time" (*The Times*, 5 October).
2. In 1804 the power on the Continent most hostile to the French government was Sweden. To retaliate, Napoleon had inserted in the *Moniteur* "an article of the most offensive and galling nature" to Gustav. The Swedish king "immediately ordered a note to be presented to the French *chargé d'affaires*, at Stockholm, announcing, that . . . all intercourse must cease between the French legation and the Swedish government; and declaring the offensive expressions in 'the *Moniteur*' to be 'the improper, insolent, and ridiculous observations which *Monsieur* Napoleon Bonaparte allowed to be inserted in his journal.' "
Gustav was now a hero to the British, *The Times*, e.g., regarding him as the noble successor to such as "Gustavus Vasa, Gustavus Adolphus, and Charles XII." See *AR* 46 (1804): 194–95; *The Times*, 2 and 10 October.
The Swedish king is Gustav Adolf IV (1778–1837), who ruled from 1796 to 1809.
For Harold the Hardy, see HLP to Q, 23 May 1801, n. 4.
3. Frotho was an early and legendary king of Denmark, grandson of Skjoldr (Scyld of *Beowulf*). Frotho figures in the Old Norse *Skáldskapavmál* in the prose *Edda*. According to Snorri in the *Edda*, he lived at the time of Augustus Caesar. See Saxo Grammaticus, *Gesta Danorum*; *Beowulf* and *The Fight at Finnsburg*, ed. Friedrich Klaeber, 3d ed. (Boston, New York, etc.: D. C. Heath, 1936), pp. 258–59, 261–62,
4. HLP's telescoping of lines 37–44 in SJ's *The Vanity of Human Wishes*.
5. *The Vanity of Human Wishes*, line 208.
6. See HLP to RG, October 1799, n. 3.

His "courage" became evident when in 1789 he was elected a member of the States General by the clergy of the bailliage de Péronne and persistently defended the monarchy. In 1792 he emigrated, traveling from Germany to Italy and Russia. All during his exile he was regarded as a martyr on behalf of king and church. He was in Rome in 1795 as an ambassador of Louis XVIII to the papal court.

Maury's "mean acknowledgment of a usurper" refers to his letter to the archbishop of Paris, which congratulated the soon-to-be-crowned emperor on his restoration of religion in France and which stated his devotion "to the present Dynasty as well as to the principles of government lately adopted in France." See *AR*, "Chronicle" 46:44; *The Times*, 10 and 11 October.

7. HLP mistakenly uses the surname of Pius VI to refer to Luigi Chiaramonti, now Pius VII. Specifically she refers to the pope's demeaning summons from Rome "to Paris, to place the imperial crown upon [Bonaparte's] head" (*AR* 46:184).

8. HLP alludes to the treaty concluded between France and William V (1748–1806), prince of Orange, announced in the Hague on 14 August 1802. According to the treaty the prince of Nassau renounced for himself, his heirs, and successors "the dignity of Stadtholder of the United Provinces which now form the Batavian Republick." But the prince, his consort, and his children "shall enjoy all permanent or annual rents which they have in the Batavian Republick, in the same manner as other possessors of rents in the said Republick." See *GM* 72, pt. 2 (1802): 771–72; Michel Richard, *Les Orange-Nassau* (Lausanne: Editions Rencontre, 1968), pp. 264–67.

TO LADY WILLIAMS AND ELEANOR WILLIAMS

Brynbella Tuesday
13: November 1804.

We cannot Dearest Ladies make a Dinner Visit on it and if we did—it should be for your Ladyship's Sake and Mrs. Williams's, without looking further for Company. I always loved *Sir John*, and now I love him more and more for seeking so sweetly to divert his charming Lady, and drive her Cares away. We shall probably have a Sight of young Roscius at Bath if they do not kill the Child with harrassing him about So:[1] and Then you'll have my Opinion who have seen so many King Richards. We have taken our House in Laura Place[2] to enter it on New Years Day—as my Master keeps surprizingly well: if Plague follows us tho'—or meets us,—we will make haste home.[3] Your Ladyship—or Dear Mama, has often heard the old Saying that whenever the Plague appeared among us——The first Alarm was always given from *Essex*. Our public papers have possibly on that Account been double diligent to assure us that all are well on Board the *Ship so named*.[4]

Mr. Clough of Glan ŷ werne says that his Letter from a Brother he has at Gibraltar, was so smoked and impregnated with Vinegar, Tobacco &c. he could hardly bear to open it:[5] We met him at Lleweney hall, and he seemed rather lowspirited upon the Occasion, as no Wonder.

Dear Ladies Adieu! We will come and make a long Morning and take your Commands before we go,—'tis all Mr. Piozzi dares venture;—and I will write you long Letters from Bath, and contribute to Mrs. Williams's Amusement everything in the Power / of Hers and your Ladyship's / ever Faithful H: L: P.

Text: Ry. 2 (1802–6).

1. Master Betty.
2. Elizabeth Garrett's house in Bath.
3. As early as 18 September, English newspapers began to report the epidemic [of yellow fever] in the Mediterranean, the *Morning Chronicle* warning readers that "No time should be lost . . . to prevent its importation into this country."
   On 3 November *The Times* announced that yellow fever, which first appeared in Malaga, had broken out in Gibraltar and Cadiz. By 22 November the epidemic, according to the same newspaper, had reached Leghorn and other parts of Italy. Four days later, *The Times* voiced a hope that "the winter . . . will most probably put an end to this terrific scourge of the human race."
4. On 7 November the *Courier* printed an extract of a letter from Gibraltar: "The *Essex* merchant ship, in which several families had embarked . . . for England, was obliged to be left behind by the convoy now arrived, the fever having discovered itself among them."
   On the 9th *The Times* refuted the report by publishing "a letter addressed to Mr. George Paton, a respectable Merchant in the City, from his friend, a passenger on board the *Essex*." The letter, dated 6 November, stated that all were healthy on board, but that they "were prevented from entering the harbour [at Spithead] by a violent gale of wind, and have been beating about ever since till last evening [the 8th], when we were so fortunate as to reach the port."
5. A son of Richard and Patty Clough, Richard Butler of Plas Clough and Min y Don, Colwyn, received a letter from his younger brother, Hugh Powell, who was to die of yellow fever prior to 12 November at Gibraltar. For the elder Cloughs of Glan y Wern, see HLP to PSP [ca. 28] August 1801, n. 13; to Q [31 December 1804], n. 7; *The Times*, 14 December 1804.

TO THE LADIES OF LLANGOLLEN

Brynbella
24: December 1804.

Ah dear Ladies! *"Hope told a flattering Tale"*[1] when She promised us a Journey to Llangollen. Mr. Piozzi has been visited with the *severest* Fit of Gout I ever knew him to suffer: and this Scrap is written by his Bedside the 15th Day of his Confinement to a recumbent Posture.

When he *can be carried*,—it must be the shortest way to Bath;[2] where if Strength and Voice and Fingers in any Degree return, he will be happy in using them for your Ladyship's and Miss Ponsonby's Amusement next May: but in the mean Time the Hands have been hideously Maltreated, and a melancholy Hoarseness still hinders his Attendants knowing how much he Suffers.

Such Dear Ladies is our dismal Christmas: That you may enjoy this, and many more with all possible Comfort; is the constant Wish and Prayer of your

Ladyship's and Miss Ponsonby's / Much Obliged / and truly faithful Servant / H: L: Piozzi.

It is long since I have seen my Husband so well, as just before this dreadful Burst came on.

Text: Wicklow MS 4238. National Library of Ireland.

1. The first line of an anonymous four-line song that appears in the *Universal Songster,* 3 vols. (London: John Fairburn, etc., 1825–26), 1:320.
2. On 24 January 1805, a *"half recovered"* GP and HLP were to "set out for Bath: *no* Valet, & our Maid Allen but *half well*: a White Snow covering the Ground, & Mr Piozzi not able to put down his Foot" (*Thraliana* 2:1065).

TO LADY WILLIAMS

Brynbella Saturday
29: December 1804.

I *thought* my dearest Lady Williams knew nothing of our Sorrows here at Brynbella: Mr. Piozzi has been for Three Whole Weeks quite in Shrieking Agony: not so much with *Gout,* as with Three frightful Abscesses in his Foot: drawing, discharging, and succeeding each other with undescribable Anguish. At length a large Chalkstone bigger than any Nutmeg, detached itself; and Mr. Moore drew it away: so now the *Labour* is over, he will I hope have a good *Getting up* as we Women Say; and then to Bath with the next Full Moon—before which time if I can get to Bodylwyddan and see Your Ladyship and all your Darlings—*I will*— and comfort Dear Mama too, so far as I shall be able. The Poppy head Poultice with Carrot used to give *my* Mother most Ease; and sometimes a Wash called Bates's Anodyne Balsam.—The best Way is for her to amuse the Pain by frequent Changes of Application,—and divert Thought by presenting other Objects to the Mind.

See how many young People She has outlived, since the first Summons was given! God Almighty has perhaps sent this sharp Weather to save her from seeing *our own* Country visited by the Fever which rages now in Spain, Portugal and Italy[1]—which *Frost* alone can stop——and which has possibly seized and destroyed our Ambassador Mr. Aufrere tho' for *that* Strange Event I rather suspect Buonaparte.[2]

The World is full of wonders. Could Master Betty's Parents have believed— had less than an Angel told them?—how their Son at 13 years old should have so interested a Million of People that for pacifying their Fears concerning his Health a regular Bulletin should be issued every Day—as in the Case of a crowned Head.[3]

How lucky has your Ladyship been in seeing him! a Pleasure I despair of, now that we cannot go to Bath before the 14th. of January with any Propriety; and he will not be spared from London certainly after he once recovers. It is very true that the Nights are very long in remote Countries now; and the Sound of a Watchman crying Past 12 o'Clock, is comfortable to one's Ears after 8 or 9 Months Absence from Social Life: but if we had been well enough to go, There is no habitation ready for us yet in that little crouded Town, which I shall feel *so* glad to make one in; before this cold Month is ended. Even Mr. Pitt can find no Place, and how should Dear Lady Williams's every faithful / H: L: Piozzi.

Let me Dear Ladies hear of you once again before our Departure; and pray present us with Respect and Affection to Sir John and his young 'Squire, and my pretty Godson and his Sisters.

Text: Ry. 2 (1802–6). *Address*: Lady Williams / Bodylwyddan / St. Asaph. *Postmark*: St. Asaph 218.

1. Newspaper reports of the yellow fever epidemic in the Mediterranean continued into December: "The accounts from *Alicant* and *Carthagena*, of [9 November], are of the most distressing kind. The spirits of the inhabitants were completely exhausted between famine and the plague. One hundred persons continued to die daily at each place, and the havock would have been greater had the disorder appeared at an earlier period of the season" (*The Times*, 7 December).
2. HLP wrote the surname of the linguist and translator Anthony Aufrere (1756–1833) for that of John Hookham Frere (1769–1846). The latter in October 1800 had been appointed envoy extraordinary and plenipotentiary at Lisbon. In September 1802 he was transferred to Madrid. By August 1804 he was recalled because of difficulties that arose between him and Manuel de Godoy (1767–1851), príncipe de la Paz (1795), and a series of letters that passed between them. These letters were printed by the *Moniteur* to insinuate "that all the British Ministers abroad were privy to the design of assassinating Buonaparte, and that Mr. Frere had declared in public company such means to be lawful; on which the Prince of Peace made a severe answer." In the correspondence that ensued, Frere asked Godoy "to contradict the calumny of the *Moniteur*" but no contradiction appeared. See *GM* 74, pt. 2 (1804): 679–80.
3. The London debut of Master Betty was carefully planned. By 1 December he played Achmet in *Barbarossa*, by Dr. John Brown (1754; 1755), at the Covent Garden, moving to the Drury Lane on 10 December. Even before his performance, "Never, perhaps, were the expectations of the public more highly raised—never was the public curiosity so intense and ardent" (*Courier*, 3 December). The reviews of his performance as Achmet were fulsome.
By 5 December the *Courier* lamented "that the health of the Boy should be so risked by thus playing every night. . . . We are under great apprehensions for him." He was to perform again in *Barbarossa* at the Drury Lane on the 18th but did not because of an "indisposition." On 22 December *The Times* commented:
"We are sorry to be compelled to notice an act of extreme affectation, to say no worse of it, on the part of the parents of the Young Roscius. The following bulletin, we understand, was yesterday put up on the door of his lodging:—
" 'The Physicians think Master Betty is much the same this morning as yesterday.' . . ."
" 'The immense crowd of enquirers,' is no excuse for the adoption of a species of notice which is seldom resorted to by even the first of our Nobility."

TO HESTER MARIA THRALE

[31: December 1804]

My dearest Girl will see from the writing of this Letter that we have outstaid all my Pens and all my Paper,—I might almost add all my Patience too. Mr. Piozzi has but just done Shrieking, and 'tis hoarseness, not happiness makes him leave off *now*. A Succession of 3 frightful Abcesses in 3 different Parts of his Feet, have set Opiates and Pacifiers all at Defiance, and kept him nine Days without our daring to move him, or change his Linen or his Bed. Two Men, Two Women and myself did however accomplish it on the 10th Morning: when he was kept with the utmost Difficulty by dint of Wine and Cordials, from bursting in our Arms with Rage and Pain united.—but I was *so* 'fraid during that Soft mild Weather, that his Attendants would get *Putrid Fevers*. Oh that we were once at Bath was all our Cry—yet when things go badly there—God send us *safe home* do I many Times exclaim—proving the Vanity of human Wishes with Johnson and with Juvenal;[1] nay and with Gilimer the Vandal Chief: who cried out Vana Vanitas, inquit Concionator; vana Vanitas, omnia sunt Vanitas.[2] And surely the Sight of a Letter signed W. H. Betty in our Paper is beyond *all Proofs*, when it shews how a Darling Son's unexpected Fame and Fortune is incapable of rendering his Father happy who in that Letter proclaims himself *miserable*, from mere Sensibility of Blame thrown on him by a Public interested almost to Frenzy in his Child's Welfare.[3]

Well! here's a Frost thank God, and I am truly glad on't—so should *you* be—for as the Phrase is—let us beware of the *Third Time*. When Garrick's superior Excellence burst upon Mankind, There was a contagious Complaint about the Town, and People called it The Garrick Fever; in Imitation possibly of what happened at Abdera in the Days of Lysimachus 2000 years before, when a new Tragic Actor—Archelaus—drove the Spectators into a Delirium accompanied by High Pulse &c. and set them all repeating in their Beds.—Tam elegans Insania says Lucian, could not have fallen except on Men of Wit and Understanding.[4]

How lucky you are in a private Box! but I suppose the *Journey* to Covent Garden is not without its Danger.[5]——shall never get Sight of him now, for how should We arrive at Bath while he remains there! and how should he not be killed by Such Exertions!

Poor Mrs. Smyth![6] I am sorry for her; but the Gibraltar Dead List contains the names of Two or three Young Men from this Neighbourhood, whose Parents are still *more* to be pitied;[7] and *all* Sorrows must yield to those of Mrs. Greathead: I have never heard a Cause assigned for Bertie's Loss, and looking for *Causes* is but Loss of Time.[8] Did you read the last Number of the Christian Observer with the Account of the Phænomenon seen by Captain Jones?[9] Davies's Celtic Researches are very entertaining:[10] but he might have said more strange Things when he had said so many.—He proves Lleweny to have been a Druid's Grove, and *that* I like exceedingly:[11] When he was gone *Tree-Mad* however,[12] He should have recollected the Old Rabbinical Story how Abraham planted a Pine, a Fir and a Cedar, so near each other, that they grew *into* each other:—and then he might have found out what others have thought before *him*, that these were Typical of the Jewish, the Mahometan and the Christian Religions which shall join together before the last Consummation of all Things.[13]

Meanwhile Pere Pezron said much in favor of the Celtic Antiquity long ago,[14] and a Literary Friend of this Country made me observe the other Day that in our Welsh Language *Nòd* means a Mark; and that the Place Cain retired to was for that Reason called the Land of Nòd, the Land of the *Marked Man*. So God bless Dear Creatures! and good Night! *You* must look to the Frank for a Date; I hardly know Morning from Evening running up and down so, all the 24 Hours: and scarcely 4 of *them* illuminated, excepting by Candles; and my Teeth ache to Distraction beside.

Why do our Ministers Send out such Fellows as Sir George Rumbold?[15] I *must* ask *that* because we all ask one another all day long: I must also beg my dear Sophia's Excuse till another Time, but do tell her that Whitehead's Essence of Mustard rubbed on her Feet after warm bathing, would be likely to quicken the Circulation;—charging her at the same time to do nothing without Dr. Vaughan's Leave:—he seems to be right in his Notions of her Case, and God give him the Success desired and prayed for[16]—by hers and Yours and Susan's ever Affectionate / H: L: P.

Text: Bowood Collection. *Address*: Miss Thrale / 13 Great Cumberland Street / London. *Postmark*: franked by Lord De Blaquiere, Denbigh December Thirty one 1804; 2 January 1805.

1. SJ's poem is an "imitation" of Juvenal's *Tenth Satire*.
2. Gelimer, who lived in the sixth century, was the last king of the Vandals in Africa. Usurping the throne of Hilderic in 530, he was himself taken prisoner by the Byzantine general Belisarius in 534. He was made to participate in Belisarius's triumph at Constantinople in the same year and spent his remaining years on an estate in Galatia, provided by the Emperor Justinian I. See *Retrospection* 1:160 and n. See also Gibbon's *History of the Decline and Fall of the Roman Empire*, ed. J.B. Bury, 7 vols. (London: Methuen, 1923), 4:45.
3. The *Morning Post*, 19 December, reported that in canceling Betty's appearance as Achmet on the 18th, "the Manager read from a letter written . . . by the boy's father, W. Henry Betty. '. . . I did not conceive yesterday that my son's indisposition would have prevented his appearance this evening, or my regard for the interest of the Theatre and my respect for the Public, who patronize him with such unparalleled generosity, would have caused me instantly to have apprised you of it.'"
A few days earlier the boy's father dismissed overtures from the Lewes Theatre to have the Young Roscius perform there. The letter of dismissal was written by a Mr. Hough (the boy's tutor): "I have conversed with the father upon the subject, the result is, that as he has been highly blamed for suffering his son's playing six successive nights in Covent-Garden, *he must decline your polite offer*, which, he confesses, is very liberal" (*The Times*, 19 December).
4. Often translated into Latin as *Luciani Samosatensis Quomodo Historia Conscribenda Sit* (e.g., in 1776), the text of the anecdote uses phrases and words like *in ridiculam, delirio, morbus*, and *febri* which were summarized in the phrase *tam elegans Insania*. For the anecdote itself, see *The Way to Write History* in *The Works of Lucian of Samosata*, trans. H. W. and F. G. Fowler, 4 vols. (Oxford: Clarendon Press, 1905), 2:109.
5. HLP was aware of the crowds and tumult attendant upon Master Betty's perform-

ances. On his first night at Covent Garden, the crowds were so great that "the Violence of the candidates for places, broke through all *decorum*, and literally carried the boxes by *storm*." Although police and guards were employed to maintain order, they could not "controul . . . the torrent which poured into the theatre. The accidents were mostly confined to the loss and destruction of apparel. . . . A number of persons *fainted* through excessive exertion, or the violence of the pressure, and were carried out of the house. . . . Some additional precautions are, however, necessary, and we suppose will be *attended to*" (*The Times,* 3 December).

6. Jane Smyth, of Heath House, near Bristol, was still grieving for her husband, Thomas, who had died 11 March 1800. In addition, she mourned the death of Thomas's brother, Sir John Hugh Smyth (ca. 1753–30 March 1802), of Long Ashton, county Somerset.

See HLP to Q [23 May 1801], n. 14; *AR* 44 (1802): 503.

7. Only on 14 December did *The Times* print the names of British officers who died of yellow fever at Gibraltar prior to 12 November 1804. Forty names appeared on the Dead List, among whom was Ensign Hugh Powell Clough (b. 1783), son of Richard and Patty Clough, and a Lieutenant "Smith" of the Queen's Regiment.

8. After an illness "of some days," Bertie Greatheed, "aged 23," died at Vicenza on 8 October. As HLP commented in *Thraliana* 2:1063 n.1: "The Mother had best die too! her Pride, her Pleasure, *her* Importance is all gone." See *GM* 74, pt. 2 (1804): 1073, 1236.

9. HLP has in mind vol. 3 (November 1804) of *The Christian Observer,* conducted by Members of the Established Church (London: John Hatchard, 1804), 3:669, 673–74. "A Lady who resides near Milford Haven" reports a vision "seen by Captain Jones, of the James Tender, lying at Milford. He says, that on Thursday the 19th July last, about six or seven o'clock in the evening, he saw the vision of seven ships in the element at the harbour's mouth in action, and could distinguish the French and English colours; after an hour's action, an angel appeared with a trumpet, which, when he blew, all vanished away. The captain called all the impressed men out of the hold, who saw them as well as himself" (p. 669).

Several pages later an explanation of the vision appears. "It is probable, that at the time when Captain Jones was contemplating with astonishment the appearance of ships in the air, several ships were passing at a distance, and these, from the particular constitution of the atmosphere at that period, were represented as being not very remote from Milford Haven. Their quick motions might be mistaken for naval manœuvres, and to a mind under the influence of surprise and consternation, a cloud in a fantastic shape might be easily metamorphosed into an angel with a trumpet" (p. 673).

10. Edward Davies (1756–1831), *Celtic Researches, on the Origin, Traditions & Language, of the Ancient Britons* (London: Printed for the Author, and sold by J. Booth, Duke-Street, Portland-Place, 1804). Davies, a cleric and an antiquarian, was known as "Celtic Davies."

11. While Davies does not mention Lleweni by name, he does write about heavily wooded lands whose owners would provide some of the leaders of ancient Wales; those he called "Bards" or "Sages." Moreover, since HLP regarded herself as part of the Celtic tradition, she would "like exceedingly" that her Druid ancestors were "the jealous preservers" of early and primitive discipline, traditions, doctrines, customs and opinions" (p. 150).

12. The thrust of his argument may be found on pp. 308–9.

"We can trace, uniformly, in the figures of speech, in the terms, the customs, traditions, and superstitions of antiquity . . . the vestiges of *symbols,* adopted from various kinds of *trees,* and communicating ideas, by *parts* of those *trees.* We find, that *rods,* and *springs,* in some way, or another, have represented the first principles of speech, learning, and science." HLP's attitude toward Davies's linguistic research was one of interest tinged with mild disbelief.

13. The story (with modification) is told by Eustace Budgell in *Spectator* 589. "There is an old Tradition, that *Abraham* planted a *Cyprus,* a *Pine,* and a *Cedar,* and that these three incorporated into one Tree, which was cut down for the building of the Temple of

Solomon." (The statement of the tradition was derived from Bayle, art. "Abraham, Remark T.")

In the margin of her *Spectator* (8:180), HLP had written: "If there is such old Tradition, it had certainly some reference to the Three Nations that sprung from him, *Jews, Tartars,* and *Gentoos.*"

14. Paul Yves Pezron, *The Antiquities of the Nations, more particularly of the Celtae or Gauls, taken to be originally the same people as our Ancient Britains* . . . Englished by Mr. Jones (London: S. Ballard and R. Burrough, 1706).

15. George Berriman Rumbold (1764–1807), second baronet (1791), had entered the diplomatic service and in 1803 became ambassador to the Hanse Towns and minister residentiary of Great Britain at Hamburg. On 25 October, a detachment of 250 French troops landed in boats on the Hamburg Berg, went to the Grindel, Rumbold's country residence, entered his house and seized his papers. Taken to Hanover in a guarded coach, he was then moved to Paris and imprisoned in the Temple for a single day. Thereafter he was put on a French cutter at Cherbourg sailing under a flag of truce and transferred to the English frigate *Niobe,* which brought Rumbold to Portsmouth.

Like other English diplomats at this time, Sir George was charged by Fouché with having masterminded an anti-Bonaparte conspiracy. See *GM* 74, pt. 2 (1804): 1063–64, 1159–60.

16. Henry Vaughan (1766–1844) graduated from Christ Church, Oxford, with a B.A. in 1788 and an M.D. in 1791. He settled in London, was elected physician to the Middlesex Hospital, and appointed physician extraordinary to the king in 1793. In the following year he was made a fellow of the Royal College of Physicians. In 1809 he was to change his name from Vaughan to Halford by act of Parliament. George III, who liked and admired him, created him a baronet in the same year.

Index

To avoid undue crowding, or repetitions from earlier volumes, dates related to individuals have at times been omitted from annotations. For ready reference, wherever appropriate, those dates are supplied within the index.

Members of the British nobility are listed under family names with cross references from titles.

Members of the French, Italian, and other European nobility are listed under the names and titles by which they are usually known, with cross references, if necessary, from other names and titles.

Names of major figures in the correspondence are designated by abbreviations (e.g. Samuel Johnson = SJ). For list of abbreviations, see pp. 41–42.

Abbess (or Abbiss), Joyce, 131, 134 n.4, 174, 203
Abercorn. *See* Hamilton
Abercromby (or Abercrombie), Sir Ralph (1734–1801), 127 n.4, 276, 277 n.4, 283, 346 n.6
Abington (Abingdon), Frances (1737–1815) (actress), 465
Aboyne. *See* Gordon
Abrahams (or Abraham), William (d. 1804), and his wife Eliza, 357, 359 n.13
Abrantes, duc d'. *See* Junot
Acerbi, Joseph: *Travels Through Sweden, Finland, and Lapland*, 469, 473 nn. 10 and 12
Achmet (sultan), 284 n.5
Adams, Jane, née Owen (fl. 1758–1810), 475, 476 n.5
Adams, Susan (ca. 1786–1804), 475, 476 n.5
Adams, Rev. Tobias (d. 1805), 476 n.5
Addington, Henry (1757–1844), first Viscount Sidmouth, 17, 19, 22, 414 n.6, 418 n.6, 429, 430 n.10, 436, 437 n.8
Addison, Joseph, 99 n.11, 338
Adolphus, John: *Biographical Memoirs of the French Revolution*, 85, 86 n.11
Albani, Alessandro (1692–1779), Cardinal: villa of, 55, 57 n.11
Albany. *See* Louisa, princess of Stolberg-Gedern, countess of Albany
Albemarle. *See* Monck (Monk)

Alberto Maria (1792–98), prince of Naples, 55, 57 nn. 9 and 10
Aldborough. *See* Stratford
Aldus (Aldo), of Aldine Press. *See* Mannucci
Alexander I (czar of Russia), 305 n.10, 329, 426, 427 n.2
Alexander IV (pope). *See* Rinaldo
Alfieri, conte Vittorio (1749–1803), 124 n.6, 128, 149; duel with viscount Ligonier, 135, 136 n.1. *See also* Ligonier, Penelope; Louisa, princess of Stolberg-Gedern, countess of Albany
Allen, Elener (maid), 121, 174, 392, 405, 407, 455, 459, 482 n.2
Alleyne, Abel, of Four Hills, Barbados (father of Jane, Lady Alleyne), 105, 107 n.5
Alleyne, Abel (d. 1812) (son of Sir John Gay Alleyne), 105, 107 n.5
Alleyne, Christian Dottin (d. 1873) (daughter of Sir John Gay Alleyne; married [1829] Rev. Henry Withy), 105, 107 n.5
Alleyne, Jane Abel, Lady (née Alleyne; second wife of Sir John Gay Alleyne) (d. 1800), 105, 107 n.5
Alleyne, Jane Gay (daughter of Sir John Gay Alleyne), 105, 107 n.5
Alleyne, Sir John Gay (1724–1801), baronet, 107 n.5
Alleyne, John Gay (1787–1800) (son of Sir John Gay Alleyne), 107 n.5

488

Alleyne, Mary Spire (daughter of Sir John Gay Alleyne), 105, 107 n.5
Alleyne, Rebecca Braithwaite (d. 1846) (daughter of Sir John Gay Alleyne; married William Bovil), 105, 107 n.5
Alleyne, Sir Reynold Abel, second baronet (1789–1870) (son of Sir John Gay Alleyne), 107 n.5
Allingham, Maria Caroline (d. 1811): marriage to Samuel Ricketts, 103, 104 n.13
Almon, John (1737–1805) (bookseller), 241 n.2
Andreaux, adjutant-general, 200–201 n.4
Andréossi, Gen. Antoine-François (1761–1828), comte, 412 n.3
Andrews, Miles Peter (d. 1814) (dramatist), 57 n.5, 308, 309 n.15, 311, 357
Angelucci, Father, 247, 248 n.9
Angoulême, Louis-Antoine de Bourbon, duc d', 372, 373 n.5
Angoulême, Marie-Thérèse-Charlotte de France, Mme d', 194, 196 n.16
Angus. *See* Douglas
Anstey, Lucretia (Light), née Luders, 293–94, 295 n.10
Anstey, Capt. Robert (ca. 1760–1818), son of Bath poet, Christopher Anstey, 295 n.10
Antigonus I (Cyclops), 380, 382 n.15
Antigonus II (Gonatas), 380, 382 n.15
Antiochus Soter, 290, 292 n.9, 297
Antoninus Pius (Roman emperor), 455, 456 n.1
Anville, Jean-Baptiste Bourguinon d' (1697–1782): *Compendium of Ancient Geography*, 290, 291 n.2, 296
Apreece, Thomas George, 88 and n.5
Araciel, Giuseppe, marchese de, 74, 77 n.11
Archelaus (ancient tragic actor), 484
Archimedes (ca. 287–212 B.C.), 184
Arden. *See* Perceval, Charles George
Argent, Mrs. (Lady Pitches's maid), 164
Armistead, Elizabeth (mistress and later wife of Charles James Fox). *See* Fox, Elizabeth
Armstrong, Sgt. Benjamin, 343–44 n.3
Armstrong, John Warneford (Irish informant), 389 n.7
Artois, Charles-Philippe, comte d' (1757–1836) (later Charles X, king of the French), 110 nn. 4, 5, and 6, 428 n.2
Astley, John, of Cheshire, 241 n.2
Aufrere, Anthony (linguist and translator), 482, 483 n.2

Augereau, Maréchal Pierre-François-Charles, duc de Castiglione (1757–1816), 432 n.2
Augusta Sophia, Princess (1768–1840), 59 n.5
Aulus Gellius: story of the lion and the slave, 293, 295 n.8
Aurelius Valerius Constantius. *See* Chlorus, Aurelius Valerius Constantius
Aventine (or Aventinus). *See* Turmair
Ayral, Bonneville, 359 n.17

Bagot, Charles Chester (later Chester) (1730–93), and his wife Catherine, née Legge (d. 1819), 282 n.2
Bagot, Lewis, bishop of St. Asaph, 106, 107 n.13, 201, 272, 273 n.5, 336, 341 n.3, 372, 373 n.2, 374, 414 n.8, 422 n.16; *Twelve Discourses on the Prophecies*, 263, 264 n.1
Bagshaw, George, 161 n.9
Bagshaw, Richard (fl. 1798–1817), of Bagshaw and Sons, London, 161, 162 n.9
Bagshaw, Thomas, 161 n.9
Baillie, Joanna: *The Election*, 348 n.1; *Ethwald*, 347, 348 n.1; *Plays on the Passions*, 85, 86 n.6, 103, 166, 167 n.12, 192, 198, 199 nn. 2 and 3, 347, 348 n.1; *The Second Marriage*, 348 n.1
Baird, Gen. Sir David (1757–1829), 304 n.1
Baker-Holroyd (formerly Holroyd), John (1735–1821), first earl of Sheffield, 403 n.1
Ball, Rear Adm. Sir Alexander John (1757–1809), baronet, 283, 284 n.3
Banks, Sir Joseph (naturalist and explorer): contributions to *Philosophical Transactions*, 78; *Voyages . . . in the Southern Hemisphere*, 80–81 nn. 12 and 13, 213, 214 n.2
Banti, Brigitta Zaccarria, née Giorgi (ca. 1756–1806) (operatic soprano), 356 and n.2
Barber, John Thomas, 410, 411 n.1
Baretti, Giuseppe, 414
Barnes, Edward: translation of Hannah More's *Village Politics* into Welsh, 282 n.4
Barras, Vicomte Paul-François-Nicolas de, of the Directory, 95 n.8, 463 n.7
Barrington, Daines: "Observations on . . . Card-playing in England," 135, 137 n.5
Barrington (Waldron), George, the pickpocket, 78, 80 n.9
Barrington, Jane, née Guise (d. 1807) (second wife of Bishop Shute Barrington), 353, 354 n.4

Barrington, Shute, bishop of Durham, 193n.6
Barry, Col. Henry, 240, 241n.3
Barry, Spranger (1719–77) (actor), 287, 289n.13, 354n.9, 435
Bates's *Anodyne Balsam* (home remedy), 482
Bath. *See* Thynne
Bath and Wells, bishop of. *See* Moss, Charles
Battles and treaties. *See* Piozzi, Hester Lynch, née Salusbury (Thrale) (HLP): on battles; on treaties
Baudiment, Agnès de, dame de Braine (Braisne), third wife of Robert, comte de Dreux (12th cent.), 118, 119n.5
Bayle, Pierre, 487n.13
Bayne, Alicia: *Memorials of the Thackeray Family* (with Jane Townley Pryme) 473n.15
Bayntun, Sophia, née Mayhew (presumably wife of Sir Henry William Bayntun), 344n.7
Beauchamp. *See* Lygon
Beauharnais, Viceroi Eugène de (1781–1824) (stepson and aide-de-camp of Napoleon), 149, 151n.2
Beauvais, bishop of. *See* Dreux, Philippe de
Beaver, Philip, of Bulama, 189, 190n.5
Beckwith, Mrs. *See* Davies, Mrs. Thomas
Beddoes, Thomas (1760–1808), M.D.: *Notice of some Observations made at the Medical Pneumatic Institution*, 185, 188
Bedford. *See* Russell
Beechey, Sir William (1753–1839): portrait of Thomas Cadell by, 208
Belgrand de Vaubois, Gen. Charles-Henri, comte de, 152, 153n.5
Belisarius (liberator of Rome), 485n.2
Bell, Capt. Alexander, 152, 153n.5
Bellamy, Thomas, 82, 83n.7
Bentinck, William Henry Cavendish (1738–1809), third duke of Portland, 141n.4, 232n.4, 390n.3
Bentley, Richard (1662–1742), 341n.6
Bentley, Richard (1748 or 1749–1831): *A Few Cursory Remarks* (on Pitt), 430–31n.10
Berain. *See* Katherine of Berain
Bere, Rev. Thomas, and Blagdon controversy, 249n.1, 301–2n.8, 307, 341n.8, 345–46n.2
Berkeley, Augustus (1715/16–55), fourth earl of Berkeley, 58, 59n.3
Berkeley, Lady Elizabeth (Craven). *See* Elizabeth Berkeley (Craven), margravine of Brandenburgh-Anspach

Bernini, Giovanni Lorenzo, 386n.2
Berquin, Arnaud (ca. 1749–91): *L'Ami des Enfans*, 322, 323n.4
Berri (Berry), Charles Ferdinand de Bourbon (1778–1820), duc de, 110n.5
Berry, Rear Adm. Sir Edward (1768–1831), first baronet, 283, 284n.3
Berthier, Gen. Louis-Alexandre (1753–1815), 206n.2, 332n.12, 346n.6
Bertie, Gen. Albemarle, ninth earl of Lindsey, 467n.2
Bertie, Charlotte Susanna, née Layard, Lady Lindsey (wife of Gen. Albemarle Bertie), 467n.2
Betty (Piozzi maid), 455
Betty, William Henry West (1791–1874) ("Young Roscius"), 435, 436n.2, 480, 482, 483n.3, 484, 485n.3
Bevan, Catherine (d. 1811) (pastry cook in Bath), 262, 263n.6
Bianchi, Francesco (composer and harpsichordist), 226n.1
Bible: Abraham, 484–85 and nn. 12 and 13; analogies between Joseph and Jesus, 290, 292nn. 8 and 10, 297; Esdras, 459
—books of: Acts, 61, 64n.16; 1 Chronicles, 97, 98n.9, 180, 182n.4, 449, 450n.2; 1 Corinthians, 400, 401n.3; Daniel, 293, 294n.3; Exodus, 180, 182n.6; Genesis, 61, 64n.14, 349, 350n.8; Habakkuk, 459; John, 383, 384n.4; Judges, 333, 335n.4; Luke, 61, 64n.10, 400, 401n.5; Matthew, 400, 401nn. 3 and 5; Numbers, 61, 64n.15; Psalms, 69, 70n.2; Revelation, 61, 64n.14, 383, 384n.4; 1 Samuel, 180, 182n.6; 2 Samuel, 97, 98n.9, 180, 182n.4
Bickerstaffe, Isaac: *The Maid of the Mill*, 300, 302n.11; *Love in a Village*, 344n.5
Biddulph, Charlotte, née Middleton (d. 1843), 141, 142n.8, 253 and n.5
Biddulph, Robert (d. 1814) (husband of Charlotte Middleton of Chirk Castle), 253n.5
Bigland, Ralph: *Historical, Monumental and Genealogical Collections, Relative to the County of Gloucester*, 377, 381n.4
Billington, Elizabeth, née Weichel (ca. 1765–1818), 342, 344n.5, 356, 358n.3, 360
Bingley, Rev. William: *Animal Biography*, 429, 430n.4
Birch, Sir Joseph (1755–1833), first baronet, 373n.6
Bird, William Wilberforce (ca. 1759–1836), M.P. for Coventry (1796–1802), 252nn. 6 and 7

Blagdon, Francis: translation of *Denon's Travels*, 400, 402 n.13
Blagdon controversy, 249–50 n.3
Blaquiere. *See* De Blaquiere
Blount, Charles, eighth baron Mountjoy, first earl of Devonshire, 420 n.4
Bobadill (Bobadil), Capt. (character in Jonson, *Every Man in his Humour*), 421 n.9
Boccaccio, Giovanni, 81, 150, 151 n.12
Boileau-Despréaux, Nicolas (1636–1711), 293, 295 nn. 5 and 6
Broisrobert, François le Métel de, abbé, 96, 98 n.4
Bompard, Commodore Jean-Baptiste-François, 107 n.7
Bonaparte, Apollyon, 298 n.1
Bonaparte, Carlo (d. 1785) (father of Napoleon), 171, 173 n.14
Bonaparte, Hortense-Eugénie-Cecile (1783–1837), daughter of Alexandre-François-Marie, vicomte de Beauharnais, 373 n.3
Bonaparte, Jérôme (1784–1860), 373 n.3
Bonaparte, Joseph (1768–1844), 373 n.3
Bonaparte, Joséphine, née Marie-Josèphe-Rose Tascher de La Pagerie (Beauharnais) (1763–1814), 194, 196 nn. 15 and 16
Bonaparte, Lucien (1775–1840), 373 n.3
Bonaparte, Maria Letizia, née Ramolina (ca. 1750–1836) (wife of Carlo Bonaparte and mother of Napoleon), 171, 173 n.14
Bonaparte, Marie-Anne-Elisha, 373 n.2
Bonaparte, Marie-Annonciade-Caroline, 373 n.2
Bonaparte, Marie-Pauline, 373 n.2
Bonaparte, Napoleon, 89, 91 n.3, 181, 333, 408, 448 and n.2, 450 n.3; advancement and titles for family members, 374; attendance at Easter services in church, 351, 352 n.8, 402; conspiracies and assassination attempts against, 287, 459, 460 nn. 4 and 5, 483 n.2; and creation of Cisalpine Republic, 206 n.2; and defeat of Danes at Copenhagen, 276; as Emperor of France, 20, 24, 113, 358, 359 n.17, 373 n.4, 396 n.9, 469, 472 nn. 3 and 5; evacuation of Malta and Egypt, 240, 241 n.6; executions ordered by, 343, 344 nn. 10 and 11, 465–66 n.2; as First Consul, 94, 95 n.8, 128 n.9, 154, 155 n.2, 373 nn. 3 and 4; global ambitions and plans to invade England, 281 and n.2, 329, 417 n.3, 431, 439, 440 n.3, 446–47; HLP's titles for, 23; letter to Gen. Jean-Baptiste Kléber, 178, 179 n.4; his name and parentage, 173 n.14, 259–60 n.2; overtures to Catholic Church, 367, 369 n.5; and peace negotiations with Britain, 158, 159 n.1, 165, 166 n.2, 426, 472 n.2; retreat from Turkey to Egypt, 109, 111 n.14; his second conquest of Italy, 330, 332 nn. 11 and 12; siege of Genoa, 194, 196 n.17; and use of actors and dancers to entertain conquered countries, 71 and n.3
Bond, Oliver, 18
Borromeo, Cardinal Federico (1564–1631), archbishop of Milan, 130 n.14
Bosanquet, Joseph (London merchant and banker): *Address* [at a] *Meeting of Merchants (1803)*, 423, 425 n.8
Bossi, Abaté Giuseppe, 74, 76 n.11
Boswell, James, the Younger (1778–1822): and third variorum edn. of *Plays and Poems* of Shakespeare, with Edmond Malone, 137 n.6
Botticini, Francesco (1446–98): illustrations for *La città di vita*, 130–31 n.15
Bourbon. *See* under individual names of royal family
Bourdieu, Anne (d. 1798), 89 n.6
Bourdieu, John (barrister), 88–89 n.6
Bourdieu, William, 88 and n.6
Bourgeois, Lewis and David (London perfumers), 431, 432–33 n.4
Bourguignon d'Anville. *See* Anville.
Boussay, Jacques-François de (1750–1810), baron de Menou, 276, 277 n.4, 280
Bovi, Marino (b. 1758): engraving of Violet's miniature of HLP, 246 n.5
Bowdler, Elizabeth Stuart (d. ca. 1800) (mother of Harriet): *Practical Observations on the Revelations of St. John*, 67 n.11
Bowdler, Harriet (Henrietta Maria) (1754–1830) (religious writer), 67 n.11, 390, 391 n.5; *Poems and Essays* and *Doctrines and Duties of Christianity*, 69 n.11, 124, 125 n.3, 422 n.18
Bowdler, John, the elder (1746–1823) (brother of Harriet): *Reform or Ruin*, 67 n.11
Bowdler, Thomas (d. 1785) (married Elizabeth Stuart, 1742; father of Harriet), 67 n.11
Bowdler, Thomas (1754–1825) (brother of Harriet): ed. *Family Shakespeare*, 391 n.5
Bowen, William (apothecary), 404 and n.2
Boycott, Philadelphia, née Cotton (aunt of HLP): bequest to HLS, 183, 184 n.2
Boyd, Walter (ca. 1754–1837) (banker): *A Letter to Pitt on . . . the Stoppage of Issues in Specie*, 269 nn. 3 and 4

Boyer, Gen. Pierre-François-Xavier de (1772–1851), 456 and n.4
Boyle, Edmund, seventh earl of Corke and Orrery, 323, 324n.2, 359n.10
Boyle, Mary, née Monckton (1746–1840) (second wife of Edmund Boyle, seventh earl of Corke and Orrery), 357, 359n.10, 382, 384n.1
Bradford, Rev. William, of Lleweni: letter to, 404n.1
Bradford. *See also* Bridgeman
Brand, John: *Observations on the Popular Antiquities of Great Britain*, 84n.11
Brandenburgh-Anspach. *See* Christian Frederick, margrave of Brandenburgh-Anspach; Elizabeth Berkeley (Craven), margravine of Brandenburgh-Anspach
Braschi, Giovanni Angelo. *See* Pius VI
Brickdale, Elizabeth (1766–1805): marriage to Dr. George Crossman, 323, 324n.4
Bridgeman, Charles Orlando (1794–1827), 226n.5, 247
Bridgeman, Elizabeth, née Simpson (1735–1806), dowager Lady Bradford (wife of Lord Henry Bridgeman), 148, 248, 264, 267; "croaker" tendencies of, 247, 450; husband's death, 199, 200n.1, 207; illnesses of, 69, 90
Bridgeman, Rev. George (1765–1832) (brother of Orlando), 324n.2
Bridgeman, George Augustus (1789–1865), 226n.5, 247
Bridgeman, Henry (1725–1800), first baron Bradford of Bradford (1794): death of, 201 and n.1, 207, 211n.13; bishop of St. Asaph on, 201
Bridgeman, Henry Edmund (1795–1872), 226n.5, 247
Bridgeman, Lucy Elizabeth, née Byng (1766–1844), Lady Bradford (wife of Orlando Bridgeman), 350, 351n.1. *See also* Bridgeman, Orlando
Bridgeman, Lady Lucy Isabella, née Boyle (wife of George Bridgeman), 323, 324n.2; death of, 323, 324n.2
Bridgeman, Orlando (1762–1825), second Baron Bradford (later Viscount Newport and earl of Bradford), 200, 201n.5, 210, 351n.1, 420n.2, 431; children of, 127n.6, 226n.5, 247; family seats of, 220, 221n.2, 267
Bridgeman, Orlando Henry (1794–1827), 226n.5, 247
Bridport. *See* Hood

Bristol. *See* Hervey
Broadhead, Theodore, letter to, 256n.2
Broadwood, John (pianoforte manufacturer), 363n.9
Brooke, Charlotte, 136, 138n.14; *Reliques of Irish Poetry*, 136, 138n.14, 150
Brooke, Henry, 138n.14
Brooke. *See also* Greville
Browne, Charlotte, née Dillon, Lady, 337n.2
Browne, Mary, née Aylmer, Lady, 337n.2
Browne, Valentine, baron of Castlerosse and viscount Kenmare [I.], 336, 337n.2
Browne, William George (1768–1813) (African explorer), 94–95 and nn. 2, 3, and 4, 105n.19
Bruce, Charles (1732–71), fifth earl of Elgin, 224n.4, 458n.13, 459, 460n.3
Bruce, Charles Andrew (1768–1810), governor of Prince of Wales Island, 354n.2
Bruce, Martha, née White, Lady Elgin (governess to Princess Charlotte Augusta, daughter of the Prince and Princess of Wales), 224n.4
Bruce, Thomas, seventh earl of Elgin and eleventh earl of Kincardine, 457, 458nn. 12 and 13, 459, 460n.3
Brunet's Hotel, Leicester Square, London, 342, 344
Bruslart, Louis Guérin, baron de (1764–1829) (émigré; aide de camp to duc de Bourbon; commander-in-chief of royal army under Condé in Normandy), 166–67n.7
Bruys, François: *Éloge historique du Prince Eugène* and *Histoires des Papes*. 149, 151n.2
Buckingham. *See* Villiers
Buckinghamshire. *See* Hobart
Budgell, Eustace: *Spectator No. 589*, 486n.13
Bull, John (bookseller in Bath), 64n.21
Bullock, Richard (1729–1809) (rector of St. Leonard's Church, Streatham, and St. Paul's, Covent Garden), 144n.8
Bunyan, John, 136
Burdett, Sir Francis, 89; and Middlesex election, 367, 368, 371n.2, 373–74n.6
Burdett, Sophia, née Coutts, Lady (wife of Sir Francis), 91n.4
Burges, Mary Anne (1763–1813): *The Progress of Pilgrim Good-Intent, in Jacobinical Times*, 186, 186–87n.6
Burney, Charles (CB), 99n.11
Burney, Rev. Charles, Jr., 61, 310, 311n.5

Burney, Frances ("Fanny") (FB) (later Mme d'Arblay) (FBA), 315
Burton, Laura (or Lora) (1740–1812): marriage to John Dawnay, 325, 326n.2
Burton, Rev. Robert (1577–1640): *The Anatomy of Melancholy*, 376, 377n.5
Burton, Sir Robert (ca. 1738–1810), M.P., 403 and n.2
Bushnell, David, 350n.10
Bute. *See* Stuart, John
Butler, Charles (1750–1832) (barrister), 185, 186n.1, 191, 193n.10
Butler, Lady Eleanor. *See* Llangollen, Ladies of
Butler, Samuel (1612–80): *The Rehearsal*, 226n.3
Byng, George (1740–1812), fourth viscount Torrington, 351n.1
Byng, George (1764–1847), M.P. Middlesex (1790–1847), 371n.2, 373–74n.6
Byron, Sophia, née Trevannion, 127n.6

Cadell, Thomas: portrait of by Beechey, 208; publishes HLP's *Anecdotes, Observations,* and *Letters,* 209n.5
Cadoudal, Georges (1771–1804) (anti-Bonapartist), 23, 25n.46, 460n.4, 465n.3, 474, 475n.1
Calder, Sir Henry (1740–92), baronet, 411n.7
Calder, Sir Henry Roddam (1790–1868), baronet, 411n.7
Calder, Louisa, née Osborne, Lady (d. post 1800) (second wife of Sir Henry), 411n.7
Callinicus (Callinicos) of Heliopolis (fl. ca. 673 A.D.), 184 and n.4
Cambacérès, Jean-Jacques-Regis de (1753–1824), duc de Parme, 95n.8
Camden, William: *Britannia Sive florentissimorum regnorum,* 328, 329n.9, 380n.3
Camelford. *See* Pitt, Thomas
Canning, George (1770–1827) (statesman, poet), 21, 414n.6
Capet, Hugh (938–96), 393 and n.3
Carless, Joseph (mayor of Shrewsbury), 173, 174–75n.4
Carleton, Hugh (1739–1826), viscount (Irish judge; lord chief justice), 389n.7
Carlo Emanuele IV (1751–1819) (king of Sardinia, 1796–1802), 55, 57nn. 7 and 8, 242, 243n.5
Carnarvon. *See* Herbert
Carnot, Lazare-Nicolas-Marguerite (1753–1823), 23, 298n.1, 469, 472n.3

Caroline Amelia Elizabeth, Princess of Wales (1768–1821), 213, 214n.1, 361, 363n.8
Carrick, Andrew (1767–1837) (M.D. in Clifton and Bristol), 182–83n.11, 245
Carrick Caroline, née Tudway (second wife of Andrew Carrick), 182–83n.11
Carrick, Elizabeth, née Hillier (first wife of Andrew Carrick), 182–83n.11
Carryll, Mary (fl. 1778–1809) (servant of the Ladies of Llangollen), 273, 274n.9
Carter (London fishmonger), 210
Casaubon, Isaac: editor of Polyaenus's *Stratagems of War* (1589), 290, 292nn. 5 and 7, 296
Case, Hester, of Ludlow (Bath visitor and friend of PSP), 155, 156n.2, 203, 215, 299, 301n.7, 390, 391n.4, 415–16n.5
Castéra, Jean Henri: *The Life of Catherine II,* 81–82, 83n.1, 89
Castiglione. *See* Augereau
Castlereagh. *See* Stewart
Castlerosse. *See* Browne
Castries, Jean-François-Anne-Henri-Louis de la Croix de Castries, duc de (1763–1817) (maréchal de camp), 110n.6
Cathcart, Charles, ninth baron Cathcart, 230n.10
Cathcart, Jean, née Hamilton, Lady, 230n.10
Cathcart, Louisa (Murray) (1758–1843), *suo jure* countess of Mansfield, 228, 229nn. 8 and 9, 230n.10
Cathcart. *See also* Greville
Catherine of Valois, daughter of Charles VI (king of France), wife of Henry V (king of England), and of Owen Tudor, 216, 217n.13, 420n.5
Catherine II (1729–96) (empress of Russia), 81, 83n.1, 89, 289–90n.18
Cator, John (1728–1806) (a guardian of the Thrale daughters), 302, 334; and Crowmarsh Battle estate, 146–47nn. 1 and 3, 197, 202
Caulfield, James, fourth viscount Charlemont, earl of Charlemont, 125n.4
Cavendish, Georgiana, née Spencer (1757–1806), duchess of Devonshire, 389n.3, 448n.1
Cervantes Saavedra, Miguel de: *Don Quixote,* 313, 314n.8
Championnet, Jean-Étienne (1762–1800), 57n.9, 71n.2, 128, 130n.5, 332n.12
Champneys, Charlotte Margaret, née

Mostyn, Lady, of Flintshire, 419–20, 421 n.15
Champneys, Sir Thomas Swymmers, second baronet, 419, 421 n.15
Champollion, Jean-François: *De l'écriture, Hiératique des Anciens Egyptiens*, 381 n.7
Chappelow, Rev. Leonard (LC): letters from, 50 nn. 1 and 2, 54 nn. 2 and 3, 66 n.1, 67 nn. 6 and 8, 70 n.1, 79 nn. 1, 2, and 3, 80 n.7, 90 n.1, 110 n.9, 112 nn. 1 and 2, 127 n.6, 141 n.1, 162 n.7, 173 n.17, 195 n.1, 196 n.15, 209–11, 211 n.6, 218 n.1, 264–66, 275 nn. 2, 5, and 6, 408, 418 nn. 8 and 9, 420 nn. 1, 2, and 3, 421 n. 9, 422 n.18, 426, 427 n.1, 430 n.3, 431, 432 n.1, 435, 436 n.1, 437 n.10, 443 nn. 1, 2, and 3, 450 nn. 1 and 3, 471 nn. 1 and 2; letters to, 23, 49–51, 52–54, 65–69 and n.12, 69–70, 70–72, 78–84, 89–91, 93–95, 96–101, 108–12, 126–28, 140–42, 148–49, 152–55, 160–62, 165–68, 170–73, 177–80, 183–84, 189–90, 193–96, 199–202, 206–15, 217–18, 220–22, 224–26, 230–32, 233, 236–37, 243–44, 247–48, 267–68, 270–71, 274–76, 293–94, 302–4, 323–24, 326–29, 350–52, 372–74, 395–96, 397–98, 408–9, 411–12, 416–18, 419–22, 426–28, 431–33, 435–37, 445–46, 449–51, 468–73
—and literature: on Bible and biblical imagery, 210, 211 n.5, 437 n.10; HLP on poetry of, 100, 101 n.10; and HLP's *Retrospection*, 11, 245; sends HLP pens, books, and toothbrush, 18, 89, 90 n.1, 154; "The Sentimental Naturalist," his poem on animal kingdom, 327, 328 n.3, 469, 472 n.6; silence in re literary news, 160–61, 162 n.7; on *strigil* and *strigilis*, 54 n.2
—on national and international events: anti-Gaelic, 19; battles of Magnano and Cassano, 112 and n.2; French defeat in Italy, 187, 188 n.2; London and parliamentary news, 140–41, 142 n.5; London poor and high cost of living, possible famine, 154, 210, 231, 232 n.4; Macdonald's defeat at the Trebbia, 112 and n.2; orders *The Times* delivered to Bath, 171, 173 n.17; possible French invasion of England, 419, 420 n.3, 449–50 and n.3
—personal life: on Lucy Elizabeth and Orlando Bridgeman, 127 n.6; coach accident of, 65; on death of Lord Bradford and Lady Bridgeman, 199, 325; derivation of his name, 171, 172 n.11; estate in Norfolk (Roydon, near Diss) and residence in London ("Mouse Trap Hall"), 67 n.8, 327, 328; HLP on, 198; illnesses of, 373; as librarian of Trinity College, Cambridge, 54 n.2; at royal review in Hyde Park, 432 n.1
—travels and visits: to Brynbella, 105, 112 n.1, 419, 420 n.2; to JSPS, 109; to Streatham Park, 70; to Weston seat of Lord and Lady Bradford, 247 and n.1, 248 n.1, 323, 350
Charlemont. *See* Caulfield
Charles of Blois (fl. 14th cent.): in Dibdin's *English Fleet*, 456 n.2
Charles II (king of England, Scotland, and Ireland), 224, 387 n.4; his restoration celebrated, 411, 412 n.1
Charles VI (king of France), 419, 420 n.4
Charles IX (king of France), 382 n.16
Charles (Karl) (archduke of Austria) (1771–1847), 84, 86 n.2, 92, 94, 113, 127 n.8, 131, 132 nn. 1, 3 and 9, 149 n.4, 182 n.7
Charles Edward Stuart, Prince (the Young Pretender), 128, 129 n.2
Charlotte Augusta, Princess (1796–1817) (daughter of Prince and Princess of Wales), 223, 224 n.4, 349, 356, 365, 366 n.4
Charlotte Sophia (queen of Great Britain): birthday celebrations, 160, 161 n.5, 453 n.2
Charlton, Edmund Lechmere (1710–1805) (father of Nicholas Lechmere), 440, 441 n.8
Charlton, Edmund Lechmere (1789–1845): letter to, 357, 359 n.8
Charlton, Elizabeth, née Whitmore (d. 1803) (second wife of Edmund Lechmere, 1710–1805; stepmother of Nicholas Lechmere), 440, 441 n.9
Charlton, Sir Francis, fourth baronet, 441 n.8
Charlton, Mary: *The Wife and the Mistress* (novel), 403 and n.4
Charlton, Nicholas Lechmere (1733–1807), 440, 441 n.9
Charlton, Susanna, née Case (wife of Nicholas Lechmere), 441 nn. 8 and 9
Chartres, duc de. *See* Louis-Philippe (1773–1850)
Chatham. *See* Pitt
Chester, Capt. Charles, 281, 282 n.3
Chiaramonti, Gregorio Luigi Barnabà. *See* Pius VII
Chichester. *See* Pelham
Chlorus, Aurelius Valerius Constantius, 61, 64 n.12, 310, 311 n.4

Choiseul, Marie-Gabriel-Florent-Auguste de (1752–1817), comte de Choiseul-Gouffier, 110 n.6
Christian Frederick, margrave of Brandenburgh-Anspach and Bayreuth, 58, 59 n.3
Churchill, Lady Louisa Augusta, née Greville, 442, 443 n.5
Churchill, William, 442, 443 n.5
Churton, Rev. Ralph (1754–1831): *A Sermon preached before . . . Oxford* (19 April 1793), 460 n.2
Cibber, Colley (1671–1757), 195 n.2
Cibber, Susannah Maria, née Arne (actress), 353, 354 nn. 8 and 9
Cicero, Marcus Tullius: *Tusculan Disputations*, 348 n.4
Cinthio. *See* Giraldi
Cisner, Nicholas, 292 n.11
Clarence, Duke of. *See* William IV
Clarges, Louisa, née Skrine, Lady (widow of Sir Thomas, third baronet), 119, 120 n.10, 477–78 and n.2
Clarges, Sir Thomas (1721–53), 92, 93 n.3
Clarges, Sir Thomas (1751–82), third baronet, 120 n.10, 477–78 and n.2
Clarges, Sir Thomas (ca. 1780–1834), fourth and last baronet (pupil of RG), 92, 93 n.3, 105, 107 n.2, 108, 120 n.10, 477–78 and n.2
Clarges, William (younger brother of the fourth baronet), 477–78 n.2
Clarke, Anne, née Powell (wife of Isaac Winslowe Clarke; died in Detroit), 245, 246 n.11
Clarke, Isaac Winslowe (deputy commissary-general, Montreal), 246 n.11
Clay, Jane, née Musgrave (wife of William), 78, 80 n.11, 243, 247, 468
Clay, William (merchant; relative of LC), 140, 141 n.1, 171, 172 n.5, 267, 397, 398 n.1, 399
Clayton, Sir William, fourth baronet, 174 n.3
Clifford, Martin (d. 1677): *The Rehearsal*, 226 n.3
Clinton. *See* Trefusis
Clough, Ensign Hugh Powell, 315 n.13, 481 n.5, 484, 486 n.8
Clough, James Henry, 315 n.13
Clough, Patty, née Butler (wife of Richard, of Glan y Wern and Plas Clough, Denbighshire), 313, 315 n.13, 481 n.5, 486 n.8
Clough, Sir Richard, knight of the Holy Sepulchre (d. 1570) (second husband of Katherine of Berain; builder of Bachygraig, 1567), 216, 217 n.12

Clough, Richard (1753–1814), of Glan y Wern and Plas Clough, Denbighshire, 315 n.13, 481 n.5, 486 n.8
Clough, Richard Butler (1781–1844), 480, 481 n.5
Clovis I ("Louis") (Frankish king), 138, 139 n.4
Cobbett, William (editor of the *Porcupine*), 259 and n.2
Cobenzl, Johann-Philippe de, count (1741–1810) (vice-chancellor of Austria), 217 n.7
Coke, Daniel Parker (1745–1825) (M.P., Derby; Nottingham), 372, 373 n.6
Colebrooke, Sir George (1729–1809) (M.P., Arundel), 391, 392 n.1
Colloredo-Mansfield, Franz, Prince of (chancellor of Austria), 216 n.7
Colman, George, the elder (1732–94) (dramatist), 362 n.6
Colman, George (1762–1836): editor of *Posthumous Letters*, 466
Columba (St. Colum). *See* Johnson, Samuel
Combermere. *See* Cotton, Sir Stapleton
Conant, Sir Nathaniel (chief magistrate, Bow Street court), 122, 123 n.6
Concanen, Matthew, Jr., of Southwark (book collector), 235, 236 n.11
Condé, John (fl. 1785–1800) (engraver), 68
Condé, Louis-Henri-Joseph de Bourbon (1756–1830), ninth and last prince of Condé, 110 n.4, 428 n.7
Condé, Louis-Joseph de Bourbon (1736–1818), eighth prince de Condé, 110 n.4
Conegliano. *See* Moncey
Congreve, Adelaide Sarah, of Shrewsbury, 176, 177 n.3
Congreve, John (d. 1783), of Shrewsbury, 177 n.3
Congreve, Col. William (burgess of Shrewsbury), 177 n.3
Congreve, William (1670–1729) (dramatist): *The Mourning Bride*, 457, 458 n.5
Constant de Rebecque, Henri-Benjamin (Benjamin Constant) (1767–1830) (politician and author), 401 n.9
Constantine I the Great (272–337) (Roman emperor), 184 n.4
Constantine (or Konstantin) Pavlovitch (1779–1831), grand duke (second son of Czar Paul), 187, 188 n.3, 287, 289–90 n.18
Conway, William Augustus (1789–1828) (actor and future correspondent) (WAC), 292 n.6, 393 n.3
Coote, Mary, of Bath, 60, 63 n.2
Copley, Anthony: *Wits, Fits, and Fancies*, 401 n.2

Copley, Capt. Joseph, 94 n.1
Corke and Orrery. *See* Boyle; Monckton
Cornwallis, Charles, first marquess and second earl Cornwallis (1738–1805) (statesman), 18, 343, 344 n.8
Cosway, Richard (1740–1821) (artist): portrait of Maria Anne Fitzherbert, 68; portrait of the Prince of Wales, 452
Cotton, Lady Anna Maria, née Pelham-Clinton (1783–1807) (daughter of third duke of Newcastle-under-Lyne; wife of Stapleton Cotton), 252, 253 n.3
Cotton, Lt. Lynch (fl. 1796–1809), 131, 134 n.3
Cotton, Philadelphia (1738–1819) (HLP's cousin), 199 n.9
Cotton, Sidney Arabella (HLP's aunt), 183, 184 n.2
Cotton, Sophia (HLP's aunt), 183, 184 n.2
Cotton, Sir Stapleton, of Lleweni Hall (1773–1865), sixth baronet (later baron and viscount Combermere) (husband of Lady Anna Maria Pelham-Clinton), 131, 134 n.3, 252, 253 n.3
Courtenay, William, viscount Courtenay of Powderham Castle, *de jure* earl of Devon, 283, 285 n.10
Coutts, Thomas (1735–1822) (banker), 287, 289 n.13
Coventry, Barbara, née St. John, countess of Coventry (second wife of the sixth earl), 81 n.14
Coventry, Lady Catherine, née Henley (daughter of earl of Northington and wife of Lord Deerhurst), 77 n.16
Coventry, George William (1722–1809), sixth earl of Coventry, 81 n.14
Coventry, George William (1758–1831), viscount Deerhurst (later seventh earl of Coventry) (son of sixth earl and his first wife, Maria [Mary]), 75, 77 nn. 16 and 17, 81 n.14, 410, 431
Coventry, John (1765–1829) (son of sixth earl and his second wife, Barbara), 81 n.14
Coventry, John (1793–1871) (grandson of sixth earl; son of John), 144 n.9, 411 n.6
Coventry, Margaret ("Peggy"), née Pitches (1760–1840), viscountess Deerhurst, Lady (wife of George William Coventry, viscount Deerhurst), 89 n.9
Coventry, Maria (Mary), née Gunning, countess of Coventry (first wife of the sixth earl), 81 n.14
Coventry, Thomas William (ca. 1779–1816) (son of the sixth earl and his second wife, Barbara), 81 n.14
Cowper, William (d. 1823), first earl Cowper (lord chancellor), 157 n.1
Cowper, William (1731–1800) (poet), 157 n.1, 465, 467–68 nn. 3 and 4
Cowper. *See also* Hesketh
Cradock (later Caradoc), Gen. John Francis (1762–1839), K.B., first baron Howden, 358 n.6
Craven, Henry Augustus Berkeley, 59 n.4
Craven, Keppel Richard, 59 n.4
Craven, William (1738–91), sixth baron Craven, 59 n.2
Craven, William (1770–1825), seventh baron Craven, viscount Uffington, first earl of Craven, 58, 59 n.4
Crawford, Stewart, M.D., of Bath, 370, 371 n.7
Crewe, Frances Anne, née Greville, 116–17 n.14
Crewe, John, first baron Crewe, 116–17 n.14
Cromwell, Oliver (1599–1658), 84 n.11
Crossman, Elizabeth, née Brickdale, 323, 324 n.4
Crossman, Rev. George: as purported suitor of Hannah More, 315, 323, 324 n.4, 327; wife Elizabeth and children of, 324 n.4
Crussol, François-Emmanuel de (1728–1802), ninth duc d'Uzès (maréchal de camp), as emigré, 110 n.6
Crutchley, Jeremiah, Jr. (1745–1805) (a guardian of Thrale daughters), 334
Cruttwell and Hazard (Bath booksellers), 175 n.4
Cumberland. *See* Ernest Augustus, duke of Cumberland and king of Hanover
Cumberland, Richard (1732–1811) (dramatist): HLP's meeting with, 457; *The Sailor's Daughter,* 457, 458 n.6, 465–66, 468 n.5; *Wheel of Fortune,* 468 n.5
Cunliffe, Sir Ellis, baronet, of Liverpool, 462 n.3
Cunliffe, Sir Foster (1755–1834), of Denbigh, third baronet (father of Mary Williams-Wynn), 326 n.7
Cunliffe, Mary, née Bennet, Lady, 461, 462 nn. 2 and 3
Cunliffe. *See also* Gosling, Margaret Elizabeth; Smith, Mary
Currie, William, M.D., of Chester Infirmary, 81 n.20
Curzon, Assheton, of Penn House, Bucks.,

and of Hagley, Staffs. (1729/30–1820), first baron and first viscount of Penn, 58, 59 n.6
Cuzzoni, Francesca (1700–70) (opera singer), 209 n.6
Cyfeiliog, Owen, prince of Powys: *Hirlas* (poem), 99, 101 n.5

Dalrymple, Hew (African colonizer), 190 n.5
Dance, George (1741–1825) (architect and artist), 378
D'Argonne, Noël Bonaventure (pseudonym: Vigneul-Marville), 386, 388 n.13
Darmarius, Andreas: transcription of Polyaenus's *Stratagems*, 292 n.5
Dashwood, Sir Francis, baronet, Lord le Despencer, 453 n.1
Davies, Edward (Brynbella farm worker), 272
Davies, Edward: *Celtic Researches*, 484, 486 nn. 10 and 11
Davies, John (d. 1785): leaves Llanerch Park to his sister Letitia Leo, 56, 57 n.14, 81 n.19
Davies, Rev. Reynold (schoolmaster, "Streatham University") (RD): character of, 431; curate of Saint Leonard's in Streatham (1777), 407 n.4; JSPS as his student, 58, 65, 70, 79 n.3, 88 and n.6, 89, 153 n.1, 154, 155 n.1, 162–65, 163 nn. 1 and 6, 202, 265, 305 n.7, 316, 392, 436 n.1, 473; on Macnamara's funeral, 165 n.1; negotiates sale of HLP's *Retrospection*, 209 n.9; letters from, 143–44 nn. 1, 2, 3, 5, and 6, 153 n. 1, 154 n.1, 163 nn. 1 and 6, 165 nn. 1 and 6, 209 n.9; letters to, 87–89, 142–44, 162–63, 175–77, 321–23, 398–99, 405–7, 410–11
Davies, Thomas (Brynbella gardener), 71 n.1, 85, 120
Davies, Mrs. Thomas (Brynbella housekeeper; formerly Mrs. Beckwith), 71 n.1, 75, 78, 85
Dawnay, Catherine (d. 1821), 325, 326 n.2
Dawnay, John, fourth viscount Downe, 326 n.2
Dawnay, Laura (or Lora), née Burton (1740–1812), 325, 326 n.2
De Blaquiere, Anna Maria. *See* Fitzmaurice, Anna Maria, Viscountess Kirkwall
De Blaquiere, Eleanor, née Dobson (wife of John Blaquiere, first baron of Ardkill), 80 n.4, 262
De Blaquiere, Elizabeth ("Bessy") (1786–1870) (sister of Lady Kirkwall), 450, 451 n.7; engagement to Rev. George Henry Glasse, 432, 433 nn. 6 and 8, 434 n.8, 434, 450, 451 n.7; wife of John Bernard Hankey, 335, 353, 363, 425, 426 n.2, 432, 433 n.8, 450
De Blaquiere, John (1732–1812), first baron of Ardkill, 80 n.4, 169, 170, 308, 309 n.15, 313, 317, 401 n.1, 429, 438
De Blaquiere, John (1776–1844), second baron of Ardkill, 418 n.10, 426 n.3
De Blaquiere, Peter Boyle (1784–1860) (naval officer), 425, 426 n.3
De Blaquiere, Gen. William (1778–1851), third baron of Ardkill, 349, 350 n.9
Debrett, John (d. 1822) (bookseller: "democrat"), 241 n.2
Deerhurst. *See* Coventry
Defoe, Daniel, *Robinson Crusoe*, 322, 323 n.7
De la Warr. *See* West
De Luc, Mrs., of Bath, 314, 340
Denbigh. *See* Feilding
Denon, Baron Dominique-Vivant: *Denon's Travels* (i.e. *Voyage dans . . . Egypte*), 400, 402 n.13
Derby. *See* Smith-Stanley
Derry, bishop of. *See* Hervey, Frederick Augustus
Desaguliers, John Theophilus (philosopher and scientist), 62, 64 n.20
Desaix, Gen. Louis-Charles, chevalier de Veygoux (1768–1800) (commander of French forces in Egypt), 179 n.2
Deseuil, Abbé Augustin (Parisian bookbinder), 234, 235 n.4
Desgenettes, Nicholas-René Dufriche (1762–1837) (French surgeon), 344 n.10
Despard, Edward Marcus (Irish-born rebel), 388, 389 n.6, 400, 402 n.15
Despencer, Le (*soi-disant* baroness). *See* Lee, Rachel Fanny Antonia
Despencer, Le. *See* Dashwood, Sir Francis, baronet
Devon. *See* Courtenay
Devonshire. *See* Cavendish
De Winter. *See* Winter
Dibdin, Charles (dramatist, actor, and singer): adapts song from *Le Deserteur*, 216, 217 n.11
Dibdin, Thomas John (dramatist): *English Fleet* (patriotic opera), 455, 456 n.2; *The Jew and the Doctor*, 346, 347 n.4
Dickinson, William, M.P., 247, 248 n.7
Dickson, Adm. Sir Archibald, baronet (d. 1803) or Adm. William (d. 1803), 308 n.8

Diderot, Denis (1713–84): *L'Encyclopédie ou Dictionnaire raisonné*, 64 n.21, 128, 130 n.7; *Le Père de Famille* (prose drama), 175 n.6

Dimond, William Wyatt (d. 1812) (Bath actor and theatrical manager): performs in *Lovers' Vows* and *The Stranger*, 166, 167 n.15; and SS, 62, 65 n.24, 279 n.2, 307, 309 n.14, 330

Dimond, William, the younger: Catholic conversion and premature death of, 475, 476 n.4

Diocletian, Gaius Aurelius Valerius, 298 n.2

Dixon, Thomas (Irish rebel), 54 n.6

Dobbs, Francis (Irish politician), 204 and n.4

Domitian, Titus Flavius (51–96) (Roman emperor), 284

Dorset. *See* Sackville

Douglas, Archibald, eighth earl of Angus (second husband of Princess Margaret Tudor), 130 n.9

Douglas, John (1721–1807), bishop of Salisbury (Sarum), 52 n.1

Drake, Elizabeth Anne, née Mackworth, 467, 468 n.10

Drake, Francis (British diplomat): friendship with Piozzis, 92, 93 n.5, 156, 158, 161, 163, 167, 168, 464, 465 n.3; marriage of to Miss Mackworth, 464, 465 n.3, 467, 468 n.10

Drax family. *See* Dreux

Drebbel, Cornelis J. (ca. 1620) (submarine inventor), 349, 350 n.10

Dreux, Philip de (d. 1217), bishop of Beauvais (son of Agnès de Baudiment de Braine [Braisne] and Robert, comte de Dreux), 118, 119 n.5

Dreux, Robert, comte de (fifth son of Louis VI), 118, 119 n.5

Ducie. *See* Reynolds-Moreton

Ducos, Consul Pierre Roger (1747–1816), 95 n.8

Dumouriez, Gen. Charles-François du Perrier (or Périer) (1739–1823): British refuge and pension for, 85, 86 n.8, 109, 188 n.3, 427, 428 n.9; *Tableau spéculatif de l'Europe* (1798), 428, 430 n.3

Duncan, Adm. Adam (1731–1804), viscount, 440–41 n.3, 477 n.1

Dundas, Lt. Gen. David, 140, 141 n.2

Dundas, Henry (1742–1811), first viscount Melville, 269 n.2

Duperrier Dumouriez. *See* Dumouriez

Du Perron, Cardinal Jacques-Davy (1556–1618), 98 n.4

Duppa, Richard: *A Journal of . . . Remarkable Occurrences . . . in Rome*, 100, 101 n.8

Duras. *See* Durfort de Duras

Durfort de Duras, Amédée-Bretagne-Malo de (1771–1838), duc de Duras, 110 n.6

Durfort de Duras, Emmanuel-Céleste-Augustin (1741–1800), duc de Duras, 110 n.6

Durham. *See* Lambton

Duroc (or du Roc), Gen. Gerard-Christophe-Michel (later duc de Frioul), 302–3, 304 n.2

Dutton, Honoria, née Gubbins: "Bacchante girl," 108, 110 n.8; marries Ralph Dutton, 391, 392 n.7, 403 and n.3; and SS, 113, 115 n.6

Dutton, Ralph, 391, 392 n.7, 457 and n.1

Earle, Sir James (1745–1817) (surgeon extraordinary to George III), 245, 246 n.4, 464, 465 n.5

Échard, Laurent (ca. 1670–1730): *Dictionnaire Geographique-Portatif*, 290, 291 n.2

Edgcumbe, Richard, second earl of Mount Edgcumbe, 358 n.5

Edgeworth de Firmont, Henry Essex (1745–1807) (confessor to Louis XVI and chaplain to Louis XVIII), 247, 248 n.3

Edgeworth, Maria: *Belinda*, 312, 314 n.6, 325; *Popular Tales*, 467, 468 n.9

Edgeworth, Richard Lovell: preface to Maria Edgeworth's *Popular Tales*, 468 n.9

Edouart, Augustin-Amant-Constant-Fidèle: silhouette of Hannah More, 272

Edward I (king of England), 151–52 n.16

Edward IV (king of England), 374 n.9

Edward's book shop, Pall Mall, 234, 235 n.2, 236, 242

Egmont. *See* Perceval

Elchingen. *See* Ney

Elgin. *See* Bruce

Elizabeth Berkeley (Craven), margravine of Brandenburgh-Anspach, 59 n.3

Elizabeth of York (queen of England; mother of Henry VIII), 130 n.9

Elizabeth, Princess, of England, and Landgravine of Hesse-Homburg (1770–1840), 59 n.5

Elovis (French emigré; harpist in Bath), 158, 159 n.3

Elphinstone, Vice-Admiral George Keith (1746–1823), later viscount Keith (future husband of Q): as Baron Keith and admiral of the Blue, 303, 305 n.4, 440, 441 n.11; advises John Salusbury Mostyn, 446 n.7

Elton, Sir Abraham, and Bristol riots, 277 and n.5, 286, 288 n.3, 301 n.8, 346 n.2
Emanuele Filippo, styled conte di Front (or Fron) (diplomat), 55, 57 n.6
Embry, Edward, rector of St. Paul's, Covent Garden, 143, 144 n.8, 164, 165 n.6
Emmet, Robert, 19, 167 n.16, 421 n.6
Enghien, Louis-Antoine-Henri de Bourbon-Condé, duc de, 23, 464–65 n.2, 478 n.4
Englefield, Sir Harry, seventh baronet, 115, 117 n.14
English, John: "Sad Memorial . . . to Jane, his most dear wife," 381 n.4
Ernest Augustus (1771–1851), duke of Cumberland and king of Hanover, 433, 434 n.2, 435 n.4, 476 n.2
Erskine, Thomas, 98 n.8, 241 n.2
Este, Charles Lambton, later baron, 350, 351 n.5
Este, Charlotte Sophie, née Smith (wife of Charles), 350, 351 n.5
Este, Harriet. See Wells, Harriet
Este, Louisa Caroline, née Smith (wife of Thomas), 351 n.5
Este, Michael Lambton, M.D. (Pavia), 351 n.4
Este, Thomas, 351 n.5
Eugène, Prince. See Beauharnais, Viceroi Eugène de
Eusebius of Caesarea (ca. 260–340): *Ecclesiastical History*, 299
Evans, William (artist, designer, engraver), 208
Evans, William, of Parc y Twll, 385 n.2
Evans, Mrs. William, of Parc y Twll, 384, 385 n.2
Ewen, John (apothecary; friend of Peter Giles at Streatham Park), 385–88 and n.1

Farmer, Rev. Richard (1735–97), 135, 137 n.6
Farquhar, Sir Walter (1738–1819), baronet, M.D., 390 and n.2
Farren, Elizabeth (or Eliza). See Smith-Stanley, Elizabeth
Farrington, Joseph, 60 n.8, 87 n.11, 422 n.17, 451 n.7, 463 n.7, 476–77 n.7
Fata Morgana: vision off the Falmouth coast, 247, 248 n.8
Feilding, Anne Catherine, née Powys (or Powis), viscountess (widow of William Robert), 261, 262 n.2
Feilding, Basil, sixth earl of Denbigh, 262 n.2

Feidling, William Robert, styled viscount Feilding, 262 n.2
Felton, William: *Treatise on Carriages*, 104 n.3
Fénelon, François de Salignac (or Salagnac) de la Mothe (1651–1715), archbishop of Cambrai: *Les Avantures de Télémaque*, 206, 207 n.4
Ferdinando IV (king of Naples and Sicily, 1759–1825; styled Ferdinando I of the Two Sicilies, 1816–25), 55, 57 n.9, 250, 332 n.12
Fermor, George, third earl of Pomfret, 358 n.4
Fermor, Mary, née Browne, countess of Pomfret, 356, 358 n.4, 361, 362 n.2
Ferrers. See Shirley
Ferriday, John: partner of Thomas Gillet, printer of *Retrospection*, 256 n.4
Ferris, Capt. (naval officer), 308 n.6
Ferronays, Eugène de la, comte de Vaudreuil, as emigré, 110 n.6
Fesch, Joseph Cardinal, archbishop of Lyons (Napoleon's uncle), 374, 375 n.2
Fielding, Henry: *Tom Jones*, 19, 66, 67 n.7
Fieschi di Masserano, Maria Christina Teresa Ferrero (wife of Giuseppe Francesco Gaetano San Martino di San Germano), 57 n.6
"Filidh": influence of an Irish cultural life, 151 n.15
Fitzherbert, Alleyne (1753–1839), baron St. Helens (diplomat), 305 n.10
Fitzherbert, Maria Anne, née Smythe (Weld) (1756–1837) ("wife" of Prince of Wales): illness of, 69, 70 n.3, 74; liaison with Prince of Wales, 70 n.3, 213, 214 n.1, 361, 363 n.7; portrait of by Cosway, 68
Fitzhugh, Charlotte, née Hamilton, 353, 354 n.5
Fitzhugh, William (merchant and M.P.), 354 n.5
Fitzhugh. *See also* Hamilton
Fitzjames (or Fitz-James), Édouard (1766–1833), fourth duc de, as emigré, 110 n.6
Fitzmaurice, Anna Maria, née De Blaquiere (1780–1843), Viscountess Kirkwall, 228, 229 n.7, 338 n.9, 414, 415 n.2, 432, 444; death of Dublin relatives in rebellion, 419, 421 n.6, 424; marriage and pregnancy of, 80 n.4, 393, 424, 426 and n.1
Fitzmaurice, John Hamilton (1778–1820), styled viscount Kirkwall (son of Thomas Fitzmaurice and Mary, *suo jure* countess of Orkney), 65, 412, 429, 434, 438, 448; accident and recovery, 71, 223 and n.1,

323, 324 n.1; betrothal to Mary Jane Ormsby rumored, 210, 211 n.6, 214, 221, 222, 262, 286, 291, 292 n.12, 337, 338 n.9; generosity of, 382, 465, 474; Lleweni Hall, 80 n.4, 214, 388, 429, 434, 435 n.6; marriage to Anna Maria De Blaquiere, 80 n.4, 376, 377 n.7; and Piozzis, 148, 474 n.1; political aspirations of, 141, 142 n.6;

Fitzmaurice, Mary, née O'Bryen or O'Brien (1755–1831), *suo jure* countess of Orkney (mother of viscount Kirkwall; wife of Thomas Fitzmaurice), 61, 79–80 n.4, 148, 181, 222, 228, 287, 353, 365, 383, 403, 414, 415 n.2, 417, 418 n.12, 425, 434

Fitzmaurice, Thomas (1742–93), 80 n.4

Fitzmaurice, Thomas John Hamilton (first son of Lord and Lady Kirkwall), 426 and n.4, 442, 474

Fitzwalter, Robert (d. 1235), lord of Dunmow and Baynard's Castle, Essex, and ceremony of "Dunmow Bacon," 408, 409 n.1

Foot, Jessé: *Life of Arthur Murphy*, 91 n.12

Fordyce, Henrietta, née Cummyng (widow of James), 174, 175 n.10

Fordyce, Rev. James, 175 n.10

Fossé, Augustin-François-Thomas du, 423, 425 n.7

Fossé, Monique du, née Coquerel, 423, 425 n.7

Fouché, Joseph (1759–1820), duc d'Otranto (Napoleon's minister of police), 23

Foulkes, Thomas (Welsh landowner), 233 n.1

Fox, Charles James (1749–1806) (politician), 16, 21, 387 nn. 7 and 9, 427 n.2

Fox, Elizabeth (Armistead), 386, 387 n.9

Francis, Rev. Clement Robert (1792–1829) (FBA's nephew), 366 n.5

Francis, Marianne (1790–1832) (FBA's niece) (MF), 393–94 n.4

Frank (embezzling Pennington servant), 156, 198, 199 n.1

Franz (or Francis) II (1768–1835) (Holy Roman Emperor, 1792–1806; emperor of Austria, as Franz I, 1804–35; king of Bohemia and Hungary, 1792–1835), 80 n.10, 89, 92 n.2, 148–49 and n.3, 188 n.2, 215, 216 nn. 6 and 8, 228, 230 n.11, 244, 247, 248 n.2

Frederica Charlotte Ulrica Catherina, duchess of York (1767–1820), 258 n.9, 279, 280 n.9, 365 n.3, 391, 392 n.7

Frederick Augustus (1763–1827), duke of York and Albany, 122 n.2, 257, 258 n.9, 279, 365 n.3, 391, 392 n.7

Frere, John Hookham (author, translator, diplomat), 482, 483 n.2

Friedrich Wilhelm III (king of Prussia; brother of Frederica, duchess of York), 280 n.9

Frioul, duc de. *See* Duroc (or du Roc)

Front (Fron). *See* Emanuele Filippo

Frotho the Fierce (legendary king of Denmark), 479 and n.3

Frotté, Louis de (1755–1800) ("Norman gentleman"; general in royalist army), 167 n.7

Fuller, Andrew: *Socinianism*, 52 n.2

Fuller, Rev. Thomas (1608–61): *History of the Worthies of England*, 182 n.8

Fuller, Thomas (1654–1734), M.D.: *Gnomologia*, 290, 291 n.3

Fulton, Robert (1765–1815) (developer of submarine *Nautilus*), 350 n.1

Ganteaume, Vice Adm. Honoré-Joseph-Antoine, comte, 304–5 n.3, 308

Garat, Dominique-Joseph, 23, 469, 472 n.3

Gardiner, Charles John, viscount Mountjoy, earl of Blesington [Blessington], 221, 222 n.7, 420 n.4

Garnerin, André-Jacques (balloonist and parachutist), 365, 366 n.2

Garnier, Charles-Georges-Thomas: *Ana* and *Vigneul-Marvilliana*, 388 n.13

Garrett, Elizabeth (HLP's Bath landlady), 331, 332 n.16, 336, 389 n.1, 467, 480, 481 n.2

Garrett, William (husband of Elizabeth), 384 and n.6

Garrick, David (1717–79), 253; adapts *Winter's Tale* as *Florizel and Perdita*, 353 nn. 8, 9, and 10; aids actress Mary Robinson, 83–84 n.8; as Bayes in *The Rehearsal*, 225 n.2, 244; death of, 353; illustration of by Dance-Holland, 133; popularity of, 132, 134 n.4, 484; recommends Hawkesworth to edit naval account, 345 n.1

Gay, John: *Beggar's Opera*, 236, 237 n.2; *Trivia*, 86, 87 n.13

Gelimer (6th cent. Vandal king), 484, 485 n.2

Genest, John: *Account of the English Stage*, 65 n.24

George III (king of Great Britain): attempted assassination of, 193, 195 n.2,

200; birthday celebration, 356; burial of, 372; cancels visit to Bath with Queen, 307, 308n.13; HLP's confidence in, 240; illness and derangement of, 278, 280n.5, 453 and n.2, 455, 456, 457, 461, 478 and n.3
—national and international affairs: dissolves Parliament and calls for general election, 366n.3; and domestic economy, 251, 266n.12; and "Preliminaries of Peace," 334; proclamation to suppress riots, 227, 229n.4; relations with Russia, 185; on slave trade, 17
George Augustus Frederick, Prince of Wales (later George IV, king of Great Britain), 78, 80n.5; caricature of by Gillray, 454; illness and excessive drinking of, 165, 166n.5, 178, 180n.10, 453; openly escorts Maria Fitzherbert, 361, 363n.7; as "Pall Mall Rake," 108, 110n.7; portrait of by Cosway, 452
Gibbon, Edward, 11, 12, 485n.2
Giles, Peter (d. 1830) (Streatham Park tenant; grain merchant): hospitality to Piozzis, 201, 202n.6, 212, 224, 239n.48, 353; liaison of with housekeeper, 194, 196n.18, 353; purchases books for Streatham Park, 231, 236, 240, 242, 363
Gillet, Thomas: printer of *Retrospection*, 179–80n.8, 256 and n.4, 258n.5, 293
Gillies, Catherine ("Kitty"), née Beaver, 323, 324n.3
Gillon, John (1748–1809) (family adviser): birthplace and residences of, 176, 270, 271n.5, 397; as book collector, 113, 115n.5, 121, 235, 240; as HLP correspondent and source of news, 67n.9, 121–22, 160, 176, 189, 203, 309, 408, 410, 441n.12, 458n.7; and HLP's litigation with John Cator, 147n.1; HLP's matchmaking for with Anne Poole, 105, 107nn. 1 and 4; illnesses of, 399; as mediator in family quarrel over Crowmarsh estate, 146–47n.3, 178, 185, 191, 193n.10, 194, 196n.2, 197nn. 1 and 3, 202
— and HLP's *Retrospection*: negotiates sale, 11, 202n.4, 267, 271n.4, 299; and printers' errors and critical controversies, 258n.5, 308n.2, 293, 295n.9; seeks second edition, 268n.2
—letters from, 67n.9, 83n.7, 110n.7, 116n.5, 117n.1, 122n.4, 147nn. 1 and 3, 177n.6, 179n.1, 193n.10, 197 and n.2, 209n.9, 214n.1, 258n.5, 260n.5, 268n.2, 271n.4, 276n.8, 316, 317n.7, 441n.12; letter to, 146–48
Gillon, William (merchant), 294, 295n.11
Gillray, James (artist), 454
Giraldi, Giovanni Battista (1504–73) (known also as Cinthio, Cintio, Cinzio, or Cynthus), 135, 137n.7
Gittins, John (tenant at Bachygraig), 231, 232n.5, 235n.2, 430n.5
Glasse, Anne, née Fletcher (first wife of George Henry), 433n.6
Glasse, Caroline. *See* Hume, Caroline
Glasse, Rev. George Henry, engagement to Elizabeth De Blaquiere, 432, 433nn. 6 and 8, 434, 450, 451n.7
Glasse, Harriet, née Wheeler (second wife of George Henry), 433n.8
Glasse, Rev. Samuel (father of George Henry), 433n.6
Gloucester, dukes of. *See* William Frederick; William Henry
Godolphin. *See* Ormsby
Godoy, Manuel de, principe de la Paz, 483n.2
Godwin, Mary, née Wollstonecraft (1759–97), 170n.6
Godwin, William (1756–1836) (philosopher and novelist): *Caleb Williams*, 225, 317n.6; *Enquiry concerning Political Justice*, 169n.5; relationships with Helen Maria Williams and Harriet Lee, 169n.3, 273n.4; *St. Leon*, 168, 169n.2, 317n.6; satirized, 170n.6
Gohier, Ministre Louis-Jérôme (1746–1830) (president of the French Directory), 95n.8
Goldsmith, Oliver (1728–74): *Deserted Village*, 235, 236n.12; *History of the Earth and Animated Nature*, 171, 172n.11; mentioned in *British Synonymy*, 340, 341n.6
Goodinge, Thomas (preacher and schoolmaster), 58, 59n.1
Gordon, Catherine, née Wallop (second wife of Lockhart), 461, 463n.6
Gordon, John, third earl of Aboyne [S.] (d. 1732), 463n.6
Gordon, Rev. Lockhart: and abduction of Rachel Lee, 451, 453n.1, 457, 458n.11, 461, 462–63nn. 5 and 6
Gordon, Loudon: and abduction of Rachel Lee, 451, 453n.1, 457, 458n.11, 461, 462–63nn. 5 and 6; *Apology for the Conduct of the Gordons*, 462–63n.5
Gosling, Margaret Elizabeth, née Cunliffe

(sister of Mary [Mrs. Drummond] Smith), 462 n.2
Gosling, William (London banker; husband of Margaret Elizabeth, née Cunliffe), 462 n.2
Gosling. *See also* Cunliffe, Margaret Elizabeth; Smith, Mary
Grantham. *See* Robinson
Gratian, Flavius (367–83) (Roman emperor), 171, 172 n.10
Graves, Richard: *The Spiritual Quixote*, 71, 72 n.9, 75
Graves (or Greaves), Adm. Sir Thomas (ca. 1747–1814), 308 n.8
Gray, Ann (1725–1817) (mother of RG; wife of Robert, the elder), 345
Gray, Elizabeth, née Camplin (d. 1841) (wife of RG): children of, 119, 120 n.11; and possible French invasion of Britain, 448; visits Piozzis at Brynbella, 92, 105, 108, 109 n.1; letter from, 119 n.1; letter to, 118–20
Gray, John (infant son of Elizabeth and Robert), 242, 243 n.2
Gray, Polly (sister of RG), 346 n.3
Gray, Robert, the elder (d. 1788) (London goldsmith and jeweler; father of RG), 346 n.3
Gray, Rev. Robert "Old Testament" (1762–1834), bishop of Bristol (RG), 89, 181; anecdote about, 252; children of, 119, 120 n.11; and death of sister, 346 n.3; and HLP's *Retrospection*, 253 n.2, 278; and possible French invasion of Britain, 25 n.43, 448, 449 n.1
—career: prebendary of Chichester, 191, 193 n.6, 213–14; receives D.D. degree from Oxford, 372, 373 n.1; tutor of Sir Thomas Clarges, 477–78 n.2
—travels: visits Shute Barrington, bishop of Durham, or Sir Henry Browne, 221–22 n.5; visits Piozzis at Brynbella, 92, 105, 108, 111, 190 n.1; visits Piozzis in Bath, 65, 67 n.3; visits Piozzis in London, 465; with HLP at Bodleian library, 234
—writings: *Catechism. . . . Principal Testimonies in Proof of the Divine Authority of Christianity*, 221 and n.4; *Key to the Old Testament*, 61, 63–64 n.8, 64 n.11; *Sermons*, 64 n.11; travel *Letters*, 64 n.11; verses for the Brynbella sundial, 119, 120 n.8
—letters from, 346 n.1, 449 n.1; letters to, 51–52, 138–40, 242–43, 255–56, 281–82, 306, 338–39, 345–46, 347–48, 449, 478–80
Gray, Sarah (sister of RG), 346 n.3

Gray, Thomas (RG's half-brother), 346 n.3
Gray, William (goldsmith and jeweler; brother of RG), 346 n.3
Gray. *See also* Norman, Anne
Greatheed, Ann, née Greatheed (ca. 1748–1822) (cousin and wife of Bertie), 206, 357, 361, 415, 417, 418 n.9, 439, 441 n.6; Continental travels of, 206, 396 n.8; death of son, 484, 486 n.8
Greatheed, Bertie (1759 or 1760–1826) (cousin and husband of Ann): *An Englishman in Paris*, 418 n.9; masked ball riot, 357; Piozzis select piano for, 361; *The Regent*, 86; visits Brynbella, 157
—on Continent, 206, 396 n.8; conversations with Junot and Bonaparte, 418 n.9; as prisoner in France, 417, 418 n.9, 436, 437 n.9, 439, 441 n.6
Greatheed, Bertie (1781–1804) (son of Bertie and Ann), 132, 206, 357, 417, 418 n.9, 439, 441 n.6; Continental travels of, 206, 396 n.8; death of, 484, 486 n.8
Greatheed, Richard Wilson (1749–1832), 134 n.10
Gregoire, Henri (1750–1831) (anti-Bonapartist), 23
Gregory, Rev. George, 263 n.8
Grenville, William Wyndham (1759–1834), baron Grenville (foreign secretary, 1791–1801), 158, 159 n.1, 160, 161 n.6, 269 n.2
Greville, Elizabeth, née Hamilton (wife of Francis, first earl Brooke), 442, 443 n.5
Greville, Francis, first earl Brooke of Warwick Castle, 442, 443 n.5
Greville, Robert Fulke (second husband of Louisa Cathcart, *suo jure* countess of Mansfield), 228, 229 nn. 8 and 9
Grey, Charles (1764–1845), baron Grey, viscount Howick, and second earl Grey (Opposition speaker), 266 n.12
Griffin, Gerald, 284 n.2
Griffith, Griffith (clergyman at Tremeirchion Church), 329 n.7
Griffith, Hugh, of Carnarvon (1724–95) (Piozzi tenant): letters to, 163 n.5, 339, 341 n.2
Griffith, John (son of Hugh; husband of Margaret, née Owen) (high sheriff of Carnarvonshire, 1813), 96 n.1; letter to, 95–96
Griffith, Margaret, née Owen, of Clenennau, 96 n.1, 180, 182 n.5
Griffith, Rev. Richard (ca. 1759–1819) (rector of Llandegfan cum Beaumaris), 105, 107 n.6

Grimani, conte Filippo Vincenzi (1755–1826) (Venetian nobleman), 234, 235 n.1
Gronovius, Abraham (1695–1775), 382 n.13
Grosvenor, John (Oxford surgeon), 457, 458 n.10
Gubbins. *See* Dutton, Honoria
Guido d'Arezzo (11th cent. composer), 256 and n.5
Gunning, Sir Robert, baronet (diplomat), 112 n.2
Gustav (or Gustavus) Adolph IV (king of Sweden), 129 n.2, 263 n.5, 479 and n.2
Guthrie, William (editor of *Critical Review*), 305 n.9

Hadfield, James (would-be assassin of George III), 193–94, 195–96 nn. 7, 8, and 9, 200 and n.3, 203
Haidar Ali Khan (Indian ruler), 293, 295 nn. 9 and 12
Halford. *See* Vaughan
Hall, John (1739–97) (engraver), 114
Halpap, Lucas: *Hialmars och Ramers Saga*, 382 n.10
Hamilton, Archibald (1673–1754) (seventh son of Anne, *suo jure* duchess of Hamilton) (governor of Greenwich Hospital; governor of Jamaica), 230 n.10
Hamilton, Lady Cecil (1770–1819), viscountess Hamilton, countess and marchioness of Abercorn, 94 n.1
Hamilton, Elizabeth: *Memoirs of Modern Philosophers* and *Letters on Principles of Education*, 262, 263 n.8, 314 n.7, 342, 344 n.6, 347
Hamilton, Emma Hart (ca. 1761–1815), Lady: and Horatio Nelson, 56, 57 n.12, 60
Hamilton, Rev. Frederick (or Frederic) (1728–1811), 228, 230 n.10, 435, 437 n.3, 442, 443 n.5, 450, 451 n.5
Hamilton, Jane. *See* Holman, Jane
Hamilton, John James (1756–1818), viscount Hamilton, ninth earl of Abercorn, and marquess of Abercorn, 94 n.1
Hamilton, Rachel (or Rachael), née Daniel (d. 1805), 230 n.11, 330, 332 n.13, 437 n.3, 450, 451 n.5
Hamilton, Sir William (1730–1803) (diplomat and archaeologist; husband of Emma Lady Hamilton), 74, 77 n.10, 395, 396 n.2
Hamilton. *See also* Fitzhugh
Hammersley's Bank, London, 361
Hankey, Elizabeth, née De Blaquiere, 432, 433 n.8

Hankey, John Bernard, of Fetcham Park, Surrey, 433 n.8
Hannibal, 164, 165 n.8, 307, 308 n.6
Hardy, Sarah. *See* Lysons, Sarah
Hardy, Thomas (1752–1832) (radical politician), 97, 98 n.8
Harington, Henry (1727–1816), M.D., 383
Harold the Hardy, 283, 284 n.4, 479 and n.2
Harold (king of the English): at battle of Hastings (1066), 307, 309 n.10
Harris, James (1746–1820), first earl of Malmesbury, 20, 453 n.1
Hase ("the Hebraist"), Christian Gottfried (d. 1766), 299
Hastings, Francis Rawdon (1754–1826), first marquess of Hastings, second earl of Moira (soldier and statesman), 295 n.9
Hathor (mythological deity), 446–3
Hawke, Adm. Edward, Baron Hawke of Towton, first lord of the admirality, 99, 100 n.2
Hawkesbury. *See* Jenkinson
Hawkesworth, John (ca. 1715–73) (author and editor): "Life. An Ode" (*Gentleman's Magazine*), 312, 314 n.5; *Voyages . . . in the Southern Hemisphere*, 80–81 n.13, 345 and n.1
Hawkins, Charlotte, 142, 144 n.3
Hawkins, Elizabeth, née Newman, 144 n.3
Hawkins, William, of Croydon, 142, 144 n.3
Hay, Alexander (Bath apothecary and surgeon), 59, 60 n.12
Hayes, Sir John (Daniel Macnamara's physician), 163 n.1
Hayley, William (biographer), 465, 468 n.4
Hayman, Rev. Henry, 237 n.3
Hayman, Susanna, née Cridland, 237 and n.3
Hayward, Abraham (1801–84) (essayist): editor of HLP's *Autobiography*, 10–11, 24 n.5
Hazlitt, William (1778–1830) (essayist): commentary on Holcroft's *Memoirs*, 170 n.7
Heathcote, Rev. Ralph (1721–95), 54 n.4
Heberden, William, M.D., 453 n.2
Hédouville, Comte Gabriel-Marie-Joseph-Théodore (1755–1825) (general and diplomat), 166–67 n.7
Hely-Hutchinson, Gen. John, first baron Hutchinson (1757–1832), 304 n.1, 314 n.9
Henley. *See* Coventry, Lady Catherine
Henri IV (1553–1610) (king of France), 292 n.7, 296
Henry III (king of England), 128, 129 n.3

Henry V (king of England), 217 n.13, 419, 420 n.4

Henry VII (king of England), 128, 129 n.10

Henry VIII (king of England), 128, 129 n.10, 130 n.9

Herbert, Henry (1741–1811), baron Porchester of High Clere and earl of Carnarvon (father of Frances Reynolds-Moreton), 55, 57 n.5

Hervey, Miss: as nyctalopic oddity, 245, 246 n.8

Hervey, Frederick Augustus (1730–1803), bishop of Derry, fourth earl of Bristol and fifth baron Howard de Walden: imprisonment of by French in Milan, 74, 76 nn. 8 and 9

Hervey family: seat of at Ickworth, West Suffolk, 74, 76 n.8

Hesketh, Lady Harriet, née Cowper (cousin of poet William Cowper, grandniece of William Cowper, first earl Cowper), 157 and n.1, 465; HLP's admiration of, 223, 314, 340, 415; as friend of PSP and Hannah More, 224 n.4, 336, 337–38 n.3, 341 n.3

Hesketh, Sir Thomas, baronet, 157 n.1

Hieronymous, Karl Friedrich, Freiherr von Münchausen (1720–97), of Bodenwerder, Hanover: *Adventures of Baron Munchausen*, 393–94 n.4

Hill, Sir Richard (1732–1808), second baronet, of Hawkstone Park: visited by Bridgemans and LC, 220, 221 n.2; visited by Piozzis, 225, 238

Hoare, Prince: *Chains of the Heart*, 347 and n.6

Hobart, Robert (1760–1816), baron Hobart, fourth earl of Buckinghamshire (statesman), 190 n.4

Hoche, Gen. Louis-Lazare (1768–97), 477 n.1

Hodgkins, Samuel (d. 1804) (GP's butler and valet): illness of, 131, 134 n.6, 310, 431, 434, 439, 445, 447, 459, 476; death of, 460 n.1

Holcroft, Thomas (author and translator): anecdote about, 168, 170 nn. 6 and 7; friend of Godwin, 169 n.5; *Memoirs . . . written by himself*, 170 n.7; *Road to Ruin*, 75, 77 n.15; *Travels*, 467, 468 n.8

Holland, Sir Nathaniel Dance (1735–1811) (artist), 133

Holman, Jane, née Hamilton (d. 1810) (daughter of Rev. Frederick and Rachel Hamilton; wife of Joseph George Holman), 383, 442; as friend of HLP, 186, 191, 201, 253 n.2, 330; her pregnancy and miscarriage, 69, 70 n.5, 222, 228, 383, 384 n.5, 388, 391, 393, 457, 458 n.7; resides in provinces, Edinburgh, and Dublin, 222, 383, 384 n.5, 422, 424 n.2, 426; visits Brynbella, 433, 435, 439

Holman, Joseph George (1764–1817) (actor and dramatist): *Love Gives the Alarm*, 422, 457, 458 n.7; marriage of, 332 n.14; performance as Harry Dornton in Holcroft's *Road to Ruin*, 75, 77 n.15; resides in provinces, Edinburgh, and Dublin, 222, 383, 384 n.5, 422, 424 n.2, 426, 450; stillborn child of, 393; visits Brynbella, 433, 435, 439; *The Votary of Wealth*, 75, 77 n.14

Holroyd, Sarah Martha: translation of Christoph Christian Sturm's *Betrachtungen*, 402, 403 n.1

Holroyd. See also Baker-Holroyd

Home, John (1722–1808): *Douglas*, 79, 81 n.17, 279, 280 n.10

Hood, Adm. Alexander (1727–1814), baron Bridport, first viscount Bridport (commander of the Channel Fleet), 91 n.13, 97, 102, 104 n.4

Hoppner, John, R. A. (1758–1810) (portrait painter), 254

Horace (Quintus Horatius Flaccus) (65–8 B.C.): *Ars Poetica*, 276, 277 n.3; *Audivere Lyce*, HLP's imitation of *Carmina*, 108, 110 n.8; *Epistles*, 297, 299 n.4

Horsley, Samuel (1733–1806), bishop of St. David's (1788–93), Rochester (1793–1802), St. Asaph (1802–6): *Charge to the Clergy of his Diocese* (1800), 215, 217 n.10; HLP dinner party for with Williams family, 416; second marriage of, 447 n.2; promotion to see of St. Asaph, 363, 364 n.1

Horsley, Sarah, née Wright (1752–1805) (second wife of Samuel), 438, 439 n.2

Houston, Tomkison (or Tomkinson) (piano manufacturer in Soho), 360, 362 n.1

Howden. See Cradock

Hufeland, Christoph Wilhelm von: *Die Kunst das menschliche Leben zu verlängern*, 281 and n.2

Hughes, Rev. Edward, of Kinmel Park, Denbighshire, 107 n.12, 178, 180 n.9

Hughes, Mary, née Lewis, of Kinmel Park, Denbighshire, 178, 180 n.9

Humbert, Gen. Jean, 18, 477 and n.1

Hume, Caroline, née Glasse, 432, 433 n.7

Hume, Rev. Thomas, 433 n.7

Humphrey, H. (engraver), 454

Hunt, Miss (sub-governess to Princess Charlotte Augusta), 223, 224n.4
Hunt, Rowland (1754–1811) (landowner of Boreatton): *A Word on the Times, to those who Buy* (food for the poor), 173, 174–75n.4
Hunter, Anne, née Home (1741–1821) (wife of the surgeon) (poetess), 167n.11
Hunter, John (1728–93) (surgeon and anatomist), 167n.11
Hutchinson. *See* Hely-Hutchinson

Ibrahim Bassa (Pasha), 436 and n. 10
Ickworth. *See* Hervey
Inchiquin. *See* O'Bryan
Innocent IV (pope). *See* Sinibaldo de' Fieschi
Iselin (Iselius), Jacob Christoph (1681–1737) (Swiss theologian and philologist), 299, 301n.6
Isis (Egyptian deity), 445, 446n.4

Jackson, Eliza E. (d. 1829 or 1830) (wrote *Dialogues on the Doctrines and Duties of Christianity*, 1806) 85, 86n.4, 465; friendship with PSW/PSP, TSW, and Hannah More, 439, 441n.5; sons of, 103, 105n.14, 441n.5
Jackson, Henry ("little Harry") (son of Eliza), 439
James I (king of England), 137n.3
James, Lady Jane, née Pratt (d. 1825) (wife of Sir Walter), 468n.12
James, Sir Walter (d. 1829), baronet, of Berkshire, 218n.4, 343, 349, 467, 468n.12
James Francis Edward Stuart, Prince (the "Old Pretender"), 128, 130n.8
Jenkinson, Robert Banks (1770–1828), baron Hawkesbury and second earl of Liverpool (foreign secretary): as forgery victim, 411–12 and n.4; and signing of "Preliminaries of Peace," 329, 331n.2
Jervis, Adm. John (1735–1823), first lord of the Admiralty, earl of St. Vincent, 60, 63n.4, 456 andn.3, 457, 458n.4
Jesse, Mary, 279, 280n.13
Jesse, Rev. William, 280n.13
Johnson, Richard: *Famous Historie of the Seven Champions of Christendom*, 322, 323n.5
Johnson, Samuel (SJ): as "Blinking Sam" in portrait by Reynolds, 406; as guardian of Thrale daughters, 334; and HLP's *British Synonymy*, 9; *Vanity of Human Wishes*, 388, 389n.4, 407 and n.1, 445, 446n.5, 479nn. 4 and 5, 484; *Works* of published by Stockdale, 241n.2
—attitudes and opinions of: on filial duty in *Anecdotes, Rambler, Rasselas*, 103, 105n.15; on indulgence, 255, 256n.1, 298, 299n.6; on lawyers, 405, 407n.3; on love and hate in *The Fountains*, 75, 77n.12, 259, 260n.4; on passage of time in *English Poets*, 74, 76n.1; on reading, 280n.6; on St. Colum and Icolmkill in *Journey to the Western Islands*, 227, 229n.1; on Shakespeare's learning, 137n.6; on Thomson's *Sophonisba*, 341n.6; on tragic heroines in "Preface" to *Johnson's Shakespeare*, 160, 161n.2; on trivial pursuits in *Anecdotes*, 201 and 202n.2
Johnstone, Thomas Crane (relative of Elizabeth Madocks), 58, 59n.7
Jones, Capt., of the *James* tender, 484, 486n.9
Jones, Ann (housekeeper and mistress of Peter Giles), 196n.18, 353
Jones, Edward (tenant of Bachygraig, 1784–1800), 100, 101n.11, 214 and n.3
Jones, Edward (b. 1787), of Bachygraig, 101n.11
Jones, Eleanor, née Owens (wife of Edward), 100, 101n.11
Jones, Esther (b. 1784), of Bachygraig, 101n.11
Jones, John ("good old Mr. Jones") (1717–1806), of Mitcham, Surrey, and London, 99, 101n.6, 113, 201
Jones, John (landowner adjacent to Brynbella), 233n.1
Jones, John (minister of Tremeirchion church), 327, 329n.9
Jones, Lewis, of Oswestry, 118, 119n.2
Jones, Manice (b. 1788), of Bachygraig, 101n.11
Jones, Peter (d. 1793), of Bachygraig, 101n.3
Jones, Samuel (d. 1794), of Bachygraig, 101n.11
Jones, Thomas Tyrwhitt (Opposition M.P.), 213n.1
Jonson, Ben: *The Alchemist*, 475, 476n.3; *Every Man in his Humour* (Bobadill), 421n.9
Jordan, Dorothea (or Dorothy) (1761–1816) (actress), 103
Joseph II (1741–90) (Holy Roman Emperor,

1765–90; king of Bohemia and Hungary, 1780–90), 148, 149n.3
Jourdan, Maréchal Jean-Baptiste, later comte (1762–1833), 93n.4
Julius Capitolinus (biographer): *Historia Augusta*, 456n.1
Junot, Gen. Jean-Andoche, duc d'Abrantes (1771–1813), 418n.9
Justinian I (Flavius Amicius Justinianus) (483–565) (Roman emperor), 485n.2
Justinus (Justin), Marcus Junianus: *Iustini historici politissimi Epitoma*, 380, 382n.13
Juvenal (Decimus Junius Juvenalis) (ca. 60–ca. 40 B.C.): *Satire 10*, 484

Katherine of Berain (Berayne) (1534/5–91) (wife of John Salusbury, d. 1566; Richard Clough, d. 1570; Maurice Wynn of Gwydir; Edward Thelwall, d. 1610), 216, 217n.12
Keith. *See* Elphinstone
Kelly, Michael (actor and musician), 116n.11
Kemble, Charles (1775–1854) (son of Roger; brother of SS): performs in Godwin's *Antonio*, 253, 255n.8, 393n.2
Kemble, John Philip (1757–1823) (son of Roger Kemble; brother of SS) (actor-manager), 198, 199n.5, 393n.2; adapts and performs in Joanna Baillie's *De Monfort*, 85, 86n.5, 166, 167n.12, 198, 199n.3; as manager of the Dury Lane Theater, 353, 354n.7; performs in Pye's *Adelaide*, 166, 167n.10; performs in Sotheby's *Julian and Agnes*, 279, 280n.11; performs in Shakespeare's *King John* with SS, 253, 255n.5; produces and performs in *Winter's Tale*, 353, 354n.10; as trustee for the Siddonses, 477n.7
Kemble, Roger (1721–1802) (father of SS, John Philip, Charles, Stephen, et al.) (actor-manager), 392, 393n.2
Kemble, Stephen, or George Stephen (1758–1822) (son of Roger; brother of SS), 393n.2
Kenmare. *See* Browne
Kentish, Rev. John (1768–1853) (Unitarian divine): *Moral Tendency of Christian Doctrine*, 52n.2
Kenyon, Lloyd (1732–1802), first baron Kenyon (lord chief justice), 98n.8
Kerr, Isabella, née Errington (d. 1794), 144n.7
Kerr, Gen. John Manners (1766–1843), 144n.7
Kerr, William (1738–1824), M.D., 144n.7

Kerr, William (b. 1794): as classmate of JSPS, 143, 144n.7, 410, 411n.6
Kerr family: and earldom of Ancram and marquessate of Lothian, 143, 144n.7
Killala, bishop of. *See* Stock, Joseph
Kilwarden. *See* Wolfe
King, Edward: *Morsels of Criticism*, 297, 299n.5; *Munimenta Antiqua*, 327, 328n.5
King, James (Bath master of ceremonies), 180, 182n.3
Kirkham's Hotel, Brook Street, London, 201, 202n.6
Kirkwall, Viscountess. *See* Fitzmaurice, Anna Maria
Kirwan, Walter Blake, 391, 392n.5
Kléber, Gen. Jean-Baptiste (French commander in Egypt), 178, 179n.2, 183n.12, 277n.4
Korsakov, Gen. Alexander Mikhailovitch Rimski (1753–1840), 127n.8
Kosciusko, Thaddeus (Polish hero): and Helen Maria Williams, 353, 354n.11, 370, 371n.5
Kotzebue, August Friedrich Ferdinand von (1761–1819) (German dramatist), 225
Kray, Gen. Paul (1735–1804), baron Kray de Krajowa (commander of Austrian forces), 53–54n.1, 182n.7
Kymer, Elizabeth: and "Blue School" in Streatham, 246n.6
Kymer, John (landowner and London merchant), 245, 246n.6, 386, 387n.10
Kymer, Mary Anne (widow of John): and "Blue School" in Streatham, 245, 246n.6

La Châtre, Claude-Louis (1745–1824), comte de (later duc de), as émigré, 110n.6
Laidley, Dr. (British trader in Africa), 189, 190nn. 2 and 3
Lalande, Joseph-Jérôme-Le Français de (1732–1807) (astronomer), 160, 161n.1
Lambton, Lady Anne Barbara Frances, née Villiers, 411n.5
Lambton, John George, later viscount Lambton and first earl of Durham: as classmate of JSPS, 410, 411n.5
Lambton, William Henry, 411n.5
Langbaine, Gerard, the younger (1656–92), 137n.6
Languet de Gergy (founder of Enfants Malades), 386–87n.2
Lanjuinais (Lanjaunais), Jean-Denis (1753–1823) (French politician), 23
Lansdowne. *See* Petty

Lanzoni (refugee from Perugia, Italy), 245, 246 n.3
Laodice (fl. third cent. B.C.) (mother of Seleucus II), 290, 291 n.2
La Revellière-Lepeaux, Louis-Marie (member of French Directory), 95 n.8
Lawrence, Sir Thomas (1769–1830) (artist): drawing of Sophia Lee, 466; drawing of Samuel Lysons, 379; intimacy with Sally and Maria Siddons, 117 n.16; intimacy with SS, 87 n.12, 476–77 n.7
Layard, Brownlow Villiers (son of Charles Peter; priest at Saint Asaph), 433, 434 n.2, 439, 441 n.7, 467 n.2
Layard, Caroline Bethia (1787–1827) (daughter of Charles Peter), 467 n.2
Layard, Charles Edward (son of Charles Peter), 467 n.2
Layard, Rev. Charles Peter, D.D., 404, 405 n.4; as dean of Bristol, 404, 405 n.4; death of, 413, 414 n.8; subscription for relief of his family, 414, 415 n.2, 465, 467 n.1
Layard, Charlotte Susanna (1780–1858) (daughter of Charles Peter), 467 n.2
Layard, Henrietta Margaret (1782–1855) (daughter of Charles Peter), 467 n.2
Layard, Henry Peter John (son of Charles Peter), 467 n.2
Layard, Louisa, née Port (wife of Brownlow Villiers), 434 n.2
Layard, Louisa Frances (1789–1851) (daughter of Charles Peter), 467 n.2
Layard, Marianne (1781–1840) (daughter of Charles Peter), 467 n.2
Leclerc, Gen. Victor-Emmanuel (1772–1802), 352 n.7
Lee, George Augustus (brother of Harriet and Sophia), 174
Lee, Harriet, 74, 155, 215, 316, 431; as author of "The Officer's Tale," 121, 122 n.5; as co-author (with Sophia) of *The Canterbury Tales*, 97, 103, 105 n.15, 113, 115 n.4, 262, 301, 302 n.13; and HLP's *Retrospection*, 253 n.2, 290 n.19, 301; "Kruitzner . . . a German Tale" and HLP, 312, 314 n.6, 315, 317 n.3, 325, 331, 332 n.15; as proprietor (with Sophia) of Belvidere House (school in Bath), 72 n.4, 204 n.2, 272, 273 n.4, 279 n.3, 337; relationship with William Godwin, 273 n.4, 316, 317 n.6; relationship with HLP, 74, 191, 240, 300, 301, 302 nn. 9 and 13, 306, 310, 311 n.8, 316, 384, 431, 467
Lee, Matthew Allen (husband of Rachel), 453 n.1

Lee, Rachel Fanny Antonia, *soi disant* baroness le Despencer, 457, 458 n.11, 461, 462 n.5; abduction of by Gordon brothers, 451, 453 n.1, 462 n.4
Lee, Sophia, 74, 155, 160, 215, 316, 431; *The Chapter of Accidents* (dramatic comedy), 174, 175 n.6; "The Clergyman's Tale," 121, 122 n.5; as co-author (with Harriet) of *The Canterbury Tales*, 97, 103, 105 n.15, 113, 115 n.4, 262, 301, 302 n.13; drawing of by Lawrence, 466; *The Life of a Lover*, 467, 468 n.7; as proprietor (with Harriet) of Belvidere House (school in Bath), 72 n.4, 204 n.2, 272, 273 n.4, 279 n.3, 337; "The Two Emilys," 273, 274 n.10
Leeds. *See* Osborne
Leheup (or Lewcup), Peter, 257, 258 n.10
Leicester. *See* Montfort
Lémery, Louis: *Traité des Aliments*, 90, 91 n.7
Leo, Daniel, of Llanerch Park (d. 1803) (sheriff of Denbigh), 57 n.14, 75, 79, 94, 169; death of, 81 n.19, 422 n.7; excessive tree-cutting of, 349, 350 n.5
Leo, Henry (illegitimate son of Daniel): as principal beneficiary of Letitia Leo, 341 n.7
Leo, Letitia, née Davies (d. 1801): as heiress of Llanerch Park, 56, 57 n.14, 81 n.19; illness and death of, 169, 340, 341 n.7, 422 n.7
Leochares (fl. ca. 366 B.C.) (Athenian sculptor), 387 n.11
L'Estrange, Sir Roger: *Fables*, 226 n.4
Lewis, Matthew Gregory (1775–1818): *Tales of Wonder*, 467, 469 n.9
Light, Lucretia. *See* Anstey, Lucretia
Ligonier, Edward, viscount Ligonier, earl Ligonier of Clonmel [I.]: duel with Alfieri, 135, 136 n.1
Ligonier, Penelope, née Pitt (wife of Edward, viscount Lignoier): affair with Alfieri, 136 n.1
Lillo, George (1693–1739): *George Barnwell*, 62, 65 n.23
Lindsey. *See* Bertie
Linley, Elizabeth Ann (first wife of R. B. Sheridan), 97, 99 n.12
Linley, Thomas (musician), 99 n.12
Linnaeus, Carolus (Karl or Carl Linné) (1707–78) (Swedish botanist), 90, 91 n.8, 275 n.5, 469, 473 n.10
Linois, Rear-Adm. Charles-Alexandre-Léon Durand, comte de (1761–1848), 308 n.6
Lissey, Mrs. (Pennington servant), 198, 199 n.1

Llangollen, Ladies of (i.e., Lady Eleanor Butler, 1745–1829; Sarah Ponsonby, ca. 1755–1831), 66, 67 n.10, 71, 123, 124 n.2, 140, 150, 173, 183, 217, 218 n.1, 220 nn. 2 and 3, 221, 397; drawings of, 470–71; and Mary Jane Ormsby and Charles Watkin Williams-Wynn, 326 and n. 7; Plas Newydd, their cottage, 118, 119 and n.3, 124, 220 and n.2, 221, 469, 471, 472 n.8; visits to by LC and Piozzis, 221, 263–64; and J. C. Walker, 123, 124 n.2, 220 and n.3; letters from, 177 n.2, 219; letters to, 187–89, 219–20, 263–64, 290–92, 325–26, 481–82

Llewelyn ap Griffith: slain with his brother David while resisting Edward I, 150, 151–52 n.16

Lloyd, Sir Edward Pryce, of Pontriffith (1768–1854), baronet (baron Mostyn, 1831): letters from regarding exchange of land with Piozzis, 232, 233 n.1, 281 and n.1

Lloyd, Hugh (Denbigh grocer), 361

Lloyd, John ("Philosopher"), of Wigfair (or Wickwor) (1749–1815): HLP on his learning, 96, 215; and HLP's *Retrospection*, 213, 384; letters to, 117–18, 205, 232–33, 281, 384–85, 416

Locke, William, the elder (art collector), 305 n.8

Lofft, Cappel (1751–1824), 327, 328 n.4

Logan, Rev. John: *Review of Charges against Warren Hastings*, 241 n.2

Longman and Rees, of Paternoster Row (booksellers), 175 n.4

Lonsdale. See Lowther

Lorges, Jean-Laurent de Durfort-Civrac, duc de (1746–1826), 110 n.6

Loughborough. See Wedderburn

Louis VI (king of France), 119 n.5

Louis XIV (king of France), 333, 385, 387 n.4

Louis XVI (king of France): death sentence and execution of, 24, 439 n.2, 469; effigy of, 64 n.13, 393, 393–94 n.4, 394, 395; spurious *Political and Confidential Correspondence*, 461–62, 463 n.1

Louis XVIII (king of France): refuses to renounce claim to throne, 419, 421 n.12; travels as exile, 109, 110 n.4, 247, 248 nn. 3 and 4, 464, 465 n.1

Louis-Antoine de Bourbon. See Angoulême, Louis-Antoine de Bourbon, duc d'

Louis-Antoine-Henri de Bourbon-Condé, duc d'Enghien: execution of under Bonaparte, 23, 464–65 n.2, 467, 478 n.4

Louis-Henri-Joseph de Bourbon, last prince de Condé. See Condé

Louis-Joseph de Bourbon, eighth prince de Condé. See Condé

Louis-Philippe de Bourbon (1773–1850), duc d'Orléans, king of the French, 110 n.6

Louisa, princess of Stolberg-Gedern, countess of Albany (wife of Prince Charles Edward Stuart), 128, 129 n.2, 135

Lovell, Dr. (Bath physician), 404 n.3

Lowther, Col., 443 n.3

Lowther, Mrs.: child of baptized by LC, 442, 443 n.3

Lowther, William, second earl of Lonsdale, 80 n.6

Luc, Jean André de, 204 n.4

Luc, Margaret de, née Cooper, 203, 204 n.4

Lucas, Robert St. John (founder of York House, Bath), 269 n.1

Lucian of Samosata: *Dialogues of the Gods*, 105 n.17; *Luciani Samosatensis Quomodo Historia Conscribenda Sit*, 484, 485 n.4

Lucullus, Lucius Licinius (1st cent. A.D.): in Plutarch's *Lives*, 287, 288 n.7

Lutwyche, William, 344 n.7

Lydgate, John: *The Churl and the Bird* (trans. from French), 150, 151 n.11; *Fall of Princes*, 151 n.13

Lygon, William Beauchamp, second earl Beauchamp, 105, 107 n.3

Lynch, James Henry (d. 1868) (artist): drawing of Ladies of Llangollen, 470

Lyons, archbishop of. See Fesch, Joseph

Lysaght, Ann, 60, 63 n.2

Lysimachus (ca. 360–281 B.C.), 484

Lysons, Rev. Daniel (1762–1834) (DL): drawing of by Dance, 378; *Magna Britannia* (with brother Samuel), 265, 266 n.8, 329 n.8; marriage to Sarah Hardy, 380 n.1; *Views of Hampton Court Palace, Account of Hampton Court Palace, and Account of Parishes in . . . Middlesex*, 265, 266 nn. 6 and 7; visit to Brynbella with brother Samuel, 328; letter from, 384, 385 n.1; letter to, 377–82

Lysons, Samuel (1763–1819) (SL), 223 n.3; drawing of by Lawrence, 379; illustrations for *Reliquiae Britannicus Romanae*, 265, 266 n.6; *Magna Britannia* (with brother Daniel), 265, 266 n.8, 329 n.8; as trustee for the Siddonses, 477 n.7; visits Brynbella (with brother Daniel), 328

Lysons, Sarah, née Hardy (d. 1808) (wife of DL), 380 n.1

Lysons, Sarah (b. 1802), 380 n.1

Macaulay, Zachary (philanthropist), 190 n. 6
Macdonald, Gen. Jacques-Étienne-Joseph-Alexandre, duc de Tarente, 109, 111 n. 13
MacGuire, Thomas (attorney general, North Carolina), 132, 134 n. 10
Mack, Gen. Karl Freiherr von Leiberich (1752–1828) (commander, Neapolitan Army of the Bourbons), 332 n. 12
Mackay family (HLP's cousins), 311, 312 n. 13
Mackworth, Sir Herbert, baronet, 468 n. 10
Maclaine (or Maclean), Rev. Archibald, 63 n. 8, 173, 174 n. 2, 404, 405 n. 2, 408; translation of Mosheim's *Ecclesiastical History*, 299, 301 n. 3
Maclaine, James, "gentleman highwayman" (brother of Archibald), 173, 174 n. 2
Macmahon, J. P.: translation of *Tableau de Paris*, 171, 173 n. 16
Macnamara, Catherine (widow of Daniel), 162, 163 n. 2, 163, 394, 395 n. 2
Macnamara, Daniel (1720–1800) (duke of Bedford's steward in Streatham), 82, 83 n. 5, 88, 162, 163 n. 1, 394
Madocks (or Maddocks), Elizabeth, née Craven, 58, 59 n. 2, 75, 420, 422 n. 16
Madocks (or Maddocks), John Edward, of Fron Iw, Denbigh (husband of Elizabeth), 56, 57 n. 13, 59 n. 2
Mahomet: and the hegira, 74
Maillé, duc de (emigré), 110 n. 6
Mainwaring, George Boulton (b. ca. 1773) (son of William), 371 n. 2
Mainwaring, William (1735–1821) (M.P., Middlesex), 368 n. 3, 370, 371 nn. 2 and 3
Malmesbury. *See* Harris
Malone, Edmond (1741–1812): *Rise and Progress of the English Stage*, 135, 137 n. 3; third variorum edn. of *Plays and Poems* of Shakespeare, with James Boswell the younger, 137 n. 3
Malthus, Thomas Robert (1766–1834): *Essay on the Principle of Population*, 469, 472 n. 9
Mandeville, Bernard (ca. 1670–1733): *Essay on Charity and Charity-Schools*, *Fable of the Bees*, and *Search into the Nature of Society*, 469, 472–73 n. 9
Mannucci, Teobaldo (Aldo Manuzio) (founder of Aldine Press), 234, 235 n. 4
Mansfield. *See* Cathcart; Greville; Murray
Manuzio. *See* Mannucci
Mara, Gertrud Elisabeth, née Schmeling (1749–1833) (vocalist and violinist), 360

Marbeuf, Louis-Charles-René, comte de: parentage of Napoleon Bonaparte incorrectly attributed to, 171, 173 n. 14
Margaret Tudor (1489–1541) (queen of James IV of Scotland; daughter of Henry VII of England), 128, 130 nn. 8, 9, and 10
Maria I (queen of Portugal), 60, 63 n. 6
Maria Isabella (1793–1801) (princess of Naples), 55, 57 nn. 9 and 10
Marianne: as symbol of acrimonious debate, 185, 186 n. 2
Marie-Antoinette-Josèphe-Jeanne (queen of France), 216, 255 n. 10
Marie Caroline (queen of Naples; sister of Marie Antoinette), 55, 57 nn. 9 and 10, 255 n. 10
Marivaux, Pierre Carlet de Chamberlain de (1688–1763): *La Vie de Marianne*, 439, 441 n. 5
Markham, William (1719–1807), archbishop of York: lines attributed to by Walpole, 375, 377 n. 3.
Marsh, Herbert, bishop of Llandaff and Peterborough: *Politicks of Great Britain and France*, 218 and n. 6
Martial (Marcus Valerius): "Ad Caesarem," 284, 285 n. 13; *Epigrammatum*, 282, 284 n. 1
Mason, David (1748–1812) (father of Mostyn maid), 192, 193 n. 7
Masséna, Maréchal André, duc de Rivoli, prince d'Essling (1758–1817), commander of French army of Italy, 127 n. 8, 131, 132 nn. 1, 3, and 9, 194, 196 n. 17, 200, 201 n. 4, 330, 331 n. 10
Masters, Charles Harcourt: as creator of Sydney Gardens, Bath, 394, 395 n. 4
Maury, Jean-Siffrein, abbé (later cardinal), 478, 479 and n. 6
Mayhew, Clementina Mary (d. 1816) (daughter of Richard), 342–43, 344 n. 7
Mayhew, Richard (Bath apothecary), 344 n. 7
Mayhew, Sophia (later Bayntun) (sister of Clementina), 344 n. 7
Mayhew and Ince (London upholsterers), 383 and n. 2
Maynard, Anthony Lax, 52, 54 n. 4
Maynard, Dorothy, née Heathcote, 52, 54 n. 4
Maurizio Giuseppe Maria (1762–99) (brother of Carlo Emanuele IV, king of Sardinia), 55, 57 n. 8
Mazzinghi, Joseph (1765–1844): composer (with William Reeve) of music for Prince Hoare's *Chains of the Heart*, 347 and n. 6

Meath, bishop of. *See* O'Beirne, Thomas Lewis.
Medhurst, Grenvil William Wheeler, 193, 195 n.3
Melas, Gen. Michael Friedrich Benoit (1729–1806), 187, 188 n.2, 194, 196 n.17
Melville. *See* Dundas, Henry
Melzi d'Eril, conte Francesco (later duke of Lodi), 128, 129–30 n.4, 135
Ménage, Gilles (1613–92): as compiler of *Ménagiana*, 88 n.2, 339 n.2
Menou. *See* Boussay
Mercier, Louis-Sébastien: *Tableau de Paris*, 164, 165 n.4, 165
Mercury, patron of thieves, 231
Merlin, Philippe-Antoine, comte Merlin de Douai (1754–1838) (jurist; member of French Directory), 95 n.8
Merry, Anthony (fl. 1799–1809) (chargé d'affaires, Copenhagen; later minister plenipotentiary and envoy extraordinary), 246 n.2
Merry, Robert ("Della Crusca") (1755–98): death of, 71, 72 n.11, 75.
Metastasio, Pietro Antonio Domenico Bonaventura Trapassi (1698–1782) (Italian poet and dramatist): *Gioas re di Giuda*, 75, 77 n.13
Methven. *See* Stuart
Meyer, Henry (ca. 1782–1847) (portrait painter and engraver; nephew of John Hoppner), 208, 254
Meyrick, James, F.R.S., F.S.A., 171, 173 n.15
Middleton (or Myddelton) family, of Chirk Castle, Denbigh. *See below*
Middleton (or Myddelton), Anne (d. 1781), 142 n.8
Middleton (or Myddelton), Charlotte (d. 1843) (daughter of Richard; wife of Robert Biddulph), 141, 142 n.8, 253 and n.5
Middleton (or Myddelton), Elizabeth, née Rushout (d.1772) (first wife of Richard), 142 n.8
Middleton (or Myddelton), Euphemia, née Crawford (1749–1825) (third wife of Richard), 142 n.8
Middleton (or Myddelton), Harriet, 141, 142 n.8
Middleton (or Myddelton), Maria (d. 1843) (wife of Frederick West), 142 n.8
Middleton (or Myddelton), Mary, née Lloyd (d. 1788) (second wife of Richard), 142 n.8

Middleton (or Myddelton), Richard (1725–95) (M.P.), 142 n.8
Milman, Sir Francis (1746–1821), first baronet, M.D.: as physician to George III, 422 n.17, 453 n.12
Milton, John: *L'Allegro*, 283, 285 n.5; "On Cyriac (or Cyriack) Skinner," 330, 331 n.5; *Comus*, 249 and n.2; Cowper's projected translation of Latin and Italian poetry of, 468 n.4; *Paradise Lost*, 83, 84 n.14, 123, 124 n.3, 291, 292 n.12, 381 n.4
Moira. *See* Hastings
Moleville, A. F. de Bertrand de: *Refutation of the spurious letters of Louis XVI*, 463 n.8
Moncey, Maréchal Bon-Adrien-Jannot de (1754–1842), duc de Conegliano, 206 n.2
Monck (Monk), George, first duke of Albemarle, 154, 155 n.3
Monckton, Mary (1746–1840), countess of Corke and Orrery (daughter of John Monckton, first viscount Galway; second wife of Edmund Boyle, seventh earl of Corke and Orrery), 357, 395 n.10, 382, 383
Monnoie, Bernard de la, French verses of, 87, 88 n.2
Montagu, Elizabeth, née Robinson (1720–1800) (bluestocking): death of, 174, 175 n.8; letter to Elizabeth (Handcock) Vesey, 84 n.9
Montagu, Lady Mary Wortley (1689–1762): HLP on *Letters* of, 413–14 n.2, 436, 437 n.10; in HLP's *Retrospection*, 413 and n.3
Montagu (formerly Robinson), Matthew, fourth baron Rokeby [I.] (nephew and heir of Elizabeth Montagu), M.P., 174, 175 n.8
Montfort, Guy of (ca. 1243–ca. 1288) (son of the earl of Leicester), 257, 258 n.3
Montfort, Simon of (ca. 1208–65), earl of Leicester, in HLP's *Retrospection*, 258 n.3
Montfort, Simon of, the younger (1240–71) (son of the earl of Leicester), 257, 258 n.3
Monti, Vincenzo (Italian dramatist), 125 nn. 6 and 7
Moore, Clementina (sister of John Moore, apothecary), 331 n.7
Moore, John (1729–1802), M.D.: *Mordaunt, Zeluco*, and *Edward*, 168, 169 n.3
Moore, John (1752–1820) (apothecary and surgeon of Bath; originally of Cocker-

mouth, Cumberland), 250; treats Hodgkins and GP, 434, 447, 459, 482
Moore, Maj. Gen. John (1761–1809) (son of Dr. Moore), 54 n.6, 131, 132–34 n.2
Moore, Sarah ("Sally") (sister of John Moore, apothecary), 330, 331 n.7
Moore, Thomas (poet and musician), 357, 359 n.12
More, Hannah, 14, 82, 187, 199 n.1, 215, 257, 299 n.7, 449 n.1; on Rev. Thomas Bere, 272–73 n.7, 300–301 n.8, 341 n.8, 345–46 n.2; and Blagdon controversy, 249–50 n.1, 327, 329, 333, 334, 337–38 n.3, 340; and Blagdon school, 249–50 n.3; books of displayed by bishop of St. Asaph, 336; friendship with T. S. Whalley, 286, 332–33; illness and depression of, 339 n.3, 370, 475, 476 n.6; *Progress of Pilgrim Good-Intent* erroneously attributed to her, 186 n.16; purported marriage to Rev. George Crossman, 312, 314 n.4, 315, 323, 324 n.4; silhouette of by Edouart, 272; sisters of, 273, 274 n.8, 314, 315; *Strictures on Female Education*, 102, 104 n.9; tale of "The Two Shoemakers," 150, 151 n.13; *Village Politics*, 375
Moreau, Gen. Jean-Victor (1763–1813), 23, 93 n.4, 109, 111 n.13, 346 n.5, 465 n.3, 474, 475 n.3
Morris (trustee for SS), 477 n.7
Mortier, Maréchal Adolphe-Edouard-Casimir-Joseph (1768–1835), duc de Trévise, 427 n.5
Mortimer, Thomas (1730–1810): *The British Plutarch*, 303; and *Critical Review*, 303, 305 n.6
Mosheim, John Lawrence: *An Ecclesiastical History . . . from the Birth of Christ*, 299, 301 nn. 3 and 4
Moss, Charles (1711–1802), bishop of Bath and Wells, 346 n.2, 414 n.8
Mostyn, Anna Maria (ca. 1778–1846) (sister of JMM), 159 and n.4
Mostyn, Cecilia Margaretta, née Thrale (1777–1857) (daughter of HT and HLT) (CMM), 190; described, 457; entertains De Blaquieres, Kirkwalls, and Piozzis in London, 467; and London vs. Wales, 160, 420, 423–24; and Piozzis' twenty-fifth wedding anniversary, 474 and n.1; pregnancy of, 79, 81 n.15; relationship with her sisters, 328; relationship with HLP, 275, 276 n.8, 442, 443 n.3; sons of, 457, 467, 474 and n.1; travels to London, Streatham, Tunbridge, Brighton, 78, 80, 214, 443 n.3
—and John Meredith Mostyn (JMM), 113; elopement with, 107 n.14; meet Prince of Wales at Streatham, 78, 80 n.5; reconciliation with and return to Wales, 415
Mostyn, Henry Meredith (1799–1840) (second son of JMM and CMM), 100, 101 n.12, 443 n.3, 457, 467, 474 and n.1
Mostyn, Rev. John (d. 1801), curate of St. Marcella's church, Denbigh, 271, 273 n.1
Mostyn, John Ellis, of Holywell, Flintshire (father of the curate), 271, 273 n.1
Mostyn, John Meredith (1775–1807) (JMM): affair with CMM's maid, 192, 193 n.7; illness of, 445–46, 457, 458 n.8; at London and Streatham, 78, 80–5; at London without CMM, 94; relationship with Prince of Wales, 80 n.5; retains estate at Segroid, 160, 161 n.4; in Wales, 328; letter to, 159 n.4
Mostyn, John Salusbury (1798–1827) (eldest son of JMM and CMM), 100, 101 n.12, 443 n.3, 457, 467, 474 and n.1; attends Davies' school, Streatham, 446 n.7
Mostyn, Margaret, née Wynn (wife of Sir Roger), 421 n.14
Mostyn, Sir Roger (ca. 1735–96), fifth baronet of Mostyn, 141, 420, 421 nn. 14 and 15
Mostyn, Samuel (1755–1819) of [Calcot] and Nantgwillim Farm (brother of Rev. John Mostyn, curate), 214, 215 n.5
Mostyn, Sir Thomas (1776–1831), sixth baronet, M.P. for Flintshire, 141, 142 n.7
Mostyn, Thomas Arthur Bertie (1801–76) (third son of JMM and CMM), 315 n.11, 443 n.3, 457, 467, 474 and n.1
Moulin, Gen. Jean-François-Auguste (1752–1810) (member of French Directory), 95 n.8
Mount Edgcumbe. *See* Edgcumbe
Mountjoy. *See* Blount; Gardiner; Stuart
Mullins, William Townshend (1761–1827), second baron Ventry (first husband of Frances Elizabeth Sage), 85, 86 n.7, 115
Münchausen. *See* Hieronymous
Murphy, Arthur (1727–1805): and Crowmarsh dispute, 146; dedicates his translation of Vanière's *Prædium Rusticum, The Bees*, to SAT, 101 n.4; illness of, 91 n.2; *Life of Garrick*, 287, 289 nn. 10, 11, and 12; temperance of, 90, 91 n.12, 176, 177 n.4, 257

Murray, David (1727–96), second earl of Mansfield, 228, 229 nn. 8 and 9

Murray, Harriott (actress at Covent Garden): marriage of to Henry Siddons, 207 n.2

Mustapha III, pacha of Belgrade, 295 n.13, 352 n.6

Myddelton, May, née Ogilvie, of Aberdeen (d. 1823) (wife of Robert, 1751–1815; mother of eight children, including Ogilvie John), 109, 110 n.10, 218 n.5, 445, 446 n.6

Myddelton, Ogilvie John (1794–99), 110 n.10

Myddelton, Rev. Robert, of Gwaynynog, Denbighshire (1729–97) (rector of Denbigh), 109

Myddelton, Rev. Robert, D.D., of Gwaynynog (1751–1815) (rector of Rotherhithe, Surrey; husband of May, née Ogilvie), 109, 110 n.10, 262

Myddelton, Rev. Robert (1795–1870) (rector of Rotherhithe, Surrey): succeeds to the Gwaynynog estate in Denbighshire, 442, 443 n.7

Naples, royal family of. *See* Alberto Maria; Ferdinando IV; Marie Caroline; Maria Isabella

Nares, Edward (1762–1841), 'ΕΙΣ ΘΕΟΣ, 'ΕΙΣ ΜΕΣΙΤΗΣ, 348 n.3

Nares, Lady Georgina Charlotte (1771–1802) (daughter of fourth duke of Marlborough; wife of Edward), 348 n.3

Nelson, Frances Herbert, née Woolward (Nisbet), Lady, 60

Nelson, Adm. Horatio, baron and viscount Nelson, and duke of Bronté, 57 nn. 9 and 12, 283 n.3; battle of the Nile, 89 n.8; blockade of Toulon, 427–28 n.6; created duke of Bronté by Ferdinando IV, 283, 285 n.7; failure at Boulogne, 310, 311 n.10, 313, 314 n.9; victory at Copenhagen, 275 n.3

Neville, Lady Cecily (daughter of first earl of Westmorland, 374 n.9

Newcastle-under-Lyne. *See* Pelham-Clinton

Newton, Thomas (d. ca. 1834) (tenant of Crowmarsh Battle), 146, 147 n.2, 178, 198

Ney, Maréchal Michel (1769–1815), Prince de la Moskowa, duc d'Elchingen, 388 n.12

Nicholls, Rev. Norton, of Blundeston, 311, 312 n.12

Nixon, Robert (fl. 1620) ("Cheshire idiot"), prophecies of, 449 n.2

Norfolk (LC's servant), 54

Norman, Anne, née Gray (wife of Samuel Norman of Taunton; sister of RG), 346 n.3

Norris, Randall (attorney for Q): and Crowmarsh lease, 146, 148 n.5, 197

Northumberland. *See* Smithson and Percy

Nugent, R. (French emigré at Bath), 157, 158 n.1, 158, 159 n.2

Oakeley, Sir Charles (1751–1826), baronet, 175 n.9

Oakeley, Helena, née Beaton, Lady (d. 1829), 174, 175 n.9

O'Beirne, Thomas Lewis, bishop of Ossory and Meath, 363, 364 n.2, 390 and n.3, 459

O'Brien, Margaret, née Macnamara (fl. 1765–1804) (niece of Catherine and Daniel Macnamara), 87, 88 n.1, 162 nn. 2 and 3, 395 n.2

O'Bryan, Mary (1755–1831), *suo jure* countess of Orkney (wife of Thomas Fitzmaurice, Lleweni Hall; mother of Lord Kirkwall), 414, 415 n.2, 457, 465

O'Bryan (or O'Brien), Murrough (1726–1808), baron Thomond of Taplow, Bucks., marquess of Thomond [I.], fifth earl of Inchiquin [I.] (grandfather of Lord Kirkwall), 326 and n.8, 338 n.9, 420, 422 n.17, 425, 426 n.1, 434, 451 n.7

O'Coighley (or Quigley), James (rebel Irish priest), 18

O'Connor, Arthur (1763–1852) (Irish rebel), 18

Odoacer (476–93) (king of Italy), 206, 207 n.1

Oldfield, John (fl. 1780–1842) (attorney): and Gittins, Bachygraig tenant, 235 n.2

Oldmixon, John (1673–1742) (whig historian and pamphleteer), 449 n.2

Ongley (navy official wounded during assassination attempt on George III), 194, 196 n.10

Orford. *See* Walpole

Orkney. *See* Fitzmaurice

Ormsby, Margaret (wife of Owen; mother of Mary Jane; heiress of William), 60 n.9, 216 n.5, 228

Ormsby, Mary Jane (daughter of Margaret and Owen), 216 n.5; HLP's cousin, 262, 263 n.9; inherits William Owen's Godolphin property, 59, 60, 216 n.5, 338 n.9; reputed fiancée of Charles Watkin Williams-Wynn, 326 n.7; reputed fiancée of

Lord Kirkwall, 210, 211n.6, 219 and n.2, 228, 286, 338n.9
Ormsby, Owen (husband of Margaret; father of Mary Jane), 60n.9, 215, 216n.5
Ormsby, William, of Porkington, Salop, 60n.9, 216n.5
Ormsby. *See also* Fitzmaurice (Viscount Kirkwall)
Osborne, Francis Godolphin (1750/51–99), fifth duke of Leeds, death of, 58, 59n.8
Osmond Bey (Mameluke leader): succeeds Murad Bey, 304n.1
Otto, Louis-Guillaume (1754–1817), comte de Mosloy (French diplomat), 331n.3
Ott von Batorkez, Field Marshal Peter Carl von (1738–1809), baron: at siege of Genoa, 194, 196n.17
Ovid: *Epistulae ex Ponto*, 148, 149n.2; *Fasti*, 138, 139n.1, 143n.1; *Heroides*, 60, 63n.3; *Metamorphoses*, 146, 147n.4, 265, 266n.9, 394
Owen, John (1741–1823) (brother of Margaret), 215, 216n.4
Owen, Margaret (1743–1816) (Shrewsbury relative of HLP), 71, 99, 228, 252–53; visit to Brynbella by, 215, 216n.4; visit to by Piozzis, 173, 176; letter to, 58–60

Pache, Jean-Nicholas (1746–1823), "Citizen Pache" (Girondist; mayor of Paris): exile of in England, 410, 411n.3
Paget (formerly Bayly), Henry (1744–1812), tenth baron Paget, third earl of Uxbridge, 276, 277n.1
Paine, John (d. 1796) (blacksmith): memorial inscription for, 377, 380n.2
Paine, Thomas (1737–1809): friend of Godwin, 169n.5; *Rights of Man* satirized, 170n.6
Palmer, Charlotte (fl. 1780–97): *Letters on several Subjects from a Preceptress to her Pupils who have left School*, 117n.15
Palmer, John (1742–1818): innovator of mail-coach system, 268
Palmer, Thomas (barrister), 262–63n.3
Palmerston. *See* Temple
Palmieri, Matteo: *La cittè di vita*, 130–31n.15
Park, Mungo: on slavery, 107n.10; *Travels in Africa*, 17, 106, 107n.9, 189, 190n.1
Parker, Master (child prodigy), 93, 94n.1
Parker, Adm. Sir Hyde (1739–1807), 281n.5
Parkinson, John (Streatham surgeon-dentist), 322 and n.2
Parr, Samuel (1747–1825) (classicist and schoolmaster), 311n.5; *A Spital Sermon*, 460n.2
Parry, Caleb Hillier (1755–1822), M.D. (Bath physician): attends GP and HLP, 346, 347nn. 2 and 3; 383, 404, 405, 408, 429; and Bath architecture, 358–59n.7
Parsons, William (fl. 1764–1807) (Della Cruscan in Italy, 1784–87): carries letter to LC, 171; carries letter from PSP, 465; contributions to *Florence Miscellany* and *A Poetical Tour*, 125 and n.5; friend of Pindemonte, 125 and n.5, 128; visits Brynbella, 157
Pasvan Oglu (Pazvantoglu or Pasvantoglu) (1758–1807) (rebel Bulgarian chieftain), 334, 335n.8, 352n.6
Paul I (Pavel Petrovich) (1796–1801) (czar of Russia): assassination of, 274, 275n.6; and embargo on British ships, 244, 246n.2, 248n.3, 268n.4; erratic behavior and defection of, 185, 186n.3, 187, 188n.3, 206n.1, 247, 263n.5; as French puppet, 247, 250; quarrel with Bonaparte, 275n.6
Paulo, Comte Jules de, 110n.4
Peart, Edward (ca. 1756–1824) (physician), 399n.1
Pegus, Charlotte Susanna, née Layard (Bertie), 467n.2
Pegus, Rev. Peter William (d. 1860), 467n.2
Pelham, Thomas (1756–1826) (later second earl of Chichester), 453n.2
Pelham-Clinton, Thomas (1752–95), earl of Lincoln and third duke of Newcastle-under-Lyne (father of Anna Maria Cotton), 252, 253n.3
Pellew, Sir Edward (1757–1833), first baronet (later admiral and first viscount Exmouth): and expedition to Quiberon, 212, 213n.8
Pemberton, Emma: letter from, 362n.4
Pennant, Thomas (1726–98) (traveler and naturalist): description of Bachygraig, 216, 217n.12; *A Tour in Wales* (Chester Cycle), 135, 136n.2
Pennington, Penelope Sophia, née Weston (PSW/PSP): conversation of, 300; on current events, 112–13, 115n.2, 279n.1, 337, 439, 440n.2; dislike of Lord Bridport, 102, 104n.5; gift of keepsake to HLP, 197; and HLP's *Retrospection*, 253n.2, 277, 290n.1, 299, 308n.2; illnesses of, 69, 70n.4, 155, 415–16n.5; letter from brother Gilbert, 371n.1; quarrel with HLP, 408n.2, 414, 415n.1, 433, 434n.1,

475, 476 nn. 1 and 2; quarrel with Anna Seward, 173, 174 n.10; on provincialism in Bristol and Bath, 358 n.1; on Q's position on Crowmarsh, 191; on SS's economic squabbles with R. B. Sheridan, 132, 134 n.13;.on TSW's *Castle of Montval*, 97, 98–99 n.10; possible insolvency of, 376 n.2, 384 n.2; visit to Brynbella, 286, 288 n.4, 340; letters from, 86 nn. 1, 2, 3, and 11, 98–99 n.10, 104 nn. 1, 5, and 9, 115 nn. 1 and 2, 117 n. 16, 122 n.1, 134 nn. 5 and 13, 149 n.3, 182 n.1, 216 n.1, 223–24 nn. 3 and 4, 277 n.5, 279 nn. 1, 2, and 3, 280 nn. 6, 7, and 10, 288 nn. 1, 3, and 4, 289 nn. 11 and 15, 290 n.19, 301 nn. 1 and 2, 301–2 n.8, 302 nn.9 and 12, 306 n.1, 306–8, 309 n.13, 312 n.6, 314 nn. 1, 3, and 7, 317 nn. 2, 3, and 4, 329, 331 n.2, 333, 336–38, 338 n.5, 339, 341 nn. 1 and 3, 358 n.1, 371 n.1, 376 n.1, 389 nn. 1 and 3, 404 n.3, 408 n.2, 415 nn. 1, 2, and 5, 424 nn. 1 and 6, 434 nn. 1 and 4, 440 n.1, 441 nn. 5 and 7, 448 nn. 1 and 4, 476 nn. 1 and 2; letters to, 72–73, 84–87, 102–5, 112–17, 120–23, 131–34, 155–58, 173–75, 180–83, 185–87, 191–93, 197–99, 202–5, 215–17, 222–24, 239–42, 244–46, 259–60, 268–70, 271–74, 278–80, 286–90, 293, 312–15, 318–21, 329–31, 336–38, 339–42, 346–47, 352–54, 356–59, 369–71, 375–77, 382–84, 388–89, 390–94, 398 n.4, 402–3, 404–5, 407–8, 414–16, 422–25, 433–35, 439–42, 447–48, 457–58, 465–68, 475–77

Pennington, William (d. 1829), 85, 122, 156, 173, 174, 180, 181, 198, 245, 301, 307, 369, 376, 434; illness of, 131, 134 n.5, 259, 279, 300, 404

Penshurst. *See* Smythe, Percy

Pepoli, Alessandro (Italian dramatist), 125 nn. 6 and 7

Pepys, Sir Lucas (1742–1830), M.D., first baronet, 453 n.2

Perceval, Bridget, née Wynn (d. 1826) (wife of John, viscount Perceval, later fourth earl of Egmont), 353, 354 n.3

Perceval, Catherine, née Compton, Lady (1731–84), baroness Arden of Lohart Castle [I.] (second wife of John, second earl of Egmont), 266 n.1

Perceval, Charles George (1756–1840), baron Arden of Lohart Castle [I.] (brother of Spencer), 266 n.1

Perceval, John (1710/11–70), second earl of Egmont, 266 n.1

Perceval, John (1767–1835), styled viscount Perceval (later fourth earl of Egmont), 354 n.3

Perceval, Spencer (1762–1812) (son of second earl of Egmont; prime minister): assassination of, 266 n.1

Percy, Lady Elizabeth, née Seymour, *suo jure* baroness Percy (wife of Hugh Percy, formerly Smithson, earl and duke of Northumberland), 74, 76 nn. 3, 4, and 5

Percy. *See also* Smithson

Perny, Rev. John Anthony (1758–1825): and Loughborough House School, near Streatham Park, 88 and n.3, 190 and n.8

Perrault, Charles (1628–1703): *Blue Beard*, 256 n.3

Perrée, Contre-Amiral Jean-Baptiste-Emmanuel (1761–1800), 344 n.10

Petty, Henry (later Petty-Fitzmaurice), third marquess of Lansdowne, 219 and nn. 1 and 3; visit to Brynbella, 10–11, 219 n.1

Petty, William (1737–1805), first marquess of Lansdowne and second earl of Shelburne (statesman), 163 and n.5

Pezron, Paul Yves: *The Antiquities of the Nations*, on Celtic antiquity, 485, 487 n.14

Phaeton (Phaethon) (son of sun god Helios and Clymene), 128, 130 n.6

Philipstal (de) (illusionist of "Supernatural Appearances"), 364, 365 n.3

Philoctetes. *See* Fénelon, François de Salignac de la Mothe

Pichegru, Gen. Jean-Charles (1761–1804): and conspiracy against Napoleon, 23, 25 n.46, 428 n.8, 460 n.4, 465 n.3, 475 n.3

Pigott, Honour, of Chetwynd, Salop (1735–1816), 59, 60 n.11

Pilâtre de Rozier. *See* Rozier

Pindemonte, Marquis Ippolito (1753–1828) (Italian poet), 125 and n.4, 128

Pine, Robert Edge (1730–89), executed portrait of HLP for *European Magazine*, wrongly attributed to Reynolds in *Piozzi Letters*, II, frontis. (portrait owned by Courage Brewery, London)

Piozzi, Gabriel (GP): charitableness of, 152, 336, 415; death of, 14; financial problems of, 186; and pianoforte for Ly W, 355; relationship with HLP, 233 and n.1; and James Robson, 92; on taxation, 22, 418 n.8; and Thrale daughters, 82; travels to London and Streatham with JSPS, 54, 56 n.1, 58; valet for, 431

—on international events: election of new pope, 178, 179 n.5; Italy's liberation from

France, 97, 154, 312 n.15; restoration of French monarchy, 178, 179 n.5
—illness of: attacks of gout, 14, 85, 92, 102, 105, 107 n.1, 108, 109 n.1, 111, 191, 200, 203, 205, 210, 281, 312, 331, 339, 409, 410 n.1, 439, 482; in Bath, 342 n.2; and "Bevanda" (pain-alleviating wine), 289 n.16; remission from gout, 65, 140, 154, 169, 197, 201, 214, 231, 275, 445; and St. Anthony's Fire, 336

Piozzi, Giovanni Batiste (Giambattista), of Brescia (fl. 1742–1813) (younger brother of GP; father of JSPS), 10, 473, 474 n.1

Piozzi, Hester Lynch, née Salusbury (Thrale) (HLP)

—on art and literature: Ambrosian Library of Milan, 129, 130 n.14, 296; Bluestocking enemies, 397; books at Streatham Park, 235, 236 nn. 9 and 10; Robert Burton's *Anatomy of Melancholy*, 377 n.5; Mary Charlton's *Wife and . . . Mistress*, 403 and n.4; Chester morality play "Christ's Passion," 137 n.3; Denon's *Travels*, 400, 402 n.13; Gay's *Beggar's Opera* and *Trivia*, 86, 87 n.13, 236, 237 n.2; Gibbon's *Decline and Fall*, 12; herself as model for Floretta in SJ's *The Fountains*, 75, 77 n.12; history vs. fiction, 313, 325, 326 n.5; Italian art works stolen by French, 149, 151 n.6; jest books, 399, 401 n.2; Jonson's *The Alchemist*, 475, 476 n.3; Harriet Lee's *Kruitzner*, 312, 314 n.6, 318, 331, 332 n.15; Sophia and Harriet Lee's "The Clergyman's Tale" and "Officer's Tale" in vol. 3 of *Canterbury Tales*, 121, 122 n.5; mistaken attribution of Baillie's *Plays on the Passions* to Ann Radcliffe, 85, 103; mistaken attribution of Burges's *Progress of Pilgrim Good-Intent* to Hannah More, 186, 186–87 n.6; modern novelists and education, 313, 314 n.7, 331, 332 and n.15; Hannah More's writings on French Revolution vs. Burke's 250 n.4; Nares's *Plurality of Worlds*, 347, 348 n.3; Pope's *Dunciad*, 307, 308 n.5; "Rural Felicity" ("Eileen Aroon"), 283, 284 n.2; Sheridan's *Pizarro*, 113, 116 nn. 7, 8, 10, and 11; *Seven Champions of Christendom* as book for JSPS, 322, 323 n.5; SJ's *Vanity of Human Wishes* and Juvenal, 484. *See also* entries under specific authors

—on battles: Aboukir (first and second), 277 n.4; Agincourt, 419, 420 n.4; Alexandria by British, supposed capture of, 440, 441 n.13; Austerlitz, 110 n.4; Camperdown, 441–42 n.3, 477 n.1; Eylau, 110 n.4; Friedland, 110 n.4; Genoa, siege of, 200 and n.4, 201 n.4, 250; Jena, 110 n.4; Marengo, 216 n.6, 307, 309–10 n.9, 332 n.11; Quiberon, 207, 208, 209 n.8, 212, 213 n.8; Surinam by British, capture of, 132, 134 n.11; Zurich (first and second), 127 n.8, 134 nn. 8 and 9

—health: chokes on bone, 140, 141 n.1; cold, 253; depression, 107 n.1, 154, 191, 408, 411; exhaustion induced by GP's illness, 484; fear of illness, 404, 435, 437 n.5, 445; influenza, 140, 141 n.4, 400, 402 n.16, 408, 409 n.1, 411; insomnia, 148; plague, 435, 437 n.5; rheumatism, 186, 278, 331; and sea bathing as therapy, 409, 410 n.2; stomach disorder, 69, 70 n.3; vaccination, 445

—houses, residences, and property of: Bachygraig, 214, 429; Bachygraig memorial stone, 216; Bath residences, 155, 257, 343; Brighton house bequeathed to HLT and then to CMT/CMM, 191, 192 n.2; Brynbella, 69, 72, 97, 98 n.6, 102, 123, 124 n.4, 232, 233 n.1, 297, 312, 323, 327, 330, 426; Crowmarsh Battle estate, 147 n.2, 175–77 and n.5, 180, 182 n.6, 183–84, 185, 187, 191–92 n.4, 257, 323; Llangwadl and Tydweiliog, Carnarvonshire, 340, 341 n.2; London residences, 352–69; London residences, temporary, 186 and n.5, 189, 194, 196 n.11, 201, 241, 243, 244, 245, 250–51, 252–53, 260; Streatham Park, Surrey, 183, 193 n.10, 338, 405 and n.2, 462

—interests in and attitudes toward: Abraxas stone, 61, 63 n.8, 309; Bath Theatre vs. Drury Lane, 166, 167 n.15; Bath weather, 158; bountiful harvest, 286, 297, 312, 321, 323, 327, 330, 422; British mutineers, 97; charity at Brynbella, 173; *concordia discors*, 469, 472 n.7; conservative patriotism, 225, 368, 450; decline of orthodoxy, 51, 52 nn. 1 and 2, 459, 460 n.2; Duchess of Devonshire's lavish balls, 214–15 n.4; Dunmow bacon, 408, 409 n.11; earthquake in North Wales, 180, 287; fire on hills near Llangollen, 220 and n.1, 221; French customs, 367–68; French emigrés, 462; galvinism, 395, 396 n.6, 397, 398 n.4, 399–400; gypsy fortune-tellers at Norwood, 73; hieroglyphics, 378, 381 n.7; high cost of living in London, 455, 464; history, 12; illness in populated areas, 160; insurrection,

188; lawyers and lawsuits, 179; Learned Pig, 94 n.1; London and London high life, 355–56, 357, 359 nn. 14 and 17, 360, 363–65, 368; London newspapers, 126, 127 n.7, 140, 141 n.4, 274, 275 n.2; marriage, 105; merchants, British, 140–41 n.4, 211, 251, 268 n.5, 270, 306; Methodism, 52 nn. 1 and 2; monarchy, 434 n.4; Hannah More's health as "public concern," 181; the poor, 15, 98 n.6, 120, 148–49 n.5, 212, 242, 243 n.3; New Jerusalem, 298 n.8; raven in "The Lay of Krakamal," 381 nn. 9, 10, and 11; religion in France, 368, 369 n.5; restoration of pope and stadholder, 140; reviewers, 339 and n.4; Rhedycina, 241–42 n.8; Secret-Society Men, 303, 305 n.4, 307, 309 nn. 11 and 12; slave trade and slave labor, 16–17, 25 n.29, 345, 346 n.4; social extravagance, 206, 231, 232 n.4, 237, 464; taxation, 22, 351, 417, 418 n.8; tobacco, 152, 153 n.4
—on legal matters: quarrel with Lady Salusbury, 260–61 n.2, 263–64, 473, 474; rejection of new plea of insanity, 195 n.8; suit against John Cator, 146, 147 n.1
—on national and international events: abolition of slave trade, 25 n.29; Act of Union and United Irishmen as conspirators, 18, 19, 54 n.6, 69, 80 n.8, 82, 84 n.10, 85, 90, 91 n.16, 102, 105, 107 n.7, 166, 167 n.16, 171, 172 n.7, 421 n.6; Addington ministry criticized by landed gentry, 435, 437 n.6; African affairs, 189; Anglo-Russian troops in Netherlands, 126, 127 n.4, 141, 142 n.2; anti-Bonaparte conspiracies, 459, 460 n.4, 474, 475 n.3; attitude toward Louis XVIII, 419, 421 n.12; British capture of Seringapatam, 132, 134 n.11; British democrats, 367, 371 n.2, 373–74 n.6; British expedition to Malta, 152, 153 n.5, 419, 421 n.13, 427 n.3; British labor unrest, 252, 253 n.1; British naval victories and losses, 226, 227 n.2, 276, 277 n.2, 307, 308 n.6; British seamen imprisoned in Siberia, 248 n.3; British subsidies for French royalty in exile, 108, 110 n.5; British triumph in India against Tippoo, 126, 127 n.3, 166, 167 n.9, 271 n.3; British West Indies wealth, 436, 437 n.7; Calais bombarded, 478 and n.2; Catholic emancipation, 18, 19, 269 n.2; Chouans in military action against French, 165, 167 n.7; Cisalpine republic created by France, 268 n.3; Clapham sect, 16; devastation of Rome by French armies, 149, 150 n.5; dissolution of Holy Roman Empire anticipated, 217 n.9; economic outlook for country gentlemen, 206; England as "Cut-Finger Club," 243, 244 n.2; European diseases, Jacobinism and food shortages, 171, 172 n.3; Flannel Acts, 429, 430 n.7; French deceit, 240; French military losses in Italy, 91 n.2, 92, 93 n.4, 95 n.8, 109, 110–11 n.12, 126–27 n.8, 132, 303; French naval fleet at Boulogne, 478, 479 n.1; French prisoners of war in England, 457, 458 n.2; French Revolution, 234, 235–36 n.8, 386–87 n.8; harvest in Wales, 286, 297, 312, 321, 323, 327, 330, 422; Hausa states in Africa, 95 n.4; Helvetian Republic counterrevolutionary movement, 387–88 n.12; high food costs, scarcities, and riots in Britain, 96 n.2, 97, 98 n.6, 102, 120, 148–49 n.5, 152, 153 n.2, 158, 160, 166, 167 n.17, 178, 179 n.7, 187, 200, 203, 222, 223 n.1, 224, 225 n.1, 226, 231, 232 n.4, 238, 239 n.3, 246 n.7, 249, 250 and nn.2 and 5, 251, 270 and n.2, 327, 328 n.2, 455; Hunters Corps disbanded by ministry, 188 n.4; influenza epidemic in Britain, 398, 399 n.1, 404 n.4, 409 n.1, 435, 437 n.5, 442, 443 n.2; Italian resistance to French invasion, 92, 95 n.8, 102, 111 n.12, 126, 127 n.8, 196 n.17, 248 n.2; Labrador Stone as predictor of French Revolution, 393–94 n.4, 395–96 nn. 3, 4 and 5; legislation to enforce residence of beneficed clergy, 414 n.7; military allies for Britain, 171, 172 n.8, 247, 247 n.2; militarism as economic benefit to Britain, 245; military news from Switzerland, 126, 128 n.9, 131, 132 n.2; Ministry of all the Talents, 316; mortality rate in England, 411, 412 n.2; naval armistice (1800), 230, 232 n.3; Old Pretender's birthday, 128, 130 n.12; overthrow and replacement of French Directory by Consulate, 94, 95 n.8, 128 n.9; Parliament's purchase of Russian troops and support, 134 n.12; peace and peace negotiations, 21, 154, 155 n.2, 160, 161 n.6, 222, 223 n.2, 230, 240, 285 n.5, 324 n.3, 325–26 n.6, 333, 352 n.8; possible division of Turkish empire and new war, 335 n.7, 351, 352 nn. 6 and 8; possible invasion of England by France, 281, 307, 308 n.8, 309 nn. 11 and 12, 315 n.12, 326–27, 446 n.2, 446–47, 448 and n.2, 449, 450 n.3, 457, 461, 462 n.1, 463; Prussian troops evacuated from Hanover, 336 n.11; Red Lion conspiracy, 84 n.13, 91 n.16, 93; Sec-

ond Armed Neutrality, 244, 246 n.2; submarines in naval warfare, 349, 350 n.10; Sugar Islands capture, 426, 427 nn. 3 and 4; Turks battle with France in Egypt and French evacuation, 183 n.12, 276 n.4, 286, 302, 304 n.1, 313, 314 n.10, 334; union of France and Spain against England, 102, 104 n.2; voluntary subscriptions for British war effort, 165, 166 n.3; yellow fever epidemic, 148, 149 n.6, 480, 481 n.3, 482, 483 n.1
—personal traits and relationships: ambivalent relationships with daughters, 10, 13, 14, 96, 100, 101 n.1, 180, 403; anger of attributable to her Welsh blood, 181; books and book lending, 252, 399, 463; commissions translation into Welsh of Hannah More's *Village Politics*, 283 and n.4; criticism of second marriage, 9; first impressions often faulty, 388; intellectual feminism, 166, 167 n.11; knowledge of proverbs, 72, 73 n.1; large dowry for HT, 183, 184 n.1, 185, 187; member of Bath literary set, 203; relationship with Streatham neighbors, 88; secretiveness, 388; as self-admitted "Croaker," 19; solitude and idleness, 377 n.5; wedding anniversaries of, 216, 225, 474 and n.1
—quarrels: with CMM, 100, 101 n.11; over Crowmarsh estate, 146, 147 n.1, 178, 179 n.1, 180, 185, 186 n.2; with duke of Bedford, 83 n.6; with Sophia Lee, 306; with PSP, 414, 415 n.1, 475; with Q, 169 n.1, 180; with RD, 142, 143 n.1
—travels and visits (with GP): Ambrosian Library, Milan, 129, 130 n.14, 296; Alnwick Castle, Northumberland, 74, 76 and n.2; Bath, 123, 148–49 n.1, 154, 170, 239, 241, 259, 337, 397, 398 n.4, 464, 480, 482 n.2; Brynbella, 172 n.2, 259, 271, 377; Carnarvonshire, 388; Hampton, 305 n.8; Hawkstone, 233, 234; Irish Channel, 477; Laura Chapel, Bath, 155 and n.4, 269; Laura Place, Bath residence owned by Elizabeth Garrett, 480; Leasowes, 118, 119; Little and Great Ormes Head on Llandudno Bay, 220, 221 n.1; Manchester Square, London, 352, 353 n.1; Oxford, 234; Prestatyn, 316, 321 n.1, 324, 478 and n.1; Shrewsbury, 172 n.3, 173; Sydney Gardens, Bath, 394, 395; their vault at Tremeirchion Church, 429; Vale of Clwydd, 72, 138; Weston Park to visit LC, 224–25, 233, 234
—on treaties: Alkmarr, Articles of, 141, 142 n.9; Amiens, 20–21, 344 n.8, 349, 350 n.6, 354 n.11, 359 n.17, 411, 412 n.3, 477 n.1; Campo Formio, 149 n.4; Congress of Rastatt (Radstat) (1797), 100, 101 n.9; "Convention" between England and Austria, 215, 216 n.7; El Arish, 181, 183 n.12; Peace of Lunéville, 216–17 n.7, 248 n.2, 268 n.3, 330, 331 n.9; Peace of Tolentino (1797), 332 n.12; "Preliminaries of Peace" (1801), 329, 331 n.2, 333
—minor works: "Anniversary Poem: An Answer to the Vipers," 423–24 n.5; "A Ballad [July 1803] when threaten'd with invasion," 428, 430 n.1; "Harvard Piozziana," 63 n.8, 289 n.8; "Hymn . . . for Dymerchion Church," 433 n.6; "Imitation of Horace's 'Audivere Lyce,'" 108; ". . .Lines on Seeing the Portraits in the Library at Streatham Park," 257–58 n.7; *Minced Meat for Pyes*, 64 n.8, 476 n.4; *Old England to her Daughters*, 22, 25 n.39, 436–37 n.6; *Satire: A Party to Richmond*, 443 n.5; satirical attempt at modern fiction, 318–21 and n.2; *Three Warnings to John Bull*, 9–10; translation of "Rex, Lex, et Pontifex," 109
—works: *Anecdotes*, 287–88 n.9; *British Synonymy*, 9, 16, 24 n.26, 203, 341 n.7; *Children's Book or rather Family Book*, 105 n.17; *Florence Miscellany*, 125 n.5; *Johnson's Letters*, 207; *Observations*, 57 n.11, 124 n.1, 125, 152 n.18, 172 n.4, 244, 245 n.1; *Thraliana*, 15, 20, 24 nn. 2, 3, and 6, 80 n.5, 89 n.7, 95, 96 n.2, 98 n.2, 105 n.19, 106 n.1, 107 n.10, 117 n.16, 476 nn. 5 and 7, 482 n.2
—*Retrospection*, 9, 10–12, 24 nn. 9–11, 52, 94, 96, 123–24 n.5, 126, 170, 178–79 n.8, 189, 203, 207 n.1, 215, 218, 240, 242, 267; advance copies of, 253 and n.2; advertising for, 203, 242 n.10; date of publication, 249; effect of Q's chancery suit on, 180; Thomas Gillet and printer's errors, 207, 208 n.4, 243, 256–57 and n.4, 293, 297; HLP's rebuttal to reviewers, 21 n.4, 298, 299, 306, 308 n.2, 376, 377 n.4; potential purchasers of ms. for publication, 201, 207 n.1; reception of, 13, 14, 24 nn. 13 and 14, 249, 272, 273 nn. 3 and 6, 290–91 and n.1, 293, 303, 305 n.6, 310, 311 n.7; reviews in William Cobbett's *Porcupine* and *The British Critic*, 259 and nn. 1 and 2, 295–96 n.14; sales of, 259, 266 n.5, 267, 271 n.4; second edition anticipated, 267; John Stockdale purchases ms. for publication, 11–12, 202 nn. 3 and 7, 240, 241 n.2

Piozzi, Teresa, née Fracasso (wife of Giambattista; mother of JSPS), 10, 473, 474n.1
Pitt, George, first baron Rivers (father of Lady Ligonier), 136n.1
Pitt, Thomas (1737–98), first baron Camelford, 461, 463n.7
Pitt, Thomas (1775–1804), second baron Camelford, 461, 463n.7
Pitt, William (1708–78), first earl of Chatham, 122n.2, 257, 258n.11
Pitt, William (1759–1806) (son of the above), prime minister, 15, 16, 19; and Henry Addington, 414n.6; ailments of, 165, 166n.6, 265, 266n.11, 390 and n.2; and expedition against Batavian Republic, 121n.2; and grain shortages, 166, 167n.11; and the Irish question, 90, 91n.16; and peace negotiations with France and Russia, 213n.7, 426, 427n.2; and possible French invasion of Britain, 307, 308n.8, 309nn. 11 and 12, 315n.12, 326–27, 419, 421n.9; resignation of as prime minister, 269n.2, 270; and slave trade, 22; and tax increases, 20
Pius VI (pope; elected 1775) (G. Angelo Braschi) (1717–99), HLP's misidentification of, 479, 480n.7; imprisonment and death of, 138, 139n.2, 140, 479
Pius VII (pope; elected 1799) (Gregorio Luigi Barnabà Chiaramonti) (1742–1823), 178, 179n.2, 212 and n.6; under Bonaparte's control, 367, 369n.5, 479, 480n.7
Plethon, Georgios Gemistos (Georgius Gemistus Pletho) (platonist), 130n.15
Plumer, Mrs. (JSPS's "preceptress" in Davies' school), 143n.1, 163n.6
Plumptre, Anne, 118n.3
Plutarch (Mestrius Plutarchus), of Chaerones. See Lucullus
Poggio Bracciolini, Gian Francesco (Italian humanist), 150, 152n.17
Polyaenus (fl. ca. 153) (Macedonian writer): Stratagems of War, 290, 291–92nn. 4 and 6, 296
Pomfret. See Fermor
Ponsonby, Sarah. See Llangollen, Ladies of
Poole, Anne, of Beaumaris (1763–1839) (daughter of Richard and Mary, née Owen): letter to, 24n.27, 105–6
Pope, Alexander: Dunciad, 307, 308n.5, 327, 333; Eloisa to Abelard, 435, 437n.4; Epistle IV: To Richard Boyle, 234, 235n.3; in SJ's English Poets, 74, 76n.1; translation of Iliad, 102, 104n.10; translation of Odyssey, 413, 414n.5

Porson, Richard (1759–1808) (Greek scholar), 311n.5
Porteus, Beilby (1731–1808) (bishop, successively, of Chester and London), 346n.2
Portland. See Bentinck
Portsmouth. See Wallop
Powell, Jane ("Jenny") (1766–1838) (friend of PSP), 131, 132, 134n.7, 241, 242n.9, 259, 279, 434; later wife of Rev. Thomas Warren, 260n.3
Powell, Margaret (ca. 1765–1835) (sister of Jane; friend of PSP), 131, 134n.7, 241, 259, 279, 434
Pownall, Thomas (1722–1805) (politican and antiquary), 134n.4
Powys, Lissey Anne, née Cooper, of Berwick House, Salop, 261, 262n.1
Powys, Thomas Henry (1776–1801) (son of Lissey Anne and Thomas Jelf), death of, 262n.1
Powys, Thomas Jelf, of Berwick House, Salop, 261, 262n.1
Pretyman (later Tomline), Sir George (1750–1827) (bishop of Winchester), 345–46n.2
Priddy, Jacob (proprietor of Italian warehouse, Soho), 83, 84n.15
Priddy, Samuel, 84n.15
Priestley, Joseph (1733–1804): satirized, 170n.6
Primrose, Mrs. (ST's maid), 310
Prior, Matthew (1684–1721), 312, 314n.2, 325, 326n.5
Procopius (b. ca. 500) (Greek historian): History of the Wars of Justinian, 184n.15
Pryme, Jane Townley, and Alicia Bayne: Memorials of the Thackeray Family, 473n.15
Psalmanazar, George: Description of Formosa, on souls of animals, 347, 348n.4
Ptolemy I Soter (king of Egypt), 290, 292n.9, 297, 380, 382nn. 14 and 15
Ptolemy II Philadelphus (king of Egypt), 380, 382nn. 14 and 15
Ptolemy V Epiphanes (210–180 B.C.) (king of Egypt): commemorated in Rosetta Stone, 372–73, 374n.10
Pulteney, Lt.-Gen. Sir James (ca. 1751–1811), 152, 153n.4
Pye, Henry James (1745–1813) (poet laureate); Adelaide (play), 166, 167n.10

Quasdanovitch, Gen. Peter (Austrian commander), 50n.3
Quigley. See O'Coighley

Radcliffe, Ann, née Ward (1764–1823): mistaken for author of *Plays on the Passions*, 85, 103
Ragnar [Regner] Lodbrok (legendary Danish king): *The Saga of Ragnar Lodbrok* (sequel to *Volsung Saga*) and *The Lay of Kraka*, 378, 381 n.9
Randolph, Rev. Francis (1752–1831) (proprietor and minister of Octagon and Laura Chapels: prebendary of Bristol), 61, 63 n.7, 73 and n.2, 215, 271, 376, 389 n.13; and Bristol riots, 277 and n.5; illness of, 404 and n.3, 415 n.2, 475; preaching of on public issues, 278, 299, 345–46 n.2, 372, 439; sermon eloquence of, 299, 300, 301 n.2, 331, 415 and n.2; letter to, 180, 181
Randolph, John (1749–1813), bishop of London (brother of Mary), 73 n.2
Randolph, Mary, née Randolph (1745–1809) (wife of Francis; sister of John), 73 n.2, 102, 122, 123 n.7, 203, 222, 299, 314, 391, 392 n.8, 415 n.2, 434; and HLP's *Retrospection*, 245; illness of, 475
Randolph, Rev. Thomas (1701–83) (father of Mary), 73 n.2
Raphael (Raffaello Santi or Sanzio) (1483–1520) (artist): his *Transfiguration* in Vatican Museum, 149, 151 n.6, 385
Rauzzini, Venanzio (1746–1810) (Italian operatic singer and composer), 443 n.6
Ray, Ann, née Barker (wife of Robert), 142, 144 n.5, 202
Ray, Edmund Barker, 144 n.5
Ray, Henry Belward, 144 n.5
Ray, Lucy, 144 n.5
Ray, Robert (d. 1833) (barrister), 200; marriage of, 142, 144 n.5, 145
Ray, Sarah, of Streatham (mother of Robert), 145 and n.2; rents Piozzi land, 405, 407 n.5
Raynal, Abbé Guillaume-Thomas-François: *Anecdotes Littéraires*, 416 and n.1
Reeve, William (1757–1815): composer of music for Prince Hoare's *Chains of the Heart* (with Joseph Massinghi), 347 and n.6
Regnard, Jean-François (dramatist and poet): account of in *Universal Museum*, 293, 295 n.7; mention of in *Retrospection* attacked, 293, 294 n.4, 469, 473 n.12; quarrel with Boileau, 293, 295 nn. 5 and 6
Rennell, James (1742–1830) (geographer), 80 n.12
Rennell, Thomas (1754–1840) (master of the Temple, dean of Winchester), 364 n.2
Rest, Maj.-Gen. (Austrian), 200 n.4
Reubell, Jean-François (member of French Directory), 95 n.8, 110 n.3
Reynier, Gen. Jean-Louis-Ebenezer, comte, 402 n.14
Reynolds, Sir Joshua, portrait of Sheridan, 114; portrait of HLP by Robert Edge Pine wrongly attributed to in *Piozzi Letters*, II, frontis. *See also* Pine
Reynolds-Moreton, Lady Frances, née Herbert (1775–1830) (daughter of Henry Herbert, earl of Carnarvon; wife of Thomas), 55, 57 n.5
Reynolds-Moreton, Thomas (1776–1840), Baron Moreton of Tortworth and earl of Ducie (husband of Frances), 55, 57 n.5, 58
Richard ("poor Reechard") (servant of JSPS and the Cloughs), 313, 315 n.13
Richard I (king of England), 118, 119 n.4
Richard III (king of England), 130 n.9, 374 n.9
Richard, third duke of York (1411–60), 372, 374 n.9
Richards, John (1767–1809) (attorney for Q), 202
Richelieu, Cardinal Armand-Jean du Plessis, duc de (1585–1642), 96
Richer (rope dancer), 166, 167 n.14
Ridgeway, William (barrister), 388, 389 n.7
Ridley (London engraver), 466
Rigaud, Gen. André, 344 n.4
Rinaldo, count of Segni (1254–61): as Pope Alexander IV, 256 and n.6
Rivers, first baron. *See* Pitt, George
Roberts, Rev. John (curate of Tremeirchion church): lodges with Gittins at Bachygraig, 429, 430 n.5; sermon *On the Necessity of a Religious Life*, 424, 425 n.10; translations into Welsh of *Book of Homilies*, a hymnary, and Hannah More's stories, 423, 424 n.4; letters to, 25 n.29, 459–61
Robertson, William (1721–93): *The History of America* (1777), 283, 285 n.6
Robespierre, Maximilien-François-Isidore de (1758–94), 230, 232 n.2
Robinson, George (1737–1801): HLP's first choice as publisher of *Retrospection*, 170, 176, 178, 180 n.8, 200, 201 and n.1, 203, 207, 209 n.9, 213, 218; and Lee sisters' *Canterbury Tales*, 105 n.16
Robinson, Mary, née Darby (mistress of the Prince of Wales): *Memoirs of Perdita*, 82, 83–84 n.8
Robinson, Morris (d. 1777) (father of Matthew Montagu), 175 n.8

Robinson, Thomas (husband of Mary), 83n.8

Robinson, Thomas Philip (later Weddell and earl de Grey), third baron Grantham, seat of at Newby Hall (Yorks.): renowned for ancient statuary, 234, 235n.6

Robinson. *See also* Montagu

Robinson-Morris, Morris (d. 1829), third baron Rokeby [I.], 175n.8

Robson, Rev. George (son of James Robson), 413 and n.2, 438 and n.1

Robson, James (1733–1806) (New Bond St. bookseller); advises HLP to answer critics, 293, 299, 306; political appointment of, 92, 93n.6; letters to, 92–93, 413–14, 438–39

Rochambeau, Gen. Donatien-Marie-Joseph de Vineur (1750–1813), 444n.2, 458n.2

Roche, John (Dublin merchant) (son of Stephen), 269 and n.1

Roche, Stephen, of Limerick, 269 and n.1

Roebuck, Elizabeth, née Tickell, 99n.11

Rogers, Samuel (1763–1855) (poet), 167n.11, 172n.3; portrait of by Hoppner, 254; presumed suitor of CMT and ST, 253, 253–55n.6; writes epilogue for SS, 255n.7

Romulus (first emperor of Rome), 139, 140n.6

Romulus Augustulus (last western Roman emperor, 475–76 A.D.), 139, 140n.6

Roscoe, William: *The Life and Pontificate of Leo the Tenth, Life of Lorenzo de' Medici, Nurse, a Poem* (translated from *La Balia* by Luigi Tansillo), 136, 138nn.10, 11, and 12, 150

Rose, George (1744–1818) (a founder of the London *Evening Sun*), 126, 127n.7

Rosenkrantz, Niels (Danish diplomat in Russia), 261, 263nn. 4 and 5

Ross, Gen. Alexander (1742–1827), 112 and n.2

Rougé, Baron Antoine, 110n.4

Rousseau, Jean-Jacques (1712–78): satirized, 170n.6

Rowe, Nicholas (1674–1718): *The Fair Penitent*, 102, 104n.7, 286, 288n.6; *Jane Shore*, 330

Rowlandson, Thomas (1756–1827): caricature of John Stockdale by, frontis.

Rozier, Jean-François Pilâtre de (balloonist), 372, 374n.7

Ruffo di Bagnara, Cardinal Fabrizio, 118–19 and n.7

Rumbold, Sir George Berriman, second baronet (diplomat), 485, 487n.15

Rusby: tried for grain price fixing, 212n.4

Russell, Lady Charlotte Anne, née Villiers (d. 1808) (wife of Lord William Russell; sister-in-law of Francis, fifth duke of Bedford), 142, 144n.4, 175, 177n.1, 410

Russell, Francis (1765–1802), fifth duke of Bedford, 82, 83n.6, 144n.4

Russell, Lord William, 144n.4, 175, 177n.1, 246, 250, 250n.1

Sacchini, Antonio Maria Gasparo (1730–86) (Italian operatic composer), 159n.2

Sackville, John Frederick (1745–99), third duke of Dorset (ambassador extraordinary to France), 401–2n.10

Sage, "Fanny." *See* Sullivan, Frances

Sainbury, Thomas (d. 1795) (alderman), 113, 115n.12

St. Apollonia (3d cent. martyr), 296, 298n.3

St. Asaph, bishop of. *See* Bagot, Lewis; Horsley, Samuel

St. Asaph, dean of. *See* Shipley, Rev. William Davies

St. Colum. *See* Columba

St. Helens. *See* Fitzherbert

St. Lucia (d. 304) (martyr), 297, 298n.2

St. Patrick, 150, 151n.15

St. Vincent. *See* Jervis

Salusbury, Catherine, née Van (or Vann), of Llanwern (d. 1836) (wife of Sir Robert), 430n.9

Salusbury, Hester Maria, née Cotton (1707–73) (mother of HLP), 183, 184n.1, 447 and n.1

Salusbury, John (d. 1566) (first husband of Katherine of Berain), 217n.12

Salusbury, John (1707–62) (father of HLP): and Bachygraig mortgage, 260n.1; as Nova Scotia colonist, 255n.11; sudden death of, 397, 398n.2

Salusbury, John Salusbury Piozzi (1793–1858) (nephew and adopted son of GP and HLP) (JSPS), 85, 97, 100, 102, 265; arrival of in England, 10; birth parents of, 143, 474n.1; the "Brescian," 79n.3; character of, 322; and GP's illness, 473; life saved by GP, 92; possible illnesses of, 152, 410; resemblance of to GP, 92; and Susan Thrale, 87, 89; letter to, 473–74

—education of, 82; at Reynold Davies' school at Streatham, 10, 53, 88n.9, 165, 216, 236, 316, 410; HLP's plans for, 100,

139, 140n.7; and idiomatic English, 52, 143, 238; and Latin, 361; and religious doubts, 163, 164, 165n.2; visits to by GP, HLP, and LC, 238, 435, 436n.1
—and HLP: heir of, 82, 189–90; impatience with progress of, 175; and place of in landed gentry, 162, 163n.4, 189; pleasure with, 357, 405
—travels and holidays of: to Brynbella, 301, 392; Christmas holidays in Streatham, 142, 152, 394, 395n.3; Easter holidays with HLP and GP, 459; to London with GP, 51, 54, 56n.1
Salusbury, Lucy, née Salusbury (ca. 1667–1745) (grandmother of HLP) (married cousin Thomas of Bachygraig), 429, 430nn. 6 and 8
Salusbury, Sir Robert (1756–1817), baronet, of Cotton Hall Denbigh (heir of Sir Thomas), 430n.9
Salusbury, Sarah, née Burrows, Lady (ca. 1721–1804) (second wife of Sir Thomas Salusbury of Offley): death of, 473, 474n.1; HLP as heiress-at-law of, 184n.1; lawsuit brought by Piozzis against, 260 and nn. 1 and 2; letter to, 260–61
Salusbury, Thomas, of Bachygraig (d. 1714) (husband of Lucy), 430n.6
Salusbury, Sir Thomas (1708–73), LL.D. (uncle of HLP) (judge, Admiralty Court): disinherits HLP, 162, 163n.4; burial of at Offley Place, 429, 430nn. 8 and 9
Salusbury, Lt. Thomas, of Cotton Hall and Llanwern (fl. 1791–1805), 131, 134n.3
Samber, Robert: translator of Perrault's *Blue Beard*, 256n.3
San Martino di San Germano, Emanuele Filippo, styled conte di Front (diplomat), 55, 57n.6
San Martino di San Germano, Giuseppe Francesco Gaetano (husband of Maria Christina) (statesman), 57n.6
San Martino di San Germano, Maria Christina Teresa Ferrero Fieschi di Masserano (wife of Giuseppe), 57n.6
Sannazaro (Sannazar, Sannazarius), Jacopo (1458–1530): *Eclogæ Piscatoriæ*, 154
Sarum (i.e. Salisbury), bishop of. *See* Douglas, John
Saxo Grammaticus (fl. 1188–1201) (Danish historian): *Gesta Danorum*, 479n.3
Schérer, Gen. Barthelemy-Louis-Joseph (1747–1804), 93n.4
Scott, Miss (reputed fiancée of Henry Siddons), 206, 207n.3, 215, 223, 377n.6

Scott, Sir Walter: and *Plays on the Passions*, 167n.11
Scrase, Charles (1709–92): as legal advisor to HLT, 82, 84n.9
Sebastiani, Gen. Horace-François-Bastien de la Porta, comte (1772–1851) (later maréchal de France), 352n.6
Sedaine, Michel-Jean (1719–97): *Le Deserteur*, 216, 217n.1
Seleucus I (Nicator) (ca. 358–281 B.C.), 291n.2
Seleucus II (Callinicus) (ca. 265–225 B.C.), 291n.2
Selim III (1761–1808) (sultan of Ottoman Empire), 171, 172n.9, 287, 352n.6
Seneca, Lucius Annaeus (ca. 4 B.C.–15 A.D.), 472n.5
Sérrant, Vicomte Walsh de (French emigré), 110n.6
Sérurier, Maréchal Jean-Mathieu-Philibert, comte (1742–1819), 93n.4
Seward, Anna (1742–1809) (Lichfield poet), 192
Seward, William (1747–99): death of, 71, 72n.8, 75, 90
Seymour, Algernon, first earl of Northumberland, seventh duke of Somerset, 76n.3
Shairp (or Sharp), Stephen (consul general at St. Petersburg), 275n.6
Shakespeare, William: on his learning and knowledge of Italian, 135, 137nn. 6 and 7, 149–50, 151nn. 8 and 9; third variorum edn. of *Plays and Poems*, 137n.6
—works of: *All's Well that Ends Well*, 476, 478n.8; *As You Like It*, 419, 421n.8; *Comedy of Errors*, 337, 338n.7; *Hamlet*, 90, 91n.5, 198, 199n.4, 218 and n.3, 336, 338n.4; *1 Henry IV*, 105n.17; *2 Henry IV*, 475, 476n.2; *Henry V*, 216, 217n.13, 419, 420n.4; *King Lear (il Rè Lear sue tre Piglia)*, 136, 137–38n.8; *Macbeth*, 316, 317n.8, 340, 341n.5, 439, 441n.4; *Measure for Measure*, 340, 341n.4; *Midsummer Night's Dream*, 223, 224n.6, 257, 258n.4; *Merry Wives of Windsor*, 353 and n.13; *Merchant of Venice*, 105n.17, 306, 308n.3; *Much Ado About Nothing*, 337, 338n.8; *Othello*, 135, 137n.7, 149–51nn. 8 and 9, 318, 321n.2; *Richard III*, 416, 418n.4; *Romeo and Juliet (Tragedià Veronese)*, 102, 104n.8, 136, 137–38n.9, 150, 192, 193n.8; *Taming of the Shrew*, 149–51nn. 8 and 9, 476, 477n.8; *Tempest*, 220 and n.4, 228, 229n.6, 450, 451n.6

Sharp, Elizabeth, née Hopkins (1756–1821) (singer) (mother of Betty), 278, 279–80 n.4
Sharp, Elizabeth ("Betty") (1793–1849) (Bath singer and pianist), 278, 279 n.4, 391, 392 n.6, 443 n.2
Sharp, Granville (1735–1813) (philanthropist), 190 n.6
Sharp, Michael (d. 1800) (oboist) (husband of Elizabeth and father of Betty), 279–80 n.4
Sharp, Michael William (d. 1840) (painter) (brother of Betty), 279–80 n.4
Sheares, Henry, 389 n.7
Sheares, John, 389 n.7
Sheffield. *See* Baker-Holroyd
Shelburne. *See* Petty
Shelley, Eleanor, née Garnier (1702–92), 198, 199 n.9
Shelley, Eleanor (1729–1813), 198, 199 n.9
Shelley, Henry (1693–1735), 199 n.9
Shenstone, William: estate of at Leasowes, 71, 72 n.10, 75, 118, 119 n.3, 357
Shepherd, R.: as translator of Polyaenus, 291–92 n.4
Sheridan, Elizabeth Ann, née Tickell, 97, 99 n.12
Sheridan, Richard Brinsley, 79, 81 n.18, 156 and n.7, 194, 195 n.7, 196 n.9; *Pizarro*, 102, 103 n.12, 113, 116 n.7, 125 n.5; portrait of by Reynolds, 114
Sherwood, John Withers (barrister) (first husband of Elizabeth Whalley), 82, 83 n.4
Shipley, Rev. William Davies (1745–1826), dean of St. Asaph, 325, 326 n.3, 436
Shirley, Anne (half-sister of Laurence Shirley, fourth earl Ferrers, and Robert, sixth earl), 193, 195 n.6
Shirley, Catherine, née Cotton (wife of Robert, sixth earl Ferrers), 193, 195 n.5
Shirley, Laurence (1720–60), fourth earl Ferrers, 193, 195 nn. 4 and 6
Shirley, Robert, sixth earl Ferrers, 193, 195 n.5
Siddons, Cecilia (1794–1868), 155, 300; escorted by Sophia Lee to parents' home in Great Marlborough Street, 160, 161 n.3; as pupil of Lee sisters in Belvidere House school, Bath, 71, 72 n.4, 262, 278, 279 n.3; with parents, 391, 392 n.4
Siddons, George John (b. 1785), 306, 308 n.4; in Bengal Civil Service, 376, 377 n.6, 393 n.2
Siddons, Harriott, née Murray (actress) (wife of Henry Siddons), 207 n.3, 377 n.6
Siddons, Henry (Harry) (1774–1815), 306, 308 n.4; as reputed fiancé of Miss Scott, 206, 207 n.3, 215, 223, 377 n.6
Siddons, Maria (1779–98): compared with Cecilia Siddons, 71; death of, 65, 317 n.2; and Thrale daughters, 85, 87 n.12, 117 n.16
Siddons, Sarah, née Kemble (1755–1831) (actress) (SS), 58, 132, 186, 201, 249, 257, 262, 271, 318, 457; as correspondent, 199 n.7, 317 n.10, 330, 331 n.8, 353, 392, 393 n.2; death of Sally, 415 and n.3; financial difficulties and "home concerns," 287, 289 n.14, 393 n.2; financial quarrels with Sheridan, 81 n.18, 103, 104 n.12, 132, 134 n.13, 156 and n.7; friendship with HLP initiated by Whalleys, 333; and GP and HLP, 271, 352–53; harassment of by admirer, 468, 471 n.2; and JSPS, 262; and Sir Thomas Lawrence, 87 n.12, 117 n.16, 476–77 n.7; marriage of, 222; physical and emotional disorders, 65, 67 n.4, 71, 80, 240, 245, 253, 255 n.9, 302 n.12, 312, 314 n.3, 315, 316, 317 n.10, 333; receives copy of *Retrospection*, 253 n.2, 258 n.3; respite in Bath, 58, 71; and Miss Scott and Henry, 206, 207 n.3., 215; separation from William, 468, 472 n.3, 475, 476–77 n.7; and Whalleys, 333
—acting career of: in Bath and Bristol, 55, 56 nn. 3 and 4, 65 nn. 4 and 23, 69, 71, 274, 275 n.1, 277 and n.6, 279 n.2; in Ireland, 358, 359 n.18, 383, 388, 389 n.2, 391, 392 n.2; in London, 340, 341 n.9; in Manchester, Birmingham, etc., 289 n.15; in Scotland, 117 n.6; cancels northern tour to be with ill husband, 198, 199 and n.1; effect of Maria's death on, 315, 317 n.2; judgments of Arthur Murphy and PSP on, 287, 289 n.14; refuses to perform in *The Fair Penitent*, 471 n.2
—performs in: Baillie's *De Monfort*, 166, 167 n.13; Congreve's *The Mourning Bride*, as Zara, 457, 458 n.5; Home's *Douglas*, as Lady Randolph, 79, 81 n.17, 279, 280 n.10; Kotzebue's *The Stranger*, 156 n.7; Lillo's *George Barnwell*, 62, 65 n.23; Rowe's *Jane Shore*, 156 n.7, 317 n.2, 330; Shakespeare's *King John*, as Constance, 253, 255 n.9; Shakespeare's *Measure for Measure*, 156 n.7; Shakespeare's *The Winter's Tale*, as Hermione, 355; Sheridan's *Pizarro*, as Elvira, 126, 127 n.5, 156 n.7,

166, 167n.13; Sotheby's *Julian and Agnes*, 279, 280n.11; Southerne's *The Fatal Marriage*, as Isabella, 156n.7; TSW's *Castle of Montval*, as the Countess, 85, 86n.6, 89, 98n.10
Siddons, Sarah Martha ("Sally") (1775–1803): death of, 415n.3; failing health of, 198, 199n.6, 223–24n.3, 228, 300; and Sir Thomas Lawrence, 198, 199n.6; on quarrels with Sheridan about money, 81n.18, 156 and n.7; on SS as Countess of Montval, 98n.10; in Scotland with SS, 115, 117n.16
Siddons, William (1744–1808) (actor) (husband of SS): financial difficulties of, 393n.2; illness and retirement of, 198, 199nn. 1, 7, and 8, 222, 223–24n.3, 228, 240, 300, 316; quarrels with Sheridan over money, 127n.5, 156n.7; with SS in Ireland, 376, 377n.6
Sidmouth. *See* Addington
Sieyès, Abbé Emmanuel-Joseph (1748–1836) (member of French Directory), 23, 95n.8, 108, 110n.3, 178, 179n.4
Simmons, Samuel Foart, M.D., 453n.2
Simpson, Elizabeth, née Tickell (Roebuck), 99n.11
Sinibaldo Fieschi (ca. 1200–54), count of Lavagna (later Pope Innocent IV), 128, 129n.3, 135
Slodtz, Michelangelo (sculptor; school of Bernini), 386n.2
Smelt, Leonard (ca. 1719–1800) (army engineer; deputy governor to the royal princes; deputy ranger of Richmond Park), 229n.9
Smith, Charlotte, née Turner (1749–1806): *Emmeline, the Orphan of the Castle*, 136, 138n.13, 150, 151n.14
Smith, Charlotte Sophia Delaval, née Blake (wife of Sir Robert), 351n.5
Smith, Drummond, 462n.2
Smith, Gen. Edward, 357, 358n.6, 376, 431n.11, 467, 468n.11
Smith, Sir George Henry, sixth baronet (son of Sir Robert and Charlotte), 351n.5
Smith (or Smyth), Joseph Bourchier, 457, 458n.9
Smith, Mary, née Cunliffe (wife of Drummond), 357, 359n.15, 360, 362n.6, 461, 462n.2
Smith, Penelope, née Bowyer (Cooke) (wife of Gen. Edward), 429, 431n.11, 467, 468n.11
Smith, Gen. Richard, M.P., 357, 358n.6

Smith, Sir Robert (Paris banker), 351 and n.5
Smith, Spencer (British envoy), 465n.3
Smith, Adm. Sir William Sidney (1764–1840): as naval hero, 178, 179n.3, 183n.12, 283, 417, 418n.13, 457, 458n.3; negotiates treaty of El Arish, 183n.13; as uncle of Gen. Edward Smith, 431n.11
Smithson (later Percy), Hugh, earl and duke of Northumberland, 74, 76n.3
Smith-Stanley, Charlotte Margaret, née Hornby (1778–1817) (wife of thirteenth earl of Derby), 395n.1
Smith-Stanley, Edward (1752–1834), twelfth earl of Derby, 70
Smith-Stanley, Edward (1775–1851), thirteenth earl of Derby, 395n.1
Smith-Stanley, Edward George Geoffrey (1799–1869) (styled Lord Stanley until 1844), fourteenth earl of Derby, 395n.1
Smith-Stanley, Elizabeth (or Eliza), née Farren (ca. 1759–1829) (second wife of twelfth earl of Derby), 70, 357
Smith-Stanley, Henry Thomas (1803–75) (second son of thirteenth earl of Derby and Charlotte Margaret), 395n.1
Smyth, Jane, née Whitchurch, Heath House, Bristol, 284, 285n.14
Smyth, Sir John Hugh, of Heath House, Bristol, 486n.6
Smyth, Thomas, 486n.6
Smythe, Percy Clinton (later first baron Penshurst and sixth viscount Strangford) (diplomat), 219 and n.1
Somerset. *See* Seymour
Sotheby, William: *Julian and Agnes*, 279, 280n.11
Southerne, Thomas (1660–1746): *The Fatal Marriage*, 156n.7
Spanheim, Friedrich (1632–1701): *Opera*, 62, 64–65n.23
Spencer, Edward: *Hannah More's Meeting-Houses*, 346n.2
Spencer, George John (1758–1834), second earl Spencer, 269 and n.2
Spenser, Edmund: *The Faerie Queene*, 453, 455n.4
Sprat, Thomas (1635–1713), bishop of Rochester and dean of Westminster: *The Rehearsal*, 226n.3
Stadholder. *See* William (or Willem) V
Staël-Holstein, Ann-Louise-Germaine, née Necker: and Bonaparte, 400, 401n.9; *Delphine*, 397, 398n.5, 399–400, 401nn. 7 and 8

Staines, Sir William (lord mayor of London), 242, 243n.6
Stanhope, Charles, third earl Stanhope, 357, 359n.9
Stanley, Col. Thomas, of the Royal Lancashire militia, M.P., 463, 464n.1
Starke, Mariana: *Letters from Italy . . . to the Expulsion of Pius VI*, 154, 155n.4
Staunton, Sir George Leonard (1737–1801), baronet: *Authentic Account of an Embassy from the King of Great Britain to the Emperor of China* (1797), 236n.14
Stawell, Henry, sixth baron Stawell, 59n.5
Stawell, Mary, née Curzon, 58, 59n.5
Steele, Sir Richard (1672–1729), 338, 339n.1
Stewart, Dugald (professor of mathematics), 418n.14
Stewart, Robert (1769–1822), second marquess of Londonderry, viscount Castlereagh, 18
Stock, Joseph, bishop of Killala, 420, 422n.16
Stockdale, John (bookseller; former blacksmith, valet, porter), 240, 241n.2, 418n.8, 432n.1, 442, 443n.1; caricature of, 2; dinner party of at London Tavern, 238, 239n.2; as publisher of Hunt's *Word on the Times*, 175n.4, as publisher of Logan's *Review of Charges against Warren Hastings*, 241n.2
—as publisher of *Retrospection*, 179–80n.8, 236, 243, 244n.1, 245, 252, 265, 418, 442, 443n.1; dilatory payments by, 275, 276n.9; "Memorandum of Agreement" with HLP, 237–38; sales of, 249, 259 and n.2; typographical errors in, 267
Stockdale, John Joseph (1770–1847): translation of Dumouriez's *Tableau spéculatif de l'Europe*, 428, 430n.3
Stockdale, Mary (wife of John, the elder), 237n.1
Stockdale, Mary R. (poet and translator) (daughter of John, the elder), 236, 237n.1
Stockdale, Rev. Percival (editor of *Critical Review*), 304, 305n.9
Stodart, John (curate of Tremeirchion Church), 327, 329n.7
Stodart, Malcolm (grandson of Robert), 363n.10
Stodart, Robert (London piano maker), 362, 363n.10
Stodart, William (son of Robert), 363n.10
Stolberg-Gedern. *See* Louisa, princess of Stolberg-Gedern
Stone, Nicholas (sculptor and master mason to James I and Charles I), 234, 235n.7
Strachey (or Strachie), Rev. John (1738–1818), D.D., 182n.9
Stratford, Elizabeth, née Hamilton (d. 1846), 450, 451n.5
Stratford, John (d. 1823), third earl of Aldborough [I.], 450, 451n.5
Stratton, Mary, 272, 273n.3, 391, 392n.9
Stratton, Samuel, 273n.3
Strickland, Cecilia, née Towneley (1741–1814), of Sizergh Park, Westmorland, 126, 227
Stuart, Prince Charles Edward. *See* Charles Edward Stuart
Stuart, Henry, later Lord Methven (third husband of Princess Margaret Tudor), 130n.9
Stuart, John, viscount Mountjoy, fourth earl of Bute, 420n.4
Sturm, Christoph Christian (1740–86); *Betrachtungen über die Werke Gottes (Reflections on the Works of God)*, 402, 403n.1
Suchet, Gen. Louis-Gabriel, 331–32n.10
Suetonius Tranquillus, Gaius: *De Vita Caesarum*, 91n.10
Sulla (Sylla) Felix, Lucius Cornelius (b. ca. 138 B.C.), 469, 472n.5
Sullivan, Frances ("Fanny") Elizabeth, née Sage (Mullins) (fl. 1772–1830) (niece of TSW), 85, 86n.7, 115
Sullivan, Rev. Robert Boyle (d. 1824) (second husband of "Fanny" Sage), 115
Suvorov-Rimniskey, Alexander Vasilievitch, count (field marshal commanding Russian troops in Italy), 93n.4, 94, 98n.7, 112n.2, 113, 115n.2, 127n.8, 165–66, 167n.8; and Czar Paul, 205, 206n.1; and second battle of Zurich, 134nn. 8 and 9
Swift, Jonathan: *Cadenus and Vanessa*, 287, 289n.9; *Gulliver's Travels*, 310, 311n.11, 410, 411n.2
Swinburne, Henry (1743–1803): *Travels in the Two Sicilies*, 247, 248n.9
Symons, John (surgeon of Bath and architectural colleague of Dr. Parry), 357, 359n.7
Sympson, Charlotte, née Hughes (b. ca. 1777), 97, 99n.14
Smpson, Robert (b. 1770), 97, 99n.14

Talleyrand-Périgord, Charles Maurice (1754–1838), 158, 159n.1, 402n.11

Tandy, James Napper (United Irishman), 18, 107n.7, 140, 141n.3
Tansillo, Luigi: *La Balia (The Nurse)*, 136, 138n.12
Tarente. *See* Macdonald
Tate, George: *History of the Borough, Castle, and Barony of Alnwick*, 76n.2
Tatham, Edward: *Sermon preached before . . . Oxford (5 Sept. 1791)*, 460n.2
Tchien Lung (d. 1799): described in Staunton's *Authentic Account*, 235, 236nn. 13 and 14
Tegg, Thomas, 371n.2
Temple, Henry John (1784–1865), third viscount Palmerston, 418n.14
Temple, Sir William (1628–99), 119, 120n.9
Terence (Publius Terentius Afer) (b. ca. 190 B.C.): *Andria*, 299n.4
Thackeray, Eliza Jones, née Wilson (d. 1833) (wife of Dr. Thackeray), 471, 473n.15
Thackeray, William Makepeace, M.D. (1769–1849): treats GP and Hodgkins, 106, 108n.18, 445, 446, 447, 471, 473n.15
Thelwall, Edward (d. 1610) (fourth husband of Katherine of Berain), 217n.12
Thelwall, John (1764–1834), 97, 98n.8
Thomond. *See* O'Bryan (or O'Brien)
Thomas, Honoratus Leigh, M.D. (1769–1846), 81n.20
Thomson, James: *The Seasons*, 223–24n.3, 271, 273n.2; *Sophonisba*, 341n.6
Thornton, Henry (1760–1815) (philanthropist and economist), 190n.6, 369n.7
Thornton, Robert John, M.D. (ca. 1768–1837), 78, 80n.7
Thou [Thuanus], Jacques Auguste de (1553–1617): *History of his Own Time*, 183, 184n.3
Thrale, Cecilia Margaretta (daughter of HT and HLT) (CMT, CMM): illness of in 1783, 89n.3; at Scarborough with Piozzis, 312n.14. *See also* Mostyn, Cecilia Margaretta
Thrale, daughters of HT and HLT: and CMT's inheritance of HT's Brighton property, 192n.2; Crowmarsh dispute described in *British Synonymy*, 204n.1; effect of peace talks on inheritance of, 333–34; visits of to Brighton and Lowestoffe, 262, 328; well-being of, 160, 171, 245, 246nn. 1, 2, and 8, 353, 396, 397, 440, 441n.11, 457, 467. *See also* Mostyn, Cecilia Margaretta; Thrale,
Cecilia Margaretta; Thrale, Hester Maria; Thrale, Sophia; Thrale, Susannah Arabella
Thrale, Henry (HT): and the Almshouse at Newington, 74, 76n.7; his daughters' view of his marriage, 183; and HLS's dowry, 183; as M.P. for Southwark (1765–81), 126, 127n.2, 282n.1; his will and marriage settlement, 187
Thrale, Hester Maria ("Queeney") (daughter of HT and HLT) (later Lady Keith) (Q), 10, 14, 74, 76n.2, 96, 107n.13, 190, 285n.12, 478, 484, 485–86n.6; and Crowmarsh dispute, 178, 180, 185, 187, 193n.10, 197 and n.1, 202; illness of, 98n.2; at Heath House, 423; and HLP's *Retrospection*, 252; at Lowestoffe, 316; residence in Cumberland Street, London, 97; visit to Scotland, 109, 127, 147n.3; letters from 59n.2, 60–65, 74–77, 120n.10, 227–30, 234–36, 252–55, 257–59, 282–85, 286–88, 296–98, 309–11, 311n.2, 399–402, 428–31, 484–87; letters to, 64n.19, 285n.10, 316, 317n.10
Thrale, Ralph (1773–75) (son of HT and HLT), 447 and n.1
Thrale, Sophia (daughter of HT and HLT) (later Mrs. Hoare) (ST), 203, 253, 257, 258n.6, 310, 357, 428
Thrale, Susanna Arabella (daughter of HT and HLT) (SAT), 85, 87, 89, 100, 101n.2, 174, 203, 257, 283, 285n.9, 357
Thugot, J. A. F. de Paula, baron (Austrian diplomat) (or possibly baron François-Marie de Thugot, 1734–1818), 216n.7
Thynne, Isabella Elizabeth, née Byng (1773–1830), marchioness of Bath, 389n.3
Thynne, Thomas (1756–1837), second marquess of Bath, 389n.3, 417n.3
Tiberius, Julius Caesar Augustus (42 B.C.–14 A.D.) (emperor of Rome), 299, 301nn. 4, 5, and 6
Tibson ("old nurse"), 70, 71n.1
Tickell, Elizabeth: as protegée of Sophia Lee, 97, 99n.11, 103. *See also* Roebuck, Elizabeth; Simpson, Elizabeth
Tickell, Mary, née Linley (wife of Richard), 99n.11
Tickell, Thomas (1686–1740) (poet; associate of Addison), 99n.11
Tickell, William (Bath surgeon; concocter of quack medicine), 79, 81n.19, 97
Tierney, George (1761–1830) (Whig M.P. for Southwark), 369n.7

Tomkison (or Tomkinson), Thomas (piano manufacturer in London, with Houston), 360, 362 n.1, 367, 368 n.1
Tomline. See Pretyman, Sir George
Tommy (Piozzi footman), 383
Tone, Theobald Wolfe (1763–98) (United Irishman), 107 n.7
Tooke, John Horne (1736–1812) (radical politician and philanthropist), 97, 98 n.8; friendship with Godwin, 169 n.5
Torlonia, Prince Alesandro [von] Civitella-Cesi (1800–1875) (Roman banker), 57 n.11
Torlonia, Giovanni Raimondo (1754–1829) (banker of Pius VI and VII), 57 n.11
Torrington. See Byng
Toulmin, Joshua (1740–1815) (dissenting historian): *Practical Efficacy of Unitarian Doctrine*, 52 n.2
Toussaint L'Ouverture, François-Dominique (ca. 1744–1803) (Haitian patriot), 344 n.4, 349, 350 n.7, 352 n.7
Travers, Benjamin (alderman and fishmonger of London), 367, 368 n.4
Trefusis, Elizabeth (ca. 1736–1808) (sister of baron Clinton): *Poems and Tales*, 245, 246 n.9
Trévise. See Mortier
Troubridge, Rear Adm. Sir Thomas, first baronet (1758–1807), 283 and n.3
Tryon, Margaret, née Wake (d. ca. 1804) (wife of William), 440, 442 n.14
Tryon, William (1725 or 1729–88) (governor of New York and later of North Carolina), 442 n.14
Tudor, Margaret. See Margaret Tudor
Tudor, Owen (husband of Katherine of Berain), 216, 217 n.13, 420–21 n.5
Tuite, Elizabeth, née Cobbe, Lady (1765–1850), 428, 430 n.2
Turmair, Johann (1477–1534) (known as Aventin, Aventinus, Aventinum): *Annales Boiorum (Annals of Bavaria)*, 291, 292 n.11, 296
Turner, Richard (Bath apothecary), 278, 280 n.7
Turner, Brig. Gen. Tomkyns Hilgrove (ca. 1766–1843) (antiquary), and Rosetta Stone, 381 n.6
Turton, Sir Thomas (Southwark politician), 369 n.7
Twiss, Frances ("Fanny"), née Kemble (1759–1822) (younger sister of SS), 316, 392 n.3
Twiss, Francis (1760–1827) (brother-in-law of SS), 316; *Verbal Index to Plays of Shakespeare*, 391, 392 n.3, 419

Unwin, Mary, née Cawthorne (1724–96), 465, 467–68 n.3
Unwin, Rev. Morley (d. 1767), 467
Uxbridge. See Paget
Uzès. See Crussol

Valens (Eastern Emperor, A.D. 364–78) (brother of Valentinian), 171, 172 n.10
Valentinian (Roman emperor, A.D. 364–75), 171, 172 n.10
Valiant London 'Prentice, Famous History of the (anon., ca. 1750), 322, 323 n.6
Vandercom, Joseph Fitzwilliam (fl. 1764–1834) (Piozzi attorney), 146, 147 n.3, 148 n.5, 175, 177 n.6, 178, 179 n.1
Vaudreuil, Jean-Louis Rigaud (1762–1816), vicomte de (French emigré), 110 n.6
Vaudreuil, Pauline-Victoire Rigaud, née de Riquet de Caraman (1764–1834), vicomtesse de (wife of Jean-Louis Rigaud), 110 n.6
Vaughan, Anna Maria, née Mostyn (wife of Sir Robert Williams), 419, 421 n.14
Vaughan (later Halford and baronet), Henry, M.D. (fellow, Royal College of Physicians): attends ST and George III, 485, 487 n.16
Vaughan, Sir Robert Williams, second baronet, of Nannau, co. Merioneth (M.P. for Merioneth), 419, 421 n.14
Ventry. See Mullins
Vernon, Francis V.: *Voyages and Travels of a Sea Officer*, 234, 235 n.5
Vesey. See Montagu, Elizabeth
Viganoni, Giuseppe (operatic tenor from Brescia), 356, 358 n.3
Vigneul-Marville. See D'Argonne
Villaret de Joyeuse, Vice Adm. Louis-Thomas, comte (1748–1812), 352 n.7
Villiers, George (1628–87), second duke of Buckingham: *The Rehearsal*, 224, 226 n.3
Vincent, William, D.D. (headmaster of Westminster School): *Defence of Public Education*, 363, 364 n.2
Violet, Pierre: and portrait for frontispiece of *Retrospection*, 245, 246 n.5
Virgil (Publius Virgilius Maro) (70–19 B.C.): *Aeneid*, 96, 98 n.5, 206, 207 n.2
Visconti, Ennio (antiquarian), 61, 63 n.8
Vitalba (Bath mercer), 425 n.9
Vitellius, Aulus (Roman emperor and glutton), 90, 91 n.10

Voltaire, François-Marie Arouet de (1694–1778): creates Dr. Pangloss in *Candide*, 395, 396 n.7; on early sources of storytelling, 150, 152 n.19; on Regnard and Boileau, 293, 294 n.5; satirized, 170 n.6

Waldron. *See* Barrington
Walker, Alethea, née James (lavish hostess of West Derby), 283, 285 n.11
Walker, George: *The Vagabond*, 168, 170 n.6
Walker, John (1739–1812) (founder of *The Times*), 89, 90 n.2
Walker, John, II (1776–1847) (son and successor of John), 84 n.12, 264, 266 n.2
Walker, Joseph Cooper, of St. Valerie, Bray, Ireland, 124 n.1, 194, 196 n.13, 220 n.3; and eighteenth-century Italian literature, 125 and n.6; *Historical Memoir on Italian Tragedy*, 123, 124 n.2; "Rappresentazioni" in *Historical and Critical Essay on the Revival of Drama in Italy*, 128, 135, 137 n.4, 150; and spirit of Irish sedition, 136; wish to return to Florence, 136; letters from, 123–24, 128–31, 149–52; letters to, 124–24, 135–38
Walker, Richard (husband of Alethea), 285 n.11
Wall, Gov. Joseph, of East India Company, 342, 343–44 n.3
Wallop, John, second earl of Portsmouth (brother of Catherine Gordon), 461, 462–63 nn. 5 and 6
Walmsley, Thomas (Bath landscape painter), 349, 350 n.4
Walpole, Horatio (or Horace) (1717–97), fourth earl of Orford, 77 n.16, 377 n.3
Walton, W. (artist), 471
Warren, Adm. Sir John Borlase (1753–1822), 107 n.7
Warren, Rev. Thomas (vicar of Tolpuddle, Dorset), 259, 260 n.3. *See also* Powell, Jane
Warton, Thomas (1728–90) (Oxford professor of poetry and ancient history): on the Chester Mysteries, *History of English Poetry*, 135, 137 n.3; on Medea's oil, 184 n.4
Watson, Robert: *History of the Reign of Philip the 2d*, 211, 212 n.3
Watts, Isaac (1674–1748): *The Art of Reading and Writing English; The Knowledge of the Heavens and Earth Made Easy; Improvement of the Mind*, 322, 322–23 n.3; name of invoked, 340
Wedderburn, Alexander (1733–1805), first baron Loughborough and earl of Rosslyn (lord chancellor), 345–46 n.2
Wells, Harriet, née Este, 350, 351 n.2
Wells, Nathaniel, 351 nn. 2 and 3
West, Frederick (ca. 1767–1852) (son of John West, second earl de la Warr; husband of Maria, née Middleton, or Myddelton, of Chirk Castle), 142 n.8
West, Jane: *A Tale of the Times*, 92 and n.2, 168, 169 n.4, 262, 263 n.7
West, John (1729–77), second earl de la Warr, 142 n.8
West, Maria, née Middleton or Myddelton (d. 1843) (wife of Frederick), 141, 142 n.8
West, Thomas (yeoman farmer) (husband of Jane), 92 n.2
Weston, Gilbert (fl. 1760–post 1802) (brother of PSP), 371 n.1, 375
Weston, Jacob (1742–1820) (steward of Streatham Park): duties of, 88, 143, 144 n.10; letters to, 144 n.10, 474 n.1
Weston, Mary (1718–ca. 1815) (mother of PSP and Gilbert), 156 n.8, 174, 192, 198, 245, 301, 434; and Gilbert's breach of trust, 369–70, 371 n.5, 375; poor health of, 181
Whalley, Augusta Utica Heathcote (second wife of TSW), 415 n.4, 475
Whalley, Elizabeth, née Jones (Sherwood) (ca. 1740–1801) (wife of TSW): on British military fortunes, 276; and her cousin PSP, 155, 156 n.6; crippling accident, illness, and death of, 215, 286, 288 nn. 1 and 2, 298, 299 n.7, 340, 340 n.10; meets LC, 82, 83 n.3; second marriage of, 82. *See also* Sherwood, John Withers
Whalley, Mary (1707–1803) (mother of TSW): death of, 339; longevity of, 93, 174, 175 n.7, 333, 335 n.1
Whalley, Rev. Thomas Sedgwick (1746–1828) (nonresident pastor of Hagsworthingham, Lincs.; prebendary of Wells) (poet, traveler) (TSW), 150; and benefit for Layard family, 465; and Blagdon controversy, 299 n.7; and Bristol riots, 277 and n.5; on *Critical Review*, 332, 334–35 n.2; and friendship, 14, 72, 181, 286, 353, 399; and HLP's *Retrospection*, 277, 288, 290 n.19; illness of, 215, 286, 288 nn. 1 and 2; marriage of to Augusta Utica Heathcote, 415 n.4, 475; meets LC with Elizabeth, 82, 83 n.3; on military events, 276, 439, 448 and n.4; and niece Fanny (Sage) Sullivan, 115; and Piozzis at Longford Cottage, 198, 277, 334; and Plu-

tarch's life of Lucullus, 286–87, 288 n.7; production of *Castle of Montval* at Drury Lane (with SS), 85, 86 n.6, 89, 97, 98–99 nn. 10 and 11, 103; letters from, 329, 334 n.2; 335 n.10; letters to, 249–50, 276–78, 332–36

Whitchurch. *See* Smyth, Jane

White, Benjamin, II (fl. 1794–1816): as possible publisher of *Retrospection*, 201, 202 n.4, 207, 209, 210, 211 n.1, 212, 213

White, Charles, F.R.S. (surgeon): and practice of midwifery, 303, 305 n.5

White, Sarah (1738–1822) (Bath shopkeeper) (sister-in-law of the mercer, Vitalba), 424, 425 n.9

Whitehead, John (ca. 1740–1804), M.D.: his "Essence of Mustard," home remedy, 485

Whitelock, John (1770–1805) (Streatham tenant), 405 and n.2

Whitworth, Arabella Diana, née Cope (Sackville) (wife of the ambassador), 400, 401–2 n.10

Whitworth, Charles, baron of Newport Pratt, co. Galway (later earl Whitworth, ambassador to France), 22, 401–2 n.10

Wilberforce, William (1759–1833) (M.P.; philanthropist): on Blagdon controversy, 346 n.2; on slave trade, 16, 190 n.6

Wilkinson, Patty (companion of SS), 198, 199 and n.1, 289 n.15

William, duke of Normandy, 309 n.10

William III (1650–1702) (king of Great Britain, 1689–1702; formerly prince of Orange and first *stadholder* or *stadhouder* of Holland, 1672), 138, 139 n.5, 479, 480 n.8

William IV (1765–1837) (king of Great Britain), 455 n.5

William (or Willem) V Batavus (1748–1806), prince of Orange and Nassau-Dietz: renounces ancestral role of *stadholder*, 139 n.5, 479, 480 n.8

William Frederick (1776–1834), styled William, second duke of Gloucester and Edinburgh, earl of Connaught, 434, 435 n.5

William Henry, first duke of Gloucester (1743–1805), 434, 435 n.5

Williams, Anne, née Hughes (1775–1837) (wife of Sir Robert Williams), 106, 107 n.12

Williams, Catherine, of Anglesey (mother of Owen), 107 n.11

Williams, Eleanor, née Hughes (d. 1810) (widow of Hugh Williams of Ty Fry; mother of Ly W), 106, 107 n.16, 343, 344 n.12, 349; fragile health of, 446–47, 464, 474, 475 n.5, 482; letter to, 443–44

Williams, Emma (1798–1889) (daughter of Sir John and Ly W), 106, 349, 453

Williams, Harriet (1797–1885) (daughter of Sir John and Ly W), 106, 349, 365, 453

Williams, Helen Maria (1762–1827): as editor of spurious letters attributed to Louis XVI, 462, 463 n.8; friendship with Godwin, 169 n.5; friendship with Kosciusko, 370, 371 n.5; friendship with Gen. John Moore, 131, 132–34 n.2; and HLP, 423; letter to PSP on "political error," 424–25 n.6; *Letters Written in France in the Summer 1790, to a Friend in England*, 424, 425 n.7

Williams, Hugh (1741–68), of Ty Fry, Anglesey, 107 n.10

Williams, Hugh (1802–76), third baronet of Bodelwyddan (second son of Ly W and Sir John; HLP's godson), 341, 343 n.2, 348, 361, 366, 367, 453, 463, 474, 475 n.6

Williams, Sir John (1761–1830) of Bodelwyddan, first baronet, 361, 409, 447, 453; and amateur theatricals, 159; on Bath prices, 169; his broken leg, 106; health of, 226; and invasion preparedness, 461; sells Cheshire estate, 327, 328 n.1

Williams (later Sir John Hay-Williams), John, II (1794–1859), second baronet (son of Sir John and Ly W) (JW), 56, 158–59, 169, 238, 239 n.1, 361, 453; letter to, 25 n.29

Williams John (Chester barrister) (great-grandfather of the elder Sir John), 328 n.1

Williams, Margaret, née Hughes (d. 1821) of Kinmel Park (wife of Owen Williams of Anglesey), 106, 107 n.1

Williams, Margaret (1759–1823), of Bath (sister of Sir John) (MW), 168, 169 n.1, 298, 349, 350 n.11

Williams, Margaret, née Williams, Lady (1768–1835), of Bodelwyddan (Ly W): on Bonaparte, 23; children of, 169, 170 n.8, 348–49 and n.1, 474, 475 nn.5 and 6 (*see also* under names of individual children); and GP's illness, 474; gifts to from HLP, 463; letters to, 54–57, 56–n.1, 168–70, 180 n.9, 205–6, 226–27, 238–39, 250–52, 261–63, 342–44, 348–50, 355–56, 360–63, 365–66, 367–69, 409–10, 446–47, 451–56, 461–63, 463–65, 474–75, 477–78, 482–83

Williams, Margaret (1799–1880) (daughter of Sir John and Ly W), 169, 170 n.8, 453

Williams, Mary Elizabeth (1803–90) (daughter of Sir John and Ly W), 442, 443, 444 n.1, 446

Williams, Owen (ca. 1764–1832), of Anglesey (husband of Margaret, née Hughes), 107 n.11

Williams, Owen Edward (b. 1798) (son of Owen and Margaret), 107 n.11

Williams, Sir Robert (1764–1830), of Nant and Caerau, M.P., 106, 107 n.12

Williams, Thomas, of Anglesey (father of Owen), 107 n.11

Williams, Thomas Peers (1795–1875) (son of Owen and Margaret), 107 n.11

Williams, Rev. William (brother of the elder Sir John) (rector of St. George's, Denbigh), 349, 350 n.11, 444

Williams family, of Bodelwyddan: letters to, 158–59, 363–65, 480–81

Williamson, Lt. Gen. Sir Adam (uncle of Jemima Wilson) (governor of Jamaica and Santo Domingo), 255 n.10

Williams-Wynn, Charles Watkin (M.P. and Tory politician), 326 and n.7

Williams-Wynn, Mary, née Cunliffe (d. 1838) (daughter of Sir Foster Cunliffe, third baronet; wife of Charles Watkin), 326 n.7

Williams-Wynn. *See also* Wynn

Willis, Thomas, M.D.: attends George III, 278, 280 n.5

Wilmot, John Eardley (1750–1815) (master in chancery), 397–98 n.7

Wilson, Rev. Bernard (or Barnard): translation of *Thou's History of his Own Time*, 183, 184 n.3

Wilson, Jemima, née Belford, of Kent, 253, 255 n.10, 257

Wilson, Sir Robert Thomas, 255 n.10; *A Narrative of the Expedition to Egypt*, 400, 402 n.14

Winter ("Xerxes"), Adm. Jan Willem de, 109, 111 n.15, 439, 440–41 n.3, 477 n.1

Wolfe, Arthur (1739–1803), first viscount Kilwarden (lord chief justice of Ireland), 19

Wolfe, Rev. Richard (d. 1803) (nephew of Arthur), 19

Wood, Henry (tutor of JSPS), 303, 305 n.7, 321–22, 394, 395 n.5, 405

Wood, John (ca. 1705–54) (Bath architect), 59, 60 n.10

Wren, Sir Christopher (1632–1723) (architect), 387 n.4

Wright, John (ca. 1770–1844) (Piccadilly bookseller), 97, 98 n.8, 161

Wynn, Anna Maria, née Meredith (Mostyn), of Llewessog (widow of Edward Watkin; mother of JMM), 71, 72 n.7, 159 and n.4, 223

Wynn (or Wynne), Anne Sobieski, née Dod (wife of Robert Watkin), 79, 79–80 n.4

Wynn, Edward Watkin (d. 1796), 72 n.7

Wynn, Maurice, of Gwydir (third husband of Katherine of Berain), 217 n.12

Wynn (or Wynne), Robert Watkin (d. 1806), of Plas Newydd and Garthmeilio, 79, 79–80 n.4

Wynn, Sir Watkin Williams (1772–1840), fifth baronet (M.P. for Denbighshire), 14, 221 and n.3, 326 and n.7

Wynn. *See also* Williams-Wynn

Yonge, Barbara (d. 1837) (sister-in-law of Rev. William Davies Shipley), 326 n.3

York, duchess of. *See* Frederica Charlotte Ulrica Catherina

York, duke of. *See* Frederick Augustus

Yorke, Charles Philip (1764–1834) (secretary at war), 417 n.3

Young, Edward (1683–1765): *The Revenge*, 80 n.9

Younge (master in Hannah More's school): Bere's attack on, 249–50 n.3